Interdisciplinary and Practical Approaches to Managerial Education and Training

Luísa Cagica Carvalho
Polytechnic Institute of Setúbal, Portugal

Nuno Teixeira
Polytechnic Institute of Setúbal, Portugal

Pedro Pardal
Polytechnic Institute of Setúbal, Portugal

IGI Global
PUBLISHER of TIMELY KNOWLEDGE

A volume in the Advances in Logistics, Operations, and Management Science (ALOMS) Book Series

Published in the United States of America by
IGI Global
Business Science Reference (an imprint of IGI Global)
701 E. Chocolate Avenue
Hershey PA, USA 17033
Tel: 717-533-8845
Fax: 717-533-8661
E-mail: cust@igi-global.com
Web site: http://www.igi-global.com

Library of Congress Cataloging-in-Publication Data

Names: Carvalho, Luísa Cagica, 1970- editor. | Teixeira, Nuno Miguel, 1974- editor. | Pardal, Pedro, 1973- editor.
Title: Interdisciplinary and practical approaches to managerial education and training / Luisa Carvalho, Nuno Miguel Teixeira, Pedro Pardal, editors.
Description: Hershey, PA : Business Science Reference, [2022] | Includes bibliographical references and index. | Summary: "This book addresses the main topics of interest regarding the best practices, laboratory methods, policies, protocols, in the areas of business education and managerial training offering topics related to practical approaches to managerial education and training"-- Provided by publisher.
Identifiers: LCCN 2021021772 (print) | LCCN 2021021773 (ebook) | ISBN 9781799882398 (hardcover) | ISBN 9781799882404 (paperback) | ISBN 9781799882411 (ebook)
Subjects: LCSH: Management--Study and teaching. | Business education. | Executives--Training of.
Classification: LCC HD30.4 .I5733 2022 (print) | LCC HD30.4 (ebook) | DDC 658.0071--dc23
LC record available at https://lccn.loc.gov/2021021772
LC ebook record available at https://lccn.loc.gov/2021021773

This book is published in the IGI Global book series Advances in Logistics, Operations, and Management Science (ALOMS) (ISSN: 2327-350X; eISSN: 2327-3518)

British Cataloguing in Publication Data
A Cataloguing in Publication record for this book is available from the British Library.

For electronic access to this publication, please contact: eresources@igi-global.com.

Advances in Logistics, Operations, and Management Science (ALOMS) Book Series

John Wang
Montclair State University, USA

ISSN:2327-350X
EISSN:2327-3518

Mission

Operations research and management science continue to influence business processes, administration, and management information systems, particularly in covering the application methods for decision-making processes. New case studies and applications on management science, operations management, social sciences, and other behavioral sciences have been incorporated into business and organizations real-world objectives.

The **Advances in Logistics, Operations, and Management Science** (ALOMS) Book Series provides a collection of reference publications on the current trends, applications, theories, and practices in the management science field. Providing relevant and current research, this series and its individual publications would be useful for academics, researchers, scholars, and practitioners interested in improving decision making models and business functions.

Coverage

- Decision analysis and decision support
- Operations Management
- Services management
- Organizational Behavior
- Production Management
- Political Science
- Computing and information technologies
- Finance
- Risk Management
- Networks

IGI Global is currently accepting manuscripts for publication within this series. To submit a proposal for a volume in this series, please contact our Acquisition Editors at Acquisitions@igi-global.com or visit: http://www.igi-global.com/publish/.

The Advances in Logistics, Operations, and Management Science (ALOMS) Book Series (ISSN 2327-350X) is published by IGI Global, 701 E. Chocolate Avenue, Hershey, PA 17033-1240, USA, www.igi-global.com. This series is composed of titles available for purchase individually; each title is edited to be contextually exclusive from any other title within the series. For pricing and ordering information please visit http://www.igi-global.com/book-series/advances-logistics-operations-management-science/37170. Postmaster: Send all address changes to above address.

Titles in this Series

For a list of additional titles in this series, please visit: http://www.igi-global.com/book-series/advances-logistics-operations-management-science/37170

Management Strategies for Sustainability, New Knowledge Innovation, and Personalized Products and Services
Mirjana Pejic-Bach (University of Zagreb, Croatia) and Çağlar Doğru (Ufuk University, Turkey)
Business Science Reference • © 2022 • 365pp • H/C (ISBN: 9781799877936) • US $215.00

Cases on Supply Chain Management and Lessons Learned From COVID-19
Ana Paula Lopes (Polytechnic of Porto, Portugal)
Business Science Reference • © 2022 • 238pp • H/C (ISBN: 9781799891406) • US $225.00

Key Factors and Use Cases of Servant Leadership Driving Organizational Performance
Maria Pressentin (International School of Management, France)
Business Science Reference • © 2022 • 368pp • H/C (ISBN: 9781799888208) • US $215.00

Handbook of Research on Innovative Management Using AI in Industry 5.0
Vikas Garg (Amity University, Greater Noida, India) and Richa Goel (Amity University, Noida, India)
Business Science Reference • © 2022 • 351pp • H/C (ISBN: 9781799884972) • US $295.00

Contemporary Challenges for Agile Project Management
Vannie Naidoo (University of Kwa-Zulu Natal, South Africa) and Rahul Verma (Delhi University, India)
Business Science Reference • © 2022 • 354pp • H/C (ISBN: 9781799878728) • US $225.00

Cases on Optimizing the Asset Management Process
Vicente González-Prida (University of Seville, Spain & National University of Distance Education, Spain) Carlos Alberto Parra Márquez (University of Seville, Spain) and Adolfo Crespo Márquez (University of Seville, Spain)
Business Science Reference • © 2022 • 457pp • H/C (ISBN: 9781799879435) • US $215.00

Handbook of Research on Current Trends in Asian Economics, Business, and Administration
Bülent Akkaya (Manisa Celal Bayar University, Turkey) Kittisak Jermsittiparsert (Henan University of Economics and Law, China) and Ayse Gunsel (Kocaeli University, Turkey)
Business Science Reference • © 2022 • 497pp • H/C (ISBN: 9781799884866) • US $295.00

Logistics and Supply Chain Management in the Globalized Business Era
Lincoln C. Wood (University of Otago, New Zealand) and Linh N.K. Duong (University of the West of England, Bristol, UK)
Business Science Reference • © 2022 • 413pp • H/C (ISBN: 9781799887096) • US $225.00

IGI Global
PUBLISHER of TIMELY KNOWLEDGE

701 East Chocolate Avenue, Hershey, PA 17033, USA
Tel: 717-533-8845 x100 • Fax: 717-533-8661
E-Mail: cust@igi-global.com • www.igi-global.com

Table of Contents

Detailed Table of Contents

The journey of business, management, and accounting education over the past decades included several teaching methods which may nowadays be considered outdated for the modern students who live, learn, and connect through technology. This study clusters the academic literature addressing online learning and b-learning applied to educational and training in the business, management, and accounting. Through the collection of all the relevant publications in Scopus, this study uses automated text mining techniques in VOSviewer software for comparing the evolution overtime of the online and blended methods in the context of scientific knowledge production. The results unveil that online-learning-related literature is grouped in nine clusters, instead of the seven clusters in case of blended learning, meaning that the first is more disperse in terms of topics. An in-depth analysis of the studies most closely related to each cluster's terms allow the authors to provide critical reflections that help professionals when choosing the accurate method and also the academics in identifying future research agendas.

Chapter 4
Key Factors for Entrepreneurial Success: A Synthesis of Earlier Research and an Agenda Proposal to Support Entrepreneurial Training 56
Teresa Gomes da Costa, Polytechnic Institute of Setúba, Portugal
Luísa Cagica Carvalho, Polytechnic Institute of Setúbal, Portugal & CEFAGE, University of Évora, Portugal

Studies about success and unsuccess factors for startups are still relevant due to the dispersion of the literature about it. Additionally, it remains important to understand how some usual tools used by the entrepreneurs could support a better diagnosis of the success conditions in an earlier phase of the business, avoiding or preventing the unsuccess. This study is a work in progress financed by EU under Erasums+ Program and aims to discuss the factors that influence the business entrepreneurial success considering several stages of the business and its maturity. Finally, it also attends to the business plan as an important tool for entrepreneurial success. The chapter organizes contributions attending to the dimensions—entrepreneurial profile, external environment, and managerial process—and presents an agenda about a set of factors in a macro perspective (public policies, infrastructures, etc.) and in a micro perspective (entrepreneurial profile, social and human capital, etc.) that allows a reflection about the success on a different stage of a business.

Chapter 5
Corporate Simulation and the Articulation of the Problem-Based Learning Methodology With the Continuous Assessment Model 73
Ana Bela Teixeira, Polytechnic Institute of Setúbal, Portugal
Nuno Delicado Teixeira, Polytechnic Institute of Setúbal, Portugal
Rosa Morgado Galvão, Polytechnic Institute of Setúbal, Portugal
Paulo José Rodrigues Costa, Polytechnic Institute of Setúbal, Portugal
Telmo Passuco Wergikosky, Polytechnic Institute of Setúbal, Portugal
Filipe Damas Bacalhau, Polytechnic Institute of Setúbal, Portugal

Academic success is a priority, and according to the literature review, it is associated with the application of problem-based learning methodologies or the continuous assessment model. The case study performed was based on the course unit Corporate Simulation (CS), part of the Accounting and Finance course academic curriculum. After describing the functioning process, objectives, and assessment model of CS, it was shown that from 2014/15 to 2019/20, the level of approval of CS was 94.8%. Also, from the results of the survey conducted with the students who completed CS, from 2007/08 to 2018/19, on a scale of 1

Highly engaged employees are central to strong organizational outcomes. Nonetheless, consistency in maintaining high levels of engagement eludes most organizations. Disengaged employees are often toxic and cultivate negativity. An in-depth analysis of the drivers of employee engagement indicates that leadership is the strongest influencer of engagement. Bass's transformational leadership and the leader-member-exchange (LMX) theories outline characteristics of transformational leaders. The theories intersect where Bass posits is the stage in the relationship between leader and follower where leader behavior inspires followers to excel with no additional incentives needed. Training and development of the transformational leader who drives high engagement must take adult learning principles into account in recognition of the unique learning needs of adults.

Following the recent measures implemented worldwide as result of the pandemic caused by COVID-19, educational institutions needed to implement online learning practices, demanding a rapid appropriation of digital skills by teachers and students. The Polytechnic Institute of Portalegre, in Portugal, was one of the higher education institutions (IES) that organized a transition process for this teaching model. The objectives of the study focused on the characterization of the online learning process, including the practice of online learning and the students' perspectives regarding the future of online learning. The results obtained, from 420 validated questionnaires, point to a positive evaluation of this pedagogical experience, with some particularities listed in certain areas of the teaching and learning process, suggesting an in-depth analysis on the level of digital skills on the part of teachers and students in order to consolidate distance learning as a true pedagogical innovation process and not just as an "emergency remote teaching" experience.

The psychological theories of leadership have a great deal to offer today's organizational leaders. Four of these theories—transactional, transformational, authentic, and servant leadership—are complementary in style, aiming to serve the self-actualization of employees as well as the greater good of the organization. This chapter explores the similarities and differences between these leadership styles, as well as the strengths and weaknesses of their basic principles and assumptions, especially as pertains to the work of diversity, equity, and inclusion (DEI) practitioners in educational settings. This chapter examines the benefits of integrating these theories, along with some newer and lesser-known theories, into a multimodal approach that can be effective for managers coaching team members toward greater organizational equity. A brief case comparison illustrates how the principles of DEI leadership can be applied.

Since the outbreak of COVID-19 pandemic, tertiary education has been mainly pursued through online teaching. This form of teaching is also associated with challenges regarding the social presence of both lecturers and the students during classes. In this context, understanding how to effectively enforce social interaction and trust in the virtual classroom is of high importance. This chapter presents various examples of social learning pursued by the Management Center Innsbruck in their blended learning degree programs. Many of these have already been established in 2014 when the first blended learning degree programs started. However, the need for physical distancing made clear that social presence and interaction are of even greater relevance than ever before. Increasing the sense of cohesion and being a proper member of a study group can also be supported by more informal interactions.

The needs of the adult learner are distinctly different from those of children. In a world where employees are becoming increasingly remote, recognizing the core concepts of adult instruction is increasingly critical. This chapter examines the foundational constructs of adult learning and instruction and factors that promote and inhibit adult learning. Theories of adult learning pioneers Knowles, McClusky, Deci, and Ryan apply in the organizational classroom and the "virtual" classroom. With this understanding, the learning practitioner may implement meaningful curriculum that appeals to the adult learner, encouraging individual growth while supporting employee retention and organizational development.

The COVID-19 pandemic has profoundly impacted the Brazilian service sector. With the health crisis, challenges and changes in the business models of car dealerships are also intensified. Creativity is discussed by several conceptual approaches. From the point of view of neuroscience, it is a response to the human need of solving problems. It is within this premise that the present work aims to enhance value proposition for a business model centered on automobile e-commerce. This purpose unfolds in an exploratory research on approaches, methodologies, and tools of creativity, as well as the application of Cristiano Alves's creative framework in this business model. The analysis of the results signals improvements in solutions for car e-commerce. With this, it is concluded that collective creativity is efficient in the discovery of potentially innovative ideas.

In this chapter, a systematic review of the literature on evaluations of service-learning projects in the area of business and economics has been carried out. The authors have analyzed the four basic parts of evaluation: who evaluates, when to evaluate, how to evaluate, and what to evaluate. Subsequently, an evaluation proposal has been made for each of the agents involved, taking into account each of these dimensions. One of the main conclusions is that reflection is a fundamental part of the evaluation process, as well as of the student learning process because it allows them to deepen the lived experience.

This chapter aims to analyze the socio-intercultural management competencies as they are integrated in any organizational setting, including individuals, groups, and communities. In the analysis, it is assumed that the development of socio-intercultural management in the organizations requires the integration of the socio-intercultural principles building competencies in transdisciplinary contents in current social issues, concerns, and solutions of problems of the organizations and society. The method employed is the analytical focusing on a reflective and comparative analysis of the literature reviewed and their achievements in practical implementation in the real managerial world. It is concluded that awareness of cultural differences for organizational management sustainability are the base for the development of socio-intercultural management competencies required in the new glocal labor market environment.

Employee engagement is defined as an employee's emotional connectedness with an organization. One of the key levers that affects employee engagement is leadership support. Leaders who effectively manage are vital to all organizations as they play a key role in helping to establish relational networks which lead to higher levels of engagement for their employees. This chapter discusses how leaders can impact engagement. Furthermore, it outlines how leaders can grow and develop in their leadership practice. Leaders who focus on creating a culture of learning and engagement experience higher levels of performance.

Preface

In the last decades, the development of innovative practices has gained considerable interest, but challenges are far from easy. New generations of students grow up in a very different environment, severally influenced by information and communications technologies (ICT). In the 2018 United Nations conference on Trade and Development, the Secretary-General of UNCTAD stated that "we live at a time of technological change that is unprecedented in its pace, scope and depth of impact". Furthermore, in a globalized world, ICT are changing the way businesses create and capture value, how and where we work, and how we interact and communicate.

These allegations were prior to the actual global pandemic, which is an event that accentuated the use of ICT like never before. Thus, some of the traditional teaching's methods are rapidly becoming obsolete, unattractive to the new generation of students or needing the complementarity of additional methodologies. In the last years higher education institutions as well as lectures individually, invested in the introduction and development of new teaching methods, including in activities of training.

More active methodologies are being incentivized, like problem-based learning (PBL), Co-creation, team-based learning (TBL) or gamification. Beside the methodologies, teaching in a more technological environment is essential for promoting digital skills of lectures and students. In the context of COVID-19, practices of e-learning or b-learning increased the adoption of digital platforms, influencing teaching practices. In addition, institutions are also giving attention to the development of soft skills as a complement of hard skills, which opens a field for different teaching contexts and experiences.

Despite the higher development of new teaching approaches in the recent years, relevant questions related to learning objectives, suitable methodologies, and impact assessment, remain unanswered. Thus, this book had the objective to receive research inputs that allow the interested community to learn with experiences as well as to access insights, discussion on new forms of teaching and training methodologies and curricular programs, in all the fields of management.

This book has an interdisciplinary nature appealing to lectures, academic management and regional development scholars, students, and practitioners. Contributions received from international authors focusing on a more practical approach for managerial education, at different levels of education and highlighting its importance for local communities and companies, provided a broader geographic overview.

In the first chapter, "Insights Into Preparing Training Courses on Financial Services for Entrepreneurs in Africa," Teixeira and Carvalho discuss the issues related to the access to financing for micro, small, and medium entrepreneurs in Africa. In this Continent, in general, financial system still evidence tendencies that not favoring the productive sector. Under the Envolver project (running in Angola), which aims to promote the development of a sustainable and inclusive private sector, based on the diversification and availability of financial services adapted to MSMEs and entrepreneurs, a diagnostic study was developed to map the financial products currently available to micro, small and medium enterprises. This study allows to outline a set of recommendations for innovative financial solutions adjusted to this audience, based on examples of success in similar contexts.

The second chapter, "Distance Education in Higher Education: Modern Applications and Management Courses," developed by Castro, Moreira and Carvalho, approached the changes introduced in the last years and underlining mainly during the Pandemic that put on the light distance learning. This chapter applied a literature review to study what exists about distance learning in higher education, with a special focus on business administration courses. To get the full benefit of online learning, new strategies and learning methodologies are applied and information and communication technology can play a fundamental role here.

The third chapter, "Blended Learning Compared to Online Learning in Business, Management, and Accounting Education: A Bibliometric Analysis and Literature Review," authored by Santos, clusters the academic literature addressing Online Learning and B-Learning applied to educational and training in the business, management and accounting. Through the collection of all the relevant publications in Scopus, this study uses automated text mining techniques in VOSviewer software for comparing the evolution overtime of the Online and Blended methods in the context of scientific knowledge production. The results unveil that Online-Learning related literature is grouped in 9 clusters, instead of the 7 clusters in case of Blended-Learning, meaning that the first is more disperse in terms of topics. An in-depth analysis of the studies most closely related to each cluster's terms allow to provide critical reflections that help professionals when choosing the accurate method and the academics in identifying future research agendas.

The fourth chapter, "Key Factors for Entrepreneurial Success: A Synthesis of Earlier Research and an Agenda Proposal to Support Entrepreneurial Training," by Costa and Carvalho, discusses success and unsuccess factors for startups. This research highlight that remains important to understand how some usual tools used by the entrepreneurs could support a better diagnosis of the success conditions in an earlier phase of the business, avoiding or preventing the unsuccess. Finally, also attend to the business plan as an important tool for entrepreneurial success. The chapter organizes contributions attending to the dimensions: entrepreneurial profile; external environment and managerial process and presents an agenda about a set of factors in a macro perspective (public policies, infrastructures, etc.) and in a micro perspective (entrepreneurial profile, social and human capital, etc.) that allows a reflection about the success on a different stage of a business.

The fifth chapter, "Corporate Simulation and the Articulation of the Problem-Based Learning Methodology With the Continuous Assessment Model," developed by Teixeira et al., considers that academic success is a priority. And, according to the literature review, it is associated with the application of problem-based learning methodologies or the continuous assessment model. The case study performed was based on the course unit Corporate Simulation (CS), part of the Accounting and Finance course academic curriculum. After describing the functioning process, objectives, and assessment model of CS, it was shown that from 2014/15 to 2019/20, the level of approval of CS was 94.8%. Also, from the results of the survey conducted with the students who completed CS, from 2007/08 to 2018/19, on a scale of 1 to 5, in options 4 and 5 (good and very good), the objectives weigh on average, 85.3%, and that, in the academic year 2019/20, the specific characteristics of functioning, as a consequence of COVID 19, did not cause changes in the trends of assessment and approval in CS.

The sixth chapter, "Transforming Tourism Education: An Interdisciplinary Approach to Sustainable Tourism Management," developed by Vasconcelos and Melo, describes an Interdisciplinary Project that was designed and implemented within the scope of a Tourist Activities Management degree and whose main topic was sustainability. Based on the use of a bilingual student blog, this project challenged students to produce multimedia content (posts, podcasts and videos) focusing on sustainable practices and behaviors in different tourism sectors. Making use of a Project Based Learning approach, the strategy used is perceived as innovative having enhanced student participation and engagement. Concurrently, a preliminary analysis also suggests that there has been a positive change in the participants' awareness towards sustainability, with the different assignments and research having prompted changes in their behavior, denoting the project's pertinence, particularly in these challenging and technology-laden times.

The seventh chapter, "Evaluation of the Potential of Ideation Tools to Create Technologies Aimed at Education," developed by Paula et al., aims to evaluate the potential of an ideation framework, which is based on the idea of collective intelligence, to develop technologies for the area of education, and to be more compatible with the current model of society. The study analyzed four tools, the empathy map, the user journey, method 6-3-5, and the Edward de Bono hat method as a validation tool for ideas. At the end of the application, it resulted in the choice of four insights to be applied, which are the virtual assistant by voice command, a video gallery and podcast, gamification for the user to be reciprocated, and individual study planning to particularize each case, and thus fostering the effectiveness in increasing learning as proposed by the project.

The eighth chapter, "Employee Engagement and Learning for the Transformational Leader," developed by Lacy, studies the importance of the engagement of employees to create strong organizational outcomes. Besides that, analyze the importance of leadership as a driver to influence the level of engagement of employees, based on Transformational Leadership and the Leader-Member-Exchange (LMX) theories, to outline characteristics of transformational leaders.

The ninth chapter, "Online Learning or Emergency Remote Teaching? Reflections on Online Learning as a Pedagogical Innovation in a Higher Education Institution," developed by Alves et al., studies the case of Polytechnic Institute of Portalegre, in Portugal, to characterize the online learning process, including the practice of online learning and the students' perspectives regarding the future of online learning. The results obtained, from 420 validated questionnaires, point to a positive evaluation of this pedagogical experience, with some particularities listed in certain areas of the teaching and learning process, suggesting an in-depth analysis on the level of digital skills on the part of teachers and students, in order to consolidate distance learning as a true pedagogical innovation process and not just as an "emergency remote teaching" experience.

The tenth chapter, "Preparing Managers to Lead for Diversity, Equity, and Inclusion," developed by Keiffer-Lewis and Berman, studies four psychological theories of leadership, namely, transactional, transformational, authentic, and servant leadership. It explores the similarities and differences between these leadership styles, as well as the strengths and weaknesses of their basic principles and assumptions, especially as pertains to the work of diversity, equity, and inclusion practitioners in educational settings. Thus, this chapter examines the benefits of integrating these theories, along with some newer and lesser-known theories, into a multimodal approach that can be effective for managers coaching team members toward greater organizational equity.

The eleventh chapter, "The Importance of Social Components in Online Learning: The Case of Business Administration Online at MCI," developed by Palan et al., studies the challenges regarding the social presence of both lecturers and the students during online classes. So, this chapter presents various examples of social learning pursued by the Management Center Innsbruck in their blended learning degree programs. The examples show that the need for physical distancing made clear that social presence and interaction are of even greater relevance than ever before.

The twelfth chapter, "Adult Learning in the Workplace: Critical Application and New Mediums," developed by Nelmark, examines the foundational constructs of adult learning and instruction and factors that promote and inhibit adult learning. Authors argue that theories of adult learning pioneers Knowles, McClusky, Deci, and Ryan, apply in the organizational brick and mortar classroom and the "virtual" online classroom. Thus, they reinforce that with the understanding of these theories, the learning practitioner may implement meaningful curriculum that appeals to the adult learner regardless of venue, encouraging individual growth while supporting employee retention and organizational development.

The thirteenth chapter, "Creativity Processes Applied to the Innovation Management of Digital Showroom for Cars," developed by Macêdo and Queiroz, discusses creativity process through several conceptual approaches, in order to respond to the effects of Covid-19 pandemic in the Brazilian service sector, especially on the intensified challenges and changes in the business models of car dealerships. Creativity, from the point of view of neuroscience, it is a response to the human need of solving problems. It is within this premise that the study, presented in this chapter, aims to enhance value proposition for a business model centered on automobile e-commerce. This purpose unfolds in exploratory research on approaches, methodologies and tools of creativity, as well as the application of Cristiano Alves' Creative Framework in this business model. The analysis of the results, signals improvements in solutions for car e-commerce, allowing to conclude that collective creativity is efficient in the discovery of potentially innovative ideas.

The fourteenth chapter, "The Role of Evaluation in the Service Learning in Economics and Business: Systematic Review and Proposal of Evaluation," developed by Ortiz-Fernández, Tarifa-Fernández, and Rambaud, performs a systematic review of the literature on evaluations of service-learning projects, in the area of Business and Economics. The authors provide an analysis of the four basic parts of evaluation: who evaluates, when to evaluate, how to evaluate and what to evaluate. Subsequently, it is developed an evaluation proposal for each of the agents involved, taking into account each of these dimensions. One of the main conclusions of the chapter is that reflection is a fundamental part of the evaluation process, as well as of the student's learning process because it allows them to deepen the lived experience.

The fifteenth chapter, "Socio-Intercultural Management Competencies," developed by Vargas-Hernández, analyses the socio-intercultural management competencies as they are integrated in any organizational setting, including individuals, groups and communities. In the analysis, it is assumed that the development of socio-intercultural management in the organizations requires the integration of the socio-intercultural principles building competencies in transdisciplinary contents in current social issues, concerns and solution of problems of the organizations and society. The authors employed an analytical methodology focusing on a reflective and comparative analysis of the literature reviewed and their achievements in practical implementation in the real managerial world. The chapter provides the conclusion that awareness of cultural differences for organizational management sustainability is the base for the development of socio-intercultural management competencies required in the new global labor market environment.

The sixteenth chapter, "Leader Effects on Engagement," developed by Walker-Schmidt, discusses how leaders can impact engagement. Furthermore, it outlines how leader can grow and develop in their leadership practice. Employee engagement is defined as an employee's emotional connectedness with an organization. One of the key levers that affects employee engagement is leadership support. Leaders who effectively manage are vital to all organizations as they play a key role in helping to establish relational networks which lead to higher levels of engagement for their employees. Thus, leaders who focus on creating a culture of learning and engagement experience higher levels of performance.

To conclude, we would like to thank the authors whose collaboration has made this project possible and express our hope that readers will find this publication inspiring and useful.

Luísa Cagica Carvalho
Nuno Teixeira
Pedro Pardal

Chapter 1
Insights Into Preparing Training Courses on Financial Services for Entrepreneurs in Africa

Nuno Teixeira
Polytechnic Institute of Setúbal, Portugal

Luisa Margarida Cagica Carvalho
https://orcid.org/0000-0002-9804-7813
Polytechnic Institute of Setúbal, Portugal & CEFAGE, University of Évora, Portugal

ABSTRACT

Access to financing for micro, small, and medium entrepreneurs continues to face obstacles and difficulties. This scenario becomes even more evident when we refer to the situation of the African continent, where the financial system still shows tendencies that do not favor the productive sector. Under the Envolver project, which aims to promote the development of a sustainable and inclusive private sector, based on the diversification and availability of financial services adapted to MSMEs and entrepreneurs, a diagnostic study was developed to map the financial products currently available to micro, small, and medium enterprises. This study allows us to outline a set of recommendations for innovative financial solutions adjusted to this audience, based on examples of success in contexts similar to Angola.

INTRODUCTION

Access to financing for micro, small, and medium entrepreneurs continues to face obstacles and difficulties. This scenario becomes even more evident when we refer to the situation of the African continent, where the financial system still shows tendencies that do not favor the productive sector.

Under the Envolver project, which aims to promote the development of a sustainable and inclusive private sector, based on the diversification and availability of financial services adapted to MSMEs and entrepreneurs, a diagnostic study was developed to map the financial products currently available to micro,

DOI: 10.4018/978-1-7998-8239-8.ch001

small and medium enterprises. This study allows us to outline a set of recommendations for innovative financial solutions adjusted to this audience, based on examples of success in contexts similar to Angola.

GENERAL CONDITIONS FOR MSME ACCESS TO FINANCING

Access to financing by MSMEs is a topic that has been studied for several decades. This is because, although these companies always represent a large part of the business context in most countries, due to their characteristics, they usually have difficulties in obtaining financing for their activity, in terms of amounts, maturity and costs, which conditions their development and the evolution of social progress and the growth of world economies.

In 2003, the report of the European Observatory for SMEs (small and medium enterprises) prepared by the European Commission, considered access to finance as one of the main constraints to the development of SMEs, which became more pronounced the smaller the size of the companies. Therefore, bank credit was the main external source of financing, and the only one for many companies. However, most of the time the financing was obtained in insufficient amounts, at high costs and with short maturities.

For the development of financial support measures for SMEs, the report stated that their heterogeneity should be considered. Thus, it defined four types of companies:

- Start-up companies;
- Enterprises in a mature phase;
- Innovative companies;
- Growth companies.

Start-ups had greater difficulties, and as well as bank credit, it was common to get financing through friends and family. They also resorted to business angels who also provided commercial, entrepreneurial, and management know-how.

Maturing companies obtained cheaper financing because they offered more equity and asset guarantees.

Innovative and growing firms were better able to access capital than SMEs in general. However, because of uncertainty about the future, their sources of financing were heavily based on business angels and venture capital. Traditional financial institutions demanded more real guarantees from companies of this type.

In 2006, in a document on the constraints for access to financing by Portuguese SMEs, IAPMEI mentioned that there were aspects to consider both on the supply and demand side.

In the following years, and until today, several international studies (for example, Kamau, 2011; OCDE, 2015; Ogoy, 2016; Magembe, 2017; Pham, 2017; Gião, 2018; SMEFINANCE, 2020; Kong et al., 2021) have been conducted that are aligned with the conclusions of the European Commission and IAPMEI and show that size is a very important variable in defining the financial structure of companies, since, normally, companies with lower turnover or assets have more limited access to credit. This is because smaller companies regularly have lower-quality financial reports, greater fluctuations in the volume of activity and lower-value assets that make it difficult to establish collateral to obtain credit.

However, it appears that even in companies considered as MSMEs, there are other variables that influence their financial structure and access to debt. Thus, several research works have identified a correlation between the types of strategy adopted by the companies and the sources of financing used

Table 1. Financing constraints

Constraints on the Supply of Financing
• Reduced number of potential financiers, which deprives companies of negotiating power; • High costs of risk analysis and administrative processing of operations, which are more easily monetized in larger projects hinders the financing of innovative projects; • High level of sophistication of credit risk analysis criteria for companies; • Primacy of real guarantees; • Reduced liquidity of capital markets, giving precedence to large companies; • Deficient coordination with proximity agents, such as venture capital companies or business angels.
Financing Demand Constraints
• Lack of perceived quality of the financial information produced and disclosed; • Difficulty in sharing market or business information, which hinders credit risk analysis; • Weak financial culture and reduced scale, with difficulty in negotiating capacity as a consequence; • Difficulties in providing guarantees, particularly in the initial phase of activity; • Excessive concentration of capital and resistance to opening new partners; • Lack of entrepreneurial culture and investment in skills with high added value (quality, innovation, customization of supply, etc.).

Source: Authors

(for example, Modigliani & Miller, 1963; Leland & Pyle, 1977; Myers, 1977; Myers, 1984; Myers & Majluf, 1984; Kane et al., 1985; Titman & Wessels, 1988; Arias et al., 2000):

- SMEs' management regarding financial structure is highly constrained by the tax effect, since the financial costs of borrowed capital are accepted fiscally unlike profit distribution;
- Companies with diversification and differentiation strategies have lower financial risk, which gives them greater ease in obtaining debt capital;
- Companies with a higher level of innovation and with large investments in research and development have longer pay-back periods, increasing the business risk and decreasing indebtedness;
- Companies with production factors that are difficult to substitute also present higher financial risk and consequently lower indebtedness;
- Companies with a better competitive position (market share), present higher indebtedness, due to the lower risk of the associated business;
- Companies with higher profitability, show less indebtedness, since they have greater self-financing capacity and thus do not need to expose their competitive situation to financial institutions.

In summary, the studies show that the business strategy (diversification, type of competitive advantage created, size adopted, level of vertical integration and markets covered) and the characteristics of each business (volumes of investments required, specificities of the assets, length of payback periods, etc.), clearly condition the types of financing sources used.

In addition to trying to explain the definition of the sources of financing, research studies conducted over time have also tried to identify the conditioning factors of the maturity of the financing adopted by firms. The variables growth rate, company size and importance of collateral assets stand out (Myers, 1977; Kane et al., 1985; Flannery, 1986; Korner, 2006):

- Pace of growth: firms with higher growth rates have greater financial needs. Medium- and long-term financing presents higher costs and, therefore, contracting it may lead to sub-investment situations for the owners, since they will not be the ones to withdraw the largest portion of the projects' profits. In this sense, they opt for the alternative of successive negotiation of short-term debt with lower remunerations;

- Company size: MSMEs have some characteristics that force them to resort more frequently to short-term debt, namely, higher volatility of profitability, less disclosure of reliable financial information and lower renown with financial institutions;
- Collateral assets: companies often present assets as guarantees for the fulfillment of their financing installments (for example, material resources such as real estate, land, inventories and third-party debts, which are part of their accounting records). As such, the more collateral assets companies can provide as guarantees, the easier it will be for them to obtain medium- and long-term financing at the desired conditions, in terms of cost and terms. Thus, medium- and long-term debt presents greater access restrictions than short-term debt. This is due essentially to the fact that longer debt maturity is associated with a greater probability of default by debtor companies. Thus, it is natural that the costs and the level of demand of the requirements for access to this type of financing are higher, requiring greater collateral guarantees than many companies are able to provide.

In other international studies (for example, Titman & Wessels, 1988; Arias et al., 2000;Teixeira & Brites, 2020), it was found that the renown of the company and the quality of its management also contributed to explain the maturity of debt:

- Companies that are recognized in the market as being of low quality resort more to medium- and long-term debt, because they fear that short-term credit agreements may not be renegotiated;
- On the other hand, companies that are a reference for high quality prefer to use short-term debt as a way to give a positive signal to investors about the future of their activity;
- In other studies, it was also found that firms with higher debt levels resort to medium- and long-term debt to avoid the pressure of bankruptcy costs.

Finally, several authors (for example, Korner, 2006; Teixeira & Brites, 2020) have also mentioned the financial principle of matching between debt maturity and the degree of liquidity of assets, which is interconnected with the rules on financial equilibrium. Thus, the decision on the maturity that the sources of financing should have is associated with the ideal combination of equity and debt capital. This minimizes the cost of financing and while putting no pressure on the treasury.

In conclusion, it should be noted that over the years several studies have been conducted, the vast majority of which have proven that there are a large number of variables that seem to condition financing decisions and access to financing sources outside the companies' activity.

ACCESS TO FINANCING FOR MSMES IN EMERGING ECONOMIES

Access to financing in emerging economies is complex, accentuating the constraints described in the previous section, both on the supply and demand side (SMEFINANCE, 2020).

In terms of financial institutions, they are not very inclined to finance MSMEs, since their business is normally ensured through financial services to public entities and large companies, clients with greater financial capacity and who guarantee financial operations of large amounts that allow a higher return on the interest charged (SMEFINANCE, 2020).

MSMEs, in addition to the higher risk associated with the activity, derived from the greater volatility of the business and the lack of collateral, compete for the negotiation of financial operations of small amounts, which are less attractive in terms of income to be generated for financial institutions. In addition, in these economies inflation rates are usually higher, which implies that interest rates have higher and prohibitive values for the financial capacity of MSMEs and, in particular, for the neediest populations such as young people, women and rural entrepreneurs (European Microfinance Network, 2012 and 2015).

On the demand side, there are also several constraints that make it even more difficult for MSMEs to access financing. In addition to the higher risk associated with the volatility of turnover, there are some strongly inhibiting contextual conditions that are associated with the informality of the activity of economic agents, which include the lack of registration of people and property (which even often belongs to the state – the case of much land in Angola), and do not allow the existence of assets that function as collateral or greater control of the business through the existence of organized accounting in companies. In addition to these aspects, there is also a deficit in financial literacy, which inhibits knowledge about business management and financial products, generating an entrepreneurial and business culture focused on solving day-to-day problems, without a medium- and long-term vision that contributes to social progress and sustained economic growth of countries (Teixeira & Rodrigues, 2013).

Thus, there are several studies (for example, Zaman, 2004; IIPM, 2006; Hulme & Moore, 2007; Beck et al., 2011; Rahman, 2011; European Microfinance Network, 2012 and 2015; Barai & Adhikary, 2013; Fal, 2013; IFC, 2014; Terano et al., 2015; Bertha Centre for Social Innovation & Entrepreneurship, 2018; Nadeem & Rasool, 2018; Chandrayanti et al., 2019; Dang & Chuc, 2019; Mollah, 2020; Rahman & Ley, 2020; SMEFINANCE, 2020; Shneor, 2020) conducted in different emerging economies in Asia, Latin America and Africa, which mention the following as the main constraints for MSMEs in accessing financing:

- Lack of capacity to provide collateral guarantees;
- Lack of capacity to prepare and control an adequate business plan;
- Complicated and demanding credit evaluation processes in terms of the dossiers to be constituted (for example, feasibility studies and necessary legal documentation);
- High interest rates;
- Lack of adequate accounting systems to control the business;
- Limited relations with banking institutions, which creates difficulties of communication and alignment of action among the different economic agents involved;
- Lack of support from the government in terms of streamlining the necessary procedures for the completion of legal documentation (for example at the level of company and asset registration) and licensing of the activity;
- Lack of management skills on the part of business owners and entrepreneurs;
- High transaction costs for the realization of financial operations (costs of the necessary legal procedures and financial services fees).
- On the other hand, international studies also address the identification of a set of bad practices in several emerging economies that, in addition to restricting the development of private initiative among the poorest populations, have further contributed to their impoverishment:
- Lack of control of project execution and repayments to the financial system;
- Practice of high interest rates to compensate for the higher risk and smaller scale of operations;

Table 2. Generic actions to improve access to credit

Entrepreneurial competencies	Financial Instruments	Transparency and cooperation	Institutional partners
Business training	Lower interest rates	Clear criteria for access to credit	Involvement of professional associations
Training in financial instruments	Delivery of amounts according to objectives	Reinforcement of the Banking - Companies dialogue	Involvement of business Associations
Collective commercialization channels	Maturities associated with business cycles	Better information on financing	Partnerships in the value chain industries
Events to publicize the offer	State credit guarantees	Limit the maximum cost of financing	Creation of business centers I incubators
Financial rewards for successful projects	Serious involvement of the financial system	Decrease administrative costs	
Programs in entrepreneurship education			
Streamlining insolvencies – 2nd chance			

Source: Authors

- Passing all the costs associated with the operations to the clients, making financing even more expensive;
- Short credit repayment terms which are poorly adjusted to the business operation cycles;
- Definition of standardized financial operations without any concern for the definition of different customer segments based on the characteristics of their income level, assets and business;
- Practices of eliminating "bad clients/bad payers" (very poor), pressure for entrepreneurs to sell personal assets to pay the installments and socio-cultural pressure for credit repayment (for example, highly practiced on women), which is creating an even greater segregation of the population.

Thus, the European Commission and several international studies (for example, Ojah & Mokoteli, 2010; Psico, 2010; European Microfinance Network, 2012 and 2015; Gustafson & Khandker, 2016; Paschen, 2016; SMEFINANCE, 2020; IFC, 2020) consider that the difficulties of access to financing in emerging economies by MSMEs require an integrated set of actions that make a sustained contribution to the development of the business context. This should be done at the level of entrepreneurs' skills, improvement of financial instruments, transparency and cooperation and the involvement of the main institutional partners, in order to disseminate good business practices by the various economic agents and involve entrepreneurs and more disadvantaged populations such as young people, women and people in rural areas. The following table summarizes these general ideas.

Thus, through these actions it is intended to contribute to greater financial literacy and greater capacity for preparing and controlling business plans and the existence of a greater and more effective network between entrepreneurs. This would allow more sharing of best practices, technologies and processes, broader dissemination of products and services and business opportunities and, finally, the existence of information systems between companies, institutions and banks, which better align the expectations of the different actors and avoid delays and failures in the processes of funding applications.

Regarding the populations most in need of access to financing, such as women, young people and the rural population, studies and reports from international organizations such as the European Microfinance Network (2012 and 2015) suggest some ways to integrate these groups more easily into the financial system.

Women play a key role in most societies in emerging economies, representing a central hub for families and children. However, they attend less of the higher education system and are largely excluded from the business sector. This implies that one of the managing members of the household earns no income, contributing to a higher level of poverty in the general population. Thus, any initiative that aims to develop the business sector in emerging economies must be able to reach women. Thus, some specific actions are suggested, such as the development of training in soft skills, business and financial instruments, the creation of prizes for successful projects, the creation of groups of beneficiaries of financial products to be co-responsible for business development and debt repayment, and the implementation of conditions which imply that the creation of their own business does not jeopardize the stability of families.

As for young entrepreneurs, their constraints are associated with the lack of collateral, business experience, and knowledge of financial products. Such characteristics come up against the rigid and demanding procedures of financial institutions and other financiers. Thus, it is equally fundamental to increase a culture of entrepreneurship and continuous training in the area of management and financial products.

The European Microfinance Network (2012 and 2015) suggests the following financial solutions that are best suited to young people:

- Bank Financing:
    - Loans on favorable terms, with low or zero interest rates without requiring collateral. However, young entrepreneurs must demonstrate commitment, responsibility and ability to repay the loan and be able to present a business plan;
    - Microloans, most appropriate in situations where there is limited business experience and no collateral;
    - Loans with guarantees provided by the state where governments assume the credit risk involved in lending to young entrepreneurs.
- Equity Financing:
    - General reduction in administrative and legal costs to foster capital investment through personal savings or family resources;
    - Involvement of business angels, linking young entrepreneurs to funding sources, but at the same time acting as management consultants and facilitators with key contacts.
- As far as rural entrepreneurs are concerned, the approach to their insertion in the financial system should include:
    - Covering territories without financial services with mobile facilities that allow communication and relationship development with rural populations;
    - Developing partnerships between governments and banks to create financial products with low interest rates;
    - Continuous training throughout the credit process (before, during and after);
    - Partnerships along the value chain and the creation of cooperatives that allow a better link between producers and urban markets;
    - Creating groups of beneficiaries of the financial products to be co-responsible for the development of the business and the repayment of the debt;

- ◦ Defining customer segments according to income and asset levels to allow for more tailored products and avoid the risk of bankruptcy;
- ◦ Introducing information and communication technologies in credit institutions to reduce the costs of their activity and lower interest rates for the rural population with special needs in terms of transportation and communication costs.

In conclusion, in general, the studies and reports of international organizations consider that a greater financial integration of these most disadvantaged groups also requires a set of more comprehensive actions that make the entrepreneurial ecosystem more friendly to private initiative, such as:

- Debureaucratization of legal processes and their costs, for example, through the creation of one-stop-shop services that allow all the procedures to be carried out;
- Streamlining insolvencies;
- State participation through guarantees on operations;
- Continuous training in business and financing and coaching to ensure the effective transmission of knowledge;
- Facilitation of operating infrastructures such as incubators or shared work spaces that contribute to greater proximity between companies;
- Creation of opportunities for the dissemination of supply and conducting business through fairs or virtual markets for buying and selling products;
- Involvement of business associations and professional associations as promoters of promotional events or links between companies.

PRODESI AND THE FINANCING OF MSMES IN ANGOLA

The vision of the PRODESI program is to accelerate the diversification of the Angolan economy by promoting domestic production and thus substituting imports and increasing exports from sectors other than oil. In this way, by stimulating private initiative and, in particular, entrepreneurship and the inclusion of the neediest population, it is intended to contribute to the sustainability of the economy and change the balance of payments, increasing the amount of money in the financial system.

To achieve this vision, it is essential to guarantee the financing of business projects and, in this sense, to define the strategic priorities in terms of national production.

As such, in order to accelerate the diversification of national production and the generation of wealth and to channel financial resources more effectively, PRODESI has defined a set of specific productions and lines to be integrated in clusters that have greater potential for value generation and export and import substitution, namely:

- Food and agroindustry;
- Mineral resources;
- Oil and natural gas;
- Forestry;
- Textiles;
- Clothing and footwear;

- Tourism and leisure.

These clusters include 54 products that represent priority in terms of the development of business projects, since they can contribute more quickly to the substitution of imports and to the increase of exports.

Thus, PRODESI presents several plans for action that intend to ensure some fundamental dynamics to guarantee its purpose of diversification and increase of national production:

1. Intensively increase priority goods and services and generate productive lines through new suppliers of national goods and services, decreasing dependence on external suppliers;
2. Increase the internationalization of production resulting from priority production lines;
3. Promote the emergence of poles and clusters, that is, geographic or sectorial concentrations of interrelated companies, to create synergies throughout the value chain of the different economic activities;
4. Encourage the establishment of strategic business partnerships, national and international, that generate employment and direct investment, national and foreign, which contribute to the increase of technology, innovation and differentiating professional skills;
5. Promote public-private partnerships that safeguard the interests of the state and contribute to greater efficiency in public services.

Bearing in mind these dynamics and the defined vision, PRODESI intends to contribute to the following objectives defined in the National Development Plan 2021-2022:

1. Average annual growth of non-oil GDP greater than 5%;
2. Average annual growth of agriculture GDP higher than 7%;
3. Average annual growth of manufacturing industry GDP higher than 4%;
4. Average annual growth of energy GDP higher than 8%;
5. Increase the relative weight of non-oil exports in total exports from 5% to 15%;
6. 75% increase in the average annual Foreign Direct Investement (FDI), in relation to the annual average registered in the period 2009-2015;
7. Rise at least 20 places in the international classification of the business environment of the "Doing Business" Report, prepared by the World Bank.

Among the initiatives and actions foreseen for the operationalization of PRODESI, at the level of financing solutions that can boost it, Transversal Initiative 2: Encourage private investment can be highlighted. This includes 14 measures that are described in greater detail below, based on the text of the respective program:

1. Encourage the creation of financial products (credit, guarantees and transactional products) in the banking and insurance sectors;
2. Structure lines of credit, guarantee funds and investment funds oriented to the program;
3. Encourage the creation of financial products traded in the securities market directed to the hedging of exchange, physical and price risks of commercial transactions;
4. Encourage the creation of credit insurance to protect businesses against the commercial risk of non-receipt;

5. Encourage the creation of financial products to support exports on consignment, positioning the storage of products made in Angola in strategic locations;
6. Encourage the creation of financial products to support internationalization projects for Angolan companies, aimed at setting up production units in other countries for products being manufactured in Angola;
7. Increase financial support for the export of services, mainly transport services and ICT services;
8. Create state financing mechanisms for specific projects, through the signing of program contracts with precise clauses on the rights and duties of each party, deadlines, productive goals, and jobs to be created;
9. Update the Angola Investe Program (PAI), renewing it and creating the Angola Investe + Program, now more focused on import substitution and export diversification, with restructured and customized financial products tailored to each of the diversification priority products;
10. Create legislation for fiscal incentives, to promote the economic interest of export-oriented local production;
11. Create tax incentive legislation to promote the economic interest of import substitution oriented local production;
12. Create incentives and concrete projects to reduce the degree of informality of economic activities, reconverting the informal economy, especially in those activities which generate a large volume of employment;
13. Implement a prioritization mechanism for the allocation of foreign exchange resources to the Priority Programs of the Diversification of the Economy;
14. Define the paradigm and implement agreements to avoid double taxation, prioritizing their gradual implementation.

In the next section, the main sources of financing which are currently available for the diversification of the national economy are presented.

FINANCIAL PRODUCTS AVAILABLE IN ANGOLA FOR THE DIVERSIFICATION OF THE ECONOMY

Figure 1 shows the main sources of financing currently available in Angola, which are more directed towards the business environment and more specifically to MSMEs.

Below a characterization is provided of each of the financial products shown in the figure above.

Project to Support Credit (PAC):

The PAC intends to contribute to the financing of business projects that aim to develop activities at the level of the 54 assets considered as priority in PRODESI.

It is noteworthy that the PAC presents an integrated vision to support access to credit, contemplating activities upstream of obtaining credit, in the process of granting credit and downstream of its granting.

Upstream of obtaining credit, the involvement of the network of business service providers is expected in supporting the preparation of dossiers and economic and financial feasibility studies of projects that

Figure 1. Financial products targeted at MSMEs
Source: Authors

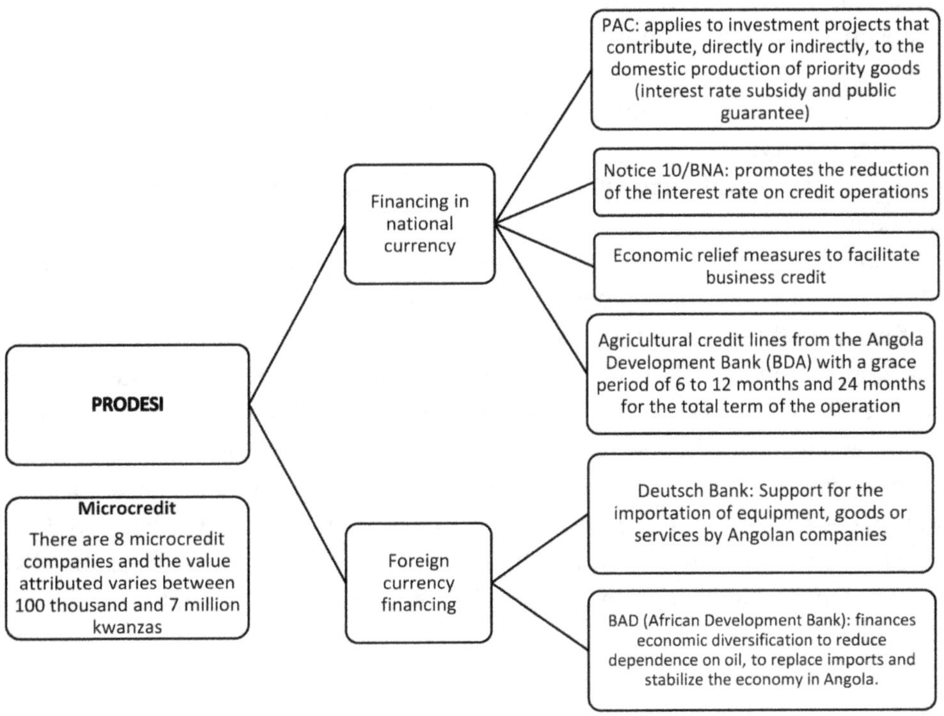

intend to access credit, as well as capacity building and training of promoters and managers of MSMEs in different skills in the area of business management.

In terms of the process of obtaining credit, the Risk Capital Fund and the Credit Guarantee Fund may be involved, should the promoters wish to access financing through venture capital and the support of credit guarantee companies to reduce the financial cost of operations. Simultaneously, the processes of obtaining credit are also analyzed by the commercial bank, with which the financial operation is contracted, and by the Development Bank of Angola (BDA), which will cover part of the value of this operation through another financial operation at a lower cost and payable later.

Finally, downstream of obtaining credit, there is expected to be a follow-up of the implementation of the projects, contributing to their physical and financial execution. In addition, the involvement of the judicial community is also foreseen, especially CREL (Center for Extrajudicial Dispute Resolution) to solve potential commercial litigation and insolvency cases more easily.

In addition to the projects having to be developed in businesses included in the list of 54 products identified in the PRODESI, the promoters must meet some eligibility conditions, such as having more than three years of activity for projects with turnover in the order of 3 million USD; in the case of start-ups the turnover should not exceed 1.5 million USD, the company must have organized accounting, the managers must have an exclusive employment contract and demonstrate good standing, and the project management team must demonstrate technical and management knowledge to drive the business.

The PAC is developed through nine protocoled banks that assure the commercial credits: BFA, BAI, BIC, Standard Bank, BMA, BNI, BCH, BIR, and BCI.

Regarding the operation of PAC support, it is based on the coordination of products from the different entities involved and mentioned above. It should be noted that, taking into consideration the 54 products referenced in the PRODESI, 16 investment areas were defined with specific financing conditions. Below are the different support that can be obtained under the PAC:

- Financing through venture capital: investment between 10% and 30% of the investment value in the companies' equity;
- Guarantee from the Credit Guarantee Fund: a public guarantee of up to 75% of the investment value can be granted;
- Financing through commercial banking: there are grace periods (between one and three years) where there are only interest payments. Afterwards, the financing obtained can be repaid over periods of between three and eight years;
- Financial support from the BDA: It finances between 50% and 75% of the interest and of the credit insurance that the company has contracted. In addition, it grants a grace period for the amount of interest charged and capital borrowed, equal to the maturity period of the operation contracted at the commercial bank. After the end of the first financial operation, the reimbursement of the loan to the BDA begins and the payment of the interest charged on the borrowed capital, calculated based on an interest rate with a value of 50% of the remuneration of the FND (National Development Fund). The repayment term of this second financial operation varies between three and five years.
  Notice nº 10:

Notice nº 10, published in the Diário da República I series nº 42 of April 3rd, defines a set of 26 priority products, of which investment projects presented by cooperatives and SMEs should be prioritized and have a maximum cost of 7.5%.

Economic Relief Measures for the Facilitation of Credit to Businesses

In order to mitigate the impact of the COVID-19 pandemic on the activity of MSMEs in the productive sector, financial resources in the amount of 488 billion kwanzas were made available, distributed by the following financial support initiatives:

- **Agrarian Development Support Fund (FADA):**

The FADA makes a line of credit of 15 billion kwanzas available for financing family farms, with interest rates no higher than 3%.

Characteristics of the financing:

- Amount of the line: 15 billion kwanzas;
- Term: negotiable case by case;
- Grace period (with interest payment): negotiable case by case;
- Interest rate: up to 3%.

- **BDA credit line for purchasing products for small and medium enterprises:**

The Development Bank of Angola (BDA), provides a credit line of 17.6 billion kwanzas to finance the purchases of trade and distribution operators from national producers of the following products: corn, wheat, rice, sugar, sugar cane, *massambala, massango, matata* rena, sweet potato, cassava, beans, *peanuts*, sunflower, soybeans, table banana, bread banana, mango, avocado, citrus, papaya, pineapple, tomato. onion garlic, carrot, eggplant, cabbage, cucumber, cabbage, beef, goat meat, sheep meat and pork, poultry, eggs (chicken), honey, horse mackerel, sardinella, sardines, tuna, *caxuxu*, corvinas, groupers, hake, *roncadore*, sole, swordfish, lobster, coastal prawn, shrimp, *alistado*, crab, cuttlefish, squid and octopus, *cacusso* (species of the genera *Oreochromis* and *Tilapia*) and catfish (*Clarias gariepinus*).

Characteristics of funding:

- Amount of the line: 17.6 billion kwanzas;
- Term: two years;
- Grace period (with interest payment): 180 days;
- Interest rate: 9%.

- **BDA credit line for product purchases by family cooperatives:**

The BDA makes a line of credit of 8.8 billion kwanzas available to finance the purchases of family producer cooperatives and small and medium-sized agribusinesses from suppliers of improved cereal, vegetable and tuber seeds, fertilizers, pesticides, vaccines and the provision of agricultural soil preparation and correction services.

Characteristics of funding:- Amount of the line: 8.8 billion kwanzas;

- Term: 2 years;
- Grace period (with interest payment): 180 days;
- Interest rate: 9%.

- **BDA credit line for modernization and expansion of family cooperatives:**

The Development Bank of Angola, BDA, is making a credit line of 13.5 billion kwanzas available to finance projects of modernization and expansion of the activities of a maximum number of 15 cooperatives per province (total of 270 cooperatives in the country), in the agriculture and fishing sectors.

- Characteristics of funding Amount of the line: 8.8 billion kwanzas;
- Limit: 50 million kwanzas per cooperative;
- Deadline: negotiable case by case;
- Grace period: negotiable case by case;
- Interest rate: 7.5%.

- **FACRA fund for cooperative equity capital:**

The Fundo Activo de Capital de Risco (FACRA), is making 3 billion kwanzas available to make equity investments in agriculture, livestock and fisheries cooperatives, participating in the payment of the equity portion required in the concession of loans, which will be made available by the BDA.

- **FACRA credit line to finance microfinance institutions:**

The Fundo Activo de Capital de Risco, FACRA, is making a credit line in the amount of 3 billion kwanzas available to finance microfinance societies, field schools, and community credit banks selected through public tender that intend to operationalize at the lowest possible cost a microcredit allocation process for women and young entrepreneurs in the following activities: agriculture, with emphasis on the production of cereals, pulses and oilseeds, roots and turmeric and vegetables; poultry farming; laying poultry; purchase of cattle for fattening and slaughter; food processing and beverage production; logistics and distribution of agri-food and fishery products, aquaculture; recycling of urban solid waste; provision of transport services; provision of professional training services; software development; tourism, cultural and artistic production. In addition, FACRA has an amount of 4 billion kwanzas available for the direct financing of startups through venture capital.

- **Stimulating lines of credit from commercial banks to cooperatives and SMEs:**

Commercial banks with net assets recorded on their balance sheet on December 31st of the year 2019, equal to or greater than 1.5 billion kwanzas, should finance a minimum number of 50 new credits during the year 2020 for cooperatives and small and medium enterprises in the production chain of one of the 54 products defined in the Credit Support Program (PAC) and PRODESI. Other commercial banks must finance a minimum number of 25 new credits for the same entities and purposes.

Agricultural Credit Lines from Banco de Desenvolvimento de Angola

The BDA has four lines of credit available directed to the agricultural sector, namely:

- Agricultural campaign credit, which aims to suppress short-term operational needs of MSMEs promoting agricultural projects, with a grace period of six to twelve months, a total repayment term of 24 months and a minimum MSME share of 5% to 20%;
- Agricultural machinery and equipment credit, which aims to meet the needs of fixed capital, such as machinery, equipment and means of transport and cargo, with a grace period of 12 to 24 months, a total repayment term of 60 months and a minimum MSME co-financing of between 5% and 20%;
- Infrastructure credit for agricultural production support, which aims to meet the fixed capital needs of agricultural holdings for the construction, rehabilitation or expansion of infrastructure and support structures for agricultural production, with a grace period of six to 24 months, a total repayment term of up to 120 months and a minimum MSME co-financing of between 10% and 20%;
- Credit for agricultural investment projects, which aims to finance root or expansion projects, with a need for fixed and working capital, with a grace period of up to 48 months, a total repayment term of up to 132 months and a minimum MSME co-financing of between 5% and 20%.

Note that access to all these types of credit requires collateral guarantees such as commercial pledges or consignment of revenues, among others.

Credit Line from Deutsch Bank

The aim is to promote and support the Angolan private sector in the import of equipment, goods or services essential to the implementation of investment projects in various sectors of activity, including agriculture, livestock, agro-industry, fisheries, manufacturing, and mining, with a minimum value of 10 million euros. The interest rate is negotiated in each operation.

Considering the amounts involved and the requirements to access the operations, it is considered that this product is not directed to MSMEs.

Credit Line from the African Development Bank Operationalized by BPC

This is a line of credit that aims to boost SMEs and business projects developed by women in the following sectors: agriculture, industry, energy and water, and sustainable fishing.

This line of credit finances up to 80% of the global value of the investment, with the following sectorial limits:

- 3,300,000.00 (farming);
- 4,400,000.00 (industry);
- 2.750,000.00 (energy and water);
- 3,850,000.00 (fishing).

There may be a grace period of up to 12 months and the repayment period ranges from two to eight years.

Regarding interest rates, there are two references:

- TB (treasury bonds) four years + margin up to 3% (Indexed to the USD);
- Luibor (Luanda's Interbank Fund Offering Rate) 12 months + margin up to 5%.

Finally, to access this credit line, collateral guarantees are required such as mortgages, pledges of equipment, or guarantors, among others.

Microcredit

There are eight micro-credit societies and the value assigned in the operations varies between 100 thousand and 7 million kwanzas. The investment projects covered by the microcredit program are: software development, food processing, agribusiness chain products and services, logistics and distribution of agri-food and fishery products, cultural and artistic production, and recycling of urban solid waste.

This program is very much associated with the formalization of the economy and had a strong boost at the time of the COVID-19 pandemic, as MSMEs suffered especially from this situation (e.g., difficulties in complying with tax obligations, availability of working capital, among others). Thus, the Angolan government has approved two micro-credit lines of 3 billion and 4 billion kwanzas. The first is directed to community credit banks and the financing is attributed through public tender and the second to MSMEs or micro-entrepreneurs in the production area of certain products considered a priority for the economy.

In the private component of micro-credit, the government has been working with commercial banks to develop specific financial products for MSMEs. These solutions are beginning to appear in a tentative way, through support for access to credit or financial inclusion.

The maximum ceiling of these operations is 7 million kwanzas. Normally the amount is paid in full at the beginning of the project. In general, the financed projects do not reach this ceiling and are normally financed in amounts between half a million and 3 million kwanzas.

Regarding guarantees, these operations normally require the domiciliation of salaries, the presentation of a bank statement for the last six months and the completion of a promissory note by the beneficiary.

The maturity of the operations varies between three and twelve months in the case of working capital, and 24 months in the case of fixed capital investments. The repayment is made in fixed monthly installments, of capital and interest automatically debited from the clients' accounts. Interest rates vary between 36% and 42.6% per year.

RESULTS OF PRODESI IN ACCESS TO FINANCING

Considering the Memorandum on Access to Credit of 3/06, until the beginning of June 2021, 1,413 projects were submitted to the bank in the scope of PRODESI, of which 784 were approved. In addition to this, 96 more projects were under negotiation with the banks. There is thus an approval rate of "PRODESI" projects in the banking sector of about 55.5%.

Regarding the 784 approved projects, these are distributed between the BNA's Aviso 10/2020 credit line with 236 approved projects, the Deutsche Bank credit line with 3 approved projects, the Credit Support Project credit line with 20 approved projects, and the line of credit for financing the purchase of agricultural (and fishing) inputs with 15 approved projects, the line of credit of financing imports of fertilizers with eight approved projects, the line of credit of the purchase of consumer goods of national origin with 212 approved projects, the line of credit of the cooperatives of the productive sector with 287 approved projects and other lines of credit with three approved projects.

From the approved projects, it was possible to obtain an approved amount of Kz649.7 billion which is distributed between the BNA's Aviso 10/2020 credit line with Kz490.25 billion approved, the Deutsche Bank's credit line with Kz82.14 billion approved, the Credit Support Project credit line with Kz35.01 billion approved, the line of credit for financing the purchase of agricultural (and fishing) inputs with Kz1.82 billion, the line of credit for financing the import of fertilizers with Kw16.69 billion, the line of credit for the purchase of consumer goods of national origin with Kw16.05 billion approved, line of credit of the cooperatives of the productive sector with Kw6.72 billion approved and other lines of credit with Kw1.02 billion approved. Table 3 summarizes this information and is presented below:

It can also be noted that there are 533 non-approved projects, i.e., projects that were rejected by the bank because they presented insufficiencies in the credit dossier, namely in terms of: inconsistencies in the business plan, lack of necessary documentation in the project, project/promoter risk. Of these, 34 projects were definitively rejected by the bank and 499 returned to the previous stage for reformulation.

In 2021, 128 projects have already been approved and are distributed across the BNA's Aviso 10/2020 credit line with 30 approved projects, the credit support project credit line with one approved project, the

Table 3. Total values of approved projects

Support Measures	Number of approved projects	Financing amounts (billion Kz)
Notice nº 10	236	490.25
Deutsche Bank	3	82.14
PAC	20	35.01
Agricultural Lines	23	18.51
Purchase of consumer goods	212	16.05
Cooperative lines	287	6.72
Other lines	3	1.02

Source: Authors

purchase of consumer goods of national origin credit line with 13 approved projects and the cooperatives credit line in the productive sector with 84 approved projects.

The projects approved in 2021 represent funding in the amount of Kz172.6 billion, distributed by the BNA's Aviso 10/2020 credit line with Kz169.52 billion, the Credit Support Project credit line with Kz0.50 billion, the credit line for the purchase of consumer goods of national origin with Kz0.93 billion and the line of credit for cooperatives in the productive sector with Kz1.66 billion approved. Below is a table with a summary of this information:

In terms of provinces, Luanda stands out as having the largest number of projects (467), representing a weight of 21.5% of the total, followed by Huíla (185) and Kwanza Sul (149) with a weight of 8.5% and 6.9%, respectively.

With regard to sectors of activity, agriculture clearly stands out as having the highest number of applications for funding, 1,180, with this sector representing 54.4% of the total number of projects submitted.

As for the analysis by the performance of the financial institutions, of the approved projects, 210 are awaiting disbursement and 574 have already been disbursed. The bank with the largest share in the number of projects disbursed is the BDA (433), followed by the BNI (24) and the BIC (20), representing 75.4%, 4.2% and 3.5%, respectively, of the total number of projects disbursed.

In terms of the amounts disbursed, the banks BIC, SCBA and BDA are the most significant, representing Kz54 billion (21.4%), Kz41 billion (16.3%), and Kz38 billion (15.1%), respectively.

Finally, according to the situation presented in the Project Management Office (PMO) of June 8th, analyzing the fulfillment of the repayments of contracted financial operations, it can be seen that there is a repayment rate of 35%, and the value of the overdue rents (1,306.75) is higher than that of the settled

Table 4. Values of approved projects in 2021

Support Measures	Number of approved projects	Financing amounts (billion Kz)
Notice nº 10	30	169,52
PAC	1	0,50
Consumer goods purchase	13	0,93
Cooperative lines	84	1,66

Source: Authors

Table 5. Amounts per microcredit institution

Microcredit Institutions	Number of approved projects	Financing amounts (billion Kz)
COOPERAFAJE	20	111 388 944
FÁCILCRED	582	537 406 515
GINGACRED	10	51 860 053
KIF CRÉDITO	21	80 708 000
KIXICRÉDITO	73	265 868 754
MULTICRÉDITO	14	52 417 570
NESPECRED	36	141 500 000
WILETE CRÉDITO	318	165 837 860

Source: Authors

rents (Kz705.91 M). These figures show high levels of default on loans granted, and there is room to optimize the design of the financial solutions available.

Still taking into account the PMO documentation of June 8, it is possible to conclude that 1,051 micro-credit projects were presented and approved in 2020, representing Kz1,207,000,000. In 2021 these values will be around 1,675 projects and Kz1,990,000,000.

Regarding the analysis by microcredit institution, the following table is presented with a summary of the data.

The table above shows that the institutions with the greatest weight in microcredit activity are Fácilcred and Wilete Crédito, as they have a much higher volume of projects than the other players (although in terms of value, Kixicrédito is the second most important). They are also the two institutions with the greatest social reach, because they also present the lowest value per operation, which means that their target audience is the most financially needy (Fácilcred assigns an average of Kz923,378 per loan and Wilete Crédito Kz521,502).

RECOMMENDATIONS AT THE LEVEL OF FINANCING SUPPORT TO MSMES IN ANGOLA

The execution of PRODESI has allowed for the dynamization of private initiative, with thousands of requests for financing already in place, both through banking and micro-finance institutions. Such dynamics are contributing to the economic diversification and to the progressive increase of national production.

However, there is some difficulty on the part of MSMEs in meeting their contractual obligations to credit institutions, which highlights the opportunity to make some adjustments in financial products and in the context conditions, allowing an improvement in the relationship between companies and the financial system.

Next, we present recommendations on the level of financing support to MSMEs, considering its framework in the two main types: credit and corporate equity.

Reinforcing Access to Credit

- Clear definition of credit product segments, dividing operations into trade finance (support for working capital needs) and the acquisition of fixed assets, enabling operations associated with the financing of companies' regular activity to have shorter maturities and, simultaneously, lower costs, reducing the banking risk and facilitating access to credit by MSMEs;
- Introduction of new financial products, factoring and leasing. On the one hand this will increase the bank's portfolio, generating more revenues for the financial sector and, on the other hand, it will allow companies to finance their normal operating cycle and acquire strategic assets in a less costly way and with further capacity to provide collateral;
- Development of the register of granted credits and a database of MSMEs involved in PRODESI in order to define customer segments according to their risk profile and project objective (e.g., business creation or expansion), contributing to the establishment of different ranges of financial operations in terms of interest rates, amounts and maturities. Financing lines with special conditions could even be created for MSMEs with the status of market leaders or excellence in order to valorize the winning projects;
- Involvement of business associations, youth institutions and cooperatives for the definition of financial operations involving groups of borrowers (both in banking and micro-credit institutions), using the Grameen Bank methodology of co-responsibility for credit management, reducing the risk of non-repayment of outstanding capital. Thus, the values of the credit operations will be higher, increasing the scale of operations, but allowing lower interest rates while maintaining the profitability of the financial institutions. On the other hand, as borrowers have the possibility of choosing the elements to be included in each credit group, they will establish relationships of trust and will try to fulfill their obligations as a way of not having their social reputation damaged regarding the rest of the group and the business associations or cooperatives of which they are part. Finally, the groups to be formed should favor players from the different stages of the value chain of the activity sectors, ensuring the creation of synergies and links between companies;
- Definition of financing modalities with an availability of capital in a logic of premium and achievement of objectives (for example, investment execution, turnover, job creation, operational results), according to a schedule defined with financial institutions. Thus, it is intended to direct the capital to the projects that are truly being carried out and contributing to the goals of PRODESI;
- Legal permission for micro-credit institutions to receive deposits, thereby increasing their income and thus being able to lower the interest rates on credits to be granted to micro entrepreneurs and the needy population;
- Definition of repayment modalities of the capital and interest payment in the credits granted to agricultural projects (which represent more than half of the approved projects) considering the seasonality of the harvests to adjust the payment of the capital and interest to the moments when the revenues are created. In these cases, repayment through constant, periodic installments may lead to default by companies at times when the business does not generate any revenue;
- Boosting the use of credit guarantee companies, so that there is greater risk sharing in financial operations negotiated with banks. Normally, the companies guarantee part of the financing value (for example, 80% or 75% of the loan value), in return for a guarantee commission and, in some cases (when the companies are mutual guarantee companies), the acquisition of a share of the

company by the company that requested the financing, thus becoming a shareholder (this reduces the company's risk and contributes to greater private involvement in the operations);

- In the case of agricultural projects or produced goods, real guarantees can also be applied based on products stored in a certain previously defined space. In addition, a provisioning receipt is issued which proves that these deposited goods are a guarantee for the creditor and that they cannot be sold or moved before the loans are repaid. Cooperatives can play an important role in making this type of guarantee more dynamic and contribute to lower interest rates on operations.

Strengthening Access to Equity Capital

- Stimulation of a network of incubators that provide acceleration programs where venture capital companies and business angels participate and entrepreneurs go through several levels of competition and presentation and development of their business plans, receiving prizes and funding according to their selection for the next stages;
- Implementation of online marketplaces where entrepreneurs will have the opportunity to present their projects and obtain funds through business angels, venture capital companies, and crowdfunding.

RECOMMENDATIONS AT THE LEVEL OF MSMES IN ANGOLA

In addition to the actions on the supply side of financing, it is essential to increase the level of business and financial literacy among MSMES in order to ensure greater effectiveness in the processes of applying for financing from banks and to ensure greater business management capacity. This will increase the survival rate of companies in the most disadvantaged groups such as young people, women and rural population.

Thus, it is essential that the MSMES ensure the sharing of knowledge on various topics related to business and finance. Some training priorities are suggested, among which the following can be highlighted:

- Conducting training actions in the topics of entrepreneurship, business models and plans, evaluation of investment projects, funding sources and internationalization;
- The program content, didactic resources and tools to be developed should be based on methodologies that favor the practice and resolution of real problems associated with business activity in Angola, reducing the complexity of the themes and optimizing the effectiveness of the sessions;
- Finally, the training actions should be complemented with a follow-up of human resources over time, contributing to greater effectiveness in the practical application of knowledge and better performance of the companies in their activity. To this end, training sessions should be complemented with mentoring sessions or on-the-job training.

CONCLUSION

In summary, it is also important to mention that on the supply side, proposals are being developed, based on an exhaustive diagnosis phase with the Angolan public and private banking sector. These will raise awareness and provide knowledge and tools that help banks support credit for Angolan MSMEs, thus promoting matching between supply and demand for credit.

In this context, the training of human resources in Angola should include the creation of tailor-made programs that include the development of a set of key skills in the field of technical knowledge. This will support effective risk analysis, as well as the ability to advise potential promoters on the most appropriate financial products, credit commitments and repayment plans.

On the other hand, the development of eminently practical training programs that favor the use of decision support tools, practical cases and examples that clearly illustrate the Angolan reality will be a pressing priority. It should be noted that much remains to be done in this area, given the scarcity of literature and studies that discuss this theme in the African continent and particularly in Angola.

ACKNOWLEDGMENT

This paper is financed by National Funds of the FCT – Portuguese Foundation for Science and Technology within the project «UID/ECO/04007/2019»

REFERENCES

Arias, C. A., Martínes, A. C., & Gracia, J. L. (2000). *Enfoques Emergentes en Torno en la Estrucutura de Capital: El caso de la Pyme*. Generalitat Valenciana.

Barai, M., & Adhikary, B. (2013). The Success of Microcredit in Bangladesh: Supplementing 'Group Lending' Explanation with Institutional Understanding. *Review of Integrative Business & Economics Research*, *2*(1), 471–490.

Beck, T., Maimbo, S., Faye, I., & Triki, T. (2011). *Financing Africa Through the Crisis and Beyond.* World Bank. doi:10.1596/978-0-8213-8797-9

Bertha Centre for Social Innovation & Entrepreneurship. (2018). *Innovative Finance in Africa*. Universidade do Cabo, África do Sul.

Chandrayanti, T., Nidar, S., Mulyana, A., & Anwar, M. (2019). Credit Accessibility Model of Small Enterprises Based on Firm Characteristics and Business Performance (Case Study at Small Enterprises in West Sumatra Indonesia). *International Journal of Entrepreneurship*, *23*(Special Issue), 1–14.

Dang, L., & Chuc, A. (2019). *Challenges in implementing the credit guarantee scheme for small and medium-sized enterprises: the case of Vietnam*. Asian Development Bank Institute.

European Microfinance Network. (2012). *EMN study for Youth entrepreneurship*. European Microfinance Network.

European Microfinance Network. (2015). *European Good Practices in rural microfinance*. European Microfinance Network.

Fal, M. (2013). Accelerating Entrepreneurship in Africa. *Innovations*, *8*(3/4).

Flannery, M. J. (1986). Asymmetric Information and Risky Debt Maturity Choice. *The Journal of Finance*, *41*(1), 19–37. doi:10.1111/j.1540-6261.1986.tb04489.x

GEM. (2013). *GEM ANGOLA 2013 – Estudo sobre o empreendedorismo*. Global Entrepreneurship Monitor.

Gião, R. (2018). *Financiamento das PME- Estudo de caso à Gomes, Sobral & Filhos, lda*. Dissertação de Mestrado manuscript. Instituto Politécnico de Setúbal.

Gustafson, S., & Khandker. (2016). *How microfinance has reduced rural poverty in Bangladesh*. IFPRI.

Hulme, D., & Moore, K. (2007). Why has Microfinance been a Policy Success in Bangladesh? In A. Bebbington & W. McCourt (Eds.), *Development Success*. Palgrave Macmillan. doi:10.1057/9780230223073_5

Hussain, A. (2019). Disciplining Microfinance Borrowers in Bangladesh. *Social Change*, *49*(3), 453–468. doi:10.1177/0049085719863890

IAPMEI. (2006). *PME na Estrutura Empresarial Nacional*. www.iapmei.pt

IFC. (2014). *CASE STUDY Garanti Bank SA: Combining SME Banking Excellence with a Proposition for Women Entrepreneurs in Turkey*. World Bank.

IFC. (2020). *Microfinance*. Available on: www1.ifc.org

IIPM. (2006). Case Study on SIDBI – A Successful Financial Institution in SME Financing. Indian Institute of Planning and Management (IIPM) Ahmedabad.

Kamau, K. (2011). *Factors influencing SMEs access to finance: A case study of Westland Division, Kenya*. Munich Personal RePEc Archive.

Kane, A., Marcus, A., & McDonald, R. L. (1985). Debt Policy and the Rate of Return Premium to Leverage. *Journal of Financial and Quantitative Analysis*, *20*(4), 479–499. doi:10.2307/2330763

Kong, X., Si, D., Li, H. & Kong, D. (2021). Does access to credit reduce SMEs' tax avoidance? Evidence from a regression discontinuity design. *Financial Innovation*, *7*(18).

Korner, P. (2006). *The determinants of corporate debt maturity structure: Evidence from Czech firms*. Czech *Journal of Economics and Finance*. Charles University Prague.

Leland, H., & Pyle, D. (1977). Informational Asymmetries, Financial Structure and Financial Intermediation. *The Journal of Finance*, *32*(2), 371–387. doi:10.2307/2326770

Magembe, Y. (2017). Credit Access by Small and Medium Enterprises in Tanzania: A Case Study of Dar es Salaam City. *International Journal of Economics & Management Sciences*, *6*(5), 1–9. doi:10.4172/2162-6359.1000459

Ministério da Economia e do Planeamento (2018). PRODESI. Available on: https://prodesi.ao/

Modigliani, F., & Miller, M. H. (1963). Corporate Income Taxes and the Cost of Capital: A Correction by. *The American Economic Review*, *53*(3), 437–447.

Mollah, M. (2020). *Loan Disbursement Procedure of Grameen Bank*. Daffodil International University.

Myers, S. C. (1977). Interactions of Corporate Financing and Investment Decisions - Implications for Capital Budgeting. *The Journal of Finance*, *29*(1), 1–25. doi:10.1111/j.1540-6261.1974.tb00021.x

Myers, S. C. (1984). The Capital Structure Puzzle. *The Journal of Finance*, *39*(3), 575–592. doi:10.2307/2327916

Myers, S. C., & Majluf, N. S. (1984). Corporate Financing and Investment Decisions. When Firms have information that investors do not have. *Journal of Financial Economics*, *13*(2), 187–221. doi:10.1016/0304-405X(84)90023-0

Nadeem, T., & Rasool, R. (2018). Marketing: the crucial success factor for Pakistan's credit guarantee scheme. Asian Development Bank Institute.

OCDE. (2015). *New Approaches to SME and Entrepreneurship Financing: Broadening the Range of Instruments*. OCDE.

Ogoy, H. (2016). *Strategies for Accessing Credit by Small and Medium Enterprises* (Unpublished master's thesis). Walden University.

Ojah, K., & Mokoteli, T. (2010). Possible Effective Financing Models for Entrepreneurship in South Africa: Guides from Microfinance and Venture Capital Finance. *African Finance Journal*, *12*(1), 1–26.

Paschen, J. (2016). Choose wisely: Crowdfunding through the stages of the startup life cycle. *Business Horizons*, 1–10.

Pham, H. (2017). Determinants of New Small and Medium Enterprises (SMEs) Access to Bank Credit: Case Study in the Phu Tho Province, Vietnam. *International Journal of Business and Management*, *12*(7), 83–99. doi:10.5539/ijbm.v12n7p83

Psico, J. (2010). *Microfinanças - Solução para o Combate à Pobreza?* Escolar Editora.

Rahman, A., & Ley, A. (2020). Micro-credit vs. Group savings – different pathways to promote affordable housing improvements in urban Bangladesh. *Habitat International*, *106*, 106. doi:10.1016/j.habitatint.2020.102292

Rahman, W. (2011). Comparison of Microcredit Models in China and Bangladesh – the Implication for Institutional Sustainability. *World Applied Sciences Journal*, *14*(2), 245–255.

Recomendação da Comissão. (2003). *361/CE, de 6 de Maio de 2003*. Comissão Europeia.

Shneor, R., Zhao, L., & Flåten, B. (2020). *Advances in Crowdfunding - Research and Practice*. Palgrave MacMillan. doi:10.1007/978-3-030-46309-0

SMEFINANCE. (2020). *Improving SMEs' access to finance and finding innovative solutions to unlock sources of capital*. World Bank.

Teixeira, N., & Brites, R. (2020). A estrutura de capital das empresas portuguesas exportadoras para o mercado comunitário. Jornadas Luso-Espanholas de Gestão Científica; Bragança.

Teixeira, N., & Rodrigues, E. (2013). Microfinanças - Sustentabilidade Financeira versus Alcance Social na África Subsariana. *XIII Congresso do Instituto Internacional de Custos*.

Terano, R., Mohamed, Z., & Jusri, J. (2015). Effectiveness of microcredit program and determinants of income among small business entrepreneurs in Malaysia. *Journal of Global Entrepreneurship Research*, *5*(1), 1–14. doi:10.118640497-015-0038-3

Titman, S., & Wessels, R. (1988). The Determinants of Capital Structure Choice. *The Journal of Finance*, *43*(1), 1–21. doi:10.1111/j.1540-6261.1988.tb02585.x

Zaman, H. (2004). The Scaling-Up of Microfinance in Bangladesh: Determinants, Impact, and Lessons. World Bank Policy Research Working Paper 3398.

KEY TERMS AND DEFINITIONS

African Countries: Countries located on the African continent.

Financial Services Curricula: Provide a set of contents to a better understanding and analyse of the Financial supply and tools for entrepreneurs and families.

Training: Series of lessons to teach the skills and knowledge for a particular job or activity.

Chapter 2
Distance Education in Higher Education:
Modern Applications and Management Courses

Carolina Nunes Castro
Polytechnic Institute of Setúbal, Portugal

Luísa Cagica Carvalho
https://orcid.org/0000-0002-9804-7813
Polytechnic Institute of Setúbal, Portugal & CEFAGE, University of Évora, Portugal

Sandrina B. Moreira
https://orcid.org/0000-0003-2124-8366
Polytechnic Institute of Setúbal, Portugal

ABSTRACT

Distance education became a reality, increasingly based on higher education. The pandemic context (COVID-19) that devastated many countries and the whole world in general proved this reality and presented a different proposal in education and even in people's lives. It has changed the educational system, and there has been much discussion about e-learning and remote teaching in digital learning environments, yet they are quite different terms. This chapter aims to study what exists to date about distance learning in higher education, with a special focus on business administration courses. To get the full benefit of online learning, new strategies and learning methodologies are applied, and information and communication technology can play a fundamental role here.

INTRODUCTION

Distance Education (DE) has already existed for more than 150 years, although its practices have been more commonly adopted in training and learning contexts during the pandemic period by Higher Educa-

DOI: 10.4018/978-1-7998-8239-8.ch002

tion Institutions (HEIs) focused on face-to-face teaching. This new context brought new challenges to the management of these HEIs, as well as to the adaptation of the academic community, teachers and students, to this new teaching-learning model (technology, assessment systems, teaching strategies, etc.).

This chapter seeks to briefly describe the main phases that gave rise to DE and, in addition, it also seeks to present this concept in a comprehensive way from the perspective of Higher education. Throughout this approach, several similar terms associated with DE are presented and a relevant distinction is also made for a term that is naturally suited to the pandemic context of Covid-19. In addition to the general definition of the concept, the characteristics that distinguish it from others are presented as well as possible barriers that may limit it. After a briefly exploration of the topic and their modern applications, this chapter seeks to contextualize theory with management courses, such as accounting, marketing, and human resource management.

The meaning of the word "teaching" highlights the role of the teacher in the learning process and comprises all activities that impart knowledge, facts, ideas or skills (Anohina, 2005). However, Higher Education has changed in recent years. In fact, teachers are no longer the center of the learning process. It is therefore important to situate teachers and students in Higher Education in time and space. Currently, students are at the center of this process, and the preference for traditional methodologies begins to be questioned and, therefore, teachers use new methodologies to stimulate creativity, teamwork and skills. Thus, within the classroom, students do their activities with due preparation beforehand, using active methodologies (Martínez-Jiménez & Ruiz-Jiménez, 2020). In this sense, throughout the approach followed in this chapter, traditional and active methodologies are presented, both of which are currently applicable in the teaching learning process. Regarding these methodologies, a clear distinction is made between the role of the teacher and the student in the process, and a parallelism is also made between the DE modality and its alternative, which naturally offers another type of advantages. Furthermore, there is an attempt to elucidate the change in thinking and resource management, especially when the more active perspective is referred to, and two different types of methodologies (flipped classroom and blended learning) are mentioned.

In the context of HEIs that offer management courses and whose relationship with the environment is a recurring practice, this teaching modality, especially during the periods of confinement in this pandemic context, proved to be particularly challenging. In fact, such context had repercussions in a set of limitations in terms of contacts within the scope of applied research in co-creation, particularly in the initial period, in which there was no established protocol of action. However, there has also been a mutual learning between the parties, in order to enable new practices that involve digitalization. It is therefore important to relate the Virtual Learning Environment (VLE) with Information and Communication Technologies (ICTs) and with the interaction and communication between teachers and students of Higher Education management. This chapter will list some possible strategies regarding the VLE, in order to make the teaching-learning process more effective.

METHODOLOGY

This chapter aims to analyze some scientific publications on DE in Higher Education, attending management courses. Initially, a list of documents was prepared in a database (Scopus), based on some criteria that justified the validation of those documents, like the procedure for choosing certain keywords in the search area. Thus, some "direct" terms to the study were used, such as "distance", "education", "online", "learning", "higher" and "e-learning", linked to an additive code "AND" ("distance" AND education" AND "online" AND "learning" AND "higher" AND "e-learning").

It was necessary to identify some highly regarded authors for the definition of DE. In order to facilitate the search, the option "Search within" in Scopus was selected: article title, abstract and keywords. In addition, it was selected some subject areas linked to the Management area, such as Social Sciences, Computer Science and Business, Management and Accounting and also some document and source types, such as articles, reviews and journals.

After a careful reading it was verified that not all search results had appropriate content, so those were automatically rejected. In addition, some articles were selected (from the most cited article to the least cited, through the option "cited by highest") and then the references were consulted and several repeated authors were detected.

After picking up some names of repeated and highly cited authors, some limitations were detected. In fact, sometimes the articles return more information than intended. For instance, the terms "remote teaching" and "distance education" have been compared lately, in particular the aspects that distinguish them and the possibility of adoption in the post-Covid-19 period. In this sense, the edit option was selected and the term "remote learning" was added as a keyword in the search area. In fact, a few articles on the subject were returned however only three articles were exclusively related to Higher Education. For this reason, only those three articles were registered and analyzed, taking into account that the remaining articles (false positives) included other academic levels, especially basic education.

These steps allowed for the exclusion and admission of articles and reviews according to the limitations mentioned above. The publications obtained through the observation of the keywords most used by the authors were grouped by contexts, in an attempt to restrict the subjects (through the "filter by keyword" option) in order to later align the authors' ideas to conduct the literature review.

DISTANCE EDUCATION – DEFINITION, ADVANTAGES AND BARRIERS

The definition of López-Pérez et al. (2011) about DE is possibly one of the most popular. The authors state that this is a teaching modality that allows individuals who are geographically separated to learn. On the other hand, Moore (1990) mentions that this geographical separation can be replaced by dialogue through electronic or printed media. One of the most assertive definitions was given by Keegan (1986), who states that DE is more than a teaching mode or method. The author goes further by saying that DE is a system. Among the definitions, theories also appear, namely the transactional distance theory formulated by Moore and Kearsley (2005), which stresses that distance is a pedagogical phenomenon and not just a matter of geographical distance.

Going back to the 1950s and 1960s, television became a new medium of instruction, which initiated a period of studies that compared it to traditional classroom instruction. Similarly, various forms of computerized instruction (1970s and 1980s), multimedia (1980s and 1990s), teleconferencing (1990s) were another means of comparison in an attempt to assess their effectiveness (Bernard et al., 2004). It should be noted that these forms of teaching presented are associated with a more traditional DE, since the non-traditional form already encompasses more advanced technology, as well as more prepared individuals (either through the experiences they have had, or by force of necessity), which only happened more notoriously from the beginning of the 21st century.

Correspondence courses began in England in the mid-nineteenth century; online and blended learning emerged in the 1990s with the advent of the Internet and the World Wide Web (Palvia et al., 2018). It is important to frame the acceptance of the DE modality in the world and, according to the authors, there are some countries that have been producing more and more scientific content and standing out:

- The United States of America (USA), after a fall in expectations for online education in 1998, took advantage of this failure and introduced blended learning a year later. In other words, from a mistake came a new experiment.
- India, one of Asia's developing countries, only experimented with online education in 2008; however, studies show that the country is looking to improve and mainstream online education and, with the active participation of the government, is expected to see continued growth in the coming years.
- Middle Eastern countries have been very reticent about online learning, which may be related to poor Internet access, disbelief in the modality and the lack of online repositories in Arabic. Currently, Saudi Arabia, in partnership with HEIs, has strongly promoted e-learning in the country.
- Australia and New Zealand have also recognized online learning as a tool with potential for learning and, in a technologically rich context, are witnessing a growing popularity of online learning programmes.
- Countries such as South Africa, Ghana and Malawi have been leading movements for online education on the continent with the support of government policies that promote the modality.

New technologies have the potential to overcome three major problems associated with traditional DE: rescuing isolated students, giving them the possibility of being able to interact with teachers and other students throughout the process; providing easy access to libraries and other information resources; and updating study materials (Guri-Rosenblit, 2005). Bernard et al. (2004) argue that DE was once seen as a reasonable alternative to face-to-face teaching, especially for students who were constrained by travel or time or circumstances. However, they agree regarding the potential of technology, stating that the expression "learning anywhere and anytime", essentially promoted by the media and by new technologies, has placed traditional education institutions in an intense competition for online education institutions.

DE is differentiated from other modes of education. Thus, Anohina (2005), Bernard et al. (2004) and Keegan (1980) agree that in DE there is a different planning and preparation of classes; the use of technical means connects teachers and students and also improves the acquisition of content; and, finally, the provision of two-way media facilitates dialogue and interaction among all.

According to Simonson et al. (2011) and Martins and Nunes (2016), DE in Higher Education, compared to face-to-face education, has several characteristics and barriers (Table 1), of which the following stand out:

Distance education, remote teaching and e-learning are different approaches that should be made clear from the outset. DE has been around for more than 150 years and has gone through several phases: first, correspondence study, with the use of printed media of instruction and communication; second, the use of analogue media; and third, the use and integration of digital technologies of instruction and communication (Simonson et al., 2011). It should be noted that, throughout the third phase, other terms like DE have emerged and are often applied out of context, as is the case of remote learning or electronic learning itself (or e-learning as it is usually called).

Table 1. Characteristics and barriers of DE in higher education

	Characteristics of DE in Higher Education	Barriers of DE in Higher Education
Simonson et al. (2011)	DE is just as effective as face-to-face when it comes to student outcomes.	Greater commitment to time management.
	Students already familiar with DE generally have a more favorable attitude towards this teaching modality than students in traditional education, because the former feel that they learn as much as if they were in a classroom.	Cash is needed to implement programs adapted to DE.
	Each form of technology linked to DE has advantages and disadvantages regarding the quality of the learning experience.	Organizational resistance to change.
	Students who are accustomed to DE tend to be intrinsically motivated and have the notions of control and flexibility very present.	Shared preconceptions about DE in the organization.
	While interaction seems intuitively important to the learning experience, interaction should always have a purpose.	Lack of strategic planning for DE.
	Focusing on collaboration and interaction in a group can be more important than focusing only on individual participation.	Slow pace of implementation.
		Compensation and/or incentives are needed for faculty.
		Difficulty in keeping up with technological changes.
		Lack of classrooms, laboratories or technology-enhanced infrastructure.
Martins and Nunes (2016)		Organizational practices are generally resistant to change.
		The pace of teaching is subject to the immediacy that is characteristic of online interaction.
		Teachers' extra work is often undervalued and they should therefore have career progression reviews and some incentives.
		Little synchronicity regarding know-how from a virtual point of view.
		Lack of knowledge about the expectations of students about the modality.

Source: Own construction based on Simonson et al. (2011) and Martins and Nunes (2016)

E-learning is a form of learning supported by digital technologies and assumes the absence of the teacher and students (Al-Qahtani & Higgins, 2013). However, it is not intended exclusively for students who attend DE, i.e. it is transversal to any level of education according to the individual's needs, either within the scope of in-class activities, seminars, laboratory activities, projects, or simply to solve online tests and exams (Guri-Rosenblit, 2005). According to Sun et al. (2008) e-learning is an alternative to traditional face-to-face teaching. Many institutions implement e-learning to meet the needs of students, especially those with full-time employment, i.e. Higher Education students.

The term "online learning" presupposes the use of a network, so the term "Internet-based learning" is considered a subset of the term "online learning", which is not the case with the term "Computer-based learning" because there is no connection to a network. E-learning occurs through any electronic medium, so online learning and computer-based learning are subsets of e-learning. The term 'distance learning' is broader than e-learning as it encompasses both non-electronic (e.g. written correspondence) and technology-based learning (Anohina, 2005).

In turn, the term remote learning differs from the term DE because the former describes a peculiar situation that poses some pedagogical and logistical challenges. To safely and innovatively deal with a peculiar situation (for example, the Covid-19 pandemic), alternative approaches and solutions have to be defined, which is not an easy task for those who transition from conventional educational settings to some form of DE or hybrid approach, one of the main concerns being the use of synchronous technologies (Barton, 2020). For some, the lack of knowledge about the evolution of DE leads to it being easily equated with the term remote learning (Bonk, 2020). In other words, remote learning is not a deliberate choice; rather, it represents a solution or an alternative to a particular circumstance. According to Johnson et al. (2020), the rapid transition that Higher Education faced during the Covid-19 pandemic differs from a mere planned online experience, with even the most experienced faculty members in DE using new teaching methods to deal with the challenges presented.

APPROACHES TO DISTANCE LEARNING - TRADITIONAL AND ACTIVE METHODOLOGIES

According to Bernard et al. (2004), some authors believe that DE is the "poor relation" of teaching modalities, especially when compared to traditional classroom alternatives. Al-Qahtani & Higgins (2013) suggest that the physical absence of a teacher can be a disadvantage in some e-learning contexts, particularly when students are more used to a traditional approach, which makes this teaching modality more limited. However, López-Pérez et al. (2011) argue against the radical nature of these facts by stating that a greater motivation to study a subject from e-learning activities brings a greater degree of motivation to face-to-face activities. And the same could be said of the reverse of the situation. In other words, traditional methodologies support and enhance active methodologies, and vice versa.

Traditional methodologies assume that direct instruction is on the teacher's side, with the student having to perform an activity to deepen his/her knowledge and, therefore, the teacher plays an active role as an information source and the student plays a passive role and needs to work at home to consolidate what has been learned (Martínez-Jiménez & Ruiz-Jiménez, 2020). Active methodologies are a more modern approach to teaching and aim to replace or complement the so-called traditional methodologies. As the methodology is called active it means that it will necessarily require more flexibility and adaptability from students and teachers. It is important to mention, however, that the adoption of this type of methodologies does not depend on the type of education (distance or face-to-face), although digital formats and tools are increasingly appearing as instruments to support its implementation.

It is true that the application and implementation of active methodologies should be very well considered, since there is some concern, to a greater or lesser extent, regarding the use of criteria related to these methodologies, namely the form of assessment. Moreover, adopting this new approach is a gradual process and this is due, above all, to the passive learning habits that are proper and residual of the traditional classroom, where learning requires a less proactive effort. In this sense, only the most motivated and proactive students perform better in relation to active methodologies (Chen et al., 2014).

One of the active methodologies is the flipped classroom methodology. In this context, Huang and Lin (2017) refer that the classrooms are free for practical work, but before the students have an online lecture of the contents. During the practical class, in the classroom, students can help each other, so it is a methodology that benefits all students. The authors Martínez-Jiménez & Ruiz-Jiménez (2020) and Ahmed & Indurkhya (2020) reinforce this idea, mentioning that students take on new roles and develop new skills. As for the teacher, he/she has more opportunities to invest time in interacting with students, answering their questions and supporting them in problem solving (Ahmed & Indurkhya, 2020).

It is difficult to integrate each student's learning styles into the classroom. The flipped classroom allows the teacher to present options that appeal to most learning styles while still maintaining control over course coverage and content (Lage et al., 2000). Still, students become the active participants and the center of the learning process. They have to learn to manage their time working online and, consequently, they become more autonomous and motivated than if they were in a traditional classroom (Lopes & Soares, 2018).

As an example, it is possible to say that the flipped classroom methodology offers a solution through remote teaching to help meet the needs arising from a global health emergency. In addition, it is a good methodology to support individual performance, through digital tools that guarantee social distancing and ensure that teachers and students stay in touch. However, the application of this methodology requires the identification of students with economic and social difficulties, as well as the provision of material resources and training focused on active methodologies for all teaching staff (Izagirre-Olaizola & Morandeira-Arca, 2020).

The flipped classroom is a change in thinking about teaching and resource management. It would be interesting for Higher Education students to be informed about this methodology in order to reflect on the opportunities it provides and the extent to which it fits and adapts to the course (Brewer & Movahedazarhouligh, 2018).

It is true that teamwork can have an impact on motivation and results in methodologies such as the flipped classroom (Huang & Lin, 2017). Shyer students feel more comfortable working in small groups, where they do not have as much resistance in bringing their ideas, than in larger groups (Martínez-Jiménez & Ruiz-Jiménez, 2020). In addition, this methodology allows Higher Education students to learn at their own pace and to have flexibility when working with electronic resources; it allows enough class time for more robust discussion and problem solving; and it allows for greater autonomy on the part of students to intervene in activities (O'Flaherty & Phillips, 2015).

The flipped classroom methodology, for example, is a methodology that involves greater attendance and participation of students compared to the traditional methodology and this may be the reason why some students do not like the change and prefer to take exams in final assessment. In this sense, teachers should moderate the amount of work proposed to students, so as not to make them feel overloaded. The implementation of this new methodology brings yet another challenge: teachers should move away from their traditional role, reducing explanations; they should thus propose more assignments such as debates (Martínez-Jiménez & Ruiz-Jiménez, 2020).

Another active methodology is blended learning. This methodology differs from the previous one (flipped classroom), since in blended learning the teaching activities are separated, sometimes in the classroom, sometimes online, without ever being obliged to follow a criterion or a specific teaching strategy in each one of them. One of the factors that is identical in both methodologies is motivation because, according to Bernard et al., (2014), it encourages and stimulates interest and, consequently, makes the results more positive. In addition, motivation makes students more willing to share knowledge and solve collective problems, which will lead them to achieve goals more effectively (Lin et al., 2020). Another formulation, now made by Rovai and Jordan (2004), states that blended learning is learning that includes the conveniences of the online world without the total loss of face-to-face contact.

Blended learning aims at least two objectives: reaching students through technologies and promoting a strong sense of community among students. In effect, this type of environment becomes more learning-centered, with a focus on active learning through collaboration (Rovai & Jordan, 2004).

According to Garrison and Kanuka (2004), a clear policy and strong leadership leads to a faster evolution regarding this methodology in HEIs. The authors point out some suggestions to increase competitive advantages:

- Monitoring the transformations resulting from blended learning, as these are important to use as measures of change. This monitoring concerns learning outcomes, students' satisfaction and achievement.
- Evaluation of the effects of blended learning in relation to critical and reflective thinking, as these are a priority.
- In addition to the evaluation of learning outcomes, the learning process should also be evaluated.
- Finally, as this methodology is explored, it is still important to evaluate its effectiveness.

LEARNING ENVIRONMENTS AND INFORMATION AND COMMUNICATION TECHNOLOGY (ICT)

There is a growing concern in dealing with diversity and equity in educational systems, especially in Higher Education. In fact, there are still many doubts about if and how equity can be improved in VLEs, especially when the flipped classroom methodology is applied (Ahmed & Indurkhya, 2020). For Chizmar & Walbert (1999), technologies do not fail to be a good starting point as they allow students to choose diverse experiences in order to find the approach that best suits the way they learn. They can collaborate in groups or work alone, free from constraints of place and time.

ICT applied in educational settings are also known by different terms, such as web-based learning, computer-mediated communication, telematic environments, e-learning, virtual classrooms, online instruction, I-Campus, electronic communication, cyberspace, computer-driven interactive communication or education without boundaries (Guri-Rosenblit, 2005).

DE is carried out through any Information and Communication Technology, as these allow remote learning: correspondence, television, telephone, audio conferencing, videoconferencing, radio, satellite broadcasts, videos or even fax (Anohina, 2005).

From the perspective of Arbaugh et al., (2010), more time online means more work and less quality of life for everyone, often leading to computer-related physical problems such as neck and back strain and eye strain, as well as symptoms associated with physical and psychological stress. Conversely, the opportunity to organize work on an "anytime, anywhere" basis can result in benefits such as flexibility to manage family commitments as well as schedule other work-related activities. However, from the teachers' perspective, the transition to a VLE in Higher Education interferes with the amount of work (it means a longer schedule in the preparation of online resources besides teaching the classes) and also some conflicts always arise regarding the modes of teaching, as they are often not synchronized with the demands of online interaction and immediacy (Martins & Nunes, 2016).

In this context, Martins and Nunes (2016) suggest some strategies that regulate e-learning learning in HEIs:

- Synchronize tasks to create courses that adapt and quickly decide which content, resources, tools, and interaction strategies best suit the needs of students at different times.
- Review the academic period (semesters and quarters), as well as the allocation of credits per subject.
- Consider the terms of performance appraisal and career progression of teachers, considering the increased workload or amount of work.
- Regulate expectations for faculty and student interaction in order to sustain productive engagement and homogeneity in the experience.

Resistance and preconception about the modality of DE could have compromised a better performance of teachers considering the unexpected context of Covid-19 pandemic, but even in the absence of an instituted protocol it's clear that HEIs have maintained the level of students' motivation. The fact that students prefer face-to-face interaction does not mean that online contact is considered a drawback in Higher Education, but rather a challenge. Moore and Kearsley (2005) follow a transactional distance theory and suggest that distance is a pedagogical phenomenon and not just a matter of geographical distance. It is possible to say that there has been mutual learning between the parties in the sense of enabling new practices that involve digitalization, such as the introduction of social media.

From the perspective of Rueda et al. (2017), the new digital world requires students, especially those in Management Higher Education courses, to determine which technological resources should be used to improve learning and student satisfaction. The authors distinguish two types of resources for a targeted use in the area of Management: traditional teaching technologies and social media applications. Traditional teaching technologies are more conventional and less interactive platforms, specific to the course (for example, the Moodle platform, email or even a teacher's web page). These technologies allow a direct connection to the course at any time (e.g. Moodle), aiming to facilitate communication and sharing of material between teachers and students. Social media applications refer to networks such as Facebook, Twitter and YouTube, which have a much more interactive and enticing side given their popularity. All of these resources can be used to enhance and complement the frequent traditional methodologies of face-to-face classes.

Currently, there are more modern distance education technology tools, such as social networks, which create opportunities to meet a global demand. But this path is often oriented to meet the needs of the technology providers themselves who focus on reducing costs and improving efficiency, which sometimes compromises quality (Anderson & Rivera-Vargas, 2020). The goal is not only to help students achieve their goals, but also to make them aware of information and digital competence as these will impact their personal and professional lives (Sales et al., 2020). The advancement of digital technologies in Higher Education is challenging traditional teaching, but on the other hand, it is also offering dynamic and innovative opportunities for student learning (O'Flaherty & Phillips, 2015).

According to Sales et al. (2020), information and digital competence should be part of the universities' strategic plan and institutional commitment. It is necessary to have teachers with continuous training related to this type of competencies, since they will be reflected in the training offered to students.

In fact, information and digital competence should be present from an early stage in Higher Education. However, the authors point out that technology may be important, but critical thinking is essential, as it allows students to progress based on personal autonomy. The prolonged use of technology, which comes from stages prior to Higher Education, configures quite technical skills and even a predisposition towards digital, but this is rarely accompanied by a solid knowledge base related to good practices in the use, management and production of information. This means that students arrive at Higher Education with a profound need to improve this critical-reflexive aspect. Anderson and Garrison (1995) agree on this issue of critical thinking. They also state that the simple use of technology ensures little at this level and that teachers should actively create opportunities to promote sustained interaction among all, in order to develop thinking skills worthy of Higher Education.

A tool such as "Zoom" was implemented and used by many educational institutions and organizations during the Covid-19 pandemic (Bonk, 2020). These types of tools can be used in learning contexts, helping to facilitate the students' learning process and improve academic achievement (Gonçalves et al., 2020). However, there are not always enough resources and technological infrastructures in full working order. In addition, teachers may not have training focused on synchronous technology and pedagogical approaches. The scenario may worsen when students have to share the Internet with family members or other people living in the same household, as well as when they have to share work space (Bonk, 2020). The inclusion of innovative technology accompanies the transition to a different learning context, as it did during the Covid-19 pandemic, and should be based on facilitating the learning process.

Podcasting supports international students in developing their skills. International students, whose first language is not English, often find it difficult to acquire these skills during their first year. These students can often record and repeat lessons. As such, podcasts are a positive reinforcement in their learning (Evans, 2008).

It is known that what increases student engagement is the quick availability of learning materials, the updating of course content information, and the quick responses to questions through ICT (e.g., Moodle and e-mail). Student engagement improves learning performance, i.e. students are more motivated to participate and learn. Student learning outcomes in turn increase student satisfaction with the teacher, the course and the teaching method. Acquiring critical knowledge and developing management skills, through simulations for example, increase student satisfaction. Going back to the example of social media, it is noticeable that using this most popular type of technology for academic purposes can increase student engagement and satisfaction with the course. Perceived usefulness occurs when an individual believes that using a specific technology will improve their performance. Ease of use occurs when an individual perceives that the technology can be used without any effort (Rueda et al., 2017).

In this sense, interaction between everyone can be promoted through the creation of social networks. Students can act as coordinators in the process and activities can be based on games and group projects, as well as debates and encouraging students to freely express their opinions to create a more interactive environment (Vlachopoulos & Makri, 2019).

According to Rueda et al. (2017), social media promotes the relationship between student engagement and learning performance since:

- They are a good platform for the exchange of ideas.
- They provide material and opportunities to turn motivation into knowledge.
- They provide enjoyment to students.

Also, according to Rueda et al. (2017), the complementary use of social media applications can effectively engage students. For example, if students do not read all the information that the teacher has sent via Moodle about a particular issue or situation, other networks such as Facebook or WhatsApp are efficient tools to communicate informally and get the latest information from other students. The teacher can use Twitter to ask questions before the case discussion class, or after class, as well as to recognize the best participants of that discussion. In this way, social media applications decrease the perception of distance and increase flexibility and time saving.

The quality of the courses varies according to the technology available and the teachers' knowledge, i.e., technology has the potential to enhance students' active learning, but it also requires a compatible pedagogy to achieve its maximum quality. Therefore, for each type of course, the sense of community among students is likely to vary depending on the teacher's values and skills (Rovai & Jordan, 2004). Course quality is the most important concern in e-learning environments. Technological design plays an important role in the perceived usefulness and ease of use of the course and will impact on student satisfaction (Sun et al., 2008).

The quality of online education should not depend exclusively on the teaching staff. Thus, institutions may need to request other professionals (some more experienced) to support the development of online courses, as well as other kinds of remote support services that may be needed and, in addition, certain services may need to be reorganized to support teaching (e.g., the management of the online library) (Johnson et al., 2020). For teachers, it is a demanding task to master these and other activities, as well as interactivity, not only from a technical point of view but also to deliberately pursue pedagogical goals when doing so (Peters, 2000).

The context of Covid-19 pandemic has forced many HEIs to reinvent teaching-learning process for the continuity of online format (most through remote technologies such as digital platforms). Such dynamic can help manage the time available for studies and professional activities.

INTERACTION AND COMMUNICATION

DE is a system, which indicates that each part interacts with the other and each part interacts with the whole, and, consequently, the idea of isolation is removed. There is a wide variety of means of teaching and communication. Teaching and communication can be addressed separately to some extent, but they are often one and the same (Simonson et al., 2011).

DE is subdivided into two groups: content production and interaction between students and teachers. Regarding the second group, it is possible to state that the interpersonal relationships established between students and teachers are fundamental in DE, since the feelings of empathy and belonging, for example, promote motivation and are conveyed by the students' involvement through a friendly interaction (Holmberg, 1997).

The first students and teachers who were subjected to DE will have been able to interact with each other, however, they were not able to do it in the best possible way, because these interactions may have been limited by the very structure of the courses and the technology linked to teaching. Therefore, institutions that intend to follow this teaching modality will not only need effective technology but also more targeted, intentional and engaging interactions (Abrami et al., 2011). Garrison (2017) emphasizes the importance of e-learning in education, referring it as a disruptive technology that is changing the way learning is approached in the educational context. This change is expected to imply a new predisposition to teaching and learning and its approach mirrors the current times, which are so unexpectedly affected by the Covid-19 pandemic.

The role of teachers is very important in this context, since they are the ones who most closely follow the students' academic path, following, supporting and regularly monitoring their results (Lopes & Soares, 2018). According to Abrami et al. (2011) and Rovai (2007), the interaction between students and teachers focuses on dialogue. This interaction aims to promote the subject under study, so as to assign it a certain meaning, relate it to personal knowledge and apply it in problem solving.

Maintaining contact at all times with the teacher through traditional teaching technologies, such as email, provides the student with greater flexibility and freedom to work and be engaged. Students may see flexibility as a benefit to effective time management, which can lead to greater autonomy and responsibility for their learning (Rueda et al., 2017). Similarly, this would need to be very well led to promote deeper dialogue and intense cooperation (Sales et al., 2020).

In virtual environments it is very important that teachers try to "reduce" the sense of distance as much as possible. In this sense, the teacher can do it through messages and quick responses to students, as well as through the integration of synchronous activities. Teachers can also reinforce this interaction by facilitating student participation in discussion forums and publications, moving into other roles within the profession, such as tutor and motivator. The description of expected outcomes at the end of the period are recognized strategies to result in a good interaction between teachers and students (Vlachopoulos & Makri, 2019), as well as the use of traditional teaching technologies and social media (Rueda et al., 2017). For Rovai (2007), discussion forums are created to form a more cohesive link between everyone and also to promote task-related discussions that are used to develop deeper debates.

Ineffective communication prevents the exchange and exploration of diverse perspectives that can enrich life, both personally and academically. In addition, the communication style of some students can silence others. Such silence may negatively influence the outcomes of these more discrete students when discussions and debates are a graded component of the course. In this way, students who do not have a predisposition to interact more expressively are, consciously or unconsciously, inhibited from learning in the same way as students who participate actively (Rovai, 2007). On the other hand, when the interaction between students becomes truly collaborative and they work together to help each other, the benefits of interactivity can be greater (Abrami et al., 2011). These situations should be moderated by teachers.

Teachers' attitudes towards e-learning impact on student satisfaction, attitude and performance. Thus, a teacher who has a negativist view of e-learning should not expect to have students with high satisfaction or motivation. Since not all teachers are predisposed to teach online, institutions should select them not only for their professional experience, but above all for their attitude towards using this technology. Students' anxiety also hinders their satisfaction with e-learning, so helping students build their confidence in using devices makes the experience more enjoyable. A computer course could be a prerequisite to better prepare students. In addition, there should be instructional knowledge and technical assistance to students in relation to e-learning in order to decrease uncertainty and frustration, leading to better learning experiences. Regarding evaluation criteria, the strategy should adequately identify different schemes to assess learning effects in a more diversified way. In addition to teachers' assessments of students' performance, self-assessment could be incorporated into the system, allowing students to monitor their own achievements (Sun et al., 2008).

MODERN APPLICATIONS - MANAGEMENT COURSES

Management is an area very rich in possibilities and covers several strands, including areas such as accounting, economics, finance and marketing. Only a few strands are transversal in terms of concepts and some are more qualitative and others more quantitative. In addition, the spectrum of management students ranges from undergraduate to the level where students participate in highly qualified executive programs. Similarly, the use of technologies in teaching covers a very broad field ranging from traditional classroom teaching, occasionally using electronic means, to fully online teaching (Müller & Wulf, 2020).

The introduction of technology in management education goes far beyond the characteristics of the technology and the students' knowledge, as it has implications for the teaching format, the teachers and the students' characteristics, all of which are interdependent. The teaching format adopted by the teacher determines his/her role and the appropriate technology. The characteristics of the selected technology (quality and reliability) and the teacher's characteristics (attitude, control and teaching style) have an impact on the students' perception. Thus, all four dimensions - student, teacher, format and technology - directly or indirectly influence the effectiveness of technology-supported instruction (Müller & Wulf, 2020).

The strategic orientation of each course in management varies depending on the area under study. If the intention is to study an area with a more qualitative weighting, the main focus is people, and strategy will have to be worked out from what is expected of social relations. On the other hand, if the expected is to work on a more quantitative side, then the strategy is more analytical and less flexible, notwithstanding all the creative possibilities for strategic organization within these areas that may arise, either on the teacher's initiative or at the suggestion of the student.

Accounting and Finance courses should bet on the most "raw" strategy, given their mostly analytical and quantitative characteristics. According to Lopes and Soares (2018), it is possible to follow this strategy through several video sessions that students watch before coming to class at different times during the semester and can do so on websites such as Khan Academy and other open resources available. In this way, students work at their own pace, re-watch the more complex parts, and skip those they already understand. From the authors' perspective, a video of just a few minutes is more accessible than reading a book on the same subject. Within the classroom, students put into practice what they have learned from the video sessions and many other resources they have previously encountered, collaborating and creating meaningful work, developing some tasks through various discussions with teacher guidance. Online quizzes and activities can enhance learning because if students are "tested" before class, it is easier to adapt the content covered in the following lessons. According to Arbaugh et al. (2009), Accounting and Finance courses, when fully online, tend to be narrative accounts of the teachers' experiences.

Marketing courses inevitably require more discussion and confrontation of ideas. When comparing online and face-to-face confrontation for the discipline of consumer behavior, Sautter (2007) states that online confrontation is more appropriate in terms of providing students with more time to gather and read the important information, which is crucial in the development of critical thinking and in the development of persuasive and convincing arguments. It can be useful to carry out an objective analysis of the comments resulting from the confrontation. Alternatively, face-to-face confrontation exercises promote oral communication skills and emphasize the need to be able to think clearly, at times when students must argue convincingly, often under time or circumstance pressure. The author adds that teachers should analyze the profile and learning styles of the students in order to combine the discussion exercises in the best possible way, so as to understand the different needs of each one.

Figure 1. Proposed active methodology for information systems management
Source: Adapted Mok (2014, p. 8)

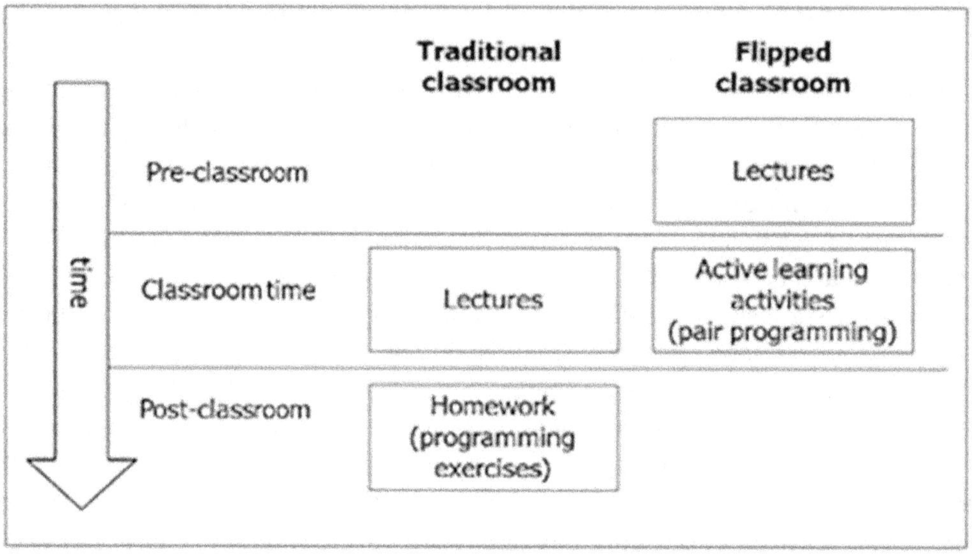

There are more and more studies on Information Systems Management focused on online and blended learning (Arbaugh et al., 2009). In fact, this is the area that is most closely linked to technologies within the Business Sciences, and programming exercises are often used to consolidate knowledge. Mok (2014) observed in one of his studies on joint programming, that if the theoretically weaker students in the course repeat at home the explainer videos on the subject they are studying, many come as prepared as their peers and therefore become much more confident in solving problems during the joint programming sessions, done in pairs. It is hoped that active methodologies such as the flipped classroom can better integrate students into these types of exercises, using face-to-face class time to enrich the collective experience. Figure 1 is a graphic representation of the differences between the traditional classroom and the flipped classroom according to this context. By the order of the arrow, which reflects time, it is possible to identify three phases in the figure, (the before, during and after classroom) and we can also verify two methodologies, which is the traditional methodology and the flipped classroom methodology. What distinguishes them is that the readings and research begin during the classroom in the traditional methodology, while these same readings and research in the flipped classroom methodology gain time to the student, because they are done at home. We can see that traditional teaching sends joint programming exercises home right after the readings in class, while in the flipped classroom methodology the student does them in class, together with classmates and the teacher in a more active condition (methodology).

Usually, responsibilities for the achievement of objectives and outcomes never lie entirely with the students on HRM courses. Students are expected to practice knowledge and skills through a structured, yet flexible framework that provides activities before, during and after class. Especially a framework that enriches their interpersonal experiences through social contact and through scenario-oriented problems and simulated cases (Huang & Lin., 2017).

It should be noted that, in order to have a more productive class time, it is necessary for students to be in tune with their work and the study done at home (Lopes & Soares, 2018). Figure 2 represents a possible strategy, proposed by Huang and Lin (2017), when implementing the flipped classroom methodology for

Human Resource Management courses, with a view to strengthening team spirit (also called *team-based learning*). In short, we can count three vertical plots (before, during and after the classroom) and three horizontal plots (first the individual activities, then the group activities and, finally, the completion of the activities). Before class, students must individually and collectively watch the videos of the subject proposed by the teacher and take notes, and in collective work students must summarize the videos and highlight the important parts of it. During the class, students must individually organize and share their ideas and, in collective group, they must take into account the summaries and propose ideas for the analysis of simulated cases, to later present to the teacher, and at this stage the teacher must be involved

in the dynamics. Following the class, each student and group should share their ideas *online,* having the groups to raise problems about them, thus fostering the debate. At this stage, the teacher should accompany and moderate the discussion.

This organization and framework proposal may be adaptable to other courses within the area of Business Sciences, such as Distribution and Logistics Management, since it is an area where it matters to study and understand the dynamics of human resources with the order and planning.

CONCLUSION

The concept of DE is not recent. There are several definitions that try to explain this concept, presenting different visions and perspectives about it. Adopting the DE modality in Higher Education is, today, a decision that seems more likely than in the past decade, however, there is still a long way to go, especially to ensure the pedagogical requirements to guarantee the quality of this modality.

There is a conflict of interests between what is practical and what is more efficient in the teaching-learning process. It is true that there are many appreciated conveniences in DE, such as the time factor, or the comfort, but then it is also necessary to take into consideration the implied disadvantages, such as the poor socialization and expectation of students who opt for a face-to-face course. Therefore, the ideal would be to find a middle ground, mainly through a deeper knowledge of the needs and profile of the students.

The "flipped" classroom and the blended learning model represent the pedagogical switch of the traditional learning method as students' first contact with the subjects is made outside the traditional classroom. In fact, both must be done carefully, monitoring their learning outcomes. While students are in classroom, the time should be consumed with open discussions, that is, with more occasions for them to interact from one another into their learning process in a collaborative environment.

The integration of modern applications into the educational process in business administration courses can be a positive change in students' motivation for learning. The repeatability of videos or exercises at home allows students to manage their own pace, meaning they can be fully prepared for classroom time.

Considering their nature, courses such as Accounting and Finance and Information Systems naturally tend to be more appreciated when students have more feedback from teachers and colleagues. On the other hand, courses such as Human Resources Management or Marketing tend to be more about open discussions and the confrontation of ideas. Therefore, it would be more efficient if some those practical courses were applied in an inverted classroom and some those theoretical courses in blended learning, depending on the active learning activities chosen for the classroom time and the agreement of all.

In fact, the *Covid-19* pandemic has highlighted the importance of socialization and the leading role that teachers have been playing because, strictly speaking, they are the real moderators of this new and

Figure 2. Strategic organization for the flipped classroom methodology
Source: Adapted Huang & Lin (2017, p. 327)

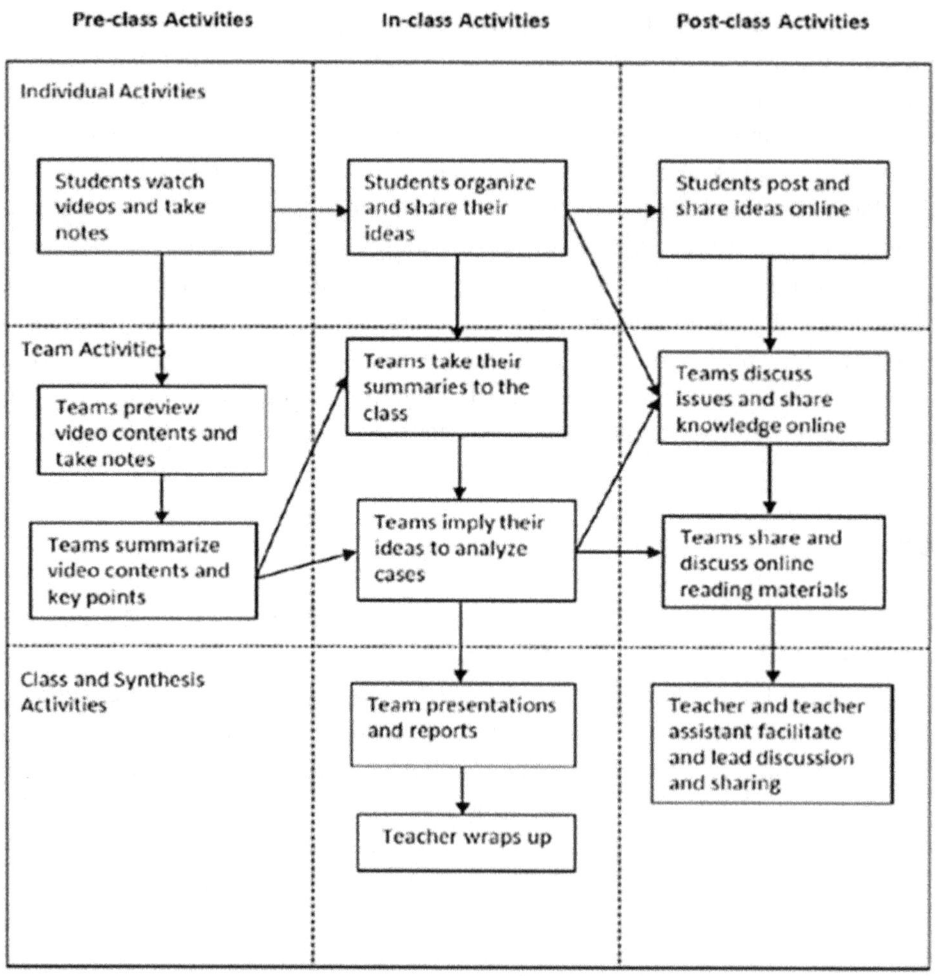

unpredictable reality in education. It is therefore important to invest more and more in their training and also to prepare them for any new challenges. As for the students, it is essential to strengthen their confidence and find a way to understand their needs and problems in order to build a better future together.

ACKNOWLEDGMENT

This paper is financed by National Funds of the FCT – Portuguese Foundation for Science and Technology within the project «UID/ECO/04007/2019»

REFERENCES

Abrami, P. C., Bernard, R. M., Bures, E. M., Borokhovski, E., & Tamim, R. M. (2011). Interaction in distance education and online learning: Using evidence and theory to improve practice. *Journal of Computing in Higher Education, 23*(2–3), 82–103. doi:10.100712528-011-9043-x

Ahmed, M. M. H., & Indurkhya, B. (2020). Investigating cognitive holding power and equity in the flipped classroom. *Heliyon, 6*(8), e04672. doi:10.1016/j.heliyon.2020.e04672 PMID:32885070

Al-Qahtani, A. A. Y., & Higgins, S. E. (2013). Effects of traditional, blended and e-learning on students' achievement in higher education. *Journal of Computer Assisted Learning, 29*(3), 220–234. doi:10.1111/j.1365-2729.2012.00490.x

Anderson, T., & Rivera-vargas, P. (2020). *A Critical look at Educational Technology from a Distance Education Perspective.* doi:10.1344/der.2020.37.208-229

Anderson, T. D., & Garrison, D. R. (1995). Critical thinking in distance education: Developing critical communities in an audio teleconference context. *Higher Education, 29*(2), 183–199. doi:10.1007/BF01383838

Anohina, A. (2005). Analysis of the terminology used in the field of virtual learning. *Journal of Educational Technology & Society, 8*(3), 91–102.

Arbaugh, J. B., Desai, A., Rau, B., & Sridhar, B. S. (2010). A review of research on online and blended learning in the management disciplines: 1994-2009. *Organizational Management Journal, 7*(1), 39–55. doi:10.1057/omj.2010.5

Arbaugh, J. B., Godfrey, M. R., Johnson, M., Pollack, B. L., Niendorf, B., & Wresch, W. (2009). Research in online and blended learning in the business disciplines: Key findings and possible future directions. *Internet and Higher Education, 12*(2), 71–87. doi:10.1016/j.iheduc.2009.06.006

Barton, D. C. (2020). Impacts of the COVID-19 pandemic on field instruction and remote teaching alternatives: Results from a survey of instructors. *Ecology and Evolution, 10*(22), 12499–12507. doi:10.1002/ece3.6628 PMID:32837715

Bernard, R. M., Abrami, P. C., Lou, Y., Borokhovski, E., Wade, A., Wozney, L., Wallet, P. A., Fiset, M., & Huang, B. (2004). How does distance education compare with classroom instruction? A meta-analysis of the empirical literature. *Review of Educational Research, 74*(3), 379–439. doi:10.3102/00346543074003379

Bernard, R. M., Borokhovski, E., Schmid, R. F., Tamim, R. M., & Abrami, P. C. (2014). A meta-analysis of blended learning and technology use in higher education: From the general to the applied. *Journal of Computing in Higher Education, 26*(1), 87–122. doi:10.100712528-013-9077-3

Bonk, C. J. (2020). Pandemic ponderings, 30 years to today: Synchronous signals, saviors, or survivors? *Distance Education, 41*(4), 589–599. doi:10.1080/01587919.2020.1821610

Brewer, R., & Movahedazarhouligh, S. (2018). Successful stories and conflicts: A literature review on the effectiveness of flipped learning in higher education. *Journal of Computer Assisted Learning, 34*(4), 409–416. doi:10.1111/jcal.12250

Chen, Y., Wang, Y., & Chen, N. (2014). Computers & Education Is FLIP enough? Or should we use the FLIPPED model instead? *Computers & Education*, *79*, 16–27. doi:10.1016/j.compedu.2014.07.004

Chizmar, J. F., & Walbert, M. S. (1999). Web-Based Learning Environments Guided by Principles of Good Teaching Practice. *The Journal of Economic Education*, *30*(3), 248–259. doi:10.1080/00220489909595985

Evans, C. (2008). The effectiveness of m-learning in the form of podcast revision lectures in higher education. *Computers & Education*, *50*(2), 491–498. doi:10.1016/j.compedu.2007.09.016

Garrison, D. R. (2017). *E-learning in the 21st Century: A Community of Inquiry Framework for Research and Practice* (3rd ed.). Routledge.

Garrison, D. R., & Kanuka, H. (2004). Blended learning: Uncovering its transformative potential in higher education. *The Internet and Higher Education*, *7*(2), 95–105. doi:10.1016/j.iheduc.2004.02.001

Gonçalves, S. P., Sousa, M. J., & Pereira, F. S. (2020). Distance learning perceptions from higher education students—The case of Portugal. *Education Sciences*, *10*(12), 374. Advance online publication. doi:10.3390/educsci10120374

Guri-Rosenblit, S. (2005). "Distance education" and "e-learning": Not the same thing. *Higher Education*, *49*(4), 467–493. doi:10.100710734-004-0040-0

Holmberg, B. (1997). Distance-education theory again. *Open Learning*, *12*(1), 31–39. doi:10.1080/0268051970120105

Huang, C. K., & Lin, C. Y. (2017). Flipping business education: Transformative use of team-based learning in human resource management classrooms. *Journal of Educational Technology & Society*, *20*(1), 323–336.

Izagirre-Olaizola, J., & Morandeira-Arca, J. (2020). Business management teaching–learning processes in times of pandemic: Flipped classroom at a distance. *Sustainability (Switzerland)*, *12*(23), 1–18. doi:10.3390u122310137

Johnson, N., Veletsianos, G., & Seaman, J. (2020). U.S. faculty and administrators' experiences and approaches in the early weeks of the COVID-19 pandemic. *Online Learning Journal*, *24*(2), 6–21. doi:10.24059/olj.v24i2.2285

Keegan, D. (1986). *The foundations of distance education*. Croom Helm /Routledge.

Keegan, D. J. (1980). On defining distance education. *Distance Education*, *1*(1), 13–36. doi:10.1080/0158791800010102

Lage, M. J., Platt, G. J., & Treglia, M. (2000). Inverting the classroom: A gateway to creating an inclusive learning environment. *The Journal of Economic Education*, *31*(1), 30–43. doi:10.1080/00220480009596759

Lin, C. Y., Huang, C. K., & Ko, C. J. (2020). The impact of perceived enjoyment on team effectiveness and individual learning in a blended learning business course: The mediating effect of knowledge sharing. *Australasian Journal of Educational Technology*, *36*(1), 126–141. doi:10.14742/ajet.4446

Lopes, A. P., & Soares, F. (2018). Perception and performance in a flipped Financial Mathematics classroom. *International Journal of Management Education*, *16*(1), 105–113. doi:10.1016/j.ijme.2018.01.001

López-Pérez, M. V., Pérez-López, M. C., & Rodríguez-Ariza, L. (2011). Blended learning in higher education: Students' perceptions and their relation to outcomes. *Computers & Education, 56*(3), 818–826. doi:10.1016/j.compedu.2010.10.023

Martínez-Jiménez, R., & Ruiz-Jiménez, M. C. (2020). Improving students' satisfaction and learning performance using flipped classroom. *International Journal of Management Education, 18*(3), 100422. Advance online publication. doi:10.1016/j.ijme.2020.100422

Martins, J., & Nunes, M. B. (2016). The temporal properties of e-learning: An exploratory study of academics' conceptions. *International Journal of Educational Management, 30*(1), 2–19. doi:10.1108/IJEM-04-2014-0048

Mok, H. N. (2014). Institutional Knowledge at Singapore Management University Teaching tip : The flipped classroom Teaching Tip. *The Flipped Classroom., 25*, 7–11.

Moore, M. (1990). Recent contributions to the theory of distance education. *Open Learning, 5*(3), 10–15. doi:10.1080/0268051900050303

Moore, M. G., & Kearsley, G. (2005). *Distance education: A systems view*. Wadsworth Publ.

Müller, F. A., & Wulf, T. (2020). Technology-supported management education: A systematic review of antecedents of learning effectiveness. *International Journal of Educational Technology in Higher Education, 17*(1), 47. Advance online publication. doi:10.118641239-020-00226-x

O'Flaherty, J., & Phillips, C. (2015). The use of flipped classrooms in higher education: A scoping review. *Internet and Higher Education, 25*, 85–95. doi:10.1016/j.iheduc.2015.02.002

Palvia, S., Aeron, P., Gupta, P., Mahapatra, D., Parida, R., Rosner, R., & Sindhi, S. (2018). Online Education: Worldwide Status, Challenges, Trends, and Implications. *Journal of Global Information Technology Management, 21*(4), 233–241. doi:10.1080/1097198X.2018.1542262

Peters, O. (2000). Digital learning environments: New possibilities and opportunities. *International Review of Research in Open and Distance Learning, 1*(1), 22–39. doi:10.19173/irrodl.v1i1.3

Rovai, A. P. (2007). Facilitating online discussions effectively. *The Internet and Higher Education, 10*(1), 77–88. doi:10.1016/j.iheduc.2006.10.001

Rovai, A. P., & Jordan, H. M. (2004). Blended learning and sense of community: A comparative analysis with traditional and fully online graduate courses. *International Review of Research in Open and Distance Learning, 5*(2). Advance online publication. doi:10.19173/irrodl.v5i2.192

Rueda, L., Benitez, J., & Braojos, J. (2017). From traditional education technologies to student satisfaction in Management education: A theory of the role of social media applications. *Information & Management, 54*(8), 1059–1071. doi:10.1016/j.im.2017.06.002

Sales, D., Cuevas-cerveró, A., & Cuevas-cerveró, A. (2020). *Perspectives on the information and digital competence of Social Sciences students and faculty before and during lockdown due to Covid-19*. doi:10.3145/epi.2020.jul.23

Sautter, P. (2007). Designing discussion activities to achieve desired learning outcomes: Choices using mode of delivery and structure. *Journal of Marketing Education*, *29*(2), 122–131. doi:10.1177/0273475307302014

Simonson, M., Schlosser, C., & Orellana, A. (2011). Distance education research: A review of the literature. *Journal of Computing in Higher Education*, *23*(2–3), 124–142. doi:10.100712528-011-9045-8

Sun, P. C., Tsai, R. J., Finger, G., Chen, Y. Y., & Yeh, D. (2008). What drives a successful e-Learning? An empirical investigation of the critical factors influencing learner satisfaction. *Computers & Education*, *50*(4), 1183–1202. doi:10.1016/j.compedu.2006.11.007

Vlachopoulos, D., & Makri, A. (2019). Online communication and interaction in distance higher education: A framework study of good practice. *International Review of Education*, *65*(4), 605–632. doi:10.100711159-019-09792-3

ADDITIONAL READING

Broadbent, J., & Poon, W. L. (2015). Self-regulated learning strategies & academic achievement in online higher education learning environments: A systematic review. *Internet and Higher Education*, *27*, 1–13. doi:10.1016/j.iheduc.2015.04.007

Burd, E. L., Smith, S. P., & Reisman, S. (2014). Exploring Business Models for MOOCs in Higher Education. *Innovative Higher Education*, *40*(1), 37–49. doi:10.100710755-014-9297-0

Gómez Galán, J. (2017). Interacciones Moodle-MOOC: Presente y futuro de los modelos de e-learning y b-learning en los contextos universitarios. *EccoS –. Revista Científica (Maracaibo)*, *44*(44), 241–257. doi:10.5585/eccos.n44.7353

Okaz, A. A. (2015). Integrating Blended Learning in Higher Education. *Procedia: Social and Behavioral Sciences*, *186*, 600–603. doi:10.1016/j.sbspro.2015.04.086

Williams, C. J., Matt, J. J., & O'Reilly, F. L. (2014). Generational Perspective of Higher Education Online Student Learning Styles. *Journal of Education and Learning*, *3*(2). Advance online publication. doi:10.5539/jel.v3n2p33

Winanti, G. F. L., Napitupulu, T. A., Soeparno, H., & Trisetyarso, A. (2019). Learning Framework in the Industrial Age 4.0 in Higher Education. *1st 2018 Indonesian Association for Pattern Recognition International Conference, INAPR 2018 - Proceedings*, 227–232. 10.1109/INAPR.2018.8627039

KEY TERMS AND DEFINITIONS

Active Learning: Teaching method that transforms learners as active participants in their learning and creates student-centered classrooms instead of teacher-centered ones.

Blended Learning: Alternative and active education method that combines digital learning and face-to-face teaching time.

Digitalization: Transformative use of technology that organizations incorporate into their vision statements and company culture.

Distance Learning: Education obtained remotely since in-person sessions between the learners and educators are limited.

E-Learning: Computer based educational tool or system (the "e" comes from electronic) that enables people to learn anywhere and at any time.

Remote Learning: Education obtained remotely since in-person sessions between the learners and educators are impossible due to a very peculiar situation.

Traditional Learning: Long-established teaching method with a very few digital interactive and innovative strategies, currently much more student-centered than teacher-centered.

Chapter 3
Blended Learning Compared to Online Learning in Business, Management, and Accounting Education:
A Bibliometric Analysis and Literature Review

Márcia R. C. Santos
ESCE, Polytechnic Institute of Setúbal, Portugal

ABSTRACT

The journey of business, management, and accounting education over the past decades included several teaching methods which may nowadays be considered outdated for the modern students who live, learn, and connect through technology. This study clusters the academic literature addressing online learning and b-learning applied to educational and training in the business, management, and accounting. Through the collection of all the relevant publications in Scopus, this study uses automated text mining techniques in VOSviewer software for comparing the evolution overtime of the online and blended methods in the context of scientific knowledge production. The results unveil that online-learning-related literature is grouped in nine clusters, instead of the seven clusters in case of blended learning, meaning that the first is more disperse in terms of topics. An in-depth analysis of the studies most closely related to each cluster's terms allow the authors to provide critical reflections that help professionals when choosing the accurate method and also the academics in identifying future research agendas.

INTRODUCTION

The journey of business, management and accounting education over the past decades included several teaching methods which may nowadays be considered outdated for the modern students who live, learn,

DOI: 10.4018/978-1-7998-8239-8.ch003

and connect at technologies. Academics have already revealed that the way educators teach in this field can contribute for increasing the value of the students and mitigate possible enrolment declines (Maher, 2000). One of the variety of ways of including technologies in teaching is using technology for providing Online Learning or a mix between on-line and on-class education (Blended-Learning or B-Learning) (Martín et al., 2008).

During COVID-19 pandemic both Online Learning and B-Learning were used massively by educators. Nonetheless, those teaching methods have been applied by business, management and accounting educators prior this pandemic. In both periods (before and after COVID-19), (Parte & Herrador-Alcaide, 2021) revealed that those methods create, in both periods, the sense of belonging of the teaching community is high.

Despite the efforts that researchers have made for contributing for this field of knowledge during COVID-19 pandemic, the volume of literature published in past decades indicates that academics have been along the years contributing for creating knowledge around Online Learning and B-Learning methods which could be placed at the service of those who teach in the entire educational system.

In this sense, the present study aims to unveil the research trends exploring Online Learning and B-Learning methods for application in educational and training in the business, management and accounting disciplines. A comparative analysis of the results in each method is conducted, which can help professionals when choosing the accurate method and also the academics in identifying future research agendas.

BACKGROUND

The learning methods changed radically when technology started to be incorporated in education. The concept of distance learning gained force as a "*system design that are effectively incorporated in delivering education to student teacher and student may communicate asynchronously and synchronously*" (Al-Arimi, 2014). The literature describes a journey in which E-learning appeared as a way of offer tools to both students and teachers for running remote training and online courses. It includes for instance the use of wiki and blogs, chats, e-mail, and multimedia CD-ROMs (Martín et al., 2008). The B-Learning method allowed to combine the distance, online and on-class education which depends on the availability of resources, which were scarce in COVID-19 pandemic (Santos et al., 2021). The term hybrid learning and B-Learning are used interchangeably, but they mean the some in literature (Hrastinski, 2019). This concept refers to a training or teaching environment combining face-to-face education with access to online learning tools (Hall & Davison, 2007). The role of B-Learning is especially relevant in the post lockdown period, in supporting the flexible learning expected in transitioning between fully online and blended (Nerantzi, 2020).

When social media become a reality, their impact was studied in order to understand how could it provoke a positive disruption in education, E-Learning and B-Learning. (King, 2012) actually confirmed that critical thinking, communication, collaboration, and creativity and innovation applied to social media tools could positively impact in educational and professional settings. E-learning tools were particularly relevant for mitigating constraints in educational sectors during the first lockdown period of COVID-19 pandemic, in which schools were closed and the contact between trainers/professors and trainees/students was exclusively online. Recent studies revealed the contribution of e-learning resources

Table 1. Number of publications per period

Period	Blended-Learning	Online Learning	Total
1997-2006	30	65	95
2007-2016	152	259	411
2017-2021	176	354	530
Total	358	678	1,036

or facilities for the students' performance, showing a positive thought among students about e-learning (Sathishkumar et al., 2020).

Several authors are looking for the future of E-learning tools, namely discussing the limitations of current E-learning systems and proposing an analysis of good practices in other E-learning ecosystems which could benefit both teachers and students (Uden & Damiani, 2007). However, this discussion by default is based on the comparation between practices in industry sector versus educational sector, or public versus private sector case-studies. In other cases, the students versus teachers' perspectives are analysed (Cardoso et al., 2019).

A review of the academic literature addressing Online Learning and B-Learning methods for application in educational and training in the business, management and accounting disciplines could benefit this discussion, considering that academic publications explore the challenges of organizations in all different sectors and from actors' views. As in other fields, literature reviews supported academics and practitioners to be provided with an overview of the main topics within the scientific knowledge, as well as designing new research (Santos et al., 2020).

MATERIAL AND METHODS

In order to achieve the aim of this study, the academic literature was collected from the major scientific database, i.e., Scopus. For this purpose, two different queries were applied. The first allowed to select academic publications addressing Online Learning in regards to education and training methods, limited to the field of business, management and accounting (see query below).

TITLE-ABS-KEY ((“education” OR “train*”) AND (“online learning”)) AND (LIMIT-TO (SUBJAREA, “BUSI”))

The second query was constructed based on the same layout, but the term Online Learning was replaced by Blended Learning (see query below).

TITLE-ABS-KEY ((“education” OR “train*”) AND (“blended learning”)) AND (LIMIT-TO (SUBJAREA, “BUSI”))

After cleaning the publications that were found in both samples, a total of 1,036 documents were analysed. Based on the date of publication, the results show that the number of studies in both Blended-Learning and Online Learning methods are increasing, as presented in Table 1.

Although this tendency was very similar until 2016, the last 4 years made the Online Learning to become the focus of researchers. Indeed, based on the absolute frequency of the number of publications in both areas, it is clear that online learning is the learning method in business, management and

Figure 1. The absolute frequency of the number of papers addressing blended or online learning in business, management and accounting field

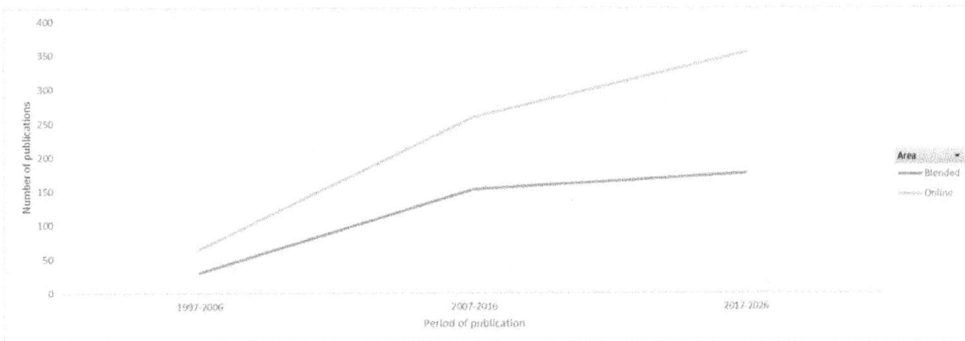

accounting fields most addressed in the literature, and this difference was accentuated in recent years from 2017 up to 2021 (see Figure 1).

In order to unveil the main topics addressed in the literature in both groups of publications, the text included in those documents have been analysed using text mining computer assisted techniques. The VOSviewer algorithm was applied, considering that a free of charge software is provided by VOSviewer developers and it is a modern tool for clustering bibliometric data that has already proved to be scientifically validated in previous similar studies (Shah et al., 2019; van Eck & Waltman, 2010; Yu et al., 2020). Additionally, considering the big data involved in the sample of the material (text included in more than a thousand publications), a manual analysis is not feasible.

RESULTS AND DISCUSSION

Clustering

Firstly, the analysis of data included the production of the network visualization, in which the main field of the publications (title and abstract) are clustered (see Figure 2).

This clustering analysis revealed that Online-Learning related literature is grouped in 9 clusters, instead of the 7 clusters of Blended-Learning. This means that the first may be more disperse in terms of topics. Regarding Online-Learning, the three most relevant clusters include the following most cited terms:

- Cluster 1: Covid, Programme, and Adoption
- Cluster 2: Massive Open Online Courses (MOOCs), School, and Attitude
- Cluster 3: Community, Participant, and Practical implication

The results on the number of the publications in the last 3 years, which exponentially increased in regarding Online-Learning, can be explained by the focus on the COVID-19 pandemic effect on the adoption of Online tools in education and training system (Cluster 1), considering the distance and lockdown measures implemented by Governments worldwide. Academics studied not only the urgent

Figure 2. Network visualization: Online (on the top) versus Blended Learning (on the bottom)

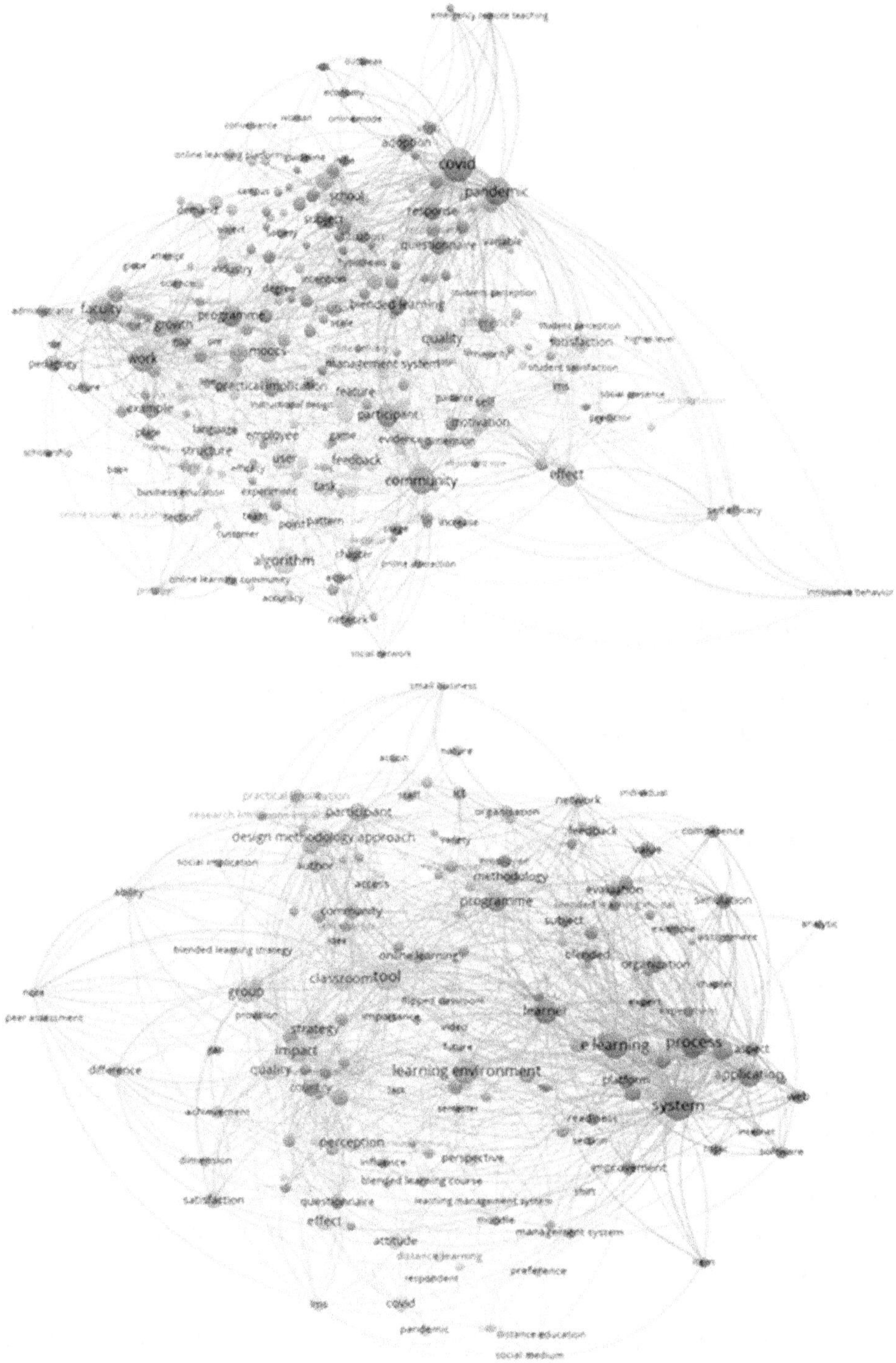

adoption of the remote teaching and virtual learning in the beginning of the COVID-19 pandemic but also in periods after the first lockdown (Anthony Jnr & Noel, 2021).

Online-Learning related literature has also a special focus on MOOCs (Cluster 2), which refer to the free online courses available for anyone to enroll. Authors in this field are trying to modeling collaborative intentions and behavior in digital environments (Razmerita et al., 2020), and analyzing the experts' perception on the feasibility of these courses (Hai-Jew, 2014).

Finally, in the Cluster 3, the academics frequently apply the Community of Inquiry Framework for assessing the sense of community on specific online tools like Moodle (Vaghjee & Panchoo, 2016) or for assessing the value of online education in higher education, technical and professional courses (Arbaugh, 2007).

In regards to the Blended-Learning related literature, the three most relevant clusters include:

- Cluster 1: System, Process, and Learner
- Cluster 2: Community, Network, and Relationship
- Cluster 3: Programme, Country, Engagement

Studies contributing for the topics addressed in Cluster 1 are focused on contributing to improve the Blended-Learning experience from the learner's point of view. Academics suggest new integrated mobile systems to monitor students' academic achievement, interaction and satisfaction (Kouninef et al., 2012; Musa Al-Momani & PILLI, 2021) and explore factors influencing the continuance intention in using Blended-Learning environments (Abidin et al., 2021).

By another hand, studies addressing Blended-Learning also explore the concept of online community building, namely through the analysis of Business Centers which support the business community in applying driven innovation projects through a network of communities and enterprises intermediaries (Porumb & Analoui, 2008). Academics also explore the virtual collaboration in higher education blended learning arrangements (Bukvova et al., 2006).

Finally, literature contributes for understating factors that influence the student engagement using learning management systems like Blackboard, WebCT and Moodle (Sanusi et al., 2019). A focus on the students' experience is also analysed to understand how the use of Blended-Learning methods can enhance the student learning experience (Poon, 2012).

Evolution of Clusters Overtime

The network visualization provides an overview of the themes addressed in the literature in all the years of publication under analysis. In order to conclude on the evolution of the themes, the overlay visualization presented in Figure 3 is useful. Regarding Online-Learning, it is evident that the two first clusters unveiled in the literature are recent trends (shown in yellow), meaning that studies exploring Online-Learning methods in business, management, and accounting disciplines addressing COVID-19 pandemic challenges for educators and students (Cluster 1) or MOOCs (Cluster 2) are areas that need further development in future research.

In regards to the Blended-Learning literature, this seems to be more mature considering that the clusters of research topics have been addressed since 2013 to 2017 (shown in blue and green).

Figure 3. Overlay visualization: Online (on the top) versus Blended Learning (on the bottom)

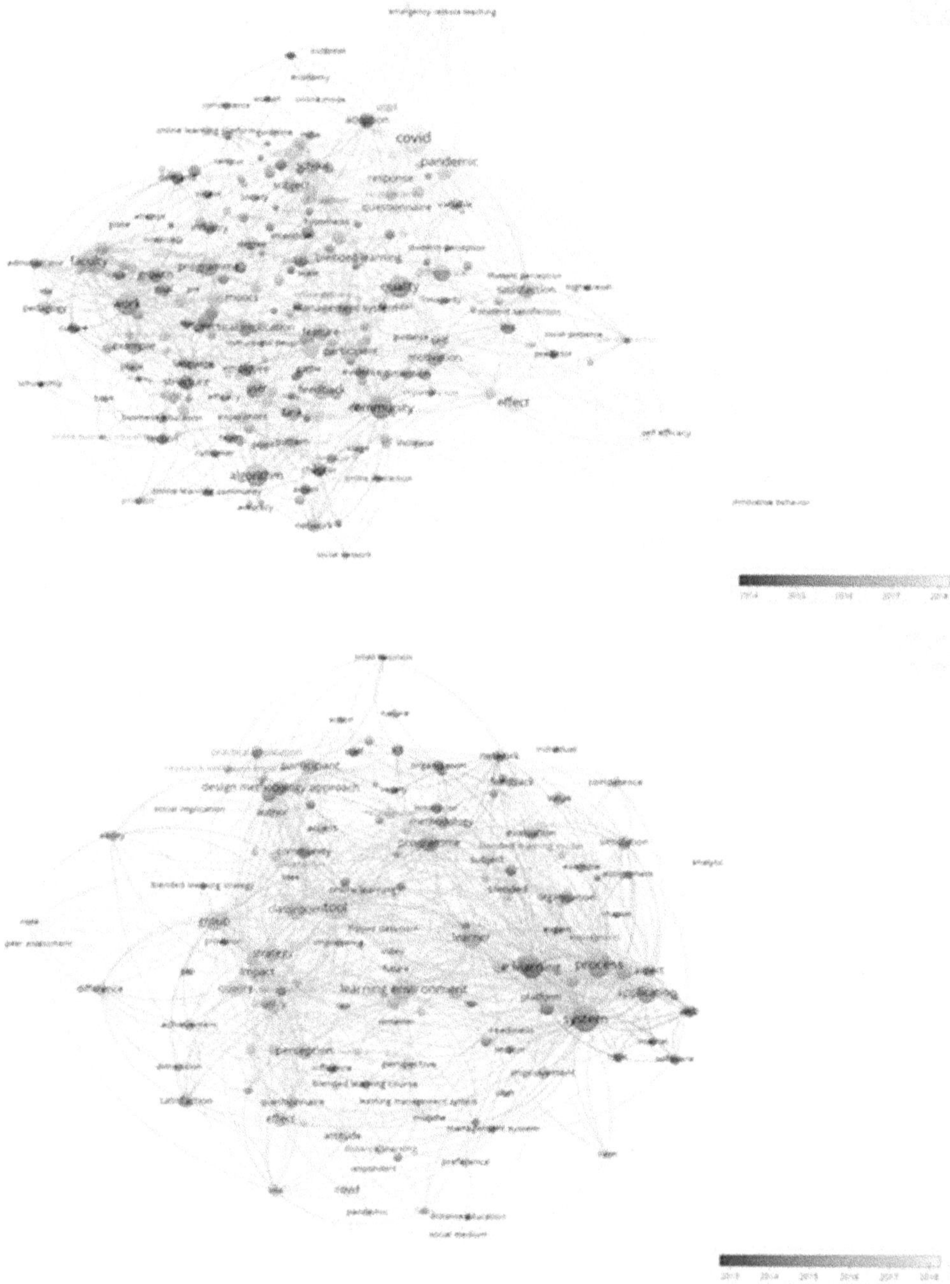

FUTURE RESEARCH DIRECTIONS

Blended-Learning related studies have been timidly published in relation to the COVID-19 pandemic. Nonetheless, this method was very frequently used after first lockdown considering that single Online-

Learning was not suffice for accomplishing educational goals. In this sense, future research could focus on addressing Blended-Learning method in the context of COVID-19 pandemic.

In regards to Online-Learning, future research should explore topics related to challenges for educators and students or MOOCs, applying different methodological approaches, as these are emerging clusters.

CONCLUSION

The present study clusters the academic literature addressing Online Learning and B-Learning methods for application in educational and training in the business, management and accounting disciplines. Through the collection of all the relevant publications in Scopus database, this study uses automated analysis in VOSviewer software to provide results on both literatures and making available material for comparing the evolution overtime of the Online and Blended methods in the context of scientific knowledge production.

The results contributed for the discussion on the status of science in both methods, which have been so relevant for educators and students apply in this COVID-19 pandemic. By one side, we have seen an exponential increase of Online-Learning related literature in recent years, proving that research in this field was not suffice for managing challenges that Online-Learning methods create for students and educators. By another hand, B-Learning methods related literature did not follow this climb, despite the fact of being a method used in COVID-19 pandemic specially after the first lockdown.

The present study's analysis is limited to the application of E-Learning and B-Learning in educational and training in the business, management and accounting disciplines. Further studies could provide insights in respect to remaining disciples. Furthermore, the results and critical analysis provided in this study provides students and educators with birds-eyes on academic contributions they can find in literature, and provide guidelines for future research agenda.

REFERENCES

Abidin, Z., Rokhman, F., & Mathrani, A. (2021). Exploring the influencing factors of learning management systems continuance intention in a blended learning environment. *International Journal of Innovation and Learning*, *30*(2), 175. Advance online publication. doi:10.1504/IJIL.2021.117221

Al-Arimi, A. M. A.-K. (2014). Distance Learning. *Procedia: Social and Behavioral Sciences*, *152*, 82–88. doi:10.1016/j.sbspro.2014.09.159

Anthony, B. Jr, & Noel, S. (2021). Examining the adoption of emergency remote teaching and virtual learning during and after COVID-19 pandemic. *International Journal of Educational Management*, *35*(6), 1136–1150. Advance online publication. doi:10.1108/IJEM-08-2020-0370

Arbaugh, J. B. (2007). Does the community of inquiry framework predict outcomes in online mba courses? *Academy of Management 2007 Annual Meeting: Doing Well by Doing Good, AOM 2007*.

Bukvova, H., Gilge, S., & Schoop, E. (2006). Virtual collaboration in higher education blended learning arrangements. *Workshop Gemeinschaften in Neuen Medien (GeNeMe) 2006*. http://www-mmt.inf.tu-dresden.de/geneme2006/

Cardoso, T., Pestana, F., & Pina, J. (2019). Assessing a b-learning teaching approach and students' learning preferences in higher education. *EDULEARN19 Proceedings*, 10007–10012. 10.21125/edulearn.2019.2502

Hai-Jew, S. (2014). *Iff and other conditionals: Expert perceptions of the feasibility of massive open online courses (MOOCs) - A modified E-Delphi study*. IGI-Global. doi:10.4018/978-1-4666-5137-1.ch013

Hall, H., & Davison, B. (2007). Social software as support in hybrid learning environments: The value of the blog as a tool for reflective learning and peer support. *Library & Information Science Research*, *29*(2), 163–187. doi:10.1016/j.lisr.2007.04.007

Hrastinski, S. (2019). What Do We Mean by Blended Learning? *TechTrends*, *63*(5), 564–569. doi:10.100711528-019-00375-5

King, K. P. (2012). Social Media as Positive Disruption in Education, E-Learning and B-Learning. In *Handbook of Research on Business Social Networking*. IGI Global. doi:10.4018/978-1-61350-168-9.ch023

Kouninef, B., Tlemsani, R., Rerbal, S. M., & Lotfi, A. (2012, July). LMS INTTIC system using mobile technology and podcasting in blended learning. *International Conference on Education and E-Learning Innovations*. 10.1109/ICEELI.2012.6360593

Maher, M. W. (2000). Management Accounting Education at the Millennium. *Issues in Accounting Education*, *15*(2), 335–346. Advance online publication. doi:10.2308/iace.2000.15.2.335

Martín, S., Gil, R., Díaz, G., Sancristobal, E., Castro, M., & Peire, J. (2008). From e-learning to m-learning through b-learning and s-learning. *50th International Symposium ELMAR-2008*, 10–12.

Musa Al-Momani, M., & Pilli, O. (2021). The Impact of Integrated Mobile System on Students' Academic Achievement, Interaction and Satisfaction. *TEM Journal*. doi:10.18421/TEM103-50

Nerantzi, C. (2020). The use of peer instruction and flipped learning to support flexible blended learning during and after the COVID-19 Pandemic. *International Journal of Management and Applied Research*, *7*(2), 184–195. doi:10.18646/2056.72.20-013

Parte, L., & Herrador-Alcaide, T. (2021). Teaching Disruption by COVID-19: Burnout, Isolation, and Sense of Belonging in Accounting Tutors in E-Learning and B-Learning. *International Journal of Environmental Research and Public Health*, *18*(19), 10339. doi:10.3390/ijerph181910339 PMID:34639635

Poon, J. (2012). Use of blended learning to enhance the student learning experience and engagement in property education. *Property Management*, *30*(2), 129–156. Advance online publication. doi:10.1108/02637471211213398

Porumb, E. M., & Analoui, F. (2008). How to use KM effectively in a European context: The case of BCT in Romania. *International Journal of Business Information Systems*, *3*(6), 609. Advance online publication. doi:10.1504/IJBIS.2008.018993

Razmerita, L., Kirchner, K., Hockerts, K., & Tan, C.-W. (2020). Modeling Collaborative Intentions and Behavior in Digital Environments: The Case of a Massive Open Online Course (MOOC). *Academy of Management Learning & Education*, *19*(4), 469–502. Advance online publication. doi:10.5465/amle.2018.0056

Santos, M. R. C., Laureano, R. M. S., & Moro, S. (2020). Unveiling Research Trends for Organizational Reputation in the Nonprofit Sector. *Voluntas, 31*(1), 56–70. doi:10.100711266-018-00055-7

Santos, M. R. C., Nunes, S., Dominguinhos, P., Mourato, J., Mata, C., & Teixeira, N. M. (2021). Financial Capacity During a Pandemic Crisis: Insights From the Non-Profit Sector. In N. M. Teixeira & I. Lisboa (Eds.), Handbook of Research on Financial Management During Economic Downturn and Recovery (pp. 59–76). IGI Global. doi:10.4018/978-1-7998-6643-5.ch004

Sanusi, N. M., Kamalrudin, M., & Mohtar, S. (2019). Student Engagement using Learning Management System in Computer Science Education. *International Journal of Recent Technology and Engineering, 8*(2S11). doi:10.35940/ijrte.B1121.0982S1119

Sathishkumar, V., Radha, R., Mahalakshmi, K., Kumar, V. S., & Saravanakumar, A. R. (2020). E-Learning during Lockdown of Covid-19 Pandemic: A Global Perspective. *International Journal of Control and Automation, 13*(4), 1088–1099.

Shah, S. H. H., Lei, S., Ali, M., Doronin, D., & Hussain, S. T. (2019). Prosumption: Bibliometric analysis using HistCite and VOSviewer. *Kybernetes, 49*(3), 1020–1045. doi:10.1108/K-12-2018-0696

Uden, L., & Damiani, E. (2007). *The future of B-learning: B-learning ecosystem.* IEEE DEST.

Vaghjee, H., & Panchoo, S. (2016, August). Applying the Community of Inquiry Framework to explore sense of community on Moodle. *2016 IEEE International Conference on Emerging Technologies and Innovative Business Practices for the Transformation of Societies (EmergiTech).* 10.1109/EmergiTech.2016.7737370

van Eck, N. J., & Waltman, L. (2010). Software survey: VOSviewer, a computer program for bibliometric mapping. *Scientometrics, 84*(2), 523–538. doi:10.100711192-009-0146-3 PMID:20585380

Yu, Y., Li, Y., Zhang, Z., Gu, Z., Zhong, H., Zha, Q., Yang, L., Zhu, C., & Chen, E. (2020). A bibliometric analysis using VOSviewer of publications on COVID-19. *Annals of Translational Medicine, 8*(13), 1–11. doi:10.21037/atm-20-4235 PMID:32793661

KEY TERMS AND DEFINITIONS

Blended Learning: This is an educational and training method that combines offline (face-to-face, traditional learning) and online learning.

Online Learning: This is an educational and training method that uses Information and Communication Technologies for remote and distance education.

Text Mining: A technique of data analysis useful for analysis of unstructured text. This is a computer-assisted text analysis technique that provides insights regarding the most cited terms in corpus.

VOSviewer: VOSviewer is a software tool for constructing and visualizing bibliometric networks.

Chapter 4
Key Factors for Entrepreneurial Success:
A Synthesis of Earlier Research and an Agenda Proposal to Support Entrepreneurial Training

Teresa Gomes da Costa
Polytechnic Institute of Setúba, Portugal

Luísa Cagica Carvalho
https://orcid.org/0000-0002-9804-7813
Polytechnic Institute of Setúbal, Portugal & CEFAGE, University of Évora, Portugal

ABSTRACT

Studies about success and unsuccess factors for startups are still relevant due to the dispersion of the literature about it. Additionally, it remains important to understand how some usual tools used by the entrepreneurs could support a better diagnosis of the success conditions in an earlier phase of the business, avoiding or preventing the unsuccess. This study is a work in progress financed by EU under Erasums+ Program and aims to discuss the factors that influence the business entrepreneurial success considering several stages of the business and its maturity. Finally, it also attends to the business plan as an important tool for entrepreneurial success. The chapter organizes contributions attending to the dimensions—entrepreneurial profile, external environment, and managerial process—and presents an agenda about a set of factors in a macro perspective (public policies, infrastructures, etc.) and in a micro perspective (entrepreneurial profile, social and human capital, etc.) that allows a reflection about the success on a different stage of a business.

DOI: 10.4018/978-1-7998-8239-8.ch004

INTRODUCTION

When we consider the sustainability of a new venture in long term, the issues related to the success or unsuccess/failure comes to the theoretical discussion. Nevertheless, the literature about it remains disperse and approach several aspects, such as, measures to capture success of a business idea, financial sustainability, entrepreneur profile, etc. persists with a lack of systematization. Attending to this dispersion this paper tries to organize the more pertinent contributions attending to the dimensions: entrepreneurial profile; external environment and managerial process.

Concerning entrepreneurial profile some studies focused this aspect as a critical success factor (Kristiansen, Furuholt, & Wahid, 2003). Business behaviour as seem like a function of the individual differences (López-Núñez et al, 2020) and personality and capacity factors can predict business activity and discriminate between 'successful' and 'unsuccessful' entrepreneurs (Rauch & Frese, 2007; Zhao & Seibert, 2006). Factors that influence the success of a new project have been discussed among academics and most of the researchers have highlighted the importance of the entrepreneur in the process of entrepreneurial success (Omri, Frika and Bouraoui, 2015).

Each year millions of new businesses started all over the world. But according with McKenzie and Paffhausen (2018) more than a quarter of these business fail within their first year, while only a small subgroup of firms grows rapidly generating value and income (Olafsen and Cook, 2016).

The capability to identify previously which firms will succeed is important either for entrepreneurs or investors. In this sense business plan is considered an important strategic tool for entrepreneurs. Planning plays a determinant role in predicting the degree of success potentially achieved by new business.

Developing an appropriate business plan can help entrepreneurs to focus on the strategies and actions that are necessary for business succeed, as well as to achieve both short-term and long-term objectives.

ENTREPRENEURIAL SUCCESS: AN EFFORT TO INTEGRATE SEVERAL CONTRIBUTIONS

The success of a startup entrepreneurial profile appears as an important issue in the literature. Some of the factors that explain the success are:

- Establishment of business goals and take timely decisions to achieve those goals in increasingly competitive and uncertain environments (Ayala and Mazano, 2014);
- Resilience i.e., a high degree of tolerance for ambiguity and a dynamic adaption to change and future, that able to learn from their mistakes (Ayala & Manzano, 2010);
- Gender and possible differences in personal characteristics between men and women that could influence the success of their business (Danes, Stafford & Loy, 2007; Danes et al., 2009). Campbell-Sills, Forde and Stein (2009) identified significant differences between the degree of resilience revealed by men and women. However, this factor is not consensual in literature and some researchers have disclosed differences between men and women in personality traits (Weisberg, DeYoung & Hirsh, 2011), emotional variables (Cabello, Sorrel, Fernández-Pinto, Extremera & Fernández-Berrocal, 2016) and entrepreneurial intention (Santos, Roomi & Liñán, 2016). According to López-Núñez et al (2020, 2) women report higher scores than men "on Big Five personality traits, less frequently perceive themselves as entrepreneurs and have lower perceptions

of self-confidence in performing entrepreneurial tasks". These findings indicate the suitability of controlling the effect of gender and age on the entrepreneur's profile. Nevertheless, the research about gender remains inconclusive and other studies did not recognize gender differences in aspects, such as the degree of resilience (Burns and Anstey, 2010; Karairmak, 2010).

- High levels of human and social capital are more likely to create business with high growth potential and profitability (Omri, Frika and Bouraoui, 2015). The social capital i.e., the resources embedded in entrepreneurs' personal networks, are considered as critical to the performance of small firms due their ability to identify new business opportunities, obtain resources at lower costs compared with market price, and increase legitimacy through external stakeholders (Stam et al., 2014). Networks are a key topic for new entrepreneurial projects because influences individuals and the ways that organizations are managed, developed, maintained, and sustained (Omri and Ayadi-Frikha, 2014; Costa & Galina, 2016).
- Motivation is also point out as an important factor for success (Alstete, 2008; Headd, 2003; Kim, Kim, & Jeon, 2018; Naffziger, Hornsby, & Kuratko, 1994; Van Praag, 2003; Van Praag & Cramer, 2001).

According to Dover and Dierk (2010) it is important to analyse this entrepreneurial profile attending to different traits that can be identified both in startups and different companies: manager (focusing on complexity – plan, organize, coordinate and control); leader (focusing on change – set direction, align, and motivate people) and entrepreneur (focusing on opportunities – identify innovate and value creation).

External environment is also important to influence business success (Huggins, 2000; Carvalho et al, 2019; Costa & Galina, 2016) and, also, the way of doing business and cooperation (Hitt & Ireland 2000; and Jarillo 1988; Paulo et al., 2017). External environment is pointed as an influence for success of new businesses: government agencies, trade unions, creditors, clients, or suppliers, on organizational activities, including strategic decisions (Child, Elbanna, & Rodrigues, 2010). Moreover, for mature companies the success criteria can be related also with the perspective of the various construction stakeholders, as client, consultants, and contractors. (Toor & Ogunlana, 2010).

Finally, managerial process is also considered a key dimension for success of new businesses and mature companies (Omri and Ayadi-Frikha, 2014). This dimension includes a set of variables, such as know-how (Swierczek & Ha, 2003), enterprise size, particularly SMEs (Kristiansen, Furuholt, & Wahid; 2003), customers and markets (William, James, & Susan; 2005), resources and finance (Swierczek & Ha, 2003; and Kristiansen, Furuholt & Wahid, 2003) and strategy (McMahon, 2001). Most of the firms born small, so dimension and especially small business are linked with success and survival. Several authors refer other factors that influence success and survival of small business, such as innovation, human, social, and financial capital of entrepreneurs (Thornhill, 2006; Unger et al., 2011), human and financial capital (Coleman, 2007; Unger et al., 2011; Baptista et al., 2013) and social capital (Luca and Presutti, 2010). Additionally, is important to highlight that the success of business for mature companies have some constraints due to the managers major concerns with daily operations neglecting the market demand and new technologies investment so important for the futures success of companies (Alam et al., 2010).

Figure 1 provides a perspective about the three dimensions and its overlays that allows a large balance to enhance the success of startups.

Figure 1. Dimensions of entrepreneurial success
Source: Authors

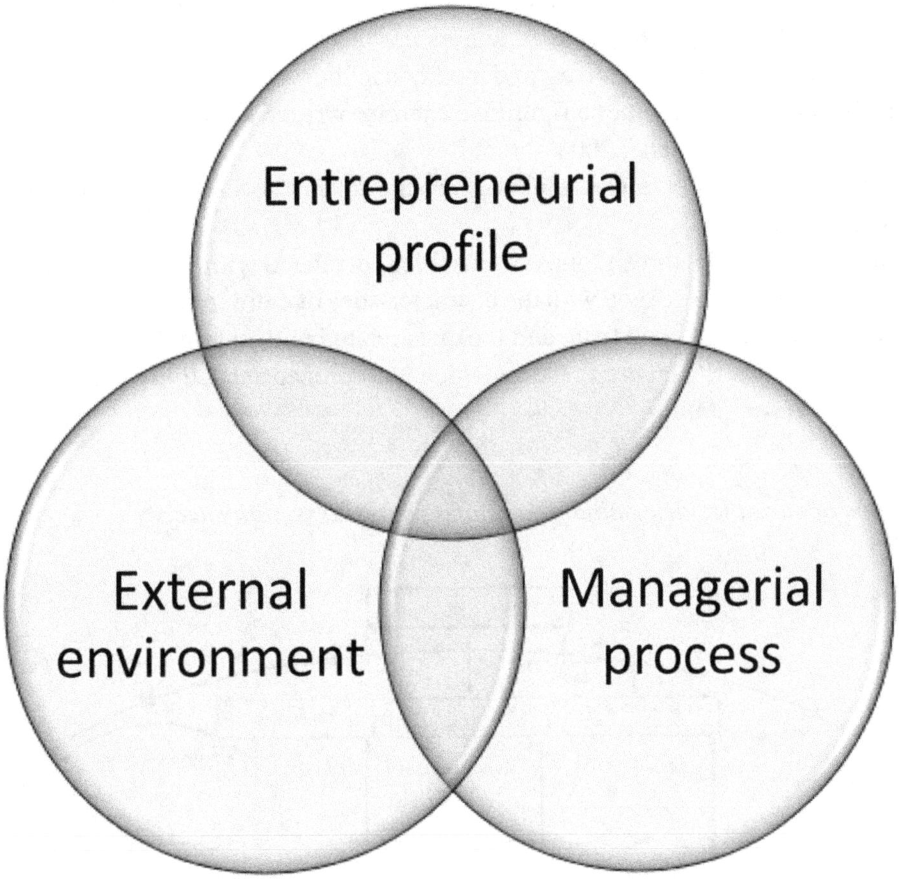

The balance between these three dimensions and variables included in each one could be tricky. In this way entrepreneurs benefit in planning their activity to identify possible risks, resources, and financial forecast. One of the more popular tools to do it is Business Plan, next section improve the discussion about business plan and their potential role to the entrepreneurial success.

THE BUSINESS PLAN AS A TOOL FOR ENTREPRENEURIAL SUCCESS

Nowadays the success of new ventures is deeply related with the opportunity exploration and innovation (Drucker, 1985; Drucker, 2015; GEM, 2019/2020). Particularly startups must born with an innovative matrix (Del Bosco, B, Mazzucchelli, A., Chierici, R. & Di Gregorio, A., 2019). But also, mature companies to compete in a complex market must have innovation in their DNA. Frequently when these companies want to expand their business, they use the business plan as a tool for planning innovative projects, as well as in case of spinoffs.

A good business plan allows entrepreneurs to respond to changes effectively and sometimes means the difference between long-term success and failure. However, some authors refer that the relation between successful business practice and the previous existence of a business plan is not clearly supported by empirical evidence and consequently some entrepreneurs choose to write business plans without actually implementing their plan's goals, objectives, and methods in their venture (Karlsson and Honig, 2009). In these cases, the business plan becomes a figurative exercise written to please stakeholders (Zimmerman and Zeitz, 2002; Delmar and Shane, 2004).

More important than write a business plan is crucial to join several factors that allows the implementation of the planning.

The literature usually refers three groups of variables correlated with innovation and determinant for business plan success: the ones related with the characteristics of entrepreneurs, the ones related with the characteristics of the newly founded firm, and the ones related with external environment depending on the geographical and industrial environment in which entrepreneurial activity occurs (Franco & Haase, 2010; Schutjens & Wever, 2000).

Figure 2. Groups of variables determinant for startups business plan success
Source: Authors

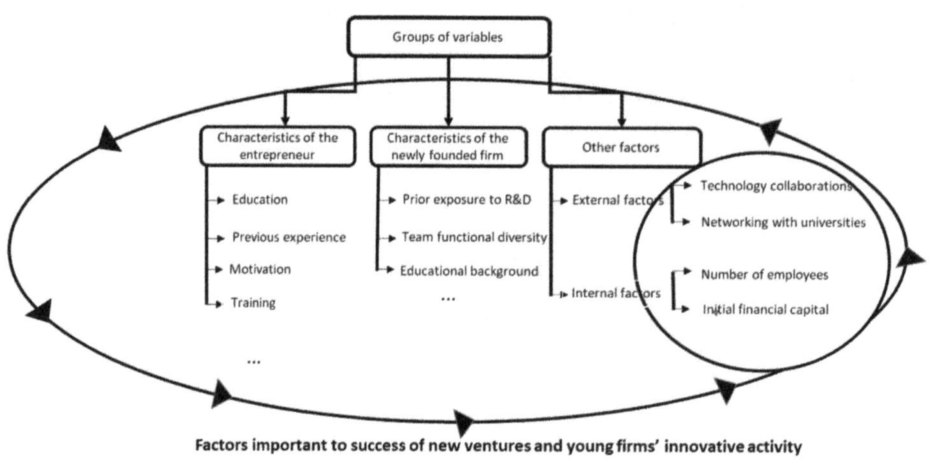

Concerning that characteristics of the entrepreneurs have a positive effect on startup success, they can influence the development and operationalization of business plan. In general education provide a set of skills that facilitate this process and this aspect is corroborate in literature by several authors that consider education as a critical success factor (Astebro & Bernhardt, 2003; Bates, 1997; Gimeno, Folta,; Headd, 2003; Jones et al, 2017; Schiller & Crewson, 1997; Smith & Clegg, 2016; Van de Ven et al., 1984). Other authors considerer the previous experience in the field or in successful business (Amankwah-Amoah, Boso, & Antwi-Agyei, 2018; Byrne & Shepherd, 2015; Cope, 2011; Doutriaux, 1992; Dyke et al., 1992; Luk, 1996; Peña, 2002; Reuber & Fisher, 1999). Finally, training and experience are also frequently referred as the determinant success of the business (Alstete, 2008; Headd, 2003; Van Praag, 2003; Van Praag & Cramer, 2001). Particularly, according to Haber and Reichel (2005) and West and Noel (2009), the training and experience of an entrepreneur are crucial for a proper formulation of the business plan and assure the ability to adapt to environmental changes and to improve the necessary implementations, and consequently increasing the chances of business success. Additionally, Headd (2003) and Ho and Wong (2007) considerer that when the entrepreneurs are motivated by the search for independence, autonomy, and the will to create their own businesses, the rigor and precision in planning are usually higher, the which also increases the willingness to make all necessary efforts to ensure that the business plan becomes a sustainable reality can be expected.

However, also the characteristics of the newly founded firm are pointed by several studies as important for business plan implementation and development. According to Protogerou, Caloghirou, & Vonortas (2017) both internal factors, especially those encapsulated in the human capital of founders such as prior exposure to R&D, team functional diversity and educational background, and external firm characteristics, such as technology collaborations and networking with universities are important in explaining young firms' innovative activity.

In addition to the characteristics of the entrepreneur, two other aspects are important, especially for the business plan operationalization, such as, the number of employees (Argawal & Audretsch, 2001; Dunne & Hughes, 1994; López-García & Puente, 2006) and initial financial capital (Brüderder et al., 1992; Headd, 2003; Schutjens and Wever, 2000). Therefore, the greater is the number of employees and the initial funding capital of startups to start its commercial activities, the better it's the chances of survival and development in long term. According with Bruëderl and Schuëssler (1990) the greater the resources that companies have at their disposal, the better their chances of survival during their initial stage of existence and their sustainability. This healthy situation in terms of resources can help the business to function long enough to identify suitable organizational routines, learn to cooperate with the various internal and external stakeholders, gain legitimacy and develop the knowledge and skills necessary for a proper implementation of the business plan, as well as to adapt their content, plans and processes, depending on the evolution of the variables relevant to the environment.

MEASURES FOR ENTREPRENEURIAL SUCCESS

In macroeconomic perspective entrepreneurship is associated with innovation (Schumpeter, 1961), economic growth (Carree and Thurik, 2003) and improvements in the country's welfare (Lumpkin & Dess, 1996; Porter, 1985). In this perspective the measure of the success is based mainly on organizational performance indicators, such as company survival, sales, profit, employee growth, market share, return of the investment (Chandler and Hanks, 1998). This organizational success indicators could be collected in the three ways (Richard, Devinney, Yip and Johnson, 2009):

1. From accounting and financial market information
2. From internal benchmarking of entrepreneurs: company growth, sales, profits, etc.
3. From external benchmarking of entrepreneurs: evaluation of the company comparing with rivals.

Moreover, financial performance, in the organizational perspective can provide other type of indicators linked with strategic direction (goals, vision, mission directed to the future results; building an effective team; and, benchmarking progress against goals) and national or global impact (market share;

expansion in national and international market; plans to enable international growth and increase impact) (Wach, 2010).

Nevertheless, other academics point out the importance of measure success using other indicators (non-pecuniary) because sometimes pecuniary indicators could be manipulated for tax reasons/earning management (Ramirez-Orellana et al, 2017) or the tendency to positively judgement of their one situation (Taylor and Brown, 1994).

This perspective highlighting the importance of consider performance concept as more than the economic dimension, such as intangible success linked with variables more associated to the entrepreneur profile, such as autonomy, independence, work-enjoyment, self-directed work and high achievement (McClelland, 1961, Schwartz and Bardi, 1997), work satisfaction (Chen et al, 2016), positive relationship with their employees and customers to achieve social recognition, to contribute to society (e.g. social entrepreneurs) or for firm continuity (e.g. family business entrepreneurs) (Gorgievski, Ascalon and Stephan, 2010). Table 1 present a taxonomy for entrepreneurial success criteria in the personal and organizational criteria.

Table 1. Taxonomy of entrepreneurial success criteria

Personal success criteria	Organizational success criteria
Self-enhancement/self- realization	Company survival
Autonomy/independence	Employee numbers and growth
Financial Security/Personal Income	Return on investment
Interesting tasks	Cash flow
Being one's own boss/influence	Sales and their growth
Reputation/prestige	Market share and expansion
Social interactions with employees and customers	General company performance and growth
Providing needed products and services	Being better then rivals

Source: Wach, 2010

CRITICAL DISCUSSION ABOUT SUCCESS FACTORS OF THE BUSINESS PLAN

The literature review about the relevance of business plan as a tool for startups and mature companies allowed the systematization of the success factors. Figure 3 provide a summary of different theorical perspective presented in previous section.

This paper considerers different types of business, namely startups, represented on the left side of the figure as well as mature companies, represented on the right side.

The center line of the figure symbolizes the course of companies since the first stage of creation until their development (planning, creation and development of business). During this course, the companies face the influence of internal and external factors. However, according with literature review, some of these factors are commons to startups and mature companies, but some of them depends on the stage of the business. This track begins in the market with the evaluation of an opportunity and the creation and capture of startup value. During planning a set of internal factors influence the success such as, size

Figure 3. A synthesis about success factors of the Business Plan
Source: Authors

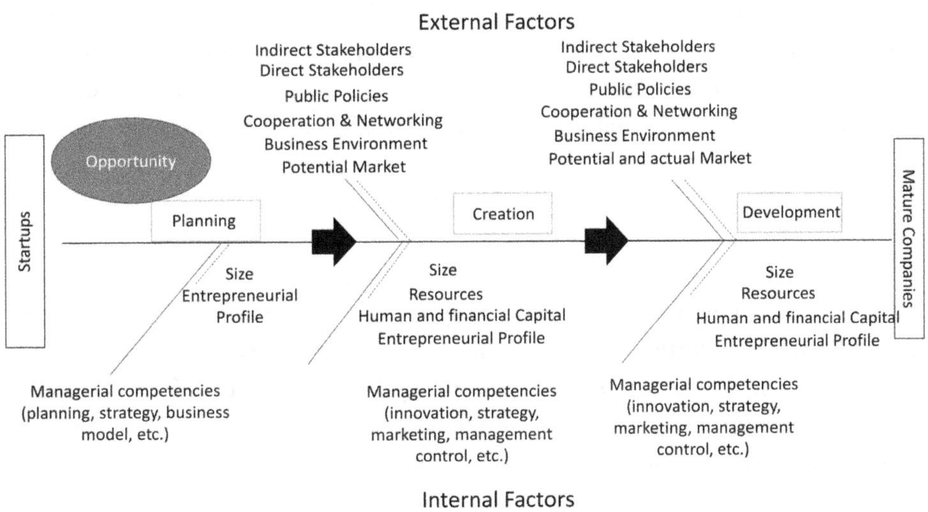

(startups born small), entrepreneurial profile (education, previous experience, motivation, resilience, training, personal characteristics such as gender, age, etc.). In the stages creation and development also, some internal factors can be added, such as resources and human and financial capital (seed capital for creation and capital for growth for development).

Transversal to all stages managerial competencies is important and reveals some particularities according to the several stages. In the creation it is important that entrepreneurs create a business model and be able to plan and formulate the strategy of the future business. In creation and development stages other managerial competencies must considerer, namely innovation, strategy, marketing and management control.

Furthermore, a set of external factors can influence the success of new business all stages: indirect stakeholders (government, universities, associations, trade unions), direct stakeholders (competitors, suppliers, distributors, customers, etc), public policies (National, European and International), cooperation and networking with several organizations, business environment (hard and software infrastructures) and potential and actual market (domestic and international).

These factors compete among them in order to achieve or not entrepreneurial success.

AGENDA PROPOSAL AND FINAL CONSIDERATIONS

The literature review suggest that is not possible to isolate the factors that influence the success of business plan from the entrepreneurial success factors in general. In fact, business plan is an important tool that can be used in different stages of business to adjust strategy to environmental changes.

In this sense, an agenda proposal can be organized according with some dimensions:

- Public policies

Public policies must be suitable to create regulation to business environment to support entrepreneurs in planning, creation, and development stages, particularly in the case of small business. Some particular focus of positive discrimination for vulnerable groups, such as young, women, immigrants should be considered, as well as policies and regulations more tailor made according with the sector in order to be able to increase the competitiveness.

- Human capital

In a macro perspective the human capital must be supported by education through a system that allows entrepreneurial skills, such as creativity, divergent thinking, critical spirit, multidisciplinary knowledge, autonomy, etc. Additionally, it is also important that in higher education students from different scientific areas have train in managerial competencies. In a micro perspective entrepreneur must attend to the importance of a long-term training and education of their collaborators.

- Financial capital

Government must create the conditions to promote the availability of the capital for different stages of business (seed capital, risk capital, micro credit, etc).

- Infrastructures

Infrastructures must be available for entrepreneurs. Some hard infrastructures such as communications, transports, but also soft infrastructures related with business are important, such as research centres, business incubators, coworking spaces, technological parks, business parks, that provide resources to the implementation and development of the business in different stages.

- Cooperation and networks

The cooperation and networks can be enhanced in different ways, externally and internally. Externally, through knowledge alliances between higher education, institutions, and companies, through competitors (coopetition), as well as through customers or suppliers. Internally, through the cooperation between companies of the same group, departments, and so on. Both externally and internally cooperation depends on the entrepreneurial profile, but not only. Also, policies can include measures to improve cooperation between different partners. For example, the access to public funding can depend on the cooperation between universities, companies, public administration, this means several parts. Technology transfer can become more effective through a close collaboration between from universities and research centres and companies. Also, education and training systems can contribute to improve the perception of positive benefits of cooperation.

In summary this paper allowed a systematization of the factors that influence the entrepreneurial success in several stages of the business. Through this research it was possible to understand that entrepreneurial success is systemic. That means, that is possible to identify some crucial factors, nevertheless these factors isolated are not sufficient to warranty entrepreneurial success in long term.

One limitation of this exploratory research is the lack of empirical research to confirm the results of the proposals of the literature review. The next step plan to validate the literature review through an empirical research collecting data about entrepreneurial success factors with entrepreneurs from the stages of the business.

ACKNOWLEDGMENT

The authors wish to thank to Erasmus+ Program of the EU I KA2-Knowledge Alliance Program-KABADA / Knowledge Alliance of Business idea Assessment: Digital Approach I 612542-EPP-1-2019-1-LV-EPPKA2-KA.

REFERENCES

Alam, G. M., Hoque, K. E., Ismail, L., & Mishra, P. K. (2010). Do developing countries need education laws to manage its system or are ethics and a market-driven approach sufficient? *African Journal of Business Management*, *4*(15), 3406–3416.

Alstete, J. W. (2008). Aspects of entrepreneurial success. *Journal of Small Business and Enterprise Development*, *15*(3), 584–594. doi:10.1108/14626000810892364

Amankwah-Amoah, J., Boso, N., & Antwi-Agyei, I. (2018). The Effects of Business Failure Experience on Successive Entrepreneurial Engagements: An Evolutionary Phase Model. *Group & Organization Management*, *43*(4), 648–682. doi:10.1177/1059601116643447

Argawal, R., & Audretsch, D. B. (2001). Does entry size matter? The impact of the life cycle and technology on firm survival. *The Journal of Industrial Economics*, *49*(1), 21–43. doi:10.1111/1467-6451.00136

Astebro, T., & Bernhardt, I. (2003). Start-up financing, owner characteristics and survival. *Journal of Economics and Business*, *55*(4), 303–320. doi:10.1016/S0148-6195(03)00029-8

Astebro, T., & Bernhardt, I. (2003). Start-up financing, owner characteristics and survival. *Journal of Economics and Business*, *55*(4), 303–320. doi:10.1016/S0148-6195(03)00029-8

Ayala, J., & Manzano, G. (2014). The resilience of the entrepreneur. Influence on the success of the business. A longitudinal analysis. *Journal of Economic Psychology*, *42*, 126–135. doi:10.1016/j.joep.2014.02.004

Baptista, R., Karaoz, M., & Mendonca, J. (2013). The impact of human capital on the early success of necessity versus opportunity-based entrepreneurs. *Small Business Economics*, *42*(4), 831–847. doi:10.100711187-013-9502-z

Baron, R. A., & Markman, G. D. (2003). Beyond social capital: The role of entrepreneurs' social competence in their financial success. *Journal of Business Venturing*, *1*(1), 41–60. doi:10.1016/S0883-9026(00)00069-0

Bates, T. (1997). *Race, self-employment and upward mobility: An illusive American dream*. John Hopkins University Press.

Bruderl, J., Preisendorfer, P., & Ziegler, R. (1992). Survival chances of newly founded business organizations. *American Sociological Review*, *57*(2), 227–242. doi:10.2307/2096207

Bruderl, J., & Schussler, R. (1990). Organizational mortality: The liabilities of newness and adolescence. *Administrative Science Quarterly*, *35*(3), 530–547. doi:10.2307/2393316

Burns, R. A., & Anstey, K. J. (2010). The Connor-Davidson Resilience Scale (CD-RISC): Testing the invariance of a uni-dimensional resilience measure that is independent of positive and negative affect. *Personality and Individual Differences*, *48*(5), 527–531. doi:10.1016/j.paid.2009.11.026

Byrne, O., & Shepherd, D. A. (2015). Different strokes for different folks: Entrepreneurial narratives of emotion, cognition, and making sense of business failure. *Entrepreneurship Theory and Practice*, *39*(2), 375–405. doi:10.1111/etap.12046

Cabello, R., Sorrel, M. A., Fernández-Pinto, I., Extremera, N., & Fernández-Berrocal, P. (2016). Age and gender differences in ability emotional intelligence in adults: A cross-sectional study. *Developmental Psychology*, *52*(9), 1486–1492. doi:10.1037/dev0000191 PMID:27570984

Campbell-Sills, L., Forte, D. R., & Stein, M. B. (2009). Demographic and childhood environmental predictors of resilience in a community sample. *Journal of Psychiatric Research*, *43*(12), 1007–1012. doi:10.1016/j.jpsychires.2009.01.013 PMID:19264325

Carree, M. A., & Thurik, A. R. (2003) The Impact of Entrepreneurship on Economic Growth. In Handbook of Entrepreneurship Research. Kluwer Academic Publishers.

Carvalho, L., Backx, A., & Galina, S. (2019). Entrepreneurs' perceptions of business incubator services in Brazil and Portugal. *International Journal of Business Innovation and Research*, *19*(1), 80–100. doi:10.1504/IJBIR.2019.099753

Chandler, G., & Hanks, S. (1998). An examination of the substitutability of founders human and financial capital in emerging business ventures. *Journal of Business Venturing*, *13*(5), 353–369. doi:10.1016/S0883-9026(97)00034-7

Chen, P., Sparrow, P., & Cooper, C. (2016). The relationship between person-organization fit and job satisfaction. *Journal of Managerial Psychology*, *31*(5), 946–959. doi:10.1108/JMP-08-2014-0236

Child, J., Elbanna, S., & Rodrigues, S. (2010). The political aspects of strategic decision making. In P. C. Nutt & D. C. Wilson (Eds.), *Handbook of decision making* (pp. 105–137). Wiley.

Coleman, S. (2007). The role of human and financial capital in the profitability and growth of women-owned small firms. *Journal of Small Business Management*, *45*(3), 303–319. doi:10.1111/j.1540-627X.2007.00214.x

Cope, J. (2011). Entrepreneurial learning from failure: An interpretative phenomenological analysis. *Journal of Business Venturing*, *26*(6), 604–623. doi:10.1016/j.jbusvent.2010.06.002

Costa, T., & Galina, S. (2016). The virtuous relationship between entrepreneurship and social capital: A study on tourism rural businesses in Portugal and Brazil. *Tourism & Management Studies*, *12*(2), 57–69. doi:10.18089/tms.2016.12207

Danes, S. M., Lee, J., Amarapurkar, S., Stafford, K., Haynes, G., & Brewton, K. E. (2009). Determinants of family business resilience after a natural disaster by gender of business owner. *Journal of Developmental Entrepreneurship*, *14*(4), 333–354. doi:10.1142/S1084946709001351

Danes, S. M., Stafford, K., & Loy, J. T. (2007). Family business performance: The effects of gender and management. *Journal of Business Research*, *60*(10), 1058–1069. doi:10.1016/j.jbusres.2006.12.013

Del Bosco, B., Mazzucchelli, A., Chierici, R., & Di Gregorio, A. (2019). Innovative startup creation: The effect of local factors and demographic characteristics of entrepreneurs. *The International Entrepreneurship and Management Journal*, 1–20.

Delmar, F., & Shane, S. (2004). Legitimating first: Organizing activities and the survival of new ventures. *Journal of Business Venturing*, *19*(3), 385–410. doi:10.1016/S0883-9026(03)00037-5

Dormann, C., & Zapf, D. (2001). Job satisfaction: A meta-analysis of stabilities. *Journal of Organizational Behavior*, *22*(6), 483–504. doi:10.1002/job.98

Doutriaux, J. (1992). Emerging high-tech firms: How durable are their comparative start-up advantages. *Journal of Business Venturing*, *7*(4), 303–322. doi:10.1016/0883-9026(92)90004-B

Dover, P. A., & Dierk, U. (2010). The ambidextrous organization: Integrating managers, entrepreneurs and leaders. *The Journal of Business Strategy*, *31*(5), 49–58. doi:10.1108/02756661011076318

Drucker, P. (1985). *Innovation and entrepreneurship* (1st ed.). Harper Collins.

Drucker, P. (2015). *Innovation and entrepreneurship – Practice and Principles*. Routledge.

Dunne, P., & Hughes, A. (1994). Age, size, growth and survival: UK companies in the 80s. *The Journal of Industrial Economics*, *42*(2), 115–140. doi:10.2307/2950485

Fernandez-Guerrero, R., Revuelto-Taboada, L., & Simon-Moy, V. (2012). The business plan as a project: An evaluation of its predictive capability for business success. *Service Industries Journal*, *32*(1), 2399–2420. doi:10.1080/02642069.2012.677830

Franco, M., & Haase, H. (2010). Failure factors in small and medium-sized enterprises: Qualitative study from an attributional perspective. *The International Entrepreneurship and Management Journal*, *6*(4), 503–521. doi:10.100711365-009-0124-5

GEM. (n.d.). *Global Report, 2019/20*. London business School.

Gimeno, J., Folta, T., Cooper, A., & Woo, C. (1997). Survival of the fittest? Entrepreneurial human capital and the persistence of underperforming firms. *Administrative Science Quarterly*, *42*(4), 750–783. doi:10.2307/2393656

Gorgievski, M. J., Ascalon, E. M., & Stephan, U. (2011). Small Business Owners' Success Criteria, a Values Approach to Personal Differences. *Journal of Small Business Management*, *49*(2), 207–232. doi:10.1111/j.1540-627X.2011.00322.x

Haber, S., & Reichel, A. (2005). Identifying performance measures of small ventures – the case of the tourism industry. *Journal of Small Business Management*, *43*(3), 257–286. doi:10.1111/j.1540-627X.2005.00137.x

Headd, B. (2003). Redefining business success: Distinguishing between closure and failure. *Small Business Economics*, *21*(1), 51–61. doi:10.1023/A:1024433630958

Hitt, M., & Ireland, D. (2000). The intersection of entrepreneurship and strategic management research. In D. Sexton & H. Landström (Eds.), *Handbook of entrepreneurship* (pp. 45–63). Blackwell.

Ho, Y., & Wong, P. (2007). Financing, regulatory costs and entrepreneurial propensity. *Small Business Economics*, *28*(2), 187–204. doi:10.100711187-006-9015-0

Huggins, R. (2000). The success and failure of policy-implanted inter-firm network initiatives: Motivations, processes and structure. *Entrepreneurship and Regional Development*, *12*(2), 211–236. doi:10.1080/089856200283036

Jarillo, J. (1988). On strategic networks. *Strategic Management Journal*, *9*(1), 31–41. doi:10.1002mj.4250090104

Jones, P., Pickernell, D., Fisher, R., & Netana, C. (2017). A Tale of Two Universities: Graduates Perceived Value of Entrepreneurship Education. *Education + Training*, *59*(7/8), 689–705. doi:10.1108/ET-06-2017-0079

Karairmak, Ö. (2010). Establishing the psychometric qualities of the Connor-Davidson Resilience Scale (CD-RISC) using exploratory and confirmatory factor analysis in a trauma survivor sample. *Psychiatry Research*, *179*(3), 350–356. doi:10.1016/j.psychres.2009.09.012 PMID:20493533

Karlsson, T., & Honig, B. (2009). Judging a business by its cover: An institutional perspective on new ventures and the business plan. *Journal of Business Venturing*, *24*(1), 27–45. doi:10.1016/j.jbusvent.2007.10.003

Kim, B., Kim, H., & Jeon, Y. (2018). Critical Success Factors of a Design Startup Business. *Sustainability*, *10*(9), 29–81. doi:10.3390u10092981

Kristiansen, S., Furuholt, B., & Wahid, F. (2003). Internet cafe entrepreneurs: Pioneers in information dissemination in Indonesia. *International Journal of Entrepreneurship and Innovation*, *4*(4), 251–263. doi:10.5367/000000003129574315

Le Bris, S., Madrid-Guijarro, A., & Martin, D. P. (2019). Decision-making in complex environments under time pressure and risk of critical irreversibility: The role of meta rules. *Management*, *22*(1), 1–29.

López-García, P., & Puente, S. (2006, April). Rasgos básicos de la supervivencia de empresas en España. *Boletín Económico del Banco de España*.

López-Núñez, M. I., Rubio-Valdehita, S., Aparicio-García, M. E., & Díaz-Ramiro, E. M. (2020). Are entrepreneurs born or made? The influence of personality. *Personality and Individual Differences*, 154.

Luca, P., & Presutti, M. (2010). The impact of social capital on the start-ups performance growth. *Journal of Small Business Management*, *48*(2), 197–227. doi:10.1111/j.1540-627X.2010.00292.x

Luk, S. (1996). Success in Hong Kong: Factors self-reported by successful small business owners. *Journal of Small Business Management*, *34*(3), 68–75.

Lumpkin, G. T., & Dess, G. G. (1996). Clarifying the entrepreneurial orientation construct and linking it to performance. *Academy of Management Review*, *21*(1), 135–172. doi:10.2307/258632

McClelland, D. C. (1961). *The achieving society*. Van Nostrand. doi:10.1037/14359-000

McKenzie, D., & Paffhausen, A. L. (2019). Small Firm Death in Developing Countries. *The Review of Economics and Statistics*, *101*(4), 645–657. doi:10.1162/rest_a_00798

McKenzie, D., & Sansone, D. (2019). Predicting entrepreneurial success is hard: Evidence from a business plan competition in Nigeria. *Journal of Development Economics*, *141*, 141. doi:10.1016/j.jdeveco.2019.07.002

McMahon, R. G. P. (2001). Growth and performance of manufacturing SMEs: The influence of financial management characteristics. *International Small Business Journal*, *19*(3), 10–28. doi:10.1177/0266242601193001

Naffziger, D., Hornsby, J., & Kuratko, D. F. (1994). A proposed research model of entrepreneurial motivation. *Entrepreneurship Theory and Practice*, *18*(3), 29–43. doi:10.1177/104225879401800303

Olafsen, E., & Cook, P. A. (2016). *Growth Entrepreneurship in Developing Countries: A Preliminary Literature Review*. The World Bank Group.

Omri, A., Frikha, M., & Bouraoui, M. (2015). An empirical investigation of factors affecting small business success. *Journal of Management Development*, *34*(9), 1073–1093. doi:10.1108/JMD-07-2013-0088

Paulo, A., Carvalho, L., Costa, T., Lopes, J., & Galina, S. (2017). Mapping Open Innovation: A bibliometric review to compare developed and emerging countries. *Global Business Review*, *18*(3), 291–307. doi:10.1177/0972150916668600

Peña, I. (2002). Intellectual capital and business start up success. *Journal of Intellectual Capital*, *3*(2), 180–198. doi:10.1108/14691930210424761

Porter, M. E. (1985). *Competitive advantage: Creating and sustaining superior performance*. Free Press.

Protogerou, A., Caloghirou, Y., & Vonortas, N. S. (2017). Determinants of young firms' innovative performance: Empirical evidence from Europe. *Research Policy*, *46*(7), 1312–1326. doi:10.1016/j.respol.2017.05.011

Ramirez-Orellana, A., Martinez-Romero, M., & Mariño-Garrido, T. (2017). Measuring fraud and earning management by a case of study: Evidence from an international family business. *European Journal of Family Business*, *7*(1-2), 41–53. doi:10.1016/j.ejfb.2017.10.001

Rauch, A., & Frese, M. (2007). Let's put the person back into entrepreneurship research: A meta analysis on the relationship between business owners' personality traits, business creation, and success. *European Journal of Work and Organizational Psychology*, *16*(4), 353–385. doi:10.1080/13594320701595438

Reuber, A. R., & Fisher, E. (1999). Understanding the consequences of founders' experience. *Journal of Small Business Management*, *37*(2), 30–45.

Richard, P., Devinney, T., Yip, G., & Johnson, G. (2009). Measuring Organizational Performance: Towards Methodological Best Practice. *Journal of Management*, *35*(3), 718–804. doi:10.1177/0149206308330560

Santos, F. J., Roomi, M. A., & Liñán, F. (2016). About gender differences and the social environment in the development of entrepreneurial intentions. *Journal of Small Business Management*, *54*(1), 49–66. doi:10.1111/jsbm.12129

Schumpeter, J. A. (1961). *The theory of economic development*. Oxford University Press.

Schutjens, V. A. J. M., & Wever, E. (2000). Determinants of new firm success. *Papers in Regional Science*, *79*(2), 135–159. doi:10.1007101100050040

Schwartz, S. H., & Bardi, A. (1997). Influences of adaptation to communist rule on value priorities in Eastern Europe. *Political Psychology*, *18*(2), 385–410. doi:10.1111/0162-895X.00062

Smith, K., & Clegg, P. (2017). Experiencing Business Start? Up Through an Enterprise Placement Year. In *Entrepreneurship Education: New Perspectives on Entrepreneurship Education. Contemporary Issues in Entrepreneurship Research London* (pp. 307–334). Emerald Group Publishing Ltd. doi:10.1108/S2040-724620170000007018

Stam, W., Arzlanian, S., & Elfring, T. (2014). Social capital of entrepreneurs and small firm performance: A meta-analysis of contextual and methodological moderators. *Journal of Business Venturing*, *29*(1), 152–173. doi:10.1016/j.jbusvent.2013.01.002

Swierczek, F. W., & Ha, T. T. (2003). Entrepreneurial orientation, uncertainty avoidance and firm performance: An analysis of Thai and Vietnamese SMEs. *International Journal of Entrepreneurship and Innovation*, *4*(1), 46–58. doi:10.5367/000000003101299393

Taylor, S. E., & Brown, J. D. (1994). Positive illusions and well-being revisited: Separating fact from fiction. *Psychological Bulletin*, *116*(1), 21–27. doi:10.1037/0033-2909.116.1.21 PMID:8078971

Thornhill, S. (2006). Knowledge, innovation and firm performance in high- and low-technology regimes. *Journal of Business Venturing*, *21*(5), 687–703. doi:10.1016/j.jbusvent.2005.06.001

Toor, S. R., & Ogunlana, S. O. (2010). Beyond the 'iron triangle': Stakeholder perception of key performance indicators (KPIs) for large-scale public sector development projects. *International Journal of Project Management*, *28*(3), 228–236. doi:10.1016/j.ijproman.2009.05.005

Unger, J. M., Rauch, A., Frese, M., & Rosenbusch, N. (2011). Human capital and entrepreneurial success: A meta-analytical review. *Journal of Business Venturing*, *26*(3), 341–358. doi:10.1016/j.jbusvent.2009.09.004

Van de Ven, A. H., Hudson, R., & Schroeder, D. R. (1984). Designing new business start-ups: Entrepreneurial, organizational and ecological considerations. *Journal of Management*, *10*(1), 89–107. doi:10.1177/014920638401000108

Van Praag, C., & Cramer, J. (2001). The roots of entrepreneurship and labour demand: Individual ability and low risk aversion. *Economica.*, *68*(269), 45–62. doi:10.1111/1468-0335.00232

Van Praag, C. M. (2003). Business survival and success of young small business owners. *Small Business Economics*, *21*(1), 1–17. doi:10.1023/A:1024453200297

Wach, D. (2010). Defining and measuring entrepreneurial success. In M. Lukes & M. Laguna (Eds.), *Entrepreneurship. A psychological approach* (pp. 89–102). University of Economics.

Weisberg, Y. J., DeYoung, C. G., & Hirsh, J. B. (2011). Gender differences in personality across the ten aspects of the Big Five. *Frontiers in Psychology, 2*, 178. doi:10.3389/fpsyg.2011.00178 PMID:21866227

West, G. III, & Noel, T. (2009). The impact of knowledge resources on new venture performance. *Journal of Small Business Management, 47*(1), 1–22. doi:10.1111/j.1540-627X.2008.00259.x

William & Susan. (2005). Fundamentals of Business: Starting a Small Business. McGraw-Hill/Irwin.

Zhao, H., & Seibert, S. E. (2006). The big five personality dimensions and entrepreneurial status: A meta-analytical review. *The Journal of Applied Psychology, 91*(2), 259–271. doi:10.1037/0021-9010.91.2.259 PMID:16551182

Zimmerman, M. A., & Zeitz, G. J. (2002). Beyond survival: Achieving new venture growth by building legitimacy. *Academy of Management Review, 27*(3), 414–431. doi:10.2307/4134387

ADDITIONAL READING

Carvalho, L., Galina, S., & Sánchez-Hérnandez, M. I. (2020). An international perspective of the business incubators' perception about business model Canvas for start-ups. *Thunderbird International Business Review, 62*(5), 503–513. doi:10.1002/tie.22112

Carvalho, L., Rego, C., Lucas, M. R., Sanchez, I., & Backx, A. (2019). *New Paths of Entrepreneurship Development*. Springer Book Series. doi:10.1007/978-3-319-96032-6

Carvalho, L. C., Rego, M. C., Lucas, M. R., Sánchez-Hernández, M. I., & Noronha, A. (2018). *Entrepreneurship and Structural Change in Dynamic Territories – Contributions from Developed and Developing Countries*. Springer Book Series. doi:10.1007/978-3-319-76400-9

Costa, T., Teixeira, N., & Lisboa, I. (2019). Perceptions of Entrepreneurial Ecosystem in Tourism Sector: A Study in Municipality of Setúbal. In N. Teixeira, T. Costa, & I. Lisboa (Eds.), *IGI Global book series Advances in Business Strategy and Competitive Advantage* (pp. 157–177). ABSCA.

Lisboa, L., Costa, T., & Teixeira, N. (2019). Managing Customers Credit to Reduce the Company's Risk and Overdue Credits. In N. Teixeira, T. Costa, & I. Lisboa (Eds.), *Handbook of Research on Entrepreneurship, Innovation, and Internationalization* (pp. 561–585). IGI Global. doi:10.4018/978-1-5225-8479-7.ch021

Teixeira, N., Lisboa, I., & Costa, T. (2019). Business Strategy and Financial Performance. In N. Teixeira, T. Costa, & I. Lisboa (Eds.), *IGI Global book series Advances in Business Strategy and Competitive Advantage* (pp. 1–59). ABSCA.

KEY TERMS AND DEFINITIONS

Business Plan: A business plan is a written document that describes in detail how a business, in general a new business) defines its objectives and how it is to go about achieving its goals.

Entrepreneur: Is an individual who creates a new business or implement changes in existing companies, taking risks. The entrepreneur is usually seen as an innovator, a source of new ideas, goods, services, and business/or procedures.

Entrepreneurship: Refers to the studies about the creation of new business. Could also be linked to opportunity and innovation. It is possible find different kinds of entrepreneurship, such as social entrepreneurship, female entrepreneurship, etc.

Startup: A startup is a company that seeks to explore a business opportunity in an innovative or untapped area. Instead of being supported by a fixed model, it has a more fluid concept, adapting to the opportunities that arise. Startups are associated to technology and innovation.

Chapter 5
Corporate Simulation and the Articulation of the Problem-Based Learning Methodology With the Continuous Assessment Model

Ana Bela Teixeira
Polytechnic Institute of Setúbal, Portugal

Paulo José Rodrigues Costa
Polytechnic Institute of Setúbal, Portugal

Nuno Delicado Teixeira
Polytechnic Institute of Setúbal, Portugal

Telmo Passuco Wergikosky
Polytechnic Institute of Setúbal, Portugal

Rosa Morgado Galvão
Polytechnic Institute of Setúbal, Portugal

Filipe Damas Bacalhau
https://orcid.org/0000-0003-1788-4618
Polytechnic Institute of Setúbal, Portugal

ABSTRACT

Academic success is a priority, and according to the literature review, it is associated with the application of problem-based learning methodologies or the continuous assessment model. The case study performed was based on the course unit Corporate Simulation (CS), part of the Accounting and Finance course academic curriculum. After describing the functioning process, objectives, and assessment model of CS, it was shown that from 2014/15 to 2019/20, the level of approval of CS was 94.8%. Also, from the results of the survey conducted with the students who completed CS, from 2007/08 to 2018/19, on a scale of 1 to 5, in options 4 and 5 (good and very good), the objectives weigh on average, 85.3%, and that, in the academic year 2019/20, the specific characteristics of functioning, as a consequence of COVID 19, did not cause changes in the trends of assessment and approval in CS.

DOI: 10.4018/978-1-7998-8239-8.ch005

INTRODUCTION

One of the current concerns regarding education in Portugal, namely in higher education, is academic underachievement and abandonment, deserving as such urgent measures to be taken. In this sense, and in opposition, academic success, when it exists, must be publicized and its origin made aware. From this perspective, it is intended, in this study, to detail and deepen the functioning of a successful course unit, which, in the teaching of Accounting and Finance, associates with the continuous assessment model, the problem-based learning methodology (Silva, Aleixo & Teixeira, 2016).

Simultaneously, higher education is currently facing another major challenge: to train graduates who respond to effective organizational needs. Etxeberria and Pike (2011) state that future accounting professionals, in addition to the technical and scientific knowledge necessary for a good performance, must acquire other skills, namely, critical thinking and analysis, the ability to work in a team, to communicate, and to have a strong sense of responsibility and ethical commitment. Referring to learning needs, Serra (2004) mentions that they should include, among others, those that allow self-learning, group learning, and the use of technologies. According to Arbrecht and Sack (2000) and Jones (2010), regarding accounting education, there has been a greater approximation between the training provided by educational institutions and employers in the last decades.

Several authors associate the success of teaching with the use of various teaching methodologies, favoring the association of traditional methods where the teacher plays a crucial role in the learning process, with the problem-based methodology, where the student is the main responsible for learning. The articulation of these methodologies points to the use of traditional methodologies at the beginning of the course and, and when the curricular structure develops, and there is the need to articulate and consolidate knowledge, the use of the problem-based learning methodology (Teixeira, Silva, Aleixo, & Mata, 2015).

Alves, Moutinho, Pires and Ribeiro (2013) report that when students attend courses in which teaching is focused on learning, they feel much more motivated and are more likely to succeed. Castillo and Abad (2003) emphasize the importance of student and teacher involvement in the teaching/learning process.

Nevertheless, the application of new teaching methodologies, driving academic success and the preparation of graduates who respond to the current needs of organizations and the systematic changes in society, has consequently posed significant challenges to educational institutions, both in adjusting the curriculum structure, as well as in the teacher's performance and the accountability of students' acquisition of learning competencies. Then, it is to be expected to articulate current and differentiating curriculum structures with the behavioral change of teachers and students and a new approach in training/teaching, with practical effects on the results and quality of education.

Thus, this study, in addition to the introduction, is organized into four sections. Section one develops the theme of successful teaching, addressing the teaching methodology problem-based learning and the continuous assessment model. Section two is dedicated to the methodology applied in the study, and section three, to the case study. The case study begins with the description of the Corporate Simulation Course Unit in the curriculum structure of the Accounting and Finance Course, where the following topics are presented: the role of the teacher/tutor and the continuous assessment model of the Corporate Simulation Course Unit, followed by different perspectives of analysis of the course unit in the period from 2014/2015 to 2019/2020. In this section dedicated to the case study, specificities arising from the impact of the COVID 19 pandemic on teaching were also highlighted, namely in the academic year

2019/2020, both regarding students and professors, as well as functioning and assessment. Section four was dedicated to the conclusions.

BACKGROUND

Successful Teaching, the Problem-Based Learning Methodology, and the Continuous Assessment Model

Focusing on higher education in Portugal, one of the problems that need to be solved is failure and school dropout. Continued academic underachievement leads to school abandonment; therefore, teaching and evaluation models are fundamental issues in education and are essential tools in searching for better results for students and the learning process (Silva, Aleixo, & Teixeira, 2016).

Balancho and Coelho (1996) consider as causes for students' failure: their way of life and family environment, and the type of learning proposals offered by the school, which usually do not motivate them to build knowledge. Barata, Calheiros, Patrício, Graça and Lima (2012) refer that a determining factor for the high level of academic failure in Portugal is associated with the idea that repeating the year favors learning. However, according to the same authors, there is no scientific evidence that retention can be a pedagogical strategy. The understanding is that may not be. Repeating the academic level can have precisely the opposite effect; repeating what did not go well demotivates and creates distance and resistance to the subject.

Gomes, Brito, and Varela (2016) emphasize the importance of new teaching models that are not based on memorization and the need to promote academic success using new teaching and learning methodologies.

The Problem Based Learning Methodology

In Portugal, traditionally, the teaching in higher education has been dominated by the predominance of theoretical models, based on a relationship between the teacher, in an active role, as the transmitter and the student as the receiver of knowledge (Alves et al., 2013)

The curriculum centered on the problem-based learning methodology shifts the focus from teaching to learning; that is, it shifts the focus from the teacher as the center of the teaching and learning process to the student, leading the student to understand that learning is not just acquiring information, but processing information and transforming it into knowledge (Sousa & Dourado, 2015).

Suárez and Ramos (2011) state, regarding the teaching methodologies, specifically in higher education, that much progress has been made, often associating traditional teaching models in which the teacher using the lecture method is the main responsible for the student's performance, with those oriented to the student's autonomous learning, where the teacher acts to facilitate the teaching process. In this last teaching method, it is expected, the student's growing responsibility in learning and of the teacher, to encourage the student to have an active role in the learning process (Ariza, 2011). Therefore, it is intended for the student to be encouraged to have an active attitude in acquiring content and in relating new content to the knowledge already acquired (Polvillo & Montaño, 2011).

Rodrigues et al. (2019) consider that when students are submitted to the problem-based learning methodology, they develop autonomy and independence during the construction of their own knowledge, as well as greater commitment, responsibility, motivation, understanding, and assimilation of content.

According to Anés and Gavira (2011), the teaching methodology problem-based learning is accomplished by presenting the students with a real and complex problem that is well defined and contextualized. The first task performed by the students is to identify the additional information they need to solve the problem.

Pasin and Giroux (2011) state that this methodology must coexist with other traditional teaching methodologies. On the other hand, Barrows and Tamblyn (1980) argue that problem-based learning methodology should not be used at an early stage of learning where the aim is knowledge acquisition, but rather at a later stage of a curriculum structure where the aim is the curriculum synthesis and learning to find solutions to the problems presented.

Hansen (2006) points out that the problem-based methodology enables students to take a critical stance, strengthen their ability to work in groups and communicate, and at the same time apply, integrate and reinforce knowledge. Anés and Gavira (2011) highlight that the student´s involvement required by this methodology motivates him, and with motivation, according to Balancho and Coelho (1996), the student can find reasons to learn and improve himself and to discover new capabilities.

This teaching model is a differentiating one regarding how teachers and students coexist in the teaching of the course units, and it is fundamental for any of them to have a different posture from that of a traditional teaching methodology. It is necessary to move from a teaching model centered on the teacher (who lectures) to learning centered on student autonomy (Etxeberria & Pica, 2011). Thus, the teacher: Guides the research; Encourages and helps the student delve deeper into the research questions; Continually asks "why so"; Involves all students in the process; Encourages group responsibility; Makes educational diagnoses. On the other hand, the student: Identifies learning needs; Plans his work; Applies previous knowledge; Acquires integrated knowledge and flexibility; Investigates and seeks answers; and Evaluates his work (Teixeira, Aleixo, & Silva, 2012).

Borochovicius and Tortella (2014) reinforce the role of the teacher in applying the problem-based learning methodology and underline it as a teaching method that inserts the student in a reality close to the one he will face in the professional world, allowing the development of conceptual and procedural content through problem-situations.

Sousa and Dourado (2015) refer that teaching, being a dynamic process, demands from the teacher a permanent updating and change in his teaching practices and in this way, having in mind the development of skills different from the ones traditionally exercised in teaching, highlights the role of the tutor, a role that, demands the ability to develop stronger interpersonal relationships with his students. It is considered that, when applying the problem-based learning methodology, the figure of the tutor is fundamental. The authors mentioned above also stated that the role of the teacher-tutor in this methodology is to stimulate students to make their own decisions, to help them define the rules that will guide the group's work. Also, to contribute for them to perform research on the critical references for the topic under study and guide them in the preparation of the final work and support those who show most significant difficulties during the process.

Thus, applying problem-based learning methodologies, especially in course units at the end of courses, is appropriate and essential, stressing the importance of the paradigm shift in teaching, focusing on the teacher/student relationship.

The Continuous Assessment Model

Changes in society and consequently in education pose new demands on teaching, namely in public higher education. It is imperative to make changes in the objectives of the training offer and implement continuous assessment models that ensure individual assessment of the student's performance.

In recent years, according to Bajaelde, Lauridsen, and Lindberg (2018), in many European countries, there has been an increased focus on assessment and assessment feedback. This trend is triggered by the development of teaching and learning methodologies that support student-centered learning. Final exams at the end of the course unit or academic year have been the order of the day, but new developments can be found mainly in continuous or formative assessment activities throughout the academic year. According to the same authors, this type of assessment seems to support learning and motivation and reduce test anxiety for most students. They also state that continuous assessment seems to lead to better results than final assessment; however, the research is not yet conclusive.

With different goals from a final assessment, which is made at the end of the course unit and aims to assess the final learning results, according to the expected output profile, the continuous assessment occurs throughout the development of the course unit. It aims to permanently monitor and provide feedback on students' performance to enable an accurate diagnosis of their evolutionary process, allowing the identification of learning difficulties and the consequent introduction of corrective measures appropriate to the recovery and acquisition of content and skills initially planned.

This evaluation model should, on the one hand, allow the evaluation of the individual participation of each student's learning path throughout the semester (if the course is semester-long) and, on the other hand, evaluate the autonomous work, eventually, through written reports that allow the assessment of the extent to which the students have learned the contents of the course. This evaluation model also allows the diagnosis of formative needs to be made according to the gaps detected globally in students and, based on them, elaborate a short-term training plan to overcome the difficulties detected.

Hernández (2012) conducted a study to determine the extent to which continuous assessment practices facilitate student learning and the challenges faced. The results of the study showed, amongst others, that continuous assessment has the potential to support student learning through feedback and increase student motivation to learn, highlighting as well the advantage of providing feedback that aims to support students throughout the learning process, rather than focusing on providing feedback on the completed task.

In the last decades, regarding the teaching of accounting in higher education institutions, several authors (for example, Bui and Porter, 2010; Jones, 2010; Arbrecht and Sack, 2000) refer that they had to restructure and innovate to meet the needs of the organizations that employ their graduates. The consensus is that this change involves articulating traditional teaching methodologies with problem-based ones. Hansen (2006) points out that this methodology stimulates and encourages group work, critical thinking, facilitates communication, integrates knowledge, and motivates the search for answers.

Therefore, using a case study approach, a course unit of the last semester of the Accounting and Finance course of the School of Business and Administration of the Polytechnic Institute of Setúbal is presented, which combines the continuous assessment model with the problem-based learning methodology.

METHODOLOGY

According to Gil (2008), the methodology is the way to obtain results related to the research developed and refers to a set of techniques and procedures carried out systematically during the development of the research.

As for its objectives, this work can be classified as exploratory research because it seeks to provide greater familiarity with the problem in order to make it more explicit (Gil, 2002:41).

In turn, scientific research is based on procedures that enable the reliability of the results and can be classified into quantitative research and qualitative research. For Marconi and Lakatos (2003), quantitative research analyzes measurable results that aim to explain the cause and effect relationships between the analyzed phenomena. In terms of approach to the problem, this study uses quantitative research as a research procedure since it involves quantifying and classifying the data for analysis. Descriptive statistical techniques and a parametric test will be used (Silva & Menezes, 2005:20).

Regarding technical procedures, the research method used is the case study. According to Smith (2003:134), the case study is an "investigation, usually confined to a single unit of analysis, which may be a single department, company, industry, or even country." "The researcher is concerned with an absolute and broad understanding of the phenomenon studied. He observes, describes, interprets, and appreciates the environment and the phenomenon as they present themselves, without seeking to control them. The goal of this research approach used to develop knowledge is to describe or interpret rather than to evaluate" (Freixo, 2010:146); thus, the case study will be used in an exploratory way, which allows a greater familiarity with the object of study. (Gil, 2002).

The single case study enables a deeper analysis of the object; however, on the other hand, it is criticized because it has some limitations, such as providing little basis for scientific generalization (Yin, 2018), and raises questions about the researcher's bias and the impossibility of generalizing the obtained results since these only represent the studied reality (Gil, 2008).

The population of the case study is the students enrolled in the course unit (CU) of Corporate Simulation of the Accounting and Finance course of the School of Business and Administration (ESCE) of the Polytechnic Institute of Setúbal (IPS).

However, as this course unit has been in ESCE since the academic year of 2002/2003, applying from the very beginning, problem-based learning methodology and the continuous assessment model, in this study, different samples and periods will be extracted from the selected population, resulting from the available information regarding the topic that is being addressed.

Thus, when talking about the objectives of the CU and whether students recognize their fulfillment, information was obtained through a survey performed among students for the period from 2007/2008 to 2018/2019. This period relates to the first and last year the survey was conducted amongst the students who completed the CU. According to the available data, the analysis of the CU success is performed regarding the period between the academic years from 2014/2015 to 2019/2020.

Furthermore, in the last analysis in which the aim is to find out if there are significant differences between the students' achievement, in the different phases of evaluation, when the CU was functioning with in-person classes and when it switched to online classes due to the confinement consequence of the pandemic, the period of the analysis is the last three academic years, that is, from 2017/2018 to 2019/2020.

CASE STUDY

Background of the Course Unit of Corporate Simulation in the Curriculum Structure of the Accounting and Finance Course

Considered since its beginning, the academic year of 2002/2003, by the Portuguese Order of Certified Accountants, as equivalent to a professional internship, Corporate Simulation is a course unit of the last semester of the Accounting and Finance Course of the School of Business and Administration (ESCE) of the Polytechnic Institute of Setúbal (IPS). It involves, on average, annually at ESCE, 100 students, 50 companies, and 12 professors, who are simultaneously tutors of a group of companies and professors in the classroom.

In the curriculum structure of the Accounting and Finance course, Corporate Simulation is assigned 21 ECTS (European Credit Transfer and Accumulation System) and a mandatory 15 hours per week in class, in person, or online.

In the 2019/2020 academic year, the CU at ESCE functioned with 106 students and 12 professors.

Corporate Simulation functions in a network comprised by six other Portuguese Public Higher Education Institutions and one other from Mozambique, which increases the size of the simulated market and the number of students involved. This simulated market reflects the characteristics and obligations of the actual market. The virtual companies are managed by two students, who, based on a virtual calendar, perform all the activities associated with creating the company, its current and strategic management, and compliance with legal and tax obligations for one financial year (CS Program 2019/2020).

Completing the simulated market value chain are the virtual financial and public institutions allowing the financial management and the fulfillment of tax and other legal obligations according to the actual legal deadlines.

For the operation of the market, technical means are used, namely, hardware and software such as the invoicing and accounting program. It should be noted that communication between companies is carried out by email and that all files associated with the documents that support each company's operation and compliance with legal requirements are physical and or digital.

Thus, following the teaching methodology problem-based learning, students in Corporate Simulation from different virtual companies connected in the virtual market develop current management tasks, such as negotiating, buying, selling, complying with legal and tax obligations, and representing the company in inspections and audits. Throughout the CU, they fulfill several steps such as commercial presentation of the company commercially, budget preparation, interim and yearly financial statements, and written and oral presentation of the activities undertaken (CS Program, 2019/2020).

Thus, respecting the defined objectives, students are provided with a practical vision of organizational activities throughout the development of Corporate Simulation. Their performance is expected to be based on an ethical approach of the accountant professional and to allow them to consolidate and reinforce the integrated training previously acquired, as well as to consolidate knowledge in the areas of financial accounting, tax, finance, and cost accounting, mainly in budgeting and inventory measurement.

Objectives and Functioning of the Course Unit of Corporate Simulation

Integrating the need to increase and consolidate the knowledge acquired throughout the Accounting and Finance Course of ESCE IPS, the students perform several tasks in the course unit of Corporate

Simulation, using virtual companies inter-related in a virtual market and reflecting the characteristics and obligations of a real market. These tasks refer to current management, compliance with legal and tax obligations, as well as the representation of the company in acts of inspection and auditing. To this end, technical means are used, particularly hardware and software, such as the TOConline Accounting program and Online Banking integrated into the simulated market platform (CS Program, 2019/2020).

Functioning of the Course Unit

Of the activities developed during the year in Corporate Simulation, amongst others, the following are highlighted:

Procedures for the creation of companies and respective initial opening accounting records; Distribution of earnings and creation of reserves; Preparation of delivery notes, invoices to customers, purchase orders to suppliers and entry notes; Purchases and stock management as well as the respective payments by bank transfer, taking into account the payment conditions agreed upon; Subcontracting; Employment contracts; Employee records, payroll processing and all procedures relating to Social Security, as well as life, work-related accidents and vehicle insurance contracts; Cash flow management; Financial applications for profitability of cash surpluses; Leasing and bank financing contracts in the short, medium and long term; Subscription of units of participation of investment funds; Financial applications in shares and bonds; Tax procedures and accounting records of Value Added Tax (VAT), Corporate income tax (CIT), Individual income tax (IIT), Stamp tax; Financial Reporting; Preparation of the formal "Tax File"; and Economic and financial analysis within the scope of financial reporting - interim and annual (CS Program, 2019/2020).

Until the 2018/2019 academic year, the business management software used in ESCE's Corporate Simulation (CS) classes was SAGE NEXT. SAGE is one of the reference management programs in Portugal, proving to be a great tool combining the support to the operation of the course unit with the purpose of training and adapting the students to the business world.

The use of SAGE, based on a server located at ESCE, was only possible in the CS classroom and, although all modules of SAGE NEXT were available, only the accounting and invoicing modules were used. The students prepared the invoicing documents in this software and made all the accounting records associated with the simulated activity. They could also extract account statements and trial balance sheets to produce financial information and prepare tax returns.

With the declaration of the Pandemic situation, it was necessary to have software that worked entirely online since the presence of the students in the classroom was not possible. The solution chosen was the TOConline software, made available by the Order of Certified Accountants. This solution had a very rapid implementation.

Similar to SAGE, regarding the associated modules, TOConline, uses two components: Commercial and Accounting. Regarding the commercial area, the main objective is to provide the student with the tools to issue autonomously all the invoicing documents (Invoices, Receipt-Invoices, Credit Notes, Debit Notes, and Receipts) associated with the operational activity of the company. Regarding the accounting component, the student, in addition to making accounting entries and extracting various types of maps (account statements, trial balances), prepares the financial statements. Thus, at any given moment, the student can know the company's real situation for which he is responsible. Associated with the Accounting module, the student must perform several periodic tasks, namely, the calculation of VAT and the calculation of activity results. These calculations are treated differently. The VAT calculation is done manually, based on the statements extracted from the accounting system, forcing the student to relate the accounting system to the VAT Periodic Statement. However, the calculation of the activity results (profit or loss) is performed automatically. The student only has to enter the estimated income tax payable manually.

The Role of the Professor/Tutor in the Corporate Simulation Operation

The successful application of the problem-based learning methodology implies rethinking the role of the professor, considering that he will have to, without solving the problems arising from the functioning of the virtual market, support and encourage the student to seek the appropriate solution, either by gathering and consolidating previously acquired knowledge, or new knowledge that will have to result from the student's research. Gomes, Brito and Varela (2016) state that, for the success of the problem-based learning methodology, the role of the tutor is essential, given the work developed in tutoring sessions with small groups, since they enable the acquisition of metacognitive skills essential to both the training process and the professional future.

Thus, based on learning obtained since the 2002/2003 academic year, following, is characterized what is implicit in the role of CS professor and after, when exercising the role of tutor.

During class (in-person or online), Corporate Simulation professors monitor the different stages of the operation of companies in the simulated market. Thus, the duties of the professor in the CS classroom include, among others:

- Fostering mutual help among students and managing possible conflicts arising from the operation of the market;
- Manage the class attendance of each student or group according to each group's schedule;
- Alert to time management (with particular emphasis on the virtual calendar) and legal and tax obligations;
- Encourage the learning process and research of different bibliographies and legal diplomas;
- Helping students to use the Corporate Simulation software platform, aware of how well the market is working;
- Participate in preparation and conference of individual audits, participate in the audits of the companies and grading the accounts reporting; and
- Participate in the oral presentation jury.

Nevertheless, usually, CS professors are also tutors of a group of students, who form the professor's tutoring group, having different responsibilities, of which is highlighted:

- Monitor the companies' activity evolution and the participation and involvement of both group members in the tasks, as well as in the preparation of the reports;
- Encourage and motivate the learning and the research of different bibliographies and legal diplomas in order to encourage the good performance of the company, support each student in tutoring, so they do not give up;
- Manage any conflicts between students in each of the tutoring companies;
- Participate in the jury of oral presentation of Corporate Simulation, but not as the arguer of the tutoring group students;

- Periodically analyze the accounting support documents (e.g., trial balance) to verify anomalous situations in the companies' accounts.

Regarding the elements of continuous assessment, the tutor also has a fundamental role and must: receive, validate and distribute them by the team of professors who will perform the audit(s) or grade the reports; must also monitor the progress of each student and promptly alert in case of risk of failure and motivate for proper preparation of the oral presentation.

In summary, the role of the tutor in CS is, in an individualized way, to encourage students to be self-sufficient and responsible in the learning process, turning their weaknesses into strengths, by identifying problems and finding solutions in such a way that they are progressively able to make informed and responsible decisions both in the course unit and in their future professional life. The tutor's role corresponds to part of the success of the course unit. The assignment of the group of students to a professor/tutor is associated with the work hours assigned to the course unit, using as guidance, assigning two companies from the simulated market for each hour of the teaching hours distribution.

Corporate Simulation Objectives

According to its Program content, the Corporate Simulation course unit has the following objectives (obj):

- obj1 – Apply and consolidate the knowledge acquired during the course
- obj2 – Strengthen integrated training
- obj3 – Provide a practical view of the profession
- obj4 – Increase the ability to work in groups
- obj5 – Encourage research
- obj6 – Enhance knowledge in preparing and presenting reports
- obj7 – Increase the ability to self-evaluate

Since the academic year 2007/2008, at the end of the semester, a survey is distributed to the students by the professor responsible for the course unit, to know if the students who attend and complete Corporate Simulation, consider that the objectives stated in the program are met. This survey questions the level of compliance of the Corporate Simulation program's objectives with the course unit's attendance. The survey used to evaluate the degree of fulfillment of the objectives of the course unit of Corporate Simulation uses a Likert scale, a 5-point options scale where:

1 = Not at all; 2 = Not much; 3 = Sufficient; 4 = Good; and 5 = Very good.

Referring to the results of the survey, table 1 shows the value resulting from the degree of importance given by students to each of the objectives, when adding up the options 4 (good) and 5 (very good), for the period from 2007/2008 to 2018/2019, that is, 12 years.

Table 1 shows that in the 12 years studied; the students always attributed a very high level of importance when adding up options 4 and 5, with the lowest value being 70.9% (in 2011/2012) and the highest 99% (in 2008/2009). On the other hand, it can also be seen that, for the 12 years analyzed, the annual average sum of all the objectives in each year ranges between 78.5% (2011/2012) and 91.6% (2013/2014).

Analyzing these same 12 years, now by objective, as evidenced in figure 1, the average obtained in each of the objectives is never lower than 82% (obj7 - increase the ability to self-evaluate) and reaches

Table 1. Weight (%) assigned to options 4 and 5 concerning the achievement of objectives from the academic year 2007/2008 to 2018/2019

%	Obj1	Obj2	Obj3	Obj4	Obj5	Obj6	Obj7	Annual mean
2007/08	76.9%	75.3%	79.5%	84.6%	75.2%	88.0%	79.1%	79.8%
2008/09	84.0%	82.0%	84.0%	93.0%	77.0%	**99.0%**	86.0%	86.4%
2009/10	83.5%	76.6%	82.5%	84.5%	86.4%	89.4%	84.5%	83.9%
2010/11	91.7%	83.3%	95.0%	88.3%	71.7%	83.3%	81.7%	85.0%
2011/12	76.6%	80.0%	76.4%	83.6%	74.6%	87.3%	**70.9%**	**78.5%**
2012/13	98.4%	90.2%	88.5%	95.1%	83.6%	90.2%	80.3%	89.5%
2013/14	95.1%	91.8%	88.5%	93.4%	95.1%	88.5%	88.5%	91.6%
2014/15	82.0%	80.9%	87.6%	78.7%	87.6%	77.5%	71.9%	80.9%
2015/16	90.9%	89.4%	90.9%	86.4%	87.9%	90.9%	89.4%	89.4%
2016/17	83.3%	79.5%	82.1%	88.5%	91.0%	89.7%	84.6%	85.5%
2017/18	87.1%	84.4%	90.9%	83.1%	87.0%	88.3%	81.8%	86.1%
2018/19	83.5%	87.1%	90.6%	89.4%	87.1%	84.7%	84.7%	86.7%
Mean per obj	86.1%	83.4%	86.4%	87.4%	83,7%	**88,1%**	82,0%	85,3%

Source: Updated from Aleixo, Teixeira and Silva (2012) and Teixeira et al. (2015).

the highest value in objective 6 (Enhance knowledge in preparing and presenting reports), with an average of 88.1%.

Next, figure 2 shows the average percentage weight of the fulfillment of the seven objectives attributed to options 4 and 5 in each academic year of the period analyzed.

The Evaluation Model of the Corporate Simulation Course Unit

The assessment of the knowledge, associated with the problem-based learning methodology, is performed using the continuous assessment model, considering to be approved the student who has a final grade (FG) equal to or greater than 10 points, resulting from the application of the following formula:

FG = 10% F I + 35% F II + 35% F III + 20% OP

Where F I = Phase I - is composed of a Report 60% and two individual evaluation instruments (audits) with a weighting of 40% of the phase's grade.

F II = Phase II - is composed of a Report which corresponds to 50% of the phase grade and the individual and company audits, to 50% of this phase;

F III = Phase III - consists of a Report worth 40% of the phase grade and individual and company audits worth 60%.

Figure 1. Analysis of the average weight (%) achievement of objectives assigned to options 4 plus 5 for the period 2007/08 to 2018/19
Source: Own elaboration

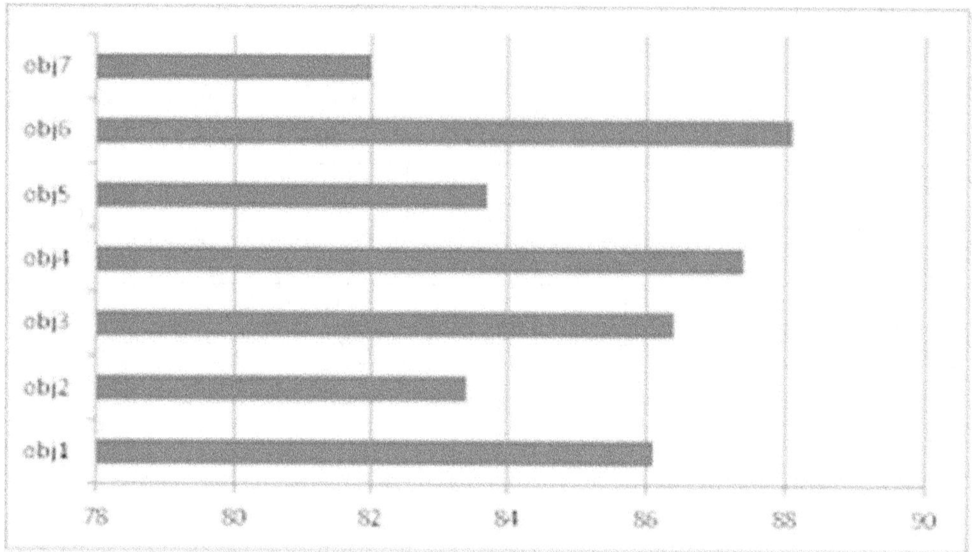

Figure 2. Analysis of the average percentage weight of fulfillment of the seven objectives, assigned to options 4 and 5, in the academic years from 2007/08 to 2018/19
Source: Own elaboration

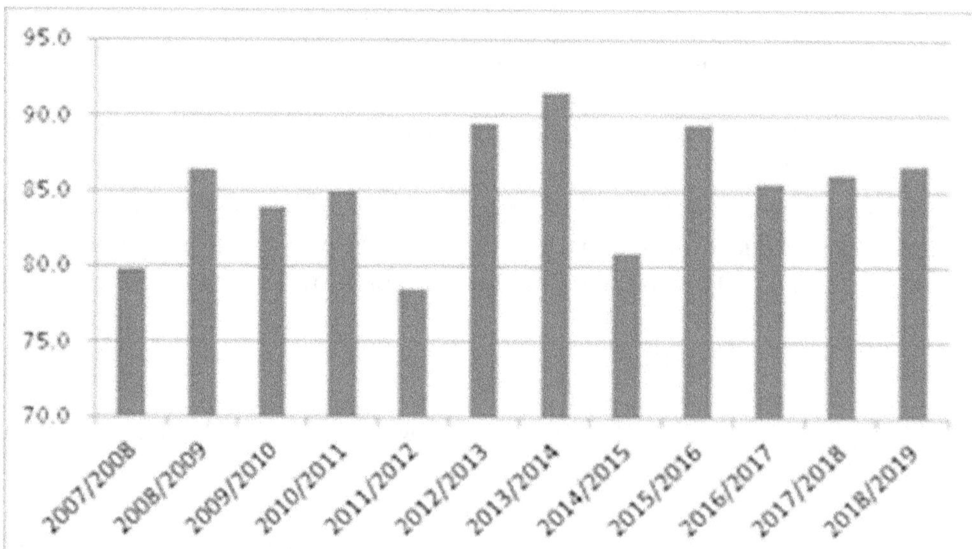

In both phase 2 and phase 3, the audits are of two types, individual and company audits. It should be noted that the Report of phase 3 has a minimum grade of 10 points, and for the oral presentation, the students must have a grade equal to or greater than 10 points in all three phases.

OP corresponds to the Oral Presentation and has a weighting in the final grade of 20%. The OP has a minimum grade of 10 points.

It is also worth mentioning that, since the random attribution of the activity of their company and the presentation of the course unit functioning, the students know the assessment model and the topics that are evaluated in any of the individual assessment moments, as well as the content of the reports to be submitted. Regarding the company audits, only the subjects that may eventually be audited are disclosed.

Thus, the course unit's assessment model publishes a total of twenty-seven assessments from 0 to 20 points throughout the semester, each one corresponding to each assessment made at different phases (3 reports, 10 individual audits, and 14 company audits). This way, the students can, at any time, self-evaluate and realize what they need to study or research to improve their performance, and the professors/tutors can, at any time, intervene and support the students in their recovery.

The themes of the individual audits are: internal control procedures, budgeting (in phase 1), bank reconciliation, buying and selling, salaries, VAT (in phase 2), withholding taxes, accruals and deferrals, financing, and per diems (in phase 3)

Phase 2 company audits are: salaries, VAT, accounting and administrative file, internal control procedures, and the complete process of the first purchase. The audits of companies carried out in phase 3 are: acquisition of tangible fixed assets (first purchase), first sale, rent and certified accountant's fee accounting records, leasing, "thoughts of the week" (measures proposed to regulate the market operation) and special operations aimed at creating conditions for extraordinary situations to occur (which the normal operation of the market does not allow).

Thus, considering the different moments and evaluation instruments, the following table 2 shows how the final grade is obtained.

Table 2. Overview of how the final grade in CS is obtained

Weight in the final grade	10.00%	35.00%	35.00%	20.00%	100.00%
Assessment phases	**Phase I**	**Phase II**	**Phase III**	**Oral P.**	**Final Grade**
Individual Assessment (audit)	40.00%	35.00%	30.00%	60.00%	38.75%
Company Assessment (audit)	0.00%	15.00%	30.00%	40.00%	23.75%
Report	60.00%	50.00%	40.00%	0.00%	37.50%
Total	100.00%	100.00%	100.00%	100.00%	100.00%

Source: Own elaboration

From the analysis of table 2, it is verified that 62.5% of the final grade is obtained in audits. 23.75% of the grade correspond to companies' audits performed in phases 2 and 3 (14). 38.75% of the grade correspond to individual audits (10), taking place throughout the 3 phases of the assessment model.

On the other hand, this table also shows that 61.25% of the final grade corresponds to group work. 37.5% results from the assessment of three reports, referring to the end of each phase and the remainder from company audits where compliance with the obligations arising from the company's activity in the simulated market throughout the simulated economic year is assessed.

Corporate Simulation - Different Perspectives of Analysis in the Period 2014/2015 to 2019/2020

Sample Characterisation

To further analyze the results obtained in the final assessment of the corporate simulation students, the mean of all students for the academic years 2014/2015 to 2019/2020 was obtained. The sample selected for this analysis consists of 534 students enrolled in the corporate simulation course unit, of which 4.7 did not complete with success or were not assessed.

Table 3. Sample characterization by gender, course, and student type

	2014/2015		2015/2016		2016/2017		2017/2018		2018/2019		2019/2020	
	Total	**%**	**Total**	**%**	**Total**	**%**	**Total**	**%**	**Total**	**%**	**Total**	**%**
Gender:												
Female	63	64.9%	51	71.8%	54	65.1%	53	62.4%	63	68.5%	73	68.9%
Male	34	35.1%	20	28.2%	29	34.9%	32	37.6%	29	31.5%	33	31.1%
Student type:												
Working student	19	19.6%	9	12.7%	17	20.5%	29	34.1%	20	21.7%	24	22.6%
Other	78	80.4%	62	87.3%	66	79.5%	56	65.9%	72	78.3%	82	77.4%
Course:												
Daytime	68	70.1%	58	81.7%	64	77.1%	61	71.8%	77	83.7%	86	81.1%
Nocturne	29	29.9%	13	18.3%	19	22.9%	24	28.2%	15	16.3%	20	18.9%

Source: own elaboration

In table 3, it is possible to see that, throughout the period analyzed, the sample consists mainly of female students, which always represents values above 60%. The percentage of working students varies between 12.7% and 34.1%. The daytime course always has a much higher number of students than the nocturne course, always standing above 70%.

Table 4. Percentage of approval

Students	2014/15	2015/16	2016/17	2017/18	2018/19	2019/20	Mean
Nº Enrolled	97.0	71.0	83.0	85.0	92.0	106.0	**89.0**
Nº Failled and NSA	5.0	4.0	2.0	5.0	6.0	6.0	**4.7**
Nº Approved	92.0	67.0	81.0	80.0	86.0	100.0	**84.3**
% of Approval	**94.8%**	**94.4%**	**97.6%**	**94.1%**	**93.5%**	**94.3%**	**94.8%**
Final grade mean (0-20 v.)	**14.4**	**13.0**	**14.2**	**13.8**	**13.7**	**13.6**	**13.8**

Source: Own elaboration

Corporate Simulation Students' Level of Success

Another possible analysis is presented in table 4 for the period from 2014/2015 to 2019/2020, which compares the number of students enrolled in the course unit with those who failed or did not submit to assessment (NSA) and those who were approved.

Analyzing table 4, which encompasses a population of 534 students, for a period between the 2014/2015 academic year and the 2019/2020 academic year, that is, for a six years period, it can be seen that, for an average of 89 students enrolled there is a successful level of 94.8%. It should also be noted that, in this period, only the 2018/2019 academic year had a success level below 94.0%, standing at 93.5%. The final grade mean obtained varies between 13.0 (2015/2016) and 14.4 (2014/2015), so it remains more or less constant throughout the analyzed period.

Figure 3 shows the evolution of the values presented in table 4 throughout the six years analyzed.

Figure 3. Comparison between the number of enrolled, approved, failed, or not evaluated
Source: Own elaboration

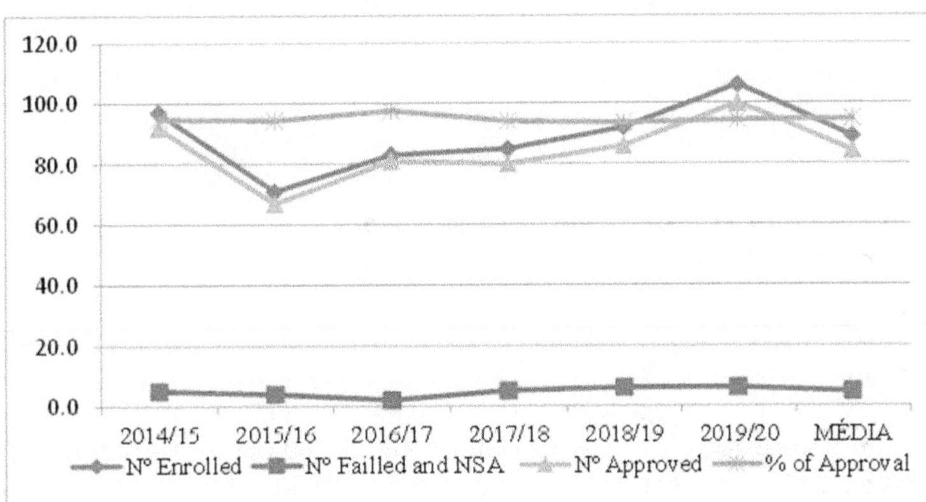

Analysis of Behavior by Gender, Student Type, and Course

For a more comprehensive analysis of the results obtained in the final assessment, according to the sample characterization, the parametric t-student test for independent samples was performed to test whether there are significant differences in the mean obtained, considering the parameters: gender, type of student and course.

The t-test for two independent samples allows verifying whether the population means of two groups are statistically equal and is used here to evaluate whether the means of the gender, student type, and course groups differ statistically. Table 5 shows the results obtained in the t-test.

Table 5. T-test results

Variable	Mean	p-value (t-test)
Gender:		
F	14.12	0.00960***
M	13.21	
Student type:		
Working student	14.04	0.52146
Ordinary	13.82	
Course:		
Daytime	13.80	0.87475
Nocturne	13.87	

*** Significant to p-value <0,01; ** Significant to p-value <0,05; * Significant to p-value <0,1
Source: own elaboration

Analyzing table 5, which presents the results obtained in the t-test, it is possible to verify that only for gender exists a statistically significant difference between means for a confidence level of 1%. Analyzing the results of the t-test for means difference leads to the conclusion that, for a significance level of 0.05, the means do not differ significantly between groups of type of student and type of course. Only gender seems to influence the final assessment results of the parameters analyzed.

Did the Pandemic Caused by Covid-19 have an Impact on Corporate Simulation?

In March 2020, the World Health Organization (WHO) declared a global pandemic due to the Covid-19 disease, first reported in December 2019 in Wuhan, China. This pandemic led governments worldwide to implement several measures to cope with it. These measures include social distancing, wearing face masks, working from home, and closing some public places, as is the case of schools at all levels.

Governments have adopted alternative solutions to manage the need to close schools and continue to provide students with quality learning. So, the COVID-19 pandemic eventually induced educational institutions to develop and implement distance learning solutions in face-to-face courses (Pesce and Hessel, 2021). This change occurred without notice, resulting in the need for teachers and students to rapidly adapt to a new reality to ensure the continuity of quality learning.

Online learning may have several definitions, but in this context is considered as an educational process that uses the internet. It is a form of distance education that allows students to access the teacher in a virtual classroom, from a remote location, usually from home (kim, 2020; Moore, Dickson-Deane & Galyen, 2011).

In Portugal, the first Covid-19 case appeared on March 2nd, 2020, leading the Government to declare an emergency state from March 19th to May 2nd, 2020, issuing a lockdown in several areas. Schools closed and remained closed for the remainder of the academic year, with classes taught online.

According to Santos 2020, despite the crisis generated by the coronavirus pandemic, which affected all areas, especially education, the moment can be an opportunity to implement changes capable of transforming educational inequality. The author highlights positive and negative aspects as a consequence of the pandemic. As the most relevant negative factors, she mentions, among others, the lack of preparation both of organizations to deal with social isolation and distance learning, and the lack of technological equipment for remote learning, and also of teachers and students. Regarding positive aspects, the author highlights the search for means to develop new skills that allow the renewal of teaching through active learning and the use of technologies to implement activities and share experiences and transmission of scientific content asynchronously.

Specifics Regarding the 2019/2020 Academic Year Functioning

Until the 2018/2019 academic year, the Corporate Simulation (CS) classes were taught face-to-face. Most of the operations were carried out using the software platform (developed and managed for this purpose by the University of Aveiro); however, the physical presence of students in the classroom was indispensable for monitoring the planned activities and the individual and company audits.

Until then, all virtual company documentation had to be filed in paper format, as well as the various reports for assessment.

In March 2020, with the declaration of the Pandemic state and the prohibition of face-to-face classes, it was necessary to restructure the operation of this course unit, which worked essentially in an “at a distance” format and totally dematerialized.

Classroom Management and Monitoring Student Activities

The classes contact period is 15 hours per week for each student, and the year 2019/2020 started with face-to-face classes, going entirely online as of March 2020, when the schools closed, by the Portuguese Government’s imposition.

For the “distance learning” CS classes, ESCE has chosen to use the Microsoft Teams software. Despite some technical difficulties due to poor network performance or the use of older equipment, which hinder its use, TEAMS proved to be a good tool for communicating with students. This software allows sound and image communication, file sharing, PowerPoint presentation, as well as knowledge sharing between teachers and students and their monitoring. Given the familiarity of teachers and students with Microsoft tools, namely Office, the adaptation process to this new app was easy and intuitive.

Microsoft Teams allows sessions with long duration, allowing the permanent contact between professors and students assigned to each session, allowing the exchange of knowledge, ideas, and suggestions, and for the students to place questions that the professors can immediately clarify. This software was also used for training sessions or seminars on important topics for students within this course unit, such as software use, taxes, and financial analysis.

Currently, for the academic year 2020/2021, classes are being held in a mixed system, face-to-face whenever possible, and the remainder online. The contact period remains 15 hours per week for each student, currently 4 hours face-to-face and the rest online. To ensure the 15 hours per week for all students, CS has an overall schedule of 57 hours per week, of which 20 are face-to-face. In the 20 face-to-face hours, the online connection is maintained to communicate with students who cannot come to ESCE.

Supplementary Student Support

To complement students' support, thus minimizing the lack of direct contact with the professors, several forums for questions and answers were created in Moodle, on the CS page, where students can post their questions, organized by topics of interest to the students, according to the problems they have to solve.

The advantage of Moodle forums over TEAMS sessions is that they are written messages and are always available to the whole student community of CS. This feature enables questions and consultation by the entire CS community, 24 hours a day, seven days a week. It also allows for greater autonomy in the support given by professors since a pre-established schedule no longer conditions them.

Instead of only one, the option for several forums has the objective of structuring the information, allowing the students to consult only the theme(s) that interest them and allowing the attribution of the management of the themes to the CS professors more specialized in each subject.

The flow of information in this type of forum is intended to circulate: Student →Professor → Student → Professor ..., until the question is completely clarified and allows the intervention of the whole community (students and professors) raising new aspects of the question or completing the information provided.

Another type of information forum was also created, where it is possible to raise questions, but whose flow is essentially Professor-Student. This forum was named "Warnings and Useful Information" and is used essentially to transmit recommendations that students should respect in their CS activity, trying to minimize the lack of direct contact with teachers in the classroom, where this type of message was transmitted.

Digital File

Throughout the assessment phases of CS, several company audits are performed. These audits consist in verifying the conformity of procedures and documentation issued by virtual companies, such as invoices, accounting records, tax returns, tax opinions, among others.

In the CS dematerialization process, it was necessary to create a filing system that simultaneously fulfilled three requirements:

- That it was entirely digital;
- That allows to know where the documents are (or should be);
- That does not allow changing documents after specific dates

Only compliance with these three requirements will allow the use of this filing system as a basis for assessing the companies' activity with efficiency and security.

In the file system created, called "Digital File", with documents exclusively in electronic format, it is possible to save the documents in any format (Excel files, Word, Zip, ...). However, the recommendation is to use PDF format (Portable Document Format, developed by Adobe System) since it is the most accessible format to read electronically without changing the original.

In order to ensure that the audit team (professors) successfully locates the documents needed for the audits, a fixed structure of folders was defined (without the possibility for changes), and the necessary training was given to the students for its correct use.

Using a fixed pre-established structure lets everyone know where the documents should be filed, avoiding using several different structures, which, although they may be correct and make sense to the person using them, are challenging to use when dealing with around fifty companies simultaneously.

After considering the various technological resources available, the Onedrive sharing system (provided by Microsoft) was chosen to create the Digital File because it seemed to be the safest and easiest resource to use. The Digital File for each company is created in the Onedrive area of exclusive management of one of the students (company partner) and then shared with the other partner and the professor tutoring. It is the file-sharing that allows professors to consult the company's documentation.

Finally, to ensure that the documents cannot be changed after the deadlines (audit dates), a mechanism has been created to make an integral copy of all company files in an area reserved for professors.

Impact on Assessment

Although the schools rapidly adapted to online teaching, it was not easy, and students were less motivated and engaged. As classes are now online, the student's continuous assessment is also performed online following several available resources. Due to the short time for adaptation, the students' online assessment still involves a lot of trial and error, using different approaches depending on teachers and convenience regarding resources available. "Appropriate measures to check plagiarism is yet to be put in place in many schools and institutions mainly due to the large number of student population" (Pokhrel & Chhetri, 2021). Another important aspect is that when students have learning difficulties, personal contact with teachers is fundamental, so academic performance is expected to decrease during this period of online teaching (Pokhrel & Chhetri, 2021).

Considering that the academic year of 2019/2020 was already taught online, so were all the continuous assessment phases. Table 6 shows the mean value of the final grade obtained in all of the continuous assessment phases for the academic year 2019/2020 (online classes) and the years 2018/2019 and 2017/2018 (face-to-face classes).

Table 6. Final grade mean of each continuous assessment phase

Acad. Year	Fhase 1	Fhase 2	Fhase 3	Oral Pres.	Final Grade
2017/2018	14.45	14.25	13.51	15.09	14.34
2018/2019	12.09	13.64	13.61	16.25	13.96
2019/2020	12.95	14.77	13,05	15.53	14.12

Source: Own elaboration

Figure 4 compares 2019/2020 academic year results with the two previous academic years. In this analysis, only the students that completed the Corporate Simulation course unit are considered.

Although the expectation is that grades decrease during online teaching, as shown in graph 4, that was not the case in every assessment moment. Comparing the academic year 2019/2020 with the previous one shows that the mean grade was lower, only in phase III and oral presentation. The final grade mean in 2019/2020 manages to be slightly higher than the one obtained in 2018/2019.

Figure 4. Corporate simulation continuous assessment results
Source: Own elaboration

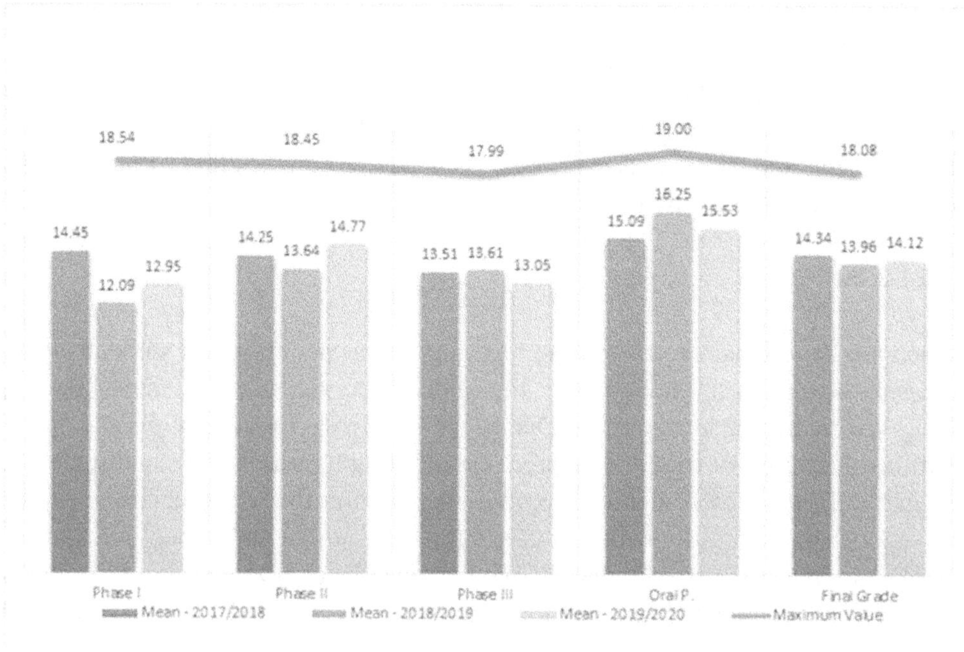

A Student's t-test was also performed to confirm the obtained analysis, from which a p-value of 0.45145 was obtained. So, any significance level leads to the rejection of the null hypothesis of the test, of equality of means, indicating that the fact that distance learning was applied to classes does not seem to have a statistically significant influence on the final average obtained for the period analyzed.

Breakdown of the Final Grade Mean Value Obtained in the Various Phases of the CS Continuous Assessment and Comparison between Two Years of Face-to-Face Classes, with One Year of Online Classes

Given that the assessment is sequential, including three distinct phases, the results obtained by phase were analyzed through descriptive statistics, according to table 7-phase I results, table 8-phase II results, and table 9-phase III results. In this analysis, the students' mean grade per phase was calculated from 2017/2018 to 2019/2020. Only students who attended CS until the final assessment moment were considered.

From the analysis of table 7, it can be seen that in phase I, in the three years studied, the mean of the individual assessment is always lower than the mean obtained in the group work, that is, in the companies' audits and the initial Report. The minimum grade in the individual assessment is equal to zero in the three years, and the maximum value, also of the individual assessment, only in 2018/2019

Table 7. Detail of the grades obtained in the continuous assessment of phase I from 2017/2018 to 2019/2020

CONTINUOUS ASSESSMENT- PHASE I				
Descriptive Statistics	Individual Assessment 40%	Initial Report 60%	Final Assessment Phase II	Academic Year
Mean	13.77	14.91	14.45	2017/2018
Mode	16.25	16.25	15.50	
Std. Dev.	4.81800	2.63833	2.97628	
Maximum	20.00	17.57	18.54	
Minimum	0.00	0.00	0.00	
Mean	7.57	14.95	12.09	2018/2019
Mode	6.88	15.25	8.59	
Std. Dev.	3.78016	2.53189	2.30409	
Maximum	16.88	18.23	16.94	
Minimum	0.00	5.00	4.00	
Mean	10.81	14.23	12.95	2019/2020
Mode	13.75	14.83	14.33	
Std. Dev.	4.19609	1.89230	2.16112	
Maximum	20.00	18.08	17.32	
Minimum	0.00	9.10	7.76	

Source: Own elaboration

has a grade lower than the maximum grade obtained in the Report. Generically speaking, in phase I, the highest mean is 14.45 in the 2017/2018 academic year. In the other two years, the mean is 12.09 and 12.95. Regarding the mode, the one obtained in the year 2018/2019, for the final result, is 8.59, while in the other two years, the values are above 14.00 points, which means they are above the passing score of 10 points, contrary to 2018/2019.

The analysis of table 8 highlights that in any of the years studied, the mean obtained in the individual assessment is always significantly lower than the mean obtained in the company's assessment and, although by a smaller difference, to the mean value obtained in the Report. As for the mean of phase II final grade, it can be seen that the highest value is obtained in the year 2019/2020. The maximum value obtained in each of the three years varies between 17.98 and 18.52 points, proving that the highest value occurs in 2019/2020.

In phase III, as in phases I and II, the group work assessment always has a mean value higher than the individual, both regarding the audits performed on the companies and the report. It is also noteworthy that in the three years analyzed, the companies' audits always have, on average, higher values than the Report. Overall, the mean values for phase III are in a concise range, with the lowest value being 13.05 in 2019/2020 and the highest 13.61 in 2018/2019. In phase III, the maximum value obtained in the three years analyzed was 17.99 in 2019/2020.

In summary, in the continuous assessment per phase, there are several types of assessment with different weightings: individual assessment through assessment tests, assessment of companies through audits performed by professors regarding various aspects of the company's activity, and preparation of

Table 8. Detail of the grades obtained in the continuous assessment of phase II from 2017/2018 to 2019/2020

CONTINUOUS ASSESSMENT- PHASE II						
Descriptive Statistics	**Individual Assessment**	**Company Assessment**	**Individual+Company Assessment**	**Intermediate Report**	**Final Assessment Phase II**	**Academic Year**
	60%	**40%**	**50%**	**50%**		
Mean	11.77	17.32	13.99	14.51	14.25	**2017/2018**
Mode	12.50	19.29	0.00	17.15	0.00	
Std. Dev.	3.91872	3.81081	3.49444	3.28811	3.24673	
Maximum	18.75	20.00	18.62	17.75	17.98	
Minimum	0.00	0.00	0.00	0.00	0.00	
Mean	11.71	16.20	13.57	13.57	13.64	**2018/2019**
Mode	9.75	9.08	19.25	12.45	15.70	
Std. Dev.	3.29090	3.27735	2.75679	3.14654	2.55433	
Maximum	18.75	20.00	19.25	18.25	18.45	
Minimum	0.00	4.41	3.63	0.00	3.88	
Mean	12.96	16.37	14.38	15.08	14.77	**2019/2020**
Mode	15.00	#N/A	16.09	15.75	15.60	
Std. Dev.	3.51550	2.44312	2.56545	1.58735	1.81472	
Maximum	20.00	19.53	19.79	17.80	18.52	
Minimum	3.33	9.72	7.56	11.10	9.99	

Source: Own elaboration

activity reports by the students. Studying the three years mentioned leads to the conclusion that students show more serious difficulty in the individual assessment where the mean values are lower. Inclusively, in the year 2018/2019, the mode is 6.88 in phase I, 9.75 in phase II, and in the year 2017/2018, it is 8.7 in phase III, therefore mean values below the passing grade. Students achieve better results in the company audits and reports, highlighting the benefits of group work.

CONCLUSION

Since academic unsuccess is a national problem, success, when it exists, by contrast, must be studied and explained.

According to the literature review, several authors advocate introducing new teaching methodologies that motivate and engage students in the learning process. There is also a consensus that associating traditional teaching methodologies with problem-based learning can help students understand the importance of traditionally transmitted knowledge when applied to solving problems closer to organizational reality.

In this way, the need to bring together the knowledge transmitted by the professors of the different course units and consolidate and deepen the different areas of knowledge is favored with the problem-

Table 9. Detail of the grades obtained in the continuous assessment of phase III from 2017/2018 to 2019/2020

CONTINUOUS ASSESSMENT- PHASE III						
Descriptive Statistics	**Individual Assessment**	**Company Assessment**	**Individual +Company Assessment**	**Final Report**	**Final Assessment Phase III**	**Academic Year**
	50%	**50%**	**60%**	**40%**		
Mean	10.76	16.12	13.44	13.62	13.51	**2017/2018**
Mode	8.70	18.86	0.00	14.04	0.00	
Std. Dev.	3.43759	3.66452	3.20163	3.22215	3.10994	
Maximum	19.40	19.16	18.31	17.58	17.32	
Minimum	0.00	0.00	0.00	0.00	0.00	
Mean	11.31	15.02	13.22	13.89	13.61	**2018/2019**
Mode	17.00	16.68	16.43	0.00	15.18	
Std. Dev.	3.63703	3.18440	2.74720	3.47672	2.59417	
Maximum	17.00	19.56	17.45	17.94	17.50	
Minimum	0.00	0.00	0.00	0.00	0.00	
Mean	12.18	19.43	12.30	13.78	13.05	**2019/2020**
Mode	12.01	20.00	11.82	15.03	12.31	
Std. Dev.	3.07432	2.81679	2.30310	3.31689	2.27873	
Maximum	20.00	20.00	17.91	18.13	17.99	
Minimum	4.01	0.00	3.40	0.00	1.36	

Source: Own elaboration

based learning methodology by involving and making the student responsible for finding the appropriate solution.

On the other hand, formal assessment based on a moment and an assessment instrument, which is easy to apply, has proven to be a potentiator of failure and dropout. Although easy to apply, this form of assessment does not allow for monitoring the student's learning evolution, leading to the accumulation of doubts, which results in failure and dropout. One of the possible solutions to avoid this outcome is the application of an evaluation model that, in a continuous way, allows to assess if the student is following the development of the content of the curriculum structure and, if necessary, take appropriate action.

Thus, in this case study, it was intended to evidence both the students' success and their own recognition of the achievement of the objectives proposed for the course unit, from the articulation of the continuous assessment model, with the problem-based learning methodology, in a course unit of the last year of the Undergraduate Degree in Accounting and Finance of the School of Business Sciences of the Polytechnic Institute of Setúbal, which is in effect since the academic year 2002/2003,

Throughout this study, it emerged that:

- Regarding the fulfillment of the objectives contained in the Course Unit Program: in the period from 2007/2008 to 2018/19, in the surveys carried out, every year, at the end of the academic year, the sum of the answers "good" and "very good", oscillated between 82% and 88,1%.

- Applying the problem-based learning methodology impacts the course unit functioning on students and professors, where the tutor's role is highlighted. And, when associated with the continuous assessment model, with twenty-seven distinct assessment moments, about 39% of the final grade is obtained in individual assessment, and the remaining percentage results from the assessment of group work, since two students manage the simulated company.
- For the analysis of the final grade, the statistical test t-test, considering gender, student type, and course, revealed a statistically significant difference between means only for gender.
- In the analysis of student success in the period from 2014/2015 to 2019/2020, it is visible that the average approval level is 94.8%, with a mean final grade of 13.8 values. In terms of pass rate, the lowest value was 93.5%, obtained in 2018/2019.
- It was also explicitly studied the 2019/2020 academic year to understand if the pandemic caused by COVID-19 had an impact on academic success. Functioning with online classes (Teams), with the transition of the accounting software from SAGE to TOConline and the digital archive, keeping the assessment model and teaching methodology, and using Moodle to support students, it was found that, both for the 3 phases of the continuous assessment and oral presentation, there were no significant changes when compared to the years 2017/2018 and 2018/2019, years that had face-to-face classes. The values obtained are not the same but do not present consistent behavior, with a trend, positive or negative.

Corporate Simulation, in face-to-face or online classes, by articulating the problem-based learning methodology with the continuous assessment model, over the years, has shown that it succeeds in making the curricular synthesis, strengthening the integrated training, providing a practical insight into the accounting profession, increasing the ability to work in groups, encouraging research, increasing the ability to self-evaluate, and strengthening the knowledge to prepare and present reports, involving students and professors, in academic success.

Therefore Corporate Simulation is a successful curricular unit, statement that can be supported in several perspectives:

- The employability of CS Graduates, which is in the range of 90% to 100% (according to studies carried out by IPS);
- The demand of our final-year students, who are attending CS by companies that annually attend the job fair organized by the IPS, to attract internships;
- The students enrolled and attending CS, either by their level of approval, either by the recognition of the knowledge acquired and the fulfillment of the objectives of the CU. Also, the low level of dropouts, which on average is around 1 to 2% of the enrolled students.

Traditionally CS has run in the ESCE of the IPS since 2002/2003 using the problem-based learning methodology and applying the continuous assessment model, with 15h weekly face-to-face. As a consequence of the pandemic, CS had to face the challenge of transforming its face-to-face operation to distance learning supported by the communication platform Microsoft Teams, the Toconline accounting software, and file sharing with Onedrive. The case study performed led to the conclusion that this challenge was successfully overcome and with similar values to the two years studied before the pandemic, considering the level of achievement, the recognition of the degree of fulfillment of the objectives, and increase of knowledge.

Referring to a higher education institution and the impact of COVID-19, Campanella and Sardinha (2021) pointed out that the suspension of face-to-face teaching activities, although it created disruptions in the development of the school year, the measures adopted to reduce the impact on teaching, learning and assessment process, were adequate as well as the platform chosen to communicate, that proved to be suitable to the needs.

REFERENCES

Aleixo, M. C., Teixeira, A. B., & Silva, S. M. (2012). Simulação Empresarial: um caso de sucesso. In XXII Jornadas Luso Espanholas de Gestão Científica. Vila Real.

Alves, J., Moutinho, N., Pires, A., & Ribeiro, N. (2013). A motivação dos alunos em Simulação Empresarial: análise de um ano letivo. *XIV Congresso Internacional de contabilidade e auditoria.*

Anés, J. A. D., & Gavira, R. L. (2011). Aprendizaje baseado en el uso de casos de estudio real. XXI Jornadas Hispano-Lusas Gestión Cientifica.

Arbrecht, W. S., & Sack, R. J. (2000). Accounting education: Charting the course through a perilous future. American Accounting Association. Sarasota.

Ariza, L. R. (2011). Enseñando a emprender. *XVI Congreso AECA.*

Bajaelde, O. E., Lauridsen, K., & Lindberg, A. (2018). *Current trends in assessment in Europe – the way forward.* White paper, Coimbra Group Education Innovation Working Group.

Balancho M. J. & Coelho, F. M. (1996). *Motivar os alunos, criatividade na relação pedagógica: conceitos e práticas* (2ª Edição). Texto Editora.

Barata, M. C., Calheiros, M. M., Patrício, J., Graça, J., & Lima, M. L. (2012). *Avaliação do programa mais sucesso escolar.* CISIUL/ISCTE/IUL Edição Direção-Geral de Estatísticas de Educação e Ciência – Ministério da Educação e Ciência.

Barrows, H., & Tamblyn, R. (1980). Problem-based learning: an approach to medical education. Springer Series on Medical Education, 1.

Borochovicius, E., & Tortella, J. C. B. (2014). Aprendizagem baseada em problemas: um método de ensino-aprendizagem e suas práticas educativas. *Ensaio: aval. Públ. Educ., 22*(83), 263-294. Retrieved 2021-12-09 from https://www.bing.com/search?q=Borochovicius%2C+E.+e+Tortella%2C+J.C.B.%2C+2014%2C

Bui, B., & Porter, B. (2010). The expectation-performance gap in accounting education: An exploratory study. *Accounting Education, 19*(1-2), 23–50. doi:10.1080/09639280902875556

Campanella, S. C., & Sardinha, L. F. (2021). *O efeito da COVID-19 na estratégia de uma instituição de ensino superior: estudo de caso.* Retrieved 2021-12-09 from https://www.researchgate.net/publication/353610866

Castillo, A. M., & Abad, I. M. (2003). Enseñanza interactiva y desarrollo de competencias directivas através de la docencia de la administración de empresas. In *XIV Jornadas Luso- Espanholas de Gestão Científica.* Açores.

Etxeberria, M. E. A., & Pike, M. E. (2011). Implantación del aprendizaje basado en proyectos en el análisis de cuentas anuales. XXI Jornadas Hispano-Lusas Gestión Científica.

Freixo, M. (2010). *Metodologia científica, fundamentos, métodos e técnicas.* Instituto Piaget.

Gil, A. C. (2008). Métodos e técnicas de pesquisa social (6ª edição). São Paulo: Editora Atlas.

Gil, A. (2002). Como elaborar projectos de pesquisa (4ª edição). São Paulo: Editora Atlas

Gomes, R. M., Brito, E., & Varela, A. (2016). Intervenção na formação no ensino superior: A aprendizagem baseada em problemas (PBL). *Interacções, 42*, 44-57. Retrieved 2021-12-09 from https://www.bing.com/search?q=Gomes%2C+R.M.%2CBrito%2C+E.+e+Varela%2C+A.%2C+2016%2C

Hansen, J. D. (2006). Using problem-based learning in accounting. *Journal of Education for Business, 81*(4), 221–224. doi:10.3200/JOEB.81.4.221-224

Hernández, R. (2012). Does continuous assessment in higher education support student learning? *Higher Education, 64*(4), 489–502. doi:10.100710734-012-9506-7

Jones, A. (2010). Generic attributes in accounting: The significance of the disciplinary context. *Accounting Education, 19*(1-2), 5–21. doi:10.1080/09639280902875523

Kim, J. (2020). Learning and Teaching Online During Covid-19: Experiences of student teachers in an early childhood education practicum. *International Journal of Early Childhood, 52*(2), 145–158. doi:10.100713158-020-00272-6 PMID:32836369

Marconi, M., & Lakatos, E. (2003). *Fundamentos de metodologia científica* (5th ed.). Editora Atlas., doi:10.1590/S1517-97022003000100005

Moore, J., Dickson-Deane, C., & Galyen, K. (2011). E-learning, online learning, and distance learning environments: Are they the same? *Internet and Higher Education, 14*(2), 129–135. doi:10.1016/j.iheduc.2010.10.001

Pasin, F., & Giroux, H. (2011). The impact of a simulation game on operations management education. *Computers & Education, 57*(1), 1240–1254. doi:10.1016/j.compedu.2010.12.006

Pesce, L., & Hessel, A. M. G. (2021). Ensino superior no contexto da pandemia da COVID – 19: Um relato analítico. *Revista Práxis Educacional, 17*(45), 1-19. Retrieved 2021-12-09 from https://periodicos2.uesb.br/index.php/praxis/article/view/8323/5692

Pokhrel, S., & Chhetri, R. (2021). A literature review on impact of COVID-19 pandemic on teaching and learning. *Higher Education for the Future, 8*(1), 133–141. doi:10.1177/2347631120983481

Polvillo, C. F., & Montaño, J. L. A. (2011): Enfoques de aprendizaje: Un estudio comparativo de las titulaciones de la escuela universitária de Osuna. XXI Jornadas Hispano-Lusas Gestión Cientifica.

Programa da Unidade Curricular de Simulação Empresarial. (2020/2021). Retrieved 10-06-2021 from http://www.esce.ips.pt

Rodrigues, F. S. M., Errante, P. R., Lima, R. Y., Carmo, A. O., Silva, E. F., Gehrke, F., Carvalho, D. S., Tikazawa, E. H., Ferraz, R. R. N., Neto, A. C., & Taha, M. O. (2019). Vantagens da utilização do método de aprendizagem baseada em problemas (MABP) em cursos de graduação na área da saúde. *RIAEE – Revista Ibero – Americana de estudos em educação, 14*(2), 340-353. Retrieved 2021-12-09 from https://www.researchgate.net/publication/348077833_Boletim_10_-_Revista_Ibero-Americana_de_Estudos_em_Educacao

Santos, Z. M. M. L. (2020). Os impactos da pandemia do Coronavirus no ensino superior. *VII Congresso Nacional de Educação*. Retrieved 2021-12-09 from https://editorarealize.com.br/index.php/artigo/visualizar/69228

Serra, F. (2004). Reorientação das actividades de ensino/aprendizagem nas instituições de ensino superior: Uma abordagem sistémica. In *XIV Jornadas Luso-Espanholas de Gestão Científica*. Açores.

Silva, E., & Menezes, E. (2005). *Metodologia da pesquisa e elaboração de dissertação* (4th ed.). Universidade Federal de Santa Catarina.

Silva, S., Aleixo, C., & Teixeira, A. B. (2016). A contabilidade e as finanças em Simulação Empresarial, um ensino de sucesso. In *I Congresso Internacional de Contabilidade Pública*. ESCE do IPS.

Smith, M. (2003). *Research methods in accounting*. Sage Publications. doi:10.4135/9781849209809

Souza, S. C., & Dourado, L. (2015). Aprendizagem baseada em problemas (ABP): Um método de aprendizagem inovador para o ensino educativo. HOLOS, 31(5). DOI: doi:10.15628/holos.2015.2880

Suárez, L. M. C., & Ramos, C. F. (2011). Um procedimento de evaluación del estilo de liderazgo en la docência. XXI Jornadas Hispano-Lusas Gestión Cientifica.

Teixeira, A. B., Aleixo, C., & Silva, S. (2012). Simulação Empresarial e as novas metodologias de ensino: Estudo de Caso. In XV Encontro AECA – Novos caminhos para a Europa, o papel das empresas e do governo. Obra digital.

Teixeira, A. B., Silva, S., Aleixo, M. C., & Mata, C. (2015). A contabilidade e as finanças na gestão empresarial: uma prática simulada. *V Congresso OTOC*.

Yin, R. K. (2018). *Case study research and applications: Design and methods* (6th ed.). SAGE Publications, Inc.

Chapter 6
Transforming Tourism Education:
An Interdisciplinary Approach to Sustainable Tourism Management

Sandra Vieira Vasconcelos
https://orcid.org/0000-0003-4062-331X
School of Hospitality and Tourism, Polytechnic Institute of Porto, Portugal & CIDTFF, ESTGA, University of Aveiro, Portugal

Carla Melo
https://orcid.org/0000-0003-3097-4108
School of Hospitality and Tourism, Polytechnic Institute of Porto, Portugal & CiTUR, Portugal & VALORIZA, Portugal

ABSTRACT

The chapter describes an interdisciplinary project that was designed and implemented within the scope of a Tourist Activities Management degree whose main topic was sustainability. Based on the use of a bilingual student blog, this project challenged students to produce multimedia content (posts, podcasts, and videos) focusing on sustainable practices and behaviors in different tourism sectors. Making use of a project-based learning approach, the strategy used is perceived as innovative having enhanced student participation and engagement. Concurrently, a preliminary analysis also suggests that there has been a positive change in the participants' awareness towards sustainability, with the different assignments and research having prompted changes in their behavior, denoting the project's pertinence, particularly in these challenging and technology-laden times.

INTRODUCTION

The tourism industry is currently experiencing an unparalleled crisis (OECD, 2020) which defies the sectors' resilience (Biggs et al., 2012) and its capacity to overcome the effects of the COVID-19 pan-

DOI: 10.4018/978-1-7998-8239-8.ch006

demic. As different researchers study the short-term social, economic and environmental effects of the pandemic, and try to foresee its long-term impacts, topics such as sustainability and sustainable development have become paramount, not only for governments and service providers as a whole, but also for tourists and the destinations themselves.

This challenge, combined with tourism's contribution for overall sustainable development – as acknowledged by the 2030 Agenda for Sustainable Development (UNWTO & UNDP, 2017) – and the continuous growth of the industry and its impacts, have raised questions regarding the sustainability of tourism activity (Arrobas et al., 2020) and the need to shift current managerial practices and priorities, paving the way for a new sustainable growth paradigm (Lalici & Weber-Sabil, 2020), something that was made more evident by the current COVID-19 pandemic.

Despite the uncertainty about the future, and the industry's ability to overcome this period and adopt more sustainable practices, tourism stakeholders will face "unlimited path-shaping opportunities (Niewiadomski, 2020, p. 654), with education for sustainability playing a pivotal role in this change (Arrobas et al., 2020). On the other hand, the pandemic has also urged a prompt reaction from the tourism higher education (THE) sector, having precipitated the ongoing digital transition, creating an opportunity for redesigning curricula and teaching methodologies, and ultimately providing tourism students with better tools to deal with their future working reality.

Based on these premises and focusing on students currently pursuing degree in Tourist Activities Management, in this chapter the authors describe a recently implemented Interdisciplinary Project (IP) aiming to further develop tourism students' awareness as to the importance of sustainable tourism, as well as to engage them in a public discussion regarding sustainable practices and behaviors, considering both the suppliers and the consumers' perspective. Taking into account recent findings, namely studies focusing on the profile of current hospitality and tourism professionals and the challenges they are currently facing (e.g., their limited levels of educational achievement and digital literacy and the resulting difficulties in adapting to new contexts and ways of working – Baum et al., 2020) this project, which involved Tourism Operations Management and English Applied to Tourism courses, made use of technological platforms and tools, namely a class blog and student-produced podcasts, to bridge the gap between theory and practice and encourage students' creativity and resourcefulness. Having been implemented in the summer semester of 2021 (while on partial lockdown, due to the COVID-19 pandemic) the project was also instrumental in promoting remote and hybrid teaching methodologies, making the most use of online collaborative approaches and tools.

Bearing this in mind, the authors start out by establishing the theoretical rationale behind the project. Based on a literature review, they provide an overview of the state of the art, focusing on tourism sustainability and sustainable practices and behaviors, as well as the role tourism education and interdisciplinarity can play within this scope. Next, they describe the teaching/learning strategy designed to achieve these goals, dividing it into three different stages: design and planning; implementation; and assessment. Given the nature of the topics explored, it was deemed necessary to collect students' initial perceptions regarding the concept of sustainability and the role it plays within the industry, as well as to introduce them to best practices and put them in contact with experts in the field. As a result, in addition to an introductory questionnaire, there was an opening webinar, which helped frame future work, namely the topics on which students should focus, as well as other webinars with practitioners from different tourism subsectors, so that students could come into contact with authentic contexts. At the end of the semester another questionnaire was applied as to collect data regarding the impacts of the project, particularly on students' perceptions regarding sustainability and whether they had evolved throughout the semester.

Given the complexity of the topic and the profusion of data, this chapter will focus mostly on the latter, drawing the participants' profile, as well as documenting their participation in the project and the ensuing transformation on their perceptions and overall insights on sustainability and its relevance within the industry. By reflecting on the participants' learning journey and the strategies used, this chapter is, therefore, expected to contribute towards the scope of managerial education by providing a different insight on new forms of teaching and hopefully inspiring future research within this field.

BACKGROUND

Defined as "[tourism] that takes full account of its current and future economic, social and environmental impacts, addressing the needs of visitors, the industry, the environment and host communities" (UNWTO, 2005, p.12), sustainable tourism relies on the need to "ensure viable, long-term economic operations" (UNWTO, 2013, p. 18) and on the engagement of stakeholders, including those working in the public and private sectors, as well as tourism education providers and tourists (UNWTO, 2013).

Given the tourism industry's importance for global economy, its relationship with sustainability is considered of particular relevance (Niñerola et al., 2019), having increasingly become more pertinent in tourism literature (e.g., Battaglia, 2017; Zika, 2017; Font & Lynes, 2018). In addition to documenting the growing awareness towards the importance of sustainability within this scope (Tolkes, 2018) and the fact it can be a crucial tool for competitiveness (Ritchie & Crouch, 2010; Cucculelli & Goffi, 2016; Goffi et al., 2019; Camisón, 2020), current research also highlights the present-day difficulties in promoting sustainable tourist development, with some researchers going insofar as describing it as a plight (Tölkes, 2018), deeming it an immeasurable and unachievable goal (Buckley, 2012; Hall, 2019; Asmelash & Kumar, 2019). In fact, several scholars have stressed the need for raising awareness towards more sustainable managerial practices and for the development of educational and training programs that improve individual and collective motivation and performance (Ji et al., 2012; Champs & García-Blandón, 2019). Although sustainable performance largely depends on individual characteristics, attributes, and behaviors (Chams & García-Blandón, 2019), educational experiences can offer transformational opportunities (Edelheim, 2020). On the other hand, even though the emergence of this new paradigm predates the COVID-19 pandemic (Saarinen 2018; Chams & García-Blandón, 2019; Higgins-Desbiolles et al. 2019; Gretzel et al., 2020), several practitioners have argued that this crisis presents itself as a "transformative moment or opportunity that will change the world" (Davies, 2020; Gills, 2020; Mair, 2020; Politico, 2020 cit in. Hall et al., 2020, p. 579), meaning changes in the whole tourism system. As argued by Brouder (2020, p. 487) – "transformation in tourism is possible (…) when there is institutional innovation on both the demand and supply side", as part of an evolutionary pathway in which THE can play a pivotal role.

Educating for Sustainability

Having emerged in the 1970s as a way of promoting environmental protection, Environmental Education has since evolved, having gradually shifted from a more nature-based approach to include cultural and social issues, making headway for other perspectives and models, including Education for Sustainable Development (ESD) (Marouli, 2021). Reflecting a new paradigm "in which environmental, social and economic considerations are balanced in the pursuit of development and an improved quality of life" (UNESCO, 2012), ESD relies on a constructivist approach "where students participate in the creation of knowledge, in interactive learning environments, and addressing real environmental problems" (Marouli, 2021, p.3) that integrates interdisciplinary and problem-solving principles. The intricate nature and key role of ESD is recognized by the United Nations with quality education currently being featured as a Sustainable Development Goal (SDG), asserting the need to "ensure that all learners acquire the knowledge and skills needed to promote sustainable development, including, among others, through education for sustainable development and sustainable lifestyles, human rights, gender equality, promotion of a culture of peace and non-violence, global citizenship and appreciation of cultural diversity and of culture's contribution to sustainable development" (UN, 2015). Given the "the breadth and the interconnectedness of the sustainable development agenda" (Annan-Diab & Molinari, 2017, p.5), ESD should, therefore, be approached from an interdisciplinary perspective (UNWTO, 2005; Luppi, 2011).

According to the Oxford dictionary, interdisciplinarity is "the quality or fact of involving or drawing on two or more branches of knowledge", i.e., addressing an issue from different perspectives, combining approaches and methods that complement each other, something that has become a staple of tourism and tourism education. In fact, having originally been studied within the scope of different disciplines, including sociology, anthropology and geography (Xiao & Smith, 2006), tourism is arguably an interdisciplinary field by nature, given "its broad framework of relationships with other areas, where tourism interaction with – for instance – economic, cultural, social, and environmental aspects is well documented." (Afifi, Atef & Al Busaidi, 2019, p. 8).

Thus, as the study of sustainable destination development emerges and becomes increasingly relevant (Persson-Fischer & Liu, 2021) there has been a deeper awareness regarding the need to adopt holistic research and managerial approaches, that integrate "knowledge, methods, theories, or disciplines" (Persson-Fischer & Liu, 2021, p.2). This integration is also stressed by Moscardo (2015, p.16) when she reinforces the need to "focus on education for sustainability which both incorporates and goes beyond education about sustainability", referring to the features that should underline this educational approach, namely the fact that it is transformative and grounded on essential human and environmental values and the core principles of sustainability; its capacity building potential; and the fact it addresses multiple stakeholders and complex issues, moving beyond traditional classroom-based approaches. Moreover, the author considers that promoting education for sustainability requires adopting a "whole system approach" (Moscardo (2015, p.16)), something complements previous findings, namely by authors such as Canziani, Sönmez, Hsieh and Byrd (2012), who compare the nature of the "sustainability movement" to that of a learning system in which "individuals are joining together in attempts to collect and systematize knowledge and guide action to protect people and the planet" (Canziani, Sönmez, Hsieh and Byrd, 2012, p.3). These complex systems include learners, communities of practice, cognition and practice, ultimately contributing towards a heightened awareness and behavioral changes, something that, in the case of future managers can help reshape future practices and decision-making processes.

In line with these ideas, a comprehensive study carried out in 2011 (Boley, 2011) outlines three main reasons for teaching sustainability within tourism programs in THE: i) its growing importance for prospective employers (namely due to consumer demand and the optimization of operational costs); ii) the need to prepare graduates to focus on triple bottom-line, aligned with the pillars of sustainability; and iii) their role as potential change agents, that can become key elements in Promoting ESD in THE. In addition to their perceived and intrinsic value, the effective development of these programs also calls for "innovation in curricula, pedagogies and technology enhanced learning" (Benckendorff & Moscardo, 2015, p. 278).

Classroom-Based Activities and Blogs

Having established the value of interdisciplinarity, collaboration and innovation, and given the scope of the current chapter, whose main goals include the description of an IP based on the development of multimedia content for a digital platform, it is important to frame and validate this approach within THE and ESD.

As Higher Education Institutions have become more aware of the need for enhancing their programs, namely by updating and diversifying their (extra)curricular offer, investing in infrastructures and technology and incorporating new pedagogical approaches (by resorting to PBL, work- integrated learning, web 2.0 platforms, and online, hybrid and mobile learning) (Airey, 2015), there has also been a growing research interest within this scope. To this effect, a review based on over 600 peer-reviewed research papers on tourism education (Hsu, Xiao & Chen, 2017), established the vital role technology has come to play in tourism education, something that has been made even more evident by the pandemic (Tiwari,Séraphin & Chowdhary, 2020; Kallou & Kikilia, 2021 & Park & Jones, 2021).

The use of web 2.0 platforms, including blogs, wikis and social media in tourism education has been the object of different studies (Lillo-Bañuls, Perles-Ribes & Fuentes, 2016) outlining their affordances, including the increase of students' participation (Liburd, Hjalager, & Christensen, 2011), the creation of enhanced and flexible teaching and learning activities (Liburd, Hjalager, & Christensen, 2011; Buhalis, Leung & Law, 2011; Sigala & Baum, 2003), and the development of technological skills, considered to be in demand in the industry (Lillo-Bañuls, Perles-Ribes & Fuentes, 2016). On the other hand, within the scope of language teaching and learning, specifically in tourism and hospitality programs, there have also been studies on the use of blogs and podcasts for developing writing and listening skills and cultural awareness (Cote & Milliner (2017); Sundgren, 2017) with digital technology being considered to support the development of linguistic and systemic competences, the integration of different areas, the possibility of delivering authentic learning (in context) and boosting student engagement (Vasconcelos & Balula, 2019).

Overall, within these contexts, blogs are considered to be effective and interactive learning tools (Cobanoglu & Berezina, 2011), particularly when they require students to produce content and/or comment on their peers' contributions, having the potential to improve academic performance, which can be attributed to "the time that students spent on reviewing the topics on the subject in order to upload their contributions" (Lillo-Bañuls, Perles-Ribes & Fuentes, 2016, p. 84) On the other hand, considering the popularity and marketing potential of travel blogs (Cobanoglu & Berezina, 2011), their use in class can also be perceived as more appealing and in line with current trends.

Adding to the growing realization that "tourism academia would benefit from embracing and developing a stronger online presence in various media, including personal websites, blogs, online publications" (Tolkach & Pratt, 2021, p. 6), the above-mentioned affordances warrant the implementation of active teaching and learning strategies that are aligned with current challenges and needs.

MAIN FOCUS

Based on these premises and the need to enhance ESD and tourism education, this chapter outlines an Interdisciplinary Project carried out with students attending the 2nd year of a Tourist Activities Management degree, focusing on sustainability and sustainable practices and behaviors in different tourism sectors. Overall, students were expected to develop a digital platform (a blog) for which they had to produce diversified content (in the form of posts and podcasts) dealing with current sustainable practices and behaviors within the scope of tourist activities. The content should focus on a specific sector, namely Accommodation, Food & Beverage, Recreation & Entertainment, Distribution and Transportation, contemplate both the supplier and demand side and be produced in Portuguese and in English. Rather than focusing on a more traditional assignment to be handed-in at the end of the semester, this interdisciplinary venture (implemented within the scope of two different courses – Tourism Operations Management and English Applied to Tourism) followed a project-based approach, i.e., it relied on student-driven, collaborative, inquiry-based learning activities carried out over an extended period of time, in which students had to engage in complex real-word challenges (Bell, 2010). Considering the main goal of Project Based Learning (PBL) is to give students the opportunity to "apply, synthesize, prioritize, summarize theoretical knowledge] (…) to arrive at an in-depth understanding of the important key concepts of [a] course" (Ab Wahid, Lee & Baharudin, 2020, p. 84), these activities were based on current challenges faced by the industry and were designed to enhance participation, creativity, and critical thinking.

Design, Planning and Implementation

After clarifying and clearly defining the general and specific goals of the project (the former focusing on fostering awareness regarding sustainable tourism practices and the development of creative ideas and campaigns, aiming to reduce the ecological footprint and promote sustainable practices and behaviors, and the latter on the previously defined learning outcomes of each of the courses involved), the teachers, taking on a facilitator role, developed a common implementation plan. Having designed this plan (which included a joint introductory session, webinars, workshops, and tutorials, they then proceeded to prepare a set of guidelines and templates to further assist the students, as well as to create a digital platform, a blog, in which they could publish the project outputs. These outputs included an informative text (blog post), a 10-minute podcast, and a final report and presentation, to be recorded as a video. As the IP resulted from the collaboration of two different courses – Tourism Operations Management and English Applied to Tourism – all publications should be bilingual and make use of adequate terminology, also reflecting students' creativity, originality and critical-thinking skills. The fact the blog was available in two languages (Portuguese and English) also broadened its reach, not limiting the audience to Portuguese-speakers.

Considering the nature of the work being developed students were provided with specific guidelines, as well as a detailed timeline, at an initial joint session. As to ensure periodical publications in the blog, groups were expected to submit the different outputs throughout the semester (Figure 1).

This segmented approach aimed to promote continuous learning and develop students' time management and decision-making skills, as they could decide which of the outputs to hand-in first. The content production process was supported by both classes involved, both in lessons and in joint discussion sessions and workshops. Finally, students were asked to write a short report in which they not only described their goals and the underlying production process, but also reflected on the affordances of technology and communication in promoting tourism sustainability, as well as their key findings and learning experience. This report was then discussed publicly.

Figure 1. Project implementation timeline

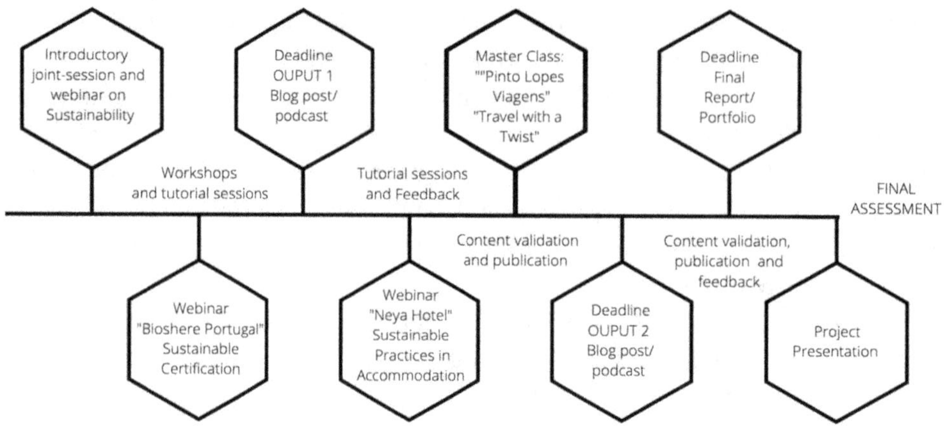

Assessment

Mimicking the approach followed throughout the project, namely the segmented assignments and spaced-out publications, assessment was perceived as a continuous process, with teachers providing timely formative feedback (both in classes and in tutorial sessions) and evaluating individual outputs, as well as the final report and presentation. All outputs were corrected and validated before publishing by both teachers, who assessed them collaboratively using rubrics. Given the differences between the courses, there were some discrepancies in the final results (with differences being mostly attributed to different levels of language proficiency and the use of terminology), however, all partial and final marks were discussed in joint sessions. The overall weight of the project was also different for each course (in compliance with institutional and departmental policy).

Methodology

As mentioned previously, the focus of this chapter was mostly placed on the general description of the IP, the participants' profile and their perceptions towards the topic of sustainability and determining if these were somehow transformed by the research and activities carried out. As a result, two questionnaires were applied at the initial and final stages of the project. As seen above, the initial questionnaire (iQ) comprised 18 questions and a comments/suggestions section aimed to collect information on the students' personal and technological profile (the latter due to the use of digital tools, not only for creating and publishing multimedia content, but also for producing the final video presentation), their perceptions on the topics of sustainability in tourism, sustainability education/training, sustainable behaviors (anticipating the possible influence of the IP), their stance and expectations on the upcoming projects and possible comments or suggestions. As a result, the semi-structured questionnaires included both closed- and open-ended questions, that were then analyzed by applying a mixed approach, including statistical and content analysis.

Table 1. Structure of the questionnaires

Section	Number of Questions	
	iQ	fQ
Informed Consent	(0)	(0)
Student Profile (gender, age, working student status)	3	3
Technological Profile (type of technological devices and frequency of use)	3	3
Students' Perceptions of Sustainability in Tourism (Degree of familiarity, concepts, agreement with statements on sustainability)	4	4
Students' Perceptions of Sustainability Training (Agreement with statements on sustainability training, interdisciplinarity)	4	4
Sustainable Behaviours (Agreement with statements on sustainable behaviours, perceived influence of the interdisciplinary project (IP))	2	2
Tourism Higher Education (Agreement with statements on tourism education, perceived obstacles regarding the development of IP.	2	2
Comments & Suggestions	1	1

In addition to a general overview of the participants, this questionnaire also made it possible to anticipate possible misconceptions and/or barriers for their participation, having helped structure the workshops to be held within the scope of the project.

As for the final questionnaire (fQ), it followed the same structure as the initial questionnaire, even though some of the questions were adapted as to cover the tools and issues addressed throughout the project's implementation.

Participant's Profile

Overall, iQ registered 39 answers (corresponding to 61.9% of students enrolled in both courses), whereas fQ was answered by 54 participants (accounting for 85.7% of students). The higher response rate upon the conclusion of the project may be interpreted as a demonstration of students' engagement and their willingness to collaborate, following the development of the project. On the other hand, drawing from the participants' profile, there was an increase of responses from working students in fQ (from 10.3% – 4 students – to 18,5% - 10 students), which seems to corroborate the previous inference, insofar as working students were initially more reticent to the methods and strategy used and unsure whether to take part in the project (as opposed to taking a final exam) (Table 2).

As for the age of the respondents, it ranges between 19 and 40 years old (average 20.6 years old), with 82.1% respondents being between 19-22 years old. As seen in Figure 2, most respondents were female (respectively, 66.7% and 64.8%), with results being consistent in both questionnaires.

Table 2. Total number of respondents (full-time students vs. working students)

	iQ	fQ
Full-time students	35	44
Working Student Status	4	10

Figure 2. Respondents by gender (%)

Findings

Sustainability and Sustainable Tourism

Having been asked to rate their degree of familiarity with concept of sustainability before and after taking part in the project, as seen in Figure 3, there was a significant increase in students' perceived awareness on the topic, with 87.3% considering they were either very or extremely familiar with the concept when answering fQ (contrasting with 12.8% in iQ). On the other hand, in iQ, 17.9% of the students considered they were only somehow familiar with the topic, whereas in fQ there is a shift towards more confident stances.

When asked to define sustainable tourism, based on the number of word occurrences, there was also a shift in students' perceptions when answering both questionnaires. Even though, as seen in Figures 4 and 5, tourism and sustainability remain the main keywords, in fQ answers were more precise and reflect the literature, namely the predominance of the pillars of sustainability (through the use of the words "environmental", "social" and "economic "– highlighted in both questionnaires, but more preponderant in fQ), as well as a more direct link to tourism, given the prevalence of the word "destination", in addition to a more balanced distribution between "local", "resources" and "activities".

This change becomes even more noticeable, when comparing the answers to the question "define sustainability using only one word" (Figures 6 and 7). Even though words such as preservation/preserving, necessary/essential and future are extensively used in both questionnaires, in fQ the concept of responsibility takes centre stage, with the words "balance" and "global" also gaining traction. Moreover, students' final answers also denote a deeper awareness of the importance of collaboration and cooperation with words such as "collective" and "team" having been used by more than one student.

Figure 3. Familiarity with sustainability (%)

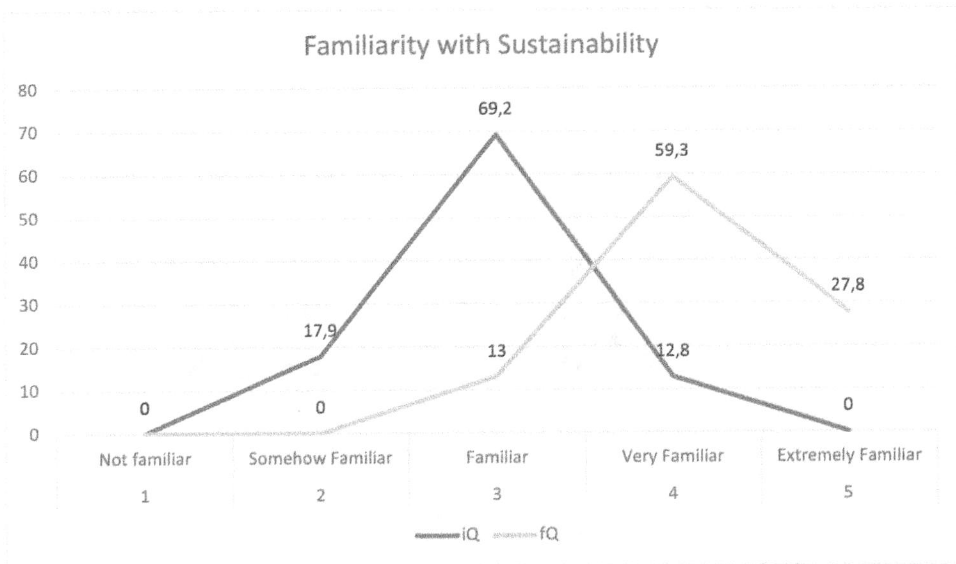

Interdisciplinary Project: Overall Perceptions

Motivation for/ Satisfaction with the IP

Initially, as shown in Figure 8, students were asked to rate their degree of motivation for undertaking the IP, according to a Likert-type scale, ranging from 1 – not at all motivated – to 5 – extremely motivated, with 82% of students describing themselves as being either highly (56.4%) or extremely motivated (25.6%). In the final survey, students were asked to rate their degree of satisfaction with the IP, also using a Likert-type scale (1 – not at all satisfied; 5 – extremely satisfied). The answers obtained indicate a

Figure 4. Sustainable tourism concept (iQ – Word Cloud)
Source: Own elaboration from webQDA/WordArt.com

Figure 5. Sustainable tourism concept (fQ – Word Cloud)
Source: Own elaboration from webQDA/WordArt.com

level of satisfaction above 98%, with 55.6% of students describing themselves as being highly satisfied, and 42.6% as extremely satisfied.

These answers are in line with previously inferred conclusion that participants were willing to participate, with the project having gained momentum throughout the semester, something that can also be

Figure 6. Sustainability in one word (iQ – Word Cloud)
Source: Own elaboration from webQDA/WordArt.com

Figure 7. Sustainability in one word (fQ – Word Cloud)
Source: Own elaboration from webQDA/WordArt.com

perceived in the answers regarding the contribution of the IP to the enrichment of the learning process (Figure 9).

When questioned about this contribution (Figure 9), in the first questionnaire 95% of the respondents gave a positive answer, while 1 respondent was unsure (having answered "maybe"). In fQ, all respondents considered that the project had contributed to their learning process, which, though not a significant change, once again suggests the overall satisfaction with the work carried out.

Figure 8. Motivation (iQ) and satisfaction (fQ) with the IP (%)

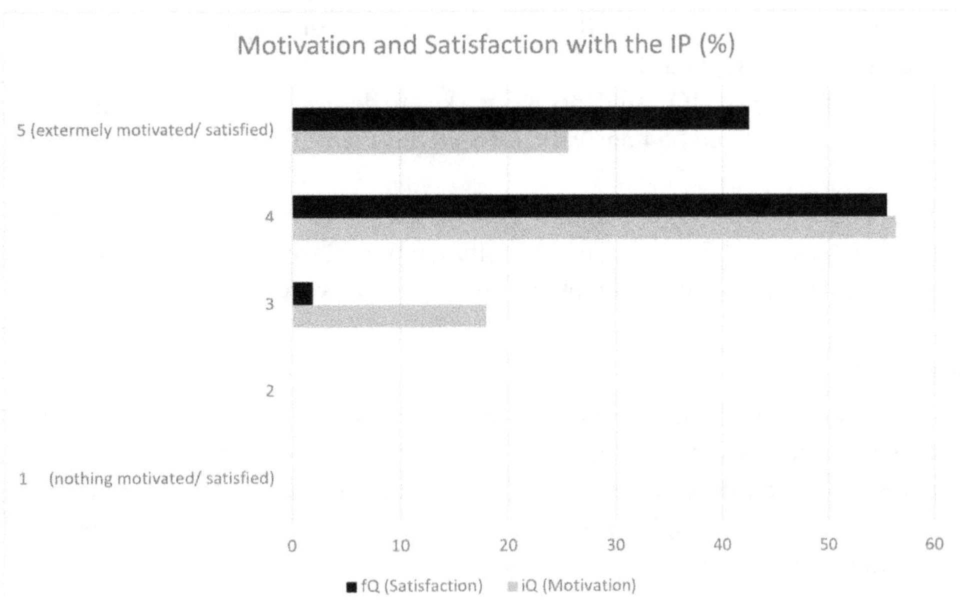

Figure 9. IP's contribution for the learning process (%)

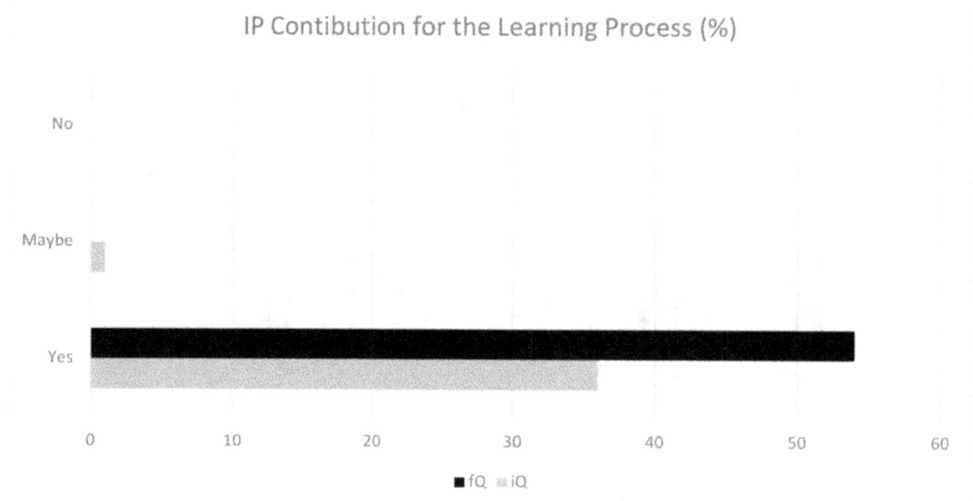

Nevertheless, despite the positive response to the project, participants also signaled what they considered to be the most significant difficulties. When initially asked to anticipate potential challenges in developing the assignments, respondents highlighted problems with managing time and balancing and planning the different tasks, rather than technical difficulties pertaining to video edition and subtitling (Figure 10). Even though time management and balancing the participation in the project with other tasks and assignments were confirmed as the most challenging aspects, the more technical side proved to be more demanding than expected. Notwithstanding, all groups were able to submit fully developed outputs that complied with the previously defined standards.

In the light of what was pointed out by Person-Fisher (2021) and Moscardo (2015), with regard to the adoption of a more holistic, integrative and multidisciplinary approach to the issue of sustainability, and considering the objectives defined for the IP, it was also considered important to analyse the students' perceptions regarding interdisciplinarity.

In both questionnaires (iQ and fQ), students were asked to describe interdisciplinarity using only one word. The results obtained (29 and 54 answers, respectively), are illustrated by the word cloud below (Figure 11).

As can be observed, the words 'cooperation' (n=6), 'useful' (n=6), 'union' (n=6) stand out as the most relevant associations, highlighting the role collaboration played within the scope of the project, in addition to its practical applications, something that is in line with the literature on SDE and PBL.

Students' Sustainable Behaviours

Reflecting on the IP influence on the adoption of more sustainable behaviors, most students consider that the development of the project influenced their own behaviors regarding sustainability (iQ=84.2%, fQ=83.3%), however, as seen in Figure 12, a residual decrease in the values recorded before and after the project can be observed. This slight difference may be due to the students' initial lack of knowledge regarding the sustainability of their own behaviors or be associated with the greater diversity/diversity/

number of respondents in the fQ. A more detailed analysis of the answers obtained regarding sustainable behaviors may, in the future, help to interpret these results in a more sustained way.

Figure 10. Main difficulties (%)

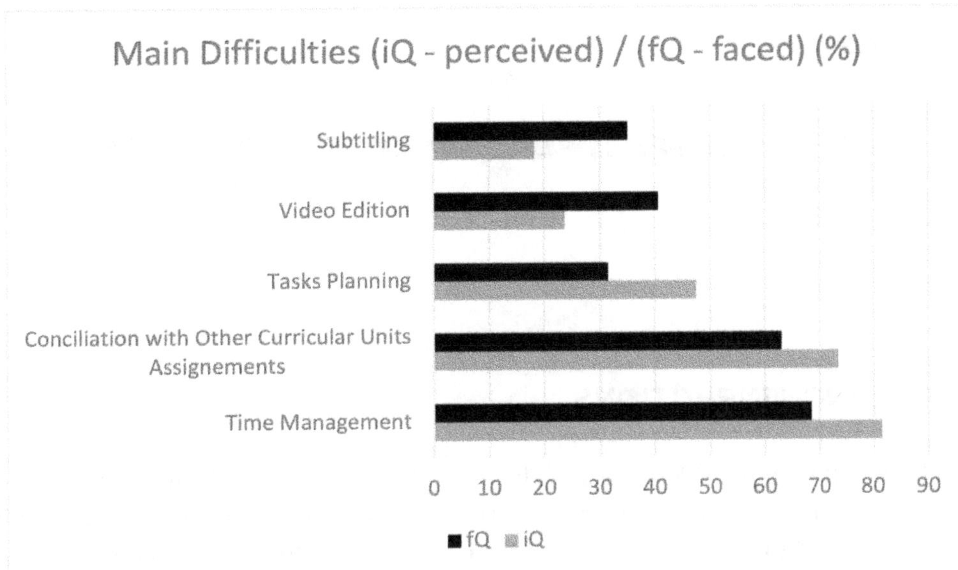

Figure 11. Interdisciplinarity in one word (%)
Source: Own elaboration from webQDA/WordArt.com

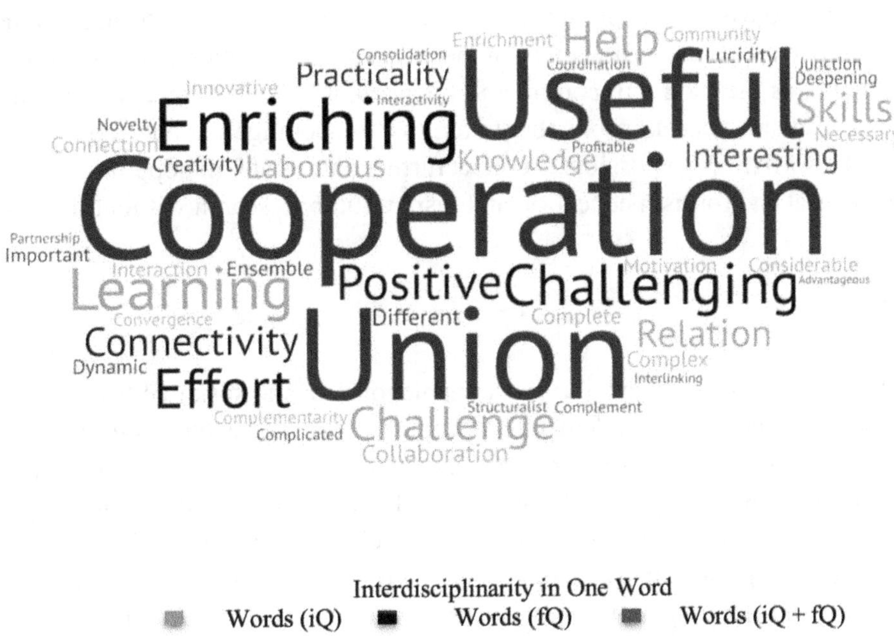

Figure 12. IP's perceived influence on student's sustainable behaviors (%)

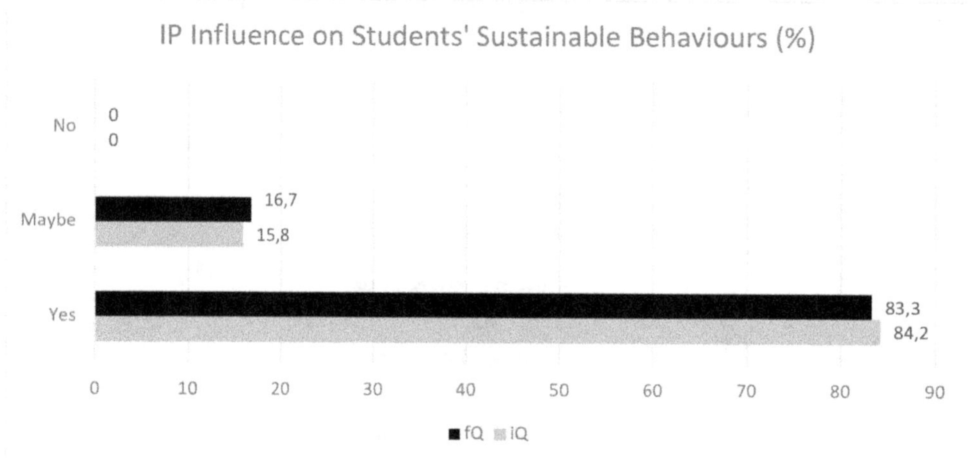

FUTURE RESEARCH DIRECTIONS

As mentioned before, the findings described are based on a preliminary and partial analysis that mostly focused on the participants' profile and their perceptions regarding the concept of sustainability and the expected outcomes regarding the IP. Considering the complexity of the topic and the data available, the authors expect to draw more specific conclusions, namely regarding different aspects of sustainability and how students perceive them, as well as on the actual outputs produced. An in-depth analysis of the posts, podcasts and videos produced will provide a more detailed insight on the sectors and sustainable practices addressed, paving the way for future publications (which can also focus on operational, educational and linguistic features). It would also be interesting to carry out a comparative study juxtaposing this strategy with more conventional approaches as to draw more precise conclusions on the advantages of collaboration and the use of technology within the scope of Education for Sustainability.

On the other hand, as the blog will continue to be available, the authors anticipate replicating the strategy in the next academic year, adjusting the strategy as to encourage students' comments and include their suggestions. This will make it possible to collect further data, that will hopefully contribute towards the scope of managerial and tourism education and inspire future research within this field.

CONCLUSION

Drawing from the premise that sustainability, sustainable tourism and sustainable development are currently key areas, whose importance and demand will continue to increase, the IP described in this chapter set out to develop students' awareness regarding these topics by using an innovative and collaborative approach. In addition to supporting the call by Wen et al. (2020) for a future-centred research agenda in the area of hospitality employment that is both multi-disciplinary in perspective, and multimethod in the tools that are used, the project also reflected the need to focus on the development of collaborative, technological and critical-thinking skills, as these are instrumental for future graduates, as well as for reshaping and updating the industry.

Based on the questionnaires applied to the participating students, the project was successful in enhancing their motivation and participation and increasing their familiarity with the concept of sustainability. Participants were overall motivated and satisfied, with the project surpassing their initial expectations, particularly in what concerns its perceived usefulness and collaborative nature.

As a result, this chapter has contributed towards the scope of managerial education by providing a different insight on new forms of teaching and hopefully inspiring future research within this field.

REFERENCES

Ab Wahid, M., Lee, W. K., & Baharudin, F. (2020). Implementing Project-Based Learning for Sustainability Management Course at Postgraduate Level. *Asian Journal of University Education*, *16*(2), 84–92. doi:10.24191/ajue.v16i2.10300

Afifi, G. M. H., Atef, T., & Al Busaidi, Y. (2019). Interdisciplinary higher education in tourism: The case of SQU, Oman. *Anatolia*, *30*(1), 6–17. doi:10.1080/13032917.2018.1494610

Airey, D. (2015). 40 years of tourism studies – a remarkable story. *Tourism Recreation Research*, *40*(1), 6–15. doi:10.1080/02508281.2015.1007633

Annan-Diab, F., & Molinari, C. (2017). Interdisciplinarity: Practical approach to advancing education for sustainability and for the Sustainable Development Goals. *International Journal of Management Education*, *15*(2), 73–83. doi:10.1016/j.ijme.2017.03.006

Aynalem, S., Birhanu, K., & Tesefay, S. (2016). Employment Opportunities and Challenges in Tourism and Hospitality Sectors. *Journal of Tourism & Hospitality (Los Angeles, Calif.)*, *5*(6), 1–5. doi:10.4172/2167-0269.1000257

Arrobas, F., Ferreira, J., Brito-Henriques, E., & Fernandes, A. (2020). Measuring tourism and environmental sciences students' attitudes towards sustainable tourism. *Journal of Hospitality, Leisure, Sport and Tourism Education*, *27*, 1–12. doi:10.1016/j.jhlste.2020.100273 PMID:33041660

Asmelash, A. G., & Kumar, S. (2019). Assessing progress of tourism sustainability: Developing and validating sustainability indicators. *Tourism Management*, *71*, 67–83. doi:10.1016/j.tourman.2018.09.020

Battaglia, M. (2017). Sustainability in the Tourism Business. Symphonya. *Emerging Issues in Management*, *3*, 122-134. doi:10.4468/2016.3.11battaglia

Benckendorff, P., & Moscardo, G. (2015). Education for Sustainability Futures. In G. Moscardo & P. Benckendorff (Eds.), *Education for Sustainability in Tourism A Handbook of Processes, Resources, and Strategies* (pp. 271–284). Springer. doi:10.1007/978-3-662-47470-9_17

Bell, S. (2010). Project-based learning for the 21st century: Skills for the future. *The Clearing House: A Journal of Educational Strategies, Issues and Ideas*, *83*(2), 39–43. doi:10.1080/00098650903505415

Biggs, D., Hall, C., & Stoeckl, N. (2012). The resilience of formal and informal tourism enterprises to disasters: Reef tourism in Phuket, Thailand. *Journal of Sustainable Tourism*, *20*(5), 645–665. doi:10.1080/09669582.2011.630080

Boley, B. B. (2011). Sustainability in hospitality and tourism education: Towards an integrated curriculum. *Journal of Hospitality & Tourism Education, 23*(4), 22–31. doi:10.1080/10963758.2011.10697017

Brouder, P. (2020). Reset redux: Possible evolutionary pathways towards the transformation of tourism in a COVID-19 world. *Tourism Geographies, 22*(3), 484–490. doi:10.1080/14616688.2020.1760928

Buckley, R. (2012). Sustainable Tourism: Research and Reality. *Annals of Tourism Research, 39*(2), 528–546. doi:10.1016/j.annals.2012.02.003

Buhalis, D., Leung, D., & Law, R. (2011). eTourism: Critical Information and Communication Technologies for Tourism Destinations. In Y. Wang & A. Pizam (Eds.), Destination Marketing and Management (pp. 205–224). CAB International.

Canziani, B. F., Sönmez, S., Hsieh, Y., & Byrd, E. T. (2012). A learning theory framework for sustainability education in tourism. *Journal of Teaching in Travel & Tourism, 12*(1), 3–20. doi:10.1080/15313220.2012.650052

Camisón, C. (2020). Competitiveness and Sustainability in Tourist Firms and Destinations. *Sustainability, 12*(6), 2388. doi:10.3390u12062388

Chams, N., & García-Blandón, J. (2019). On the importance of sustainable human resource management for the adoption of sustainable development goals. *Resources, Conservation and Recycling, 141*, 109–122. doi:10.1016/j.resconrec.2018.10.006

Cobanoglu, C., & Berezina, K. (2011). The impact of the use of blogs on students' assignment engagement. *Journal of Hospitality, Leisure, Sports and Tourism Education, 10*(1), 99.

Cote, T. J., & Milliner, B. (2017). Preparing Japanese Students' Digital Literacy for Study Abroad: Is More Training Needed? *The JALT CALL Journal, 13*(3), 187–197. doi:10.29140/jaltcall.v13n3.218

Cucculelli, M., & Goffi, G. (2016). Does sustainability enhance tourism destination competitiveness? Evidence from Italian Destinations of Excellence. *Journal of Cleaner Production, 111*, 370–382. doi:10.1016/j.jclepro.2014.12.069

Edelheim, J. (2020). How should tourism education values be transformed after 2020? *Tourism Geographies, 22*(3), 547–554. doi:10.1080/14616688.2020.1760927

Font, X., & Lynes, J. (2018). Corporate social responsibility in tourism and hospitality. *Journal of Sustainable Tourism, 26*(7), 1027–1042. doi:10.1080/09669582.2018.1488856

Goffi, G., Cucculelli, M., & Masiero, L. (2019). Fostering tourism destination competitiveness in developing countries: The role of sustainability. *Journal of Cleaner Production, 209*, 101–115. doi:10.1016/j.jclepro.2018.10.208

Gössling, S., Scott, D., & Hall, C. (2021). Pandemics, tourism and global change: A rapid assessment of COVID-19. *Journal of Sustainable Tourism, 29*(1), 1–20. doi:10.1080/09669582.2020.1758708

Gretzel, U., Fuchs, M., Baggio, R., Hoepken, W., Law, R., Neidhardt, J., Pesonen, J., Zanker, M., & Xiang, Z. (2020). E-tourism beyond covid-19: A call for transformative research. *Information Technology & Tourism, 22*(2), 187–203. doi:10.100740558-020-00181-3

Guan, Y., Deng, H., & Zhou, X. (2020). Understanding the impact of the covid-19 pandemic on career development: Insights from cultural psychology. *Journal of Vocational Behavior, 119*, 103438. Advance online publication. doi:10.1016/j.jvb.2020.103438 PMID:32382162

Hall, C. (2019). Constructing sustainable tourism development: The 2030 agenda and the managerial ecology of sustainable tourism. *Journal of Sustainable Tourism, 27*(7), 1044–1060. doi:10.1080/09669582.2018.1560456

Hall, M., Scott, D., & Gössling, S. (2020). Pandemics, transformations and tourism: Be careful what you wish for. *Tourism Geographies, 22*(3), 577–598. doi:10.1080/14616688.2020.1759131

Higgins-Desbiolles, F., Carnicelli, S., Krolikowski, C., Wijesinghe, G., & Boluk, K. (2019). Degrowing tourism: Rethinking tourism. *Journal of Sustainable Tourism, 27*(12), 1926–1944. doi:10.1080/09669582.2019.1601732

Hsu, C. H. C., Xiao, H., & Chen, N. (2017). Hospitality and tourism education research from 2005 to 2014: "Is the past a prologue to the future? *International Journal of Contemporary Hospitality Management, 29*(1), 141–160. doi:10.1108/IJCHM-09-2015-0450

Kallou, S., & Kikilia, A. (2021). A transformative educational framework in tourism higher education through digital technologies during the COVID-19 pandemic. *Advances in Mobile Learning Educational Research, 1*(1), 37–47. doi:10.25082/AMLER.2021.01.005

Lalicic, L., & Weber-Sabil, J. (2020). Stakeholder engagement in sustainable tourism planning through serious gaming. *Tourism Geographies, 23*(1), 185–205. doi:10.1080/14616688.2019.1648543

Liburd, J., Hjalager, A. M., & Christensen, I. M. F. (2011). Valuing tourism education 2.0. *Journal of Teaching in Travel & Tourism, 11*(1), 107–130. doi:10.1080/15313220.2011.548745

Lillo-Bañuls, A., Perles-Ribes, J. F., & Fuentes, R. (2016). Wiki and blog as teaching tools in tourism higher education. *Journal of Teaching in Travel & Tourism, 16*(2), 81–100. doi:10.1080/15313220.2015.1118367

Lugosi, P., & Jameson, S. (2017). Challenges in hospitality management education: Perspectives from the United Kingdom. *Journal of Hospitality and Tourism Management, 31*, 163–172. doi:10.1016/j.jhtm.2016.12.001

Luppi, E. (2011). Training to education for sustainable development through e-learning. *Procedia: Social and Behavioral Sciences, 15*, 3244–3251. doi:10.1016/j.sbspro.2011.04.279

Marouli, C. (2021). Sustainability Education for the Future? Challenges and Implications for Education and Pedagogy in the 21st Century. *Sustainability, 13*(5), 2901. Advance online publication. doi:10.3390u13052901

Mei, X. (2019). Gaps in tourism education and workforce needs: Attracting and educating the right people. *Current Issues in Tourism, 22*(12), 1400–1404. doi:10.1080/13683500.2017.1402870

Moscardo, G. (2015). The Importance of Education for Sustainability in Tourism. In G. Moscardo & P. Benckendorff (Eds.), *Education for Sustainability in Tourism A Handbook of Processes, Resources, and Strategies* (1st ed., pp. 1–24). Springer. doi:10.1007/978-3-662-47470-9_1

Niewiadomski, P. (2020). COVID-19: From temporary deglobalization to a re-discovery of tourism? *Tourism Geographies*, *22*(3), 651–656. doi:10.1080/14616688.2020.1757749

Niñerola, A., Sánchez-Rebull, M., & Hernández-Lara, A. (2019). Tourism Research on Sustainability: A Bibliometric Analysis. *Sustainability*, *11*(5), 1377. doi:10.3390u11051377

OECD. (2020). *Mitigating the impact of COVID-19 and preparing for recovery.*. doi:10.1787/23071672

Park, M., & Jones, T. (2021). Going virtual: The impact of COVID-19 on internships in tourism, events, and hospitality education. *Journal of Hospitality & Tourism Education*, 1–18.

Persson-Fischer, U., & Liu, S. (2021). What Is Interdisciplinarity in the Study of Sustainable Destination Development? *Sustainability*, *13*(7), 3639. doi:10.3390u13073639

Ritchie, J., & Crouch, G. (2010). A model of destination competitiveness/ sustainability: Brazilian perspectives. *Brazilian Public Administration Review*, *44*(5), 1049–1066. doi:10.1590/S0034-76122010000500003

Saarinen, J. (2018). Beyond growth thinking: The need to revisit sustainable development in tourism. *Tourism Geographies*, *20*(2), 337–340. doi:10.1080/14616688.2018.1434817

Sigala, M., & Baum, T. (2003). Trends and issues in tourism and hospitality Higher Education: Visioning the future. *Tourism and Hospitality Research*, *4*(4), 367–376. doi:10.1177/146735840300400409

Sheldon, P., Fesenmaier, D., & Tribe, J. (2011). The Tourism Education Futures Initiative (TEFI): Activating change in tourism education. The Critical Turn in Tourism Studies: Creating an Academy of Hope, 75-95.

Sundgren, M. (2017). Blurring time and place in higher education with bring your own device applications: A literature review. *Education and Information Technologies*, *22*(6), 3081–3119. doi:10.100710639-017-9576-3

Tiwari, P., Séraphin, H., & Chowdhary, N. R. (2020). Impacts of COVID-19 on tourism education: Analysis and perspectives. *Journal of Teaching in Travel & Tourism*, 1–26.

Tolkach, D., & Pratt, S. (2021). Travel Professors: A YouTube channel about tourism education & research. *Journal of Hospitality, Leisure, Sport and Tourism Education*, *28*, 100307. doi:10.1016/j.jhlste.2021.100307

Tölkes, C. (2018). Sustainability communication in tourism – A literature review. *Tourism Management Perspectives*, *27*, 10–21. doi:10.1016/j.tmp.2018.04.002

UNESCO. (2012). *Sustainable Development*. Retrieved from: https://en.unesco.org/themes/education-sustainable-development/what-is-esd/sd#:~:text=Sustainability%20is%20a%20paradigm%20for,an%20improved%20quality%20of%20life

United Nations. (2015). *Sustainable Development Goals*. Retrieved from: https://www.un.org/sustainabledevelopment/education/

UNWTO. (2005). *Making tourism more sustainable – A guide for policy makers*. UNWTO.

UNWTO. (2013). *Sustainable Tourism for Development Guidebook*. UNWTO.

UNWTO & UNDP. (2017). *Tourism and the Sustainable Development Goals – Journey to 2030*. UNWTO.

Vasconcelos, S., & Balula, A. (2019). Do You Speak Digital? A Literature Review on Language and Digital Competences in Tourism Education. *ToSEE – Tourism in Southern and Eastern Europe, 5*, 729-737.

Xiao, H., & Smith, S. L. J. (2006). The making of tourism research: Insights from a social sciences journal. *Annals of Tourism Research, 33*(2), 490–507. doi:10.1016/j.annals.2006.01.004

Zika, L. (2017). Student perceptions of ethics, CSR, and sustainability (ECSRS) in hospitality management education. *Journal of Teaching in Travel & Tourism, 17*(4), 254–268. doi:10.1080/15313220.2017.1399497

KEY TERMS AND DEFINITIONS

Education for Sustainable Development: Also referred to as Sustainability Education, the concept is used by the UNESCO to describe teaching and learning approaches that support the development of knowledge, skill and values pertaining to sustainability at all levels.

English for Specific Purposes (ESP): A subset of English as a Foreign Language. It refers to the teaching of English that focuses on developing communicative skills in a particular field or occupation. ESP courses are designed to meet specific needs of the learners, with reference to the particular vocabulary and register they require.

Interdisciplinarity: Activity/strategy involving or drawing on two or more branches of knowledge/academic courses.

Pillars of Sustainability: Usually represented by a diagram, this expression is used to describe the tenets of sustainability, specifically, the environment (or environmental protection), society (referring to social equity), and the economy. If one of those pillars is weak, the system will become unsustainable.

Podcast: A digital audio/video file, that can be available as a series. Podcasts can be downloaded by users who can subscribe them and/or listen to them anytime, anywhere.

Portfolio: A compilation of academic work that can be used for assessing coursework or learning progress. Digital or in other formats it can include different types of assignment and evidence (e.g., photos, texts, links, videos, etc.).

Project-Based Learning (PBL): A student-centred learning approach that implies the development of a project oriented towards the solution of a real-world problem/ challenge, with the teachers assuming a facilitating role, and the students' engagement being the key for the construction of their own learning.

Chapter 7
Evaluation of the Potential of Ideation Tools to Create Technologies Aimed at Education

Maria Eduarda Franklin da Costa de Paula
Federal University of Rio Grande do Norte, Brazil

Orivaldo Vieira de Santana Júnior
https://orcid.org/0000-0003-4918-3162
Federal University of Rio Grande do Norte, Brazil

Zulmara Virgínia de Carvalho
Federal University of Rio Grande do Norte, Brazil

Cristiano Alves
Federal University of Rio Grande do Norte, Brazil

ABSTRACT

This project aims to evaluate the potential of an ideation framework, which is based on the idea of collective intelligence, to develop technologies for the area of education, and to be more compatible with the current model of society, having more student adherence. The framework analyzed four tools, which are the empathy map, the user journey, method 6-3-5, and the Edward de Bono hat method was to use as a validation tool for ideas. At the end of the application, it resulted in the choice of four insights to be applied in the system, that is, the amount of system functionalities expanded by 50%, which are a virtual assistant by voice command, a video gallery and podcast, gamification for the user to be reciprocated, and individual study planning to particularize each case, and thus fostering the effectiveness in increasing learning as proposed by the project. However, after the ideas were validated using the hat method, only three of them remained. Finally, this framework has both a versatile, low-cost character and a relatively low application time.

DOI: 10.4018/978-1-7998-8239-8.ch007

INTRODUCTION

According to the Universal Declaration of Human Rights, approved on December 10, 1948, through the United Nations General Assembly Resolution No. 217, access to education in its entirety is a right of all citizens because it is important for the consolidation of democracy and allows individuals to have effective participation in society's decisions. Besides, the Brazilian Federal Constitution of 1988 indicates, in its article 205, that education is a right of all Brazilians and an obligation of the family and the government. Although according to the most recent (2018) International Student Assessment Program (PISA), carried out by the Organization for Economic Cooperation and Development (OECD), Brazil occupies the 66th position in the performance of students in science, 57th place in reading and interpreting texts, the situation of the scenario becomes more alarming when evaluating students' performance in mathematics as the position drops to 70th. When compared to the countries of Latin America, students' performance in science, reading, and mathematics is, respectively, 6th, 5th and 7th positions.

This performance is the result of the stagnant education model, which still tests students four times a year, and uses a tool created by T'sai Lun in 105 AD, better known as paper (Hayasaka & Nishida, 2020), although globalization has several tools that assist in the active learning process such as the personal computer. In addition, this scenario is the result of the evaluation of education professionals. The Ministry of Education (MEC) stated in 2019 that teachers receive around two and a half minimum wages for a 40-hour workweek. In addition, according to the analysis of the OECD report (2018), Brazilian teachers receive the worst salaries among those of 48 countries surveyed.

That is why there are many projects that aim to increase Brazilian educational quality, such as the Support Program for Teaching Systems for Attending Youth and Adult Education (EJA), a youth and adult education program integrated with professional education, among others. However, OECD points out that Brazil maintains a tendency of stagnation when analyzing the results of seven editions of Pisa in reading, six in mathematics, and five in science. Therefore, this project aims to evaluate the potential of the ideation framework, which is strongly based on the idea of collective intelligence, to develop technologies for the area of education, and, in addition to this, being a tool compatible with the current model of society, with this, having more student adherence, making it easier and reducing the workload of teachers. Moreover, it is configured to generate active learning which leads to the creation of long-term memories, that is, to the increase in the level of knowledge of students. Therefore, it is an effective substitute for a visibly stagnant model. In addition to this, this research takes into account that ideation uses tools that show more effectiveness to create projects, such as the empathy map, the user journey, method 6-3-5, and as a validation tool for ideas the Edward de Bono hat method was used in order to generate solid results in a shorter process time, that is, lasting hours instead of days, as well as using less human capital in order to analyze the ability of dynamics to devise systems with more targeted features to solve the problem. Also, based on active learning, to create more sustainable and scalable solutions. So, this project explains how to apply an interactive framework and its fundamentals to generate solutions. This chapter is structured around a theoretical review of active learning and tactics for designing learning. Then, the modeling of an ideation framework and its application.

Literature Review

Within the investigation of the strategic potential of the Ideation framework´s application in the qualification of teaching-learning processes, the basis of collective intelligence was studied, as well as raising information about the creative process and also conducting a theoretical review of the triggers involved in the solution of problems. In addition, the entire creative framework´s methodology will subsequently assess effectiveness as a tool to assist in the ideation process of educational systems.

COLLECTIVE INTELLIGENCE

Throughout human history, technology has always opened up new possibilities, and this is confirmed with models of societies that emerged as a result of the agricultural, industrial, and recently digital revolutions (Costa, 2019; Canut, 2005). Currently, society is marked by the popularization of social networks on the web 2.0 environment, which values users' collaboration, sharing, and interactions with information (Costa, 2019; Roesler, 2012; Canut, 2005). As a result, this widespread interconnection between people has been focused on by many theorists who try to compare the effects of individual relationships with those generated by collective behavior in high-density networks (Costa, 2019; Canut, 2005).

In this way, it brought up again the discussion about collective intelligence, which since the 5th century BC was widely discussed by Aristotle who believed that collective intelligence was superior to individual intelligence. Pierre Lévy (2003) classified collective intelligence as an intelligence that is distributed to everyone, and not just restricted to a few. Costa (2019) defined it as something that adds value to each participant, through sharing and creating knowledge. But, before defining collective intelligence, one must first return to what is considered intelligence, in which it is strongly correlated with the creation of memories and consequently with learning, that is, the creative process starts from the need for problem-solving individuals. This condition is strongly linked to the evocation of explicit and implicit long-term memories, which can be reactivated through sensory appeals such as visual, auditory, among others (Kandel et al., 2014). It is important to mention that the precursor of memories is experiencing, which is linked to how the individual interprets and relates to the environment. Therefore, in a society that shares the same culture, there will still be multiple learnings (Kandel et al., 2014). In this way, collective intelligence can be defined as the sum of multiple learnings.

So, as it refers to a sum of multiple memories, both in different areas and in the same, this knowledge will tend to the infinite, whereas individual intelligence is restricted to the limited group of memories and restricted to individual experiences. Thus, collective intelligence is better able to solve different problems in a more efficient time. However, as approached by James Surowiecki in the book "The wisdom of the crowds" (2004) in order for these diverse opinions to converge in a viable solution, it is necessary to obey some restrictions such as the diversity of opinions, independence of thoughts and the decentralization of power at the time of solving the problem – a very pertinent fact because if the power is applied in the collective, the solution will tend to the one chosen by the individual who has the power thus being an individual intelligence practice.

For this reason, the information technology industry has appropriated this theory to create open-source systems such as Arduino, open vibe, Linux, among others that are built by the collective. In addition, social networks use this to create computational models capable of identifying the user's profile and classifying it in a specific group, and thus, providing them with more information about their preferences and contents of people who are in the same group. Thus, generating much more interaction with the platform.

CREATIVITY PROCESSES

Creativity can be explained in many ways. For example, from the point of view of neuroscience, it is defined as a condition that begins with the need for man to solve problems, and is strongly linked to the evocation of memories, which can be reactivated through sensory appeals such as visual, auditory, among others (Kandel et al., 2014). According to Pontes (2020), creativity can be defined by mental processes that result in new ideas, that is, the ability of an individual to create new things, think differently and be innovative. In turn, Pearce's academy (2011) described it as a skill that can be learned.

However, all of these definitions agree that the real goal of creativity is to solve problems. That, for this, there must occur external stimuli which are capable of evoking a memory, which will be used to correlate with the current obstacle. It is extremely important to mention that if this process depends on memories, soon it will be modulated by individual experiences, culture, and the way in which the individual interacts with the world (Kandel et al., 2014).

In addition, this mental process is strongly linked to the ability to be innovative, that is, to create new ideas or to increase existing ones. This fact leads institutions to go deeper and deeper in training people to be more inventive, and thus, to generate more efficient results. It is noteworthy that innovation, in turn, is the result of a creative process, which aims to solve a problem and, for that, is associated with a new combination of existing knowledge and resources (Pietry, 2019). This process was defined by Pontes in 2020 as mental mechanisms that enable the generation of new ideas. Furthermore, according to the book "Creativity and innovation", published by Pearson's academy in 2011, creativity is a characteristic that is learned, that is, the so-called creative people only acquire their abilities through training, acquiring dual vision, being curious and inventive, and most importantly being open to learning new things.

CREATION APPROACHES

An approach that has been expanding in the industry is Universal Design, which proposes to obtain products that can be used by as many people as possible. Thus, it aims to use methodologies and tools to create products and promote the inclusion of people in relation to the use of the product (Alvarenga, 2006). It is of utmost importance to understand that in order to create an inclusive project, it is necessary to identify the user's needs and desires, then to identify the project requirements, so as to expand and evaluate them, and finally present a more inclusive product design (Alvarenga, 2006).

An approach that has been widespread in industries such as automotive is collaborative innovation (Bueno & Balestrin, 2012) because, due to the high price to create their products, some companies, such as BMW and Toyota, adopted this concept in order to establish partnerships for the development of technologies with their suppliers, taking the first steps towards inaugurating the innovation process and, furthermore, reducing production costs (Bueno & Balestrin, 2012). For this to happen, both companies perform case and data analyses that favor them (Bueno & Balestrin, 2012).

The main difference between these approaches is that Universal Design is applied to the company locally while collaborative innovation is done through the exchange of information between companies. However, both are aimed at creating innovative products, but universal design focuses on inclusion, which is not necessarily the focus of collaborative innovation. In addition, they use collaborative tools and methodologies to make ideation more efficient and make it a more agile process (Bueno & Balestrin, 2012). The tools, in turn, can be defined as a technique that will help in the solution of the process. It can be a mind map that has diagrams to make correlations with the person's previous knowledge, and for that reason, it may be wrong and susceptible to false-positive and false-negative (Miranda, 2011).

Ideation Creative Framework

The frameworks are structured by a set of tools aimed at clarifying the researcher's perspective in several ways, from the understanding that people will be affected by the researcher's project to the deepest pains of its users. The Creative Framework, developed by designer Cristiano Alves, uses 3 tools, which are the empathy map, the user journey, and the 6-3-5 method. The empathy map aims to understand users' pains – with this, using empathy, which is a multidimensional construct that requires the ability to perceive and understand the perspective of the other, in addition to feeling their emotional state (Peixoto & Moura, 2020). For this, it involves three components: the affective, the cognitive, and a regulator of emotions. The affective is based first on the understanding of the emotional states of others, and then, in the next step, sharing (Peixoto & Moura, 2020). It is worth mentioning that this is due to mirror neurons (Peixoto & Moura, 2020). The cognitive component, in turn, refers to the ability to reason about the mental states of other people, and finally the regulatory component of emotions, which is responsible for managing and explaining the empathic response (Peixoto & Moura, 2020).

Therefore, for this to happen, it is necessary to choose a user and then answer four key questions, which are "How would you feel if you were in the person's shoes?", "What is your perception of the person's current desires, needs, and fears? and futures? ", "How do you feel about knowing that person's story? ", and finally "how can I help that person?". As explained in the following model (Figure 1).

The next technique that will be used is the user's journey that allows, from a real or ideal journey, to perceive and record all customer-product interactions, thereby enabling the team to understand what the customer does, thinks, and feels, in addition to indicating emotional ups and downs and their interactions with the product at these times (Mendonça et al., 2017). Thus stimulating the generation of potential inspirations for innovations that can really add value (Mendonça et al., 2017). For this, one must map the daily journey or in a specific space of their day, analyzing the actions, thoughts, and feelings triggered by each action (Mendonça et al., 2017).

Finally, the 6-3-5 method will be applied, which aims to bring together a group of six people to think about a certain problem, then every 5 minutes create three ideas to solve the problem, that is, each member at the end of the dynamics will have brought up 18 ideas or more (Paldês, 2017). After that, discussion is generated in order to choose the most viable and innovative ideas. This method is based on the idea that more people thinking about a certain obstacle will generate an effective resolution more quickly (Paldês, 2017).

METHODOLOGY

Object of Study

In this case study, the object of study consisted of a system based on machine learning, which performs continuous analysis of the student's profile, informing where their greatest difficulty is in the course and, thus, choosing the best model of active learning to solve their problems. This system consists of a web platform, which aims to manage activities and send content to individuals enrolled in the course.

Figure 1. Empathy map model
Image source: Sarah Gibbons, 2018.

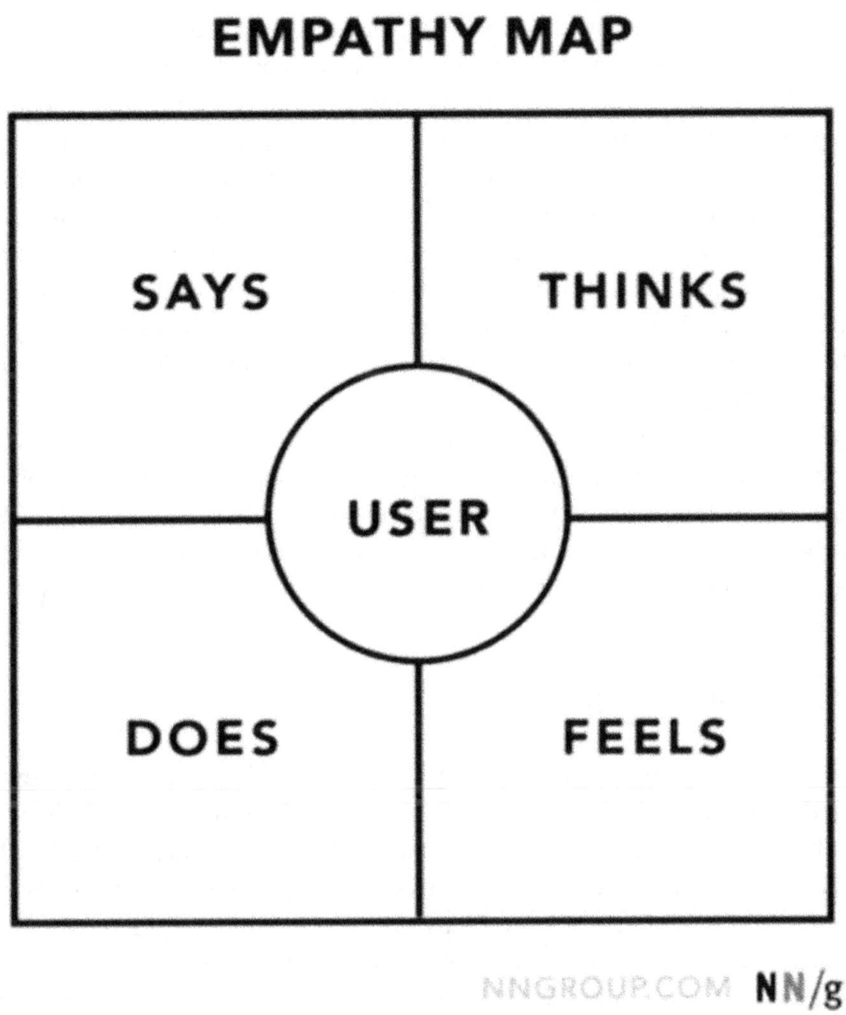

From this point, it is possible to extract the student's margin of correctness in each activity, and the interactions of each user with the system – a fact that pointed out that the only mass use of the platform takes place one day before the test.

With that, one must list which the syllabus contents of the course are. Then, using a supervised learning model which performs the classification of a dependent variable from a set of independent classes with labels (Zhang et al., 2019), the system will be able to predict the degree of difficulty of each question, and thus, classifying them as key issues and training issues. Therefore, using the unsupervised learning model, which is applied to a set of data that does not have any type of label (Zhang et al., 2019), it will be predicted in every access to the platform what the performance status the student presents, using as a metric the number of activity submissions correlated with the activity's margin of accuracy.

Thus, according to the user's performance, questions will be recommended, noting that as the student increases their performance in a given topic, the degree of difficulty of the questions asked available will also increase proportionally. Thus, allowing students who have a good performance to become increasingly better and helping to improve those who have a poor performance. It is worth noting that more active learning models were chosen, as well as the choice of carrying out more frequent and spaced evaluative activities on the same subjects to strengthen the creation of explicit long-term memories, given that this type of memory is highly flexible and allows the association of multiple fragments of the information under different circumstances. Furthermore, for processing it, four steps are taken into account, and one of them is coding, which associates observed and pre-existing information. And this is highly correlated to the intensity of this process, which is important to determine how well the learned content will be remembered. It also involves the stages of storage, consolidation, which involves the expression of genes and protein synthesis to stabilize memories and thus requiring learning to be spaced in time, and finally the evocation stage (KANDEL et al., 2014).

Finally, the system will evaluate the student by obtaining the average performance on all topics. In addition, it will be restricted to the student to comply with 75% of the syllabus, considering that this requirement is made by several institutions as specified in the general regulations of the Federal University of Rio Grande do Norte (2019). In order to validate this system, dropout rate, class attendance, and grades will be measured, and these indicators will be compared with the traditional educational model applied at the institution.

Application of the Framework

The frameworks equipped with tools aim to clarify the researcher's perspective in several ways, from the understanding that people will be affected by the researcher's project to the deepest pains of its users. In addition, it helps to understand the strengths and weaknesses of the project, thereby enabling the creation of more grounded ideas with the potential to solve the problems precisely. And in this way, an evaluation of the project was obtained and new ideas were created that will add positively to the project. In addition, it helped understanding the weaknesses, as well as with the best solutions.

The framework was applied by a group of five professionals from different areas, which were Law, Multimedia, Social Work, Neuroscience, Engineering, and Administration, which resulted, in the first moment, in two maps of empathy (Figures 1 and 2) - one of a young student and another of a middle-aged teacher, that is, profiles that fit the profile of the end-user of the system. That way you can find their pains such as lack of time, need to do activities faster, and to be more assertive.

Subsequently, the user's journey map (Figures 3 and 4) was applied, which reaffirmed the need for personas to have more time, and to use tools that help them in the first case to study effectively, and in the second case both in the study and at work.

Taking into account the reality of users, and understanding their pains and desires better, the 6-3-5 technique (Figure 5) was applied to gather new ideas for projects, from improvements to totally disruptive innovations, that is, respecting the freedom of expression of the applying group.

However, after the end of the application of the framework, the key ideas chosen do not undergo any validation, a fact that opens space for choosing ideas that are not easily applicable, do not match the alignment of the project, or whose benefit does not exceed the costs. To overcome this obstacle, the

Figure 2. Empathy map made for the project
Image source: image captured by the author, 2020.

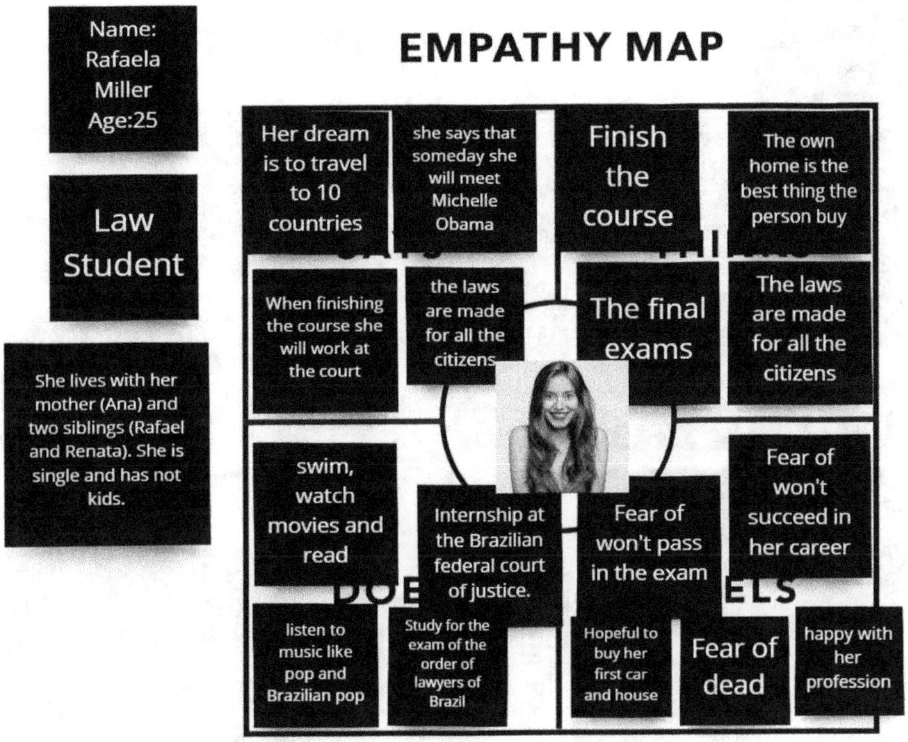

six-hat method was applied (Fig. 1), which aims to properly assess what was exposed, and thus, to be able to make a decision, as the individual starts to see the problem from 6 different perspectives and not just one (Ponzio & Machado, 2015). This dynamic contains six hats, which are based on a feeling and a way of positioning thoughts.

So, white represents a neutral position, that is, being based only on facts (Ponzio & Machado, 2015). The red one is based on feelings and intuition. Black makes punctual criticisms of the work, yellow is for optimism, green for creativity and, finally, the blue hat (Mediator) organizes and coordinates all dynamics (Ponzio & Machado, 2015).

It is worth mentioning that all members of the group must have the experience of wearing all hats, excluding the mediator's, and everyone must have a predetermined time, in addition to focusing on a hat, to maximize the snowball effect (Ponzio & Machado, 2015). Thus, all the key ideas were analyzed taking into account their feasibility within the scenario that is inserted, that is, if the reality of the School of Science and Technology of the Federal University of Rio Grande do Norte is applied. Pertinence and ease of implementation were also taken into consideration.

Figure 3. Empathy map made for the project
Caption: image captured by the author, 2020.

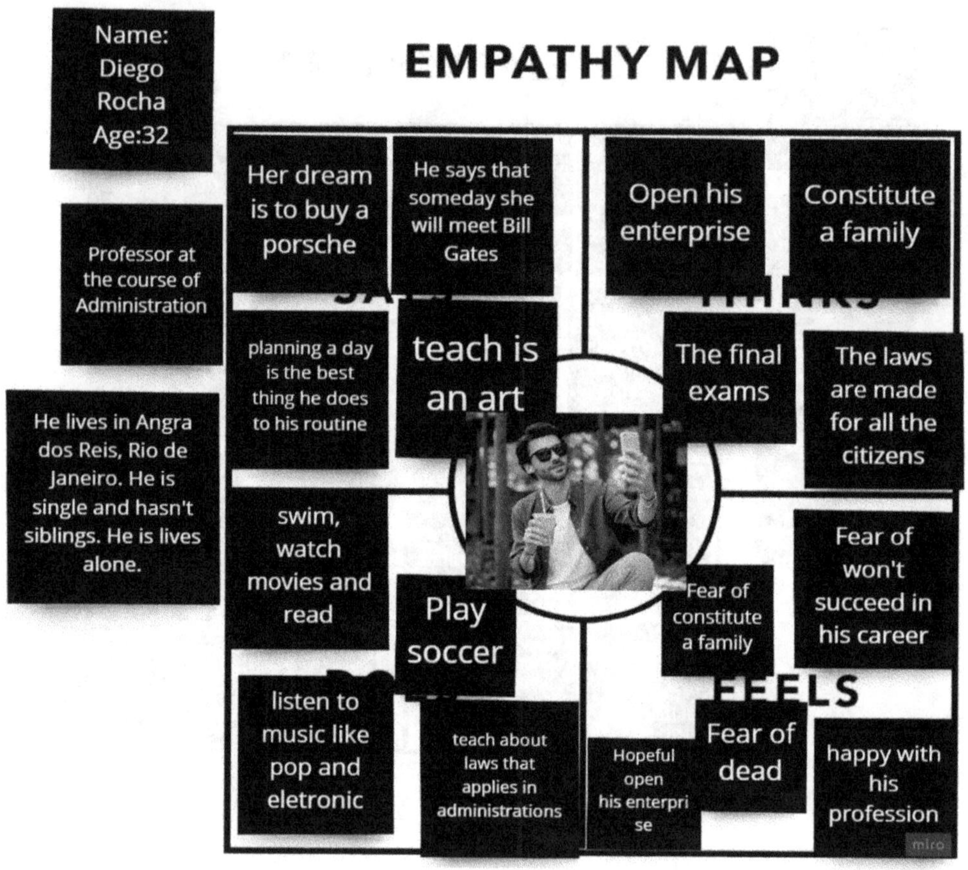

Figure 4. User journey map - Persona Rafaela Miller
Image source: image captured by the author, 2020.

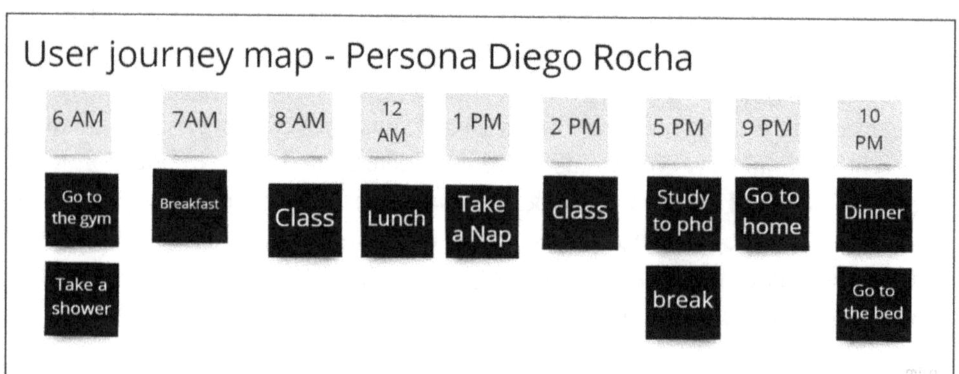

Figure 5. User journey map - Persona Diego Rocha
Image source: image captured by the author, 2020.

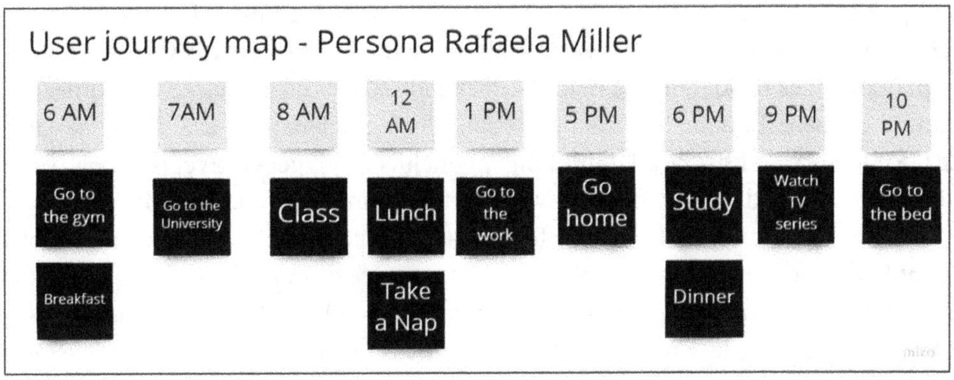

Figure 6. Ideas generated using the 6-3-5 method
Image source: image captured by the author, 2020.

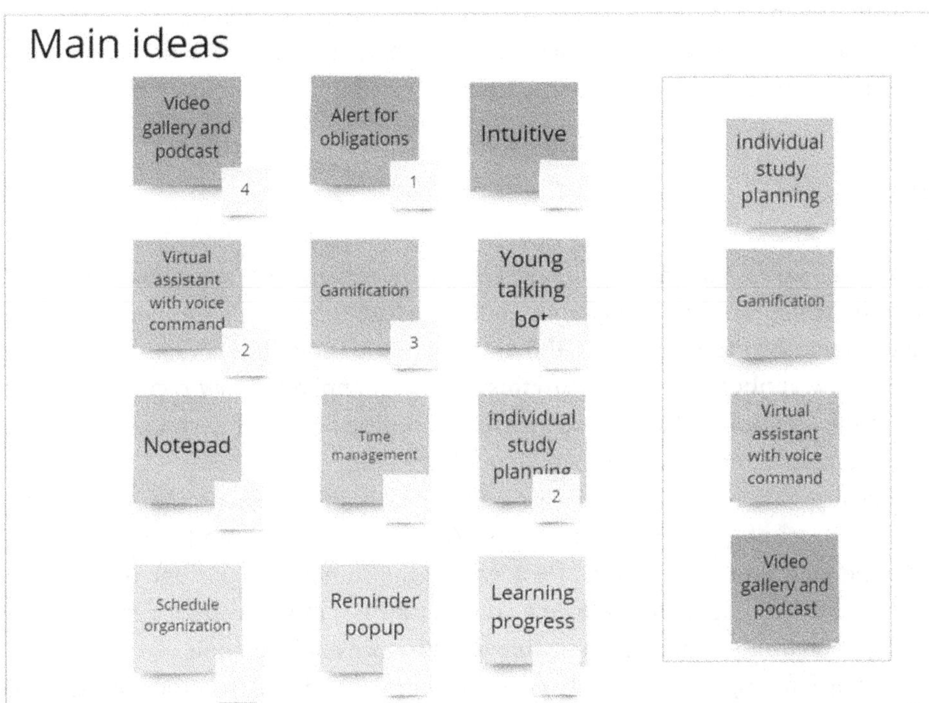

RESULTS AND DISCUSSION

The frameworks equipped with tools aim to clarify the researcher's perspective in several ways, from the understanding that people will be affected the researcher's project to the deepest pains of its users. In addition, it helps to understand the strengths and weaknesses of the project, thereby enabling the creation of more grounded ideas with the potential to solve the problems precisely. And in this way, an evaluation of the project was obtained and new ideas were created which will add positively to the project. In addition, it helped understanding the weaknesses, as well as with the best solutions. In this dynamic, the Edward de Bono hat method created in 1980 was also added, which is used in various fields of work and teaching, from companies to schools (Ponzio & Machado, 2015). Its purpose is the ordering of thought by neutralizing the "mental confusion" that can occur during a debate or evaluation session (Ponzio & Machado, 2015). It works with "parallel thinking", which is more generative, provocative, exploratory, probabilistic, non-sequential which contrasts with vertical thinking which is more selective, analytical, conventional, finite, sequential, in the search for a change in patterns (Ponzio & Machado, 2015).

The first application of the framework resulted in the choice of four ideas to be applied to the system, that is, the amount of system functionalities was expanded by 50%, which are virtual assistant by voice command that will help people with visual impairments, a video gallery and a podcast to make more materials available for users to use, gamification for the user to be rewarded, and individual study planning to particularize each case, thus increasing the effectiveness in learning as proposed by the project. It is important to note that none of the existing features were excluded at the end of the process.

Again, the framework was applied in a group composed of 5 people and was started using the four ideas resulting from the first session, and at the end of the application, only 3 remained since it was agreed that the benefits did not meet the costs, in addition to being difficult creation. In addition, 2 ideas were modified to align more strongly with the research. As such, there was a 25% decrease in the number of new features and a drop in general features that reached 11.11%.

CONCLUSION

Based on the analyzes carried out during the development of the work, it is concluded that this framework goes through all stages of creation, from understanding the client's problems and pains, through the creation and choice of ideas to their validation. It has a versatile character, of low cost, besides having a relatively low application time. With this, it can be applied to any business, in any area, from school projects to the creation of large company functionalities, as well as the solution and generation of strategies for management problems of small and large companies.

In addition, because this framework is based on the theory of collective intelligence, it is noted that it presents a greater amount of disruptive ideas, in addition to being more targeted and more likely to be applied and generate more solid results. Besides that the framework presented a versatile character, making it possible to be generalized to create a solution for the most diverse areas in a more pertinent way although it is not a limiter, that is, being able to add more analysis tools.

However, it is worth noting that this study needs further validation from other areas, considering that it is summarized in the idea of a solution for education in the scenario of Brazil, and contains only a validation method that does not take into account the opinion of users. For this reason, surveys will also be carried out with users to validate the public acceptance of the chosen features, in addition to developing the prototypes of each feature to assess pertinence and whether the proposed problem is solved.

ACKNOWLEDGMENT

This work was carried out with the support of the Coordination for the Improvement of Higher Education Personnel - Brazil (CAPES) - Financing Code 001.

REFERENCES

Alvarenga, F. B. (2006). *A Methodological Approach to the Inclusive Products Project* (Doctoral thesis). State University of Campinas, Campinas, SP, Brazil.

Bembem, Santos, & Plácida. (2013). Collective intelligence: A look at the production of Pierre Lévy. *Perspectives in Information Science, 18*(4), 139-151.

Bueno, B., & Balestrin, A. (2012). *Collaborative innovation: an open approach to new product development. Business Administration Journal.*

Costa, M. A. (2019). *Maturity in the Use of Web 2.0 Technologies in the Banking Sector in Portugal.* APNOR.

Costa, R. D. (2005). For a new concept of community: Social networks, personal communities, collective intelligence. Interface-communication, health, education. *Scielo, São Paulo, Brazil, 9*, 235–248.

Cruz, L. M., By, M., & Muller, F. (2016). *Social Epistemology And Democracy Wisdom Of The Crowds X Specialist*. Editora Fi.

Formoso, J., Jacubovich, S., Injoque-ricle, I., & Barreyro, J. P. (2018). Resolution of Arithmetic Problems, Processing Speed and Working Memory in Children. Trends in Psychology.

Jung-beeman, M., Bowden, E. M., Haberman, J., Frymiare, J. L., Arambel-Liu, S., Greenblatt, R., Reber, P. J., & Kounios, J. (2004). Neural activity when people solve verbal problems with insight. *PLoS Biology, 4*(2), 97. doi:10.1371/journal.pbio.0020097 PMID:15094802

Kandel, E. (2014). Principles of Neuroscience. McGraw-Hill.

Kandel, E. (2014). *Principles of Neuroscience*. MCGRAW Hill.

Kornis, G. (2013). *Culture in thought (and in action) by Celso Furtado: Development, creativity, tradition and innovation*. CEBRAP.

Mendonça, M. C., Schmiegelow, S. S., Almeida, F. S., Filho, F. A. P., & Sousa, R. P. L. (2017) Design Thinking, Media, Knowledge and Innovation: Reflections on a Didactic Activity Applying Persona Design and the User Journey Map. *VII International Congress on Knowledge and Innovation Proceeding*.

Morozini, A. (2013). *Adding Individual Intelligences Does Not Always Result In Collective Intelligence.* Academic Press.

Paldês, R. (2017). Method 6-3-5: A productive format for Brainwriting. *Networking Requirements.*

Peixoto, J. M., & Moura, E. P. (2020). Map of Empathy in Health: Elaboration of an Instrument for the Development of Empathy. *Brazilian Journal of Medical Education*.

Petry, J. F., Sebastiao, S. A., Martins, E. G., & Barros, P. B. A. (2019). Innovation and Diffusion of Technology in Lowland Agriculture in the Amazon. *Rev. Adm. Contemp., 23*(5), 619-635.

Pontes, S. A. E. (2020). Mathematics in early childhood education: An educational look from the perspective of creativity. *Diversitas Journal, 5*(2), 1166–1176.

Ponzio, A. P, & Machado, A. S. (2015). *Use of Creative Methods Envisioning Innovation on Teaching Architectural Design*. LUME.

Roesler, R. (2012). Web 2.0, social interactions and knowledge building. *VII SIMPED - Pedagogical Symposium and Research in Education*.

Siqueira, J. (2010). *Creativity and innovation*. http: // creativity.com

Zhang, A. (2020). Dive into Deep Learning. Academic Press.

Chapter 8
Employee Engagement and Learning for the Transformational Leader

Debra L. Lacy
Baylor University, USA

ABSTRACT

Highly engaged employees are central to strong organizational outcomes. Nonetheless, consistency in maintaining high levels of engagement eludes most organizations. Disengaged employees are often toxic and cultivate negativity. An in-depth analysis of the drivers of employee engagement indicates that leadership is the strongest influencer of engagement. Bass's transformational leadership and the leader-member-exchange (LMX) theories outline characteristics of transformational leaders. The theories intersect where Bass posits is the stage in the relationship between leader and follower where leader behavior inspires followers to excel with no additional incentives needed. Training and development of the transformational leader who drives high engagement must take adult learning principles into account in recognition of the unique learning needs of adults.

INTRODUCTION

Data from companies across a broad spectrum of industries suggests far-reaching challenges in meeting employee engagement objectives. A Gallup survey of a random sampling of United States employees indicates a "high" engagement score in the last twenty years of only 34% compared to lows in the mid-twenties in 2000 and 2005 (Harter, 2018). A highly engaged workforce produces many benefits for organizations. As Parent and Lovelace (2018) posit, companies with higher levels of engagement experience lower turnover (25 percent), less absenteeism (37 percent), fewer safety incidents (48 percent), and fewer quality incidents (41 percent). Nonetheless, high employee engagement eludes most companies (Harter 2018). Kaye and Jordan-Evans (1999), Baumruk (2006), and Gyensare et al. (2019) submit that employee engagement is most prominently influenced by leadership. The breadth and depth of a leader's influence are palpable and far-reaching given leaders' responsibility to their followers to not only share

DOI: 10.4018/978-1-7998-8239-8.ch008

an organization's vision but also provide guidance and direction in executing the vision. Organizations experience a significant variance in employee engagement that is directly related to how employees see, experience, and interact with their leaders (Sinyan, 2018).

To remain competitive locally and globally, Arokiasamy (2013) asserts, that companies must extend themselves and generously invest in motivating their employees. Central to addressing this need is understanding the implications of leadership in engaging employees. Leaders guide an organization, its practices, processes, protocols, and people. Leaders at all levels have the power to influence engagement on a sustained basis. Specifically, however, transformational leadership inspires a level of enthusiasm in followers that takes the achievement of goals and objectives to a higher level (Schuckert et al., 2018). Transformational leadership is defined by Antonakis and House (2014) as the "intellectual stimulation" and attention to individual needs, inspiration, and...ideals of employees or followers (p. 750). This meta-analysis critically examines Leader-Member-Exchange (LMX) Theory and Bass' Transformational Leadership Theory to argue that transformational leadership is the panacea for attaining and sustaining strong employee engagement results on a long-term basis. Consequently, focusing on a combination of elements of transformational leadership—from interaction with employees to theories of leadership to training and development—are pivotal in understanding how organizations can successfully address employee engagement outcomes. This chapter explores transformational leadership as a curiously overlooked long-term solution.

The ensuing argument unfolds in three steps. First, this chapter defines engagement, looks at disengagement, then surveys the high stakes and impact of employee engagement. Second, two theoretical leadership frameworks—Bass' Transformational Leadership and Leader-Member-Exchange (LMX) Theories—that anchor this research are discussed. Third, this chapter provides a practical application of adult learning theories that inform a training and development plan for transformational leaders.

Employee Engagement

In his seminal work, Kahn (1990) defines employee engagement in terms that reflect how employees connect with others and engage physically, cognitively, and emotionally. Kahn (1990) posits that engagement is "the simultaneous employment and expression of a person's preferred self in task behaviors that promote connections to work and to others..." (p. 700). Schaufeli and Bakker (2004) expound on Kahn's definition in their description of three dimensions that make up engagement: vigor, dedication, and absorption. They define vigor as "high levels of energy and mental resilience while working, the willingness to invest effort in one's work, and persistence also in the face of difficulties" (p. 295). For employees in customer-facing roles, whether in-person, on the phone, or online, vigor is evident in how they act, react, interact, and respond to customers and how they act, react, interact, and respond to their coworkers. The customer experience reflects the elevated level of enthusiasm of an employee with vigor. Schwartz (2010) asserts that customers who engage with highly enthusiastic employees feel heard, seen, valued, and appreciated and give high marks when expressing their satisfaction with a company.

On the other hand, employees with moderate to low vigor, as Schaufeli and Bakker (2004) note, are more likely to receive moderate to low customer satisfaction results because moderate to low vigor is viewed unfavorably by customers who want and, in some cases, need to feel appreciated to continue conducting business with a company. Dedication is "a sense of significance, enthusiasm, inspiration, pride, and challenge..." (Schaufeli & Bakker, 2004, p. 295). Absorption is another element of engagement and is defined as being fully concentrated and happily engrossed in one's work where time passes by quickly and one has difficulties with detaching oneself from work (p. 295). Employees that exhibit vigor, dedication, and absorption connect to an organization's vision and mission and engage in the work in meaningful ways as posited by Shuck and Wollard (2010). High engagement is the pinnacle of organizational success given the outcomes of customer experience when engagement is high. As Goffee and Jones (2013) note, organizations with highly engaged employees "outperform firms with the most disengaged folks by 54% in employee retention, by 89% in customer satisfaction, and by fourfold in revenue growth" (p. 98). The economics of engagement speaks to its criticality in driving companies' bottom line. Engaged employees wield significant power in defining the degree to which companies achieve their goals. The impact of engagement is staggering yet continues to elude organizations globally. Equally as concerning, and a challenge for transformational leaders is disengagement. It is incumbent upon transformational leaders to not only understand what drives high employee engagement, but also what disengagement is to recognize disengagement and facilitate change among followers.

Disengagement Comes at a Cost

There are various levels of engagement that extend beyond the work performed by employees. The levels range from the passionately engaged to the impressionably disengaged. Disengagement is costly given its negative impact on the customer experience and the workplace. Understanding the continuum from the highly engaged to the highly disengaged can serve as a problem-solving guide for companies seeking to understand solutions to low engagement and strategies for maintaining high engagement.

Levels of engagement are reflected in employees' attitudes and interactions toward one another and toward customers. Attridge (2009) and Harter (2018) describe the passionately engaged employee who readily connects to the mission and vision of an organization. These highly engaged employees are an organization's heroes. They are foundational to strong customer satisfaction, innovation, enthusiasm, and commitment that drive strong organizational outcomes (Mannelly, 2008). Customers who experience the warmth, high energy, and vigor of an engaged employee tell others about their experience (Manthiou et al., 2020). Customer retention as well is another benefit.

The moderately engaged employee does not leave an impression on customers. Satisfaction ratings for the moderately engaged employee in customer-facing roles are also moderate. Results are neither high nor low. Employees who fall in the middle category between the highly engaged and the actively disengaged are "generally satisfied but…not cognitively and emotionally connected" to their work and workplace (Harter, 2018, p.1). The employee in the middle presents the greatest risk for mediocre to average performance and outcomes.

On the opposite end of the spectrum are unhappy, disengaged employees. Their unhappiness is reflected in their negativity which drains others in the organization and undermines leadership. Harter (2018) describes them as the "actively disengaged" (p. 1). They are easy to spot in an organization because their unhappiness is on display. Disengagement occurs when a person detaches and consequently withdraws from a role without physically leaving the role (Gupta & Mahajan, 2012). Disengagement is especially problematic for organizations given the toxicity of disengaged employees. Disengaged employees not only hurt productivity but also put others at risk of injury in certain roles and occupations (Mannelly, 2008). They negatively affect morale and a team's sense of belonging (Bee, 2013). Additional behaviors by disengaged employees include "acting confused and floundering, low quality work, doing the minimum to survive, taking no initiative, and…attendance problems" (Mannelly, 2008, pp. 104–105). Such effects undermine the work of entire teams and organizations of every size.

The costs of disengagement are staggering. Losses in the United States alone are in the billions of dollars with annual losses calculated at $2.3 million for every 100 employees (Lear, 2016). Actively disengaged employees are often toxic, miss the mark on productivity, and are the basis of poor customer satisfaction and shortfalls in meeting goals and objectives (Bee, 2013). Disengagement is equally as impactful as engagement and warrants leadership's attention in the same way sales and revenue warrant leadership's attention. In any environment, for any organization, the impact of employee engagement is tangible. Focus on the disengaged is paramount for transformational leaders at all levels of an organization who desire the benefits of a highly engaged workforce.

Understanding the High Stakes: The Impact of Employee Engagement

The benefits of high engagement and the risks of low engagement are why organizational and leadership focus on engagement are paramount. Leaders at all levels of an organization must possess the capacity to manage the engaged and the disengaged alike. The costs of low employee engagement and the benefits of high employee engagement justify the need for investing in leadership strategies that cultivate a culture that prioritizes employee engagement as a business imperative. The fiscal and organizational stakes of employee engagement are high. According to Gallup, Inc. (2017), "the global aggregate from...data collected in 2014, 2015 and 2016 across 155 countries indicates that just 15% of employees worldwide are engaged in their job" (p. 22). Low engagement presents many "barriers" to creating high performing cultures, which Gallup (2017) notes "implies a stunning amount of wasted potential, given...business units in the top quartile of [their] global employee engagement database are 17% more productive and 21% more profitable than those in the bottom quartile" (p. 5). This data, which covers a broad spectrum of industries, suggest enormous challenges in meeting employee engagement objectives.

Engaged employees are productive and pivotal in helping an organization achieve or exceed critical strategic business goals. Companies struggle with low employee engagement, dissatisfied employees, and additional business-specific consequences that follow. Employees expect a culture that is authentic, socially responsible, and safe along with employee-specific antecedents such as learning opportunities, feedback, recognition, and rewards (Wollard & Shuck, 2011, p. 433). Lack of or deficiencies in these areas correlates to negative employee engagement outcomes.

Every organization seeks to achieve exceptional results. Whether for-profit or not-for-profit, a thriving organization captures the world's attention with its superior products and services. Moreover, a thriving organization—whether it is a running club, a parent-teacher organization, a church, or a multinational insurance company—excels and achieves at a level that outperforms others. Organizations that fully engage their people are well-positioned to excel regardless of the economy, competition, or other factors considered limiting. One leading factor as Baumruk (2006) notes, is the depth and breadth of leaders' impact, at every level, on employee or team member engagement. Organizations seeking high employee engagement have the solution within their leadership team. Too often, however, there are disconnects and silos among leaders. Poor engagement results are accepted as someone else's responsibility and someone else's problem. Pellicer (2008), nonetheless, puts responsibility for making a company a great place to work in the hands of leaders. Leaders who themselves are disengaged from the realities of poor engagement contribute to the problem. Disengaged leadership teams disenfranchise their people, often unknowingly, as concerns deepen for management teams that miss opportunities to know an organization from the inside out.

Harter et al. (2002), after analyzing results from 7,939 business units in 39 companies, asserted that both quantitative and qualitative data show managers' specific influence over employee engagement. Leaders affect every aspect of the employee experience, whether it is the front-line supervisor who gives insight and direction into day-to-day job responsibilities, the operations manager who has oversight of day-to-day macro-level activities, or the CEO who gives insight and direction to the vision and mission of an organization. Every level of leadership impacts the employee experience and engagement.

Assessing the Problem Through the Lens of Leadership Theory

Sinyan (2018) posits leadership as the strongest influencer on employee engagement. This influence extends to other drivers of engagement and affects individual and organizational performance. Two theoretical frameworks also shaped this study—Bass' Transformational Leadership Theory and the Leader-Member-Exchange (LMX) Theory which together define relationship-based, follower-focused leader behaviors and characteristics that inspire employees to excel in ways that increase employee engagement. This section examines the Leader-Member-Exchange (LMX) Theory and Bass' Transformational Leadership Theory. These theories signify the key role leadership plays in cultivating strong employee engagement. The LMX and Bass' Transformational Leadership theories offer frameworks that speak to ways leader attributes and effectiveness influence and impact employee engagement. Both frameworks give rise to the essential role leaders play in employees' interest in their roles and their drive or lack thereof to perform well in their roles (Bass, 1990). These theories also support the premise that engaged employees drive organizational results and are driven by leaders, whether transformational or transactional (Bass, 1990). Both Bass' Transformational Leadership and the Leader-Member Exchange (LMX) theories highlight the impact relationship has on engagement. The stronger the relationship, the greater the engagement (Bass, 1990; Graen & Uhl-Bien, 1995). Because of the impact of engagement on companies' bottom line and the people companies serve, the cultivation of relationships within organizations and across leadership levels makes a difference in outcomes.

The LMX and Bass theories intersect at the point of inspiration where leaders inspire or transform followers who extend themselves in deference to the relationship with the leader. Every aspect of the employee-leader relationship, or at least how an employee perceives that relationship, shapes the employee experience. The LMX theory posits a reciprocal relationship between leaders and followers where high-quality exchanges between the two influence organizational outcomes (Graen & Uhl-Bien, 1995). The leader and follower in this three-stage exchange begin as strangers in a relationship best described as transactional and driven primarily by deference given to a leader's title (Bass, 1990; Graen & Uhl-Bien, 1995). In the second stage of the LMX theory, the relationship between leader and follower becomes more personal and the exchanges between the two are less transactional (Graen & Uhl-Bien, 1995). In the third stage, the exchanges between leader and follower are more frequent and anchored in loyalty, mutual respect, and trust. Bass' Transformational Leadership theory and the LMX theory intersect in the relationship-focused third stage of the LMX theory. Bass (1990) posits that leader behavior that cultivates the relationship between leader and follower inspires followers to excel with no additional incentives needed. Leaders also mentor and consider followers who, in return, achieve higher organizational results.

The LMX and Bass' Transformational Leadership theories offer frameworks that speak to ways leader attributes and effectiveness influence and impact employee engagement. Both frameworks give rise to the essential part leaders play in employees' interest in their roles and their drive or lack thereof to perform well (Bass, 1990). These theories also support the premise that engaged employees drive organizational results and are driven by leaders, whether transformational or transactional (Bass, 1990).

Cultivating Leaders Who Cultivate Engagement: A Practical Approach

Whether a leader is born or made, training and development must be constant because people evolve, organizations evolve, and change is perpetual (Merriam & Bierema, 2014). A leader's responsibility to maintain high engagement is also ongoing as people and organizations evolve. Clarity of company values, respectful treatment of employees, and the company's standards of ethical behavior are all management principles and practices that together create a culture that favorably impacts employee engagement. Employees find their voice in an organization at the intersection of leader effectiveness and engagement.

Leader effectiveness is the most salient of solutions to the engagement issue given the power managers at all levels have in addressing factors that affect engagement. Managers are well-positioned to cultivate a climate where both primary (safety, training, onboarding) and "secondary indicators of engagement" (Shuck et al., 2011, p. 313). Feeling valued and feeling the freedom to express oneself is foundational to the culture of a thriving organization. As Gupta and Mahajan (2012) point out, how managers treat employees is predictive of employee motivation levels. Transformational leaders, as posited by both Bass' Transformational Leadership Theory and the Leader-Member-Exchange Theory focus on and never lose sight of the importance of their relationship with their followers.

Transformational Leadership

Transformational leadership, defined by Antonakis and House (2014) as the "intellectual stimulation" and attention to individual needs, inspiration, and...ideals of employees or followers (p. 750) "boosts employees' optimism and in turn enhances their work engagement" (Tims et al., 2011, p. 129). Transformational leaders inspire, are the source of intellectual stimulation, maintain a finger on the pulse of individual needs, and know their people in a way that engages their ideals (Antonakis & House, 2014). Therefore, an important starting point for any organization seeking to engage its people is leadership that is aware and capable of achieving goals and outcomes through transformational leadership. The transformational leader understands the multidimensionality of leadership.

Transformational leaders lead with authenticity (Wei, 2018). Transformational leaders affect and influence change through firsthand knowledge of the ins and outs of the organization at a strategic and tactical level. Culture, the capabilities of the organization and its people, and as Antonakis and House (2014) note maintaining and monitoring the internal and external environment in a way that is visible to employees creates employee confidence in the leader. A transformational leader influences people and outcomes in the most positive ways. Transformational leaders draw people in. They are charismatic and inspire people to achieve for both themselves and the organization. Being intentional in creating a culture focused on employee engagement inspires employees. Nonetheless, the relationship between leader and follower is reciprocal; the way leaders view employees is equally as important as the way employees view leaders. Transformational leadership transforms people and organizations. Transformational leadership is a skill, one that can be taught and cultivated within every level of leadership.

Learning Leaders

Building capabilities in leaders involves principles of adult learning, also known as andragogy, to anchor any learning strategy for adults. Merriam and Bierema (2014) posit the impact and importance of understanding adult learners and the deference that must be given to their experience, their ability and need to problem-solve, and the recognition of internal motivators. These principles of learning are central to the transformational leader's people-centered learning and development journey. Leveraging the capabilities and strengths of transformational leaders begins with a learning strategy anchored in andragogy. Whether leaders are born or made, ongoing learning that is understandable, well-thought-out, and continuous is essential to the development of successful transformational leaders.

DeAngelis and Penney (2015) draw on several learning theories that build on the transformational leader-learner's training curriculum which are based not only on the cultivation of relationships but also on the acquisition of new ideas or building on the knowledge they already have. Learning begins with an introduction or review of the theories behind each of the topics or skills. Facilitators build on these theories and position the transformational leader-learner to retain the information through the execution of active learning experiences that include small-group and project-based activities that call for collaboration, problem-solving, conflict resolution, and other learning and skill development areas (DeAngelis & Penney, 2015).

DeAngelis and Penney (2015) speak to three effective steps for connecting understanding to learning. The first step is the establishment of a learning curriculum geared toward the adult learner and his or her experiences. The second step is the connection to the learning through direct application activities and assignments that go in-depth in relationship-focused topics like conflict resolution and change management. Focus on a leader's relationship with their followers is central to Bass' Transformational and the LMX Exchange theories of transformational leadership. The third step is the synthesis, application, and ongoing assessment of the learning outcomes to confirm understanding and a transfer of knowledge (DeAngelis & Penney, 2015).

Active learning is the incorporation of the transformational leader-learner's experiences, collaboration with others, and reflection (DeAngelis & Penney, 2015) and is an essential element of a successfully executed adult learning curriculum and experience. Taken together, these elements foster engaging learning, build on prior learning, are affirming and inclusive, and build great leaders. The transformational leader-learner further explores each of these elements through active learning, performances of understanding, and other essential elements of leader development.

Active learning fully engages a transformation leader-learner. Chickering and Camson (1987) posit that the most effective learning "is collaborative and social, not competitive and isolated…and sharpens thinking [while deepening] understanding" (p. 3). Bonwell (1991) further expounds on this premise and contends that "in-class writing" (doing and thinking), "cooperative learning, debates, drama, role-playing and simulation, and peer teaching" (p. v) are additional elements that promote active learning. Whether designing a curriculum for leaders in a for-profit or not-for-profit organization, a classroom, or any other leadership or another role, active learning is a way to maximize learning and increase understanding of the engaged transformational leader-learner.

Transformational leaders first learn the theories behind each of these areas of learning before taking steps toward active learning. For a transfer of knowledge to take place, learners need "sufficient background knowledge to appreciate the context" (Deans for Impact, 2015, p. 6). Skill development, storytelling, participating in leaderless teams of six to eight individuals brought together to address real issues, along with self-discovery (DeAngelis & Penney, 2015) are the four components that allow for active learning.

Transformational leader-learners work with subject matter experts and interact with leaders from different organizations in a wide range of industries to promote rich discussions with leader-learners. Interaction with other leaders is where stories emerge and where understanding expands. Deans for Impact (2015) reinforces the idea that storytelling is a way to help learners learn, citing storytelling as "particularly effective at helping" learners retain new information (p. 4). Real-world projects that actively involve and engage the learner in direct problem-solving opportunities put theories to the test. Learners collaborate with other learner-participants. They also give and receive ongoing feedback. Learning benefits include hands-on experiences that provide opportunities to practice skill-building in a "safe space" (DeAngelis & Penney, 2015, p. 129). Conflict resolution, navigating difficult conversations, change management, inclusion, and authentic leadership (DeAngelis & Penney, 2015) are essential to effective leadership. The lessons learned and feedback provided help to develop skills and identify both strengths and areas of opportunity for the transformational leader-learner.

Transformational leader-learners focus on learning that is "reinforced and assimilated through the practice of self-reflection" (DeAngelis & Penney, 2015, p. 129). Self-reflection allows for introspection which is important for understanding individual strengths and weaknesses (DeAngelis & Penney, 2015). A leader with this level of self-awareness can build and sustain a workplace of highly engaged employees. Taking time for self-reflection and introspection also presents an opportunity for self-discovery. Self-reflection reinforces the teaching and shines a light on the level of understanding attained and learning that may require more time and attention. Self-reflection also builds understanding and awareness that is important to active learning and skill-building.

DeAngelis and Penney (2015) draw on several learning theories that connect understanding to the learning and the learner. Leader-learners attain innovative ideas or build on the knowledge they already have. Learning begins with an introduction or review of the theories behind each of the topics or skills. Facilitators build on these theories and position the leader-learner to retain the information through the execution of active learning experiences that include small-group and project-based activities that call for collaboration, problem-solving, conflict resolution, and other learning and skill development areas (DeAngelis & Penney, 2015).

Active learning is essential to the adult learning experience. The learner engages in the learning, versus passively listening. The learner can also express, assess, and apply the learning followed by feedback that builds skills and motivation for the learner. As noted by The National Academies of Sciences, Engineering, and Medicine (2018), "Motivation to learn is fostered for learners of all ages when they perceive the school or learning environment is a place where they 'belong' and when the environment promotes their sense of agency and purpose" (p. 6). One of the biggest challenges to overcome, particularly for leaders, are the "giants" of competing priorities and time. For transformational leaders to effect change in an organization, they must be learning leaders who actively engage in every learning opportunity.

Teaching Transformational Leaders

The ability to leverage the capabilities and strengths of an organization's people, in a way that builds purposeful relationships (DeAngelis & Penney, 2015), creates and sustains efficient processes. This ability also takes advantage of technologies and learning principles and practices. Whether leaders are born or made, ongoing learning that is understandable, well-thought-out, and continuous is essential to the development of successful leaders.

An organization that focuses on and commits to transformational leadership skills positions itself for favorable employee engagement outcomes. Transformational leadership skills are teachable and with the right strategy reach leaders at all levels of an organization. DeAngelis and Penney (2015) speak to the following effective approaches for connecting understanding to learning: First is the establishment of a learning curriculum and a set of experiences geared toward the adult learner. Another consideration is the connection through the direct application of the learning. Finally, the synthesis, application, and ongoing assessment of the learning outcomes are central to understanding (DeAngelis & Penney, 2015). This approach garners both understanding and learning which, combined with the application of the principles taught transforms leaders.

Components of an Effective Adult Learning Curriculum and Experience

Active learning, the incorporation of the leader-learner's experiences, collaboration with others, and reflection (DeAngelis & Penney, 2015) are the essential elements of a successfully executed adult learning curriculum and experience. Taken together, these elements foster engaging learning, build on prior learning (constructivism), are affirming and inclusive, and build great leaders. The leader-learner further explores each of these elements through active learning, performances of understanding, and other essential elements of leader development.

Active learning fully engages a leader-learner. A curriculum designed for the active learner extends beyond listening, or the appearance thereof. Chickering and Camson (1987) posit that the most effective learning "is collaborative and social, not competitive and isolated…and sharpens thinking [while deepening] understanding" (p. 3). Bonwell (1991) further expounds on this premise and contends that "in-class writing" (doing and thinking), "cooperative learning, debates, drama, role-playing and simulation, and peer teaching" (p. v) are additional elements that promote active learning. Whether designing a curriculum for leaders in a for-profit or not-for-profit organization or a classroom or online, active learning maximizes learning and increases understanding of the engaged transformational leader-learner. Leaders focus first on the theories behind each area of learning to provide "sufficient background knowledge to appreciate the context" (Deans for Impact, 2015, p. 6) and facilitate a transfer of knowledge. As DeAngelis and Penney (2015) posit, skill development, storytelling, and participating in leaderless teams of six to eight individuals address real issues and self-discovery for learners. Members of teams with no defined leader give each person an opportunity to develop, enhance, and hone individual leadership skills with each learning exercise and breadth of topics.

Conflict resolution, navigating difficult conversations, change management, inclusion, and authentic leadership (DeAngelis & Penney, 2015) are essential to effective leadership. Leaders work with subject matter experts and interact with leaders from different organizations in a wide range of industries to promote rich discussions with leader-learners. Interaction with other leaders is where stories emerge and where understanding expands. Deans for Impact (2015) reinforces storytelling as a way to help learners learn, citing storytelling as "particularly effective at helping" (p. 4) learners retain new information. Skill-building also occurs through case studies and ongoing individual or small group assignments. Real-world projects that actively involve and engage the learner in direct problem-solving opportunities put theories to the test. Learners collaborate with other learner-research participants. They also give and receive ongoing feedback. Leaderless teams that work together assign roles and responsibilities for projects.

Benefits to learners include hands-on experiences that provide opportunities to practice skill-building in a "safe space" (DeAngelis & Penney, 2015, p. 129). The lessons learned and feedback provided help to develop skills and identify both strengths and areas of opportunity for the transformational leader-learner.

Connecting Understanding to Learning and the Transformational Leader

DeAngelis and Penney (2015) draw on several learning theories that connect understanding to the learning and the learner. Leader-learners attain innovative ideas or build on the knowledge they already have. Learning begins with an introduction or review of the theories behind each of the topics or skills. Facilitators build on these theories and position the leader-learner to retain the information through the execution of active learning experiences that include small-group and project-based activities that call for collaboration, problem-solving, conflict resolution, and other learning and skill development areas (DeAngelis & Penney, 2015).

Active learning is essential to the adult learning experience. The learner engages in the learning, versus passively listening. The learner can also express, assess, and apply the learning followed by feedback that builds skills and motivation for the learner. As noted by The National Academies of Sciences, Engineering, and Medicine (2018), "Motivation to learn is fostered for learners of all ages when they perceive the school or learning environment is a place where they 'belong' and when the environment promotes their sense of agency and purpose" (p. 6). One of the biggest challenges to overcome, particularly for leaders, are the "giants" of competing priorities and time. For transformational leaders to effect change in an organization, they must actively engage in learning. Harter et al. (2002) define engagement as "the individual's involvement and satisfaction with as well as enthusiasm for work" (p. 269). There is a level of cognitive expression by the most highly engaged members of a team or organization that permeates throughout the organization. Engaged employees or team members are essential to an organization's success because engaged employees are productive, caring, and committed to excellence. They also stand ready and are always willing to go above and beyond. Pellicer (2008) posits that "when workers are highly engaged with their work, they are happier and more productive and the organizations that employ them are, in turn, more productive and more successful" (p. 27). Engaged employees are innovators who embrace change and are willing to challenge the status quo and are effective. Engaged employees leave a positive footprint wherever their steps take them. They speak up, they speak out, they make things happen.

Conversely, disengaged employees who are deliberate in their attempts to hurt an organization, influence the most engaged employees or team members. As Mannelly (2008) notes, "managing an actively disengaged employee is time-consuming…often emotionally painful, frightening, draining, and a lonely unsupported experience" (p. 116). Equally as disconcerting as the disengaged employee or team member, however, is the employee or team member who sits in a neutral space of indifference. As a result, the actions, or inactions of disengaged or indifferent employees or team members negatively affect customer perceptions and satisfaction and other employees' and team members' perceptions of the organization. Disengaged or indifferent employees get in the way of organizations maximizing their potential in whatever field or industry they are in. Transformational leaders who not only understand the distinctions between an engaged and disengaged employee but also possess the skills to change, inspire, or re-direct behaviors drive culture and business outcomes.

Transformational leader-learners constantly reflect on the learning journey, verbally, and in writing. Self-reflection is instrumental in reinforcing learning as it allows for introspection which is essential in understanding individual strengths and weaknesses (DeAngelis & Penney, 2015). A leader with this level of self-awareness can build and sustain a workplace of highly engaged employees. Taking time for self-reflection and introspection also presents an opportunity for self-discovery, which is an important constructivist principle. Self-reflection reinforces the teaching and shines a light on the level of understanding attained and areas of self-development. Self-reflection also builds understanding and awareness central to skill-building and the active learning theory.

CONCLUSION

Harter et al. (2002) define engagement as "the individual's involvement and satisfaction with as well as enthusiasm for work" (p. 269). There is a level of cognitive expression by the most highly engaged members of a team or organization that permeates throughout an organization. Engaged employees or team members are essential to an organization's success because engaged employees are productive, caring, and committed to excellence. Engaged employees leave a positive footprint wherever their steps take them. They speak up, they speak out, they make things happen. Engaged employees are behind exceptional customer experiences and organizational results that exceed objectives.

Conversely, the inattentiveness and actions of disengaged employees result in errors, lower customer satisfaction, and missed or poor organizational results. Mannelly (2008) notes, "managing an actively disengaged employee is time-consuming…often emotionally painful, frightening, draining, and a lonely unsupported experience" (p. 116). Disengaged or indifferent employees hamper an organization's ability to excel.

Leadership is the strongest driver of employee engagement. Leaders create a sense of belonging driven by inclusive practices known, based on several research studies, to have a strong correlation to employee engagement. The role of transformational leaders in achieving sustained employee engagement becomes even more paramount considering the costs. Meeting the challenge of addressing low engagement and attaining and sustaining high engagement includes cultivating a feeling of connectedness and a sense of belonging and inclusion by employees. Harter (2018) notes a 70 percent variance in engagement based on leader quality. Leaders who are present in their employees' eyes, who communicate regularly and often, and who respond to employee opinion in a way that leaves employees feeling heard (Sinyan, 2018, p. 1) represent the hallmarks of a transformational leader and are the reason this study focused on the implications, impact, and necessity of transformational leadership at all levels of an organization.

The transformational leader whose skills are built through an engaging learning experience and ongoing accountability reshapes an organization's outcomes through leadership practices that engage employees and strengthen organizational outcomes. Companies with a desire for strong employee engagement that is achieved and sustained on a long-term basis need transformational leaders. Transformational leaders need a learning path that guides them toward success that closes organizational gaps in engagement that have long eluded organizations.

Whether looking at the goals of a multinational company for-profit or a local non-profit organization seeking to attain and sustain strong engagement levels, it is the responsibility of the leaders in an organization to effect change in this critical space. Leaders at all levels have the power and influence to affect changes not only at the strategic level but at the tactical level as well. Leaders, at all levels of an organization, who are aware of both the employee and customer experience, based on firsthand experience, have the information, the training, and the power needed to change the trajectory of the employee experience. Absent a transformational leader's engagement and first-hand knowledge and understanding of an organization's people, an organization suffers.

REFERENCES

Antonakis, J., & House, R. J. (2014). Instrumental leadership: Measurement and extension of transformational–transactional leadership theory. *The Leadership Quarterly*, *25*(4), 746–771. doi:10.1016/j.leaqua.2014.04.005

Arokiasamy, A. (2013). A qualitative study on causes and effects of employee turnover in the private sector in Malaysia. *Middle East Journal of Scientific Research*, *16*(11), 1532–1541.

Attridge, M. (2009). Measuring and managing employee work engagement: A review of the research and business literature. *Journal of Workplace Behavioral Health*, *24*(4), 383–398. doi:10.1080/15555240903188398

Bass, B. M. (1990). From transactional to transformational leadership: Learning to share the vision. *Organizational Dynamics*, *18*(3), 19–31. doi:10.1016/0090-2616(90)90061-S

Baumruk, R. (2006). Why managers are crucial to increasing engagement: Identifying steps managers can take to engage their workforce. *Strategic HR Review*, *5*(2), 24–27. doi:10.1108/14754390680000863

Bee, J. (2013). How to keep toxic employees from harming your practice. *Medical Economics*, *90*(23), 38–39. PMID:25272629

Bonwell, C. C. (1991). Active learning: Creating excitement in the classroom. School of Education and Human Development, George Washington University.

Chickering, A. W., & Gamson, Z. F. (1987). Seven principles for good practice in undergraduate education. *AAHE Bulletin*, *39*(7), 3–7.

DeAngelis, L., & Penney, S. (2015). Teaching leaders. *Journal of Leadership Education*, *14*(4), 126–137. doi:10.12806/V14/I4/A3

Deans for Impact. (2015). *The Science of Learning*. Deans for Impact.

Gallup, Inc. (2017). *State of the Global Workplace*. Gallup Press.

Goffee, R., & Jones, G. (2013). Creating the best workplace on earth. *Harvard Business Review*, *91*(5), 98–107. https://hbr.org/2013/05/creating-the-best-workplace-on-earth PMID:23898736

Graen, G. B., & Uhl-Bien, M. (1995). Relationship-based approach to leadership: Development of leader-member exchange (LMX) theory of leadership over 25 years: Applying a multi-level multi-domain perspective. *The Leadership Quarterly*, *6*(2), 219–247. doi:10.1016/1048-9843(95)90036-5

Gupta, S., & Mahajan, T. (2012). An analytical study of drivers of employee engagement among executives of a manufacturing organization with special reference to handicraft industry in the Moradabad region. *Saaransh RKG Journal of Management*, *3*(2), 87–92.

Gyensare, M., Arthur, R., Twumasi, E., & Agyapong, J.-A. (2019). Leader effectiveness – the missing link in the relationship between employee voice and engagement. *Cogent Business & Management*, *6*(1), 1–20. doi:10.1080/23311975.2019.1634910

Harter, J. (2018, August 26). Employee engagement on the rise in the U.S. (Survey). *Gallup Poll News Service*. https://news.gallup.com/poll/241649/employee-engagement-rise.aspx

Harter, J. K., Schmidt, F. L., & Hayes, T. L. (2002). Business-unit-level relationship between employee satisfaction, employee engagement, and business outcomes: A meta-analysis. *The Journal of Applied Psychology*, *87*(2), 268–279. doi:10.1037/0021-9010.87.2.268 PMID:12002955

Kahn, W. A. (1990). Psychological conditions of personal engagement and disengagement at work. *Academy of Management Journal*, *33*(4), 692–724. doi:10.2307/256287

Kaye, B. L., & Jordan-Evans, S. (1999). *Love 'em or lose 'em: Getting good people to stay*. Berrett-Koehler.

Lear, G. (2016, February 18). *The cost of low employee engagement continues to increase*. http://resourcedevelopmentsystems.com/seblog/2016/02/the-cost-of-low-employee-engagement-continues-to-increase/

Mannelly, P. K. (2008). *Managing highly engaged or actively disengaged employees: A phenomenological study of first-level supervisors* (Publication No. 305122694) [Doctoral dissertation, University of Phoenix]. ProQuest Dissertations and Theses.

Manthiou, A., Hickman, E., & Klaus, P. (2020). Beyond good and bad: Challenging the suggested role of emotions in customer experience (CX) research. *Journal of Retailing and Consumer Services*, *57*, 102218–102218. doi:10.1016/j.jretconser.2020.102218

Merriam, S. B., & Bierema, L. L. (2013). *Adult learning: Linking theory and practice*. John Wiley & Sons.

National Academies of Sciences. (2018). *How people learn II: Learners, contexts, and cultures*. The National Academies Press. doi:10.17226/24783

Parent, J. D., & Lovelace, K. J. (2018). Employee engagement, positive organizational culture, and individual adaptability. *On the Horizon*, *26*(3), 206–214. doi:10.1108/OTH-01-2018-0003

Pellicer, L. (2008). *Caring enough to lead: How reflective practice leads to moral leadership* (3rd ed.). Corwin Press.

Schaufeli, W. B., & Bakker, A. B. (2004). Job demands, job resources, and their relationship with burnout and engagement: A multi-sample study. *Journal of Organizational Behavior*, *25*(3), 293–315. doi:10.1002/job.248

Schuckert, M., Kim, T., Paek, S., & Lee, G. (2018). Motivate to innovate: How authentic and transformational leaders influence employees' psychological capital and service innovation behavior. *International Journal of Contemporary Hospitality Management*, *30*(2), 776–796. doi:10.1108/IJCHM-05-2016-0282

Schwartz, G. (2010). Marrying employee engagement with customer satisfaction. *Strategic HR Review*, *9*(3), 40–41A. doi:10.1108hr.2010.37209cab.010

Shuck, B., & Wollard, K. (2010). Employee engagement and HRD: A seminal review of the foundations. *Human Resource Development Review*, *9*(1), 89–110. doi:10.1177/1534484309353560

Shuck, B. M., Rocco, T. S., & Albornoz, C. A. (2011). Exploring employee engagement from the employee perspective: Implications for HRD. *Journal of European Industrial Training*, *35*(4), 300–325. https://doi.org/10.1108/03090591111128306

Sinyan, P. (2018). *Gallup: The holy grail of employee engagement in 2018*. https://www.servicefutures.com/gallup-holy-grail-employee-engagement-2018

Tims, M., Bakker, A. B., & Xanthopoulou, D. (2011). Do transformational leaders enhance their followers' daily work engagement? *The Leadership Quarterly*, *22*(1), 121–131. doi:10.1016/j.leaqua.2010.12.011

Wei, F., Li, Y., Zhang, Y., & Liu, S. (2018). The interactive effect of authentic leadership and leader competency on followers' job performance the mediating role of work engagement. *Journal of Business Ethics*, *153*(3), 763–773. doi:10.100710551-016-3379-0

Wollard, K. K., & Shuck, B. (2011). Antecedents to employee engagement: A structured review of the literature. *Advances in Developing Human Resources*, *13*(4), 429–446. doi:10.1177/1523422311431220

Chapter 9
Online Learning or Emergency Remote Teaching?
Reflections on Online Learning as Pedagogical Innovation in a Higher Education Institution

João Emílio Alves
https://orcid.org/0000-0003-3019-3176
VALORIZA, Portugal

Adelaide Marques Proença
VALORIZA, Portugal

Alexandre Cotovio Martins
VALORIZA, Portugal

Sofia Maria Veríssimo
Polytechnic Institute of Portalegre, Portugal

Isabel Mourato
Polytechnic Institute of Portalegre, Portugal

Helena Carrilho Morgado
Polytechnic Institute of Portalegre, Portugal

ABSTRACT

Following the recent measures implemented worldwide as result of the pandemic caused by COVID-19, educational institutions needed to implement online learning practices, demanding a rapid appropriation of digital skills by teachers and students. The Polytechnic Institute of Portalegre, in Portugal, was one of the higher education institutions (IES) that organized a transition process for this teaching model. The objectives of the study focused on the characterization of the online learning process, including the practice of online learning and the students' perspectives regarding the future of online learning. The results obtained, from 420 validated questionnaires, point to a positive evaluation of this pedagogical experience, with some particularities listed in certain areas of the teaching and learning process, suggesting an in-depth analysis on the level of digital skills on the part of teachers and students in order to consolidate distance learning as a true pedagogical innovation process and not just as an "emergency remote teaching" experience.

DOI: 10.4018/978-1-7998-8239-8.ch009

INTRODUCTION

The technological means that revolutionized the daily life of societies in the last decades of the 20th century and the beginning of the 21st century have recently assumed an essential role in different areas of society, as a consequence of measures that have been implemented on a global scale to deal with the pandemic caused by the COVID-19. Among these measures is the implementation of rules of social distance and the change in behavior, aspects that were also reflected in the teaching and learning processes, across several educational institutions, including higher education institutions.

The Polytechnic Institute of Portalegre, while Higher Education Institution (HEI), in Portugal, has been investing in the last few years and strategically in a quality management system based on a path of continuous improvement of the services provided by the institution, with a view to the satisfaction of the interested parties, namely students, staff and institutional partners.

In this way and considering the importance of the self-assessment process as an instrument for monitoring the quality of the performance of a higher education institution, a questionnaire survey was applied to students ofat the Polytechnic of Portalegre, in the academic year of 2019/2020, with the intention to evaluate the online learning process implemented in the schools that integrate this HEI, following the interruption of face-to-face lessons, due to the lockdown imposed by the Portuguese government due to the pandemic COVID19, corresponding, almost entirely, to the second semester of the academic year 2019 / 2020.

This text seeks to demonstrate that, although online learning is not an innovative practice in the context of training provided in higher education, it has gained broader and generalized outlines following the "forced" migration in the period identified above, leading to a reflection process that mobilized the educational community of this HEI, including professors, students, non-teaching staff and management structures.

The objectives inherent to this research are fundamentally related to the intention of gathering a set of empirical and theoretically informed data regarding the advantages, difficulties and potentialities arising from a pedagogical practice in the context of online learning, especially when this practice was prepared and implemented in record time.

On the other hand, as suggested in the title of this text, we seek, based on the information collected, to reflect on whether we are facing a real process of online learning and pedagogical innovation or if the implemented experience is closer to a practice that we designate for "remote emergency teaching" (Grilo, 2020).

The relevance and the empirical and theoretical implications that we believe to have achieved with this research, centered on an HEI, are in the learning that this process induced with its protagonists, in particular professors and students, leading to a more in-depth reflection which aiming to correct aspects that, in the context of online learning, became visible from the evaluation that the students themselves carried out, by completing the aforementioned questionnaire, applied to the universe of students enrolled in the various study cycles offered by the Polytechnic of Portalegre.

Thus, at first, a brief incursion into the literature on the topic of online learning is carried out, to then present a set of empirical information, whose focus is to demonstrate the singularities inherent to a generalized pedagogical practice, largely implemented over a reduced period of time.

After a sociodemographic characterization of the students participating in the study, some quantitative data are presented. These data are centered on the online learning process, seeking to capture the evaluation that the students directed to the organization of the online learning practices, with special focus on the issue of learning assessment.

Parallel to the quantitative data presented, a qualitative analysis is presented, directed to the open responses expressed by the students, gathering the information in two ways: on the one hand, through a set of graphs with aggregated information of the same open responses, accompanied by another graphic design ("word clouds"); and on the other hand, through an analysis of contingency matrices represented graphically through associative pathfinder networks.

The results obtained point to a positive evaluation of this pedagogical experience, with some particularities listed in certain areas of the teaching and learning process, especially with regard to the assessment modalities, across the curricular units attended, suggesting an in-depth analysis of the level of competences and their usability, either by professors or by students, in order to consolidate online learning as a true pedagogical innovation process in higher education.

LITERATURE REVIEW

As a result of the impacts induced by the pandemic COVID19 in the activity developed by the HEIs, among which the replacement of the classroom teaching system by online learning stands out, some of the central actors in this process, namely professors and students, needed to adapt, in little time, to a new model of teaching and learning. It is in this context that the implementation of online learning using technologies appears, in order to guarantee the continuity of the school curriculum and the teaching and learning process in order to lessen deeper impacts, resulting, for example, from the interruption of the teaching component, as it has been practiced universally, that is, through the face-to-face regime in a physical space / classroom.

In fact, the urgency to implement online learning practices forced the reformulation of pedagogical practices and required professors to rapidly develop computer skills, often appealing to their creativity, both in adapting the content to the new teaching model and in use of technological means and tools that they had at their disposal.

Also in terms of equipping the computer devices and communication networks present in the classrooms and in the educational spaces inside the schools, an increased financial effort was required by the management structures of the educational organizations, with a view to update and improve the necessary equipment for the implementation of online learning.

Despite its limits and limitations, distance learning has emerged as a viable alternative to help overcome the mobility constraints imposed by the pandemic (Mishra et al., 2020). Even before the sudden transition to distance emergency education, the advantages and disadvantages of this modality were already being discussed within the scientific community.

As advantages of distance learning, Mussio (2020) highlights the possibility of a greater number of students per course; of a greater diversification in the supply of courses; of allowing a greater management of time and place in the rhythm of study; to favor the participation of people from different places; to be centered on the needs of students; to allow a rapid updating of content, as well as a personalization of the transmitted content; to have lower costs when compared to face-to-face training; to raise the possibility of detailed monitoring of student participation; to reduce logistical and administrative costs (travel, food, ...) and trigger the development of self-learning competencies.

On the other hand, Salum, Gomes and Ramires (2018) identify several disadvantages in the distance learning modality, namely, the fact that it reduces the controlled supervision by teachers in the learning process; greater difficulties on the part of students to establish a study routine autonomously, a factor that drives the lack of attention and dedication necessary to make learning efficient and effective. On the other hand, Martínez (2017) highlights the fact that several studies register a higher dropout rate of students compared to face-to-face learning:

The most precise definition varies from one institution to another, but its meaning is clear: students who drop out of a course, mostly it is because they find many difficulties in understanding the subjects, they are underserved and, in short, they feel unable to finish the studies they started. (Martinez, 2017)

Another drawback indicated by Martinez (2017) concerns the need, in distance education, for a reliable identification of the student at times of assessments. This situation, in general, is not solved and is one of the aspects that causes concern within the institutions.

Regarding the disadvantages of distance learning, Mussio (2020) points out that:

There may be technical problems related to the internet, which makes it impossible to access services or difficulties in adapting to the tool and the digital environment. Added to this, since teaching takes place only virtually, there is also a greater demand not only from the teacher-tutors responsible for the mediation of a given course, but also from the formulation and diversification of the materials made available, in order to promote greater attention and motivation of students. On the other hand, it is also necessary to demand greater discipline and self-organization on the part of the students, because studying "alone", when planning and designing the routes of their own time, distances them from the existence of complicity and relational bonds that the process of face-to-face interaction allows, thus promoting possible limitations in the development of student socialization (Mussio, 2020, p. 122).

In Europe, in general, HEIs were able to implement a strategic plan as a response to the challenges caused by the pandemic (Rumbley, 2020). The report of the International Association of Universities (IAU, 2020) reveals, however, that this response was not uniform across all HEIs and its success depended on various factors such as available means, experience and area of training. Some institutions, universities or courses were better able to face and manage the consequences arising from the closure of the institutions due to the continuity of a line of investments and previous experiences in distance teaching and learning. The report highlights the existence of a greater tendency to offer distance learning courses and training in the areas of education, management, and economics. Although most institutions recognize the importance in strategic terms of distance learning, in reality even before the pandemic, only a few institutions had this type of offering available, mainly in the sciences and engineering (IAU, 2020).

Some studies recognize that the response presented to the challenges caused by the pandemic was positive, considering that emergency solutions were successfully implemented (IAU&ESN, 2020) and there are "signs that Higher Education is more innovative and flexible than we could have imagined, especially with regard to teaching and learning" (Major, 2020, p. 265). However, Flores et al. (2021), in their study, note that

The literature also points to a 'forced preparation' for online teaching, highlighting concerns about assessment and equity issues, but also affective aspects that helped overcome the challenges encountered, namely humility, empathy, and even optimism. (Flores et al., 2021, p.5)

Also the development of 'pedagogical agility' as well as feelings of similarity and difference in pedagogical innovation in online learning contexts (Kidd & Murray, 2020) and also different types of responses from higher education institutions in the sudden transition to remote learning (Flores & Gago, 2020; la Velle et al., 2020; Quezada et al., 2020; Osman, 2020) were aspects reported in other studies.

As negative aspects mentioned by higher education students, Aucejo et al. (2020) identify delays and losses in terms of training, internships, job offers, and salaries (Aucejo et al., 2020). These last authors also refer to the fact that the pandemic has caused a very heterogeneous effect in the experience and expectations of students, reflected in variations in the time dedicated to study and the influence of the socioeconomic status of young people. Hadar et al. (2020) also identify a lack of preparation of students in terms of socio-emotional skills.

According to Flores et al. (2021), a study conducted by Bao (2020) in the Chinese Higher Education context presents interesting findings that may be similar to the pandemic context in other countries. Bao (2020) identified five principles that impacted distance learning motivated by the pandemic:

1. appropriate relevance of distance learning and student learning;
2. effective communication of information needed to conduct distance learning activities;
3. adequate support provided by faculty;
4. quality participation to enhance and deepen student learning;
5. a contingency plan to deal with unexpected situations that may arise in distance learning.

Bao (2020), in the same study, alerts to an aspect that can be an enemy of an active and effective involvement in the learning process by students: the need to combat anxiety caused by a sudden transition to the distance learning process. Another work, developed by Baloran (2020) also refers to an increase in anxiety levels of Filipino university students during the pandemic period. As aspects to be taken into account, this work identifies the need to prepare students and teachers for a combined approach between online and face-to-face teaching modality, to improve the resources and skills of students and teachers regarding the use of computer media and equipment. In short, in order to try to reduce as much as possible the effects of the absence of face-to-face interaction and to take advantage of the potentialities of the implementation of distance learning and teaching platforms, more and better preparation, training and adequate resources are needed (Lim, 2020).

The path of pedagogical innovation with the integration of technologies in the classrooms, prior to the pandemic, was still a process under construction, with advances and setbacks that required an in-depth reflection on the

Establishment of efficient, fruitful and sustainable processes of naturalizing the technologies and digital environments in school dynamics (Pedro & Matos, 2018, p. 296).

In the text "Technologies in Schools: (require) new tools, new spaces and new dynamics", published in the report "State of Education 2018" of the Portuguese National Education Council (CNE), the same authors show that "digital technologies are strategic resources to design and create innovative learning spaces, create conditions for the adoption of active pedagogies and improve students' learning ", being essential that

Educators, teachers, teacher trainers, policy makers and civil society take a systematic critical stance in relation to practices implemented in schools with digital technologies. (p. 302).

The same report further highlights that

If school pedagogical practices are at the heart of educational transformations that improve culture, initiative, civic responsibility and democratic participation by citizens, it is essential to assume that these transformations must be strongly induced by school activities. (p. 302).

The recent context that educational institutions faced, after the emergence of the pandemic caused by COVID19, contributed to the acceleration of a transformation process whose path was still being traced in an attempt to create sustainable foundations for the integration of technology in educational practices.

In fact, the urgency of moving to an online learning model also called "remote emergency education" (Grilo, 2020, p.184), emphasizing, in this case, some differences in face of true online learning, which presupposes the existence of planning and production of its own materials and specific techniques, but both dependent on the use of technology, led Unesco (2020) to disseminate, through an information note, a set of recommendations that focus on equity concerns, on inclusion and on the need to ensure that the design and offer of online learning does not aggravate existing educational and social inequalities, emphasizing the importance of more open, and long-term, more inclusive and flexible educational systems. In the same text, the importance of several factors that can condition the success of online education are highlighted, among which the following stand out: i) the adaptation of curricular objectives to the use of technological means; ii) the choice of relevant and appropriate technological means to the curricular contents; iii) the need to increase technological skills to guarantee the continuity of the teaching and learning process; iv) ensuring equity and the inclusion of all students; v) the protection of privacy and the security of personal data; vi) support for teachers and parents in the use of technological means; vii) the articulation between appropriate approaches depending on the resources used; viii) the definition of strategies that regulate, develop and implement online learning.

The implementation of online learning was a process that occurred in an unexpected way after

The abrupt interruption of classes in physical spaces imposed to the educational institutions quick decision-making, without the completion of fundamental steps for the initiatives of online education to be successful. (Moreira et. al., 2020, p. 2).

In the perspective of these authors, with vast experience in online education processes, the urgency to implement this type of teaching has prevented the achievement of fundamental stages such as:

The planning, the training of all those involved, the preparation of the technological infrastructure (hardware and software), (...), the adaptation or reformulation of curricula, in addition to promoting inclusion and equity (idem).

The Polytechnic of Portalegre was one of the portuguese HEI that quickly transitioned to an online learning model on March 16, 2020, adapting the teaching activity of its courses to the new conditions, which involved, to a large extent, the use of technological means and tools. This situation motivated the application of a questionnaire survey to students of the different study cycles taught in the schools of the Polytechnic of Portalegre with the aim not only of characterizing the way in which the online learning process was conducted, but also to help identify aspects positive and less positive aspects highlighted by the students, in the perspective that they can be improved. The results obtained with the application of this questionnaire suggest a directed reflection, both on the adequacy of the technological tools used, as well as on teaching methodologies, and in particular on learning assessment, adopted by the professors in different curricular units.

These results are mirrored in the following sectionschapters, using an analysis strategy that combines data of quantitative and qualitative nature.

METHODOLOGY

To achieve the objectives of this study, a methodological strategy was created based on the dissemination of an inquiry through an online questionnaire, aimed at the universe of students enrolled at the Polytechnic of Portalegre in June 2020, in different training cycles (Courses of 1st and 2nd cycles, Higher Professional Technical Courses, Erasmus, Individual Curricular Units and courses within the scope of protocols with other entities), in operation at the date of the application of the survey by questionnaire, totaling two thousand, one hundred and twelve (2112) students.

This extensive methodology was the most appropriate option given the central objective, which was largely based on listening to students regarding the experience carried out on migration, even if temporary, from face-to-face education to online learning, motivated by the issues raised above.

The questionnaire survey addressed to students included a diverse set of questions, which are translated into variables of a quantitative and qualitative nature, having been made available between June 19 and July 9, 2020, by email.

At the end of the listening of the student community, 420 questionnaires were received and validated, resulting in a response rate of approximately 20%, a reference value for the analysis developed in the meantime and which is noted in this text. The response totals of each school were also considered as a reference value, an option that proved to be very useful for a more detailed analysis, by school, for internal reflection in the institution and, in particular, in the respective scientific-pedagogical bodies.

The treatment of the collected information was carried out in a global and not individualized way, with the concern of guaranteeing the confidentiality of the answers, as well as the anonymity of the respondants. For this purpose, several software (Excel and SPSS) were used for the quantitative analysis and WebQDA for the qualitative analysis of the open answers included in the questionnaire.

The questionnaire was structured taking into account two dimensions of analysis. In the case of the first dimension, several issues were focused on the practice of online learning, from the beginning of the period of lockdown to the phase of evaluations, including a set of indicators related to the use of computer equipment, the characterization of the process teaching and learning, and also several issues related to the students' perspectives regarding the future of online learning at the Polytechnic of Portalegre. The second dimension of the analysis was aimed at the sociodemographic characterization of the students surveyed.

Table 1. Gender of the inquired students

	N.º	%
Female	314	74,8%
Male	106	25,2%
Total	420	100,0%

Source: IPP (2020), (self made)

In this text it is privileged an analysis mainly of a qualitative character, centered on a set of empirical data and relationships between variables, based on the open answers reported by the students, although some quantitative results are also presented, whether related to the sociodemographic characteristics of the inquired students, or related to some relevant issues inherent to the different aspects of the teaching and learning process.

RESULTS AND DISCUSSION

Sociographic Characterization of the Inquired Students

From the data obtained for the sociographic characterization of the students involved in the study, we highlight some contextualization variables, which are presented below. Thus, of the 420 respondent students, 314 (74.8%) are female and 106 (25.2%) are male (table 1). They are between 18 and 63 years old, and most students are between 18 and 23 years old, corresponding to a total of 73% of the sample considered.

In the overwhelming majority, students are of portuguese nationality (95.2%), and with regard to the regime in which they are enrolled, 88.8% are on a full-time basis and 10.5% on a part-time basis, with the remaining categories considered ("mobility student - Erasmus in/out" and "external student attending isolated curricular units") obtained very residual values.

Regarding the condition towards education, 79.8% of students are on a regular basis, against only 20.2% who have a working student regime. The overwhelming majority of them attend the daytime regime (90.5%) and, to a lesser extent, the post-employment regime. Its distribution among the four schools of the Polytechnic of Portalegre (table 2) reveals a participation in the cross-sectional study, although with some differences in terms of participants, with greater weight in the Higher Schools of Health and Technology and Management.

In the universe of respondents, undergraduate students were those who answered the questionnaire in a more significant way (84.3%), followed by students attending CTeSP (9.8%), then students in the second cycle of training (5.5%), with a residual number of students attending postgraduate courses (0.5%). Also in this regard, the most expressive year of undergraduate degrees refers to the 1st year (48.1%), followed by the 2nd year (31.9%) and 3rd year (17.4%) students. Regarding the variety of courses attended by students responding to this study, the Nursing course stands out as the one that gathers the most significant percentage of validated responses (29.3%). However, it is important to mention that almost all of the training offer currently available at the Polytechnic of Portalegre was included in the scope of the universe of students who responded to this study.

Table 2. Respondents per school

	N.º	%
ESECS - Superior School of Education and Social Sciences	88	21,0%
ESTG - Superior School of Management and Technology	127	30,2%
ESAE - Agrarian Superior School of Elvas	61	14,5%
ESS - Superior School of Health	144	34,3%
Total	420	100,0%

Source: IPP (2020), (self elaboration)

Online Learning Practice(s): Tools Used and Assessment Systems

In this section, we look at the online learning practices used by the teaching staff across the four schools of the Polytechnic of Portalegre, seeking to list the different online learning modalities implemented, the most used tools, the type of sessions and the modalities of evaluation of the most used learning.

Overall, teaching practices converged very significantly towards the use of video classes in the overwhelming majority of curricular units, constituting the ZOOM-Colibri platform, the modality pointed out by students as the most usual, being referred by 59.3% as having been the dominant option in CU.

Regarding the type of sessions given, the fact that 87.1% of respondents recognize the modality of synchronous session (using the video class), as the prevailing one, stands out, against only one use in the order of 12.9% based on asynchronous sessions (including, for example, viewing videos with educational content, developing educational activities, online research, among other activities).

With regard to the tools used in the context of distance learning, Table 3 and Figure 1 bring together the different options used and the degree of frequency of use of them, across the universe of curricular units attended by the students surveyed.

As seen, the answers obtained focus more frequently on the Zoom-Colibri options (video lessons), the "e-mail" solution and using the PAE platform (created at the Polytechnic of Portalegre and used by the academic community even before the pandemic). Conversely, the solutions "skype", "moodle platform", "facebook groups" and "WhatsApp" were less used options. As "other tools" indicated by students, they are, above all, the use of the mobile phone, the Discord platform and Instagram, though with residual values.

In the specific domain of the evaluation of the online learning process, students tend to consider that the tools used by the teachers were appropriate to the nature of the curricular units and that the teachers were available to monitor the students' work. They also mostly mention that they prefer face-to-face teaching sessions and that in online learning, it was not easy to maintain interaction with colleagues and teachers.

Table 4 and Figure 2 objectively reflect the positioning of students concerning the evaluation process carried out by professors within their curricular units.

As an extension of the previous analysis, in the assessment directed by the respondents to the implemented assessment system, 80.5% of the students report that there were changes to the assessment system in most CUs, against 19.5% who expressed an opinion to the contrary. On the other hand, 74.6% consider that the evaluation system used was suitable for online learning, although for a quarter of the total of respondents (24.9%), the opinion was in the opposite direction.

Table 3. Use of tools (Nº of responses)

	1 – Not frequent (less than 10%)	2 – Less frequent (between 10% and 50%)	3 – About 50%	4 - Frequent (between 50% and 90%)	5 – Very frequent (more than 90%)	Doesn't apply
Zoom-Colibri (vídeo lessons)	8	10	24	72	304	2
PAE platform	17	48	41	106	202	6
Moodle platform	125	47	26	33	27	162
Skype	149	31	17	17	9	197
E-mail	21	39	45	91	207	17
Facebook Groups	118	33	26	58	39	146
WhatsApp	92	51	39	62	70	106
Others	105	7	8	10	1	289

Source: IPP (2020), (self elaboration)

Through another indicator, "Adequacy of tasks proposed by the professors", the data revealed that 61.9% of students consider that the number of tasks proposed by the professors was adequate for the weekly load (contact and autonomous work), across the board CU, although 38.1% registered a contrary opinion. Also with regard to taking the tests in the online system, 70.2% of students tend to recognize

Figure 1. Frequency of use of tools (% of responses)
Source: IPP (2020), (self elaboration)

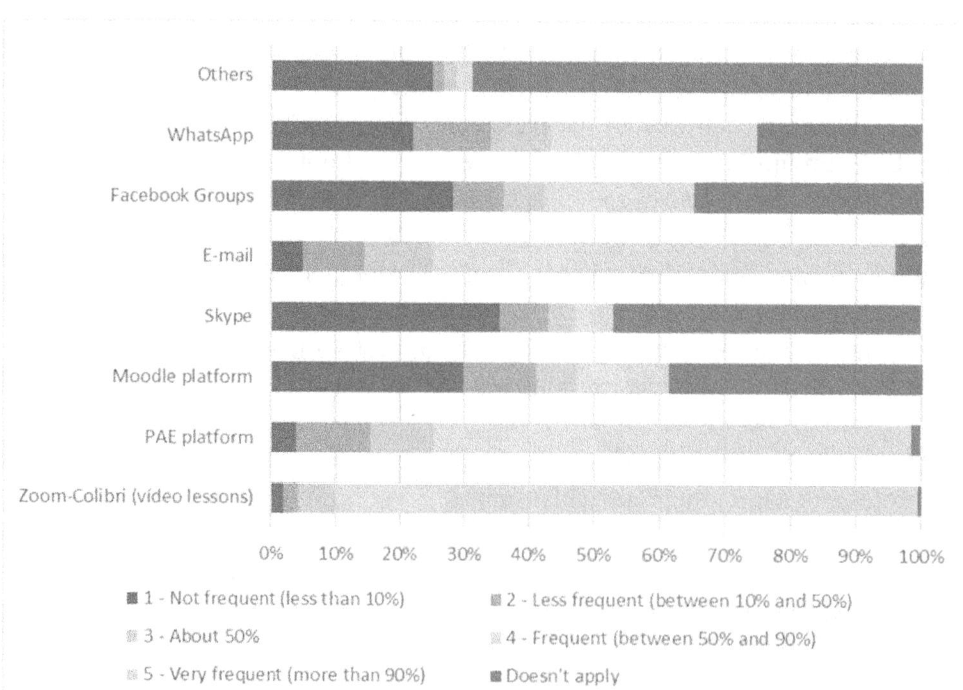

that they took place in an appropriate manner, a positive assessment that also extends in the case of the assessment directed to the deadlines for the delivery of the proposed tasks by the professors, who deserved a positive evaluation (85.2%) by the students.

Table 4. Online learning process evaluation (Nº. of responses)

	1 – Strongly disagree	2 – Partially disagree	3 – Neither agree nor disagree	4 – Partially agree	5 – Strongly agree	Doesn't know/ doesn't answer
The tools used by the professors were adapted to the nature of the CU (curricular Unit)	19	36	55	180	128	2
Synchronous classes were held at CU timetable	30	69	45	128	142	6
Professors were available to monitor the students' work	13	37	60	127	182	1
In the online learning process, it was easier to maintain interaction with colleagues and teachers	105	84	91	86	52	2
I prefer presential teaching sessions over online learning sessions	27	23	50	63	244	13

Source: IPP (2020), (self elaboration)

Figure 2. Online learning process evaluation
Source: IPP (2020), (self elaboration)

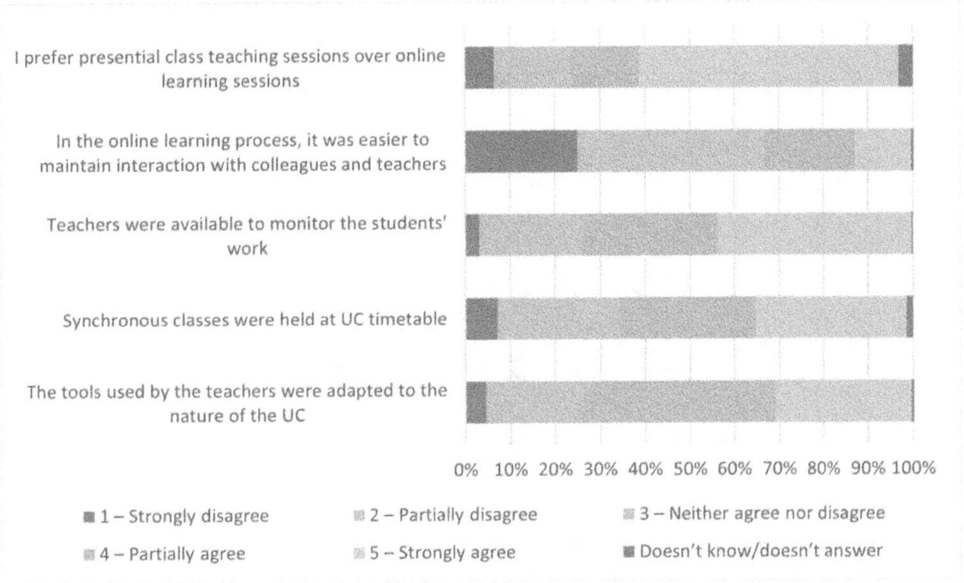

Table 5. Importance of online learning (Nº. of responses)

	1 Less important	2	3	4	5 More important	Doesn't known/ doesn't answer
Ease of reconciling academic and personal life	24	31	78	118	156	13
Ease of managing self-employed work	15	25	85	144	138	13
Easy access to CU documents	15	16	89	163	127	10
Ease of contact with professors	21	14	111	129	136	9
Computer skills development	28	22	93	145	123	9
Reduction of expenses (related to travel, food,...)	32	20	58	96	195	19

Source: IPP (2020), (self elaboration)

In a global sense, and in a transversal way to several analyzed indicators, 79.3% of the respondents consider that the distance learning modality ran positively in the curricular units attended, thus contributing to an overall evaluation favorable to its implementation.

From this analysis, we sought to assess the importance of several situations related to the development of online learning activities. Most students consider that the most important was the reduction of expenses (related to travel, food, ...), the ease in reconciling academic life with personal life and the ease in managing autonomous work in Curricular Unit (CU). Table 5 and Figure 3 show the positioning of the inquired students in relation to various aspects inherent to the implementation of online learning.

In addition to the more positive aspects, it is still significant to point out that in the domain of the difficulties experienced, during the process in which online learning was generally applied, the greatest difficulties manifested are related to time management (for example, reconcile personal life with aca-

Figure 3. Importance of online learning (% of responses)
Source: IPP (2020), (self elaboration)

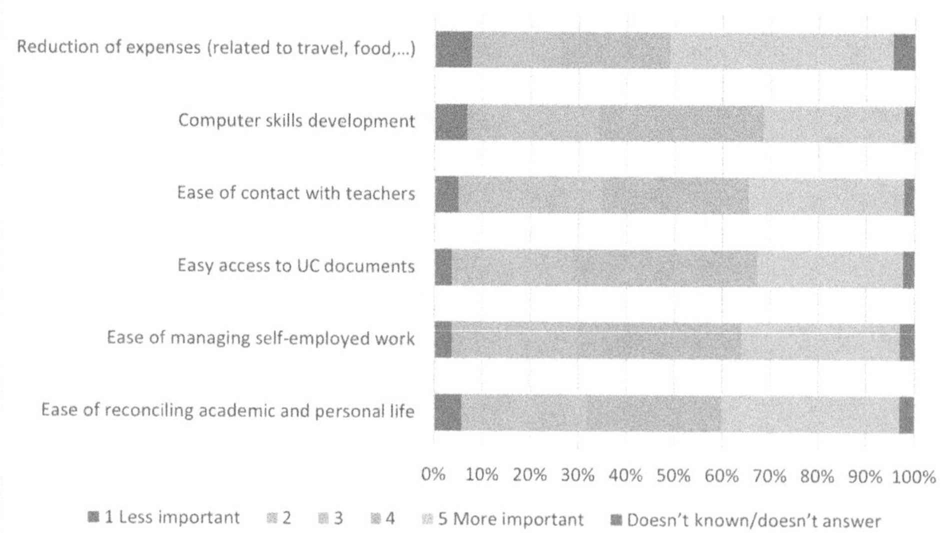

Table 6. Difficulties felt (Nº. of responses)

	1 Less difficulty	2	3	4	5 Greater difficulty	Doesn't know/ doesn't answer
Technical difficulties (problems related to obsolete computer, the internet network,...)	108	56	100	71	78	7
Time management difficulties (for example, reconciling personal and academic life)	66	59	86	88	118	3
Learning difficulties	53	78	115	89	82	3
Difficulties in fulfilling and carrying out the tasks proposed in the CU	77	99	121	75	44	4
Difficulties in carrying out the evaluation products (eg written tests, papers,...)	53	82	134	75	69	7
Difficulties in accessing the documentation provided by the professors	155	99	101	43	18	4
Difficulties in contacting the professors	118	85	119	50	46	2

Source: IPP (2020), (self elaboration)

demic life), with learning difficulties and with technical difficulties (problems related to the obsolete computer and the internet network,...). With a lesser degree of difficulty, the students referred to the access to the documentation provided by the teachers and the contact with them (Table 6 and Figure 4).

In a general way, the online learning modalities implemented by the professors deserved a globally positive balance from 83.8% of the students. Conversely, only 1.2% rated the process as very bad and 11.2% as bad, corresponding to a minority of opinion.

When faced with the possibility of online learning going on in the future, 40.7% of the universe of student respondents considers that it should be adopted only as a resource solution (Table 7). However, for 33.1%, online learning can be a more regular practice, but always maintaining the face-to-face regime as the main modality. Only 3.8% consider that this model should definitely replace face-to-face classes.

In a synthetic perspective, there is a globally positive and receptive attitude from the students towards the online learning process, accompanied by the solutions found and implemented by the professors, across schools and CUs. But, when faced with the maintenance of the online learning regime in the near future, they reveal a conservative perspective, expressing preference for the face-to-face regime as the first option, while not neglecting online learning as a resource or as a more regular practice, but always maintaining classroom teaching as the main modality. Only a small part defends the reinforcement of this practice in the future (8.6%), and the percentage of students who defend their non-return (11.4%) is not to be neglected.

A closer look at each school, however, reveals some nuances, which should be taken into account. For example, at the Higher School of Education and Social Sciences (ESECS), of the 84 students who expressed their opinion regarding the future of distance learning 48.81% consider that this type of teaching should be reinforced in all the CU or be a more regular practice, but maintaining the face-to-face regime as the main modality. In the Higher School of Management and Technology, (ESTG), the students who have the same understanding total 55 (44%); in the Agrarian Higher School of Elvas (ESAE) there are 30 (50.85%) and, finally, in the Higher School of Health (ESS) there are 49 (34.51%). With the opposite

Figure 4. Difficulties felt (% of responses)
Source: IPP (2020), (self elaboration)

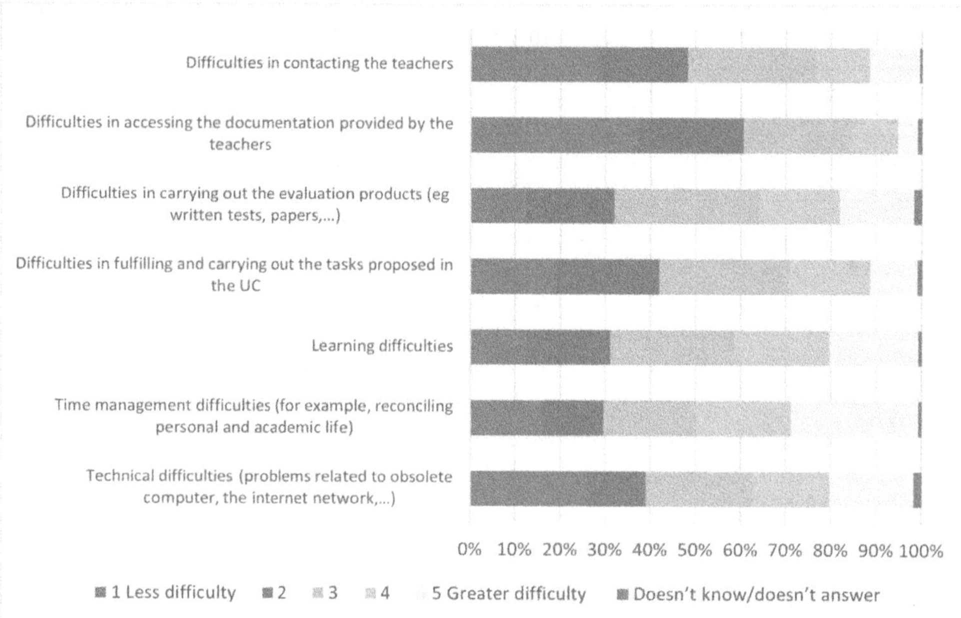

opinion, there are 38 (45.24%) students in ESECS, 64 (51.2%) in ESTG, 24 (42.37%) in ESAE and 92 (64.79%) in ESS.

In order to assess the possible association between these two variables, "distance learning in the near future" and "attended school" (as nominal variables), the chi-square test was used, considering the total of 410 responses (table 8).

The test result indicates that there is statistical evidence of an association between the variables "online learning in the near future" and "school attended" ($p < 0.05$), which means that the students' opinion about the continuity of the online learning modality in the near future is not distributed in an identical way in the four schools of the Polytechnic of Portalegre.

Table 7. Online learning model in the near future

	N.º	%
Be reinforced in all CUs	36	8,6%
To be a more regular practice, but always maintaining face-to-face as the main modality	139	33,1%
Replacing face to face lessons definitely	16	3,8%
Being a fallback sollution only	171	40,7%
Not to be considered again	48	11,4%
Doesn't know/doesn't answer	10	2,4%
Total	420	100,0%

Source: IPP (2020), (self elaboration)

Table 8. Distance learning in the near future by school attended **(Chi-square test)**

	Value	d.f.	Asymptotic significance (Bilateral)
Pearson Chi-square	22,799[a]	12	0,029
Nº of valid cases	420		
a. 3 cells (15.0%) have an expected frequency less than 5. The minimum expected frequency is 2.30.			

Source: IPP (2020), (self elaboration)

Qualitative Analysis: Word Clouds and Associative Networks Pathfinder between Pairs of Variables

As a complement to the previous analysis, the results obtained from a set of qualitative indicators are presented below, using a series of open questions included in the applied online questionnaire.

The information obtained in this way was analyzed in detail and recoded a posteriori, allowing an aggregation of answers useful for the deepening of some dimensions of analysis inherent to the study. For this, and using the WebQDA software, the development of finer analyzes was carried out, with the purpose of obtaining a more in-depth evaluation framework, as complete as possible, of the students' appraisal. In this regard, the meaning inherent in the expressions and comments shared by students gains special interest.

Thus, in a first stage, the information obtained within the scope of open responses is exposed, organized by aggregated analysis categories and accompanied by associated graphics in the form of a "word cloud", elucidating the expressions and ideas most often expressed by students.

To complete this analytical exercise, a set of connections between pairs of variables is presented, using "Pathfinder Associative Networks", generated from explanatory matrices of the relationships and connections between certain variables of interest for a more incisive and in-depth analysis of the complex web of relations between the students' various expressions of opinion. In this regard, the last open question of the questionnaire survey was taken as the central variable for this analysis, in which students were invited to express, in a free and optional way, comments regarding the distance learning process carried out at the Polytechnic of Portalegre, including suggestions for improvement to be implemented in the future.

The results obtained are represented graphically through "pathfinder associative networks", in which the contingency relations between response categories are analyzed, having analyzed the open answer questions mirrored in the questionnaire survey and of which only a few are presented in the following subchapter.

Categories of Aggregate Response and Word Clouds

We started this last chapter of the analysis by recovering an open question, of general scope, against which students were invited to comment on the process and online learning, through comments and/or proposals for improvement, with 87 comments obtained, representing a global response rate of 20.7%, compared to the total sample.

Figure 5. Students' opinion on the online learning process
Source: IPP (2020), (self elaboration)

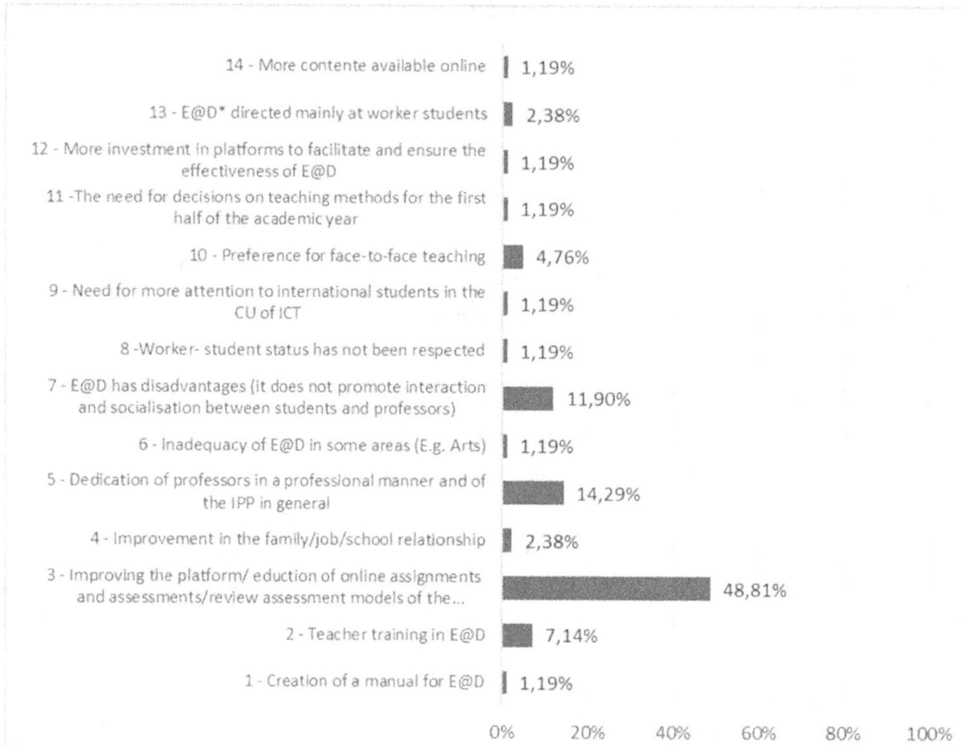

Figure 5 shows the responses obtained, recoded by more aggregated analysis categories. From the set of valid responses, the highest percentage (approximately 50%) stands out, the content of which refers to situations that students relate to the need for "improving the platform / reducing work and online assessments / reviewing assessment models of CUs / keep to schedules "(by the professors).

On a next level, about 14% of students made a point of registering a recognition for the "dedication of the professors in a professional way and the Polytechnic of Portalegre in general", as well as regarding the way in which everyone adapted to a new and still incipient reality. On the other hand, approximately 12% of the students who answered this question identified several types of disadvantages of the online learning modality, namely the lack of interaction and socialization between students and professors, as well as the lack of expense reduction provided by online learning.

In the corresponding word cloud resulting from the answers to this question (Figure 6), in addition to the expressions "classes", "students", "professors" and "teaching", other words such as "jobs", "time" and "home" stand out, translating the main difficulties that students identify in the online learning modality.

The least successful aspects, based on the 49 valid responses (Figure 7), translating limitations or difficulties in the scope of the online learning implementation process pointed out by the students, are directed, above all, to questions related to the "pedagogical effectiveness" (aspect with the highest percentage of responses), revealing students' discontent with learning in online learning. Then, there is the "adequacy of teaching practices" that students consider were not the most appropriate.

Figure 6. Word cloud from the students' opinion about the online learning process
Source: IPP (2020), (self elaboration)

Aspects related to "deficits in motivation and/or interaction", the emergence of negative factors (stress…)" with 10% and the "workload in online learning to 8% were also mentioned by approximately 12% of students, to mention only the aspects most often referenced.

The corresponding word cloud for this variable (Figure 8) corroborates the previous reading resulting from the analyzed graph. In fact, in addition to the word "presential", which acquires a central role in the range of responses obtained, other expressions stand out that suggest difficulties and problems in the online learning modality that may be associated with the "platform" used, the "motivation", "monitoring" and "communication".

With the same purpose of obtaining a generic framework of appraisals in relation to online learning, students were also asked about the advantages that they could point out resulting from this experience. Figure 9 gathers student comments on this variable, organized by analysis categories based on the listed benefits.

In this way and in addition to the advantages listed on the pages above, in a closed response mode, 38 valid responses were obtained, with a greater percentage standing out for the existence of "more favorable conditions to support the family". This is followed, with an equal percentage, by the ease of "reconciling work / school", as well as "more detailed content / tasks and more time of dedication". About 16% of the 38 responses state that the quality of online learning is lower, and there are not many advantages in relation to the face-to-face modality.

Figure 7. Negative aspects in the way online learning took place
Source: IPP (2020), (self elaboration)

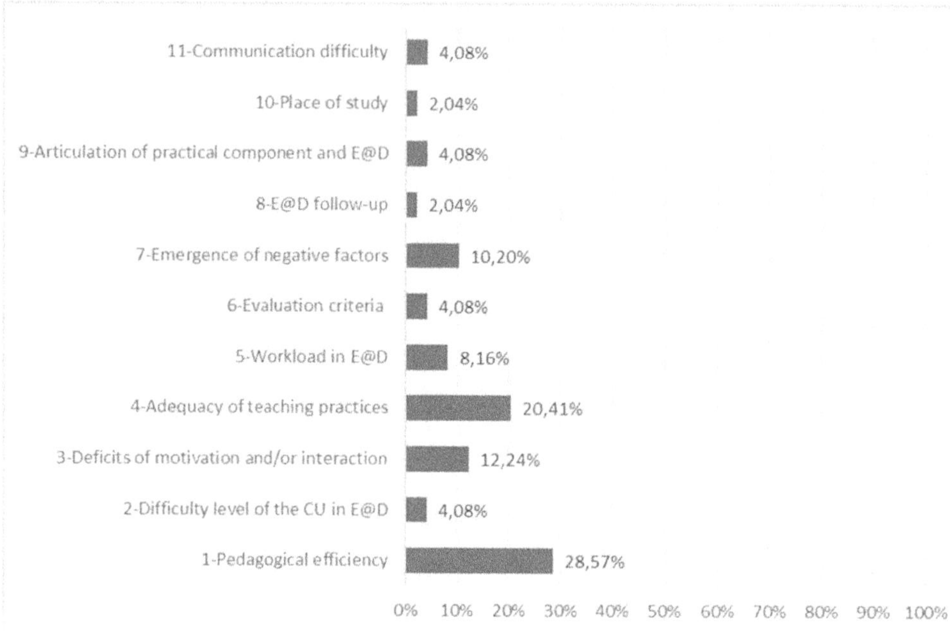

With less weight in the set of responses obtained, there are other positions that should also be analyzed. This is the case of the reference to "more work and tasks: it would be more effective if used in differently" (approximately 8%) and, with the same proportion, two other ideas: "better grades for CU / work-based assessment" and "easier understanding of contents /subject taught", both with 5.26% of the answers.

The word cloud obtained for this variable complements the previous observations regarding this issue (Figure 10).

The terms most often referenced by students refer, as advantages identified in online learning, in: "jobs", "availability", "time", "schedules" and "home"; but also, with a lesser degree of preponderance, "matter", "theoretical", "notes" and "ease".

According to the same line of reasoning, we sought to obtain from students a reference to other possible difficulties not identified *a priori* through the closed questions contained in the questionnaire. Figure 11 gathers the information obtained.

In addition to the difficulties identified and described previously, the students revealed another type of difficulties, being obtained 35 valid responses in total. In this context, with an equal percentage, "difficulties in accessing the PAE platform and the use of different types of platforms", as well as difficulties related to "reconciling work, school and family", both with 20% of responses, stand out. The "time limit on responses in online assessment" was pointed out by about 17% of students, followed by difficulties related to the monitoring of the syllabus and many assessment works, with 11.43%.

The word cloud inherent to this variable (Figure 12) brings together a set of expressions that are in line with the previous analysis, through which expressions such as "time" and "platform", such as the difficulties identified in the online learning modality, gain relevance.

Figure 8. Word cloud from the negative aspects in the way online learning took place
Source: IPP (2020), (self elaboration)

In the scope of qualitative analysis, a set of results is presented below, based on some associative networks between pairs of variables that allow an analytical deepening in the context of the evaluation of online learning by the students of the Polytechnic of Portalegre.

Associative Networks between Variable Pairs

To analyze the relationship between different response categories, an analysis based on contingency matrices (content analysis technique) was used, which assumes that two categories that appear associated in the responses of the same individuals will be equally present in the individuals thoughts (Verissimo et. Al., 2017).

The results of the matrices were represented graphically using a technique called Pathfinder Associative Networks, whose aspect is that of a network made up of nodes and connections between them. The nodes represent the categories and the links show the presence of contingency relations. The absence of a link between two categories, that is, of a contingency value equal to zero, means that there is no contingency relationship between them.

Next, an exercise is presented, crossing the open question of the questionnaire, related to comments / opinions / suggestions for improvement and a set of other questions, in complement to the analysis

Figure 9. Advantages of online learning
Source: IPP (2020), (self elaboration)

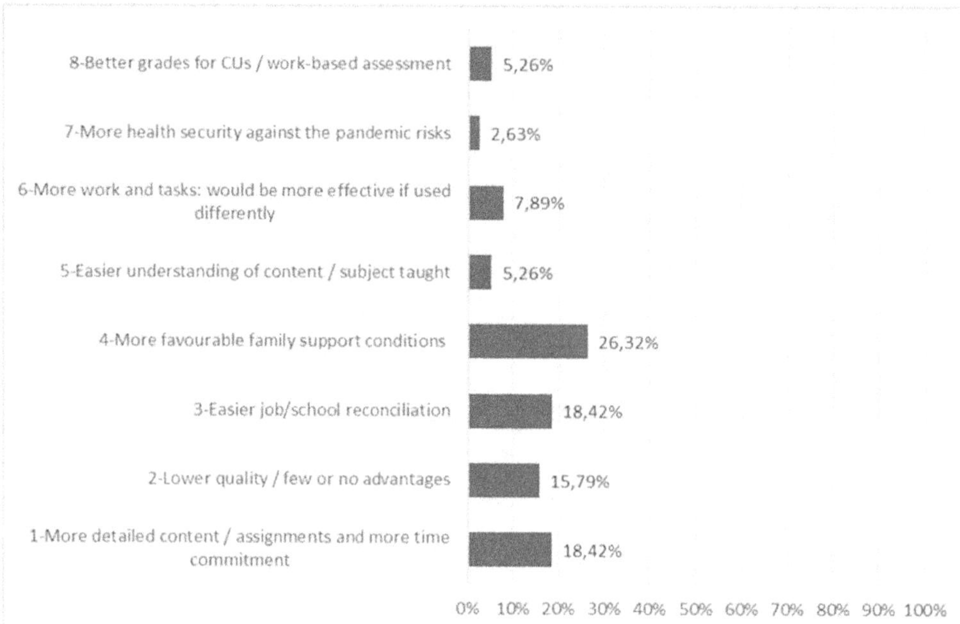

Figure 10. Word cloud from the advantages of online learning
Source: IPP (2020), (self elaboration)

Figure 11. Difficulties in online learning
Source: IPP (2020), (self elaboration)

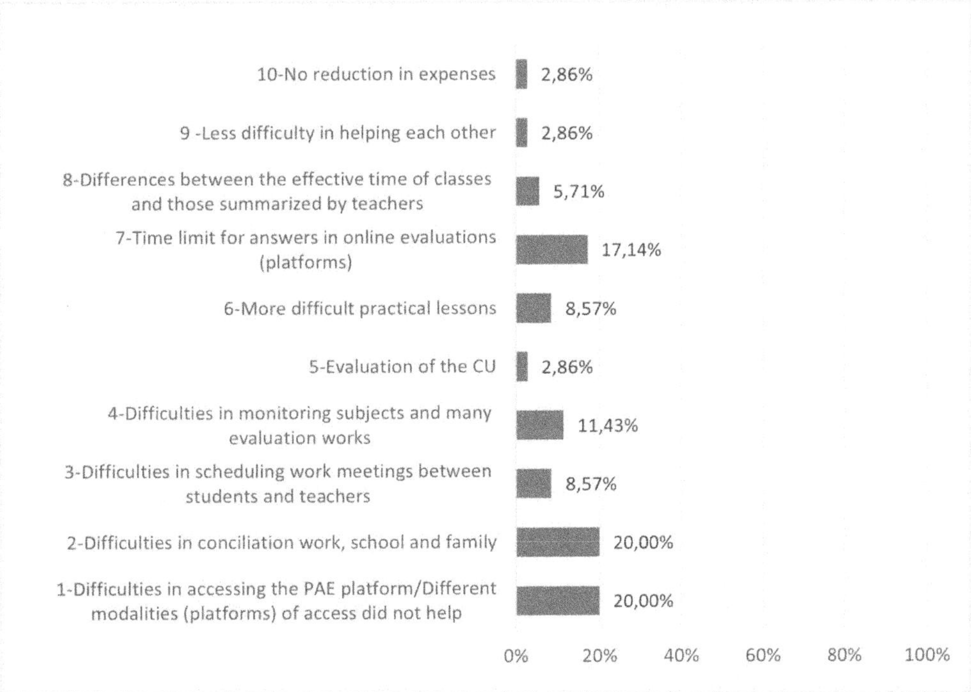

presented above, now focused specifically on aspects related to the different modalities of evaluation of the learnings.

The connections between the categories of these two questions are presented in the next Pathfinder Associative Network (Figure 13), representing the connections between the categories of the open question regarding comments, opinions and improvements, and the categories of the question concerning the aspects that justify the fact that consider that the distance learning modality did not go in a positive way.

With the observation of this network, the association that students establish between the "improvements in the platform / reduction of jobs and online assessments / reviewing assessment models of the CU / meeting schedules" and the different categories of the question related to the less well achieved aspects within the scope is evident. the practice of distance learning. These students present, above all, situations related to pedagogical effectiveness, with the adequacy of teaching practices, with deficits in motivation and / or interaction, with the emergence of negative factors such as stress and / or inadequacy and also with the evaluation criteria defined in this modality.

There is also a connection between the "teacher training on online learning" and the adequacy with teaching practices and the volume of work, which may suggest that students consider it necessary to have teacher training at the level of the teaching modality a distance so that they can develop appropriate practices with an equally adequate workload.

As an extension of the previous analysis, it was also sought to deepen the connections between the comments, opinions and improvements suggested by the students and the categories of the question related to the aspects that may justify the inadequacy of the evaluation system in online learning. The Pathfinder Associative Network, shown in Figure 14, reveals the connections between these two variables.

Figure 12. Word cloud from the difficulties in online learning
Source: IPP (2020), (self elaboration)

In the observation of the previous figure, it can be seen that the category "improvements to the platform / reduction of jobs and online assessments / reviewing CU assessment models / meeting schedules" is the one that most establishes connections with categories of the other issue under analysis, namely, "criteria evaluation","evaluation accessibility","evaluation modalities "and" articulation of the practical component with the E@D (online learning)".

These connections suggest that students who demonstrate aspects related to the platform and pedagogical questions that involve evaluation associate, in their answers, situations related to evaluation (modalities, accessibility and criteria) and also with the articulation of the practical component.

On the other hand, it is possible to note that students who referred to situations related to the assessment modalities present, in their response reports, situations related to the preference for face-to-face teaching, the need for teacher training in the area of online learning and the existence of disadvantages in this modality.

CONCLUSION

The experience of online learning prepared in a short period of time and implemented in a transversal way to the various schools and curricular units of the different study cycles at the Polytechnic of Portalegre, paid off, in general, in a positive way, having obtained a globally favorable appraisal by the student

Figure 13. Connections between comments, opinions and improvements **and the less positive aspects of online learning**
Source: IPP (2020), (self elaboration)

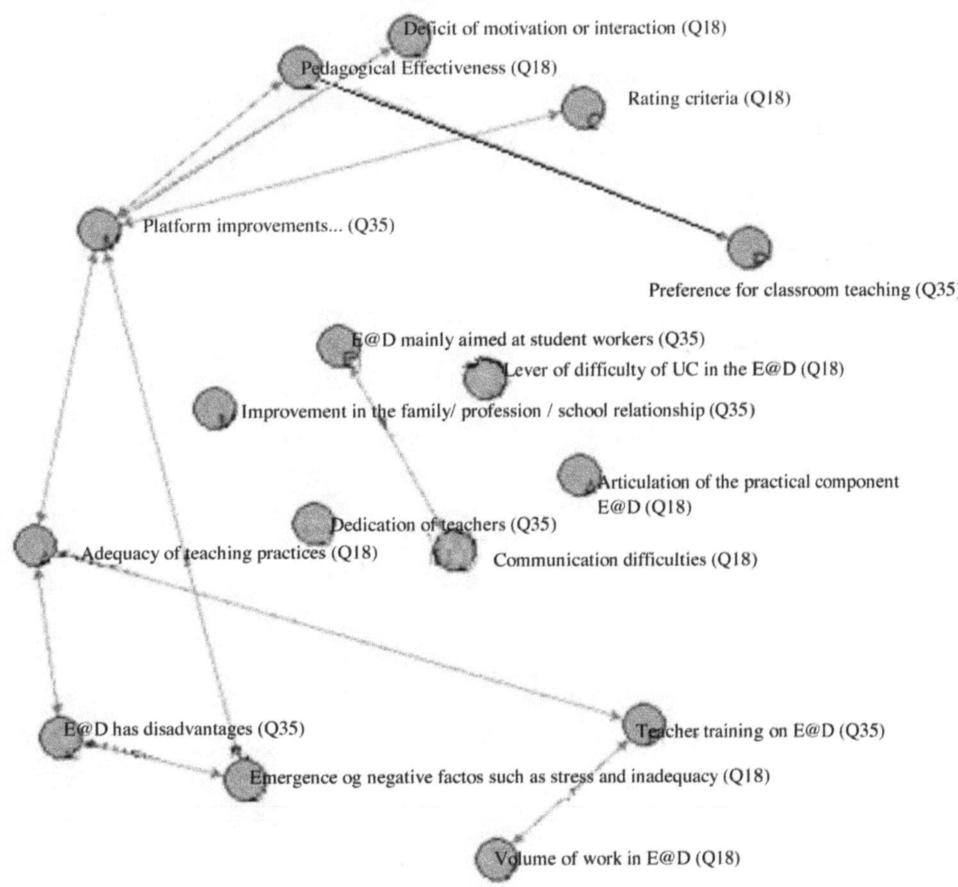

body, although there were slightly different values between the four schools of the Polytechnic, without prejudice to maintaining an overall positive evaluation in all of them (always above 75%), directed at the online learning process implemented in this higher education institution.

However, this reading with a positive scope should not overlook a set of equally relevant aspects, signaled by the students, regarding the less well-succeeded situations, resulting from the somewhat "compulsive" experience, generated by external factors related to the pandemic caused by COVID19, and which motivated the implementation of online learning at the Polytechnic of Portalegre.

The results of the present study, overall, are in line with the aspects highlighted in the literature on distance learning modality. Similarly to what happened to other institutions, namely in what was evidenced by the International Association of Universities (IAU, 2020), also the Polytechnic Institute of Portalegre was able to put into operation the distance learning modality in an emergency situation, demonstrating the flexibility with which the institution was able to adapt to an innovative and different teaching and learning process. Despite this globally positive assessment by the students of the Polytechnic Institute

Figure 14. Connections between comments, opinions and improvements and the justifying aspects of a possible inadequacy of the evaluation system in online learning
Source: IPP (2020), (self elaboration)

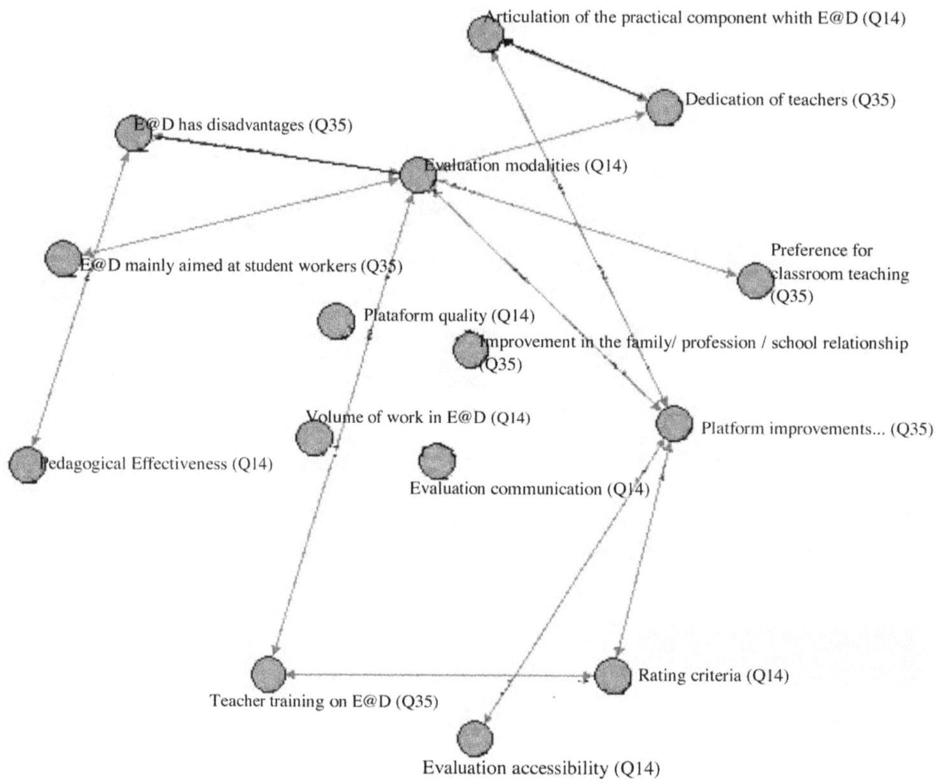

of Portalegre, some less positive aspects were identified in the teaching and learning process, such as, for example, the difficulty in managing the autonomous working time in the different CUs, a situation also described by Aucejo et al. (2020), and also identified by Mussio (2020) as one of the disadvantages of the distance learning process. Difficulties related to technical aspects such as computer means and tools are also mentioned by Mussio (2020), this being a sensitive issue revealed by the results of our study, which suggests the need for improvement of this type of conditions whose access also reverts to a reflection to be made in terms of equity. Evaluation and the need to improve evaluation methodologies is an aspect that also merited the attention of the students and that is highlighted in the study developed by Martínez (2017).

Although the students of the Polytechnic Institute of Portalegre defend the prevalence of the face-to-face teaching modality, some of them accept a combined modality with the distance learning modality, in very particular and complementary situations, something which is corroborated by Baloran (2020) who, in his work, mentions that this type of methodology can help to improve the resources and the competencies of students and professors regarding the use of computer resources and equipment.

Indeed, despite the global perception expressed by students converging towards a favorable appreciation across the entire process, several calls for attention stand out that invite a more careful and in-depth reflection on the part of the academic community, including students, professors and leaders of the HEI.

Among the various conclusions that can be drawn from the data obtained, there is one in particular that stands out and is clearly expressed in the cloud of problems generated from an open question to students (see figure 2) and that underlines the preference for the face-to-face process of the admission process, teaching and learning, not concealing the use of online learning, as long as it is assumed in a perspective of complementarity to face-to-face teaching.

This position, expressed by the student body of the Polytechnic of Portalegre, translates, in a synthetic way, the central importance that is recognized to classroom teaching, even though online learning has been globally valued, even for the commitment, dedication and professionalism that the institution and their professors impressed this experience, as evidenced by the opinions expressed by the students involved in the study.

The results obtained suggest a set of tips for reflection that invite a broad debate on online learning as a pedagogical innovation in HEIs. For this broad debate, other educational agents and protagonists involved in online learning should be involved, including professors, leaders and pedagogues, with a view to an in-depth analysis of the real place and impact of online learning strategies and modalities in the context of teaching higher education in general and polytechnic higher education in particular.

This debate should be oriented, not so much towards future punctual and similar responses as the one described here (as a result of an experience carried out in a particular HEI), but, above all, towards the construction of a broader and more politically assumed strategy as possible and true teaching alternative, within a broader framework of pedagogical innovation that is desired for higher education today, attentive and sensitive to the imperatives of social and cultural change that characterize contemporary societies in general and the educational and training sphere in particular.

Bearing in mind that, to date, there are not many studies and reflections of a scientific nature centered on experiences and online learning motivated by a process of rapid change in teaching and learning practices (MEC, 2015), following the pandemic COVID19, the case study presented shows that, although the data point to a positive evaluation of this experience within the scope of this HEI in Portugal, it is debatable whether it truly fits the theoretical assumptions inherent to a true pedagogical innovation. In fact, the information collected and the description of the process carried out tends to be closer than we can call "remote emergency teaching", although it is relevant to point out a set of progress, experienced by students and teachers, in what it respects, for example, the greater and better use of digital resources at the service of teaching and learning, essential aspects for a true and continuous process of pedagogical innovation within the higher education institutions.

REFERENCES

Alves, J. E., Proença, A., Martins, A., Veríssimo, S., Mourato, I., & Morgado, H. (2021). *Distance Learning as pedagogical innovation. Evaluation of a recente practice in Polytechnic Institute of Portalegre* [Paper presentation]. V International Forum on Management: Connected in a Multipolar world - Everything becomes smart and digital, Instituto Politécnico de Setúbal. http://ifm2021.esce.ips.pt/pt/proceedings

Aucejo, E. M., French, J., Araya, M. P., & Zafar, B. (2020, November). The impacto f COVID-19 on student experiences and expectations: Evidence from a survey. *Journal of Public Economics*, *191*, 104271. doi:10.1016/j.jpubeco.2020.104271 PMID:32873994

Baloran, E. T. (2020). Knowledge, Attitudes, Anxiety, and Coping Strategies of Studentes during COVID-19 Pandemic. *Journal of Loss and Trauma*, *25*(8), 635–642. doi:10.1080/15325024.2020.1769300

Bao, W. (2020). COVID-19 and online teaching in higher education: A case study of Peking University. *Human Behavior and Emerging Technologies*, *2*(2), 113–115. doi:10.1002/hbe2.191 PMID:32510042

Conselho Nacional de Educação. (2019). *Estado da Educação 2018.* Lisboa: Conselho Nacional de Educação. https://www.cnedu.pt/content/edicoes/estado_da_educacao/Estado_da_Educacao2018_web_26nov2019.pdf

Flores, M. A., Veiga Simão, A. M., Barros, A., Flores, P., Pereira, D., Lopes Fernandes, E., Costa Ferreira, P., & Costa, L. (2021). Ensino e aprendizagem à distância em tempos de COVID-19: Um estudo com alunos do Ensino Superior. *Revista Portuguesa de Pedagogia*, *55*, e055001. doi:10.14195/1647-8614_55_1

Grilo, E. M. (2020). *Não tenham medo do futuro. Ideias para o desenvolvimento de Portugal. As novas oportunidades e desafios do nosso país*. Clube do Autor.

Hadar, L. L., Ergas, O., Alpert, B., & Ariav, T. (2020). Rethinking teacher education in a VUCA world: Student teachers' social-emotional competencies during the Covid-19 crisis. *European Journal of Teacher Education*, *43*(4), 573–586. doi:10.1080/02619768.2020.1807513

Instituto Politécnico de Portalegre. (2020). *Ensino a Distância no Politécnico de Portalegre. Resultados do questionário dirigido aos estudantes*. Relatório final, Observatório Académico, Portalegre: Dezembro.

International Association of Universities. (2020). *Regional/National Perspectives on the Impacto of COVID-19 on Higher Education.* Consultado em 18 de novembro de 2021 em https://www.iau-aiu.net/IMG/pdf/iau_covid-19_regional_perspectives_on_the_impact_of_covid-19_on_he_july_2020_.pdf

International Association of Universities & Erasmus Student Network. (2020). *Joint paper: IAU and ESN COVID-19 impact on Higher Education: Institutionak and Students' Perspectives.* Consultado em 18 de novembro de 2021 em https://www.iau-aiu.net/IMG/pdf/joint_paper_iau_and_esn_-_institutional_and_students_perspectives_of_covid-19_impact_on_higher_education.pdf

Kidd, W., & Murray, J. (2020). The Covid-19 pandemic and its effects on teacher education in England: How teacher educators moved practicum learning online. *European Journal of Teacher Education*, *43*(4), 542–558. doi:10.1080/02619768.2020.1820480

la Velle, L., Newman, S., Montgomery, C., & Hyatt, D. (2020). Initial teacher education in England and the Covid-19 pandemic: Challenges and opportunities. *Journal of Education for Teaching*, *46*(4), 596–608. Advance online publication. doi:10.1080/02607476.2020.1803051

Lim, M. (2020). *Educating despite the Covid-19 outbreak: Lessons from Singapore*. The World University Rankings. Consultado em 18 de novembro de 2021 em https://www.timeshighereducation.com/blog/educating-despite-covid-19-outbreak-lessons-singapore

Major, C. (2020). Innovations in Teaching and Learning during a Time of Crisis. *Innovative Higher Education, 45*(4), 265–266. doi:10.100710755-020-09514-w PMID:32836726

Martínez, V. (2017). Educación presencial versus educación a distancia. *La Cuestión Universitaria, 9*, 108–116.

MEC – Ministério de Educação e Ciência. (2015). *Experiências de Inovação Didática no Ensino Superior*. Lisboa: Setembro.

Mishra, L., Gupta, T., & Shree, A. (2020). Online Teaching-Learning in Higher Education during Lockdown Period of COVID-19 Pandemic. *International Journal of Educational Research Open, 1*, 100012. Advance online publication. doi:10.1016/j.ijedro.2020.100012 PMID:35059663

Moreira, J., Henriques, S., Barros, D., Goulão, M. F., & Caeiro, D. (2020). *Educação Digital em Rede: Princípios para o design pedagógico em tempos de pandemia*. Universidade Aberta.

Mussio, S. (2020). Reflexões sobre as modalidades de estudo na educação a distância: Benefícios e limitações. *Revista EDaPECI São Cristóvão (SE), 20*(1), 119–129. doi:10.29276/redapeci.2020.20.112187.119-129

Osman, M. E. (2020). Global impacto f COVID-19 on education systems: The emergency remote teaching and Sultam Qaboos University. *Journal of Education for Teaching, 46*(4), 463–471. doi:10.1080/02607476.2020.1802583

Quezada, R. L., Talbot, C., & Quezada-Parker, Q. B. (2020). From Bricks and Mortar to Remote Teaching: A Teacher education Programme's Response to COVID-19. *Journal of Education for Teaching, 46*(4), 472–483. doi:10.1080/02607476.2020.1801330

Rumbley, L. (2020). *Coping with COVID-19: International higher education in Europe. European Association for International Education*. Acedido em 18 novembro de 2021 em https://eaie.org/our-resources/library/publication/Research-and-trends/Coping-with-COVID-19-International-higher-education-in-Europe.html

Salum, M., Gomes, M. & Ramires, D. (2018). As desvantagens do ensino à distância para curso de graduação em Direito. *Revista Electrónica Científica da FAESB, 1*(5), 135-150.

Unesco. (2020). *Suspensão das aulas e resposta à COVID19. Unesco - Organização das Nações Unidas para a Educação, a Ciência e a Cultura*. Acedido em 15 outubro de 2020 em https://unesdoc.unesco.org/ark:/48223/pf0000373305_por

Veríssimo, S., Godinho, V., Casas, L., & Luengo, R. (2017). Evaluation of Changes in Cognitive Structures after the Learning Process in Mathematics. *International Journal of Innovation in Science and Mathematics Education, 25*(2), 17–33. https://openjournals.library.sydney.edu.au/index.php/CAL/article/download/11295/11122

Chapter 10
Preparing Managers to Lead for Diversity, Equity, and Inclusion

Veronica Keiffer-Lewis
Allied Path Consulting, LLC, USA

Jude Berman
Allied Path Consulting, LLC, USA

ABSTRACT

The psychological theories of leadership have a great deal to offer today's organizational leaders. Four of these theories—transactional, transformational, authentic, and servant leadership—are complementary in style, aiming to serve the self-actualization of employees as well as the greater good of the organization. This chapter explores the similarities and differences between these leadership styles, as well as the strengths and weaknesses of their basic principles and assumptions, especially as pertains to the work of diversity, equity, and inclusion (DEI) practitioners in educational settings. This chapter examines the benefits of integrating these theories, along with some newer and lesser-known theories, into a multimodal approach that can be effective for managers coaching team members toward greater organizational equity. A brief case comparison illustrates how the principles of DEI leadership can be applied.

INTRODUCTION

Interest in leaders as well as in leadership styles, approaches, and personal traits continues to draw attention across the behavioral and social sciences. However, leadership is not solely the interest of academics; indeed, a quick Google search of the term leadership results in some 200 possible definitions. One definition of leadership frequently referenced in the literature is by Northouse (2019), who said that "leadership is a process whereby an individual influences a group of individuals to achieve a common goal" (p. 5). With this definition in mind, much investigation has taken place to uncover the best processes for influencing individuals, as well as ways leaders can identify common goals and strategies for bringing out the best in others, while creating as little interpersonal harm as possible. Moreover, the

DOI: 10.4018/978-1-7998-8239-8.ch010

hunger for ethical and authentic leaders is widespread, especially considering the continuing distrust in and dissatisfaction with—as well as corruption among—many of today's leaders (Covelli & Mason, 2017). However, despite this high level of general interest in the development of good leadership, while surveying the literature related specifically to answering the question of what style of leadership is best for organizational change aimed at facilitating diversity and equity within institutions of higher learning, Adserias et al. (2017) found that little such direct research has been conducted. It is currently unclear what link, if any, exists between different leadership styles and the effectiveness of diversity agenda implementation.

What leadership is and what makes a good leader remain critical questions, especially as pertains to the work of diversity, equity, and inclusion (DEI) practitioners in educational and managerial settings. This chapter seeks to examine four approaches to leadership that center on ethical, just, and inclusive leadership behaviors: transactional, transformational, authentic, and servant leadership. A definition, core assumptions, and principles are provided for each theory, concluding with a discussion about their cultural considerations and relevance to DEI practitioners. The chapter does not provide an exhaustive review of these leadership theories; rather, the focus is on key concepts and linkages to inclusion and on their potential for individual, institutional, and broader social transformation. The authors make the case that, when integrated with several additional relevant theoretical approaches, these theories have the potential to serve as a diversity-centered, equity-advancing, inclusive approach to managerial leadership and leadership development.

The first author draws on close to three decades of facilitation, professional coaching, action research, and field study specializing in DEI leadership; management communication; and group dynamics. Her field research on leading for equity provides the theoretical underpinnings for this chapter. She posits that equity leadership theory has a vibrant role to play in the development of a more radically inclusive managerial style, one that incorporates other humanistic, people-centered, and empowerment models of management. This new conceptual framework leaves room for team-based operationalization that meets teams where they are (i.e., not a one-size-fits-all approach), while highlighting best or promising practices in equity leadership. The objectives of this chapter are (a) to provide an overview of the relevant existing leadership approaches, (b) to propose a multimodal approach to DEI leadership that integrates the best aspects of the existing approaches, and (c) to briefly illustrate what such a DEI leadership approach might look like when managers apply it as a tool for coaching leaders toward organizational equity.

THEORETICAL OVERVIEW OF LEADERSHIP

Leadership definitions, theories, and approaches abound. In a literature review on leadership theories and styles, for example, Khan et al. (2016) highlighted the following seven theories that have shaped many corresponding leadership frameworks: (a) great-man theory, (b) trait theory, (c.) contingency theories (situational), (d) style and behavior theory, (e) process leadership theory, (f) transactional theory, and (g) transformational theory. These authors also supplied a comparative analysis of transformational leadership and transactional leadership theories. Northouse (2019) mentioned as many as 65 classifications systems used over the decades to define leadership styles.

In the behavioral and social sciences, theories can be used to shape ideas and observations into research questions that can be tested and proved or disproved. Sole and Landrum (2016) further explained the importance of theories in general as follows:

Theories serve several useful functions in thinking about meaningful patterns of behavior. First, theories help us organize the results of numerous studies. Tens of thousands of journal articles are published each year, and these articles contribute to our knowledge of human behavior. Theories help to organize these findings into more coherent groups of ideas. Second, theories often stimulate others to do research. (sec. 3.2)

In addition, and perhaps more importantly, theories help people make sense of the world and give researchers ideas about where to begin their search for truth, facts, correlations, and cause and effect. Theories on leadership are not different from theories in general; they try to explain the nature of how to develop a leader, what makes a good leader, how leaders motivate workers, and more. Finally, theories matter to psychologists seeking to understand human dynamics, which have real-world implications for leadership development.

Four Main Theories of Leadership

While there are numerous theories of leadership, this chapter focuses on four well-known theories the authors have determined to have the greatest relevance for preparing managers to lead for DEI: transactional leadership, transformational leadership, authentic leadership, and servant leadership.

Transactional Leadership

Transactional leadership is a highly structured, directive-oriented, and outcome-driven leadership style. Transactional leadership theory "is that in which leader-follower associations were grounded upon a series of agreements between followers and leaders" (House & Shamir, 1993, as quoted in Khan et al., 2016, p. 3). These agreements are often thought of as rewards and punishments; however, the process of transactional analysis suggests that transactions are not solely based on extrinsic rewards and punishments but are unique "units of social exchange." Psychologist Eric Berne (1964), the creator of transactional analysis, described the process as follows:

The unit of social intercourse is called a transaction. If two or more people encounter each other… sooner or later one of them will speak, or give some other indication of acknowledging the presence of the others. This is called transactional stimulus. Another person will then say or do something which is in some way related to the stimulus, and that is called the transactional response. (p. 29)

In sum, the stimulus (reward or punishment) is important, but so are the response and overall context of the "social intercourse." This approach also helps participants understand power relationships through ego states, which the transactional analysis lexicon identifies as those of a parent, adult, and child.

Cultural Relevance of Transactional Leadership

According to Berne (1964), the easiest transactions are those that occur between two adult ego states that have shared power; these transactions contrast with the "power over" transactions that characterize an adult-to-child or parent-to-adult social exchange. Transactional analysis can expand the understanding of transactional leadership beyond simple rewards and punishments, providing a useful analysis of social interactions, discourse, and facilitation of transformational possibilities. For example, Ciucur and Pîrvut (2012) studied the effects of a transactional analysis training program for leaders and found an increase in emotional stability and social boldness among teams.

However, some have questioned the cultural relevance and effectiveness of transactional leadership. In his review research, Martin (2020) found that transactional leadership is associated with an approach to diversity that can be described as "conservative multiculturalism, or a culture-deficit approach," which is "characterized by assumptions of one's own cultural superiority and a deficiency in culturally different 'others'" (p. 125). Similarly, Montgomery (2020) equated transactional leadership with "gatekeeping," which is an inherently exclusive intention, and which contrasts with what she terms "groundskeeping-centered leadership." The latter aligns with the framework of transformational leadership. To be effective, she argued, transactional leadership may need to be combined with transformational leadership in a manner that brings forth the strengths of both and that allows practitioners to maintain a focus on the individual drives that are negotiated through social interactions and discourse. Moreover, leaders must determine when transactional engagement is needed and what is the most beneficial way to ease transactions, to stay in alignment with the overarching goal of transformation.

Challenges of Transactional Leadership

In addition to the limitations just mentioned, on challenge of the transactional approach is tailoring transactional engagement to include the beneficial aspects of transactional analysis. According to McCleskey (2014), this approach can produce "shallow, temporary exchanges of gratification and often create resentment between participants" (p. 122). He further explained that while this approach is widely used and has positive attributes (e.g., allowing followers to explore self-interests, strategies for minimizing workplace anxiety, ways to improve organizational efficiency), it falls short in terms of considering important situational and contextual inputs. Thus, to use transactional leadership successfully, leaders must fully address the dehumanizing potential embodied in this leadership style, allowing for more informed and meaningful transactions.

Transformational Leadership

Transformational leadership theory has the potential to change the lives of leaders and of employees, and the overall organizational system. Unlike transactional leadership, it asks that followers move beyond self-interest or organizational goals. Introduced by James MacGregor Burns in the 1970s, this theory postulates that, through positive leadership exchanges centered on inspiration, flexibility, and the creation of a sense of belonging, individuals and the organization can create meaningful cultural change for the benefit of all (Kotlyar & Karakowsky, 2007). When viewed as a continuum, transformational leadership sits on the opposite end from transactional leadership praxis. Looking at the continuum, leaders can reflect on what is the best approach for the team, given the situation, in both the short and long term. In their meta-analysis of leadership styles, Abbas and Ali (2021) found that transformational leadership had a stronger effect on project success than transactional leadership did.

Dittmar (2016) supplied a framework for transformational leadership that consists of the "four I's" (or guiding assumptions): idealized influence, inspirational motivation, intellectual stimulation, and individualized consideration (03:55). Idealized influence and inspirational motivation share commonalities with referent leadership power (Harper, 2015), wherein followers "idealize" the leader and try to emulate that leader's behaviors, attitudes, and so on. Inspirational motivation captures the aspects of charisma, vision, and passion that also characterize referent leadership power. Dittmar described the third "I" (intellectual stimulation) as a sincere interest in and recognition of the skills and abilities of followers (06:24). This leadership factor shares commonalities with expert power in that the leader's knowledge and ability garner respect and power by way of the group's acknowledgment. Thus, when a group has deep respect for the expertise of the leader (e.g., when encouraged to engage, partner, or identify new opportunities and ways to use individual strengths within the team), the transformational leader benefits from the existing commitment and engagement of the group, further solidifying the leader's expert power. Finally, Dittmar summarized the fourth "I" as individual consideration in which the leader wants to know the personal and professional goals, desires, strengths, perspectives, and so on of followers (07:29).

Taken together, these I's and the overall goal of transformational leadership create an exemplary model. Transformational leadership is more than just wielding power and authority; it is a leadership model rooted in the right use of power, for the benefit of the group and the larger good of the organization. Dittmar (2016) further detailed this approach, explaining that this is "a process that changes and transforms people. It is concerned with emotions, values, ethics, standards, and long-term goals, and it includes assessing follower motives satisfying needs and treating them as full human beings" (03:22–41). For these reasons, this leadership theory sets itself apart from other models, especially when viewed as part of a transactional-transformational continuum. At times, transformation is not needed, and a simple transaction is the best approach. Moreover, transformational leadership is not without challenges; it requires authentic care for and commitment to the group, beyond the mere desire to get things done or manipulation disguised as transformation.

Cultural Relevance of Transformational Leadership

Transformational leadership theory shares similarities with both the authentic and servant leadership styles, discussed later in this chapter. Given the many ways these theories overlap, it is important to highlight the unique contributions of the transformational leadership style, while distinguishing the approach from transactional leadership. Brown et al. (2019) framed this distinction by saying that "transformational leaders underscore social justice while transactional leaders favor procedural justice" (p. 12). The assumptions and principles that define transformational leadership align with the commitments of DEI leadership. For example, transformational leadership "seeks to satisfy higher needs… engages the full person… converts followers into leaders and moral agents" (Echols, 2009, p. 94). These guiding principles are also consistent with the commitments of diversity leadership and inclusive leadership. When considering the possibilities of a DEI-centered leadership approach, Chin et al. (2016) argued that "knowing yourself" is important; "to be a leader takes being aware of your surroundings, where you're at, and what people think of you" (sec. 8), which is a guiding premise of transformational leadership.

Casa et al. (2021) conducted a survey of leaders in organization in 77 countries and confirmed the cultural universality of transformational leadership. Both the followers' perceptions of transformational leadership behaviors and their extent of satisfaction derived from those behaviors did not differ across multiple cultures. However, this research did not address the effectiveness of transformational leadership in situations characterized by cultural diversity (i.e., where the leader and followers are from different cultures). According to Khan et al. (2016), transformational leadership presupposes an "alignment with the greater good as it entails involvement of the followers in processes or activities related to personal factor towards the organization and a course that will yield certain superior social dividend" (p. 3). Khan et al. explained that leaders are follower-focused as they "set aside their personal interests for the benefit of the group" (p. 3); look to empower the group; and understand the group's needs, beliefs, values, and goals. In many ways, this type of participatory, strengths-based approach suggests a type of servant leadership, albeit while still staying centered on the goals of the organization at large (Boyum, 2006).

Challenges of Transformational Leadership

Like all leadership theories, transformational leadership is not without challenges. One challenge previously mentioned is that the overarching goal of this approach is the organization's needs rather than the individual needs of those working within the system. Additionally, limited empirical evidence exists on the effect of this approach on groups, teams, and organizations; situational influences; and the "underlying mechanism of leadership influence" (McCleskey, 2014, p. 120).

Authentic Leadership

Authentic leadership falls under the transformational leadership umbrella and offers another means of understanding leadership identity, leader development, and practices that empower others and serve the greater good. While authentic leadership continues to garner vast interest among research scholars, leadership gurus, and organizational systems, a consensus about the definition of authentic leadership as well as the best developmental approach to deepening authentic leadership across the lifespan is still lacking.

To "be authentic" means knowing oneself and acting according to those beliefs, values, morals, and so on—or as Harter (2002) said, "owning one's personal experiences, be they thoughts, emotions, needs, preferences, or beliefs, processes captured by the injunction to know oneself" (p. 382). Authentic leadership rests on the assumption that the leader is starting from a positive psychological disposition. In this regard, positive mental habits of mind include confidence, hope, optimism, and resilience (Northouse, 2019). Moral reasoning is the assumption that authentic leaders strive to "do the right thing" and have an internal moral compass that results in judgments and behaviors that help the greater good, while also inspiring followers' ethical practices and an organizational culture of moral courage (Datta, 2015; Onyalla, 2018). Finally, a guiding assumption of this approach is that personal narratives or life experiences that are processed and integrated make for a more mindful, compassionate, and empathetic leader. In other words, authentic leaders are self-aware and critically reflective; they have taken time to understand and make sense of their lived experiences, which deepens their cultural humility and empathic resolve toward others.

Authentic leadership is further delineated through four primary components: self-awareness, internalized moral perspective, balanced processing, and relational transparency (Avolio et al., 2009). Self-awareness, or the process of deep self-knowing and understanding, is central to the authentic leader and raises the question of what it means to lead from one's authentic self. One way to authentically lead is to invest in self-discovery, based on the assumption that critical life experiences matter and provide filters and schemas for making sense of future experiences and interpersonal engagements. Covelli and Mason (2017) described self-awareness is a skill leaders and followers can learn to engage in, along with emotional self-regulation, unbiased processing or decision making, open communication and transparency, and "action planning" for life-long learning. In these ways, processing life events leads to a moral center or a more authentic self as well as to a clearer understanding of both positive and negative triggers. Without such reflection on the influence of past experiences on self-perception, authentic leaders may not be leading from their most honest, healed, and authentic self.

Northouse (2019) named three developmental perspectives (i.e., intrapersonal, interpersonal, and lifespan development) that are relevant to the principle of self-awareness. These perspectives can inform authentic leadership development by offering a framework to help leaders identify areas of strength and growth. For example, leaders can assess their authentic leadership approach at the intrapersonal level by evaluating their skills and abilities for naming personal values, roles, strategies for deeper self-reflection, and emotional self-regulation. Together, these three developmental perspectives offer a learning pathway for authentic leadership development.

Cultural Relevance of Authentic Leadership

Lee (2017) stated that "issues of identity, diversity, and inclusion are core to … authentic leadership" (p. 349). Carayol (2011) summarized the three essentials of leadership as (a) managing less and leading more, (b) understanding that culture is more powerful than strategy, and (c) understanding that one's heritage is not destiny. The authentic leader is one who understands these essentials fully; the authentic leader stresses leading over managing by focusing on deeper understanding, connections, intrinsic motivations, and doing the right thing. The authentic leader creates a culture of inclusion, trust, and empowerment that supersedes strategic interventions. Trustworthiness has been cited as "an intrinsic feature of authentic leadership" and an antecedent to authenticity (Hassan & Ahmed, 2011, p. 165) and is critical to leading across differences, leader-follower interdependence, and equity work (Chin et al., 2016). Finally, the authentic leader understands and holds past experiences as a guide for future opportunities; authentic leaders are not wed to the past but are open to the future.

Challenges of Authentic Leadership

The authentic approach does not adhere to a specific style of leadership; rather, it encourages leaders to know themselves and their team first, and then to determine which of the styles and approaches feel authentic and workable for the group. Furthermore, this approach recognizes that for leadership to be authentic, individuals must demonstrate mindfulness and intentionally engage from deep self-awareness, personal ethics, positivity, care, flexibility, and an understanding of the real-time context (Covelli & Mason, 2017). Thus, one of the challenges to this approach is the degree to which leaders are being their authentic self rather than claiming authenticity and self-awareness in an effort to connect and manipulate followers. Alvesson and Einola (2019) warned about the pitfall of "excessive positivity" that authentic leadership can generate.

A related challenge of authentic leadership is its working assumption that a leader's internalized moral perspective must be rooted in values, beliefs, morals, and fairness that uphold the greater good and reduce harm. Onyalla (2018) pointed out that one cannot assume that the values, beliefs, and morals of a given leader come from an ethically legitimate perspective. Instead, scholars must define authentic leadership to necessarily mean that a leader's ethical "virtuous acts" refrain from "behaviors that harm others" (p. 7). The same reasoning can be applied to balanced processing. Leaders who seek out differing opinions and who are humble and open to new ideas do so from a place of ethical leadership and not for self-serving outcomes. Finally, according to Onyalla, positive psychological habits of mind are revealed in the act of transparent communication because that act shows openness to reaching out, courage, honesty, and desire to connect with others—all of which require confidence, optimism, and trust in others. Thus, the challenge is to determine what is driving the leader's process, behaviors, and decisions—that is, to determine if the leadership decisions come from positive or negative intentions.

Servant Leadership

Servant leadership, which holds parallels to transformational leadership, is a term coined by Robert Greenleaf in 1970. The Center for Servant leadership (n.d.) described the theory:

A servant-leader focuses primarily on the growth and well-being of people and the communities to which they belong. While traditional leadership generally involves the accumulation and exercise of power by one at the "top of the pyramid," servant leadership is different. The servant-leader shares power and puts the needs of others first and helps people develop and perform as highly as possible. (para 4)

The following underlying assumptions of the servant leadership theory were identified by Greenleaf (1977): (a) the leader desires to serve the follower first; (b) the servant leader ensures the needs of others are the highest priority, before the organization; (c) success is determined by the health, satisfaction, self-efficacy, and work autonomy demonstrated by the follower; and finally (d) followers seek to be of service as they become leaders, maintaining the focus on serving others (p. 13). In the video Ten Leadership Theories in Five Minutes, Zigarelli (2013) explained further that:

Servant leadership theory, which is kind of a blend between transformational and transactional leadership. Boiled down to its essentials, it says that if a leader makes a priority of identifying and meeting followers' needs—serving rather than being served—that leader creates an environment of trust and cooperation and reciprocal service... and ultimately higher performance.... People follow out of love and gratitude rather than out of compulsion or fear. (04:16–52)

Boyum (2006) described this approach as rooted in the "process of serving" others in ways that elevate the followers' "esteem, self-fulfillment and self-actualization" (p. 3). She said the fundamental principles guiding this approach include addressing social disparities, serving the follower from an innate desire or calling, meeting the individual needs of others over the organization's needs (a critical distinction from transformational leadership), in addition to a willingness to "act" in service and a commitment to relationship trust (p. 2). Boyum went on to explain that, in part, the inspiration for the development of this approach was Greenleaf's (1977) belief that leadership was in "crisis" due to the humanist movement (p. 5).

Although Greenleaf (1977) might have resisted the humanist movement, his approach shared a similar goal: self-actualization, or meeting one's highest potential. Self-actualization, a concept put forward by Abraham Maslow, was very influential in understanding both personal and professional development, along with human motivation (Leahey, 2014, p. 76). Similarly, Carl Rogers and other psychologists looking to center the client, follower, or individual held perspectives that seem congruent with Greenleaf's theory of servant leadership. Zigarelli (2013) explained that servant leadership is a people-centered approach and underscores the importance of trust, empathy, and authentic care for employees: "Servant leadership theory... says that if a leader makes a priority of identifying and meeting followers' needs—serving rather than being served—that leader creates an environment of trust and cooperation and reciprocal service... and ultimately higher performance" (04:16-04:52). Echols (2009) added that servant leadership creates a "synergy" in which those the leader serves (e.g., employees) feel more connected, safe, and endeared to the leader, resulting in increased motivation, productivity, and morale (p. 97).

Servant leadership also has the potential for enhancing meaningful work, which is a strong motivational factor. Van Wingerden and Stoep (2018) found that the belief in and experience of doing meaningful work is related to increased use of strengths, engagement, and high performance, including guarding against burnout, while adding to a sense of well-being. The meaningful-work theory, taken together with research on human emotional drives and motivation, provides a holistic approach to a grounded transformational servant-leadership model. Lee and Raschke summarized the human drives theory of motivation, saying, "Lawrence and Nohria (2002) propose the 'human drive' theory, which states that employees are guided by four basic emotional drives that are a product of common human evolutionary heritage: the drives to acquire, bond, comprehend, and defend" (p. 165). In fact, determining what followers need, and how best to meet those needs, becomes a challenge for the servant leader.

Cultural Relevance of Servant Leadership

Servant leadership offers a valuable multi-modal approach to leading that, regardless of Greenleaf's (1977) assertions, sheds light on humanism, existentialism, and transpersonal psychological perspectives. Early (n.d.) explained that the servant leadership approach, which grew out the contingency theory movement (1967–1990), was one of the few approaches that continues with great interest and applicability (para. 10). Early further pointed out that one of the components of this approach is the desire of the leader to serve followers as a means of "empowering them to live and work to their full potential" (para. 11). In the words of Nart et al, (2018), "The servant leader serves his followers without discriminating based on language, religion, race, color and gender. In this direction, servant leadership understanding is the most appropriate leadership style for the spirit of management of diversities" (p. 34).

Challenges of Servant Leadership

Eaton (2020) offered a feminist critique of servant leadership. While acknowledging the altruistic orientation of servant leadership, she pointed to the "undeniable power, control, and injustice issues embedded in service," which tends to be overlooked by scholars in the field. Her critique centered on the negative connotation of "servant" to those for whom it equates with "servitude" and evokes oppression, poverty, and inequity.

ADDITIONAL THEORIES OF LEADERSHIP

In addition to the preceding four theories, several less widely known theoretical orientations are more specifically relevant to a DEI leadership framework: equity leadership theory, radical inclusion, and inclusive leadership.

Equity Leadership

Equity leadership theory was introduced by John S. Adams in 1963 and argues that fairness is essential to employees' motivation and overall satisfaction (MindTools, n.d.). Equity leadership ensures fairness and justice, which requires courageous dialogues, reflective inquiry, and awareness of systems oppression. Equity leaders look to meet people where they are and to address inequities in all their forms. They listen deeply and strive to understand. Equity leadership suggests that to develop a harmonious and mutually beneficial workforce, employers must ensure balance between inputs and outputs. In short, when employees feel respected, valued, and treated fairly, they are more productive, motivated, and happy.

Radical Inclusion

Radical inclusion was popularized by Dempsey and Brafman (2018) as a style of leadership that de-emphasizes the leader and stresses the need for power sharing, trust, and confidence building among followers and participants. This approach can also be seen as an extension of equity leadership that aims to create a more equitable workplace for all. Rhodes (2019) contrasted radical inclusion with radical exclusion, whereby the former is characterized by "Workplace protections from harassment, bullying, discrimination and violence…. [A] collaborative process….. Equal compensation….[Respect] and [value] for the differences you bring that make the organization stronger, [and] set up to succeed in your role by receiving sponsorship to advance in the organization" (para 6). Leaders who practice radical inclusion are committed to everyone a workplace environment feeling culturally safe, heard, supported, and affirmed.

Inclusive Leadership

Inclusive leadership has been described by Echols (2009) as a complementary outgrowth of the transformational and servant leadership styles. He distinguishes inclusive leaders from participative leaders, in that the former are proactively alert to the potential marginalization of any participants, whereas the latter merely seek to get participants involved. As described by Wuffli (2016), inclusive leadership has four main principles: it is dynamic and change oriented, horizontal, holistic and broadly applicable, and explicitly normative (p. 3). Notably not all discussion of inclusive leadership theory places it in the context of DEI initiatives (Roberson & Perry, 2021). Bourke and Titus (2020) conducted research in diverse workplaces and found that inclusive leaders had six traits: visible commitment, humility, awareness of bias, curiosity about others, cultural intelligence, and effective collaboration. They concluded that "while all six traits are important and operate as a cluster, a leader's awareness of personal and organizational biases is the number one factor" (para 5).

DEVELOPING A DEI LEADERSHIP FRAMEWORK

Existing widely known and accepted leadership theories (e.g., transactional, transformational, authentic, and servant leadership) that center on understanding individual team members' drives and providing authentic care, compassion, and a sense of belonging aim to increase the probability of more successfully attending to individual needs. When individual team members' needs are met, their feelings and needs are affirmed, and their work is valued (i.e., seen and experienced as meaningful), they do better on the job. They go to work as full, complex human beings with feelings, needs, and desires. Good leaders do their best to understand the individual and collective drives of their team; they communicate the value and meaningfulness of each person's contribution or work, while themselves staying humble, inspirational, compassionate, and genuinely open to new possibilities. However, these existing leadership theories have not necessarily been applied to and evaluated in the field in an integrated manner. More importantly for the purposes of this chapter, they have not necessarily been applied to DEI leadership. While DEI trainings and DEI education efforts in general have proliferated over the past decade plus (Johnson-Mallard et al., 2019), the specific focus of DEI leadership has been notably lacking.

Among the few existing approaches to DEI leadership development is the competency model for diversity and inclusion practitioners (Lahiri, 2008). This model includes leveraging personal and social identities, using a global and diverse mindset, leveraging community and organizational contexts, and promoting a diversity-supporting and inclusive climate. These competencies appear when identifying the barriers or challenges that those with multiple marginalized identities navigate when leading in organizations. In other words, participants experience challenges when working in an organizational culture that does not recognize or value intersectionality; cultivate or apply a global and diverse mindset; recognize the influence of history and context on relationships and job performance; and celebrate or promote diverse ways of knowing, offering support, or creating a sense of inclusive belonging.

As an equity practitioner with close to 30 years of experience and field study, the first author found that highly effective and inclusive teams can be cultivated through a DEI leadership model that successful integrates relevant approaches. Such inclusive leadership, which is rooted in leveraging diversity and advancing equity, is not only a career choice but a way of being in the world. Thus, leading for equity transcends the workplace and career objectives and instead aims for the creation of new healing human interactions and social transformation. Although this might not be every leader's goal, it is the authors' goal in arguing for an inclusive leadership framework.

Figure 1 is a visual map of the diversity-centered, equity-advancing, and inclusive approach to leadership proposed in this chapter. All of the theoretical approaches discussed are incorporated. Note that the transactional component has been subsumed under transformational leadership.

CASE COMPARISON

With the intention of better integrating the various relevant leadership approaches, the authors conducted a case comparison that looked at two different management models: (a) the DEI leadership model and (b) conflict coaching and mediation support.

Grounded theory was employed in the analysis because it allows for the uncovering of new information or knowledge from data, which can then guide new theoretical considerations (Smith, 1999). Smith identified some of the benefits of grounded theory in conjunction with oral history. First, the phenomenon under investigation (i.e., in this case, cultural humility development) remains primary, allowing the researcher to honor the fact that reality is always much more complex than the data collected. Second, this approach appreciates that the researcher provides a unique perspective through which the data are viewed. Third, this approach is developmental, inviting interpretations "from the beginning of the project, not from an arbitrary point 'after' the data have been collected" (p. 8). For these reasons, grounded theory is uniquely suited to help make sense of case studies.

The following case examples were taken from leadership management training sessions. The managers in both cases were working for small to mid-size nonprofit social justice and educational equity advocacy organizations. In both cases, the managers were supervising team members who were working directly with educational institutions, legislatures, and their constituents in the field. Manager 1 received direct training and coaching on DEI leadership, while manager 2 opted out of the training and received

Figure 1. The DEI Leadership Framework

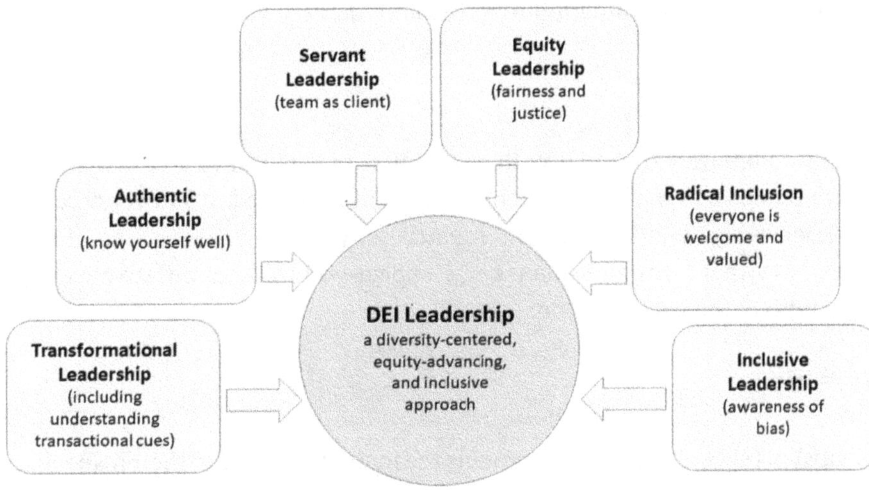

only conflict coaching and mediation support. Both managers self-identified as White women in their late 30s to early 40s and had similar educational backgrounds and family compositions. Both managers supervised small teams of no more than four people, all of whom identified as people of color (POCs) within their organization or as women of color.

The following case snapshots were taken from in-person or virtual coaching sessions and debrief meetings in which managers met with team members. They are organized under three of the theoretical themes that contribute to the DEI leadership framework proposed in this chapter: servant leadership, equity leadership, and radical inclusion.

Servant Leadership

In the first set of snapshots, the first manager (i.e., the DEI manager) exhibits servant leadership by listening to and attending to the needs of the team member. She makes the team member's needs her highest priority, even if it will mean extra work for herself going forward. She puts herself on level with (thus "serving") the team member by suggesting they redo the evaluation together, working as equals. In contrast, the other manager says she "understands," but her tone and explanation put the full onus for correcting the situation on the team member. Even though both team members ask their managers for support, only the DEI manager offers it.

Snapshot 1

Team Member 1: My annual evaluation said I'm not meeting the organizations performance standards. I am a first-generation professional and asked for mentoring, which was promised to me when hired but I haven't received any help.

Manager 1: [kindly] I understand your frustration and as your new manager, I will make sure you receive mentoring and coaching. I want you to excel and not feel pressure to perform to someone else's standards; let's redo your annual evaluation together and identify your strengths and growth areas.

Snapshot 2

Team Member 2: I completely disagree with my annual evaluation that says I am not performing to expectations. I have requested coaching, which was promised to me but I never received any support.

Manager 2: [defensively] I understand, but regardless, you know your scope of work and what you are expected to do. Now that I am your manager, I expect you to take initiative to improve your work and meet the expectations for your position.

Equity Leadership

These next two snapshots show follow-up comments the managers made to their respective team members in the previous snapshots. The DEI manager responds by focusing on the equity issues she perceives as salient to this team member. She offers to engage in an open dialogue and expresses her awareness of systems oppression. She attempts to meet the team member where they are—including the possibility they are not comfortable proceeding with the conversation—and to do her best to address any inequities. In contrast, manager 2 stresses the team member's discomfort, in effect blaming that individual for it. Her apology comes across as insincere since she does not offer support, but instead shifts the responsibility for support to others. She does not appear to be motivated by an interest in promoting fairness and justice with her team member.

Snapshot 1

Manager 1: [supportively] You said that you are a first-generation professional, can you tell me more about that experience? I am aware that as a White woman I might be having a quite different experience in our organization. I want to make sure I understand your experience and any issues you're facing so I can support you. Are you comfortable with having this conversation?

Snapshot 2

Manager 2: [dismissively] You have mentioned on several occasions that you feel isolated and unsupported as a woman of color in our organization. I'm sorry you feel that way… Maybe you can join the diversity committee. They meet at lunch and it will not interfere with your work.

Radical Inclusion

The final set of snapshots focuses on discussions the team members had with their manager about another individual on their respective teams. The DEI manager demonstrates radical inclusion by asking to hear more and to work toward a solution for this gender equity issue. Her words convey a commitment to having everyone in their workplace environment feel culturally safe, heard, supported, and affirmed. In contrast, manager 2 is dismissive of the race equity issue the team member has brought to her attention.

By insisting the third individual bring any issue to her directly, she discourages radical inclusion and instead asserts the power dynamic of her leadership role.

Snapshot 1

Team Member 1: I wanted to tell you that [one of our team members] is not feeling comfortable at our staff meetings because he feels you focus more on what the women are saying and never really include him. I told him it was safe to talk to you about it but he's afraid of ramifications. He said I could talk to you about what I am experiencing, and I have noticed it myself.

Manager 1: [disappointedly and curiously] Thank you for bringing this to attention. I am so sad to hear this and want to stay open to your experiences and not get defensive. Can you tell me more? I would also like to hear any ideas you have for how I can change this dynamic. However, I don't want you to feel that you have to teach me or fix this; I will definitely do my personal work and come up with some new meeting strategies.

Snapshot 2

Team Member 2: I think you should know that [one of our team members] feels like an outsider in our meetings. She doesn't feel like you respect her input because she's a POC and admin, and you don't seem to ever speak to her. I have noticed this myself and when I brought it up to her, she agreed it's an issue but she's afraid to talk to you about it. I told her I would try and talk to you.

Manager 2: [disappointedly and defensively] I don't think that's what's going on. She is still somewhat new and needs time to learn about our team and her role. There is nothing about her race or position that is impacting our relationship. If she has an issue or wants to participate in meetings more, she should bring this to me directly and we can talk about it.

FUTURE RESEARCH DIRECTIONS

The DEI leadership framework discussed in this chapter is rife with potential for future research. Specific suggestions can be drawn from the literature on the various leadership theories reviewed. For example, in their work on authentic leadership, Covelli and Mason (2017) found several cultural considerations that deserve further research. They noted that "leadership is culturally constructed," which includes how people interpret their own life experiences and how they then embody cultural influences. Furthermore, an individual's authentic leadership may not translate across cultural systems (Sanchez-Runde et al., 2011). Gardiner (2011) pointed out one of the flaws of the authentic leadership framework is that it does not account for the social and historical factors that inform one's ability to lead. Finally, Covelli and Mason pointed out the lack of cross-cultural understanding, which can lead to further misunderstandings. Thus, more research is needed to understand the generalizability of the DEI leadership framework.

The literature on transformational and servant leadership also offers strengths and some challenges. Echols (2009) argued for five characteristics of inclusion that are identified across both of these approaches:

1. Creating opportunities for maximum leadership across constituents
2. Empowering individuals to reach their full potential and pursue a shared goal

3. Integrating high moral standards and reducing the possibility of authoritarianism
4. Modeling authentic inclusion and commitment to leadership develop in others
5. Developing boundaries and maintaining integrity for the full appreciation and inclusion of marginalized community members (p. 68)

While this list of characteristics can guide DEI leaders, it is not without challenges as well. Leaders may run the risk of being seen as "manipulative," weak, indecisive, or biased (p. 103). Followers may also feel skeptical of or resistant to a leadership approach that moves beyond transactional engagement and requires more self-reflection and disclosure. Regardless, these approaches have the potential to set the stage for a DEI multimodal approach to inclusive leadership and leadership development. More research on what a blended approach might entail and how to apply such a framework to leadership development is still needed.

CONCLUSION

Transactional, transformational, authentic, and servant leadership are complementary in their approaches and aim to serve the self-actualization of employees as well as the greater good. While this chapter explored the similarities and difference between these and other leadership styles, it also argued for an integrated, inclusive, diversity-centered leadership approach that draws from all of them. Given the limited research on diversity leadership models, increasing employees' diversity, and the organizational equity imperative, the authors conclude that leadership psychology can offer managers meaningful guidance. Moreover, this chapter argued for the integration of leadership styles that are people centered; empowering; and mindful of bias, past experiences, and individuals' developmental needs. Such a DEI leadership approach can help leadership psychologists as well as diversity and inclusion practitioners when coaching organizational leaders and managers to bring out the best in themselves and their teams.

REFERENCES

Abbas, M., & Ali, R. (2021). Transformational versus transactional leadership styles and project success: A meta-analytic review. *European Management Journal*. Advance online publication. doi:10.1016/j.emj.2021.10.011

Adserias, R. P., Charleston, L. J., & Jackson, J. F. L. (2017). What style of leadership is best suited to direct organizational change to fuel institutional diversity in higher education. *Race, Ethnicity and Education*, *20*(3), 315–331. doi:10.1080/13613324.2016.1260233

Alvesson, M., & Einola, K. (2019). Warning for excessive positivity: Authentic leadership and other traps in leadership studies. *The Leadership Quarterly*, *30*(4), 383–395. doi:10.1016/j.leaqua.2019.04.001

Avolio, B. J., Walumbwa, F. O., & Weber, T. J. (2009). Leadership: Current theories, research, and future directions. *Annual Review of Psychology*, *60*(1), 421–449. doi:10.1146/annurev.psych.60.110707.163621 PMID:18651820

Berne, E. (1964). *Games people play*. Grove Press.

Bourke, J., & Titus, A. (2020, March 6). The key to inclusive leadership. *Harvard Business Review*. https://hbr.org/2020/03/the-key-to-inclusive-leadership

Boyum, G. (2006). *The historical and philosophical influences on Greenleaf's concept of servant leadership: Setting the stage for scientific theory building*. https://www.regent.edu/acad/global/publications/sl_proceedings/2006/boyum.pdf

Brown, M., Brown, R. S., & Nandedkar, A. (2019). Transformational leadership theory and exploring the perceptions of diversity management in higher education. *Journal of Higher Education Theory and Practice*, *19*(7), 11–21. doi:10.33423/jhetp.v19i7.2527

Carayol, R. (2011, June 9). *René Carayol: Authentic leadership* [Video]. YouTube. https://youtu.be/g1ACR-odNR4

Caza, A., Caza, B. B., & Posner, B. Z. (2021). Transformational leadership across cultures: Follower perception and satisfaction. *Administrative Sciences*, *11*(32), 32. Advance online publication. doi:10.3390/admsci11010032

Center for Servant Leadership. (n.d.). *The servant as leader*. Robert K. Greenleaf Center for Servant Leadership. https://www.greenleaf.org/what-is-servant-leadership/

Chin, J. L., Desormeaux, L., & Sawyer, K. (2016). Making way for paradigms of diversity leadership. *Consulting Psychology Journal*, *68*(1), 49–71. doi:10.1037/cpb0000051

Ciucur, D., & Pîrvut, A. F. (2012). The effects of a transactional analysis training programme on team leadership factors in automotive industry. *Procedia: Social and Behavioral Sciences*, *33*, 667–671. doi:10.1016/j.sbspro.2012.01.205

Covelli, B. J., & Mason, I. (2017). Linking theory to practice: Authentic leadership. *Academy of Strategic Management Journal*, *16*(3), 1–10.

Datta, B. (2015). Assessing the effectiveness of authentic leadership. *International Journal of Leadership Studies*, *9*(1), 19–32. https://www.regent.edu/acad/global/publications/ijls/new/vol9iss1/2-IJLS.pdf

Dempsey, M., & Brafman, O. (2018). *Radical inclusion: What the post-9/11 world should have taught us about leadership*. Missionday.

Dittmar, J. (2016, June 30). *Transactional vs. transformational leadership definition* [Video]. YouTube. https://www.youtube.com/watch?v=FtnFKLqhL-Y

Early, G. (n.d.). A short history of leadership theories. *Leaders' Quest*. https://leadersquest.org/content/documents/A_short_history_of_leadership_theories.pdf

Eaton, S. E. (2020). Challenging and critiquing notions of servant leadership: Lessons from my mother. In *Women negotiating life in the academy* (pp. 15–23). Springer. doi:10.1007/978-981-15-3114-9_2

Echols, S. (2009). Transformation/servant leadership: A potential synergism for an inclusive leadership style. *Journal of Religious Leadership*, *8*(2), 85–116. http://arl-jrl.org/wp-content/uploads/2016/02/Echols-Transformational-Servant-Leadership-2009-Fall.pdf

Gardiner, R. (2011). A critique of the discourse of authentic leadership. *International Journal of Business and Social Science*, *2*(15), 99–104.

Greenleaf, R. K. (1977). *Servant leadership: A journey into the nature of legitimate power and greatness*. Paulist Press.

Harper, T. (2015, July 16). *Leadership types of power* [Video]. YouTube. https://www.youtube.com/watch?v=2jW1batb_pM&feature=youtu.be

Harter, S. (2002). Authenticity. In C. R. Snyder & S. J. Lopez (Eds.), *Handbook of positive psychology* (pp. 382–394). Oxford University Press.

Hassan, A., & Ahmed, F. (2011). Authentic leadership, trust and work engagement. *International Journal of Humanities and Social Science*, *6*(3), 164–170.

Johnson-Mallard, V., Jones, R., Coffman, M., Gauda, J., Deming, K., Pacheco, M., & Campbell, J. (2019). The Robert Wood Johnson nurse faculty scholars diversity and inclusion research. *Health Equity*, *3*(1), 297–303. doi:10.1089/heq.2019.0026 PMID:31289788

Khan, J., Jaafar, M., Javed, B., Mubarak, N., & Saudagar, T. (2020). Does inclusive leadership affect project success? The mediating role of perceived psychological empowerment and psychological safety. *International Journal of Managing Projects in Business*, *13*(5), 1077–1096. doi:10.1108/IJMPB-10-2019-0267

Khan, Z. A., Nawaz, A., & Khan, I. (2016). Leadership theories and styles: A literature review. *Journal of Resources Development and Management*, 16.

Kotlyar, I., & Karakowsky, L. (2007). Falling over ourselves to follow the leader: Conceptualizing connections between transformational leader behaviors and dysfunctional team conflict. *Journal of Leadership & Organizational Studies*, *14*(1), 38–49. doi:10.1177/1071791907304285

Lahiri, I. (2008). *Creating a competency model for diversity and inclusion*. The Conference Board Council on Workforce Diversity. https://www.conference-board.org/pdf_free/councils/TCBCP005.pdf

Leahey, T. H., Greer, S., Lefrancois, G. R., Reiner, T. W., Spencer, J. L., Wickramasekera, I. E., & Willmarth, E. K. (2014). *History of psychology*. Bridgepoint Education.

Lee, M. (2017). Interrogating authentic leadership: Identity does matter. *Advances in Developing Human Resources*, *19*(4), 347–349. doi:10.1177/1523422317728730

Lee, M. T., & Raschke, R. L. (2016). Understanding employee motivation and organizational performance: Arguments for a set-theoretic approach. *Journal of Innovation & Knowledge*, *1*(3), 162–169. doi:10.1016/j.jik.2016.01.004

Martin, D. (2020). Exploring the relationship between the framing of cultural diversity and the strategies used in its management among educational leaders. *Canadian Journal for New Scholars in Education*, *11*(2), 125–129.

McCleskey, J. A. (2014). Situational, transformational, and transactional leadership and leadership development. *Journal of Business Studies Quarterly*, *5*(4), 117–130.

MindTools. (n.d.). *Adams' equity theory: Balancing employee inputs and outputs.* https://www.mindtools.com/pages/article/newLDR_96.htm

Montgomery, B. L. (2020). Academic leadership: Gatekeeping or groundskeeping? *The Journal of Values Based Leadership, 13*(2), 135–151. doi:10.22543/0733.132.1316

Nart, S., Yaprak, B., Yildirim, Y. T., & Sarihan, A. Y. (2018). The relationship of diversity management and servant leadership with organizational identification and creativity in multinational enterprises. *Finans Politik ve Ekonomik Yorumlar, 55*(637), 31–47.

Northouse, P. G. (2019). *Leadership: Theory and practice.* Sage Publications.

Onyalla, D. B. (2018). Authentic leadership and leadership ethics: Proposing a new perspective. *The Journal of Values Based Leadership, 11*(2), 1–10. doi:10.22543/0733.62.1226

Rhodes, P. (2019, September 19). *What is radical inclusion?* The Good Men Project. https://goodmenproject.com/featured-content/what-is-radical-inclusion-kvnw/

Roberson, Q., & Perry, J. L. (2021). *Inclusive leadership in thought and action: A thematic analysis. Group and Organization Management.* Sage Publications., doi:10.1177/10596011211013161

Sanchez-Runde, C., Nardon, L., & Steers, R. M. (2011). Looking beyond Western leadership models: Implications for global managers. *Organizational Dynamics, 40*(3), 207–213. doi:10.1016/j.orgdyn.2011.04.008

Smith, N. (1999). *Expansive data collection, focused analysis: Combining oral history and grounded theory procedures as research methodology for studies in race, gender and class* [Conference paper]. Race, Gender, and Class Project Conference, Southern University of New Orleans.

Sole, K., & Landrum, R. E. (2015). *Academic research and writing: A guide for the social sciences.* Bridgepoint.

Van Wingerden, J., & Van der Stoep, J. (2018). The motivational potential of meaningful work: Relationships with strengths use, work engagement, and performance. *PLoS One, 13*(6), 1–11. doi:10.1371/journal.pone.0197599 PMID:29897935

Wuffli, P. A. (2016). *Inclusive leadership: A framework for the global era.* Springer. doi:10.1007/978-3-319-23561-5

Zigarelli, M. (2013, August 17). *Ten leadership theories in five minutes* [Video]. YouTube. https://youtu.be/XKUPDUDOBVo

ADDITIONAL READING

Carucci, R. (2016, October 24). Organizations can't change if leaders can't change with them. *Harvard Business Review.* https://hbr.org/2016/10/organizations-cant-change-if-leaders-cant-change-with-them

Fisher, E. S. (2020). Cultural humility as a form of social justice: Promising practices for global school psychology training. *School Psychology International, 41*(1), 53–66. Advance online publication. doi:10.1177/0143034319893097

Greene-Morton, E., & Minkler, M. (2020). Cultural competence or cultural humility? Moving beyond the debate. *Health Promotion Practice, 21*(1), 142–145. doi:10.1177/1524839919884912 PMID:31718301

Hook, J. N., & Davis, D. E. (2019). Cultural humility: Introduction to the special issue. *Journal of Psychology and Theology, 47*(2), 71–75. doi:10.1177/0091647119842410

Linton, C. (2011). *The equity framework.* Corwin.

Miller, F., & Katz, J. (2007). *The Path from exclusive club to inclusive organization: A developmental process.* http://www.kjcg.com/news/articles/documents/The_Path_from_Exclusive_Club.pdf

Rodriguez, F. C. (2015). Why diversity and equity matter: Reflections from a community college president. *New Directions for Community Colleges*, (172), 15–24. doi:10.1002/cc.20160

KEY TERMS AND DEFINITIONS

Authentic Leadership: An approach to leadership that emphasizes self-awareness, an internalized moral perspective, empathetic engagement, and relational trust.

Equity Leadership: An approach to leadership that emphasizes fairness and justice.

Inclusive Leadership: An approach to leadership that emphasizes responding to diverse scenarios with a nonjudgmental mind, humility, and awareness of both one's own and others' bias.

Radical Inclusion: An approach to leadership that deemphasizes the leader and stresses the need for power sharing, trust, and confidence building among followers and participants.

Servant Leadership: An approach to leadership that emphasizes the leader intentionally serving the follower(s).

Transactional Leadership: An approach to leadership that is based on understanding social interactions as a series of agreements between the leader and follower(s).

Chapter 11
The Importance of Social Components in Online Learning: The Case of Business Administration Online at MCI

Nicole Palan
University of Graz, Austria

Julia Waldegger
https://orcid.org/0000-0003-4712-9541
Management Center Innsbruck, Austria

Maria Pammer
Management Center Innsbruck, Austria

ABSTRACT

Since the outbreak of COVID-19 pandemic, tertiary education has been mainly pursued through online teaching. This form of teaching is also associated with challenges regarding the social presence of both lecturers and the students during classes. In this context, understanding how to effectively enforce social interaction and trust in the virtual classroom is of high importance. This chapter presents various examples of social learning pursued by the Management Center Innsbruck in their blended learning degree programs. Many of these have already been established in 2014 when the first blended learning degree programs started. However, the need for physical distancing made clear that social presence and interaction are of even greater relevance than ever before. Increasing the sense of cohesion and being a proper member of a study group can also be supported by more informal interactions.

INTRODUCTION

The Management Center Innsbruck (MCI) | The Entrepreneurial School®, as a pioneer in Austrian tertiary online education, started with blended learning programs combining online and face-to-face teaching

DOI: 10.4018/978-1-7998-8239-8.ch011

in 2014 due to the increased demand of students to study while working. The faculty at MCI has thus acquired expertise in teaching online already well before the outbreak of the COVID-19 pandemic and the switch to fully online teaching. For this chapter, the authors will focus on experiences from the very first blended learning program implemented at MCI, the undergraduate program Business Administration Online. This degree program is offered both in German and in English and thus can also shed light on specific requirements when teaching online in a setting with many international students in contrast to an environment where most students come from German speaking regions only.

The MCI has established high standards to assure and maintain a high level of quality of the online teaching formats: For instance, every faculty member must complete a mandatory online teaching training before starting their online teaching. This ensures that lecturers are aware of the specific needs regarding social interaction in online settings and to be well prepared for the didactical challenges stemming from distance learning. In addition to continuously improve the quality in online teaching, MCI regularly offers further training for online teaching for advanced topics of online teaching, such as tools to increase interaction among students during class and to establish also social presence in online teaching. Moreover, four teaching assistants at the department act as quality managers and instructional designers, providing informal support for all lecturers to help improve the instructional design of every single online course in the curriculum, the use of software for teaching, smart grading practices, and tips for quick and effective feedback for students.

Altogether, faculty members at MCI were thus already trained well in teaching in an online environment before the outbreak of the COVID-19 pandemic. As an instantaneous response to the challenges of the COVID-19 pandemic on teaching classes in a high-quality manner, further asynchronous training modules were designed and implemented by the learning solutions department, a unit that supports (online) teaching at MCI, immediately after the first lockdown in March 2020. Since then, these additional training possibilities have facilitated the switch to full online teaching for all lecturers and have ensured the active participation of students in online formats and to raise awareness for the various social components in online teaching.

BACKGROUND

In this chapter, the authors focus on the degree program Business Administration Online, which is tailored for students who are looking to combine studying a high-quality program and working in their jobs. The degree program takes 6 terms and requires passing courses valuing 180 ECTS points. The program is facilitated in a blended learning format comprising both synchronous and asynchronous aspects. The synchronous lectures consist of six live webinars and one full day residency in the middle of the course. The asynchronous aspect is flexible online study time and thus ideal for working students. The weekly workload for students amounts to 20-25 hours in total. This weekly workload is divided into 70 per cent for asynchronous study time, 20 per cent for live webinars and ten per cent for the one-day residency per course[1].

On average, Business Administration Online students are 29 years at the start of their studies and can look back on a profound professional experience in business and management or beyond. The majority of the students chose the blended learning format due to work reasons, however, some decided on this format due to other motives, such as a career as a professional athlete, or family commitments. Even though the blended learning program requires only up to 10 days per term in Innsbruck, most students in the German track are from the DACH region (i.e. Germany, Austria and Switzerland). The students enrolled in the English track have more diverse backgrounds. Still, most students live in continental Europe. Besides the different nationalities of students, the size of the German and English track differs as well. Every winter term, 60-75 students start in the German and 35-40 students in the English track. The structural differences between the German and the English track also affect aspects of social presence and must be considered in designing online teaching units. Even though the group size is larger in the German track, students develop group cohesion quicker than the smaller English track. The students in the German track have more homogenous cultural backgrounds and mostly speak German as their first language. However, the students in the English track might face communication barriers stemming from having to use a foreign language and different cultural backgrounds. Language barriers can significantly impact the trust formation (Jonsen et al., 2011). Thus, building social presence is likely to require more effort in the English track. Another challenge for group cohesion between students in the English track is that students from the DACH region tend to switch to German for informal communication even though they participate in an English language program. While this is easily managed for formal communication in class by reminding students to talk English when in break-out sessions as well, non-German speakers might be excluded from informal talks during breaks which might disturb forming an overall group cohesion. This issue is even more important the higher the share of German speaking students is in the English program and thus the majority is less aware of the negative side effects of talking in their mother tongue rather than in the common language of the study program.

Often, the same lecturers teach the course for the German and English group, which makes it necessary to adapt content and teaching style for the two different groups. In one of the first courses, students are not only made familiar with the learning management system and the MCI e-campus and strategies for online learning, but team building and fostering group cohesion is one of the main goals. When comparing the two tracks, the students in the German group are quicker to organize themselves in groups during this course without much assistance of the lecturer. The English group, however, is more hesitant to organize themselves in groups and more hesitant in their communication with each other. Often, the lecturer and the teaching assistant in the first course "Digital Competence & Self-Leadership" have to spend more time for group building and offer more support in the English track.

Lecturers teaching the same courses in both tracks report different activity levels of the German and English track. From livelier discussions in break-out sessions and the willingness to present the results in the main group, raising content-related questions and participation in group discussions, the German track seems to show less reluctance to actively participate. Interestingly enough, the administrative staff can also observe this difference in information sessions related to administrative processes (e.g. mandatory internship, elective courses, optional semester abroad, etc.).

To fully exploit the limited time for student-lecturer as well as peer interaction, the program often follows a flipped classroom principle. Hence, students prepare content before the webinars, which leaves more time during the synchronous online phases for student interaction, such as discussions or group work. Several studies show that a flipped classroom approach can have the additional advantage of contributing to social presence (Ferreri & O'Connor, 2013; Jia et al., 2021; Kay et al., 2019; Lage et al., 2000; Wu et al., 2017). For the preparation, students must work through the learning path provided on the learning management system Sakai. The learning path starts with an overview of the course, learning goals and detailed structure of the course, the study schedule, and assessments to help students stay engaged and plan. Every week, students find tasks to prepare for the webinars as well as tasks to fulfil after the webinars. The tasks are not necessarily graded, yet teachers incentivize students to fulfil the tasks in time. Moreover, students also find different multimedia learning materials on Sakai, ranging from (academic) texts, (self-recorded) micro lectures, slide sets, podcasts, self-evaluation tests, etc. The structure of the learning path is identical for every course throughout the program.

As the sequence of courses follows a fixed structure,students beginning their studies together stay in the same group until graduation (barring a voluntary interruption of studies or the exclusion from the degree program), which facilitates the social component of a degree program. Students are used to work together online with the same people over the course of three years, establishing strong bonds and trust in group work relations, facilitating social interactions.

Structure, transparency, and predictability characterize not only the time model but also the faculty's teaching philosophy. Teaching in a part-time degree program requires a highly structured course design and transparency regarding the distribution of the workload. Alternatively, it also provides ample opportunity to focus on the student-centred learning approach and turn students into collaborators on their own learning journey and co-facilitators for their peers' journeys.

Even though faculty can look back on a vast experience in online teaching, moving to a fully online program due to the closure of the campus in March 2020 comes with challenges. The residencies have been appreciated for their possibility of knowledge transfer and practical applications. While these aspects are more easily transferable to an online environment, aspects of social presence and fostering group cohesion and building as well as strengthening the learning community are much more difficult to substitute in a fully online environment.

The trend to shift teaching from face-to-face to online lectures in higher education has started well before the COVID-19 pandemic due to advances in technology that increased the quality of both the online access and synchronous online teaching as well as the increased demand of students for more flexibility in time and place.

This is also reflected by the fact that theoretical and empirical research has addressed the shift from the focus of "social presence" and "presence" in the traditional classroom to one in the online learning environment (Cobb, 2009). The first to address the importance of social presence in the learning environment and thus founding social presence theory are Short, Williams, and Christie (1976). The importance of social presence in computer-based learning environments has already been analyzed in the 1990s, when online degree programs were implemented only rarely. Gunawardena and Zittle (1997), for instance, showed that social presence is significantly contributing to audience satisfaction and thus highlight the importance of adjusting teaching programs to account for the need of interaction in an online environment.

In more recent times, the Community of Inquiry model is widely used for examining and evaluating a learning community. The community of inquiry model, distinguishes three interacting elements; cognitive presence, social presence and teaching presence (Garrison, 2007). The first element refers to students' progressive development of learning from understanding the problem to exploring, integrating and applying (Garrison, 2007, p. 65). It can be conceptualized as "an iterative relationship between a learner's personal understanding and shared dialogue with others" (Dilling et al., 2020, p. 856). Cognitive presence is necessary to develop critical thinking skills (Scherer Bassani, 2011). Regarding this component, the authors will focus on the interplay of social and teaching presence in this chapter only.

Social presence in this context is defined as "the extent to which persons are perceived to be real and are able to be authentically known and truly connected to others in mediated communication" (Bentley et al., 2015, p. 494). Social presence thus consists of (a) effective communication, (b) open communication and (c) group cohesion (Garrison, 2007, p. 63). Social presence moves beyond open and effective communication to build relationships between individuals towards creating a cohesive and respectful group. Students must be able to present themselves as humans with individual thoughts, feelings, and interests to fully enter human connection with their peers. Thus, social presence can be conceptualized as "the degree to which students feel connected and comfortable interacting in the online classroom" (Dilling et al., 2020, p. 856). This, in turn, positively influences their engagement on the subject and thus helps sustain content-related communication (Rourke et al., 2001).

Research suggests mixed findings related to the comparison of social presence in fully online, blended learning and traditional face-to-face settings. Some studies find higher perceptions of social presence in the blended learning environment compared to online programs (Akyol et al., 2009), whereas Bowers and Kumar (2015) report higher perception of social presence in an online environment compared to a face-to-face setting. Bowers and Kumar's study shows that weekly announcements, e-mails, discussion summaries, and the use of online discussion in small groups foster social presence in an online setting as interaction takes place at a more continuous level compared to face-to-face teaching environments. According to Dilling et al. (2020), however, affective expression relating to interpersonal relationships are higher in a face-to-face setting compared to a fully online learning environment. This can be attributed to a lack of direct contact with the instructor and other students (Priego & Peralta, 2013). Thus, instructors must carefully design the course and facilitate interaction between students in the best and most effective way to ensure a high level of motivation and facilitate study success for students.

The third element is teaching presence, including course design, facilitation and direct instruction (Garrison, 2007, p. 67). In educational settings, social presence helps to create an environment where educational goals can be reached through inquiry and quality interaction (e.g., reflective and threaded discussions). Students' feeling connected as a "sense of belonging or presence, feelings of support, and level of interaction with the instructor" (Gallien & Oomen-Early, 2008, p. 468). Akyol et al. (2009) report that students in blended learning programs perceive a higher teaching presence and social presence compared to fully online programs. This can be attributed to personal interaction during face-to-face teaching. In contrast, Bowers and Kumar (2015) find students' perception of teaching presence to be higher in an online environment compared to a traditional face-to-face setting. Communicating the course goals clearly, being responsive to students' needs and providing timely feedback are crucial for fostering teaching presence in an online setting. A more recent study suggests that an equally strong teaching presence and social presence can be found in the online and face-to-face learning environment (Dilling et al., 2020).

Due to the spread of the COVID-19 pandemic, schools, colleges and (applied) universities worldwide had to move to online teaching in March 2020. Since then, most on-campus sessions or face-to-face teaching opportunities had to be cancelled. For many institutions, which had not established online teaching formats before, the switch to the fully online mode could be compared to Hodges et al.'s (2020) definition of emergency remote teaching, i.e. "the temporary shift of instructional delivery using distance education strategies due to crisis circumstances". For the MCI, however, it was helpful that this switch could be based on several years of online teaching experience. Instructors were already familiar with course design as well as facilitating and instructing in an online environment. Still, as the full day face-to-face sessions were invaluable for further building rapport between instructors and students and between students themselves, challenges had to be met also in curricula that have relied on online teaching well before the pandemic.

MAIN FOCUS OF THE PAPER

In this chapter, the authors thus describe some of the best practice examples of Business Administration Online that have been established over recent years to facilitate social presence and to maximize students learning development:

ESTABLISHING LEARNING COMMUNITIES AND SOCIAL COHESION IN ONLINE LEARNING

Settings

In the synchronous phases of online learning, both teaching and social presence play an important role throughout the course of our degree programs. Building learning communities throughout the program is guided by the goal "to achieve meaningful learning" (Dilling et al., 2020, p. 856), and is an incremental part of social presence. As developing a learning community is a continuous process, every single course of the curriculum implements both elements of social and teaching presence and thus plays an important role in fostering and deepening them. Starting with the first course of the bachelor program, "Digital Competence and Self-Management" where students deal with online learning from a theoretical perspective, but where they can also apply their acquired knowledge about online learning and reflect on their individual learning strategies. Based on the digital competence framework (Carretero et al., 2017), the course addresses digital competencies and digital literacy as a foundation for the courses to come. Therefore, the learning goals comprise aspects like the following:

- Being able to explain what is different between online communication and interaction and traditional communication;
- Being able to describe the characteristics and different phases and roles in virtual team building;
- Being familiar with the Sakai learning management system and the course site set-up and learning paths;
- Being able to use the various functions in Sakai and have practiced using them; for example, students are encouraged to embed videos and pictures or to create an online post in their first assignments to learn how to connect with their fellow students and establish a group feeling;
- Being familiar with the functions of Adobe Connect to communicate with the lecturer and fellow students during the webinars and knowing what to expect in webinars.

Furthermore, each student cohort is encouraged to develop their common code of conduct addressing – among other aspects – their communication and interaction in the courses, the (digital) communication outside the official channels (e.g., WhatsApp groups, Facebook group, etc.), the behavior in group work, and their mutual support. This helps the group to build an online learning community. Thus, the students do not only introduce themselves to each other and engage in group work, but they also work on codes of conduct for their learning community. The codes of conduct typically regulate that the students should actively participate in the course by bringing in their own experiences and actively asking questions. They commit to working together respectfully, following the netiquette, responding to each other in time, and work on open and appreciative communication. In later courses, faculty typically picks up the codes of conduct again to remind the students of their agreements regarding their ownership of their learning journey and the rules for working together. This helps show the students that they are (also) responsible for building and caring for their learning community. After completing this first course, students have thus acquired the necessary skills to successfully engage in online communication and activate social presence during the degree program.

After setting the stage with this first course, different elements of teaching and social presence are included in every following course. Therefore, the degree program invites faculty to reserve time for this in all synchronous learning phases and to consider it in the asynchronous self-paced phases. In the following, practical examples show some easy to implement and successful possibilities to increase social presence. The suggestions are based on experiences and successful applications and are structured according to the point in time they might be used, before the course, during the first webinar/synchronous phase, and later in the course.

Before the Course Starts

Faculty members can start building social presence even before the official course start. A written message, including a course outline, expectations, and a short personal note can be an easy and quick way to give students an idea of what they can expect. Providing a current picture and a short CV including hobbies on the webpage also helps students to establish a relationship of trust between the lecturer and students.

Instead of using a written message, faculty members can also reach out to their students with a short video message. Borup et al. (2012, p. 199) report that asynchronous videos support teaching presence and show that there is a "real" person behind the screen, especially when the videos are shot from home and instructors offer glimpses from their personal life. The video can be used to mention course highlights, expectations, or to explain the first assignment. Sometimes, faculty members are hesitant when it comes to videos because they fear it might be too time-consuming. However, there are tools, like Loom, that make it very easy also for novices to record individual videos. The advantage of using a short introductory video is that students can both see and hear the lecturer and non-verbal communication can be transported more easily. Altogether, it is thus easier for lecturers to transport also less formal, social elements in this note, allowing the lecturer to become more tangible to the prospect student group. The department Business Administration Online invites every lecturer teaching an online course to record a "Meet the lecturer video" in a professional recording studio at MCI.

Similarly, forum posts can be used to get in touch with students before the course start. One possibility is to ask about their experience with the course topic, which can also be beneficial for aligning group activities according to these results. A short task before the course start encourages students to engage with the course already. Besides reminding students to read the syllabus, short questions about the students' course expectations help show that the faculty wants to support their learning journeys. The answers to these questions can then be referred to in a message or the first webinar.

During the First Webinar

If the lecturer has not introduced themselves before the first webinar, social presence can be increased by taking time for a proper introduction on the faculty's as well as the students' side at the start of the course. For teaching presence, it is important, that also the faculty members are seen as humans with individual thoughts, feelings, and interests (Dilling et al., 2020). Hence, the faculty introduction is not limited to their professional background, but they are encouraged to emphasize their relation to the respective subject, and some private insights, like hobbies, as well. As lecturers should feel comfortable with the information they reveal to students, also lecturers at MCI are free to decide how much and specifically which information they want to reveal about themselves. The possibilities for the students' introductions heavily depend on the group size. For bigger groups, a shared note board like Padlet can be used where every student answers some (course-related or general) questions and where pictures or short introduction videos can be shared as well. Digital whiteboards, like Miro, can be used for living statistics where students, for example, "line up" according to certain criteria, like their age or their distance to the university location. When using introduction methods for students, it has to be kept in mind that even if the information is new to the teachers, students might have exchanged this sort of information before. To avoid redundancies, it might help to build a course introduction on one of the previous courses. Also, it has to be considered, that these activities can be time-consuming and that curricula normally do not consider the needs for building up social presence. Here, introducing elements of flipped classroom (Bergmann & Sams, 2012) can be useful for freeing up time to establish social presence. In this respect, it can also be an advantage for online degree programs if the same lecturers teach more courses as the students are already familiar with the lecturer.

In addition to the introduction, various ice-breaker activities (Honeycutt, 2016) can be used during the first webinar. For example, students can be asked to articulate their expectations for the course, their prior experience in a certain field, or their work links to the respective topics. Furthermore, starting with a quote or a picture related to one's background or a personal story related to the course can be used to catch the student's attention. Besides, it helps students get a glimpse of the "person behind the teacher".

Throughout the Course

Video and audio elements can be helpful support of social presence throughout the course. Through the use of videos, students feel more engaged and connected to the lecturers because it increases their social presence in the course (Scagnoli et al., 2019). Non-verbal communication elements broadcasted by video conferencing tools also foster social presence and connectedness among students (Jia et al., 2021). Hence, video elements, like (group) discussions, where students are encouraged to switch on their cameras, are frequently used in the respective programs. When working with big student groups, having all cameras on might be too twitchy on the screens and too challenging for the bandwidth of the participants' internet connections. Here, it can help to split the group in half, have one-half work on a task while discussing with the other half, and switch afterward. Although students are sometimes hesitant when it comes to using their cameras and microphones in class, the effort of convincing them is worth it. The involved non-verbal communication elements, such as eye contact and smiling or other facial expressions, simulate face-to-face communication and increase intimacy, one of the key elements of social presence (Jia et al., 2021). From the authors' experience, it helps if students know in advance that cameras and microphones will be used during a webinar. Furthermore, regular usage from the first course onward helps overcome the barriers of using these tools.

Particularly, when no video elements are in use, lecturers report the lack of instant feedback to their teaching style due to missing body language and facial expressions. Student response systems, also known as clickers, can be an easy-to-use help in these situations. In their simplest form, student response systems are polling systems that allow to collect students' answers and give access to the results immediately (Hung, 2017). Several conferencing software programs, such as Adobe Connect or Big Blue

Button, have them already integrated with their systems. For more advanced polling versions, additional tools that offer various question and answer formats, for example, multiple-choice, find on image, rating, open question, word cloud, matching, prioritization, sorting, fill in the blanks, and brainstorming, can be used (e.g. by Wooclap). If the polling tool is not integrated with the conferencing software, it can also be used in the asynchronous phases, for example, in the preparation of a webinar. The variety of questions allows seeing whether the students can follow the content or the pace of the lecture is appropriate. Furthermore, it can also be used to emphasize social perspectives when asking for students' preferences (e.g. whether they want to work on an assignment in groups or individually) or for their well-being (whether they need a break). Additionally, student response systems offer great potential for quick feedback on teaching methods. Since these tools are anonymous, the barrier to participate is low and often, students appreciate the quick break from the lecture by having an active element during class.

Despite the positive impacts that active learning elements have on the students' learning outcomes (Honicke & Broadbent, 2016), they have to be implemented carefully, particularly in an online learning setting. Some instructional practices bear the threat of triggering anxiety, especially when the risk for social evaluation is involved. For example, "cold calling", which describes the common practice of selecting a student to answer instead of waiting for volunteers, is particularly anxiety-provoking because of its danger of negative judgment by fellow students in the (online) classroom (Hood et al., 2021). Since the fear linked to socially-oriented anxiety may have a negative impact on student engagement, other approaches might be more fruitful. To ease the frightening aspects of "cold calls", good experiences were made by giving students a short heads-up prior to addressing them with a question ("warm calling"). A short notice before a group or an individual work, or a hint for a particular student can reduce the stress and gives the students time to organize their thoughts and can consequently reduce the risk of anxiety. Furthermore, the better the students know each other, the easier it is for them to speak up, which reinforces the need to invest in social presence.

One additional way that students get to know each other better is to invite selected students for a short "guest speech" in their field of expertise. Especially, when working students are among the participants, these short speeches can add valuable industry insights in addition to the social aspect. Furthermore, real life challenges from the students' working backgrounds can be used during courses. The following example from a change management class should illustrate this idea: Prior to the course start, students were asked to post their experience with the change in their work environment in the forum and discuss it with their peers. Based on these posts, the lecturer invited five students to present their case in a 5-minute pitch at the beginning of an online change management workshop. Based on their interest, the other 20 students could choose a case they wanted to work on during the workshop. In groups, the students could further discuss the case and apply various change methods to the specific challenge. Next to interesting practical insights, the students hereby had the chance to get to know each other and their respective work backgrounds better.

In addition to elements that mainly refer to synchronous online phases, social presence can also be enhanced in the phases in between. A useful example is accompanying a course with regular announcements. They can be used to summarize what happened, to give an outlook of what will happen next, or to add details to certain course elements. The announcements can be written messages, and video or audio statements. However, independent of the format, the lecturers can use them to emphasize their presence and accessibility in asynchronous phases.

A final example of social presence that is often used toward the end of a course during asynchronous phases is personalized feedback. Giving feedback has a social dimension, even when it is focused on content (Evans, 2013). What is more, instructor feedback plays a vital role in building a relationship between lecturers and students (Boling et al., 2012). Research shows that feedback provided with a high social presence is considered to be more useful . Therefore, using audio and video feedback offers great potential, as it shows slightly more social presence indicators than written feedback (Walter et al., 2015). In the respective degree program, a possibility for audio feedback is included in the learning management system, which makes it easy to comment on assignments or forum posts verbally. However, there are various audio recording apps for smartphones available that can be used for feedback. Similarly, screencasting software, which shows the student-paper and the lecturer's face simultaneously, can be used (e.g. Screencast-O-Matic, Loom). Surveys showed, that students enjoyed hearing their instructor's voice (Wallace & Moore, 2012) and that it felt more personal, more supportive, and more interactive. From a lecturer's perspective, audio and video feedback are also appreciated. It gives them the possibility to make their feedback more detailed and personalized. Besides, there is no reason to worry about one's time resources for this sort of feedback, text feedback is shown to be much more time-consuming than other formats (Kirschner et al., 1991).

To sum up, for a comprehensive implementation of social and teaching presence, both need to be frequently considered in every course design and there are plenty of possibilities to do so. Swan (2002), as well as Dennen et al. (2007), emphasize that not only the frequency but the type and quality of interaction between students and lecturers is decisive for shaping social presence and ensuring study progress – and thus the feeling of interconnectedness and belonging to the learning group.

Creating a Formal Framework for Informal Communication with an Online Cocktail Party

In the blended learning format, social and teaching presence especially occur during and after on-campus lectures in a face-to-face setting. The experience in the last years showed that on-campus days at MCI were crucial to promote a learning community. Effective and open communication, as well as group cohesion, are enhanced in a face-to-face setting. The on-campus days typically take place after three synchronous webinars. Even though students had time to get to know the lecturer in the first half of the course in a synchronous and asynchronous online setting, the group dynamic and the interaction with the lecturer often develops after spending a day together in person in the classroom. Students tend to ask more questions about the subject area out of interest during breaks or after the official lecture, even if there is no close connection to the content of the course.

Since the switch to fully online teaching, students no longer spend their breaks chatting with each other and getting to know each other on a personal level so easily. It was a common occurrence for the faculty to join students for a coffee during the break or after the official end of a lecture as well and to discuss personal experiences of students. Not only faculty but also administrative staff members missed the opportunity to interact with the students during the on-campus sessions. Moreover, also students reported a decreased group cohesion and less opportunity to interact with each other more informally. It is thus of increased importance to design a formal framework for social and teaching presence in the purely online learning environment. Opportunities for informal interactions arise manifold in a face-to-face setting without consciously planning them. For the online setting, however, informal interaction requires planning.

To improve communication and group cohesion informally after not having seen each other in person for a year (two terms), the department organized an online cocktail party for every year group. The aim of this online cocktail party was threefold: a) fostering social presence within the student group, b) enhancing the social presence of faculty, and c) fostering the social presence of the Head of Department and Studies as well as the administrative staff at the department. Thus, faculty and administrative staff joined the students for this online cocktail party as well.

A relationship based on mutual understanding and trust between the students and the Head of Department and Studies is invaluable for the smooth running of the degree program. The Head of Department's social presence increases student satisfaction with the degree program and helps to keep the dropout rate low. In addition to official feedback instruments implemented at MCI (e.g., course evaluations, regular meetings with the class representatives), students do not hesitate to contact the Head of Department and Studies directly in case any problems might arise. Thus, the Head of Department and Studies must show social presence to ensure that the students feel cared for and as more than a mere matriculation number. Before the event, the administrative staff sent out an invitation to all students including a shopping list for alcoholic and alcohol-free cocktails. For facilitating the online cocktail party, the department intentionally did not use the conferencing software that is used for the synchronous webinars. This should highlight that the event is not part of the formal aspects of the degree program. The tool Wonder allows participants to move their avatar around a virtual room and to connect with other people. As soon as one avatar gets close to another, a video chat pops up. Up to 15 participants can meet in one circle and chat with each other. The host can also broadcast video messages, which interrupt all conversations in the different circles for the duration of the broadcast. To further increase group cohesion, the department facilitated a cocktail party for every year group in a separate Wonder room. The department members remained with every group for 45-50 minutes. While an exchange across the groups is desirable for networking purposes, the focus was on offering a formalized frame for informal communication between one respective year group.

On the evening of the online cocktail party, the Head of Department and Studies welcomed every year group in their Wonder room. Moreover, she also showed every year group individually how to prepare the cocktail from her kitchen at home. Thus, she expressed a more personal side and invited the students to connect with her. The students could follow along with the instructions or stick to their drink of choice. After this short official introduction, the Head of Department and Studies, other faculty and administrative staff joined the students in their circles for video conversations. The department members intentionally engaged not only in study-related conversations to engage with students on a more personal level. After approximately 45-50 minutes, faculty and administrative staff left the year group and joined the next one in their respective Wonder room. Whereas the year groups had one cocktail party in one Wonder room, the department members joined the cocktail party for every year group. With this organization, the year groups enjoyed more one-on-one time with the Head of Department and Studies, faculty, and administrative staff. Moreover, students could engage in more conversation without any department members present, which further underlined the informal character of the meeting. In principle, students were free to lock their conversation circle so that department members could not join their conversation and overhear exchanges that are more private. This option was mentioned in the official welcome to the event.

This virtual cocktail party was especially a great opportunity for the first-year students to engage with each other informally as they only had briefly met in person on their introduction day at the very beginning of their studies. Thus, this group of students did not have many chances to connect and embrace the feeling of a study group. Moreover, also second-year students could benefit from this part as they only had spent three on-campus days in their first term together and thus valued the informal exchange with each other and the department members highly. In addition, for the third-year students, who have had more opportunities to get to know each other during the first two years joined the cocktail party for their year group as well as it was unclear if they would meet each other in person again for an on-campus day at MCI before finishing their studies. Student feedback suggests that the students from the various year groups enjoyed spending time with each other and having a more formalized framework where they could meet their fellow students.

Moreover, the students felt valued and appreciated by the department members. The individual conversation showed that the department cares about students' well-being and social aspects and not only about their academic success and formalized learning. The online cocktail party also offered the opportunity to show teaching presence already before the start of the course. Naturally, students also talked about their study experience so far in general and about specific courses as well.

While this formal framework for informal communication was widely accepted and valued by the students, other attempts proved less successful. During the beginning of the campus closure in March 2020, the administrative staff of the department offered weekly virtual office hours for students. On one side, administrative staff wanted to support students in the switch to fully online teaching at a time where many were faced with professional and private challenges during the first lockdown. On the other side, the staff also wanted to consolidate questions related to organizational matters of the degree program. For the virtual office hour, students could enter an online meeting room without prior registration in the evening. Only a few students used this opportunity and the department decided to phase out the virtual office hours after two months. Perhaps for students, writing an e-mail or calling requires less effort and reaches the same goal. Moreover, the switch from blended learning to fully online learning did not cause any organizational problems for the students, which were not already solved by faculty when teaching the courses.

CONCLUSION

Social presence seems to be especially important for students at the beginning of their studies when they have not yet established trust to other students or the lecturers. In this regard, the establishment of trust in student relationships is of great importance for successful collaboration within a group and the satisfaction of students – even more so in a complete online learning environment. It is thus crucial for lecturers and departments to enhance social presence and teaching presence in online teaching programs to increase both the satisfaction of students as well as the quality of their education programs.

When establishing social presence activities in online degree programs, one must distinguish between programs that were transferred online due to external factors such as the COVID-19 pandemic and those programs originally designed as (partly) online programs. For students who deliberately decided on an online program, online interaction is one element influencing their satisfaction out of many, such as organization, convenience, and flexibility (Preisman, 2014). However, for students who unintendedly ended up in an online learning environment, social presence can be even more important. In face-to-face settings, opportunities for informal communication and thus promoting social presence arise naturally – during breaks, or before and after the lecture. Therefore, in online settings, the lecturer has to establish a framework for informal conversation. Finding a formal framework that works for the students is connected with trial and error. Some formal frameworks like a virtual cocktail party during a global pandemic work, whereas others like the virtual office hour with administrative staff are less accepted by students.

However, "unintendedly" does not only refer to students but also lecturers. When switching to online teaching on short notice, many aspects must be considered, which does not put teaching and social presence first on the priorities list. Therefore, this paper wants to raise awareness of its importance for successful learning processes - maybe even more in times where people are forced to keep their distance. Furthermore, it should highlight that the ways to increase social and teaching presence are manifold. Hence, before lecturers start teaching online, teacher training that addresses the issue and presents a selection of tools and methods can help lecturers to increase their students' learning outcomes in online environments.

REFERENCES

Akyol, Z., Garrison, D. R., & Ozden, M. Y. (2009). Online and blended communities of inquiry: Exploring the developmental and perceptional differences. *The International Review of Research in Open and Distributed*, *10*(6), 65–83. doi:10.19173/irrodl.v10i6.765

Bentley, K. J., Secret, M. C., & Cummings, C. R. (2015). The Centrality of Social Presence in Online Teaching and Learning in Social Work. *Journal of Social Work Education*, *51*(3), 494–504. doi:10.1080/10437797.2015.1043199

Bergmann, J., & Sams, A. (2012). *Flip your classroom: Reach every student in every class every day* (1st ed.). International Society for Technology in Education.

Boling, E. C., Hough, M., Krinsky, H., Saleem, H., & Stevens, M. (2012). Cutting the distance in distance education: Perspectives on what promotes positive, online learning experiences. *The Internet and Higher Education*, *15*(2), 118–126. doi:10.1016/j.iheduc.2011.11.006

Borup, J., West, R. E., & Graham, C. R. (2012). Improving online social presence through asynchronous video. *The Internet and Higher Education*, *15*(3), 195–203. doi:10.1016/j.iheduc.2011.11.001

Bowers, J., & Kumar, P. (2015). Students' perceptions of teaching and social presence: A comparative analysis of face-to-face and online learning environments. *International Journal of Web-Based Learning and Teaching Technologies*, *10*(1), 27–44. doi:10.4018/ijwltt.2015010103

Carretero, S., Vuorikari, R., & Punie, Y. (2017). *DigComp 2.1: The digital competence framework for citizens with eight proficiency levels and examples of use. EUR, Scientific and technical research series* (Vol. 28558). Publications Office.

Cobb, S. C. (2009). Social Presence and Online Learning: A Current View from a Research Perspective. *Journal of Interactive Online Learning*, (8), 241–254.

Dennen, V. P., Aubteen Darabi, A., & Smith, L. J. (2007). Instructor–Learner Interaction in Online Courses: The relative perceived importance of particular instructor actions on performance and satisfaction. *Distance Education*, *28*(1), 65–79. doi:10.1080/01587910701305319

Dilling, J., Varga, M. A., & Mandernach, B. J. (2020). Comparing Teaching and Social Presence in Traditional and Online Community College Learning Environments. *Community College Journal of Research and Practice*, *44*(10-12), 854–869. doi:10.1080/10668926.2020.1752852

Evans, C. (2013). Making Sense of Assessment Feedback in Higher Education. *Review of Educational Research*, *83*(1), 70–120. doi:10.3102/0034654312474350

Ferreri, S. P., & O'Connor, S. K. (2013). Redesign of a large lecture course into a small-group learning course. *American Journal of Pharmaceutical Education*, *77*(1), 13. doi:10.5688/ajpe77113 PMID:23459199

Gallien, T., & Oomen-Early, J. (2008). Personalized Versus Collective Instructor Feedback in the Online Courseroom: Does Type of Feedback Affect Student Satisfaction, Academic Performance and Perceived Connectedness With the Instructor? *International Journal on E-Learning*, *7*(3), 463–476. https://www.learntechlib.org/p/23582

Garrison, D. R. (2007). Online Community Inquiry Review: Social, cognitive, and teaching presence issues. *Journal of Asynchronous Learning Networks*, *11*(1), 61–72. doi:10.24059/olj.v11i1.1737

Gunawardena, C. N., & Zittle, F. J. (1997). Social presence as a predictor of satisfaction within a computer-mediated conferencing environment. *American Journal of Distance Education*, *11*(3), 8–26. doi:10.1080/08923649709526970

Hodges, C., Moore, S., Lockee, B., Trust, T., & Bond, A. (2020). The difference between emergency remote teaching and online learning. *Educause Review*. https://er.educause.edu/articles/2020/3/the-difference-between-emergency-remote-teaching-and-online-learning

Honeycutt, B. (2016). *Flip the first 5 minutes of class: 50 focusing activities to engage your students*. Flip It Consulting.

Honicke, T., & Broadbent, J. (2016). The influence of academic self-efficacy on academic performance: A systematic review. *Educational Research Review*, *17*, 63–84. doi:10.1016/j.edurev.2015.11.002

Hood, S., Barrickman, N., Djerdjian, N., Farr, M., Magner, S., Roychowdhury, H., Gerrits, R., Lawford, H., Ott, B., Ross, K., Paige, O., Stowe, S., Jensen, M., & Hull, K. (2021). "I Like and Prefer to Work Alone": Social Anxiety, Academic Self-Efficacy, and Students' Perceptions of Active Learning. *CBE Life Sciences Education*, *20*(1), ar12. doi:10.1187/cbe.19-12-0271 PMID:33600218

Hung, H.-T. (2017). The Integration of a Student Response System in Flipped Classrooms. *Language Learning & Technology*, *21*(1), 16–27.

Jia, C., Hew, K. F., Bai, S., & Huang, W. (2021). Adaptation of a conventional flipped course to an online flipped format during the Covid-19 pandemic: Student learning performance and engagement. *Journal of Research on Technology in Education*, 1–21. doi:10.1080/15391523.2020.1847220

Jonsen, K., Maznevski, M. L., & Schneider, S. C. (2011). Diversity and its not so diverse literature: An international perspective. *International Journal of Cross Cultural Management*, *11*(1), 35–62. doi:10.1177/1470595811398798

Kay, R., MacDonald, T., & DiGiuseppe, M. (2019). A comparison of lecture-based, active, and flipped classroom teaching approaches in higher education. *Journal of Computing in Higher Education*, *31*(3), 449–471. doi:10.100712528-018-9197-x

Kirschner, P. A., van den Brink, H., & Meester, M. (1991). Audiotape feedback for essays in distance education. *Innovative Higher Education*, *15*(2), 185–195. doi:10.1007/BF00898030

Lage, M. J., Platt, G. J., & Treglia, M. (2000). Inverting the Classroom: A Gateway to Creating an Inclusive Learning Environment. *The Journal of Economic Education*, *31*(1), 30–43. doi:10.1080/00220480009596759

Preisman, K. A. (2014). Teaching Presence in Online Education: From the Instructor's Point-of-View. *Online Learning*, *18*(3). Advance online publication. doi:10.24059/olj.v18i3.446

Priego, R. G., & Peralta, A. G. (2013). Engagement factors and motivation in e-Learning and blended-learning projects. In F. J. García-Peñalvo (Ed.), *Proceedings of the First International Conference on Technological Ecosystem for Enhancing Multiculturality - TEEM '13* (pp. 453–460). ACM Press. 10.1145/2536536.2536606

Rourke, L., Anderson, T., Garrison, R., & Archer, W. (2001). Assessing Social Presence In Asynchronous Text-based Computer Conferencing. *Journal of Distance Education*, *4*(3), 51–70.

Scagnoli, N. I., Choo, J., & Tian, J. (2019). Students' insights on the use of video lectures in online classes. *British Journal of Educational Technology*, *50*(1), 399–414. doi:10.1111/bjet.12572

Scherer Bassani, P. B. (2011). Interpersonal exchanges in discussion forums: SStudy of learnitudy of learning communities in distance ng communities in distance learning settings. learning settings. *Computers & Education*, *56*, 931–938. doi:10.1016/j.compedu.2010.11.009

Swan, K. (2002). Building Learning Communities in Online Courses: The importance of interaction. *Education Communication and Information*, *2*(1), 23–49. doi:10.1080/1463631022000005016

Wallace, I., & Moore, C. (2012). Providing in-depth and personalised feedback to online students using audio recording. *IPEDR*, *27*, 53–58.

Walter, N., Ortbach, K., & Niehaves, B. (2015). Designing electronic feedback – Analyzing the effects of social presence on perceived feedback usefulness. *International Journal of Human-Computer Studies*, *76*, 1–11. doi:10.1016/j.ijhcs.2014.12.001

Wu, W.-C. V., Hsieh, J. S. C., & Cang, J. C. (2017). Creating an Online Learning Community in a Flipped Classroom to Enhance EFL Learners' Oral Proficiency. *Journal of Educational Technology & Society*, *20*(2), 142–157. https://www.jstor.org/stable/10.2307/90002170

ENDNOTE

1 Details on the degree program can be found on the program webpage www.mci.edu/en/study/bachelor/business-administration.

Chapter 12
Adult Learning in the Workplace:
Critical Application and New Mediums

Scott Nelmark
Baylor University, USA

ABSTRACT

The needs of the adult learner are distinctly different from those of children. In a world where employees are becoming increasingly remote, recognizing the core concepts of adult instruction is increasingly critical. This chapter examines the foundational constructs of adult learning and instruction and factors that promote and inhibit adult learning. Theories of adult learning pioneers Knowles, McClusky, Deci, and Ryan apply in the organizational classroom and the "virtual" classroom. With this understanding, the learning practitioner may implement meaningful curriculum that appeals to the adult learner, encouraging individual growth while supporting employee retention and organizational development.

INTRODUCTION

The learning practitioner's understanding of adult learning principles is essential for effective employee instruction and avoiding methodological contradictions that inhibit learning. Employees as adult learners have unique learning requirements that require attention for active learning and engagement. Detail of these requirements follows, but for a moment, imagine a Monday morning "staff development" meeting driven by a slide presentation in a dark room. The instructor steps forward and establishes the ground rules for the session. Participants are to put phones away or on mute, hold all questions until the end, and hang on; there are 350 slides to grind through during the eight-hour session. One might argue that medieval torture devices are preferable to such inhumane treatment. The human mind chained to a droning, omniscient orator and endless bullet points is prone to mentally exit such an environment frequently, negating the workshop's intended purpose - the transfer of knowledge. Furthermore, such experiences minimize the probability of employee anticipation for the next "learning event" as many conveniently scheduled calendar conflicts arise to prevent further personal distress.

DOI: 10.4018/978-1-7998-8239-8.ch012

Successful implementation of adult learning in the classroom through virtual meeting platforms also requires the adult learning practitioner to command an understanding of adult learner needs. The COVID-19 global pandemic, taking hold in early 2020, has either stressed or enabled adult learning, depending on the perspective. The learning practitioner, prepared or not, was suddenly required to extend adult learning for employees beyond the corporate classroom. A wealth of research exists on adult learning requirements; a summation of core findings follows in this chapter with additional consideration of their application within the new "normal" of remote employees and Internet-driven business. Following COVID-19, the paradigm of remote workers is likely to stay, reinforcing the need to engage employees in effective online learning sessions. While the delivery modes have shifted hard right from the classroom to the virtual learning environment, employees' need for purposeful engagement as adult learners persists.

The modern learning practitioner in the workplace must overcome the challenges of distance, restriction, and new learning environments, as continuous learning is essential to personal and organizational advancement. Thoms and Burton (2016) advised:

Growth entails learning throughout life. This learning offers a diversity of learning styles; diversification of ideas; enhanced measurements and aspects to knowledge assembly, construction, and production; attainment of competencies; in addition to avenues of change to transform from one way of thinking and acting to another. (p. 88–9)

Continuous learning supports adult performance (and ultimately, organizational growth) in the workplace, yet the wrong type of education is detrimental for employees. The failure to offer meaningful adult learning in the workplace is a problem that affects individual job performance and organizational profitability. Organizations with long-term goals focus on their most valuable assets—their employees—from the first day of onboarding and throughout their tenure. Englehardt and Simmons (2002) suggested, "The emphasis on training may be captured by a distinct and defined program; however, supporting the full range of these factors implies something more… an environment for learning" (p. 41). Beyond offering career-based education, compelling growth opportunities must support the employee's needs as an adult learner.

This chapter includes three sections drawn from scholarly research to promote the understanding and purposeful application of adult learning methods for employees in the modern context. The first section examines the discovery of employees' needs as adult learners to support impactful organizational outcomes. The second section surveys the factors that inhibit adult learning in support of active participation. Lastly, this chapter explores the application of andragogical concepts in local and virtual settings with additional considerations for meaningful distance-based learning and engagement.

EMPLOYEES AS ADULT LEARNERS AND ORGANIZATIONAL IMPLICATIONS

Employees are the greatest asset of organizations, though trends in management practices often oppose creating a high-performance learning culture as organizations downsize or outsource tasks to minimize overhead, destroying organizational culture along the way (Pfeffer & Veiga, 1999). Such actions are counterintuitive to earning profits that shareholders demand. Employees surviving these layoffs are stymied in active contribution and productivity within their roles, wondering if they are next (Pfeffer & Veiga, 1999). Rather than laying off employees for short-term cost savings, efficient organizations invest in their employees for exponential returns in the long term (Pfeffer & Veiga, 1999). Despite the critical need for learning as an essential element of organizational health, organizational leadership may consider learning a frill and, as a result, is among the first programs reduced or eliminated during times of economic challenge (Pfeffer & Veiga, 1999). Pfeffer and Veiga (1999) implored, "Knowledge and skill are critical, and too few organizations act on this insight" (p. 43). Employees empowered with knowledge as contributors enable an organization to succeed during inevitable trials and thrive during economic challenges. Educated and inspired employees are the foundation of a successful organization and are a vital competitive differentiator (Pfeffer & Veiga, 1999). Failing this commitment suggests immediate inefficiencies and expense as employees are ill-equipped to handle routine and exceptional tasks.

The commitment to an environment of continuous learning is challenging to sustain, but it is essential to organizational adaptation and survival. It is also a vital individual choice. Mahan and Stein (2014) implored:

Learning occurs from assimilation of experiences and information—neuronal networks are formed—but motivation and attention are powerful enhancers of the learning process. Learning is important for living and action; apparently there is no easy way to make important neuronal networks and no easy transfer of learning where learning in one area converts to enhanced learning in unrelated areas. The physiology of learning requires energy and effort. Behavior change requires motivation and commitment. (p. 145)

Despite the importance of learning in life, many adults hesitate to commit the energy and effort required to change behaviors and enhance their lives. The adult learner in the professional context requires the fulfillment of particular psychological needs before engaging in learning.

ADULT LEARNING NEEDS WITHIN THE ORGANIZATIONAL CONSTRUCT

The learning organization paradigm begins at the individual level. Senge (2006) offered, "Organizations learn only through individuals who learn. Individual learning does not guarantee organizational learning. But without it, no organizational learning occurs" (p. 129). The institution of individual learning begins with care, patience, and acknowledging the learner's needs. In describing automaker Toyota's perspective on employee education, Liker and Meier (2006) examined their culture of people development, likening the process to a garden:

The soil is tended and prepared, the seeds are watered, and when the seeds grow, the soil is maintained, weeded, and watered again until finally the fruit is ready. This image is one of dedication, patience, and caring. You must be dedicated to the seeds for the entire time, be patient in waiting for the reward, and care for and nurture the plants. (p. 129)

In this analogy, front-end effort and ongoing care enable positive results. In the organizational sense, carefully planning appropriate learning, delivering learning through appropriate andragogical instructional methods, and remaining persistent in this effort is essential.

Learning, Onboarding, and Attrition

The quality of the onboarding process and available learning influences an employee's future interests. West (2018) suggested that employee onboarding experiences often determine their perception of the organization and, ultimately, their decision to remain on the job or leave. This process often needs improvement, with an average of 50 percent attrition rate of hourly employees within four months (West, 2018). Dismal abandonment figures suggest that the onboarding process is challenging to implement effectively. Cable et al. (2013) stated, "the process of recruiting, hiring, and training new employees is expensive and time-consuming" (p. 28). The alternative is not economical. Employee turnover, often connected to frustration within role assignments (Chiu & Francesco, 2003), is very costly; up to $100,000 to replace an account executive (Moore, 2006). Sriram et al. (2019) offered that attaining substantial organizational health requires the minimization of employee attrition.

The manufacturing sector affords an excellent case study of the necessity of appropriate learning as a new employee. Will (2017) offered that new manufacturing employees require 65 hours of training and two months on the job to become effective in their role. Training hours represent direct competition with available production hours and require careful implementation (Mockus, 2015). Planning is essential to illustrate an investment and value in a new employee rather than sending them to a task without direction (Putre, 2015). Traditional onboarding in manufacturing consisted of completing forms with Human Resources and observing a senior employee in operation (Putre, 2015); this archaic practice is ineffective. Senior operators tasked with training the recruits resort to pedagogical teaching methods from their earlier school experiences (Davidson, 1997) and often cannot commit the time to recruits due to other responsibilities. Davidson (1997) suggested that such methodology disregards employees as adult learners, is not consistent, and results in outcomes that do not always align with those of the organization. Older methods such as written materials are ineffective, as many of today's workers use digital technology for communications and learning (Mockus, 2015). Offering new employees learning access on a digital platform before their first day onsite drives efficiencies and affords more hands-on learning when they arrive (Simer, 2017). Most new employees already use devices (such as Apple iPhones, iPads, and Android devices) that are suitable for pre-employment learning.

Generational Considerations

The support of generational preferences supports employee engagement. Simer (2017) offered, "turnover rates tend to be higher for younger generations... the more efficient the (onboarding) process, the better the experience and the more likely it is that new hires will stay at a company longer" (p. 2). Peer mentoring, coupled with self-directed learning, is of interest to millennial employees (Putre, 2015). Where guidance is not possible, an insider's tour of the various work areas may pique the millennial's interest (Putre, 2015). Millennials often decide to remain long-term within the first day (Putre, 2015); appropriate planning promotes the desire to engage. Putre (2015) suggested that 52% of millennials prefer gamification or simulation in their learning. As the first digital natives, Millennials expect technology integration in their education (Simer, 2017). Mockus (2015) implored that allocating training time is difficult, and micro-learning sessions and short videos may supplement training efforts without consuming much time. In all cases, accessible training increases the opportunity to learn where and when it is convenient.

Enhancing Retention

Challenges occur at many levels as new employees leave an organization. Sriram et al. (2019) indicated that employee attrition, or company exit, is costly to the organization and indicates overall organizational health. Attrition affects product quality and operational continuity and is an issue globally in manufacturing organizations (Kokubun, 2017; Sriram et al., 2019). Aside from employee replacement's direct cost, production losses and safety concerns are prevalent with increased attrition (Sriram et al., 2017). Sriram et al. (2019) added that "lack of career advancement and ineffective utilization of their knowledge and skills" (p. 23) are frequent reasons for voluntary departure and suggested that older workers are engaged in their roles through "career satisfaction, training, and development" (p. 24). From a managerial perspective, the desire to enhance status is a factor in deciding to leave when the enhancement is impossible within the same company (Krausz & Reshef, 1992). Sriram et al. (2019) outlined the relationship between employee education and tenure; educated employees are more stable in their roles than their uneducated counterparts. Employees may seek to enhance their status in the workplace through educational pursuits. However, Krausz and Reshef (1992) cited that only 2.8 percent of the respondents in their study attempted to improve their position through study. Pre-Internet values trends by Krausz and Reshef (1992) may differ significantly since the broad introduction of formal and informal learning opportunities online following their research.

Minimizing excessive employee attrition, an inefficient workforce, and low employee morale is possible through appropriate employee learning and career development that respects employee needs as adult learners. Employers must strive to support substantial onboarding and commit to continuous learning and improvement both individually and at the organizational level.

Understanding Andragogy

The learning practitioner's understanding of the fundamental tenets of adult learning theory is the foundation of a thriving adult learning environment in the workplace. Over the last several decades, the adult learner's unique requirements became the focus of significant research. One of the pioneers of understanding adult learning, Malcolm Knowles, offered vital distinctions between the learning needs of children and adults. Successful learning in the organization acknowledges the adult learner's needs as differentiated from models of instruction experienced in the early years of education. The traditional educational system serves children's education and focuses on achievements such as SAT scores or job acquisition and was described as "progressively regressive" by Knowles (1973). Knowles (1973) assured that proper learning for adults must violate pedagogy practices and consider andragogy. The term andragogy, founded in the Greek language, translates to "leader of adults" (Knowles, 1973; Finn, 2011). Distinctly different from pedagogy ("leading children"), andragogy suggests that adult education has dramatically different requirements from pedagogy. In the pedagogical model, the learner maintains dependency, while successful andragogy supports learner progression from dependence to self-directedness (Knowles, 1977). Children benefit from subject-centered learning that prepares them for future education, college, and the workplace; the adult requires task-oriented learning and immediacy of application (Knowles, 1973). Knowles (1970) described this difference as innate needs shift from childhood to adulthood:

Table 1. Pedagogical vs. andragogical assumptions (Knowles, 1977, p. 211).

	Pedagogical	**Andragogical**
About	Teacher-directed learning	Self-directed learning
Concept of the Learner	Dependent personality	Increasingly self-directed organism
Role of Learner Experience	To be built on more than used	A rich resource for learning
Readiness to Learn	Varies with levels of maturation	Develops from life tasks & problems
Orientation to Learning	Subject-centered	Task or problem-centered
Motivation	External rewards and punishments	Internal incentives, curiosity

The first and by far the most important difference between adults and youths as learners... is that of their self-concept. A child first sees himself as a completely dependent personality. During the course of his childhood and youth, that dependence is reinforced as decisions are made for him in the home, at school, in church, on the playground... But at some point, he starts experiencing the joy of deciding things for himself... and by adolescence he is well along the way toward rebelling against having his life run by the adult world. He becomes an adult psychologically at the point at which his concept of himself changes from one of dependency to one of autonomy... Now at the point at which this change occurs, there develops in the human being a deep psychological need to be perceived by himself and by others as being indeed self-directing. Andragogy is based upon the deep insight that the deepest need an adult has is to be treated as an adult, to be treated as a self-directing person, to be treated with respect. (p. 86)

Knowles (1977) offered that many adults have been conditioned for pedagogically-based dependency learning so intently that leaders and decision-makers often revert to this dependency mindset in instructional situations. Therefore, learning initiatives must respect the adult learner's needs rather than reliance on pedagogical instructional methods by default in the organizational context. Table 1 illustrates the divisions in pedagogical and andragogical learning practices.

Many authors cite Eduard Lindeman's adult learning assumptions in the analysis of adult learning. For example, Knowles et al. (2005) outlined beliefs of Lindeman that serve as foundational elements of adult learning theory:

1. Adults are motivated to learn as they experience needs and interests that learning will satisfy; therefore, these are appropriate starting points for organizing adult learning activities.
2. Adults' orientation to learning is life-centered; therefore, the appropriate units for organizing adult learning are life situations, not subjects.
3. Experience is the richest resource for adults' learning; therefore, the core methodology of adult education is the analysis of experience.
4. Adults have a deep need to be self-directing; therefore, the role of the teacher is to engage in a process of mutual inquiry with them rather than to transmit his or her knowledge to them and then evaluate their conformity to it.
5. *Individual differences among people increase with age; therefore, adult education must make optimal provision for differences in style, time, place, and pace of learning.* (p. 39-40)

Expanding on Lindeman's foundational elements, Knowles et al. (2005) offered five assumptions of the model of andragogy:

1. The need to know. Adults need to know why they need to learn something before undertaking to learn it.
2. The learner's self-concept. Adults have a self-concept of being responsible for their own decision, for their own lives… they develop a deep psychological need to be seen by others and treated by others as being capable of self-direction. They resent and resist situations in which they feel others are imposing their wills on them… the minute adults walk into an activity labeled "education" or "training"… they hark back to their previous school experience, put on their dunce hats of dependency, fold their arms, sit back, and say "teach me."
3. The role of the learners' experience. Adults come into an educational activity with both a greater volume and a different quality of experience from that of youths.
4. Readiness to learn. Adults become ready to learn those things they need to know and be able to do so in order to cope effectively with their real-life situations.
5. *Orientation to learning. Adults are motivated to learn to the extent that they perceive that learning will help them perform tasks or deal with problems that they confront in their life situations.* (p. 64-7)

Understanding the concepts of andragogy is vital when creating meaningful and relevant instruction in support of the adult learner. Attempting to teach adults with methods of pedagogy is likely to meet resistance as it contradicts the needs of employees as adult learners. Of equal significance is learning established on principles of constructivism. As a construct of effective adult learning, constructivist-based learning promotes applying new knowledge to actively solve problems, build, and create. The immediate reinforcement of new concepts through active application supports retention and application long after the session and far beyond the rote memorization required for an antiquated multiple-choice exam. Adult learners become engaged when tasks are directly applicable to their needs and are encouraged to learn through the immediate and active application of new skills.

MOTIVATION AND CONFLICTING PRIORITIES

Despite content design aligning with these principles, learning efforts may fail to get off the ground if learners fail to engage; an unwilling or unable participant is unlikely to benefit from well-intentioned instruction. Unlike children attending compulsory education, adults ultimately choose learning participation (Knowles, 1977), suggesting that adult educators must support and encourage adult learner engagement. Employee motivation to learn is affected by internal and external factors. Learning motivation is a complex and continually changing force, founded in early learning experiences, and modified through social interactions (Hubackova & Semradova 2014). Motivation cumulates from personal and situational factors that promote action or withdrawal; this paradigm shifts over a lifetime (Lukianova, 2016).

Poupore (2014) offered that learner interest includes motivation, cognition, and emotional factors. Combined, these factors represent a "powerful motivational conglomerate" for the adult learner (Poupore, 2014, p. 87). Remedios and Richardson (2012) suggested that learners' perception of their abilities mirrors their motivation. Comparably, Siegle, Rubinstein, Pollard, and Romey (2010) offered that extensive research suggests a "positive correlation between self-efficacy beliefs and academic performance and persistence" (p. 93). Self-efficacy relates to locus of control or the belief that one can change outcomes based on their actions (Hegarty, 2011; Hsia et al., 2014). Hegarty (2011) offered, "those with an internal locus of control believe they have a strong influence over particular events. Their behavior, in essence, determines outcomes" (p. 147). In this case, the learner may control their success level on the job and future opportunities based on effort and agency. The most potent motivation occurs internally rather than externally within a specific context and the realization of the necessity of the knowledge (Finn, 2011). The belief of the self as a "fixed entity," such as the notion that basic abilities are unchangeable, is negatively related to high performance (Siegle et al., 2010) and may further inhibit learning commitment. Even as the employee as an adult learner understands that outcomes correlate with results, various reasons exist for adults to engage in or avoid learning. Hubackova and Semradova (2014) suggested that receiving a degree or qualification (goal attainment) is of utmost importance to the adult.

Goal Attainment

Participating in education and earning a degree, certification, or gaining mastery suggests that the learner desires achievement but must delay gratification and endure the defined academic or occupational learning workload, producing results before award realization. In the independent (intrinsic) context, the learner wishes to engage in the content as it is enjoyable, exciting, or challenging in support of self-determination (Elliot & Harackiewicz, 1996; Deci & Ryan, 2008), and serves as "a means to an end" (Wellrad et al., 2013, p. 517). Moustakas (2018) offered, "Approximately 50% (of adults) consider that it is important to acquire knowledge and skills for everyday life but also because it is compelling either in the sense of obtaining a certificate (48.6%) or as a workplace requirement (18.1%)" (p. 48). The desire for favorable judgments or avoiding negative judgments (extrinsic motivation) promotes learner participation, although learners that internalize objectives (intrinsically motivated) are more engaged and equipped to navigate setbacks (Remedios & Richardson, 2013). Activities directly connected to extrinsic rewards tend to undermine the support of intrinsic motivation (Deci & Ryan, 2008). In the context of adult learning in the workplace, intrinsic motivation is key to learner engagement and reinforcement of mastery goals. Knowledge of motivations aligned with mastery goals, performance-approach goals, and performance-avoidance affords the educator to create the most effective learning experience.

Performance Avoidance

Organizations that commit to employee learning programs over the long term face the employee's potential to reject learning opportunities. Performance avoidance is a common reason for learning non-participation to evade the perception of incompetence, affecting nearly 49% of workers (Deci & Ryan, 2008; Remedios & Richardson, 2013). When performance evaluation occurs after learning, some adults choose to escape the failure potential by declining to engage in learning altogether (Elliot & Harackiewicz, 1996; Siegle et al., 2010). Adult learners with low self-efficacy disengage more quickly and may allow competing priorities to support dropping out (Remedios & Richardson, 2012).

In support of the subversion of post-course examination fears, meaningful instruction does not "teach to the test" but challenges the learner to properly apply course knowledge in new applications and scenarios in the constructivist paradigm. Assessments comprised of rote memorization are stress-inducing and do not reinforce the usable internalization of concepts. Knowles (1977) offered that fifteen-minute interviews with learners provided a more robust understanding of their knowledge than possible through a response-limited exam. An informed, remedial plan for inadequate performance reinforces a supportive learning atmosphere and reduces hesitancy to engage.

Cognitive Margin and Stress

Life conditions and demands on an individual frequently change. Some changes may necessitate an adult to partake in learning to successfully navigate the shifting landscape (Hubackova & Semradova, 2014). Everyday events during the human lifecycle, including births, deaths, gaining or losing employment, and marriage represent "choice points" that cause adults to re-evaluate their lives (McClusky, 1970; Ng, 2010). Cognitive margin considers the capacity to learn as affected by life circumstances, competing commitments, and other factors that consume intellectual processing capacity. McClusky (1970) offered that adults often decline to participate in learning due to "attitudes and circumstances rather than the loss of innate learning ability" (p. 10). As a foundational element of the conceptual framework of this study, McClusky (1970) suggested that "margin," or "surplus power available to a person beyond what is required to meet the demands imposed by oneself and by society" (p. 10) and considers cognitive resources that affect the ability of the adult learner to engage in learning. Societal and personal demands exist as a "load" and contradict the "power" required to engage in exploratory learning activities (Knowles, 1973). Akin to Knowles' assertions that adult learners feel comfortable and safe in the learning context, McClusky (1970) indicated that those with margin in reserve might take on the exploration and creativity required in the learning process, permitting ascension "above a plateau of mere self-subsistence" (p. 82). Consideration of learner margin encourages innovation, engagement, and excellence on the job; these elements are critical to organizational success.

Learning can be a stressor to adult learners. LePine et al. (2004) offered that the psychological response to stress may contribute to or challenge the ability to engage in learning, suggesting, "The psychological response… reflects emotions that occur as the situation is appraised with respect to whether it is potentially challenging (beneficial) or threatening (harmful)" (p. 883). Learners that experience stress through the challenge apply more effort towards learning viewed as worthwhile, while those who believe that education is a negative experience exert less effort (LePine et al., 2004). As considered in McClusky's writing, LePine et al. (2004) suggested that exhaustion and competing life events (hindrance stress) challenge the learner to push through and put forth the effort for employer-required training. When on-the-job learning is optional, employees may expend minimal energy towards completion or decline participation altogether (LePine et al., 2004). LePine et al. (2004) offered that purposeful instructional design and appropriate support reduce ambiguous learning perceptions.

Self-Determination

Adults have choices. They choose significant others, vocations, and career paths. Deci et al. (1989) offered, "self-determining means to experience a sense of choice in initiating and regulating one's own actions" (p. 580). Adult learners also choose to work or not and learn or avoid learning. The composition of an adult's consciousness and output of a belief system is a personal resolution. In this sense, the requirements of the employer and that of the learner may be at odds. Tasks or concepts deemed critical to the employer but not meaningful to the employee may be disregarded, often harmful to the employer's compulsory outcomes. The viability of corporate goal achievement suggests that concepts, beliefs, and relevant knowledge to support these goals must also become valuable to the employee. Of critical interest in this matter is the transition of such objectives from outwardly arranged to inwardly important.

Deci and Ryan (1985) organized Self-Determination Theory (SDT) within two orientations: intrinsic (associated with topic interest) and extrinsic (linked to working towards a defined goal). Expressly, "SDT assumes that people are by nature active and self-motivated, curious and interested, vital and eager to succeed because success itself is personally satisfying and rewarding… (or) alienated and mechanized, or passive and disaffected" (Deci & Ryan, 2008). When the learning process turns intrinsic, outcomes become engrained in the learner as they allocate internal resources towards successful outcomes. The intrinsic orientation model affords ongoing and meaningful engagement towards the satisfaction of current and future objectives.

SDT suggests three levels of extrinsic motivation, including introjection (taking external demands without acceptance), identification (accepting the importance of the external demands as necessary), and integration, as with the assimilation of new content with their existing self, becoming a new entity (Deci & Ryan, 2008). Of these categories, the latter two appear acceptable for the work environment. Deci and Ryan (1985) defined amotivation as the lack of internal and external motivation. In the context of the adult in the workplace, amotivation represents the employee's rejection of external demands, believing that such requests are unimportant. Without intervention, this paradigm represents a misalignment with company values at best, though the continued demonstration of amotivation is not compatible with functional role performance or sustained employability.

Ideally, intrinsic motivation or the internalization of external motivators guides adults within the workplace. Poupore (2014) suggested that subject matter interest drives intrinsic motivation towards learning. In this sense, the self-selection into an employer's industry implies a level of interest in that industry, ideally making the employee available to the reception of related learning opportunities. Deci and Ryan (2008) offered that the facilitation of basic psychological needs, including inclusion into a family or group, along with the encouragement of value internalization, may support this paradigm. Perceived competency on an individual level is also vital to internalized regulation (Deci & Ryan, 2008). Deci and Ryan (2008) noted that acceptance of activities perceived as uninteresting improves by including the rationale behind the endeavor and providing appropriate support. However, this model does not suggest that learners provided a poor experience shall accept it with the condition of an explanation. Human beings seek autonomy; this ideal is powerful when supported by an authority figure (Deci & Ryan, 2008). The provision of independence supports "initiation, supporting a sense of choice, and being responsive to their thoughts, questions, and initiatives… (people) often feel free to follow their interests and consider the relevance and importance for themselves of social values, morals, and norms" (Deci & Ryan, 2008, p. 18). When adults attain a level of autonomy in their learning efforts, the realization of positive effects occurs in performance, well-being, and development (Deci & Ryan, 2008). Baeten et al. (2013) suggested that the learning environment affects the shift towards autonomous learning, with lecture transitioning into "case-based learning" as influential in learner autonomy support. As learners move beyond the basics, it is reasonable to apply new knowledge in a constructivist context that is rewarding and meaningful in maximizing knowledge acquisition.

Age-Related Factors

Adult learning practitioners must consider the ages and educational backgrounds of adult learners. Sriram et al. (2019) also suggested that older workers are engaged in their roles through "career satisfaction, training, and development" (p. 24) while "lack of career advancement and ineffective utilization of their knowledge and skills" (p. 23) are frequent reasons for voluntary departure. Those distanced from their diplomas carry different perceptions of learning than recent graduates. Entering the workforce should not suggest a hard shift from "learner" to "worker," rather, a purposeful transition to a continuum of growth and enrichment. McClusky (1970) urged, "It is the adult condition and not the irreversible loss of ability which feeds the conventional view that aptitude diminishes with passing years" (p. 91). At the time of McClusky's writings, society viewed learning as a child's role and working as the role of adults. McClusky (1970) discovered that after age 50, some adults believe that time is running out and that learning is not possible, suggesting that adults often fall back to maintenance and repetition following the mastery of skills required to survive. Arguably, this age division has likely advanced due to longer life expectancies and the availability of remote learning in both formal and informal environments. However, the prevalence of maintenance as an adult does not preclude the necessity of discovery (McClusky, 1970) and continuous improvement in the organizational context.

Gegenfurtner and Vauras (2012) examined employees' motivational factors to learn at various career stages, finding that older adults seek social learning opportunities while avoiding those perceived as threats. Motivation to learn does not decline with age, and in some cases, motivation increases (Gegenfurtner & Vauras, 2012). Conversely, Gegenfurtner and Vauras (2012) offered that learning motivation is often challenging for younger employees. Older learners display enhanced emotional regulation in social learning situations; a trait that improves with maturity (Gegenfurtner & Vauras, 2012). Self-regulation is personal causation, which Hegarty (2011) suggested correlates particular behaviors with results.

Confidence Levels and Reengagement

Past learning experiences influence an adult's perception of learning opportunities. Apps (1970) indicated that many adults are "products of an educational system where they (existed) as A or D students, as achievers or underachievers, or as dropouts. The wholeness of the self—their total personality—as reduced to a symbol suggesting average, superior, or mediocre" (p. 97). This outwardly imposed self-perception can pose a challenge to taking on additional learning. Life events such as divorce or job loss trigger learners to engage in less learning and programs with low failure risks (Ng, 2010). Siegle et al. (2010) offered that learners' perception of their intelligence defines their views of performance and mastery goals. These goals are often contradictory, as the performance goal suggests intelligence, while mastery goals require submission to the learning content (Siegle et al., 2010). The employee may never become comfortable with this vulnerability in a competitive workplace. Cramer et al. (2019) implored:

Some employees may experience imposter syndrome in which they juggle perceived failures and mistakes that make us question our priorities and next steps. We feel like we are faking our success or are haphazard winners in the lottery... both undeserving of the success we have achieved and at risk of losing it all when someone wises up to our charade. (p. 36)

When learners have competition-based personal insecurities, preemptive support may lessen these perceived inadequacies in the learning environment. Werner and Weckenmann (2012) considered reducing task difficulty to comfortably meet the worker competence versus upgrading employee abilities through adequate training that enables process variance management during production. The former is unacceptable as it "might lead to unnoticed or uncared for the propagation of erroneous measurement results, as working steps may easily be carried out wrongly or half-heartedly if the reason is not understood" (Werner & Weckenmann, 2012, p. 1535). Aversion of the phenomenon connects learning to a "staff development cycle rather than as a unique event" (Werner & Weckenmann, 2012, p. 1536). This initiative considers developing a "network of competencies," followed by appropriate worker assignment and outcome assessment (Werner & Weckenmann, 2012, p. 1538). The following section explores sample applications and exercises that engage the learner and empower the educational practitioner in the quest for organizational growth and stability.

Additional Barriers to Learning

Many of the defined barriers to adult learning interfere with the andragogical principles examined in this chapter. Knowles (1973) suggested that adult learning's voluntary nature presents unique challenges that do not exist in pedagogy. Boeren (2011) categorized common barriers into situational, institutional, and dispositional categories. Situational barriers suggest time imbalance between personal and work commitments, institutional barriers occur when courses occur at inopportune times or locations, and dispositional barriers suggest insufficient self-confidence to engage (Boeren, 2011). Falasca (2011) further segmented the impediments of adult learning into internal and external categories. Internal barriers include a fear of failure (often leading to performance-avoidance behaviors), reliance on old knowledge, and myths such as "rote memorization is the only way" (Falasca, 2011; Finn, 2011; Apps, 1970; Knowles, 1977). Falasca (2011) outlined external barriers as physical challenges such as loss of vision and hearing that occur with aging, pain, and fatigue that affect energy and motivation, life role changes including marriage, children, and work role changes.

Adults are generally receptive to friendly learning atmospheres and learning that provides a challenge that is not overwhelming, particularly with essential task-based subjects (Falasca, 2011). Adults also enjoy participating in learning content in which they are interested and topics they have adequate knowledge to contribute (Poupore, 2014). However, perceptions of "heaviness, seriousness, complexity, and difficulty" tend to deter learner engagement (Poupore, 2014, p. 83).

Adults exhibit rapid success expectations and at an acceptable "opportunity cost" when invested in a learning program (Finn, 2011). Opportunity cost considers whether the program provides a more significant perceived benefit than money, time, or effort expended (Finn, 2011; Moustakas, 2018). Moustakas (2018) also suggested that learners consider cost, timing, location, teaching methods, and support. Other factors include family support, health reasons, psychological issues, and existing perceptions of the learning content provided (Moustakas, 2018). Disengagement (amotivation) may create an imbalance with this consideration, weighing heavily towards inaction. When such programs are optional and not actively encouraged by leadership, the disengaged adult employee refuses such opportunities. The learning institution must recognize these potential barriers and align learning opportunities appropriately with employee needs to minimize such inhibitions (Falasca, 2011; Knowles et al., 2005).

APPLICATION OF ANDRAGOGY IN THE WORKPLACE AND DISTANCE LEARNING

Learning professionals and managers of adult employees are pivotal in employee career progression and job satisfaction. Appropriate application of andragogical models in this context is key to employee growth and engagement. Armed with this knowledge, managers can support the employee as an adult learner and enhance retention and performance. This section offers practical application of earlier concepts, emphasizing andragogical principles through Internet-based video conferencing platforms such as Zoom and Microsoft Teams supporting remote learning.

Ideal classrooms support active learning environments that minimize discomfort and distraction while learners feel safe and supported (Finn, 2011). Within the classroom space in-person or virtually online, adult learners require environments where their life experiences are relevant and free to contribute without risk (Finn, 2011; Knowles et al., 2005). Successful classroom facilitation in the context of andragogy includes the active adaptation of the curriculum based on the input, experiences, and interests of adult learners (Finn, 2011). The learning facilitator in the adult learning environment serves as a guide and never the "sage on the stage." All facilitators, regardless of tenure, have much to gain from the input of adult learners; these gains include sustaining meaningful discussions in the classroom and promoting further discussion and commentary from participants. In addition, the adept facilitator maintains a welcoming ear to clarify and improve the curriculum for future sessions; employees as adult learners are pleased to share their relevant experience in this effort.

Technology in Instruction

Learners of today have information more readily available than ever before. A Google search provides answers in seconds, whereas fifty years ago, a learner went to the library searching for a non-published answer (Graesser, 2013). Online learning, thoughtfully designed, is particularly useful to the adult learner, supporting self-direction, social interactions, and purposeful inquiry (Hashim et al., 2015). The adult learner expects an intuitive and quality medium to reinforce their knowledge construction (Hashim et al., 2015), with content that supports engagement and reduced cognitive load (Jones, 2013). In this effort, organizations may enhance online learning motivation through adequate support and expectation, minimize mental overload, and provide encouragement throughout the course (Jones, 2013). Regardless of the delivery mode, successful training includes human interaction, which "advocates the active engagement of people with resources in communication with others, rather than the transfer of knowledge from educator to learner" (Thoms & Burton, 2016, p. 98). This concept of connectivism parallels theories of adult learning offered by Knowles, including the participatory paradigm. Adults have experiences to share, and all involved (including the facilitator) become absorbed in learning content while appreciating new perspectives.

Technology-driven programs are now at the forefront of the consumer realm, and technology in business is also the standard. The expectation from employees as consumers is that learning technology in the workplace follows. When appropriately applied, Internet-based learning environments emulate in-person classroom learning atmospheres without geography or campus-bound technology limitations. Online coursework is a prevailing offering at most universities, with online college enrollees in the United States exceeding seven million in 2016, four times that of a decade prior (Thoms & Burton, 2016). This trend further accelerated in 2020 with the COVID-19 global pandemic restrictions. Businesses have followed suit. In the corporate environment, many companies believe that employees possess baseline technology skills, although some employees do not embrace technology (Hsia et al., 2012; Thoms & Burton, 2016). Therefore, workplace learning practitioners must remain aware of emergent and relevant technologies to support their employees (Thoms & Burton, 2016) while providing applicable support and encouragement. Aside from educational advantages, technology implementation has cost-savings potential, such as transitioning from costly printed materials to an always-current version pushed to the mobile devices that customers and employees already own.

Li et al. (2017) contemplated the implications of technology-based learning on long-term retention, the effectiveness of error reduction, and the economic viability of implementation. Such questions are relevant. Technology-based learning, such as virtual and augmented reality, has become readily available and affordable. The adult learning practitioner must consider the impact of implementation and sustainability versus third-party developer and platform costs. Above all, direct applicability to the learner's needs is paramount. The learning practitioner must consider the desired outcomes as the basis of curriculum design decisions aside from the potential "wow factor" of new technologies. An expensive shiny new virtual or augmented reality application without substance is soon forgotten while ineffectively consuming learning and development budgets.

Virtual Meeting Facilitation

Virtual meeting applications such as Zoom and Microsoft Teams attained unprecedented popularity in recent years, and exponentially so with the COVID-19 pandemic. Face-to-face meetings in the classroom have shifted to virtual, webcam-driven meetings to the benefit or deficit of the learners. While in-person events were restricted, the dramatic expansion of online meeting technology has increased outreach as never before. Just as with modern educational environments (K-12, colleges), the expectation in organizations is that learning is delivered online. This paradigm is here to stay even after the eradication of COVID-19.

Online meetings have a reputation as time-wasters that invite attendee multitasking. Old practices, including "sit and get" instruction and "hold your questions until the end," are dated and ineffective. Quality interaction and engagement are possible in the virtual learning space with appropriate planning and learner encouragement. When actively involved, participants believe their time is well-spent and leave with a positive, confident feeling about the course material. Well-executed, virtual online meetings are an excellent opportunity to connect with learners across geographical limitations, cultures, and time zones. Physical technology concerns (connection speeds, lighting, detailed hardware information) are intentionally absent in this discussion. Instead, the focus here considers critical adult learning concepts supporting the successful facilitation of virtual online learning sessions with adults.

Engagement in the Virtual Space

Knowles' core assumptions of andragogy are explained earlier in this chapter and apply to adult learning initiatives, whether in person or in an online virtual meeting space. Virtual learning often occurs in an online "classroom." This term may promote adult recollection of childhood learning experiences that directly conflict with their current needs as experienced adults. Honoring the needs of the employees as adult learners removes subconscious barriers to learning while encouraging participation in virtual learning sessions. The rules of andragogical engagement in the physical classroom also apply in virtual sessions. An appropriate instructional environment supports adults' need to feel safe in contributing knowledge in collaboration with others, minimizing threats to the sense of self, and when they believe in the importance of the subject matter.

A live, in-person discussion includes eye contact when appropriate. In the virtual space, the eyes of the learners are in the facilitator's camera. When not sharing screen content, the facilitator looks directly into the camera while speaking, just as with participants in the classroom. Eye contact is engaging and drives attention, though in the virtual environment, bi-directional eye contact is not possible as viewing participants on-screen requires taking one's eyes off of the camera. The camera used for presentations requires proper positioning and distance from the speaker. It should be at eye level with the presenter, with the top of the presenter's head reaching approximately 75-90% of the vertical frame space. With all participant cameras on, facial expressions and body language cues add meaning to the conversation. Meetings without this visual engagement invite incomplete conversations, disinterest, and multitasking.

When connecting with adult learners online, the facilitator must strive for a welcoming and friendly demeanor. A sincere smile and a friendly tone of voice transmit very well in the online classroom. As in the physical classroom, earn the right to present as the subject matter expert, however, not as the omniscient "sage on the stage." When asked a known question, reply with genuine enthusiasm, and encourage the participation of others. When asked a question with an unknown answer, it is always acceptable to reply that the answer is unknown and commit to finding the answer and informing all attendees of the response as soon as feasible. Nobody expects the course facilitator to know everything about everything, and the follow-up creates a sense of caring and trust. In this instance, another option considers polling the group to determine if the answer is present in the room while negotiating participant consensus through additional inquiry. Adults have experiences to share, and active contribution to an ongoing discussion promotes ongoing learning commitment.

Virtual instruction with adult learners demands a new tact aside from the 350-slide onslaught mentioned at the beginning of this chapter. Hale and Grenny (2020) suggested,

Nothing disengages a group more reliably than assaulting them with slide after slide of mind-numbing data organized in endless bullet points. It doesn't matter how smart or sophisticated the group is, if your goal is engagement, you must mix facts and stories... select the least amount of data you need to inform and engage the group. Don't add a single slide more. (n.p.)

Never attempt to "get through" a pile of slides, leaving little time to hear learner input and challenges. Instead, consider providing all essential data in advance, leaving critical time for vital concepts and discussion. Create opportunities for discussion surrounding key topics. Many virtual meeting tools have breakout room functions. Build time for breakout room discussions and small group work, and bring the groups back to the primary virtual meeting room to report their findings. Select critical points for discussion, and consider offering the reference material for the audience to read later. During the presentation, distribute these must-have documents to participants in real-time in Microsoft Teams or Zoom by dragging and dropping the document(s) into the chat window.

Each presentation is an opportunity to open meaningful dialog and never a "lecture." Lecturing adults contradicts their innate need to maintain their self-concept. Engagement tools such as Kahoot and Mentimeter, when used consequentially, add interest (and perhaps a bit of friendly competition) to virtual course sessions. Use them to support and instigate ongoing conversations, but never as a novelty. Discover which interactive tools enhance the discussion and implement them skillfully. Innate familiarization with the selected tools prevents taking an otherwise fantastic lesson off track; take the time to fully master the selected engagement tools before use in a live session.

Virtual courses must support the adult learners' need to recognize the direct applicability of the course content and understand how the learning content affords personal benefit. In pre-session communications, identify the application of the course content. Consider including an example of how the new knowledge enhances their day-to-day work experience. Summarize the session content and how the learners may apply new knowledge to support professional advancement.

Adult learners need to be viewed by others as "capable of self-direction" (Knowles et al., 2005, p. 65). Learners must view the subject matter as worthwhile and that the learning session is appealing and interactive. The meeting leader must ensure that the learning environment is not lecture-based but one that encourages collaborative knowledge creation. In this mode, the instructor serves as a facilitator or guide and not a lecturer. The facilitator introduces vital concepts with the discussion progressing through input and collaboration from participants. Reward and encourage continuing dialog as others offer their experience and perspectives.

Adult learners have experience to share, and a degree of subject expertise likely exists within the virtual classroom. Consider the creation of a few problems or situations for resolution by the application of the new knowledge. Blondy (2007) suggested, "Facilitators should craft discussion questions that require learners to think about how the course content can or should be applied to situations in their own lives" (p. 122). Within the virtual environment, use breakout rooms for small-group discussions and problem-solving. When high-knowledge contributors are present, consider separating them and guide their group discussions, supporting their engagement. Following the breakout room discussions, return to the larger group where each sub-group reports their problems and findings. In this way, all can actively participate and learn from the experience and perspectives of others.

Adults benefit from learning when they are ready and able to do so; advanced courses provide no benefit for the novice. Ensure that the course topics and expected outcomes are readily available to potential course enrollees. Further confusion is negated through a "test-out" option to confirm readiness for particular level coursework to confirm the presence of functional knowledge of the expected outcomes from the previous level. The analysis of an adult learner's understanding effectively commences outside of rote memorization, the traditional examination method of pedagogy. Recognizing adult aversion to examinations, Knowles (1977) offered that fifteen-minute interviews with learners provided a more robust understanding of their knowledge than possible through a response-limited exam. An open dialog with the learner permits knowledge expansion confirmation as they apply learned concepts to new applications. Herein lies a dual-factor enhancement in reducing adult learner performance-avoidance hesitation and reinforcing learned content through active application.

Effective adult learning demands that learning is life-, task-, or problem-centered and presented in the context of real-life situations (Knowles et al., 2005). Knowles et al. (2005) offered an example of university extension courses that failed when made available to adults in the evenings. Success occurred when "Composition I" became "Writing Better Business Letters" (Knowles et al., 2005, p. 68). Another example considered a slate of reading, writing, and arithmetic courses designed to reduce illiteracy in the United States; this program failed as the learner's everyday experience negated the vocabulary and the arithmetic examples had no practical application (Knowles et al., 2005). Enhanced results followed when the curriculum was relatable and practical in the lives of the learners (Knowles et al., 2005). In all instances, the course level is appropriate for the learners, with content directly relatable from the learner's perspective.

ADULT LEARNING THEORY: A UNIVERSAL PARADIGM

Whether formal learning occurs in the classroom or online, quality learning in the workplace is essential to personal and organizational success. Acknowledging the findings of adult learning researchers who have come before affords a strong base in encouraging personal growth, development, and employee engagement in the workplace. The workplace learning practitioner must also understand the learner's level of subject-matter knowledge before the commencement of coursework. Such knowledge enables the application of specialized attention for those that need it and identifies advanced participants for additional input and insight during live course sessions. Establishing an engagement strategy for all session participant ability levels promotes interest and learning regardless of subject matter experience. With a proper understanding of the adult learner's needs, the learning practitioner can establish workplace learning conditions conducive to active commitment, meaningful discourse, appropriate learning activities, and continued support to help employees thrive.

This chapter considered many classic and contemporary theories that differentiate the adult learner's needs from "traditional" instructional methods designed to support the learning dependencies of children. Applying adult learning principles in the virtual learning environment removes geographical restrictions and, when implemented correctly, can match or surpass the quality of learning possible in the traditional classroom. Adult learning practitioners must inspire employees as adult learners in a learning environment not of pedagogical lecture but one which enhances understanding through relevance, collaboration, and practical application. Engraining these principles purposefully and thoughtfully throughout workplace learning serves as the basis of organizational advancement, efficiency, and sustainability.

ACKNOWLEDGMENT

The author would like to acknowledge Dr. Sandi Cooper as Faculty Advisor for guidance on dissertation research that led to the publication of this chapter. The author also acknowledges Dr. Nicholas Werse, Director of the Ed.D. Writing Center, for support and encouragement in the chapter proposal and submission.

REFERENCES

Apps, G. (1970). Fundamentals of adult learning. In S. M. Grabowski (Ed.), *Adult learning and instruction* (pp. 96–109). Adult Education Association of the U.S.A.

Baeten, M., Dochy, F., & Struyven, K. (2013). The effects of different learning environments on students' motivation for learning and their achievement. *The British Journal of Educational Psychology, 83*(3), 484–501. doi:10.1111/j.2044-8279.2012.02076.x PMID:23822533

Blondy, L. (2007). Evaluation and application of andragogical assumptions to the adult online learning environment. *Journal of Interactive Online Learning, 6*(2), 116–130. www.ncolr.org/jiol/issues/pdf/6.2.3.pdf

Cable, D. M., Gino, F., & Staats, B. R. (2013). Reinventing employee onboarding. *MIT Sloan Management Review, 54*(3), 23–28.

Chiu, R. K., & Francesco, A. M. (2003). Dispositional traits and turnover intention: Examining the mediating role of job satisfaction and affective commitment. *International Journal of Manpower, 24*(3), 284–298. doi:10.1108/01437720310479741

Cramer, R. A., Alexander-Floyd, N. G., & Means, T. (2019). Balance is a fallacy: Striving for and supporting a life with integrity. *PS, Political Science & Politics, 52*(1), 35–38. doi:10.1017/S1049096518001154

Davidson, B. A. (1997). *Application of adult learning principles for employee training in small manufacturing organizations* [Ph.D. Dissertation, Walden University]. ProQuest.

Deci, E., & Ryan, R. (2008). Facilitating optimal motivation and psychological well-being across life's domains. *Canadian Psychology, 49*(1), 14–23. doi:10.1037/0708-5591.49.1.14

Deci, E., & Ryan, R. M. (1985). *Intrinsic motivation and self-determination in human behavior*. Plenum. doi:10.1007/978-1-4899-2271-7

Deci, E. L., Connell, J. P., & Ryan, R. M. (1989). Self-determination in a work organization. *The Journal of Applied Psychology, 74*(4), 580–590. doi:10.1037/0021-9010.74.4.580

Elliot, A. J., & Harackiewicz, J. M. (1996). Approach and avoidance achievement goals and intrinsic motivation: A meditational analysis. *Journal of Personality and Social Psychology, 70*(3), 461–475. doi:10.1037/0022-3514.70.3.461

Englehardt, C. S., & Simmons, P. R. (2002). Creating an organizational space for learning. *The Learning Organization, 9*(1), 39–47. doi:10.1108/09696470210414818

Falasca, M. (2011). Barriers to adult learning: Bridging the gap. *Australian Journal of Adult Learning, 51*(3), 583–590.

Finn, D. (2011). Principles of adult learning: An ESL context. *MPAEA Journal of Adult Education, 40*(1), 34–39.

Gegenfurtner, A., & Vauras, M. (2012). Age-related differences in the relation between motivation to learn and transfer of training in adult continuing education. *Contemporary Educational Psychology, 37*(1), 33–46. doi:10.1016/j.cedpsych.2011.09.003

Graesser, A. C. (2013). Evolution of advanced learning technologies in the 21st Century. *Theory into Practice, 52*, 93–101. doi:10.1080/00405841.2013.795446

Hale, J., & Granny, J. (2020). *How to get people to actually participate in virtual meetings*. https://hbr.org/2020/03/how-to-get-people-to-actually-participate-in-virtual-meetings

Hashim, K. F., Tan, F. B., & Rashid, A. (2015). Adult learners' intention to adopt mobile learning: A motivational perspective. *British Journal of Educational Technology, 46*(2), 381–390. doi:10.1111/bjet.12148

Hegarty, N. (2011). Adult learners as graduate students: Underlying motivation in completing graduate programs. *The Journal of Continuing Higher Education*, *59*(3), 146–151. doi:10.1080/07377363.2011.614883

Hsia, J.-W., Chang, C. C., & Tseng, A. H. (2014). Effects of individuals' locus of control and computer self-efficacy on their e-learning acceptance in high-tech companies. *Behaviour & Information Technology*, *33*(1), 51–64. doi:10.1080/ 0144929X.2012.702284

Hubackova, S., & Semradova, I. (2014). Research study on motivation in adult education. *Procedia: Social and Behavioral Sciences*, *159*, 396–400. doi:10.1016/j.sbspro.2014.12.395

Jones, A. R. (2013). Increasing adult learner motivation for completing self-directed e-learning. *Performance Improvement*, *52*(7), 32–42. doi:10.1002/pfi.21361

Knowles, M. (1970). Andragogy, not pedagogy! In S. M. Grabowski (Ed.), *Adult learning and instruction* (pp. 71–80). Adult Education Association of the U.S.A.

Knowles, M. (1973). *The adult learner: A neglected species*. Gulf Publishing Company.

Knowles, M. (1977). Adult learning processes: Pedagogy and andragogy. *Religious Education (Chicago, Ill.)*, *72*(2), 202–211. doi:10.1080/0034408770720210

Knowles, M. (2016). Andragogy: Adult learning theory in perspective. *Community College Review*, *5*(3), 9–20. doi:10.1177/009155217800500302

Knowles, M., Holton, E. F., & Swanson, R. A. (2005). *The adult learner: The definitive classic in adult education and human resource development* (6th ed.). Elsevier. doi:10.4324/9780080481913

Kokubun, K. (2017). Education, organizational commitment, and rewards within Japanese manufacturing companies in China. *Employee Relations*, *40*(3), 458–485. doi:10.1108/ER-12-2016-0246

Krausz, M., & Reshef, M. (1992). Managerial job change: Reasons for leaving, choice determinants, and search processes. *Journal of Business and Psychology*, *6*(3), 349–359. doi:10.1007/BF01126770

LePine, J. A., LePine, M. A., & Jackson, C. L. (2004). Challenge and hindrance stress: Relationships with exhaustion, motivation to learn, and learning performance. *The Journal of Applied Psychology*, *89*(5), 883–891. doi:10.1037/0021-9010.89.5.883 PMID:15506867

Li, K., Hall, M., Bermell-Garcia, P., Alcock, J., Tiwari, A., & González-Franco, M. (2017). Measuring the learning effectiveness of serious gaming for training of complex manufacturing tasks. *Simulation & Gaming*, *48*(6), 770–790. doi:10.1177/1046878117739929

Liker, J., & Meier, D. (2006). *The Toyota Way fieldbook: A practical guide for implementing Toyota's 4ps*. McGraw-Hill.

Lukianova, L. (2016). Motivation factors of adult learning. *The New Educational Review*, *44*(1), 223–229. doi:10.15804/tner.2016.44.2.18

Mahan, J. D., & Stein, D. S. (2014). Teaching adults: Best practices that leverage the emerging understanding of the neurobiology of learning. *Current Problems in Pediatric and Adolescent Health Care*, *44*(6), 141–149. doi:10.1016/j.cppeds.2014.01.003 PMID:24981663

McClusky, H. (1965). Psychology and learning. *Review of Educational Research, 35*(3), 191–200. https://www.jstor.org/stable/1169825

McClusky, H. (1970). An approach to a differential psychology of adult potential. In S. M. Grabowski (Ed.), *Adult learning and instruction* (pp. 80–95). Adult Education Association of the U.S.A.

Mockus, H. (2018). Training beyond onboarding: Filling the gaps in food manufacturing. *Food Manufacture, 31*(2), 11.

Moore, H. (2006). Employee retention: The high cost of turnover: Attracting, retaining good staff key to success. *Automotive Body Repair News, 45*(10), 46.

Moustakas, L. (2018). Motivation and obstacles to adult participation in lifelong learning programs: The effect of gender and age. *Open Journal for Educational Research, 2*(1), 45–56. doi:10.32591/coas.ojer.0201.04045m

Ng, S. (2010). Motivation for lifelong learning: Role of positive environments and supportive relationships. *International Journal of Learning, 16*(12), 417–429.

Pfeffer, J., & Veiga, J. F. (1999). Putting people first for organizational success. *The Academy of Management Executive, 13*(2), 37–48. doi:10.5465/AME.1999.1899547

Poupore, G. (2014). The influence of content on adult L2 learners' task motivation: An interest theory perspective. *Canadian Journal of Applied Linguistics, 17*(2), 69–90.

Putre, L. (2015). Onboarding for the "on demand" generation or, how to keep millennials from bailing on day one. *Industry Week, 264*(6), 27.

Remedios, R., & Richardson, J. T. E. (2013). Achievement goals in adult learners: Evidence from distance education. *The British Journal of Educational Psychology, 83*(4), 664–685. doi:10.1111/bjep.12001 PMID:24175688

Senge, P. (2006). *The fifth discipline: The art and practice of the learning organization*. Crown Business.

Siegle, D., Rubenstein, L., Pollard, E., & Romey, E. (2010). Exploring the relationship of college freshmen honors students' effort and ability attribution, interest, and implicit theory of intelligence with perceived ability. *Gifted Child Quarterly, 54*(2), 93–101. doi:10.1177/0016986209355975

Simer, D. (2017). *Onboarding the next generation workforce in manufacturing. In Manufacturing Business Technology*. ProQuest.

Sriram, K., Joseph, J., Mathew, A., & Rai, A. (2019). Factors affecting high employee attrition in manufacturing firms: A case study. *Calitatea, 20*(169), 23–28.

Thoms, C. L. V., & Burton, S. L. (2016). Learning, development, and training: The influence of synergies through educational evolution. *International Journal of Adult Vocational Education and Technology, 7*(4), 85–104. doi:10.4018/IJAVET.2016100106

Werner, T., & Weckenmann, A. (2012). Sustainable quality assurance by assuring competence of employees. *Measurement, 45*(6), 1534–1539. doi:10.1016/j.measurement.2012.02.025

West, J. T. (2018). *Organizational socialization: The role of onboarding in employee longevity* [Ph.D. Dissertation, University of Texas at Arlington]. ProQuest.

Will, E. (2017). *Onboarding in the manufacturing boom. In Manufacturing Business Technology*. ProQuest.

ADDITIONAL READING

Charungkaittikul, S., & Henschke, J. A. (2017). Applying andragogical concepts in creating a sustainable lifelong learning society. *International Journal of Adult Vocational Education and Technology, 8*(4), 38–51. doi:10.4018/IJAVET.2017100104

Jacobs, D. (2009). *The art of the possible: Create an organization with no limitations*. Federal Market Publishing.

Jeno, L. M., Raaheim, A., Kristensen, S. M., Kristensen, K. D., Hole, T. N., Haugland, M. J., & Mæland, S. (2017). The relative effect of team-based learning on motivation and learning: A self-determination theory perspective. *CBE Life Sciences Education, 16*(4), ar59. Advance online publication. doi:10.1187/cbe.17-03-0055 PMID:29146665

Kotter, J. (2012). *Leading change*. Harvard Business Review Press.

Merriam, S., & Caffarella, R. (1999). *Learning in adulthood: A comprehensive guide*. Jossey-Bass.

KEY TERMS AND DEFINITIONS

Andragogy: Derived from the Greek language, andragogy translates to "leader of adults" and is used in reference to learning methodologies suitable for adult learning.

Cognitive Margin: The available mental resources which enable learning.

Empowerment: One's belief that they can control their destiny through selected actions.

Locus of Control: The extent of control that people believe they have over live outcomes.

Motivation: The desire to do something and the actions that support it.

Pedagogy: The implementation of learning methodologies intended for children.

Personal Causation: The belief that chosen behaviors provide specific outcomes.

Chapter 13
Creativity Processes Applied to the Innovation Management of a Digital Showroom for Cars

Francelma Maria de Moura Macêdo
Federal University of Rio Grande do Norte, Brazil

Jamerson Viegas Queiroz
Federal University of Rio Grande do Norte, Brazil

Zulmara Virgínia de Carvalho
Federal University of Rio Grande do Norte, Brazil

Cristiano Alves
Federal University of Santa Catarina, Brazil

ABSTRACT

The COVID-19 pandemic has profoundly impacted the Brazilian service sector. With the health crisis, challenges and changes in the business models of car dealerships are also intensified. Creativity is discussed by several conceptual approaches. From the point of view of neuroscience, it is a response to the human need of solving problems. It is within this premise that the present work aims to enhance value proposition for a business model centered on automobile e-commerce. This purpose unfolds in an exploratory research on approaches, methodologies, and tools of creativity, as well as the application of Cristiano Alves's creative framework in this business model. The analysis of the results signals improvements in solutions for car e-commerce. With this, it is concluded that collective creativity is efficient in the discovery of potentially innovative ideas.

INTRODUCTION

The advent of the health crisis of the new coronavirus has impacted world economy. Even the historically resilient Brazilian service sector showed an unprecedented 11.7% decline in income generation,

DOI: 10.4018/978-1-7998-8239-8.ch013

compared to the Covid-19 pandemic, which make up the country's GDP of 11.9% in the first two quarters of 2020 (Brazilian Institute of Economics [IBRE], 2020). In this direction, Brazilian vehicle sales in the first quarter recorded a 27% decline (Infomoney, 2020). The prospects for recovery from this crisis are dominated by uncertainty and heterogeneity in sectoral performance (IBRE, 2020), bequeathing the certainty of the demand for the development of solutions.

In fact, the most basic need to be a modern knowledge-producing society are educated individuals equipped with critical and creative thinking skills who make new inventions and discoveries and would like to initiate social change (Durnalı, Orakcı, & Aktan, 2019; Orakcı, Durnalı and Aktan, 2019; Orakcı, 2020). In this context, creativity is discussed by several conceptual approaches. From the point of view of neuroscience, it is a response to the human need of solving problems. (Kandel et al., 2014). In this direction, in the creation of new ideas in business projects for the development of mobile applications, the collective through framework enables the diversity of opinions and customization, according to the needs of the projects. According to Lévy (2003), Collective Intelligence is disseminated, valued, supervised in real time, which derives effective association of its know-how.

Searching before purchasing a car has always been common among consumers. According to the National Confederation of Shopkeepers (2019), 97% of internet users search for information online before buying in physical stores. With the measures of social isolation and other consequences resulting from the Covid-19 pandemic, consumers not only research, but also buy virtually (National Federation of Motor Vehicle Distribution [FENABRAVE], 2019).

It is believed that the main reason a buyer visits a store is the search for information and experiences that contribute to decision-making. Solomon (2016) states that every purchase decision is an attempt to solve a problem, but being different needs, they require different efforts as well. It is difficult to apply a standard analysis to the complex consumer behavior.

Within this premise, how could creativity help the development of innovative solutions for car e-commerce? This question will be used to prove the following hypotheses regarding the benefits of generating ideas by creative processes in collectivity: (i) collective creativity can generate more diverse and achievable ideas; (ii) scientifically undertaking an application for automotive e-commerce will contribute to more assertive decisions; (iii) the purchase research would become more comfortable and faster optimizing the time of consumers, since the application can also identify other technological deficiencies in this field.

Thus, this study aims to investigate how collective creativity can be a conductor of new ideas, using the Creative Framework developed by designer Cristiano Alves of the Federal University of Santa Catarina, an element of interaction to increase creativity and new ideas, from its application to a business model aimed at the car sales sector.

BACKGROUND

Creativity, Creation of Ideas and Innovation

Concept of Creativity

In the conceptual search, the difficulty to establish an exact definition of the term 'creativity' is evident due to its multifaceted nature that distances itself from the idea of being only remarkable or defined accurately (Sharma & Teper, 2008). According to Karkockiene (2005), there is no exact concept. However, similarities can be found in investigative studies on a global scale. This is what happens with the correlation between creativity and innovation.

For Jean Piaget (2011), creativity is a driving spring that varies from person to person. It values not only the new idea, but the possibility that materializes in practice. The author also argues that three factors are indispensable to the manifestation of creativity: (i) working alone, (ii) reading a lot of things in other areas rather than reading only works from the area itself and, finally, (iii) always having in mind an opponent, that is, analyzing someone's ideas as a contrast.

Burroughs et al. (2011) also advocate the individual effort to create ideas and add that creativity would depend on motivation and skill. The authors' point of view is that without attention there is no concentration. And, therefore, individuality contributes positively to good results in the creative process.

Piaget and Burroughs' theses are contrary to the other possibility of creating an idea: Collective Intelligence. According to Lévy (2003, p. 28), "Collective Intelligence is distributed everywhere, incessantly valued, coordinated in real time, which results in an effective mobilization of competencies". The main objective of this method is to recognize and enrich each other for the benefit of the collective. Malone (2018) defends that "collective intelligence happens when individuals collectively act intelligently." He brings this concept to companies and states that, in order to thrive, they need to adopt more democratic and less hierarchical systems, also valuing the positive result of integration between people and artificial intelligence tools.

Creation of Ideas and Innovation in Business

In the Future of Work report (2018) published by the World Economic Forum, creativity is one of three essential skills for work and professions, along with complex problem-solving and critical thinking. Every day in countries around the world companies make conscious decisions to innovate, using formats and programs such as digital and physical resources, skills-based training applied individually and collectively. Virtual Frameworks are ways to explore human creativity entirely online.

According to the World Economic Forum (2021) in its report on Technology Futures, education is being digitized and virtualized in the face of the 10% year-on-year growth of massive open online courses. Growth is due to access to information, which promotes the emergence of technological innovations. Companies like Google Expeditions, VR Education and zSpace AR are pioneers in innovating in the way they create and exude their ideas.

Creativity and the creation of ideas that are, at the same time, new and useful (Revila 2019; Amabile,1996) are closely linked to innovation, which involves converting ideas into new products, services or ways of doing things in creative environments.

For Minuano (2020), the Covid-19 pandemic, in addition to accelerating the growth of collective intelligence online, also brought another evidence: leadership models need to update themselves together with new trends, in order to bring different stakeholders closer to the creation of innovative solution.

APPROACHES, METHODOLOGIES AND TOOLS OF CREATION

Creation Approaches

One dimension of important decisions to be made in relation to the innovation process refers to which approaches to use throughout the process. These approaches support understanding, analysis, decision and action throughout the innovation process (Phaal; Farrukh; Robert, 2012). The term "approach" may have different interpretations according to the context in which it is applied. In general, it refers to "theory", while method refers to "practice". Leffa (1988) states that the term method was used for a long time as a synonym for both philosophy (theory) and ways of acting (practice) through this philosophy. Creation approaches assume the role of a solution to a given problem. Actions, steps and tools of creative approach stimulate such ideas and solutions.

Creation Methodology

Methodology is understood as the study of the method to find knowledge. "Methodology is an instrumental concern. It's about the ways to do science. It accounts for procedures, tools, paths" (Demo, 2003, p.19). The research comprises the recognition of results and means, the methodology helps in the understanding of the products of scientific research and mainly of its own process, because its requirements are not of rigorous submission to rigid procedures, but of fecundity in the production of results (Bruyne, 1991). According to the author, the methodology is the logic of scientific procedures in its beginning and development, and is not reduced to a technology of measuring scientific facts.

The use of effective methodologies can reduce the risks of these uncertainties in the choices of what a piece of technology should be like. This work used the technique 6-3-5, which is commonly known as brainwriting:

The 6-3-5 technique involves the participation of a group of people who use a specific method in the idealization of solutions to a specific problem.

Creation Tools

The term tool refers to any instrument that is used to perform a job. It plays an important role in the development of new products. Methods are tools of the scientific approach universally employed to encourage creativity and help the designer or project team generate a wide variety of new ideas (Hsiao; Chou, 2004).

Among the tools of collaborative creation, Miro is a virtual tool that has existed since 2011, a whiteboard, which allows the interaction of several people at the same time. An essential tool for those who are working remotely. In addition to the numerous applicabilities, it is free in the basic version which allows access to any individual. The interaction allows the insertion of videos, notes, links and figures.

For Altshuller (1999), the greatest difficulty in generating ideas is to free the mind to come up with original concepts. For this to happen, it is necessary to overcome the blockages to creativity, which arise as a result of conventional thoughts (Baxter, 2011). The freedom of expression of the collective in the Creative framework combines with the brainstorming approach.

According to Carreta (2019), the result of a Brainstorming session generates a high number of solutions. Many of them are unfeasible or devoid of logic. In agreement with the author's theory, this actually

Figure 1. Method 6-3-5
Source: InnoSkill (2008)

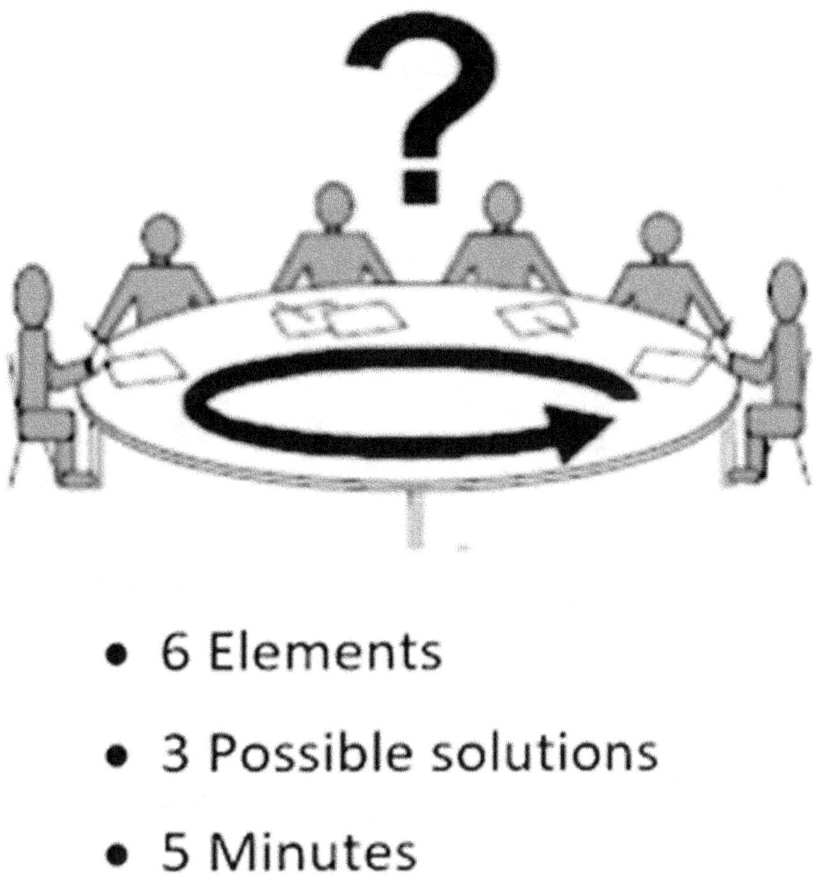

happens. Participants put countless ideas with or without logic in digital tickets. The advantage is to find creative ideas by eliminating the possibilities of innovations for a project.

Creative Framework

In Portuguese, framework means "structure" or synonymously "frame". The Creative Framework, developed by designer Cristiano Alves consists of three steps: (i) Company (Figure 2), (ii) Customers (Figure 3) (iii) Activation (Figure 4). The first phase of the creative process is the Company Stage:

In the first stage, called Step — Company, the participants, within 30 minutes, briefly describe the Central Activities. In the time of up to 45 minutes, through discussion, the team organizes the ideas taking into account the relevance of the core activities to create value for the client.

The Benchmarking of Values aims to survey competition in the market about what already exists and trends. Benchmarking, therefore, is an attempt to improve business practices and achieve superior performance. For this activity the team has up to 40 minutes to think and present the research.

Figure 2. Business stage
Source: Adapted from Alves (2020)

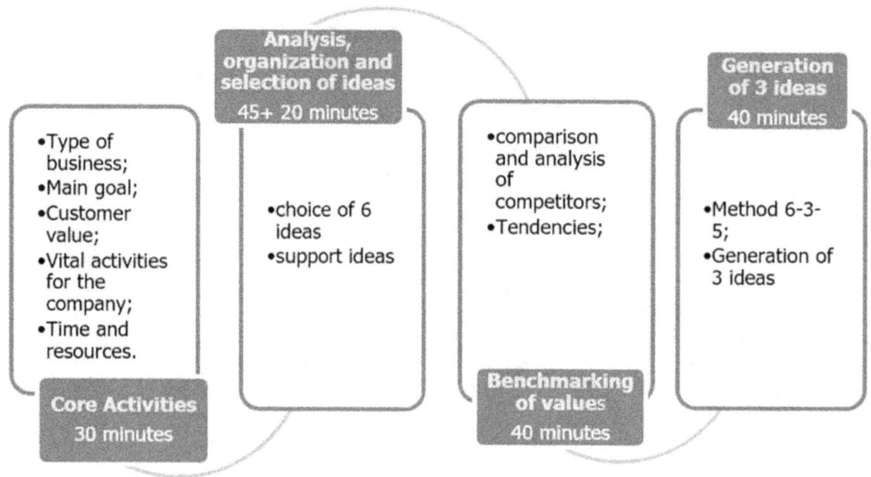

The first step is completed with a brainstorming technique, method 6-3-5, Brainwriting, which consists of a round of generation of ideas in a very short period of time. Each participant, clockwise, writes ideas based on recreating previous ideas or new ideas:

Figure 3. Customers step
Source: Adapted from Alves (2020)

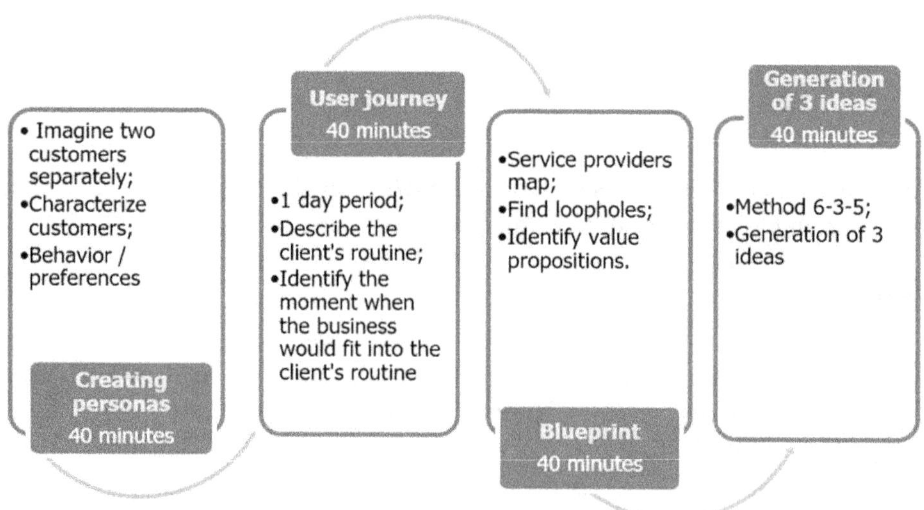

After imagining and describing a possible end consumer, the consumer's journey is carried out, a means of understanding the moment when the product or service would fit into the consumer's life.

Figure 4. Activation step
Source: Adapted from Alves (2020)

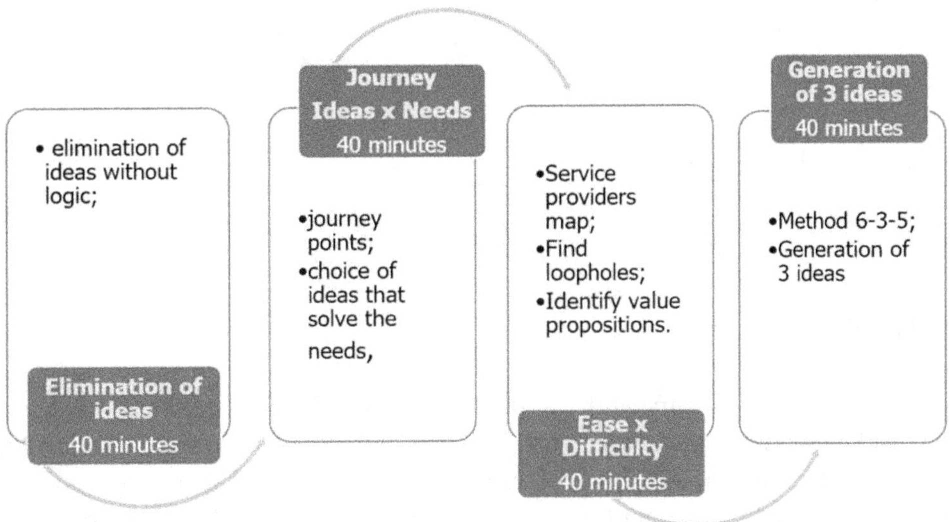

From this, plan for business strategies. In the Blueprint technique, the members refer to ideas using images. Finally, again, there is a new cycle of Brainwriting. (Muzzio, 2017) In this sense, it is important to highlight that creative environments can be present in organizations operating in the so-called creative economy (Bendassolli, Wood, Kirschbaum, & Cunha, 2009; Newbigin, 2010) or organizations that base their competitive actions on innovation.

Blueprint plays out the importance of differentiation or similarity in the interaction map using figures. By the way, Blueprint according to Fieb and Kleinaltenkamp (2004), is usually understood as a useful method in investigating facts in order to investigate and develop the process mapping of a service or product. At this stage of the framework the backstage actions, or actions that the client does not witness, are correlated with all the steps. After the realization of Blueprint, a new cycle of generation of ideas is proposed. What is observed is more and more participants have more ideas and affinity with the theme. According to Carreta (2019) methods originated from Brainstorming generate a high number of solutions, but many of them are unfeasible or devoid of logic. These ideas are no longer prioritized and are discarded. In the following steps, pains and ideas are confronted in the consumer's journey. More viable, short-term ideas gain relevance:

The third and final step is one of the most relevant. The method of selecting ideas by discarding irrelevant ideas is done by the whole team in a consensual way. This is due to the large number of ideas that one has at this stage.

The team chooses one of the created personas and this time lists only the main points of their daily journey. And, from filtering "surviving" ideas at disposal, one analyzes which ones can supply the pain in the short term. With an assessment of how much pain the idea can solve, the team elects the three with the highest score.

To finish the last stage, they use Bono Hats, which according to Bono (1985) is a method that analyzes ideas, having been consolidated around the world by extracting the maximum experience and intelligence from the participants of a discussion.

Table 1. Expressions used to perform queries on databases

Database	Expression
Capes Journals	(TITLE-ABS-KEY (creativity AND e-commerce)
Scielo	TOPIC:(creativity ecommerce)
Google Academic	creativity ecommerce AND sales apps

Source: Authors (2020)

METHODOLOGY

The role of the methodological framework of creating this work is to enhance the value proposition of the business model by directing the investigative itinerary and thereby achieving a determined end. The methodology is based on exploratory research of scientific, technological and marketing character on the role of creativity in the innovation of purchase applications, specifically the purchase of cars.

Regarding research databases, we used bases such as Capes Journals (exclusive access eCafe), Scielo and Google Scholar, as well as reliable sources in books and magazines to conduct scientific and marketing survey. Capes Journals and Scielo present a more refined search engine than Google Scholar, which facilitates the location of works more related to subjects of interest:

After exploratory research, the Creative Framework was applied with a team composed of six people, one team coordinator and five guests:

Table 2. Profession and age group of the members

Participants	age
1 Administrator- team coordinator	30 years old
1 Municipal Civil Servant	35 years old
1 Student - PhD student in Environmental Sciences	33 years old
1 Student - Elementary School	14 years old
1 Entrepreneur/ Electrical Engineer	41 years old

Source: Authors (2020)

The aim is to obtain, in real time and online, different perceptions about the business. Considering that a creative process could only happen in person, that is, physically would be an outdated idea. Amid challenges such as lack of time to move around, risks of a pandemic among other obstacles that reinforce and accelerate the deployment of all kinds of virtual interaction. The "Miro" tool is an excellent option, since it is possible to insert videos, notes and employ all the material that is normally used in person, but virtually. Research, designer, agile work, strategic planning, diagramming, funnels are several possibilities to create without getting your hands dirty or wasting paper.

Figure 5. Overview of the creative framework
Source: Authors (2020)

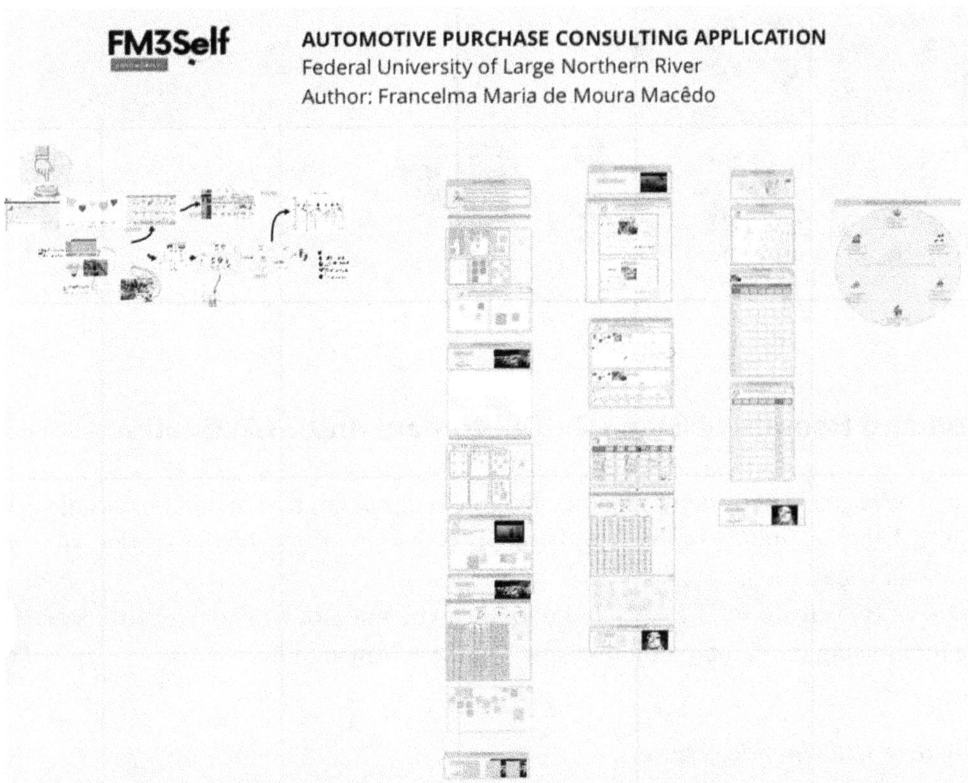

SOLUTIONS AND RECOMMENDATIONS

In the development of mobile application software, the framework aims to abstract code between several projects providing generic functionality. In the case of this research, the concept is more focused on understanding the possible needs and generating creative ideas to increase the business model of the case study whose purchase application is innovative.

In Figure 2, Figure 3, and Figure 4, you can see a schema of all the stages of the Creative Framework application to the e-business car sales business model. Below you can also see, in practice, a complete framework.

Applied to e-business for car purchases, the framework is not properly affixed to more technical developer concepts, since it is first understood which problem to solve and later what development tools to use.

Discussion and Results of Step 1- Company

The creative process of the first stage results in three ideas that arise from the core activities. The definition of three main ideas resulted in the business perception more focused on the social inclusion of People with Physical Disabilities, methodologies of product classification, and trends in researching products virtually:

Figure 6. Results of creative framework enterprise step ideas
Source: Authors (2020)

Discussion and Results of Steps 2 - Customers and 3- Activation

Consumers can be segmented by demographic, geographic, psychographic, or behavioral variable. With globalization, it becomes more complex to distinguish the segments. In the second step the product consumer persona is designed.

For Muzzio (2017) creativity is associated with the generation of new and useful ideas. The generation of three ideas using the 6-3-5 method resulted in the following ideas:

Figure 7. Creative structure ideas results
Source: Authors (2020)

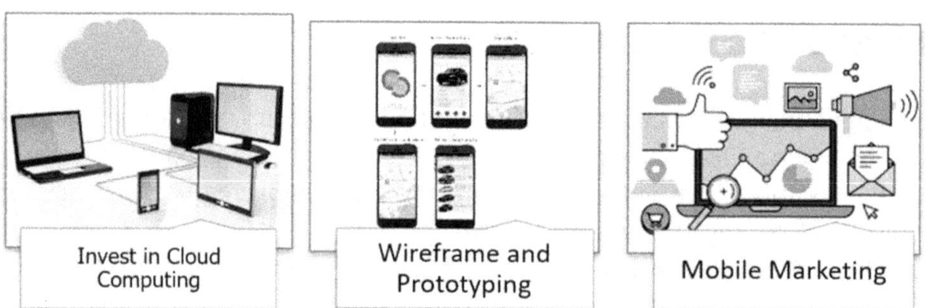

In the third Activation Stage these three ideas were validated, and it was confirmed that the three ideas found in the second stage were the best. After completing the three stages, the ideas are evaluated with the dynamics of Edward Bono's 6 Hats (1985). The author suggests each member assumes a personality type and reacts to an idea. By consensus the team chooses the idea they think is the most interesting for the product. Already a trend a few years ago, it was decided to bet on the Cloud Computing cloud. The team considers that the cloud allows good use of space, security as to the physical losses of physical devices. Marston (2011) conceptualizes Cloud Computing:

Cloud Storage or Cloud Computing is an IT service model, where computing services (hardware and software) are delivered on demand to customers via a self-service, device-independent, location date network. The resources required to provide the required quality of service levels are shared, dynamically scalable, quickly provisioned, virtualized, and released with minimal interaction with the service provider. Users pay for the service as an operating expense, without incurring significant up-to-equity expenses, with cloud services employing a measurement system that divides the appropriate block computing resource. (Marston et al., 2011, p. 2)

Thus, being used in mobile technologies as applications, it reduces the risk of loss due to hardware failure and reduces the need for physical space in memory of the devices.

FUTURE RESEARCH DIRECTIONS

The analysis of the results signals improvements in solutions for car e-commerce. With this, it is concluded that collective creativity is efficient in the discovery of potentially innovative ideas that imply direct or indirect benefits for society (customers), companies (concessionaires) and even governments because the more sales, the higher taxes of a country.

Creativity helps in the development of innovative solutions for car e-commerce by obtaining creative ideas from participants with varied profiles. This translates into benefits of the generation of ideas by creative processes in collectivity proving the following hypotheses: (i) collective creativity can generate more diverse and achievable ideas; (ii) scientifically undertaking an application for automotive e-commerce will contribute to more assertive decisions; (iii) purchase research would become more comfortable and faster optimizing consumers' time.

Collective creativity can be a generator of new ideas, using the Creative Framework developed by designer Cristiano Alves of the Federal University of Santa Catarina, an element of interaction to increase creativity and new ideas, from its application to a business model aimed at the car sales sector. It is worth mentioning the implication regarding its applicability because this model of development of ideas can also be applied to other sectors of the economy.

CONCLUSION

Within the demand for solutions to rescue the dynamics of car sales, the creation procedure studied and applied in this work, the Creative Framework by Cristiano Alves, proved effective in generating new ideas to meet the needs in the development of mobile applications. It can be seen that the ideas generated are diverse due to the different profiles of the participants. The brainwriting approach has led to a storm of ideas, mostly somewhat inapplicable at the time, since more research would be needed to adopt certain ideas. However, there were insights into good solutions, previously unimaginable. This enhanced the value proposition of the business model centered on car e-commerce. With this, it is concluded that collective creativity is efficient in the discovery of potentially innovative ideas. Quantitatively, a significant volume of ideas was presented. The members belonged to the age group and different types of professional qualification, that is, while one was an engineer with programming experience another member had no mastery of the subject of automobiles or technologies. However, in the end it is concluded distinct perspectives are necessary because in daily life it is believed that customers can be as varied as the members who collaborated in the framework. With this, it is notorious that there are benefits in the generation of ideas in collectivity. It can be affirmed that even ideas discarded in dynamics can be evaluated again in the future. It is understood that the Creative Framework model used could certainly be applied to the most varied business models because objective results, that is, innovative ideas would be achieved following the order of the steps with the highest possible level of fidelity in the participants' responses. The success of an application depends on several factors, and luck is not one of them. As for the digital showroom business for cars, the team proposes improvements and greater attention to storage technologies through Cloud Computing that is relevant to allowing space saving on the app, requiring consequently less memory in the devices of its users. Another important perception of ideas in collectivity is the use of wireframe tools for product prototyping and integrating technologies to improve decision-making. Therefore, scientifically undertaking an application for automotive e-commerce in order to create a digital showroom contributes to the new reality of the world during and after the pandemic. The digital showroom on smartphones and with virtual reality glasses and other technologies are trends.

ACKNOWLEDGMENT

This work was carried out with the support of the Coordination for the Improvement of Higher Education Personnel — Brazil (CAPES) — Financing Code 001.

REFERENCES

Altshuller, G. S. (1999). *Innovation Algorithm. Worcester: Technical Innovation Center.* (Original work published in 1969)

Baxter. (2011) *Product design: Practical guide to the design of new products* (3rd ed.). Edgard Blucher.

Bruyne, P. (1991). *Dynamics of Research in Social Sciences.* Francisco Alves.

Carreta, F. (2019). *Creativity tools for product development* [Master's thesis]. Faculty of Mechanical Engineering, State University of Campinas. Unicamp repository. http://repositorio.unicamp.br/bitstream/REPOSIP/334583/1/Carretta_Fernanda_M.pdf

CGI-Brazil. (2016, September 13) *Mobile Becomes the Main Internet Access Device.* https://www.cgi.br/noticia/releases/celular-torna-se-o-principal-dispositivo-de-acesso-a-internet-aponta-cetic-br/#:~:text=Entre%20os%20usu%C3%A1rios%20da%20network,e%2076%25%20by%20phone%20cellular

Consulting, I. (2018) *VersionOne launches the 12th Annual Report of the State of Ágile.* https://explore.versionone.com/state-of-agile/versionone-12th-annual-state-of-agile-report

Demo, P. (2003). *Educating by research (6th ed.).* Associated Authors.

Durnalı, M., Orakcı, Ş., & Aktan, O. (2019). The smart learning potential of Turkey's education system in the context of FATIH project. In A. Darshan Singh, S. Raghunathan, E. Robeck, & B. Sharma (Eds.), *Cases on Smart Learning Environments* (pp. 227–243). IGI Global. doi:10.4018/978-1-5225-6136-1.ch013

Fenabrave, I. C. D. P. (2019). *The Future of the Concessionaires' Business.* https://online.fliphtml5.com/ordey/wzhl/#p=1

Gallagher, J. M., & Reid, D. K. (1981). The learning theory of Piaget and Inhelder. Academic Press.

Getúlio Vargas Foundation IBRE. (2020, October 5) *The difficult resumption after falling: a magnifying glass on the Service Sector during the covid-19 pandemic.* https://blogdoibre.fgv.br/posts/dificil-retomada-apos-tombo-uma-lupa-sobre-o-setor-de-servicos-durante-pandemia-de-covid-19

Hsiao, S. W., & Chou, J. R. (2004). A creativity-based design process for innovative product design. *International Journal of Industrial Ergonomics, 34*(5), 421–443. doi:10.1016/j.ergon.2004.05.005

Infomoney. (2020, May 19). *The impact of COVID-19 on vehicle sales by state.* https://www.infomoney.com.br/colunistas/o-mundo-sobre-muitas-rodas/o-impacto-do-covid-19-nas-vendas-de-veiculos-por-estado/

Kandel, E. (2014) Principles of Neuroscience (5th ed.). McGraw Hill.

Karkockiene, D. (2005). *Creativity: Can it be trained? A Scientific Educology of Creativity. International Journal of Educology.*

Leffa, V. J. (1988). Methodology of language teaching. In Topics in applied linguistics: the teaching of foreign languages. UFSC.

Lobos, J. (1993). *Charming Customer: External and Internal* (9th ed.). Hamburg Publishing House.

Malone, T. W. (2018). *Superminds: The Surprising Power of People and Computers Thinking Together.* Little, Brown Spark.

Marston, S., Li, Z., Bandyopadhyay, S., Zhang, J., & Ghalsasi, A. (2011). Cloud Computing: The business perspective. *Decision Support Systems, 51*(1), 176–189. doi:10.1016/j.dss.2010.12.006

Minuano, C. (2019, October 3). *Power of collective intelligence will increase.* Folha de São Paulo. Press Observatory. https://www.observatoriodaimprensa.com.br/e-noticias/poder-da-inteligencia-coletiva-vai-aumentar/

Miro. (2020, October 10). *Car APP, by Francelma Macêdo.* https://miro.com/app/dashboard/

Muzzio. (2017). *Individual, Leadership and Culture: Evidence of Creativity Management.* https://www.scielo.br/scielo.php?script=sci_arttext&pid=S1415-65552017000100107

Orakcı, Ş. (2020). The future of online learning and teaching in higher education. In Global Approaches to Sustainability Through Learning and Education. Hershey, PA: IGI Global. doi:10.4018/978-1-7998-0062-0.ch003

Phaal, R., Farrukh, C. J. P., & Robert, D. R. (2006). Technology management tools: Concept, development and application. *Technovation, 26*(3), 336–344. doi:10.1016/j.technovation.2005.02.001

Sharma, K., & Teper, Y. (2008) The Gifted and Talented: Creativity, Cultural Perspectives and Skills. *International Conference on Creativity in Mathematics and the Education of Gifted Students*, *5*, 211-215.

Solomon, M. (2016) *Consumer Behavior: Buying, Owning and Being*. Bookman Editora ltda.

World Economic Forum. (2018). *The Future of Jobs Report 2018*. https://es.weforum.org/reports/the-future-of-jobs-report-2018

World Economic Forum. (2021). *Technology Futures: Projecting the Possible, Navigating What's Next*. https://www3.weforum.org/docs/WEF_Technology_Futures_GTGS_2021.pdf

KEY TERMS AND DEFINITIONS

Collective Intelligence: Obtaining creative ideas through a group of two or more people in favor of the recognizement and enriching the mutuality of those involved. The collective intelligence applied the generation of ideas for new business allows diversity of opinions and personalization, according to the needs of the project.

Consumer Journey: Summary of the consumer's routine, taking into account a short period of time, i.e., day, week or month. It describes the routine of the consumer attending to the moment when the product or service of the business would have the opportunity to participate. From this, plan for business strategies.

Creative Framework: It can be said that it is the tool that makes possible the interaction of collective creativity to increase new ideas, from its application to a business model. Composed of three steps: (1) company, (2) customers, and (3) activation.

Creative Ideas: Correlation of thoughts in response to human needs in order to solve problems. It varies from person to person, presenting the solution according to the type of business.

Cycle of Generation of Ideas: The originated by brainstorming, refers to the cycle practiced in the 6-3-5 Method. Six participants in a short period of time, usually in five minutes, write at least three ideas. After the end, clockwise, ideas are placed on the sheet/screen from existing ideas. At the end of the dynamic a large number of unviable and viable solutions. Viable ideas are selected for short-term application in the business, unviable ideas are no longer prioritized and are discarded.

Digital Showroom for Cars: Digital space dedicated to reception, demonstration, negotiation and closing of business with the consumer. Tool that targets virtual reality of traditional car dealerships.

Personas: It is the imaginary embodiment of what a possible consumer of the product or service would look like. Characterization through the definition of physical, psychological and social attributes.

Chapter 14
The Role of Evaluation in Service Learning in Economics and Business:
Systematic Review and Proposal of Evaluation

Piedad Ortiz Fernández
Universidad de Almería, Spain

Jorge Tarifa-Fernández
https://orcid.org/0000-0002-6031-8526
Universidad de Almería, Spain

Salvador Cruz Rambaud
https://orcid.org/0000-0002-1318-1221
Universidad de Almería, Spain

ABSTRACT

In this chapter, a systematic review of the literature on evaluations of service-learning projects in the area of business and economics has been carried out. The authors have analyzed the four basic parts of evaluation: who evaluates, when to evaluate, how to evaluate, and what to evaluate. Subsequently, an evaluation proposal has been made for each of the agents involved, taking into account each of these dimensions. One of the main conclusions is that reflection is a fundamental part of the evaluation process, as well as of the student learning process because it allows them to deepen the lived experience.

DOI: 10.4018/978-1-7998-8239-8.ch014

INTRODUCTION

Service-Learning is a learning methodology that has begun to be strongly implemented in recent years. This methodology stands out for its great potential in the educational field because it allows students to learn theoretical concepts through a meaningful service to the community. Additionally, it allows students to develop both transversal and civic skills, which makes it a very useful tool in Business education. Some research has shown that there are certain skills that are essential for good job development (for example, see Bovinet, 2007; Clarke, 1997; Done, 2011). One example are civic skills, which allow students to develop greater global and cultural awareness; another example is entrepreneurial skills, which include critical thinking, technological skills, lifelong learning, flexibility, adaptation to change, teamwork, initiative, problem solving, and communication skills, among others. All these skills have become highly prized in the labor market due to the scarcity of candidates who possess them. Among the reasons for this situation, we can find the shortcomings of traditional education. This education has been heavily influenced by passive methodologies in which lectures and memorization of concepts prevail. However, numerous studies have confirmed that these skills are developed when active methodologies, such as service-learning, are used (Sandmann, et al., 2009; Smith-Tolken, 2013).

Service-learning is sometimes confused with activities such as volunteering because of the community service it offers, or with Business internships because of the practical learning of theoretical concepts. However, this tool combines the benefits of both, i.e., the learning of theoretical concepts, and the development of moral and entrepreneurial skills.

A fundamental aspect of this methodology is the evaluation of the projects. In this phase of service-learning is quite important to know whether the proposed objectives have been achieved. One of these objectives is to know if the student has really learned. Numerous tools are used for this purpose, such as the reflective journals, focus group, surveys, interviews, and written reflection, among others. Most of the works in the existing literature are about the implementation of this methodology; however, very few works have analyzed the evaluation process of service-learning (Ruiz-Corbella and García-Gutiérrez, 2019). That is why the aim of this chapter is to propose an evaluation tool, as complete as possible, in the field of Economics and Business. In order to achieve this goal, the authors will carry out a systematic review of the literature on service-learning evaluation procedures, in which the different evaluations applied in projects will be reviewed.

With this review, the authors will classify the works based on the following dimensions: What to evaluate (students, project, community), who evaluates (students, teachers, social organizations, beneficiaries), when to evaluate (before, during and/or after project) and how to evaluate (quantitative/qualitative methods and direct or indirect methods). In this way, it will be shown what has been done in the area of economics and business; this will allow the authors to make an evaluation proposal, as complete as possible, which encompasses all these dimensions.

The structure of this chapter begins with a background section in which we will review the concept of service-learning in the existing literature, its benefits and drawbacks, examples of application of this tool in the area of economics and business, as well as the process of evaluation of this methodology and the importance of reflection in learning. In the next section, a systematic literature review of the evaluation process in the area of economics and business will be carried out. Specifically, the methodology followed by the systematic review is described, the preliminary findings of the review are described and, finally, the general results of the study are presented. Subsequently, an evaluation proposal for this teaching tool will be made. In this section, the authors propose an evaluation for the project students, the community or beneficiaries and the project organizers, based on the results obtained in the review. Finally, some future lines of research and the main conclusions and limitation of paper are presented.

BACKGROUND

Throughout the history of education, there are numerous approaches and theories that attempt to improve student learning, as well as the assessment of this learning. One of these theories stated that active learning was extremely important for the retention of lessons and the deepening of experience (Dewey, 1938). On the other hand, Piaget (1976) asserted that experience was a key factor influencing the development of cognitive structure and, in addition, pointed out the importance of social interaction in creating engaging learning scenarios. Later, Kolb (1984) defined learning as the process by which knowledge is created through the transformation of experience and emphasized the importance of using concrete experience and reflective observation, which allows for discovering and reflecting on social interactions and relationships (Godfrey, 2005; Kolb, 1984). All these definitions are an integral component of Service-Learning.

Concept of Service-Learning

The definition of Service-Learning has been an arduous task throughout history due to the breadth of its application, and the different implications it has shown. Therefore, it is necessary to highlight some of the different perspectives that have been forming the body of work of this methodology (see Table 1 in Appendix 1).

The analyzed definitions of service-learning have five key components: educational experience, community service, civic responsibility, problem solving and reflection. The most prominent components in the definitions are educational experience (Bringle and Hatcher, 1995; Chong, 2014; CNCS, 2006; Goldberg et al., 2006; Jacoby, 1996; NCSA, 1990 and NSLC, 2009) and community service (Bringle and Hatcher, 1995; CNCS, 2006; Goldberg et al., 2006; Jacoby, 1996; NCSA, 1990; and NSLC, 2009). Another important component of the concept is reflection (Bringle and Hatcher, 1995; Goldberg et al., 2006 and NSLC, 2009) as a means of acquiring knowledge. Some authors also include in their definitions two of the objectives of this methodology, that is, the need to improve student civic responsibility (NSLC, 2009 and TAAHE, 2003) and real-world problem solving (AAHE, 2003; Chong, 2014 and Goldberg et al., 2006).

Based on these key components, it can be stated that one of the most complete definitions is the one provided by NSLC (2009), although it does not incorporate problem solving. Therefore, a broader definition could state that service-learning is a teaching and learning strategy that integrates meaningful community service with instruction and reflection to enrich the learning experience, teach civic responsibility, and resolving the real problem of the communities.

Benefits and Disadvantages of Service-Learning

Service-learning methodology stands out for the numerous benefits it generates for both students and the community. Among the most important are the academic development of students (McAndrew, 2001) and the development of both transversal and civic skills (Berle, 2006; Bringle and Hatcher 1996; Carver 1997; Chong 2014; Felten and Clayton, 2011; Meyers, 2009; Opazo, et al., 2016). These benefits have improved the student's chances of being able to contribute to society as a whole in the future (McAndrew, 2001; Steinberg, et al., 2011; Sullivan and Rosin, 2008) and also allow them to develop other types of skills such as professional skills (Bovinet, 2007; Clarke, 1997; Done, 2011).

The development of these skills is key in the Business context. It has been shown that they are essential for a good development of jobs, becoming a requirement highly demanded by companies (Bovinet, 2007; Clarke, 1997; Done, 2011). Table 1 shows these skills classified into civic skills (Bovinet, 2007; Done, 2011) and Business skills, understood from two perspectives: personal and social.

Table 1. Skills required in the organizations

Author	Skills	Skill type
Bovinet (2007) and Done (2011)	Global and cultural awareness	Civic skills
	Critical thinking	Professional skills
	Cross-functional competence	
	Full competence in a self-disciplined discipline	
	Technological competencies	
Clarke (1997)	Long-term learning	
	Flexibility	
	Adaptation to change	
	Teamwork	
	Initiative	
	Problem solving	
	Decision making	
Bovinet (2007), Clarke (1997) and Done (2011)	Communication skills	

Source. Own elaboration.

The lack of professional skills in the workplace outlines great challenges for educational centers (O'Meara and Niehaus, 2009). Traditional education has been strongly criticized and it has been claimed that it has become ivory towers isolated from the world. According to O'Meara and Niehaus (2009), it is necessary to implement service-learning programs within higher education organizations to counteract this claim. The reason given by these authors is that this methodology allows developing of Business skills that the labor market requires (Basardien, et al., 2013 and Giles and Eyler, 1998).

Despite the benefits of this educational methodology, the projects implementing presents several disadvantages also collected in the literature. Among the drawbacks, two types can be found (see Table 3): on the one hand, the "learner frustration", caused by the ambiguity and uncertainty of the tasks (Bush-Bacelis, 1998) and, on the other hand, by the "lack of collaboration of the beneficiaries". This last inconvenience occurs when grantees do not deliver on time the resources requested by students (Madsen and Turnbull, 2006), and consequently it can become a threat to students' learning objectives, as they face the challenge of "doing without learning" (Kolenko, et al., 1996). In addition, another disadvantage of this methodological tool is the strong investment of time outside the traditional academic activities of both the student and the project organizer. This disadvantage can generate a poor implementation of the project, and therefore a weakening of the curriculum. This can result in students not learning and wasting their time (Gray et al., 2000).

Although the benefits abovementioned outweigh the disadvantages of this methodology, it is still marginalized in terms of its application, especially in the field of Economics and Business.

Table 2. Disadvantages and consequences of service-learning

Authors	Disadvantages		Consequences
Bush-Bacelis (1998)	Learner frustration	Task	Ambiguity and uncertainty
Madsen and Turnbull, (2006)		Lack of collaboration (beneficiaries)	Doing without learning
Gray et al., (2000)	High preparation time		Weaken the curriculum, waste of time students, no learning.

Source. Own elaboration.

Services-Learning in Business and Economics

The great financial scandals produced in the last 15 years have led to questioning the business ethics of companies or, rather, of people who run companies. This has focused the attention on business education, which has been heavily criticized because of its limited scope and lack of ethical commitment. That is why the Association to Advance Collegiate Schools of Business-International (AACSB) has advised schools and universities to contemplate an ethical education in their curriculum (AACSB, 2004, p. 7), which allows students to obtain certain moral and professional skills very demanded nowadays. For this reason, service-learning becomes a powerful tool to achieve these goals.

In the literature there are numerous examples to apply this methodology in economics and business. Next, we will proceed to give some examples in the main sub-areas of the aforementioned fields:

- Administration: It has been observed that the activities carried out helped students to understand concepts such as corporate social responsibility (Lamb, et al.,1998; Wittmer, 2004; Marques, 2016), sustainable development (Hull et al., 2016) or to learn to perform business consulting activities (Nikolova and Andersen, 2017; Paphitis and Pearse, 2017) and administrative tasks (Ide and Thomas, 2011). These activities are mainly aimed at companies and non-profit associations (community) and, to a lesser extent, other students and the population in general.
- Accounting and finance: The activities in this sub-area have a similar community, and the student's learning is related to advice on microfinance (Griner et al., 2015), auditing (Wooldland, 2009), financial concepts (Delaune et al., 2010; Sabbaghi, et al., 2013), practical accounting (Guajarathi et al., 2002) and economic viability (Colakoglu and Sledge, 2013).
- Economics: In this case, the predominant community is the general population, other students and non-profit associations. As for the concept of learning or activity carried out, they are usually devoted to the analysis of the economic and social context (Claassen and Blaauw, 2019; García-Conteras, et al., 2013), economic concepts (López, 2009) and the analysis of the impact of women in the community (Govekar and Rishi, 2007).

- Marketing: The community to which these projects are aimed are once again companies, non-profit associations and disabled people, being the main works carried out by students, advertising campaigns (Akpabio, 2012), communication plans (Bush-Bacelis, 1998; Kincade and Gibson, 2012; Braybsberger and Flamm, 2013; Hardin-Ramanan et al., 2018; Scholtz, 2018) and marketing plans (Littlefield, 2006).
- Human resources. This subarea is one of the least developed and the works with this methodology are aimed at the evaluation and description of the workstation (Madsen, 2004) as well as the training and selection of workers (Kenworthy, 1996). In this case, the communities are non-profit associations and homeless people.
- Tourism: This area is the least developed and is focused on analyzing tourism companies (Mokoena, 2018).

The following table exhibits a summary of what was developed above:

Table 3. Examples of service-learning in economics and business

Area	Student Learning	Community
Administration	Concept of Corporate Social Responsibility	Non-profit association (Marques, 2016; Wittmer, 2004)
		Students (Lamb, et al.,1998)
	Business Consulting	Enterprises (Nikolova and Andersen, 2017; Paphitis and Pearse, 2017)
	Sustainable development	Population (Hull et al., 2016)
	Administrative tasks	Non-profit association (Ide and Thomas, 2011)
Accounting and Finance	Microfinance counselling	Enterprises (Griner et al., 2015)
	Audit	Non-profil association (Wooldland, 2009)
	Financial concepts	Students (Delaune et al.,2010; Sabbaghi, et al.,2013)
	Practical accounting	Non-profit association (Guajarathi et al.,2002)
		Enterprises (Yu, 2011)
	Economic viability	Non-profit association (Colakoglu and Sledge, 2013)
Economics	Analysis of the economic and social context	Population (García-Conteras, et al.,2013; Claassen and Blaauw, 2019)
	Economic concepts	Students (López, 2009)
	Impact of women in the community	Non-profit association (Govekar and Rishi, 2007)
Marketing	Advertising campaigns	Enterprises (Akpabio, 2012)
	Communication plan	Non-profit association (Bush-Bacelis, 1998; Braybsberger and Flamm, 2013)
		Enterprises (Kincade and Gibson, 2012; Scholtz, 2018)
		Disabilities people (Hardin-Ramanan et al.,2018)
	Marketing Plan	Non-profit association (Littlefield, 2006)
Human Resources	Evaluation and description of workstation	Non-profit association (Madsen, 2004)
	Training and selection of workers	Homeless (Kenworthy, 1996)
Tourism	Analysis of tourism companies	Enterprises (Mokoena, 2018)

Source. Own elaboration.

Evaluation of Service-Learning

A common theme in much of the literature is the importance of assessing students' learning as well as their perceptions of their lived experience with the community (Ruiz-Corbella and García-Gutiérrez, 2019). However, evaluation also allows identifying areas for improvement in this methodology (Cooks and Scharrer, 2006; Sheafer, 2014). To understand the impact of service-learning, it is necessary to answer the following questions: what to evaluate, who evaluates, when to evaluate and how to evaluate (Ruiz-Corbella and García-Gutiérrez, 2019) (see Figure 1).

Figure 1. Service-learning evaluation
Source: Own elaboration.

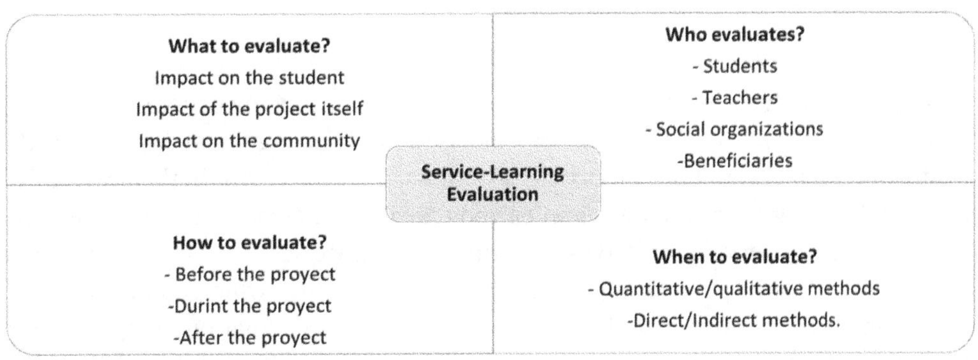

- **What to evaluate**: Knowing the purpose of the evaluation is essential for designing an evaluation. Some studies have focused the evaluation on issues such as the impact of students (e.g., development of competencies, self-esteem, development of prosocial values or theoretical content) (Eyler and Giles, 1999; Mpofu, 2007); the impact of the project on the community (e.g., democratization of knowledge, community development and empowerment) (Martinez-Odriá, 2007); the development of the project itself (e.g., adjustment of expectations, possible mismatches in times and failures in coordination) (Martínez, et al., 2013); and effective reflection throughout the process (Páez and Puig, 2013). Due to the impossibility of measuring everything, it is necessary to be clarify from the beginning what is to be evaluated.
- **Who evaluates:** In order to answer this question, it is necessary to know which the agents are involved in the project. It is possible that the only way to ensure coherence with the philosophical and pedagogical principles of service-learning is the participative evaluation of all the agents involved. In this way, a relationship of horizontality, reciprocity and mutual recognition is built (Fawcett, et al., 2003; Rivas and Donova, 2001). These agents can be classified into Students, Teachers, Social Organizations, and Beneficiaries.
- **When to evaluate:** According to Coll et al., (2001), three different moments can be distinguished: the initial evaluation, which is usually a diagnostic, predictive or prognostic evaluation; the continuous evaluation, which refers to the evaluation during the process; and the final evaluation, which is the evaluation carried out once the project is finished.

- **How to evaluate:** There are numerous evaluation tools for service-learning programs. The use of one or the other depends on what is to be evaluated. Jacoby (2014) classifies these evaluation methods into qualitative versus quantitative, and direct versus indirect. Quantitative methods are used to compare results from different groups of students and extract different types of statistics. Instead, qualitative methods are used to go deeper into the data collected by providing details and nuances. On the other hand, direct evaluation is obtained by examining the different types of work that students have handed in, and on the other hand, indirect evaluation is obtained through self-assessment questionnaires where students themselves evaluate their achievements and learning. The most relevant instruments identified in the literature are quantitative: surveys; and qualitative: reflective journals, portfolios, work submitted, written reflections, interviews, focus groups, observation (Jacoby, 2014; Steinke and Fitch, 2007).

The Reflection

The most widespread method in the evaluation of service-learning incorporates student reflection (Jenkins and Sheehey, 2012). The importance of reflection in the pedagogical approach is that students learn by reflecting on their community experiences (Eyler and Giles, 1999). In this way, reflection is the key to consider the learning process as service-learning, as it distinguishes it from other concepts such as volunteer or community service initiatives. (Gardner, 1997). Reflection, according to Ewell (1997), can be considered as a mental process applied to the act of learning, which can challenge students to use critical thinking. In doing so, the students could examine the information presented to them, questioning its validity, and allowing them to draw conclusions based on the resulting ideas. This ongoing process allows students to narrow down possible solutions and come to a conclusion. The result of this discussion allows for a better understanding of the concept, making reflection a fundamental element of this methodology.

There are numerous tools that allow the learner to reflect. The most used in service-learning are reflective journals, portfolios, written reflections, interviews and focus groups. These tools can be designed with more or less rigidity. However, there is controversy as to whether reflections should be structured or unstructured. On the one hand, some authors stated that learners should have the opportunity to engage in guided reflection. It is the basis for learning (Ash and Clayton, 2004) and allows participants to gain personal beliefs and self-awareness (Furze et al., 2011). On the other hand, other authors consider that guided reflections cover only the learning objectives and outcomes intended by the process organizers, leaving aside other interesting inputs from learners (Fullerton et al., 2015). In this line, other scholars state that this type of reflection may fall into the danger of instrumentalizing reflection (Van Beveren et al., 2018), and thus fulfilling only purely academic outcomes (Eyler and Giles, 1999; Kiely, 2005). There is, therefore, a dilemma as to how to measure the results obtained from service-learning assessments.

So far, the benefits and ways in which reflection can be presented have been raised.

Table 5 shows that the three definitions show two aspects; on the one hand, what the reflection is about and, on the other hand, what the objectives of the reflection are. Regarding the first, it can be stated that reflection is done both on the service activity (Bringle and Hatcher, 1995 and NSLC, 2009) and on problem solving (Goldberg et al., 2006). In relation to the purpose of reflection, it can be observed that it is intended to achieve a greater understanding of the course (Bringle and Hatcher, 1995 and NSLC, 2009) and an improvement in civic responsibility (Bringle and Hatcher, 1995; Goldberg et al., 2006 and NSLC, 2009).

Table 4. Reflection in services-learning

Author	Definition	Reflection about		Objective of Reflection	
		Service Activity	Problem	Course Content	Civic Responsibility
Bringle and Hatcher (1995)	*"... reflect on the service activity in such a way as to gain further understanding of course content, a broader appreciation of the discipline, and an enhanced sense of civic responsibility".*	Yes	No	Yes	Yes
Goldberg, Richburg and Wood (2006)	*"as experiential (real-life) and reflective problem-based learning in which students enrolled in an academic course provide a needed service to a community partner".*	No	Yes	No	Yes
NSLC (2009)	*"...that integrates meaningful community service with instruction and reflection to enrich the learning experience, teach civic responsibility and strengthen communities".*	Yes	No	Yes	Yes

Source. Own elaboration.

SYSTEMATIC LITERATURE REVIEW

Methodology

A systematic review of the available evidence on the implementation of service-learning projects in the field of Economics and Business has been carried out. A literature review establishes the state of current knowledge in a field (Tranfield et al., 2003). This process has been successfully carried out in medical fields as it helps to synthesize empirical evidence from a large number of studies. Thus, according to Perkmann et al., (2013), the implementation of this process in social science is due to its utility to identify areas of consensus and disagreement between researchers. For the current paper, a simplified version of the process outlined by Tranfield et al., (2003) was followed as detailed below.

Planning the Process

The first step consisted of searching for empirical studies on service-learning in studies related to Economics and Business in two large databases such as "Web of Science" and "Scopus". These have been chosen because of the important impact of their publications since they are the two most important international academic databases with interdisciplinary coverage. They represent a significant strength for the study and comparison of different scientific fields (Archambault et al., 2006).

The keywords chosen were classified into three groups: the first related to the main concept (service-learning), the second to the subject matter (management, financial, marketing, Business, human resources, Economics) and the third to the field of application (school, university, high school, classroom, secondary school, college, faculty). The keywords were chosen in such a way as to have the widest possible coverage of the subject matter. The criterion chosen for this classification has been the choice of keywords from the broadest concept to the most restricted concept based on logical operators (and, or, not). This criterion is based on Tranfield et al. (2003) and Denyer and Tranfield (2009) in which they emphasize the importance of carrying out the first search without any type of restriction or study area. From this first search with the least restrictive keywords, we proceed to introduce some criteria which begin to delimit it. All articles without date restriction in the databases were taken into account.

Conducting the Review Process

In this section, we will explain the steps followed in the search process for the articles. This search was carried out at the end of September 2019. Table 6 shows the main results of the systematic review process:

- The main keyword in this work was "service-learning", belonging to the first group of keywords related to the concept. This was entered in both databases, obtaining a total of 7,243 articles in English, with no date restriction.
- The second group of keywords was the subject, which limited the search to words related to the field we are dealing with, that is, Economics and Business. The following criteria were used: Title-Abs-Key ("Management" or "Financ*" or "Marketing" or "Business" or "Human Resources" or "Econom*"). Since the objective is to find the connection between the first and the second group, both were connected with the "and" operator. The addition of this keyword combination narrowed the search to 1,442 articles.
- Subsequently, the search was filtered with the third group of keywords, corresponding to the scope of application. This allowed the relevant articles in this study to be those that have been applied in the field of education. Therefore, the following restriction was included: Title-Abs-Key ("School" or "University" or "High School" or "Classroom" or "Secondary School" or "College" or "Faculty"). This search narrowed the number of articles to 925.
- Once the searches were narrowed down by the three groups of keywords, we proceeded to eliminate the articles that were not related to our subject matter. In particular, it could be seen that there was a large number of studies in the field of health, so papers related to this field were eliminated, including the criterion Not "Health". As a result, a total of 567 articles were found. Subsequently, the search was filtered by related areas and a total of 508 studies were obtained.
- The next step was to eliminate duplicate articles in the two databases, leaving a total of 386 articles to be analyzed.
- Once the final articles were obtained, they were analyzed one by one to check if they fit the topic, i.e., if they were service-learning articles in the subject of Economics and Business and in the field of education. This analysis narrowed down the relevant articles to 93.
- These 93 articles were divided between empirical and theoretical studies, resulting in 46 empirical and 47 theoretical studies.
- Finally, empirical articles that did not include an evaluation of the project were eliminated. This left 33 studies for analysis.

Table 5. Systematic review process

Search	Web of Science	SCOPUS	Total
"Service-learning"	3785	3458	7243
"Management" or "Financ*" or "Marketing" or "Business" or "Human Resources" or "Econom*"	590	852	1442
"School" or "University" or "High School" or "Classroom" or "Secondary School" or "College" or "Faculty"	356	569	925
Not "Health"	241	326	567
Filtered from related areas	214	294	508
Elimination of duplicate articles	-122		386
Elimination of articles not related to the subject of Economics and Business.	-293		93
Elimination of theoretical articles	-47		46
Elimination of articles that do not incorporate evaluation.	-13		33
Total of empirical articles analysed	**33**		

Source. Own elaboration.

Results

Preliminary Findings

Figure 2 shows the increasing evolution of publications of service-learning projects implemented in the area of Economics and Business. As can be seen, most of the articles have been published in the last decade, specifically 63% of the articles found.

The analyzed articles have been classified into different areas of knowledge (Business administration (BA), accounting and finance (C&F), Economics, marketing, human resources (HR), and tourism), and in turn have been divided by study methodology (implementation and case study). Table 7 shows the classification of service-learning studies according to the area of knowledge and the methodology used. The relevant results show, on the one hand, the greater weight of project implementation as a study methodology, and on the other, that the areas that have implemented this methodology the most are the areas of Business administration, marketing and accounting and finance.

Regarding the evaluation of the projects, the following findings have been found:

- **Who evaluates?** In all the assignments the student evaluates, 6% of the assignments are evaluated by the teacher and 21% of the assignments are evaluated by the beneficiary.
- **When is it evaluated?** 15% of the projects evaluate at the beginning and at the end of the project, 3% at the beginning, during and at the end of the project, and 81% only evaluate at the end of the project.
- **How is it evaluated?** 60% of the papers use qualitative methods and the remaining 40% use mixed methods, so that, qualitative and quantitative methods.
- **What is evaluated?** Regarding the impact of the project, 52% of the articles have evaluated the existing opinion about the event, and 30% what are the possible improvements for subsequent edi-

tions. Regarding the impact of the student, 73% of the papers evaluated the didactic learning of the students, 55% the development of soft skills, and 58% the development of civic skills.

Figure 2. Evolution of the numbers of articles
Source. Own elaboration.

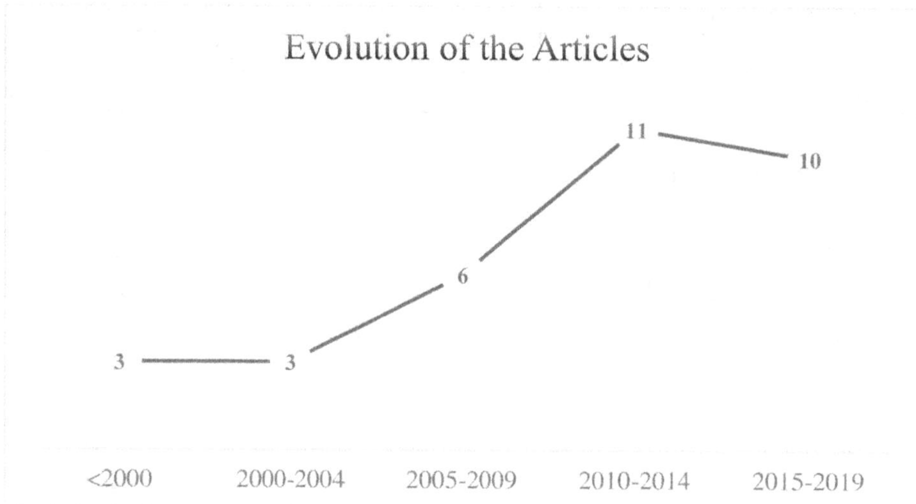

Table 6. Service-learning by area of knowledge and study methodology

Area of knowledge	Articles	Implementation	Case study
Business administration	26%	75%	25%
Accounting and finance	24%	82%	18%
Economy	13%	67%	33%
Marketing	26%	75%	25%
Human Resources	7%	67%	33%
Tourism	4%	50%	50%
Total		**74%**	**26%**

Source. Own elaboration.

General Results

In order to analyze the evaluation of service-learning in the area of Economics and Business, each of the above questions will be studied in the analyzed articles:

- **Who has evaluated?** Several authors argued the need for a participatory evaluation of all the agents involved in the service-learning project (Fawcett et al., 2003; Rivas and Donova, 2001). However, among the analyzed works, only the paper by Sholtz (2018) performs an evaluation of the three involved agents (students, teachers and employers as beneficiary agents of the project).

In other studies, the evaluators were the students and the beneficiaries themselves (Akpabio, 2012; Delaune et al., 2010; Guajarathi and McQuade, 2002; Ide and Thomas, 2011; Lamb et al., 1998; Littlefield, 2006 and Mokoena, 2018), or students and teachers (García-Contreras et al., 2013). In the remaining papers the only evaluators are the students (Bush-Bacelis, 1998; Coffey and Wang, 2006; Colakoglu and Sledge, 2013; France-Harris et al., 2019; Govekar and Rishi, 2007; Griner et al., 2015; Hardin-Ramanan et al., 2018;; Hull et al., 2016; Killian et al., 2019; Kincade and Gibson, 2012; Lopez, 2009; Madsen, 2004; Mancuso et al., 2009; Marques, 2016; McGoldrick, 1998; Paphitis and Pearse, 2017; Poon et al., 2011; Sbbaghi et al., 2013; Wiese and Sherman, 2011; Wittmer, 2004; Woodland, 2009; Yu, 2011; Zamora, 2012).

- **When have they evaluated?** In the works analyzed, the three moments of evaluation have been found, but the most used is the final evaluation. As for the initial or diagnostic evaluation, it has been observed that it is carried out through quantitative surveys whose results are compared with the results obtained in the same surveys at the end of the project. The objectives of these surveys are twofold, on the one hand, to know the degree of development of soft skills (Poon et al., 2011; Govekar and Rishi, 2007; Sbbaghi et al., 2013 and Killian et al., 2019) and civic skills (Poon et al., 2011) of the students, and on the other hand, to know their theoretical learning after the project (Delaune et al., 2010). As for evaluation during the project, we have found only two works that carry it out. This evaluation makes it possible to become aware of the development of the project and of the development of the person him/herself, and it allows offering the necessary help to the student for the successful completion of the project (Ruiz-Corbella and García-Gutiérrez, 2019). the first work that incorporates this continuous evaluation asks the student to deliver a written report and oral presentation before starting the project, during the project and at the end of it (Bush-Bacelis, 1998). In this way, students receive feedback throughout the process, allowing them to improve their learning (Mateo and Martinez, 2008; Sanmartí, 2007). In the second work the students do not make periodic deliveries of the projects but have weekly meetings with the tutor (Marques, 2016). This author states that in this way the quality of the presentations and papers is much higher, and the students' involvement seems much more intense, so that when there is close supervision there is a greater involvement of the student than when the guidance is intermittent. The rest of the papers perform a final evaluation that will be analyzed in greater detail in the following sections. Another aspect to be highlighted is the moment of evaluation of the agents involved. In all the studies analyzed, the beneficiaries and teachers are evaluated at the end of the project, while the students are the only agents in which different evaluation moments are observed.
- **How have they evaluated?** Numerous tools are available to evaluate service-learning projects. The classification of Jacoby (2014) will be used for the analysis of the work done. One of this author's classifications was the distinction between qualitative and quantitative methods. In the analyzed works it is possible to differentiate evaluations that use mixed methods and qualitative methods, but in no case have been found works that only use quantitative methods. In the evaluations of students using mixed methods, it is observed that for the quantitative evaluation they use closed questionnaires (Likert scale) at the end of the project (France-Harris et al., 2019; Lamb et al., 1998; Littlefield, 2006; Mokoena, 2018; Scholtz, 2018; Woodland, 2009; Yu, 2011), and pre- and post-project questionnaires (Delaune et al., 2010; Govekar and Rishi, 2007; Killian et al., 2019; Poon et al., 2011; Sbbaghi, 2013). Closed-ended questionnaires have also been used for community assessments (Lamb et al., 1998; Mokoena, 2018). As for qualitative tools, a wide variety of them have been observed. The most widespread is the open-ended questionnaire, in

which evaluators must answer a series of questions on aspects determined by the project organizer This tool has been used for student evaluation (Colakoglu and Sledge, 2013; Delaune, 2010; García-Contreras et al., 2013; Govekar and Rishi, 2007; Gujarathi and McQuade, 2002; Hull et al., 2016; Lopez, 2009; Sholtz, 2018; Woodland, 2009; Yu, 2011; Zamora, 2012), teacher evaluation (García-Contreras et al., 2013) and community evaluation (Gujarathi and McQuade, 2002; Lamb et al., 1998 and Mokoena, 2018). Another widely used tool is written reflection. Reflection allows us to go deeper into the lived experience, and thus learn more from it (Piaget, 1976). In this work, written reflection is referred to as the agents' written comments on a certain topic or free content. In the analyzed works, there are reflections by students (Coffey and Wang, 2006; France-Harris et al., 2019; Griner et al., 2015; Ide and Thomas, 2011; Kincade and Gibson, 2012; Lamb et al., 1998; Marques, 2016; Mokoena, 2018; Poon et al., 2011; Sabbaghi, 2013; Wittmer, 2004; Zamora, 2012) and beneficiary reflections (Delaune et al., 2010; Ide and Thomas, 2011; Littlefield, 2006; Sabbaghi, 2013;). Another method used is the interview which has been used for both students (Madsen, 2004; McGoldrick, 1998; Mokoena, 2018), teachers (Sholtz, 2018) and for beneficiaries (Mokoena, 2018; Sholtz, 2018). The remaining tools used have been applied only to students. These include the journal reflection (Govekar and Rishi, 2007; Hull et al., 2016; Killian et al., 2019; McGoldrick, 1998; Paphitis and Pearse, 2017; Wiese and Sherman, 2011), the portfolio (Bush-Bacelis, 1998; Lamb et al., 1998; Littlefield, 2006), and the focus group (France-Harris et al., 2019; Hardin-Ramanan et al., 2018; Wiese and Sherman, 2011).

- **What have they evaluated?** There are many aspects that can be evaluated in service-learning projects. However, three main categories stand out: the impact of the project on the student (theoretical content and the development of soft and civic skills), the impact on the community, and the evaluation of the project itself. In the works analyzed, it has been observed that the impact on the student's theoretical learning, as well as the development of soft and civic skills, is measured with various tools: the most commonly used is written reflection (Coffey and Wang, 2006; France-Harris et al., 2019; Ide and Thomas, 2011; Kincade and Gibson, 2012; Lamb et al., 1998; Zamora, 2012), followed by qualitative surveys (Colakoglu, 2013; Govekar and Rishi, 2007; Woodland, 2009; Zamora, 2012) and quantitative surveys (Govekar and Rishi, 2007; Killian et al., 2019; Lamb et al., 1998; Poon and Zhou, 2011; Yu, 2011). The least used tools to assess learning are Journal Reflection (Govekar and Rishi, 2007; Killian et al., 2019; Paphitis and Pearse, 2017), Focus group (France-Harris et al., 2019; Hardin-Ramanan et al., 2018), portfolio (Bush-Bacelis, 1998) and interview (McGoldrick, 1998). However, Mokoena, 2018 used different tools to measure each of these dimensions. He used reflection to measure learning and civic skills, and quantitative questionnaire and interview to know the development of civic skills. On the other hand, other authors only analyze student learning without studying the impact of the project on the development of soft and civic skills. These authors evaluated student learning from reflection (Marques, 2016; Scholtz, 2018; Wittmer, 2004), qualitative survey (Delaune et al., 2010; Guajarathi and McQuade, 2002; Lopez, 2009), journal reflection (Wiese and Sherman, 2011), focus group (Wiese and Sherman, 2011) and quantitative survey (Delaune et al., 2010; Scholtz, 2018). Another important dimension found in the evaluations of the analyzed works has been the impact of the project itself. This dimension could be classified into three sections, the opinion of the project, the possible improvements that could be incorporated in subsequent editions, and the feelings that the project has generated in the students. Regarding the opinions of the project the most used tool has been the qualitative survey (Colakoglu and Sledge, 2013; Delaune et al., 2010;

France-Harris et al., 2019; Gujarathi and McQuade, 2002; Lopez, 2009; Scholtz, 2018; Zamora, 2012), followed by written reflection (France-Harris et al., 2019; Mokoena, 2018; Poon et al., 2011; Zamora, 2012), quantitative surveys (Delaune et al., 2010; Scholtz, 2018; Woodland, 2009) and focus group (France-Harris et al., 2019; Hardin-Ramanan et al., 2018). The least used to know the opinion of students is the portfolio (Bush-Bacelis, 1998) and the interview (McGoldrick, 1998). The most used tools that allow to know which improvements can be implemented in subsequent editions of the project are qualitative surveys (Delaune et al., 2010; Lopez, 2009; Woodland 2009; Yu, 2011), written reflection (Lamb et al., 1998; Mokoena, 2018), reflection journal (Paphitis and Pearse, 2017), Focus group (Hardin-Ramanan et al., 2018) and quantitative surveys (Delaune et al., 2010). To conclude, the most used tools to know the students' feelings about the project are the written reflection (France-Harris et al., 2019; Marques, 2016; Mokoena, 2018), the quantitative survey (France-Harris et al., 2019; Woodland, 2009), the portfolio (Bush-Bacelis, 1998) and the focus group (France-Harris et al., 2019). Another noteworthy aspect is that they evaluate the rest of the agents (teachers and beneficiaries). As for the beneficiaries of the project what they evaluate are the benefits that the project has on the community, and their opinion about the students' work. For this purpose, quantitative and qualitative surveys were used to complement the results of the first ones. They also used an interview to further deepen the results (Mokoena, 2018). Another work assessed the same dimensions but used other tools such as qualitative survey (Gujarathi and McQuade, 2002) or written reflection (Delaune et al., 2010). In another study they used reflection as a community assessment tool. In this work, beneficiaries provided unstructured feedback on project success and student perceptions (Scholtz, 2018). In relation to teacher evaluations, there was only one study in which they used interview as an evaluation tool. The purpose of this evaluation was to learn about the object and rationale of the project (Scholtz, 2018).

SOLUTIONS AND RECOMMENDATIONS

One of the main problems encountered in the review was the diversity of evaluation methods implemented in the works analyzed. It has been observed that in most of the studies only the students are evaluated, in others the students and the communities, and in a minority the three agents involved (students, teachers and communities). Differences have also been found regarding the moment of evaluation, most of the studies do it at the end of the project, while others do it at the beginning and at the end or at the beginning, during and at the end of the project. In terms of how it is evaluated, we also found a great diversity of tools, which are classified as quantitative and qualitative. However, all tools incorporate to a greater or lesser extent the component of reflection. In this section, we will make an evaluation proposal as broad as possible to help researchers in their future projects to implement this methodology. Following the recommendations of Fawcett et al., (2003) and Rivas and Donovan (2001), the evaluation of service-learning should involve all the agents. For this reason, the following are evaluation proposals for each of these agents (Figure 2).

Evaluation for Students

Smith et al., (2010) advocate the use of reflection as part of the evaluation of service-learning projects. In this way students become reflective practitioners and allow academics to know the outcome of their learning. Most of the works reviewed incorporate qualitative methods to evaluate the projects. However, authors such as Hull et al., 2016 stated that these qualitative methods are very useful for student learning but, insufficient to measure and evaluate the degree of the transformative dimension of the project. For this reason, a mixed evaluation methodology is proposed in this work.

- **Quantitative evaluation method:** Closed evaluation surveys are proposed. The purpose of these surveys is to measure students' theoretical learning, the development of soft skills and the development of their civic skills after the project. For their measurement, pre-surveys and post-surveys are proposed for the project that assesses the same items. In this way, a comparison of results will be obtained that will allow us to know the impact of the project on the students. For data analysis, the methodology followed by Sabbaghi et al., (2013) is proposed. These authors designed a closed survey with statements in which students had to rate the degree of agreement or disagreement with each statement, using a 5-point Likert-type scale (i.e., 1 = Strongly disagree, 5 = Strongly agree). First, they perform arithmetic means for each of the items (z_i) in the pre ($r_{1,i}$) and post ($r_{2,i}$), surveys, and then perform the difference of means between each item pre and post:

$$z_i = r_{2,i} - r_{1,i}$$

Finally, they perform an aggregate index of averages ($\bar{z}$) to know the increase in each of the measured categories (learning, soft skills development and civic skills development). The mathematical expression of the calculation is as follows:

$$\bar{z} = \frac{1}{N}\sum_{I=1}^{N} z_i$$

Where N is the number of items in each category.

- **Qualitative evaluation method:** Qualitative tools make it possible to obtain more information on the subjective perceptions of the evaluators, thus complementing to a greater extent the results obtained in quantitative surveys. The fundamental aspect that these tools should incorporate is the student's reflection. After analyzing the works, the following qualitative tools are proposed:
  - Qualitative questionnaires: These are a series of open-ended questions that students must answer in writing at the end of the project. To do so, students must go through a process of reflection. This tool allows for structured student reflection. Smith et al., (2010) suggest that reflection must have a conceptual framework; otherwise, students' reflections would become internal and uncritical. Therefore, it is proposed that a questionnaire of open-ended questions be conducted to complement the data obtained in the quantitative surveys (impact of the project on the student). In addition, questions should be asked about the project process, i.e., what problems have you encountered during the project? What would you change in the implementation of the project, among others?
  - Written reflections: Many of the papers analyzed incorporated written reflections by the students as a method of evaluation. In some cases, these were free and in others their topics were usually guided by the teacher. An example of this is the work of Hull et al., (2016)

who incorporated an unguided and unstructured reflection obtaining as a result uncritical reflection, so they recommend that these should be guided. However, there are authors who defend the opposite position such as Fullerton et al., (2015). This author states that structured reflections lose interesting insights from learners. For this reason, in this paper we propose an option with both approaches. We propose qualitative questionnaires as structured reflection and, within them, a free content question for the student to expose any other problem, feeling or appreciation that he/she considers appropriate. In this way, the benefits of both approaches would be obtained.

- Journal reflection: It is a good tool to learn about student learning according to Hubbs and Brand (2005). These journals allow students to write down their experiences, thoughts, beliefs, assumptions, opinions about the service or the project, etc. during the course. This provides a pedagogical perspective on the service and the process. This tool can be interesting not only for the final evaluation of the student, but also for an evaluation during the process. If teachers carry out a periodic evaluation of the diaries, they can provide feedback to the student that allows them to further improve learning (Sanmartí, 2007; Mateo and Martinez, 2008). It is important that the elaboration of these diaries has a guided component by the teacher to avoid the same problems of free written reflection.
- Focus Group: It is a qualitative reflection tool that allows students to exchange opinions with their peers. Focus groups allow students who may find direct one-on-one interaction intimidating (Madriz, 2000) to obtain a safe environment with their peers to share their personal experiences. The group setting helps stimulate thinking and verbal input into the specific personal experiences of the participants. This tool can be used during the project and at the end of the project. Because the moderator is usually the teacher, he/she can give the students the necessary feedback to increase their learning. In addition, due to the direct interaction with the students, it is possible to expand on issues that have not been clear in the reflections made by the students in the open surveys, as well as in written reflections or in the journal reflection themselves.
- The interview: This tool has a similar use to the focus group because it complements the information obtained in the previous qualitative and quantitative tools. For the same reasons as the written reflections, it is recommended that they have a structured part. This tool consists of asking questions individually to the students in oral format. They can be carried out during and at the end of the project. In the same way as the focus group, it allows for feedback from the teacher. One of the main disadvantages of this tool is the time involved in carrying it out.

Evaluation for Beneficiaries

The project beneficiaries are other agents involved in the project. Considering the results obtained in the literature review, we propose the evaluations of these agents to be carried out at the end of the project. Evaluations should be carried out on what benefits the community has obtained from the project, as well as the shortcomings of the process and possible solutions for future projects. This chapter proposes mixed evaluation methods for the community. These mixed methods are composed of quantitative tools (closed questionnaire rated from 1 to 5), and qualitative tools. The latter would be divided into a qualitative questionnaire with open-ended questions to complement the results of the quantitative survey and a written reflection question in which the beneficiaries could express any other issue not covered by the previous questions. Finally, it might be interesting to conduct an interview with the beneficiaries involved to discuss and expand on the information obtained from the written evaluations. All this will depend on the time available to both the project organizers and the beneficiaries themselves.

Evaluation for Teachers or Project Organizers

In the works analyzed, the teachers or project organizers hardly ever carried out project evaluations. However, they are also agents involved in the project and no less important than the students or beneficiaries. The authors of this chapter recommend incorporating evaluations of project organizers or teachers. They propose evaluations at the end of the project on the project implementation process. In this way they will obtain the inconveniences encountered in the organization of the project and a different perspective of the student's learning. As for the evaluation methods, they will depend on the number of organizers involved. If there is enough number of studies, it would be interesting to use mixed methods. Otherwise, only qualitative methods such as the open-ended questionnaire and written reflection should be used to avoid losing information not covered by the questions asked.

Figure 3. Service-learning evaluation proposal.
Source. Own elaboration

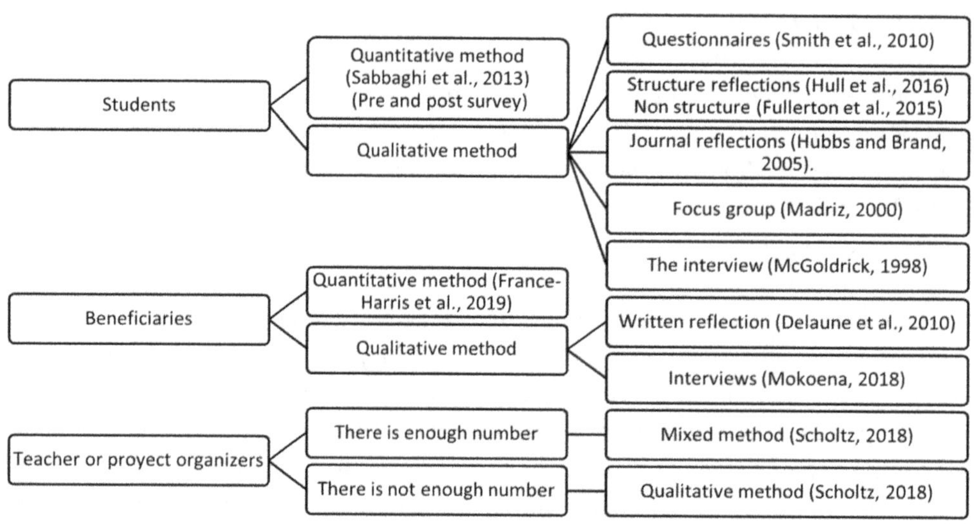

FUTURE RESEARCH DIRECTIONS

In recent years, this methodology has increased in Economics education; however, it is still scarce despite the great benefits it brings. It is necessary to continue research in this line but taking care in the evaluation of the projects. It is important to continue contributing to the literature with projects that evaluate all the agents involved. It would also be interesting to find a method to study the impact of reflection on students. That is, to incorporate questions in the evaluations that allow us to know how the reflection process has contributed to student learning. Another future line of research is to implement the proposed evaluation in projects at other academic levels, i.e., non-university. In this work the authors have been able to observe that in Economics and Business there are only works in university environments and they consider it necessary to extend the research to other academic levels related to Economics and Business.

CONCLUSION

In this book chapter, a systematic review of evaluations of service-learning projects in the area of Economics and Business has been carried out. In this review, the four basic parts of the evaluations have been analyzed: who evaluates, what they evaluate, when they evaluate and how they evaluate. It has been observed that most of the evaluations are carried out by the students, while the perspective of the project benefits and the project organizers are hardly analyzed. It was also found that in some projects the students are evaluated before starting the project and at the end, while the rest of the agents (beneficiaries and organizers) are evaluated only at the end. The main issues evaluated are related to three main categories: the involvement of the project in the student, in the community and the evaluation of the project itself. In terms of how it is evaluated, a wide variety of quantitative and qualitative tools have been found. However, the main aspect is the component of reflection as a tool for evaluation and learning by the student. All the tools analyzed make the student reflect in one way or another. According to Piaget (1976), reflection is a mechanism that allows to deepen the lived experience, and therefore, to learn more from it. In both quantitative and qualitative tools, the student must analyze the experience he has lived in order to carry out the evaluation, and that is precisely what allows him to learn. The tools that incorporate more reflection are the qualitative ones, because before answering, the student must analyze the answer well and then write it down, which improves the student's reflection. It is evident that each type of tool has its pros and cons, therefore, the evaluation with a mixed methodology allows to obtain the benefits of both quantitative and qualitative methodology. In this work, an extensive evaluation has been proposed for each of the agents involved according to the results obtained in the review carried out. However, the authors of this chapter are aware of the time constraints that usually exist in this type of project. Therefore, the project organizers will be responsible for deciding the number and type of tools to be implemented, as well as deciding what they want to evaluate, based on their time availability.

The main limitation of this work is the exclusion of other papers related to service-learning in other areas of study which could have enriched the discussion of this work.

REFERENCES

Akpabio, E. (2012). Beneficiaries' Perspective on Service Learning: Case Study of Advertising and Public Relations Campaign Course. *SAGE Open*, *2*(3). doi:10.1177/2158244012460694

Archambault, É., Vignola-Gagné, É., Côté, G., Larivière, V., & Gingrasb, Y. (2006). Benchmarking scientific output in the social sciences and humanities: The limits of existing databases. *Scientometrics*, *68*(3), 329–342. doi:10.100711192-006-0115-z

Ash, S. L., & Clayton, P. H. (2004). The articulated learning. An approach to reflection and assessment. *Innovative Higher Education*, *29*(2), 137–154. doi:10.1023/B:IHIE.0000048795.84634.4a

Association to Advance Collegiate Schools of Business-International (AACSB). (2004). *Ethics Education in Business Schools: Report of the Ethics Education Task Force*. AACSB.

Basardien, F., Friedrich, C., & Parker, H. (2013). The relationship between planning strategies and entrepreneurial success for start-up entrepreneurs in the Western Cape: A psychological approach to entrepreneurship. *International Journal of Entrepreneurship and Innovation*, *14*(4), 281–288. doi:10.5367/ijei.2013.0128

Berle, D. (2006). Incremental integration: A successful service-learning strategy. *International Journal on Teaching and Learning in Higher Education*, *18*(1), 43–48.

Bovinet, J. W. (2007). Different skill-set views: A four-year study of marketing students, practitioner and educators. *Journal of Business and Public Affairs*, *1*(1), 1–8.

Braunsberger, K., & Flamm, R. O. (2013). A mission of civic engagement: Undergraduate students working with nonprofit organizations and public sector agencies to enhance societal wellbeing. *Voluntas*, *24*(1), 1–31. doi:10.100711266-012-9289-6

Bringle, R. G., & Hatcher, J. A. (1995). A service-learning curriculum for faculty. *Michigan Journal of Community Service Learning*, *2*(1), 112–122.

Bush-Bacelis, J. L. (1998). Innovative pedagogy: Academic service-learning for business communication. *Business Communication Quarterly*, *61*(3), 20–34. doi:10.1177/108056999806100303

Carver, R. L. (1997). Theoretical underpinnings of service learning. *Theory into Practice*, *36*(3), 143–149. doi:10.1080/00405849709543760

Chong, C. S. (2014). Service-learning research: Definitional challenges and complexities. *Asia Pacific Journal of Cooperative Education*, *15*(4), 347–358.

Clarke, A. (1997). Survey on employability. *Industrial and Commercial Training*, *29*(6), 177–183. doi:10.1108/00197859710178737

Coffey, B. S., & Wang, J. (2006). Service learning in a master of business administration (MBA) integrative project course: An experience in China. *Journal of Education for Business*, *82*(2), 119–124. doi:10.3200/JOEB.82.2.119-124

Colakoglu, S. N., & Sledge, S. A. (2013). The development of critical thinking skills through a service-learning oriented entrepreneurship course. *Journal of Entrepreneurship Education*, *16*, 115–124.

Coll, C., Martin, E., & Onrubia, J. (2001). La evaluación del aprendizaje escolar: dimensiones psicológicas, pedgógicas y sociales. In C. Coll, J. Palacios, & A. Marchesi (Eds.), *Desarrollo psicológico y educación. Psicología de la educación escolar* (2nd ed., pp. 549–572). Alianza Editorial.

Cooks, L., & Scharrer, E. (2006). Assessing Learning in Community Service Learning: A social Approach. *Michigan Journal of Community Service Learning*, *13*(1), 44–55.

Delaune, L. D., Rakow, J. S., & Rakow, K. C. (2010). Teaching financial literacy in a co-curricular service-learning model. *Journal of Accounting Education*, *28*(2), 103–113. doi:10.1016/j.jaccedu.2011.03.002

Denyer, D., & Tranfield, D. (2009). Producing asystematic review. In D. A. Buchanan & A. Bryman (Eds.), *The Sage Hand-Book of Organizational Research Methods* (pp. 671–689). Sage Publications.

Dewey, J. (1938). *Experience and education*. Simon and Schuster.

Done, A. (2011). *Supply chain knowledge management: A conceptual framework* (Working paper WP-900). IESE Business School, University of Navarra. Retrieved from https://www.iese.edu/research/

Ewell, P. T. (1997). *Organizing for learning: A point of entry*. National Center for Higher Education Management Systems (NCHEMS).

Eyler, J., & Giles, D. E., Jr. (1999). Where's the Learning in Service-Learning? Jossey-Bass, Inc.

Fawcett, S. B., Boothroyd, R., Schultz, J. A., Francisco, V. T., Carson, V., & Bremby, R. (2003). Building capacity for participatory evaluation within community initiatives. *Journal of Prevention & Intervention in the Community*, *26*(2), 21–36. doi:10.1300/J005v26n02_03

Felten, P., & Clayton, P. (2011). Service Learning. *New Directions for Teaching and Learning*, *128*(128), 75–84. doi:10.1002/tl.470

France-Harris, A., Burton, C., & Mooney, M. (2019). Putting Theory into Practice: Incorporating a Community Engagement Model into Online Pre-Professional Courses in Legal Studies and Human Resources Management. *Online Learning*, *23*(2), 21–39. doi:10.24059/olj.v23i2.1448

Fullerton, A., Reitenauer, V. L., & Kerrigan, S. M. (2015). A grateful recollecting: A qualitative study of the long-term impact of service-learning graduates. *Journal of Higher Education Outreach & Engagement*, *19*(2), 65–92.

Furze, J., Black, L., Peck, K., & Jensen, G. M. (2011). Student perceptions of a community engagement experience: Exploration of reflections on social responsibility and professional formation. *Physiotherapy Theory and Practice*, *27*(6), 411–421. doi:10.3109/09593985.2010.516479 PMID:20946070

García-Contreras, R., Faletta, J. P., Krustchinsky, R., & Barnes, P. (2013). A Microcredit Program, a Math Education Initiative and Service-Learning: Matching a University's Mission to Greater Community Needs. *New Horizons in Education*, *61*(1), 11–22.

Gardner, B. (1997). The controversy over service learning. *NEAToday*, *16*(2), 17–22.

Giles, D. Jr, & Eyler, J. (1998). A service learning research agenda for the next five years. *New Directions for Teaching and Learning*, *73*(73), 65–72. doi:10.1002/tl.7308

Godfrey, P. C., Illes, L. M., & Berry, G. R. (2005). Creating breadth in business education through service-learning. *Academy of Management Learning & Education*, *4*(3), 309–323. doi:10.5465/amle.2005.18122420

Goldberg, L. R., McCormick Richburg, C., & Wood, L. A. (2006). Active learning through service-learning. *Communication Disorders Quarterly*, *27*(3), 131–145. doi:10.1177/15257401060270030201

Govekar, M. A., & Rishi, M. (2007). Service learning: Bringing real-world education into the B-school classroom. *Journal of Education for Business*, *83*(1), 3–10. doi:10.3200/JOEB.83.1.3-10

Gray, M. J., Ondaatje, E. H., Fricker, R. D. Jr, & Geschwind, S. A. (2000). Assessing service-learning: Results from a survey of "Learn and serve America, Higher Education. *The Magazine of Higher Learning*, *32*(2), 30–39. doi:10.1080/00091380009601721

Griner, L., Herron, P. J., & White, S. (2015). Study abroad partnerships: Librarians, business faculty, and in-country facilitator develop an innovative experiential learning program. *Journal of Business & Finance Librarianship*, *20*(3), 189–208. doi:10.1080/08963568.2015.1046782

Gujarathi, M. R., & McQuade, R. J. (2002). Service-learning in business schools: A case study in an intermediate accounting course. *Journal of Education for Business*, *77*(3), 144–150. doi:10.1080/08832320209599063

Hardin-Ramanan, S., Soupramanien, L. D. B., & DeLapeyre, D. (2018). Project# NuKapav: A Mauritian service-learning case study. *Equality, Diversity and Inclusion*, *37*(2), 167–181. doi:10.1108/EDI-01-2017-0008

Hubbs, D. L., & Brand, C. F. (2005). The paper mirror: Understanding reflective journaling. *Journal of Experiential Education*, *28*(1), 60–71. doi:10.1177/105382590502800107

Hull, R. B., Kimmel, C., Robertson, D. P., & Mortimer, M. (2016). International field experiences promote professional development for sustainability leaders. *International Journal of Sustainability in Higher Education*, *17*(1), 86–104. doi:10.1108/IJSHE-07-2014-0105

Ide, C., & Thomas, T. (2011). Business students' experience of community service learning. *International Journal of Work-Integrated Learning*, *12*(1), 51–66.

Jacoby, B. (1996). *Service-Learning in Higher Education: Concepts and Practices*. The Jossey-Bass Higher and Adult Education Series. Jossey-Bass Publishers.

Jacoby, B. (2014). *Service-learning essentials: Questions, answers, and lessons learned*. John Wiley & Sons.

Jenkins, A., & Sheehey, P. (2012). A Checklist for Implementing Service-Learning in Higher Education. *Journal of Community Engagement and Scholarship*, *4*(2), 52–60.

Kenworthy, A. L. (1996). Linking business education, campus culture and community: The Bentley service-learning project. *Journal of Business Ethics*, *15*(1), 121–131. doi:10.1007/BF00380268

Kiely, R. (2005). A transformative learning model for service-learning: A longitudinal case study. *Michigan Journal of Community Service Learning*, *12*(1), 5–22.

Killian, S., Lannon, J., Murray, L., Avram, G., Giralt, M., & O'Riordan, S. (2019). Social Media for Social Good: Student engagement for the SDGs. *International Journal of Management Education*, *17*(3), 100307. doi:10.1016/j.ijme.2019.100307

Kincade, D. H., & Gibson, F. Y. (2012). Retail Classroom Meets Business Practice through a Service-Learning Component. *Journal of Textile and Apparel, Technology and Management*, *7*(3), 1-14. Recuperado de: https://ojs.cnr.ncsu.edu/index.php/JTATM/article/view/2044/1408

Kolb, D. A. (1984). *Experiential Learning*. Prentice Hall.

Kolenko, T. A., Porter, G., Wheatley, W., & Colby, M. (1996). A critique of service learning projects in management education: Pedagogical foundations, barriers, and guidelines. *Journal of Business Ethics, 15*(1), 133–142. doi:10.1007/BF00380269

Lamb, C. H., Swinth, R. L., Vinton, K. L., & Lee, J. B. (1998). Integrating service learning into a business school curriculum. *Journal of Management Education, 22*(5), 637–654. doi:10.1177/105256299802200506

Littlefield, H. (2006). Service learning in business communication: Real-world challenges develop real-world skills. *Business Communication Quarterly, 69*(3), 319–322. doi:10.1177/108056990606900311

Lopez, M. (2009). Incorporating service-learning into the economics curriculum. *The Review of Black Political Economy, 36*(2), 137–149. doi:10.100712114-009-9040-8

Madriz, E. (2000). Focus groups in feminist research. Handbook of Qualitative Research, 2, 835-850.

Madsen, S. R. (2004). Academic service learning in human resource management education. *Journal of Education for Business, 79*(6), 328–332. doi:10.3200/JOEB.79.6.328-332

Madsen, S. R., & Turnbull, O. (2006). Academic service learning experiences of compensation and benefit course students. *Journal of Management Education, 30*(5), 724–742. doi:10.1177/1052562905283710

Mancuso, L. C., Alijani, G. S., Kwun, O., & Smith, L. D. (2009). Successful outcomes of teaching minority undergraduate students entrepreneurial business planning concepts using andragogy and service learning. Academy of Entrepreneurship, 15(1), 33.

Marques, J. (2016). Shaping morally responsible leaders: Infusing civic engagement into business ethics courses. *Journal of Business Ethics, 135*(2), 279–291. doi:10.100710551-014-2465-4

Martínez Domínguez, B., Martínez Domínguez, I., Alonso Sáez, I., & Geruzaga Amundarain, M. (2013). *El aprendizaje-servicio, una oportunidad para avanzar en la innovación educativa dentro de la Universidad del País Vasco*. Academic Press.

Mateo, J., & Martínez, F. (2008). *Medición y evaluación educativa*. Editorial La Muralla.

McAndrew, A. (2001). *Service-learning: Benefits, challenges, and strategies for success.* Recuperado de: http://www.unco.edu/ AE-Extra/2001/1/ServiceLearning.html

McGoldrick, K. (1998). Service-learning in economics: A detailed application. *The Journal of Economic Education, 29*(4), 365–376. doi:10.1080/00220489809595929

Meyers, S. A. (2009). Service learning as an opportunity for personal and social transformation. *International Journal on Teaching and Learning in Higher Education, 21*(3), 373–381.

Mokoena, P. P. (2018). Analysis of the research design used in a Tourism Management service learning project. *African Journal of Hospitality, Tourism and Leisure, 7*(4), 1–13.

Mpofu, E. (2007). Service-Learning Effects on the Academic Learning of Rehabilitation Services Students. *Michigan Journal of Community Service Learning, 14*(1), 46–52.

National Service-Learning Clearinghouse. (2009). What is service-learning? Nikolova, N., & Andersen, L. (2017). Creating shared value through service-learning in management education. *Journal of Management Education*, *41*(5), 750–780.

O'Meara, K., & Niehaus, E. (2009). Service learning is… How faculty explain their practice. *Michigan Journal of Community Service Learning*, *16*(1), 1–16.

Odria, A. M. (2007). Service-learning o aprendizaje-servicio: la apertura de la escuela a la comunidad local como propuesta de educación para la ciudadanía. *Bordón. Revista de pedagogía, 59*(4), 627-640.

Opazo, H., Aramburuzabala, P., & Cerrillo, R. (2016). A review of the situation of service-learning in higher education in Spain. *Asia Pacific Journal of Cooperative Education*, *17*(1), 75–91.

Páez Sánchez, M., & Puig Rovira, J. M. (2013). La reflexión en el aprendizaje-servicio. *Revista internacional de educación para la justicia social.*

Paphitis, S. A., & Pearse, N. J. (2017). Developing and implementing a service-learning course into an MBA programme: Critical perspectives from students. *Journal for New Generation Sciences*, *15*(1), 140–156.

Perkmann, M., Tartari, V., McKelvey, M., Autio, E., Broström, A., D'Este, P., Fini, R., Geuna, A., Grimaldi, R., Hughes, A., Krabel, S., Kitson, M., Llerena, P., Lissoni, F., Salter, A., & Sobrero, M. (2013). Academic engagement and commercialisation: A review of the literature on university industry relations. *Research Policy*, *42*(2), 423–442. doi:10.1016/j.respol.2012.09.007

Piaget, J., Lazarsfeld, P., & Castrillo, P. (1976). Tendencias de la investigación en las ciencias sociales. México. *Alianza*, *42*(001), T43.

Poon, P., Chan, T. S., & Zhou, L. (2011). Implementation of service-learning in business education: Issues and challenges. *Journal of Teaching in International Business*, *22*(3), 185–192. doi:10.1080/08975930.2011.653746

Rivas, M. T., & Donovan, P. (2001). La evaluación participativa. Ediciones Abya-Yala, segunda edición, Quito.

Ruiz-Corbella, M., & García-Gutiérrez, J. (2019). *Aprendizaje-Servicio: los retos de la evaluación* (Vol. 155). Narcea Ediciones.

Sabbaghi, O., SJ, G. F. C., & SJ, T. H. (. (2013). Service-learning and leadership: Evidence from teaching financial literacy. *Journal of Business Ethics*, *118*(1), 127–137. doi:10.100710551-012-1545-6

Sandmann, L. R., Kiely, R. C., & Grenier, R. S. (2009). Program Planning: The Neglected Dimension of Service-Learning. *Michigan Journal of Community Service Learning*, *15*(2), 17–33.

Sanmartí, N. (2007). 10 ideas clave: Evaluar para aprender. Coleccion ideas clave (España).

Scholtz, D. (2018). Service Learning: An Empowerment Agenda for Students and Community Entrepreneurs. *International Journal of Work-Integrated Learning*, *19*(1), 69–79.

Sheafer, V. (2014). Using service learning to teach classic learning theories. *Psychology Journal*, *11*(2), 77–82.

Smith, J., Kielly-Coleman, N., & Meijer, G. (2010). Assurance of learning: The role of work-integrated learning and industry partners. *Australian Collaborative Education Network National Conference: Work Integrated Learning (WIL)-Responding to Challenges (ACEN 2010),* 409-419.

Smith-Tolken, A. R., & du Plessis, J. M. J. (2013). *Service-Learning across the globe-Paper Series.* Academic Press.

Steinberg, K., Hatcher, J. A., & Bringle, R. G. (2011). The civicminded graduate: A north-star. *Michigan Journal of Community Service Learning, 18*(1), 19–33.

Steinke, P., & Fitch, P. (2007). Assessing service-learning. *Research & Practice in Assessment, 2,* 24–29.

Sullivan, W. M., & Rosin, M. S. (2008). *A new agenda for higher education: Shaping a life of the mind for practice.* Jossey-Bass.

Tranfield, D., Denyer, D., & Smart, P. (2003). Towards a methodology for developing evidence-informed management knowledge by means of systematic review. *British Journal of Management, 14*(3), 207–222. doi:10.1111/1467-8551.00375

Van Beveren, L., Roets, G., Buysse, A., & Rutten, K. (2018). We all reflect, but why? A systematic review of the purposes of reflection in higher education in social and behavioral sciences. *Educational Research Review, 24,* 1–9. doi:10.1016/j.edurev.2018.01.002

Wiese, N. M., & Sherman, D. J. (2011). Integrating marketing and environmental studies through an interdisciplinary, experiential, service-learning approach. *Journal of Marketing Education, 33*(1), 41–56. doi:10.1177/0273475310389154

Wittmer, D. P. (2004). Business and community: Integrating service learning in graduate business education. *Journal of Business Ethics, 51*(4), 359–371. doi:10.1023/B:BUSI.0000032514.05498.2b

Woodland, A. M. (2009). Using service-learning in graduate auditing courses: A standards-based framework. *Advances in Accounting Education, 10,* 61–80. doi:10.1108/S1085-4622(2009)0000010005

Yu, D. D. (2011). Achieving Service-Learning Goals in a Financial Accounting Class Project. *New Horizons in Education, 59*(1), 95–105.

Zamora, V. L. (2012). Using a social enterprise service-learning strategy in an introductory management accounting course. *Issues in Accounting Education, 27*(1), 187–226. doi:10.2308/iace-50102

KEY TERMS AND DEFINITIONS

Beneficiaries: These are the people in the community who benefit from the service-learning projects.

Civic Skills: Are people skills that enable people to gain a greater global and cultural awareness of the society around them.

Community: It is the group of people who benefit from the project. It is a synonym for beneficiaries.

Project Organizers: People in charge of designing service-learning projects, as well as their implementation, evaluation, and analysis of results.

Reflection: It refers to the general concept of reflection. It is a mechanism that allows to deepen the lived experience.

Soft Skills: It refers to people skills, among which are professional skills. Civic skills are not included in this classification in this work.

Written Reflection: It is a particular form of reflection. It refers to a qualitative tool in which the agents must write down their impressions, feelings, opinions, etc. on a given topic in a specific space.

APPENDIX

Table 7. Definitions of service-learning

Author	Definition	Educational Experience	Community Service	Civic Responsibility	Problem Solving	Reflection
NCSA (1990)	*"a method under which students learn and develop through active participation in thoughtfully organized service experiences that meet actual community needs".*	Yes	Yes	No	No	No
Bringle y Hatcher (1995)	*"a course based, credit-bearing educational experience in which students (a) participate in an organized service activity that meets identified community needs and (b) reflect on the service activity in such a way as to gain further understanding of course content, a broader appreciation of the discipline, and an enhanced sense of civic responsibility.".*	Yes	Yes	No	No	Yes
Jacoby (1996)	*"a form of experiential learning in which students engage in activities that address human and community needs together with structured opportunities intentionally designed to promote student learning and development".*	Yes	Yes	No	No	No
AAHE (2003)	*"the intellectual and civic engagement of students by linking the work students do in the classroom to real-world problems and world needs".*	No	No	Yes	Yes	No
Goldberg, Richburg and Wood (2006)	*"as experiential (real-life) and reflective problem-based learning in which students enrolled in an academic course provide a needed service to a community partner".*	Yes	Yes	No	Yes	Yes
CNCS (2006)	*"a method of teaching and learning that connects classroom lessons with meaningful service to the community. Students build academic skills while strengthening communities through service".*	Yes	Yes	No	No	No
NSLC, (2009)	*"a teaching and learning strategy that integrates meaningful community service with instruction and reflection to enrich the learning experience, teach civic responsibility, and strengthen communities".*	Yes	Yes	Yes	No	Yes
Chong (2014)	*"it is a form of experiential education that offers students opportunities to experience real-world learning and address genuine problems".*	Yes	No	No	Yes	No
Source: Own elaboration						

Chapter 15
Socio-Intercultural Management Competencies

José G. Vargas-Hernández
https://orcid.org/0000-0003-0938-4197
University Center for Economic and Managerial Sciences, University of Guadalajara, Mexico

ABSTRACT

This chapter aims to analyze the socio-intercultural management competencies as they are integrated in any organizational setting, including individuals, groups, and communities. In the analysis, it is assumed that the development of socio-intercultural management in the organizations requires the integration of the socio-intercultural principles building competencies in transdisciplinary contents in current social issues, concerns, and solutions of problems of the organizations and society. The method employed is the analytical focusing on a reflective and comparative analysis of the literature reviewed and their achievements in practical implementation in the real managerial world. It is concluded that awareness of cultural differences for organizational management sustainability are the base for the development of socio-intercultural management competencies required in the new glocal labor market environment.

INTRODUCTION

In the economic globalization processes, these socio-intercultural entrepreneurial interactions become inevitable in any type of business transactions and analysis. The study of international entrepreneurship is current in emerging economies (Kiss, et. al., 2012) and is a holistic organizational process that integrates the organization immersed in several cultures to explore opportunities in the international market and generate value (Dimitratos & Plakoyiannaki, 2003).

However, socio-interculturalism in international entrepreneurship is a neglected issue not even explored, as it has been social and intercultural entrepreneurship. In developing countries, the activities of social entrepreneurship are supported by those who promote social changes in politics and in the media to solve problems of social inequality, poverty and environmental sustainability (Dey, 2006; Dancin, et. al., 2011).

DOI: 10.4018/978-1-7998-8239-8.ch015

The countries with the greatest socio-intercultural entrepreneurial exchanges are those that have the tendency towards economic, trade and financial liberalization and integration policies. Various organizations and social networks support the contribution of social entrepreneurs to society (Bernard, 2012), although still the issue of social intercultural entrepreneurship is neglected.

Socio-intercultural entrepreneurship is in reality a complex issue to study and analyze, however, it brings a framework for negotiation in global and international business, trade and commerce.

This analysis allows the transformation of the type of social and cultural entrepreneur to a new type of socio inter-cultural entrepreneur whose main difference is having high visibility of the business in diversity context. In the first place, the study begins with the socio-intercultural concept to continue with the analysis of the relationship between social and cultural entrepreneurship to center on socio-interculturalism entrepreneurship. From this point, it is proposed a creative socio-intercultural entrepreneurship integration policy model. It's briefly exemplified with the case of the postgraduate program in economy and international business of an indigenous university in Mexico and finally, the analysis presents some concluding remarks.

THE SOCIO-INTERCULTURAL CONCEPT

In order to specify the socio-intercultural concept is necessary to start from Bourdieu (2007), who conceives that society is structured with two types of relationships: socials, the ones of *strength*, referring to the value of uses and changes and that encompasses, entwined, other types of relationships such as the ones of *sense*, which are responsible for the organization of the relationships of meaning in social life; these last ones, in his perspective, are the ones that constitute culture. Society "is conceived as the ensemble of structures somewhat objectives that organize the distribution of the production media and power between individuals and social groups, and that determine social, economic and political practices" (García, 2004, p. 32).

On the other hand, culture is the result of the interactions between society and nature, through social processes of material and spiritual production. Culture manifests itself in the behavior of human beings that belong to the same culture. In fact, the cultural, intracultural and intercultural processes are phenomena that the dynamics of societies cannot control; In other words, the cultural relationship between peoples as an equitable, congruent, responsible and tolerant act is a noble intention and an elusive purpose. Furthermore, interculturalism and multiculturalism are polysemic concepts that have acquired different meanings and connotations, depending on the context and policies of the welfare state (Vargas-Hernández, et. al., 2017).

On this basis, it's understood that society and culture are two interrelated concepts. In an allusion that culture also refers to a collective, in a society there are cultures who relate with each other (interculturality), but none of them are static and are modified within time (intraculturality); even so, there are forces who affect all cultures (intrasocial) and that impress that strength that Bordieau mentions.

The socio-interculturality concept goes beyond culturalistic postures which leave aside social power, but also of economy-centered postures, where culture and its relationships are minimized. It refers to processes that involve a multitude of variables in continuous interrelation between societies and that occur in many situations in violent opposition (Guerra-García, 2005, 2004a, 2004b). Socio-interculturalism is also a process that notices the intimate relationship between nature, society and culture (Ochoa-Zazueta, 2006) and that allows identifying the relationship of meanings as a fundamental component of other cultures, such as the indigenous worldview with understanding, explanation and, where appropriate, the possession of assets that are required for the interaction of natural forces and that explain cultural practices.

Socio-interculturalism is the dynamic relationship that overcomes the history of modern politics in which the fight for equality was developed, but adding the consideration of differences, in other words, in this posture is considered what Touraine (2000) proposes, conjugating equality and difference in human coexistence. That brings together and interrelates several societies with their respective cultures in an indivisible socio-intercultural process (Figueroa-Rivera, 2016). This perspective connects social, cultural, genetic, psychological and anthropological elements, with a focus on gender, ethnicity, culture and social class, inclusiveness of masculinity and femininity values and their power relations, in its search for symmetrical egalitarian interaction and in favor of the integration of the socio-cultures that coexist and cohabit in the same territorial space.

As Vargas-Hernández, et al. (2017), have argued, the notion of intercultural citizenship is critical to the concept of interculturalism because it considers the differentiated rights of small groups and minorities in such a way that they are oriented to create the social cohesion that liberalism rejects. This notion of differentiated intercultural citizenship that is based on the individual and collective rights of native cultures is resumed in socio-interculturality.

But interculturality is just an aspect of socio-interculturality; studying comprehensively reality through culturalistic postures that focus only to interculturality and minimize socio-economic aspects can bring naïve concepts distant from what's actually happening.

The socio-interculturalism implicit in welfare regimes should not be an institutionalized process of structural intersocial violence exercised by monocultural, hegemonic, colonialist, asymmetric and acculturating nationalist structures, but on the contrary, that favors the integration and assimilation of all minority cultures of society through the recognition of their rights and the development of a multicultural and poly-ethnic citizenship agenda that fosters social cohesion (Vargas-Hernández, et al., 2017).

SOCIO-INTERCULTURAL DYNAMICS AND ENTREPRENEURSHIP

Entrepreneurship opportunities are perceived differently in different cultures, but this also depends on the economic opportunities that social forces present. In one hand the intercultural dynamic can be an interpretive framework relevant in any dimension of entrepreneurship that make sense of the individuals and groups own behavior and determines their attitudes; and a specific culture supporting entrepreneurship can develop more potential and activities. But in a more extensive way, the socio-intercultural dynamic indicates the level of entrepreneurial behavior, the opportunities and exploitation in the specific society. In any specific society, the socio-intracultural dynamic indicates how it is considered entrepreneurial behaviors such as innovativeness, risk-taking, opportunity recognition, growth orientation and exploitation.

If talking about a single national culture were possible, this could be defined in terms of shared values and practices in one country (House et. al., 2004). Culture is related to entrepreneurial behavior at the individual level as a manifestation of belonging to a culture, but the intracultural, intercultural and intrasocial dynamics influence, positively or negatively, in the individual's behavior (Hayton, et. al., 2002). There are factors that encourage or discourage the entrepreneurial activity subject to the different countries, regions and cultures, requiring further recognition of differences and their causes. The entrepreneurial activities are considered to be the action of individuals y collectivities innovating and taking risks. Negative activities attached to entrepreneurship sometimes are inevitable transitional development that may not be well accepted and may foster anti-entrepreneurial values.

According to the current economic structure, social forces have oriented the individuals to generate an entrepreneurial attitude, but there are examples of collectivities who have taken their risks and generated ventures in a regional matter; for example, El Pochotal in El Fuerte, Sinaloa, a yoreme-mayo community whose women decided to elaborate an artisanal bread in the face of their husband's lack of work; this community have sold this product for over 50 years. Another example is the entrepreneurship of the Mennonites in Mexico, who produce cheese and other products and have been able to successfully maintain themselves over hundreds of years.

The entrepreneurial culture can be driven by individuals and collectivities that exhibit entrepreneurial behaviors such as making decisions, having initiatives and actions to create new opportunities. To driving a culture of empowerment and entrepreneurship requires organizational commitment and encouraging individuals to become confident.

Culture influences personal values and behaviors of individuals and groups that are related to practices of people in terms of intracultural dimensions that are relevant for entrepreneurship. The authors conclude that some cultural dimensions have more influence on creating social entrepreneurial activities and are more involved in social economy. The cultural dimensions proposed by anthropologists are related to cultural characteristics, an intercultural vision and actions of social enterprises (Urbano, et, al., 2010; Dancin, et. al., 2011, Dey, 2006). But more broadly, socio-intercultural elements, such as cultural values, entrepreneurial activity and the economic level of a country are able to explain entrepreneurial activity (Jaén, et. al., 2013).

The intracultural and intercultural dynamics have a significant effect on entrepreneurial behavior and values. Comparing cultural values and entrepreneurial behavior can partially explain why some cultures are more sensitive, conducive and supportive of entrepreneurship. In several occasions, a clash of cultural values between population and entrepreneur groups may drive self-employed into actual self-employment (Baum et al., 1993). In a wider sense, entrepreneurial behavior is incentivized in specific socio-intercultural dynamics in societies where a combination of individualism and collectivism promote the creation of ideas and innovations of major social benefit. Until today, capitalism has promoted individualism as the only entrepreneurial form, but benefits to society haven't been maximized, while collectivism, characteristic of cultures and ethnic groups, in the current social structure hasn't shown entrepreneurial effectivity, but represents an option that could provide to society.

There's a difference between socio-intercultural entrepreneurship and cultural or social entrepreneurship. Social entrepreneurs can be cultural entrepreneurs and vice versa (Dancin et al., 2011). The social entrepreneur is committed to society guided by innovative practices to solve social problems in different ways beyond the established margins (Dancin, et. al., 2011, Mitchell et al, 2007, Tracey et al., 2011; Gaglio, 2004). The emergence and development of the cultural entrepreneur has a purpose of its action, the creation of healthy habits with a creation of social value that, unlike social entrepreneurs, have a greater economic orientation in the market (Lounsbury & Glynn, 2001). Cultural entrepreneurs are oriented to change behaviors, mentalities and attitudes through the use of persuasive communication (Witter, 2011).

Recent research highlights entrepreneurs with the profiles of social entrepreneurship and cultural entrepreneurship differentiated by the purpose of their actions (Lounsbury & Glynn, 2001). While the social entrepreneur is oriented to systems and the market, the cultural entrepreneur is oriented to the creation of healthy habits and the promotion of value creation to society through the use of persuasive communication to change attitudes, beliefs and behaviors, etc., in the change of mentalities towards a better world (Witter, 2011). The cultural entrepreneur uses persuasive communication to influence each other to change behaviors, attitudes, and beliefs. Of course, these entrepreneurs can assume social or cultural roles indistinctly, (Dancin, et. al., 2011) conforms to the circumstances and conditions that require it.

The social entrepreneur is characterized by the ability to recognize social value, create opportunities and make decisions based on finding innovative solutions to social problems (Gaglio, 2004) through proactive actions that go beyond margins and assumption risk (Tracey et al., 2011; Sullivan, et. al., 2003). Social entrepreneurship is characterized by the creation of value in society as a whole (Austin, et. al., 2003; Mair & Martí, 2006).

The objective of social entrepreneurship is the creation of value through social innovation processes to solve problems in society (Urbano, et. al., 2010, Zadek & Thake, 1997; Kramer, 2005; Austin, et al., 2003; Leadbeater, 2007; Harding, 2006, Westall & Chalkley, 2007). Social entrepreneurship solves social problems with the development of entrepreneurial activities that are innovative that are directed to create a positive social impact with the reasonable obtaining of a financial profit. Social entrepreneurship works in its habitat without having geographical limits for its global growth in its activity of solving social problems. It goes beyond the social and cultural entrepreneur and provides opportunities and resources across cultures.

Social entrepreneur focuses on markets and systems, and the cultural is oriented to change the mentalities of individuals (Witter, 2011). Social entrepreneurs can carry out activities of cultural entrepreneurs and vice versa, so the behavior of the entrepreneur can be analyzed from a socio-intercultural perspective.

Socio-intercultural entrepreneurs are able to understand intracultural, intercultural and intrasocial dynamics in order to make decisions to benefit individually, culturally and socially. They establish a relationship of respect and dialogue with the diversity of cultures that it recognizes as a complex enrichment process by collaborating in the promotion of values related to social plurality and diversity of gender, race, ethnicity, etc. Socio-intercultural and ethnic diversity, multiculturalism and interculturalism are a phenomenon and a constant historical fact in the development processes of human societies and cultures with differentiated specifications and conceptualizations in different contexts.

Socio-intercultural entrepreneurship is a notion beyond the professional relationship in individuals from diverse cultures in which intercultural groups relationships and contacts play a relevant in the plural societies and the intercultural business and companies. The models that explain the socio-intercultural relations focus on the efficacy of the results (Kim 1989), centered on socio-intercultural communication and on the complexity of adaptive processes of socio-intercultural relations between individuals, collectivities and contexts (Ward, 1996). From a microsocial perspective, the content of the determinants of socio-intercultural relationships are structured around the reception of intra- and intergroup and interpersonal relationships.

An entrepreneur has the function of understanding socio-intercultural dynamics to reinforce and revolutionize the creation and production patterns by innovating, inventing or proving a technical possibility to design, develop and produce a new product or an old one in a new process, to provide new sources of materials and inputs, new organizational forms, etc. (Duarte & Ruiz, 2009). The entrepreneur develops the skills of visualization, conceptualization and implementation based on a leading foundation of emerging activities and maintains communication and empathy with society to determine the skills required by the proactivity of the markets. The entrepreneur must perform socio-intercultural entrepreneurial activities as a career option to achieve personal goals in the midst of socio-intercultural diversity. In relation to his nature and particularities, the entrepreneur is a person with determination and drive to meet his proposed goals despite adversity but considering diversity.

Additionally, to play their role, entrepreneurs need social acceptance to legitimate the activities and have access and control of financial, material and human resources to initiate new ventures (Backes–Gellner y Werner, 2007). The classic role performed by the entrepreneur find reasons to put his or her resources at risk and expose himself or herself to failure. The outcome of entrepreneurial activities depends on personal effort (Mueller and Thomas 2001, 2000).

With a socio-intercultural perspective entrepreneurs anticipate the problems taking into account all the possible foreseeable pros and cons, the (private and social) costs involved in the activities, determines the equilibrium points of all the operations of the company, makes decisions based on vital information and data analysis for strategic planning, the business plan with the initial investment required, finds financing sources, convince potential investors and take measures on the best time on cost control, price of products and services, sales planning, profits, etc.

The role of an entrepreneur is central to any new emergent business. They determine the worth of going into business and provide and explanation step by step, the work process being done in manufacturing and production, the materials needed to be used, the machinery and equipment used, the time used and the responsible person to accomplish it.

Entrepreneurship is the attitude that an individual takes on objectives to advance new projects, innovating or adding value to existing businesses, products and services. It is assumed as a tool of social technologies to achieve innovation and competitiveness, that fosters productive socio-organizational environments and consolidates the creation of companies that promote job creation in national, regional and local contexts. Entrepreneurship is a tool that strengthens the social capital of citizens based on the satisfaction of their needs and improvement of the quality of life (Garrido, 2007; Peredo and McLean, 2006; Arenas, et. al., 2012).

Framed by the socio-intercultural diversity, the entrepreneurial orientation is divided into risk taking, innovation and proactivity (Lumpkin & Dess, 1996), and its relationship with performance is influenced by contingent variables such as the organizational structure (Slevin & Covin, 1990), resources of the organization (Ostgaard & Birley, 1994), characteristics of the industry (Eisenhardt & Schoonhoven, 1990), culture (Stuart & Abetti, 1987), environment (Covin and Slevin, 1989) and strategy (Venkatraman, 1989). Performance orientation is the society encouraging and rewarding individuals for improvement based on the achievement and high quality of entrepreneurship (Hayton et al., 2002).

Cross-national socio-intercultural differences of entrepreneurial activities are related to socio-economic, cultural and psychological motives and values. The diversity of relationships, practices and activities are beyond the cultural economy, produced and embedded in small social groups and collectives, communities, ethnic and aboriginal groups, minorities and social organizations, urban cultures and subcultures, etc. which make relevant contributions to socio-intercultural entrepreneurship.

A relevant factor that classifies the profile of the entrepreneur is the socio-intercultural sensitivity. People who are socio-intercultural sensitive based on the acceptance of cultural differences and have the will to understand, appreciate and accept cultural differences (Vásquez, et.al., 2014). This sensitivity is enriched with the traditions, customs, beliefs, conceptions, values and norms of each society in its place where it is interacting and is directly connected to the human abilities of each different inhabitant. But it also generates understanding of the cultural differences in a wider society where economic forces are ineludible.

Individually, emotional development is an essential capacity of the entrepreneur to strengthen their own self-esteem and moral autonomy to make the best decisions from among several options that require evaluation processes in terms of social responsibility and commitment to global sustainability

(Del Solar, 2010). Socio-intercultural relationships and interactions between individuals from different cultures, is a factor that ramps up innovation, creativity, entrepreneurial activities and more successful at solving problems.

The diversity initiatives are related to the inclusion of different and divergent cultural subgroups and small groups not represented by the majority culture, which are not necessarily involved to achieve competitive advantages and more favorable results. One of these initiatives is that practicing socio-intercultural communication in international business is part of achieving success in your projects. It requires an open mind, without prejudice or paradigms, the ability to adapt to different environments and contexts, and the ability to integrate differentiated groups and in diversity, in plural communities and with inclusive identities.

Organizational socio-intercultural diversity breeds entrepreneurship and innovation leverage from diverse cultures, genders, ethnic backgrounds, perspectives, etc. Corporate socio-intercultural entrepreneurial diversity policies and programs at the organizational workplace already emphasize ethical socio-intercultural values such as tolerance, loyalty and solidarity, but it is required more than that, a new approach to make innovative and creative solutions to create new business projects and ventures. In the management of social entrepreneurship, the valuations of the specificities of each culture (Zait, 2002) and their diversity are considered to achieve socio-intercultural objectives of multinational organizations.

Any entrepreneurial action like start a venture or establishing a business is considered a means for generating self-employment and income has important socio-intercultural dimensions playing a role in entrepreneurship (Lounsbury & Glynn, 2001).

The socio-intercultural vision of entrepreneurship is based on the analysis of the mentioned intracultural, intercultural and intrasocial dynamics, which explain the intensity of the social practices of different cultures (Shane & Venkataraman, 2000; Schwartz, 1999). Cultural features favor the development of an area with Hofstede's cultural dimensions for social entrepreneurship with the performance of social economy activities (Hofstede, 2007). From a socio-intercultural perspective, they should be considered beyond the borders of their own culture, with a more global vision, considering social and environmental values and the satisfaction of needs that the economy cannot satisfy by itself.

Socio-intercultural entrepreneurial management is beyond awareness using different approaches, an understanding and interactions of respect to differences in adjusting behaviors and attitudes within diverse socio cultures in the global and international contexts. The analysis of social entrepreneurship can be done from a socio-intercultural management perspective based on the cultural characteristics of entrepreneurs that can be explained from cultural dimensions, that is, social entrepreneurship actions are examined from an socio-intercultural perspective, considering that culture explains human behavior (Hofstede, 2001).

Socio-intercultural entrepreneurship is a perspective that recognizes socio-intercultural features such as the cultural dimension of the distance of power between the entrepreneur and his followers and that measures the interpersonal relationship tends to promote innovation (Hofstede, 2001).

Socio-intercultural entrepreneurship influences patterns of thought and mindset as a response to solving problems at any level, space, activity or process; it refers to the design, creation and development of business involving interactions and interrelationships between people from different cultures, but considering social forces. It allows to become self-aware and to step outside of comfortable and usual cultural reference framework gaining more perspective about the issues and leading to avoid the internal struggles and external conflicts. Its development requires self-awareness for a frame shifting of references and routines in the sense of thinking outside-the box based on creativity and innovation.

The Socio-intercultural entrepreneur is oriented to solve social problems in his environment and add value to society in the cultural dimension of individualism - collectivism (Hofstede, 2001). Countries with high social entrepreneurship activity have a partially proven relationship showing a level of inclination to find innovative solutions (Sullivan, et al., 2003; Tracey, et. al., 2011) but not fully testing their social entrepreneurship activities and the socio-intercultural dimension.

The Socio-intercultural entrepreneur develops the capacities to recognize social value, make innovative decisions to create opportunities, be proactive, take risks (Sullivan, 2003) and can carry out activities of social and cultural entrepreneurs and vice versa. It refers to competent entrepreneurs with a greater sense of self-efficacy are more willing to engage in new experiences with goal setting in novel cross-cultural settings. The competencies configuration model allows identifying and analyzing the socio-intercultural requirements of a competent entrepreneurship in terms of the individuals, functions and activities that make up the socio-intercultural organizational system, the coordination of the components of the socio-technical system and the interdependence with the environment (Aneas, 2005).

SOCIO-INTERCULTURAL ENTREPRENEURSHIP

The socio-intercultural entrepreneurship approach examines the variables of the social and cultural environments influencing the entrepreneur behavior and personality, including the thinking and emotional processes in the interrelationships, contacts and connections with other people and social groups in which is part of. Some of these variables are the gender, ethnicity, religion, social class, etc. According to the contact hypothesis elaborated by Allport (1955) and Pettigrew (1971), it is the nature of the socio-intercultural contact that generates favorable attitudes in intergroup behaviors to participate and cooperate in common goals in a climate of acceptance and support (Cook & Reichardt, 1986).

The operationalization of the socio-intercultural concept registers the relations of the encounter of societies and their cultures in a context of reality of the interaction of society, culture and nature. The dynamic interaction of socio-interculturalism manifests itself at the macro level in the economic, social, political and cultural spheres, at the same time at the micro level in the interrelationships of gender, class and ethnicity. However, the socio-intercultural approach is a multidimensional approach to the diversity of social classes, popular culture, technological tools, poverty and problems of humanity according to Guerra-García, (2004b).

Socio-interculturalism for Guerra-García (2004b) is the source to derive principles that combine the social, technological and economic in the face of diversity, through the will and performance of each actor, individual or collective. The sense of individual and collective action that social actors construct based on socio-intercultural attributes delimits individual and community identities (Vargas-Hernández, 2005). An example of an analysis of socio-interculturalism is found in Guerra-García, et. al. (2020), who have examined socio-intercultural dynamics of the Topolobampo colony, Sinaloa, Mexico, described from the intercultural relations where the aspects of feminism, racism, discrimination and the ideas of limited and utopian socialism, as well as the political intention and economy for the urban and agricultural development of the region.

Socio-intercultural dimensions of entrepreneurship refer to how the different cultures are interrelated in societal organizations enhancing the different levels of entrepreneurial activities contributing to competitiveness, economic growth and job creation. It produces positive interactions between the members of any community, whether at the diplomatic, academic, business or administration levels (Maldonado,

2007). Socio-socio-intercultural entrepreneurship facilitates individuals to consider multiple point of view and challenges to learn through communicative interactions about other cultures and avoiding the obstacles of an ethnocentric perspective. It is a two-way of sharing the burden of communications and responsibility of cultural awareness (Ferraro,1994) to accommodate themselves to cultural practices.

Socio-intercultural entrepreneurship communication is supported by the understanding of the specific cultural elements that influence the sociocultural interactions between individuals with different cultural backgrounds that have an impact on global business environment. According to the Merriam-Webster (n.d.) sociocultural is defined as related too involving a combination of social and cultural factors. The socio-interculturalism of entrepreneurs involves other people with different cultures that help to achieve the objectives of undertaking business in other countries motivated to learn from other cultures beyond those with which language is shared that facilitate communication.

The sociocultural theory explains the individual mental functioning focusing on the participation in social interactions and cultural activities in relation to social, cultural, historical and institutional contexts. This theory stresses the interactions between people and culture in the context of a socio ecosystem environment. Sandoval et. al., (2008) explains a case in which the socio-intercultural context creates tensions in such a way that aboriginal students are forced to be absent intermittently from their studies at the Mexico´s Autonomous Indigenous University requiring to change its policies to adjust to the reality of its aboriginal target population. He concludes that all exogenous causes come from intrasocial, intercultural and socio-cultural dynamics in which the institution cannot have a decisive impact in the face of this social and cultural macro dynamics where the search for the culprits becomes idle.

The awareness of the socio-intercultural entrepreneurial process facilitates the communication and understanding processes between people from different cultural backgrounds in the context of effective interactions. Startup and pre-accelerator programs are based on the facilitation of socio-intercultural entrepreneurial relationships to create business and social outcomes, as the result of the facilitators socio cultural background experiences, innovation and creativity.

Socio-interculturalism makes it possible to compare western and eastern cultural perspectives to conclude that at the level of societies, socio-interculturalism raises the existence of internal cultural relations and produces identities that after each unit that enters into coalition with the others becomes part of something that is larger than the previous cultural configuration (Medina, 2006). The activities across borders of nations and regions are linked to differences in values and beliefs the diverse groups of population and entrepreneurs. In this way, socio-interculturalism manifests itself as the reciprocal learning of the various ethnic groups and other human groups

CREATIVE SOCIO-INTERCULTURAL ENTREPRENEURSHIP INTEGRATION POLICY MODEL

Entrepreneurship is related to the willingness to commit resources to create and develop uncertain opportunities. As a tool, entrepreneurship develops and strengthens social capital in regional contexts through the creation of alternatives that generate employment while satisfying market needs and improving society's quality of life and from inside society to cultures, specially to diverse localities, cities and communities, families and individuals. When enterprises are scarce in societies, unemployment increases. The creation of companies generates opportunities for the implementation of business projects that include the participation of other producers in the sector and families that improve their living conditions and contribute to the development of their community.

Entrepreneurship is considered a need for self-fulfillment that, as an intrinsic and systemic factor of the entrepreneur, compromises an entrepreneurial dynamic between education and employment. Higher university education is responsible for responding to the promotion of an entrepreneurial attitude based on social needs in terms of business development and job creation (Dehter, 2001; Formichella, 2004).

Socio-intercultural creative entrepreneurship has a strong foundation on the small groups forming micro socio cultures that share common heritage, behaviors, cultural values, beliefs, customs traditions, etc., as the basis of the entrepreneurial activities. Micro cultures manifested in small socio-intercultural entrepreneurial practices develop socio-intercultural assets expressed through inter- and intracultural creativity, innovation and value creation as the key processes of the creative economy.

The use of entrepreneurial skills between intrapreneurs and entrepreneurs present differences when starting a company or when working in a company in such a way that levels of entrepreneurship can be established that range from non-existent, minimal to the option of starting and establishing their own company or project. Start-up entrepreneurs deal with the uncertainty of possible outcomes.

Intrapreneurship is the entrepreneurial spirit within the companies themselves (Pinchot III, et. al., 1999 y Formichella, 2004) that is produced by a business vision committed to research and action of initiatives and projects that contribute to the growth and development of the company. The intrapreneur transforms dreams and ideas into projects focusing on innovation and creativity to operate profitably within an organizational environment (Koontz, et. al., 2008), and uses their entrepreneurial abilities within organizations as employees or members. Intrapreneurs who operate within companies as employees, as well as independent entrepreneurs create, develop and renew management and production structures and processes (Kundel, 1991; Dehter, 2001 an Formichella 2004).

In this manner, the focus of socio-intercultural entrepreneurship in business is on interacting with people to find solutions to problems thorough the processes such as the co-constructing better.

The socio-intercultural entrepreneurship integration policy model should be based on the collective input of the best practices in other socio socio-intercultural environments and considering the legal instruments to manage cultural diversity advantage and addressing conflicts. This integration model approach must be aimed to facilitate the design, development and implementation of socio-socio-intercultural entrepreneurial strategies.

Socio-interculturalism denotes the attitude of different cultures to practice dialogue from equality and in a self-critical conception of their own culture (Besalú, 2002). The critical thought and analysis of socio-intercultural entrepreneurship surfaces a fundamental topic of the ethical identity in business culture engaged with the environment that is becoming increasingly complex, uncertainty and challenging because the expectations and the different standards to meet, language patterns, etc. (Chaney & Martin, 2007).

The condition of a successful individual is the image of the stereotype that the neoliberal economy promotes as an entrepreneur, dynamic, efficient, aggressive, etc., which in some way has given undesirable results in terms of the dysfunctionalities of the meritocracy, increasing economic inequalities, social and cultural, etc. Therefore, a new proposal for entrepreneurship is required that abandons these traditional values in such a way that it overcomes institutional and cultural limitations, contributes to the valorization of diversity and inclusion, the opening towards new forms of human integration, etc.

Regardless of the representations and social scenarios provided with stereotypes that operate as barriers, socio-intercultural prevent the development of innovative and constructive ways to undertake the creation of new projects and new companies (Del Solar, 2010).

The strategic design of an entrepreneurial ecosystem that fosters entrepreneurship must be based on the specifications and socio-intercultural differences of the different cultural spaces that interact; these, have direct influence on socio-intercultural entrepreneurial orientation and behaviors among members of a specific cultural community. The design, adoption and implementation of socio-intercultural entrepreneurial strategies must facilitate socio-intercultural encounters, interactions and exchanges responding to the needs of diverse people while promoting inclusive, fair and active participation of individuals, organizations and communities involved in economic growth, social development and environmental sustainability.

PROGRAM IN ECONOMICS AND INTERNATIONAL BUSINESS

At the Autonomous Indigenous University of Mexico (UAIM, in spanish), a postgraduate program in economy and international business was created. Being an institution oriented to the attention of students originated from different ethnic groups and of young people with limited economic resources in the country, the creation of the program may seem strange.

UAIM was born in 2001 in the yoreme-mayo ethnoregion (one of the autochthonous ethnic groups of the country), but it brings attention to yaqui, raramuri, ch'ol, tzotzil and tzeltal students to name some of the over 25 indigenous groups where the students come from. It's part of the intercultural universities of the country. Because of its nature, culturalist postures have tried to orient the curricula to attending only cultural aspects such as languages and indigenous tourism, but UAIM's socio-intercultural posture is that there exist social aspects that go beyond the cultures, international understanding, international business, information technologies and communication, they are matters of a wider society where the cultures are immerse. That is why, the program in economy and international business and other academic programs such as accounting and computational systems engineering are offered.

The program offers the advantage of positioning in a local and international intercultural context in a way that intercultural competencies are acquired during daily coexistence; furthermore, entrepreneurship's problems, which are themes of the academic program, are discussed in relation to the participating cultures and the difficulties of the Mexican and global society.

Socio-Interculturality is a concept that allows to observe the dynamics in this educational program, in one hand the intrasocial aspects that go beyond culture, the macroeconomy, the international institutions, TICS, among others, generate adaptive changes in students who come from other cultures, in other words, intracultural changes are provoked to generate adaptation to emergent environments; likewise, interchanges are generated between students that come from different cultures, in other words, intercultural relations favor educational dynamics.

Also, the understanding that the place, which is part of an international negotiation, requires of the understanding of the intracultural dynamics, is reinforced. In other words, what happens inside each culture, the interculturals, the relationship between them and the intrasocials, the economic forces that go beyond cultures.

Therefore, not only economic aspects must be considered, but that the cultures present forces that should be explained in order to fulfill the established objectives.

There is an intracultural dynamic in the indigenous students of this program that comes of their interest of learning management and negotiate online with an international reach; that's why is a mistake to see these groups as static. Most indigenous communities in Mexico haven't economically developed because indigenous politics have tried to maintain their population in poverty despite all the political speeches. The intercultural interchange in the program have been practically between indigenous and non-indigenous people, and between entrepreneurs and non-entrepreneurs, which have enriched the themes and thesis that are addressed.

The program tries to incorporate students from the lowest economic levels that are able to understand global economy and to manage ventures with international business to the International Labour Market; socio-intercultural sensibility from students is one strength, since each of them belong to cultures and communities and are able to understand local and global dynamics.

CONCLUSION

The value of socio socio-intercultural entrepreneurial interactions results in new businesses, ventures, projects, products, markets, etc., meeting the needs of people. Entrepreneurial activities require support programs designed and implemented based on the specific intracultural, intercultural and intrasocial dynamics of the environment, as it has been confirmed.

The increasing global business transactions requires the development of new forms of socio-socio-intercultural entrepreneurship such as multinational strategic alliances and joint ventures. The entrepreneur needs to understand and practice socio-interculturalism in internationalization processes to develop the ability to break down the barriers that exist between the various cultures of the world.

The relationship from a socio-intercultural perspective between innovation and social entrepreneurship has been partially proven, as it has been confirmed by Sullivan et al., (2003), and Tracey et al., (2011), although the relationship between the cultural dimension and social economy activities has not been proven. But it can be concluded that economies with social activities show a high degree of innovation.

The relationship between the cultural dimension and the activity of the social economy is not proven. The cultural dimensions have relationships with the entrepreneurship orientation and its behaviors although the entrepreneurial practices may vary in different cultures, in such a way that the same entrepreneurial practices may be successful in one culture but dysfunctional in other.

An academic program in economy and international business is a good example of socio-interculturality, intrasocial forces are found explicit in the intention of looking into the economic knowledge and in international business; in the program, students from very diverse Latin-American ethnic groups where relationships between their cultures are promoted (the interculturality) can participate, but at the same time this dynamic provokes changes, not only from the individuals who participate in the program but in the communities where they come from (intraculturality).

Socio-intercultural entrepreneurship is a proposal that presents a methodological frame to understand society in which the enterprise is immerse and to take more assertive decisions, not only for the enterprise's benefice, but to maximize social benefits and minimize environmental damage.

The intracultral, intercultural and intrasocial dynamics allow to understand what happens in a determined business context and help the socio-intracultural entrepreneur to be more assertive at making decisions.

REFERENCES

Allport, G. W. (1955). *Becoming: Basic Consideration for a Psychology of Personality*. Yale University Press.

Aneas Álvarez, M. A. (2005). *Competencias interculturales transversales en la empresa: un modelo para la detección de necesidades formativas*. Universitat de Barcelona. Departament de Mètodes d'Investigació i Diagnòstic en Educació https://www.tdx.cat/handle/10803/2343#page=1

Arenas, C., Arenas, R., Ureña, Y., Carruyo, N., & Mejía, A. (2012). *Emprenderismo: Una Herramienta para el Desarrollo de Tecnologías Sociales. III Jornadas Internacionales FING UJGH 2012, Universidad Dr.* José Gregorio Hernández - Decanato de la Facultad de Ingeniería.

Austin, J., Stevenson, H., & Wei-skillern, J. (2003). *Social Entrepreneurship and Commercial Entrepreneurship: Same, Different, or Both?* Working Paper Series, No. 04-029, Harvard Business School.

Backes–Gellner, U., & Werner, A. (2007). Entrepreneurial Signaling via education: Success factor in innovative start-ups. *Small Business Economics*, *29*(2), 173–190. doi:10.100711187-006-0016-9

Baum, J. R., Frese, M., Baron, R. A., & Katz, J. A. (2007). Entrepreneurship as an area of psychology study: an introduction. *The Psychology of Entrepreneurship*, 1-18.

Bernard, C. (2012). *Surveying networks of social entrepreneurs*. Retrieved from http://www.kpmgfamilybusiness.com/surveying-networks-of-social-entrepreneurs/

Besalú, X. (2002). *Diversidad cultural y educación*. Síntesis.

Bourdieu, P. (2007). *El Sentido Práctico*. Siglo XXI.

Chaney, L. H., & Martin, J. (2007). *Intercultural Business Communication*. Pearson Prentice Hall.

Cook, T., & Reichardt, C. (1986). *Métodos cualitativos y cuantitativos en la investigación educativa*. Morata.

Covin, J. G., & Slevin, D. P. (1989). Strategic management of small firms in hostile and benign environments. *Strategic Management Journal*, *10*(1), 75–87. doi:10.1002mj.4250100107

Dancin, M. T., Dancin, D. A., & Tracey, P. (2011). Social Entrepreneurship: A Critique and Future Directions. *Organization Science*, *22*(5), 1203–1213. doi:10.1287/orsc.1100.0620

Dehter, M. (2001). *Intrapreneurship*. Retrieved from http://www.justoahora.com/nws/iv02.htm

Del Solar, S. (2010). *Emprendedores en el aula. Guía para la formación en valores y habilidades sociales de docentes y jóvenes emprendedores*. Fondo Multilateral de Inversiones del Banco Interamericano de Desarrollo.

Dey, P. (2006). The rhetoric of social entrepreneurship: Paralogy and new language games in academic discourse. In C. Steyaert & D. Hjorth (Eds.), *Entrepreneurship as Social Change: A Third Movements of Entrepreneurship* (pp. 121–144). Edward Elgar. doi:10.4337/9781847204424.00015

Dimitratos, P., & Plakoyiannaki, E. (2003). Theoretical foundations of an international entrepreneurial culture. *Journal of International Entrepreneurship, 1*(2), 187–215. doi:10.1023/A:1023804318244

Duarte, T., & Ruiz, M. (2009). Emprendimiento, una opción para el desarrollo. *Scienta Et Technica, 15*(43), 326–331.

Eisenhardt, K. M., & Schoonhoven, C. B. (1990). Organizational growth: Linking founding team, strategy, environment, and growth among us semiconductor ventures, 1978-1988. *Administrative Science Quarterly, 35*(3), 504–529. doi:10.2307/2393315

Empresate. (2011). *Emprender en Venezuela.* Retrieved from: https://www.empresate.org/

Ferraro, G. P. (1994). *The cultural dimension of international business.* Prentice Hall.

Figueroa-Rivera, A. N. (2016). *Antología de antropología social.* Unideal Universidad Matías Romero de Avendaño.

Formichella, M. M. (2004). *El concepto de emprendimiento y su relación con la educación, el empleo y el desarrollo local.* Tres Arroyos.

Gaglio, C. M. (2004). The role of mental simulations and counterfactualthinking in the opportunity identification process. *Entrepreneurship Theory and Practice, 28*(6), 533–552. doi:10.1111/j.1540-6520.2004.00063.x

García-Canclini, N. (2004). *Diferentes, desiguales y desconectados: mapas de la interculturalidad.* Gedisa.

Garrido, F. (2007). *Pensamiento estratégico: la estrategia como centro neurálgico de la empresa.* Editorial Deusto.

Guerra-García, E. (2004). La sociointerculturalidad y la educación indígena. In *Cuestión étnica, culturas, construcción de identidades.* México: Universidad Autónoma Indígena de México, Asociación Latinoamericana de Sociología y ediciones el Caracol.

Guerra-García, E. (2005). La Anerogogía de la Voluntad, propuesta educativa sociointercultural de la Universidad Autónoma Indígena de México. *Ra Ximhai, 1*(1), 15–38. doi:10.35197/rx.01.01.2005.02.EG

Guerra-García, E., Caro-Dueñas, M. A., & Corrales-Baldenebro, A. L. (2020). Dinámica sociointercultural del surgimiento del puerto de Topolobampo en México. *Revista CoPaLa, Construyendo Paz Latinoamericana, 10*(5), 102-125. Retrieved from http://revistacopala.net/index.php/ojs/article/view/22

Harding, R. (2006). *Social Entrepreneurship Monitor.* London Global Entrepreneurship Monitor. Retrieved from https://scholar.google.com/citations?user=IKAsBdIAAAAJ&hl=en

Hayton, J. C., George, G., & Zahra, S. A. (2002). National culture and entrepreneurship: A review of behavioral Research. *Entrepreneurship Theory and Practice, 26*(4), 33–52. doi:10.1177/104225870202600403

Hofstede, G. (2001). *Cultures and Organizations. Software of the Mind.* McGraw-Hill.

Hofstede, G. (2007). *Geert Hofstede Cultural Dimensions.* Retrieved 11/23/2007 from www.geert-hofstede.com

House, R., Hanges, P., Javidan, M., & Dorfman, P. (2004). *Culture, Leadership and Organizations: the GLOBE Study of 62 Societies*. Sage Publications.

Jaén, I., Fernandez-Serrano, J., & Liñan, F. (2013). Valores culturales, nivel de ingresos y actividad emprendedora. *Revista de Economía Mundial, 35*, 35–52.

Kim, Y. (1989). Intercultural Adaptation. In M. K. Asante & W. Gudykunst (Eds.), *Handbook of International and Intercultural Communication* (pp. 275–294). Sage.

Kiss, A. N., Danis, W. N., & Cavusgil, S. T. (2012). International entrepreneurship research in emerging economies: A critical review and research agenda. *Journal of Business Venturing, 27*(2), 266–290. doi:10.1016/j.jbusvent.2011.09.004

Koontz, H., Weihrich, H., & Cannice, M. (2008). *Administración una perspectiva global y empresarial*. McGraw-Hill Interamericana.

Kramer, M. R. (2005). *Measuring innovation: evaluation in the field of social entrepreneurship*. A Publication for Skoll Foundation by Foundation Strategy Group. Retrieves form https://community-wealth.org/content/measuring-innovation-evaluation-field-social-entrepreneurship

Kundel, S. W. (1991). *El impacto de la estructura de la estrategia y de la industria en nuevo funcionamiento de la empresa* (Doctoral Dissertatión). University of Georgia Dissertation Abstracts International.

Leadbeater, C. (2007). *Social enterprise and social innovation: strategies for the next ten years*. Cabinet Office of the Third Sector. Available from: http://www.charlesleadbeater.net/cms/xstandard/social_enterprise_innovation.pdf

Lounsbury, M., & Glynn, M. A. (2001). Cultural entrepreneurship: Stories, legitimacy, and the acquisition of resources. *Strategic Management Journal, 22*(6-7), 545–564. doi:10.1002mj.188

Lumpkin, G. T., & Dess, G. G. (1996). Clarifying the entrepreneurial orientation construct and linking it toperformance. *Academy of Management Review, 21*(1), 135–172. doi:10.2307/258632

Mair, J., & Martí, I. (2006). Social entrepreneurship research: A source of explanations, prediction, and delight. *Journal of World Business, 41*(1), 36–44. doi:10.1016/j.jwb.2005.09.002

Maldonado, K. (2007). La interculturalidad de los negocios internacionales. *Universidad Empresa Bogotá (Colombia), 6*(12), 261–291.

Medina, A. (2006). El reto de la interculturalidad: Adaptaciones del centro y del currículo. *Revista Currículo*, (19), 17–57.

Merriam-Webster. (n.d.). Sociocultural. In *Merriam-Webster.com dictionary*. Retrieved January 2, 2021, from https://www.merriam-webster.com/dictionary/sociocultural

Mitchell, R. K., Busenitz, L. W., Bird, B., Marie Gaglio, C., Mcmullen, J. S., Morse, E. A., & Smith, J. B. (2007). The central question in entrepreneurial cognition research 2007. *Entrepreneurship Theory and Practice, 31*(1), 1–27. doi:10.1111/j.1540-6520.2007.00161.x

Mueller, S. L., & Thomas, A. S. (2000). Culture and entrepreneurial potential: A nine country study of locus of control and innovativeness. *Journal of Business Venturing*, *16*(1), 51–75. doi:10.1016/S0883-9026(99)00039-7

Mueller, S. L., & Thomas, A. S. (2001). Culture and entrepreneurial potential: A nine country study of locus of control and innovativeness. *Journal of Business Venturing*, *16*(1), 51–75. doi:10.1016/S0883-9026(99)00039-7

Ochoa-Zazueta, J. Á. (2006, March). Entrevista personal. *Los Mochis, Sinaloa*, (Mayo), 16.

Ostgaard, T. A., & Birley, S. (1994). Personal networks and firm competitive strategy: A strategic or coincidental match? *Journal of Business Venturing*, *9*(4), 281–305. doi:10.1016/0883-9026(94)90009-4

Peredo, A. M., & Mclean, M. (2006). Social entrepreneurship: A critical review of the concept. *Journal of World Business*, *41*(1), 56–65. doi:10.1016/j.jwb.2005.10.007

Pettigrew, T. F. (1971). *Racial separate or together?* McGraw-Hill.

Pinchot, G. III, & … . (1999). *Intrapreneuring in Action*. Berrett-Koehler Publisher.

Sandoval-Forero, E. A., Guerra-García, E., & Delgado-Buelna, R. A. (2008). Una visión sociointercultural del ausentismo intermitente de yoremes y mestizos en la UAIM. *Tiempo de Educar*, *9*(17), 9–34.

Schwartz, S. H. (1999). A Theory of Cultural Values and Some Implications for Work. *Applied Psychology*, *48*(1), 23–47. doi:10.1111/j.1464-0597.1999.tb00047.x

Shane, S., & Venkataraman, S. (2000). The promise of entrepreneurship as a field of research. *Academy of Management Review*, *25*(1), 217–226. doi:10.5465/amr.2000.2791611

Shapero, A. (1975). The Displaced, Uncomfortable Entrepreneur. *Psychology Today*, *9*(6), 83–88.

Slevin, D. P., & Covin, J. G. (1990). New venture strategic posture, structure, and performance: An industry life cycle analysis. *Journal of Business Venturing*, *5*(2), 123–135. doi:10.1016/0883-9026(90)90004-D

Stuart, R., & Abetti, P. A. (1987). Start-up ventures: Towards the prediction of initial success. *Journal of Business Venturing*, *2*(3), 215–230. doi:10.1016/0883-9026(87)90010-3

Sullivan, G., Weerawardena, J., & Carnegie, K. (2003). Social entrepreneurship: Towards conceptualization. *International Journal of Nonprofit and Voluntary Sector Marketing*, *8*(1), 76–88. doi:10.1002/nvsm.202

Thompson, J. L. (2002). The world of the social entrepreneur. *International Journal of Public Sector Management*, *15*(5), 412–431. doi:10.1108/09513550210435746

Touraine, A. (2000). *Igualdad y diversidad: las nuevas tareas de la democracia*. Fondo de Cultura Económica.

Tracey, P., Phillips, N., & Jarvis, O. (2011). Bridging institutiona lentrepreneurship and the creation of new organizational forms: A multilevel model. *Organization Science*, *22*(1), 60–80. doi:10.1287/orsc.1090.0522

Urbano, D., Toledano, N., & Soriano, D. R. (2010). Analyzing social entrepreneurship from an institutional perspective: Evidence from Spain. *Journal of Social Entrepreneurship, 1*(1), 54–69. doi:10.1080/19420670903442061

Vargas-Hernández, J. G. (2005). Emergencia de la nueva cultura institucional: Impacto en la transformación del escenario de la globalización económica. *Economía, Sociedad y Territorio, 5*(17), 27–61. doi:10.22136/est002005316

Vargas-Hernández, J. G., Guerra García, E., & Zepeda, V. (2017). *La nueva gobernanza instrumental del estado de bienestar: transformaciones y retos*. Editorial Universitaria: Universidad de Guadalajara, Centro Universitario de Ciencias Económico Administrativas, Guadalajara, Jalisco.

Vásquez, O., Fernández, M., & Álvarez, P. (2014). La aportación de los grados al desarrollo de la sensibilidad y competencia intercultural. Perspectiva comparada entre Trabajo Social y Psicología *Revista. Cuadernos de Trabajo Social, 27*(2), 307–317.

Venkatraman, N. (1989). The concept of fit in strategy research: Toward verbal and statistical correspondence. *Academy of Management Review, 14*(3), 423–444. doi:10.2307/258177

Ward, C. (1996). Acculturation. In D. Landis & R. Bhagat (Eds.), *Handbook of intercultural training* (pp. 124–147). Sage.

Westall, A., & Chalkley, D. (2007). *Social enterprise futures*. Retrieved from: http://www.smith-institute.org.uk/pdfs/social_enterprise.pdf

Witter, M. (2011). *Financing sustainable development in small island developing states*. Tools for Mainstreaming Sustainable Development in Small States.

Zadek, S., & Thake, S. (1997). *Practical people, noble causes. How to support community-based social entrepreneurs*. New Economics Foundation.

Zait, D. (2002). *Management intercultural. Valorizarea diferenţelor culturale*. Editura Economică, Bucureti.

Chapter 16
Leader Effects on Engagement

Wendi Walker-Schmidt
Baylor University, USA

ABSTRACT

Employee engagement is defined as an employee's emotional connectedness with an organization. One of the key levers that affects employee engagement is leadership support. Leaders who effectively manage are vital to all organizations as they play a key role in helping to establish relational networks which lead to higher levels of engagement for their employees. This chapter discusses how leaders can impact engagement. Furthermore, it outlines how leaders can grow and develop in their leadership practice. Leaders who focus on creating a culture of learning and engagement experience higher levels of performance.

WHAT IS EMPLOYEE ENGAGEMENT?

Human beings have a desire to achieve and form lasting relationships with others. Through establishing connections, humans create an environment that engages others and facilitates success. In the workplace, leaders play a key role in helping to establish relational networks which lead to higher levels of engagement for their employees. Engagement can be defined in many ways. Eldor and Vigoda-Gadot (2017) define engagement as creating a link between emotions, the people within the organization, and the work (Eldor & Vigoda-Gadot, 2017). Kruse (2012) defines engagement as an emotional tie an employee has to the organization. To expand upon this definition, engagement is an emotional connectedness with an organization that allows the employee to bring their whole self to work each day (Cooper-Thomas et al., 2018). Each of these definitions has a key element of similarity, the emotional connection of the employee. Leaders can have a direct effect on the emotional connectedness an employee feels. Additionally, leaders who understand this influence are more likely to have employees who are highly engaged (Smith et al., 2016).

Employee engagement occurs at the individual and organizational level. Organizations must understand that increasing engagement will help employees work at their maximum level (Byham & Wellins, 2015). By encouraging employees to bring their whole selves to work, employers are ensuring engagement begins from day one. Personal growth, leadership support, and communication are vital to engagement. The evidence proves that employees with higher levels of engagement are more productive. Organiza-

DOI: 10.4018/978-1-7998-8239-8.ch016

tions that ensure employees are emotionally engaged in their work will increase the probability of their length of service intention (Ormrod, 2020).

Employee engagement is the cornerstone of the relationship between the organization and the employee. Many professionals in the corporate space use the terms engagement and satisfaction interchangeably, but they are not the same concept. Employee satisfaction is how content an employee is with the organization. Satisfaction is a part of the engagement, but engagement encompasses much more. Engagement is how content an employee is with their position but also includes the level of commitment and discretionary effort employees place into their role. Discretionary effort is the level of effort that employees put forth going above and beyond their normal workload. This level of effort stems from an intrinsic motivation that is internal to the employee of what they find enjoyable (Ormrod, 2020). Highly engaged employees regularly put forth higher levels of discretionary effort. However, most US employees are not within this space. Gallup cites that only 33% of US workers are highly engaged (Gallup, 2007). Employee engagement allows the employee to bring their whole selves to work in a trusting, supportive environment (Cooper-Thomas et al., 2018). When employees feel engaged in their workspace the individual employee and organization will experience success (Smith et al., 2016).

Leaders can affect employee engagement positively or negatively. As a result, leaders need to keep engagement top of mind. If leaders do not focus on engagement, the employee may disengage and leave. This can be costly to the leader, their team, and the organization. Employee turnover can be detrimental. Research confirms that twenty percent of new hires leave their role within the first 45 days on the job (Leung, 2018). Estimates cite replacing one employee can cost 90-200% of the employee's annual salary based on their role (Allen, 2008; Cascio, 2006). Heathfield (2019) asserts that exit interview data explains employees leave because of poor onboarding, lack of recognition, relationships with leaders, relationships with coworkers, and lack of contribution and meaningful work. Leaders can impact all these elements, leading to positive or negative levels of engagement. This chapter will first discuss how leaders can affect engagement levers of onboarding, ensuring employees are developing, making contributions, and engaging in meaningful work, recognition, and finally maintaining relationships with their leaders and co-workers. Secondly, the chapter will focus on how leaders must be taught the skills of creating engaging environments to incorporate into their leadership practice.

HOW LEADERS CAN AFFECT ENGAGEMENT LEVERS

Leaders' Engagement Effects on Onboarding

The definition of onboarding varies throughout the literature. However, most definitions include the element of integrating with the organization. Effective onboarding extends benefits to the new employee and organization by ensuring an emotional connection is established, thereby beginning the path to higher employee engagement. Onboarding programs are designed to acclimate the new employee to the culture and expectations of the organization. Onboarding is the program or process that assimilates new employees into the organization by creating a psychological contract between the organization and new employees based on the unique needs of the new employee (Caldwell & Peters, 2018). The most effective onboarding programs focus on "personal identity socialization" (Cable et al., 2013, p. 24). This concept emphasizes uncovering the new employee's strengths and interests to channel into their work for ultimate success (Cable et al., 2013). Research shows that onboarding is a vital part of establishing a connection between the new employee and the organization. Starting a new job can produce high levels of anxiety. When roles are not clearly defined, and the employee is uncertain about their duties it can hinder the employee's ability to connect with the organization (Collins, 2019). Therefore, creating an onboarding experience that connects to an employee's emotions is critical. A study from an i4CP 2018 report that states "when new hires experience effective employee onboarding, it will establish a sense of engagement connectedness with the organization and help new hires become productive at a much faster rate" (2018). Onboarding is fundamental to beginning the engagement and retention of a new employee (Krasman, 2015). Research shows that a comprehensive onboarding program leads to increased engagement, productivity, and overall retention (Snell, 2006). The first 45–60 days of employment are critical. Studies show that employees that do not receive thorough onboarding leave within this timeframe (Llarena, 2013).

Effective onboarding can begin a positive association between an organization and employee by setting expectations for success. At every employee's core is a desire to succeed. Organizations can help or hinder this desire during the onboarding phase of their development. Bauer (2010) describes the goals of an onboarding process to help new employees establish relationships, improve performance, and reduce turnover. Through the onboarding process, leaders can provide the employee information about their role to help align the new employee with business strategies and explain how their role will impact the organization. Within onboarding Bauer (2010, 2015) defines 4 core elements: compliance, clarification, culture, and connection. Compliance is the action of teaching policies and procedures. Clarification is setting job-related expectations. Culture provides employees with the cultural norms of the organization. Connection is creating a network of relationships within the organization (pg. 2). Building connections and relationships within an organization create a bond for employees that can increase job performance and satisfaction (Bauer & Erdogan, 2011). Thus, a psychological contract between an organization and a new employee begins to develop. When an employer establishes trust and treats employees as valued partners, employees will demonstrate higher levels of performance (Caldwell & Peters, 2018). Therefore, onboarding creates a successful partnership for both new employees and the organization. Leaders are a critical part of helping the new employee integrate with the team and organization.

A primary kcy to success for the new employee is providing the right tools and resources. Leaders support compliance by providing role clarity and the right tools for the job for the new employee to remain within policy and procedure guidelines. Additionally, leaders can provide human resources to provide support to the new employee and begin indoctrinating them into the culture. Tools are the technical pieces for job accuracy and resources include personalized support such as providing a mentor. Before the employee enters the organization on day one, leaders must begin preparation on what they need to be successful. One such tool for success is a written onboarding plan created by a cross-functional team. This team should include the leader, fellow employees, and stakeholders. The onboarding plan should encompass all the tools (hardware, software, training-technical and soft skills) that the new employee will need in their role (Bauer, 2020). Stakeholders, people with an interest or concern in the new employee's future, are a vital part of the new employees' transition into the organization. They should not only be a part of the meetings to design the onboarding plan but be a part of the ongoing development for the new employee. The new employee should meet with all stakeholders in their first two weeks (Graybill et al., 2013). Stakeholders will serve a dual purpose as influencers of the onboarding plan and as an ongoing resource for the new employee throughout their tenure.

Clarification are the details of an employee's role and how it connects to the larger picture (Bauer, 2015). In direct opposition to role clarity, is role ambiguity. Employees who experience ambiguity within their environment lose touch with the impact they can have on business strategies. They question how their role makes an impact and ambiguity begins to impact their performance. Employees that have role clarity experience the opposite effect. They have a greater understanding of their role and how it connects to the bigger picture (Hallak, 2016). Furthermore, Bauer states (pg. 5) that "measures of role clarity are among the most consistent predictors of job satisfaction and organizational commitment during the onboarding process" (Bauer, 2020). Within role clarity, Leaders guide employees to gain perspective on what tools and resources are available to them to help them be successful.

While tools are items that will help a new employee execute tasks, resources are a human element that provides mentoring, support, and creates cultural and network connections. Leaders can provide ongoing support through coaching and creating networks for the new employee. They can serve as role models and help the new hire maneuver through the corporate path. Mentors also serve in a capacity to provide coaching and support more at the job-task level to scaffold the new employee's knowledge (Merriam & Bierema, 2014). Mentors are generally a job grade above the new employee such as a team lead. The mentor-mentee relationship creates a sense of psychological safety for the new employee to ask questions they might be hesitant to address with their leader (Bauer, 2020). New employees with strong mentors have a stronger relationship to promotion and career satisfaction. Many new employees have multiple mentors throughout an organization. These mentors may or may not be in their direct business unit. Having multiple mentors increases the social networks the new employee builds and enhances their cultural connection to the organization. A community of mentors catapults the new employee into expanded opportunities throughout the organization (Dong et al., 2014). Mentorship focuses on social constructivism that enables people to work together to form new knowledge (Ormrod, 2020). New employees who have the benefit of a mentor are more likely to integrate into the corporate culture more quickly than those without this support (Bauer, 2020). Cultural integration is a key part of becoming an employee who transitions from new employee to high-performing team member. In a survey conducted by Bamboo HR (pg. 7), new employees who received culture integration training were twelve times more likely to feel emotionally committed to their organization (Fica, 2018). Entering a new organization is not always easy. External change has occurred, a new job begins. Transition is the internal emotional mechanism to adjust to change. New employees who have a difficult time transitioning are not successful. There is a strong relationship between internalizing the corporate culture and the new employee's long-term success (Saks et al., 2007). Leaders who guide new employees through cultural integration help them to transition more easily and successfully to an organizational insider.

Many resources discuss best practices; however, no organization has landed on the exact solution of how to help new employees transition successfully to being an organizational insider. However, the common elements in the literature center around creating an emotional bond with the organization, aligning the new employee with business strategies, and explaining how their role will impact the organization, understanding performance expectations, providing tools and resources that will impact success, and cultural integration. Leaders are an integral part of each of these elements. Bauer and Erdogan (2011) describe the process of employees creating an emotional bond with an organization as organizational socialization. Organizational socialization is defined as the process of moving from being an outsider to being an insider (Bauer & Erdogan, 2011). In this transition, establishing relationships is key. Leaders help their new employees facilitate relationships in the workplace by helping the employee balance their new day-to-day work and having a support system they can call upon. By helping the employee understand their role and how they impact the organization, emotional connectedness increases. Leaders who help facilitate an effective onboarding experience will have more highly engaged employees. As the employee begins to settle into their role, leaders engaging in ongoing development with their employees is vital to continue engagement.

Leaders' Engagement Effects on Developing, Making Contributions, and Engaging in Meaningful Work

After onboarding, development is key to keeping employees engaged and retaining them. Personal development is a key lever to engagement. Leaders who focus their time and energy on an employee's development will impact engagement. By focusing time with their employees, leaders show support of the employee in their professional development. Leaders align their employee's activities with the organization's mission. Daily communication with employees can help ensure they understand their individual goals and objectives, as well as how they connect and support the organizational objectives. Additionally, leaders must focus on communicating with authenticity, being clear, and transparent in relaying their message (Northouse, 2019). When employees feel informed and supported they are far more likely to put forth a discretionary effort and work collaboratively as a team (Cooper-Thomas et al., 2018). Leaders who focus on development, support, and communication create a bond with their employees. When employees experience this bond, they become better performers and put forth a higher level of discretionary effort (Gallup, 2007).

Training and development are essential components in engagement for employees to feel as though they are making contributions. Organizations that invest in their employees through providing development opportunities are providing elements for success (Studer, 2003). In the development step, leaders begin to encourage professional development and outlining a career path for their employees. One of the most impactful levers that influence engagement is an employee's personal growth. Leaders have a critical role in helping guide personal growth and development. Fullan (2011) states "the organization becomes effective because leaders are investing in employees, and this investment increases employees' individual and collective commitment to their work" (p. 50). Leaders impact employee engagement by focusing on how the team member wants to develop (Northouse, 2019). Employees who do not engage in personal growth opportunities at work are destined to leave. Each year on employee engagement surveys training and development is one of the top items on the employee wish list. In a study of three million employees, the second most significant driver for employee engagement was a need for personal growth opportunities (Nelson, 2018). Organizations that ensure employees are emotionally engaged in their work and are continuing to develop will increase the probability of their length of service intention (Ormrod, 2020).

An important step in development is first discovering where an employee's skills are currently, where they want to go in their career, and the gaps they may have. The creation of an individual development plan can serve as a guide for the employee's development. A key consideration for leaders is ensuring that the development plan continues to connect back to the broader organizational purpose. In doing so, they will help their employee in being successful throughout their time with the organization (Studer, 2003). As a leader, committing yourself to the development of your team should be one of the top priorities. Creating the development plan should not be a set-it and forget-it action, rather one that requires constant support, positive feedback when they have achieved a goal, and developmental feedback to help them learn from mistakes (Altman et al., 2011). A development plan will help employees achieve their ultimate goals and objectives. A leader's job is to empower employees to develop their fullest capacity (Maxwell, 2007). Within the individual development plan, there can be formal and informal opportunities. Most employees only consider formal training as development, such as attending a conference or training class. While these methods are important keys to development, they are not the only pathways. Leaders can help employees discover that development opportunities can be formal or informal.

Formal programs consist of classroom training and development courses, e-learning courses, workshops, conferences, and webinars as examples. Training and development must be offered to all employees to help broaden their organizational and individual competency. Aligned with performance, training and development can help the employee reach their goals and become a high-performing team member, impacting the company's outcomes. Leaders who help their employees blend formal and informal training can be powerful levers of development.

Informal programs are more impromptu in nature such as mentoring or delegation. As previously mentioned, new employees need to have mentors in the onboarding process to help them build their network and initially gain skills more quickly through support. However, mentors can continue to help employees build capacity throughout their careers. Leaders can help their employees find mentors to help them achieve the goals of their development plan. These mentors can be micromentors who stay engaged for a short period while the employee is on a special project or can serve on a long-term function for ongoing career development (Byham & Wellins, 2015). In addition to mentors, leaders can use delegation to help their employees develop in an informal capacity.

Leaders must understand how to achieve objectives through others (Altman et al., 2011). Delegation is another informal development tool a leader can institute. As a leader and their employee build the development plan, areas of interest will surface from the employee. Leaders should capitalize on this opportunity to find tasks to delegate to the employee. The leader must stay vigilant, seeking opportunities to delegate to the employees to help them build new skills and capacity (Byham & Wellins, 2015). Not only will the help employees build their skill set, but it also increases their self-esteem through making valuable contributions to the team and organization (Byham & Wellins, 2015; Studer, 2003). A blend of formal and informal may also be instituted by a leader such as placing a team member on a specific project to increase their learning and skills, aided by their mentor (Cooper-Thomas et al., 2018). Formal and informal training is linked to overall employee engagement and can affect long-term retention.

Employees and leaders should engage in a synergetic relationship between growth and development. Employees should be able to verbalize where they want their career to go, and leaders should be their guide on the side. While leaders are not solely responsible for an employee's development, they will help in driving the process. In conjunction with developing, ensuring employees are engaging in meaningful work is a driver of engagement.

Employees have a high need to feel as though they are contributing to the organization. A leader must align employees with what they do matters. By giving the employee meaningful work it gives them a sense of purpose (Byham & Wellins, 2015). When employees see how their work impacts the organizational goals, they become energized. This energy leads to higher forms of retention (Kaye & Jordan-Evans, 2014). It is the leader's role to help the employee see how their work is making a difference. Employees grow and develop, often beyond the competencies that align with their current role. A leader who provides employees the opportunity for stretch assignments can enhance their alignment with meaningful work (Adkerson, 2000). Opportunities to contribute meaningful work and see their direct contributions are an important part of keeping top talent within your organization (Corporate Leadership Council, 2004). Leaders have the responsibility to create a space of meaningful work that will let employees engage in what they are passionate about (Kaye & Jordan-Evans, 2014). Leaders that focus on what employees are contributing will help drive retention. In today's marketplace, employees want to have meaningful experiences and work in a positive environment.

Leaders' Engagement Effects on Recognizing Employees

Recognition is a key lever that influences employee engagement. Leaders play an important role in taking the time to recognize their employees. Leaders who recognize excellent performance create a positive culture on their team. Recognition is very personal to each employee and encourages behavior to be repeated. Recognition is public recognition of a job well done by an employee. Leaders can recognize using e-cards, verbal recognition in meetings, or a points-based system within a recognition platform (Cooper-Thomas et al., 2018). Recognition is a large part of many organization's budgets. A Gallup poll cites 72% of U.S. businesses provided $22.9 billion in non-cash rewards in 2015 (Gallup, 2007). Corporate events can also increase engagement. These events can help build community within an organization. Such events may be a fall festival, a celebration of achieving a corporate target goal or celebrating a company anniversary. Finally, employees maintaining relationships with their leaders and co-workers can be powerful levers to drive engagement.

Leaders' Engagement Effects on Relationships

A positive work environment is one of respect, collaboration, and trust (Byham & Wellins, 2015). Employees perform higher when there is mutual respect between them, their leader, and organization. Engaging employees in conversations about how they work best and ensuring that leaders adhere to these suggestions can influence an employee's stay decision (Byham & Wellins, 2015). How an employee integrates with their team can also influence a decision to stay. Collaboration or lack of within team dynamics can engage or disengage an employee. Being connected with a team in a collaborative environment can impact morale, pride, and team identity (Corporate Leadership Council, 2004). Positive collaboration teams can increase positive interactions and decrease negative exchanges (Ma et al., 2018). Trust is a vital part of a positive working environment. Whether it is the leader or organization, keeping one's word goes a long way with employees. Employees want to know the good, bad, and ugly about the organization (Kaye & Jordan-Evans, 2014). After all, they too have an emotional investment that centers on trust. Even when the news is bad, leaders being transparent with an employee will help them better manage the change and transition that may ensue. When leaders and organizations build trust, employees are more likely to stay. Trust creates an emotional bond that establishes an individual connectedness.

Conclusion

Leaders who focus on onboarding, development, employee contributions, meaningful work, recognition, and relationships establish higher levels of engagement for their employees. When employees feel valued, they will have higher levels of engagement. Leaders who create the right environment, connect their employees to purpose and making a difference in the organization. The research demonstrates that effective onboarding is associated with long-term engagement. Leaders play a key role in ensuring new employees have all the tools and resources they need to be successful in the onboarding process. Ongoing training and development serve as critical pieces for employee engagement. Leaders who commit to assisting employees with discovering formal and informal areas of development have overall higher performing teams. Recognition by leaders create a positive culture and lead to an environment of high performance. Employees who are regularly recognized by their leader for a job well done are more likely to stay with the organization long-term. Finally, leaders must concentrate on the factors that are most important for building a relationship with the employee. These factors are very personal and different for each employee. Only through constant conversations and active listening can a leader know these individual elements. When employees feel valued by their leader, they will have higher levels of engagement (Cattermole, 2019).

TEACHING LEADERS ABOUT CREATING ENGAGEMENT

Rome wasn't Built in a Day, Neither are Great Leaders

The question is often posed are great leaders born or bred? To answer abruptly, yes. John Maxwell (1998) states there are people who are born with more natural leadership skills than others, but leadership skills can be learned over time. Leaders must be in a constant state of learning. Organizational environments continue to evolve; therefore, leaders must continue to learn and sharpen their skills (King, et al, 2011). Leaders are faced with a plethora of choices, decisions, and change each day. In an ever-growing global environment, diversity, generational differences, technology, team member's personal and practical needs, the list could go on. Leaders must remain nimble and maintain an agility to pivot at a moment's notice to respond to change. How does a leader do it? How do they keep up? The foundational skill leaders must focus on is emotional self-awareness.

It Starts with Emotional Self-Awareness

The concept of employee engagement and knowing how to engage employees does not always occur intuitively for leaders. If leaders do not have a base level of emotional awareness, they will be out of touch with their employees and not be able to engage. Korn Ferry Hay Group research found that among leaders with multiple strengths in emotional self-awareness, 92% had teams with high energy and high performance. Great leaders create a positive emotional climate that encourages motivation and extra effort, and they are the ones with good emotional self-awareness. In sharp contrast, leaders low in emotional self-awareness created negative climates 78% of the time. Emotional awareness is defined as knowing when feelings are present in ourselves and others. It is closely related to emotional literacy, which means being able to label feelings with specific feeling words. At its highest level it means being able to predict feelings in advance. Emotional awareness is the ability to be aware of and make sense of your emotions and how it can impact others, positively and negatively. The best leaders are mindful of how their actions influence the performance of others. Northouse (2019) states "people who are more sensitive to their emotions and the impact of their emotions on others will be leaders who are more effective (p.29).

As a Leader, How Do I Learn about Emotional Awareness?

Leaders must learn and grow each day to improve their leadership practice. Part of this growth centers around learning to be emotionally aware. To begin this journey most leaders need to engage in an assessment to measure their level of emotional self-awareness. There are many assessments in the market that can provide a baseline of the emotional self-awareness competency. Once you have established a baseline, work can begin on improving the skill. This work will not be a one and done opportunity, rather an ongoing daily self-reflection of what went well and what could have been improved upon. Bradberry & Greaves (2009) state "people in high self-awareness are remarkably clear in their understanding of what they do well, what motivates and satisfies them, and which people and situations push their buttons (p. 25). The literature is replete with many sources to help leaders increase their emotional self-awareness. One commonality each of the literature pieces holds is creating an action plan from the baseline data and remeasuring at certain intervals, such as an annual reassessment to see movement. It is also helpful to share the data with someone who can serve as a trusted advisor. Often others can provide developmental feedback on our growth we may or may not see. Research demonstrates that a leader's level of emotional self-awareness has a direct impact on employee engagement. If an employee does not have a good relationship with their leader because of their leader's inability to control emotions, the employee's engagement and job performance will be affected (Eisenberger, et al., 2002). While it all begins with emotional self-awareness, there are other areas we must expand to affect engagement as leaders.

If You're Not Growing, You're Going

Vince Lombardi, an American professional football coach was quoted as saying "Leaders aren't born, they are made; and they are made just like anything else though hard work." Leaders must adopt a constant state of learning to be effective. Maxwell (1998) states "Successful leaders are learners. And the learning process is ongoing, a result of self-discipline and perseverance. The goal each day must be to get a little better, to build on the previous day's progress" (p. 24). Successful leaders keep learning journals and engage in self-reflection. Leaders need to have the ability to understand themselves. The best way to do this is to keep notes on situations and reactions to those situations. Record reactions that are positive and record reactions that are negative. As leaders, do not be afraid to label the emotions. It is only through pure reflection that we allow ourselves to grow. Leaders must engage in constant growth to become and remain great. Employees are astute observers of their leaders. If they see their leaders engaged and seeking growth opportunities, they will as well. Identify items that are challenging and decide if that is an area in which you would like to grow. Additionally, identify areas of strength and decide if that is an area in which you would like to grow. Learning is a personalized journey that must excite the learner about the subject matter. Decide what is your passion and create your learning journey in that direction. Leaders can influence employee engagement by showing their team members that they embrace challenges and continue to learn.

Trust is Everything

As previously mentioned, part of employee engagement is allowing the employee to bring their whole selves to work in a trusting, supportive environment (Cooper-Thomas et al., 2018). For employees, a positive work environment is based on respect, collaboration, and trust (Byham & Wellins, 2015). When leaders and organizations build trust, employees are more likely to be engaged. Trust creates an emotional bond that establishes an individual connectedness. So how do leaders build trust with their employees?

Leaders must create connections with their employees and demonstrate solid character. Employees must know that they can count on their leader, this is the foundation of trust (Maxwell, 1998). Leaders who communicate openly and honestly with their employees build connection and trust. Communication creates alignment for an employee and their leader. Employees want to know what is happening with their organization and expect their leaders to be transparent (Iliev & Stoyanova, 2017). When leaders are transparent, they exhibit the traits of making good decisions based on data, admitting their mistakes, keeping their promises, giving credit where it belongs, treating employees with respect, and putting others needs before their own (Byham & Wellins, 2015; Maxwell, 1998). Leaders also must be authentic in their interactions with their employees to create connections and demonstrate character.

Leaders who exhibit authentic leadership characteristics increase employee engagement (Northouse, 2019). Authenticity at its core means ensuring your actions and words match. Byham & Wellins (2015) cite "authenticity is fueled by integrity, which in turn fosters trust" (p. 33). The authentic leader is one who creates an environment of trust and confidence among their employees. To focus on becoming an authentic leader, one must concentrate on their emotional self-awareness and self-regulation. As previously mentioned, it all begins with emotional self-awareness. Obtaining and maintaining this skill is not an overnight matter, it is one that must be continually honed. Self-regulation is using the internal compass to guide decisions. When leaders have a strong sense of emotional self-awareness, they use self-regulation to make decisions and drive their behavior instead of letting outside forces influence the outcome (Northouse, 2019). Leaders can build this skill by ensuring in all interactions they communicate honestly and maintain authenticity in their relationships with their employees. By showing the leader's authentic self, engagement anchors with their employees. Leaders must learn to listen and communicate with empathy to truly connect with their employees

Can You Hear Me?

Listening to and responding to your employees enhance relationships and help to increase engagement. When leaders actively listen to their employees, it shows that they care about them and helps to remain open-minded about situations. Listening shows a level of respect for your employees. Leaders who engage in listening and communication thrive in their roles.

Effective leaders focus on listening, understanding, and communicating with their employees (King, et al, 2011). Communication consists of sending and receiving messages (Northouse, 2019. Successful leaders ask more than they tell, they lead with a question seeking to understand, rather than leading with an opinion. This is generally an uncomfortable skill for leaders to master. Asking questions and not telling the employee what to do takes courage and confidence as a leader. Additionally, as a leader how we understand the employee and communicate back to them is a vital competency. One of the critical element's leaders need to integrate into conversations is responding with empathy (Byham & Wellins, 2015). Empathy is defined as "attempting to see the world from another person's point of view" (Northouse, 2019, p.229). Using empathy in communication validates what an employee is saying but does not necessarily indicate you agree with the statement. Leaders must reflect on and summarize the statements they have heard, keeping the focus on the employee. Once employees know you have heard them and understand, they can focus on the issue rather than feelings (Byham & Wellins, 2015). Ensure communication is framed as listening and using empathy to align with employees to keep engagement high. Becoming effective at listening, understanding, and communicating are foundational skills in influencing employees.

Leading through Influence and Change

Leading through influencing employees is an essential skill of leaders. Influence is having an impact on behaviors and actions of your employees. To effectively influence, leaders need to focus more on leading through instinct rather than policy. Leading through influence must come from the heart. Influence takes a balance of all the skills of emotional self-awareness, trust, listening and communicating. Leaders engage employee's hearts and minds when using their influence skill. John Maxwell (1998) states "Leadership is influence, nothing more, nothing less." To master the art of influence, leaders must be forward-thinking, build connections and trust, and remain mindful of their emotional self-awareness. When leaders focus on these elements, they not only transform themselves, but they also transform their employees through engagement.

Leaders must be adept in guiding their employees through change, but first they must understand change. Organizational change is a two-part process consisting of change and transition management. Change management takes organizations through the change process using a systematic approach to implement change. Change is situational, external to us, and occurs quickly. Something old stops and something new begins such as a process, procedure, new technology, leadership change, or shift in culture due to a merger or acquisition (Armenakis, 1999; Bridges, 1980; Karambelkar & Bhattacharya, 2017). A subset of the change process is transition management which helps individuals evolve through change. Leaders need to especially be proficient in reading their employees and helping them through transition. Transition is more personal and internal. It is the personal adjustment that happens inside us as we try to adapt to change. Transition is psychological and processed based and occurs more slowly (Bridges, 1980; Miller, 2017). It is the transition, not the change that people often resist. When in change people often fear a loss of identity in their current world, confusion about what is to come, and a risk of failing in the new world (Bridges, 1980).

Once a leader determines an employee is experiencing change, they need to diagnose where the employee is at in Bridge's Transition curve. Bridges' model begins with endings. The organizational population begins to suspect the change and anxiety sets in. Word will leak out to the organization, despite the best-laid plans of organizations to keep plans quiet until official communication launches. Productivity starts to decline as more uncertainty surfaces about how the change will affect the employee and their work. The organization informs the employee base of the change. Messaging at this stage must be clear and concise. As previously mentioned, the organization already suspects something is happening, the official communication will confirm this. The organization will communicate the change vision. In Bridges' model, the employee enters the neutral zone where they begin to feel fear, frustration, and potentially anger over the external change. This is a critical point in the model as employees will pass or fail in this area. Leaders must intervene to help their employees through the neutral zone. As previously stated, it is often the transition, not that change employees' resist. If the employee cannot synchronize with the external change they will fail and most likely be left behind. Those who accept the change, begin to feel a sense of loss and resolution to begin seeing the change as constructive. Employees experience new beginnings in the Bridges' model and feel cautious optimism. Employees encounter role clarity, and their production increases. Finally, employees feel acceptance and their productivity is higher than when the change was first suspected. Leaders are critical to helping their employees through change by coaching and influencing them during the transition (Bridges, 1980; Miller, 2017). Communication is a key lever to successful change and transition. From the organizational perspective it is important to keep communications simple yet create a compelling story for employees to embrace (Kotter, 2012). Commu-

Figure 1. Bridges transition model
Adapted from Transitions: Making sense of life's changes, by W. Bridges, 1980.

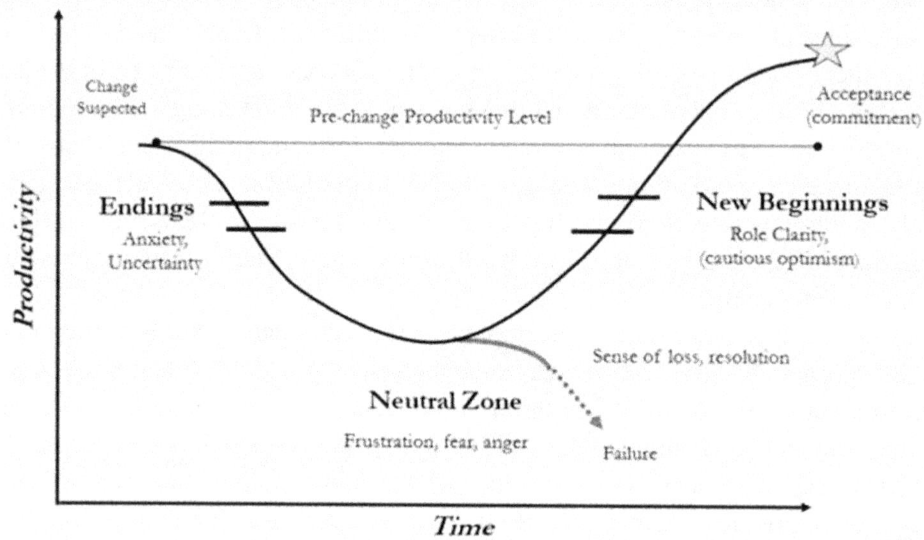

nication creates alignment between employees and the organization. Employees crave information about their organization and expect transparency (Iliev & Stoyanova, 2017). One element of communication is feedback. Leaders who provide feedback have a more committed employee base (Byham & Wellins, 2015). However, feedback is a two-way street. Employees also expect to be able to provide feedback on how the change is affecting them. Leaders that accept feedback throughout the change process will be better suited to shift during the change deployment (Meyer, 2018).

Everyday leadership has elements of influence and change woven through the fabric of each interaction leaders have with their team members. Leadership is a skill that develops over time, and leaders must be open to lifelong learning. Leaders not only will have continuous learning about themselves but will learn through each interaction with their team members. Organizational change is driven by strong leaders. Leaders serve as change agents who can help an initiative prosper or fail based on how they coach and influence their teams. To ensure that change permeates throughout an organization, leaders must be proficient in relationship building, communication, and feedback. These three elements are vital to integrating everyday leadership and organizational change. Each element, influence and organizational change, can survive on its own, but when combined they produce a synergy that thrives. By fusing influence and change, leaders ensure high levels of engagement and create a plethora of change agents throughout their organization.

CONCLUSION

Leadership is an ever-evolving state. Great leaders realize that their leadership practice is one of progress, not perfection. Leaders must constantly give themselves challenges and maintain a growth mindset. Being a leader by no means indicates you have all of the answers. Sometimes the answer of I don't know can be one of the most humbling phrases we can utter. As long as it is followed with, but I can find out, leaders are open to grow and learn. Leaders must be willing to take a deep reflective look at themselves and understand where their strengths and opportunities lie. It can also be very helpful to gain an outside perspective of you as a leader. Human beings only act in ways that are consistent with their world view and their perspective derived from experiences. Having another person look at us through their lens gives us additional perspective. Leadership coaches are great resources for this very activity. Moreover, we can begin to see the level of emotional self-awareness through reflection and other perspectives.

Emotional self-awareness is a key skill for leaders. It serves as the foundation for total emotional intelligence. To be aware of how our actions and reactions impact others is vital to influence the way we lead. Leaders who continually work on this skill have higher levels of success with their teams and within the organization itself. The ability to be able to recognize, name, and understand the emotions we are feeling brings equanimity to our leadership practice. As previously mentioned, it takes work to maintain emotional self-awareness, which is part of lifelong learning for a leader.

Learning stimulates the brain. Leaders face different obstacles each day they must have a high level of meta-cognition to solve. Engaging in lifelong learning helps leaders to better be able to process information and arrive at creative solutions. Research best practice cites leaders should engage in 4-8 hours of learning a week. If this is not in your normal cadence currently, start slow with 4-8 hours a month and begin to increase. Manage your time, don't let your time manage you. Schedule time to learn and make it a priority. Employees will model this behavior; this helps to form high functioning teams. Furthermore, it will demonstrate your humanness as a leader and create emotional connection with your employees.

Leaders should be authentic to create emotional connectedness with their employees. This level of connection engages employees and inspires them to do their best work. Authentic leaders lead with their heart, focusing on people over profits. Additionally, authentic leaders have high levels of emotional self-awareness. These leaders reflect on their emotional and actions and how they affect others. Leaders that engage the authentic style use empathy as a key indicator to create emotional connectedness with their employees. They do this by engaging in listening and responding to their employees' words and actions.

Listening and responding to employees is a powerful skill to engage employees. Leaders earn trust by listening and responding to employees in an empathetic and proactive way. Furthermore, leaders lead influence and change. Through listening and responding, leaders help to impact behavior. Effective leaders use influence to impact employee's attitudes, values, and beliefs. Likewise, leaders must be familiar with change and how people transition to change. When leader's help employees to go in the right direction, motivate them, and gives them developmental feedback individuals, teams and the organization's performance thrive.

REFERENCES

Adkerson, M. (2000). *The company you keep: Four key tools for employee retention*. Academic Press.

Altman, D., Lee, R., & King, S. (2011). *Discovering the leader in you*. Jossey-Bass.

Armenakis, A. A., & Bedeian, A. G. (1999). Organizational change: A review of theory and research in the 1990s. *Organizational Change*, *25*(3), 293–315. doi:10.1177/014920639902500303

Arthur, D. (1998). *Recruiting, Interviewing, Selecting & Orienting New Employees* (3rd ed.). Amacom.

Bauer, T. (2015). *Onboarding: Maximizing role clarity and confidence.* Success Factors.

Bauer, T. (2020). *Onboarding new employees.* https://www.shrm.org/foundation/ourwork/initiatives/resources-from-past-initiatives/Documents/Onboarding%20New%20Employees.pdf

Bauer, T., & Erdogan, B. (2011). Organizational socialization: The effective onboarding of new employees. In S. Zedeck (Ed.), APA handbook of industrial and organizational psychology, Vol 3: Maintaining, expanding, and contracting the organization (pp. 51–64). American Psychological Association. doi:10.1037/12171-002

Bearden, C., Mahan, T., & Nelms, D. (2019). *Work institute 2019 retention report.* https://info.workinstitute.com/hubfs/2019%20Retention%20Report/Work%20Institute%202019%20Retention%20Report%20final-1.pdf

Bradberry, T., & Greaves, J. (2009). *Emotional intelligence 2.0.* Talentsmart.

Bridges, W. (1980). *Transitions: Making sense of life's changes.* Addison-Wesley.

Byham, T., & Wellins, R. (2015). *Your first leadership job: How catalyst leaders bring out the best in others.* John Wiley & Sons. doi:10.1002/9781119153849

Cable, D., Gino, F., & Staats, B. (2013). *Reinventing employee onboarding.* https://sloanreview.mit.edu/article/reinventing-employee-onboarding/

Caldwell, C., & Peters, R. (2018). New employee onboarding – psychological contracts and ethical perspectives. *Journal of Management Development, 37*(1), 27–39. doi:10.1108/JMD-10-2016-0202

Cardy, R., & Lengnick-Hall, M. (2011). Will they stay or will they go? Exploring a customer-oriented approach to employee retention. *Journal of Business and Psychology, 26*(2), 213–217. doi:10.100710869-011-9223-8

Career Builder. (2017). *Exclusive Insights From 2017 Candidate Experience Study.* https://resources.careerbuilder.com/guides/candidate-experience-guide

Collins, H. (2019, October 3). *Take employee onboarding to the next level with the best self kickoff.* 15Five. https://www.15five.com/blog/best-self-kickoff/

Cooper-Thomas, H. D., Xu, J., & Saks, A. (2018). The differential value of resources in predicting employee engagement. *Journal of Managerial Psychology, 33*(4/5), 326–344. doi:10.1108/JMP-12-2017-0449

Corporate Leadership Council. (2004). *Driving performance and retention through employee engagement.* https://www.stcloudstate.edu/humanresources/_files/documents/supv-brown-bag/employee-engagement.pdf

Dachner, A. M., & Makarius, E. E. (2021). Turn departing employees into loyal alumni. *Harvard Business Review, 99*(2), 88–97.

Dong, Y., Wei, J., & Li, M. (2014). The influence of mentor network to new employees' career success. *2014 International Conference on Management Science Engineering 21th Annual Conference Proceedings,* 1064–1069. 10.1109/ICMSE.2014.6930346

Du Toit, C. (2019). *On-boarding: A practical guide to creating extraordinary new employee experiences*. KR Publishing.

Eisenberger, R., Stinglhamber, F., Vandenberghe, C., Sucharski, L., & Rhoades, L. (2002, June). Perceived supervisor support: Contributions to perceived organizational support and employee retention. *The Journal of Applied Psychology, 87*(3), 565–573. doi:10.1037/0021-9010.87.3.565 PMID:12090614

Eldor, L., & Vigoda-Gadot, E. (2017). The nature of employee engagement: Rethinking the employee–organization relationship. *International Journal of Human Resource Management, 28*(3), 526–552. doi:10.1080/09585192.2016.1180312

Fica, T. (2018). *The new definitive guide to onboarding*. Bamboo HR.

Gallup. (2007). *Gallup state of the American workplace report*. Gallup.

Gerard, V. (2019). Get on board with offboarding. *Association for Talent Development (ATD) Talent Development, 73*(7).

Goleman, D. (2018). *What is emotional self-awareness?* Korn Ferry Hay Group. https://www.kornferry.com/insights/this-week-in-leadership/what-is-emotional-self-awareness-2019

Graybill, J. O., Hudson Carpenter, M. T., Offord, J., Piorun, M., & Shaffer, G. (2013). Employee onboarding: Identification of best practices in ACRL libraries. *Library Management; Bradford, 34*(3), 200–218. doi:10.1108/01435121311310897

Hallak, D. (2016). Take control of your new job: Proactive development and onboarding success. Academic Press.

Iliev, I., & Stoyanova, T. (2017). Employee engagement factor for organizational excellence. *International Journal of Business and Economic Sciences Applied Research, 10*(1), 23–29. doi:10.25103/ijbesar.101.03

Kahn, W. A. (1990). Psychological conditions of personal engagement and disengagement at work. *Academy of Management Journal, 33*(4), 692–724.

Karambelkar, M., & Bhattacharya, S. (2017). Onboarding is a change: Applying change management model ADKAR to onboarding. *Human Resource Management International Digest, 25*(7), 5–8. doi:10.1108/HRMID-04-2017-0073

Kaye, B., & Jordan-Evans, S. (2014). *Love 'em or lose 'em: Getting good people to stay*. Berrett-Koehler Publishers, Incorporated. https://ebookcentral.proquest.com/lib/bayloru/detail.action?docID=1407851

King, S., Altman, D., & Lee, R. (2011). *Discovering the leader in you*. Wiley.

Kotter, J. P. (2012). *Leading change*. Harvard Business Review Press. https://books.google.com/books?id=xpGX1EWL_EMC

Krasman, M. (2015). Three must-have onboarding elements for new and relocated employees. *Employment Relations Today, 42*(2), 9–14. doi:10.1002/ert.21493

Llarena, M. (2013). How not to lose your new employees in their first 45 days. *Forbes*. https://www.forbes.com/sites/85broads/2013/07/19/how-not-to-lose-your-new-employees-in-their-first-45-days/#ff6e9a33be35

Ma, Q. K., Mayfield, M., & Mayfield, J. (2018). Keep them on-board! How organizations can develop employee embeddedness to increase employee retention. *Development and Learning in Organizations; Bradford, 32*(4), 5–9. doi:10.1108/DLO-11-2017-0094

Maxwell, J. (2007). *The 21 irrefutable laws of leadership: Follow them and people will follow you*. Harper Collins.

Mayer, K. (2019). When quitting doesn't have to be a bad breakup: The importance of offboarding - and other vital lessons I've learned during my time at EBN. *Employee Benefit News, 33*(4), 8.

Merriam, S., & Bierema, L. (2014). *Adult learning: Linking theory and practice*. Jossey-Bass.

Meyer, S. (2018). Continuous feedback during change supports success. *Bonfyre*. https://bonfyreapp.com/blog/continuous-feedback-during-change

Miller, J. L. (2017). Managing Transitions: Using William Bridges' Transition Model and a Change Style Assessment Instrument to Inform Strategies and Measure Progress in Organizational Change Management. *Scholarship and Professional Work, 74*, 9.

Nelson, B. (2018, September 25). How learning & development impacts employee engagement. *Training Industry*. https://trainingindustry.com/blog/performance-management/how-learning-development-impacts-employee-engagement/

Northouse, P. (2019). *Leadership: Theory and practice*. Sage Publications.

Ormrod, J. (2020). Human learning (8th ed.). Pearson Education.

Saks, A. M., Uggerslev, K. L., & Fassina, N. E. (2007). Socialization tactics and newcomer adjustment: A meta-analytic review and test of a model. *Journal of Vocational Behavior, 70*(3), 413–446. doi:10.1016/j.jvb.2006.12.004

Sears, L. (2017). 2017 Retention report: Trends, reasons & recommendations. Workinstitute.com/retentionreport

Smith, S. S., Peters, R., & Caldwell, C. (2016). Creating a culture of engagement—Insights for application. *Business and Management Research, 5*(2), 1–11. doi:10.5430/bmr.v5n2p70

Snell, A. (2006). Researching onboarding best practice: Using research to connect onboarding processes with employee satisfaction. *Strategic HR Review, 5*(6), 32–35. doi:10.1108/14754390680000925

Studer, Q. (2003). *Hardwiring excellence: Purpose, worthwhile work, making a difference*. Fire Starter Publishing.

Compilation of References

Ab Wahid, M., Lee, W. K., & Baharudin, F. (2020). Implementing Project-Based Learning for Sustainability Management Course at Postgraduate Level. *Asian Journal of University Education, 16*(2), 84–92. doi:10.24191/ajue.v16i2.10300

Abbas, M., & Ali, R. (2021). Transformational versus transactional leadership styles and project success: A meta-analytic review. *European Management Journal.* Advance online publication. doi:10.1016/j.emj.2021.10.011

Abidin, Z., Rokhman, F., & Mathrani, A. (2021). Exploring the influencing factors of learning management systems continuance intention in a blended learning environment. *International Journal of Innovation and Learning, 30*(2), 175. Advance online publication. doi:10.1504/IJIL.2021.117221

Abrami, P. C., Bernard, R. M., Bures, E. M., Borokhovski, E., & Tamim, R. M. (2011). Interaction in distance education and online learning: Using evidence and theory to improve practice. *Journal of Computing in Higher Education, 23*(2–3), 82–103. doi:10.100712528-011-9043-x

Adkerson, M. (2000). *The company you keep: Four key tools for employee retention.* Academic Press.

Adserias, R. P., Charleston, L. J., & Jackson, J. F. L. (2017). What style of leadership is best suited to direct organizational change to fuel institutional diversity in higher education. *Race, Ethnicity and Education, 20*(3), 315–331. doi:10.1080/13613324.2016.1260233

Afifi, G. M. H., Atef, T., & Al Busaidi, Y. (2019). Interdisciplinary higher education in tourism: The case of SQU, Oman. *Anatolia, 30*(1), 6 17. doi:10.1080/13032917.2018.1494610

Ahmed, M. M. H., & Indurkhya, B. (2020). Investigating cognitive holding power and equity in the flipped classroom. *Heliyon, 6*(8), e04672. doi:10.1016/j.heliyon.2020.e04672 PMID:32885070

Airey, D. (2015). 40 years of tourism studies – a remarkable story. *Tourism Recreation Research, 40*(1), 6–15. doi:10.1080/02508281.2015.1007633

Akpabio, E. (2012). Beneficiaries' Perspective on Service Learning: Case Study of Advertising and Public Relations Campaign Course. *SAGE Open, 2*(3). doi:10.1177/2158244012460694

Akyol, Z., Garrison, D. R., & Ozden, M. Y. (2009). Online and blended communities of inquiry: Exploring the developmental and perceptional differences. *The International Review of Research in Open and Distributed, 10*(6), 65–83. doi:10.19173/irrodl.v10i6.765

Alam, G. M., Hoque, K. E., Ismail, L., & Mishra, P. K. (2010). Do developing countries need education laws to manage its system or are ethics and a market-driven approach sufficient? *African Journal of Business Management, 4*(15), 3406–3416.

Al-Arimi, A. M. A.-K. (2014). Distance Learning. *Procedia: Social and Behavioral Sciences, 152*, 82–88. doi:10.1016/j.sbspro.2014.09.159

Aleixo, M. C., Teixeira, A. B., & Silva, S. M. (2012). Simulação Empresarial: um caso de sucesso. In XXII Jornadas Luso Espanholas de Gestão Científica. Vila Real.

Allport, G. W. (1955). *Becoming: Basic Consideration for a Psychology of Personality*. Yale University Press.

Al-Qahtani, A. A. Y., & Higgins, S. E. (2013). Effects of traditional, blended and e-learning on students' achievement in higher education. *Journal of Computer Assisted Learning*, *29*(3), 220–234. doi:10.1111/j.1365-2729.2012.00490.x

Alstete, J. W. (2008). Aspects of entrepreneurial success. *Journal of Small Business and Enterprise Development*, *15*(3), 584–594. doi:10.1108/14626000810892364

Altman, D., Lee, R., & King, S. (2011). *Discovering the leader in you*. Jossey-Bass.

Altshuller, G. S. (1999). *Innovation Algorithm. Worcester: Technical Innovation Center.* (Original work published in 1969)

Alvarenga, F. B. (2006). *A Methodological Approach to the Inclusive Products Project* (Doctoral thesis). State University of Campinas, Campinas, SP, Brazil.

Alves, J. E., Proença, A., Martins, A., Veríssimo, S., Mourato, I., & Morgado, H. (2021). *Distance Learning as pedagogical innovation. Evaluation of a recente practice in Polytechnic Institute of Portalegre* [Paper presentation]. V International Forum on Management: Connected in a Multipolar world - Everything becomes smart and digital, Instituto Politécnico de Setúbal. http://ifm2021.esce.ips.pt/pt/proceedings

Alves, J., Moutinho, N., Pires, A., & Ribeiro, N. (2013). A motivação dos alunos em Simulação Empresarial: análise de um ano letivo. *XIV Congresso Internacional de contabilidade e auditoria.*

Alvesson, M., & Einola, K. (2019). Warning for excessive positivity: Authentic leadership and other traps in leadership studies. *The Leadership Quarterly*, *30*(4), 383–395. doi:10.1016/j.leaqua.2019.04.001

Amankwah-Amoah, J., Boso, N., & Antwi-Agyei, I. (2018). The Effects of Business Failure Experience on Successive Entrepreneurial Engagements: An Evolutionary Phase Model. *Group & Organization Management*, *43*(4), 648–682. doi:10.1177/1059601116643447

Anderson, T., & Rivera-vargas, P. (2020). *A Critical look at Educational Technology from a Distance Education Perspective.* doi:10.1344/der.2020.37.208-229

Anderson, T. D., & Garrison, D. R. (1995). Critical thinking in distance education: Developing critical communities in an audio teleconference context. *Higher Education*, *29*(2), 183–199. doi:10.1007/BF01383838

Aneas Álvarez, M. A. (2005). *Competencias interculturales transversales en la empresa: un modelo para la detección de necesidades formativas*. Universitat de Barcelona. Departament de Mètodes d'Investigació i Diagnòstic en Educació https://www.tdx.cat/handle/10803/2343#page=1

Anés, J. A. D., & Gavira, R. L. (2011). Aprendizaje baseado en el uso de casos de estudio real. XXI Jornadas Hispano-Lusas Gestión Cientifica.

Annan-Diab, F., & Molinari, C. (2017). Interdisciplinarity: Practical approach to advancing education for sustainability and for the Sustainable Development Goals. *International Journal of Management Education*, *15*(2), 73–83. doi:10.1016/j.ijme.2017.03.006

Anohina, A. (2005). Analysis of the terminology used in the field of virtual learning. *Journal of Educational Technology & Society*, *8*(3), 91–102.

Anthony, B. Jr, & Noel, S. (2021). Examining the adoption of emergency remote teaching and virtual learning during and after COVID-19 pandemic. *International Journal of Educational Management, 35*(6), 1136–1150. Advance online publication. doi:10.1108/IJEM-08-2020-0370

Antonakis, J., & House, R. J. (2014). Instrumental leadership: Measurement and extension of transformational–transactional leadership theory. *The Leadership Quarterly, 25*(4), 746–771. doi:10.1016/j.leaqua.2014.04.005

Apps, G. (1970). Fundamentals of adult learning. In S. M. Grabowski (Ed.), *Adult learning and instruction* (pp. 96–109). Adult Education Association of the U.S.A.

Arbaugh, J. B. (2007). Does the community of inquiry framework predict outcomes in online mba courses? *Academy of Management 2007 Annual Meeting: Doing Well by Doing Good, AOM 2007.*

Arbaugh, J. B., Desai, A., Rau, B., & Sridhar, B. S. (2010). A review of research on online and blended learning in the management disciplines: 1994-2009. *Organizational Management Journal, 7*(1), 39–55. doi:10.1057/omj.2010.5

Arbaugh, J. B., Godfrey, M. R., Johnson, M., Pollack, B. L., Niendorf, B., & Wresch, W. (2009). Research in online and blended learning in the business disciplines: Key findings and possible future directions. *Internet and Higher Education, 12*(2), 71–87. doi:10.1016/j.iheduc.2009.06.006

Arbrecht, W. S., & Sack, R. J. (2000). Accounting education: Charting the course through a perilous future. American Accounting Association. Sarasota.

Archambault, É., Vignola-Gagné, É., Côté, G., Larivière, V., & Gingrasb, Y. (2006). Benchmarking scientific output in the social sciences and humanities: The limits of existing databases. *Scientometrics, 68*(3), 329–342. doi:10.100711192-006-0115-z

Arenas, C., Arenas, R., Ureña, Y., Carruyo, N., & Mejía, A. (2012). *Emprenderismo: Una Herramienta para el Desarrollo de Tecnologías Sociales. III Jornadas Internacionales FING UJGH 2012, Universidad Dr.* José Gregorio Hernández - Decanato de la Facultad de Ingeniería.

Argawal, R., & Audretsch, D. B. (2001). Does entry size matter? The impact of the life cycle and technology on firm survival. *The Journal of Industrial Economics, 49*(1), 21–43. doi:10.1111/1467-6451.00136

Arias, C. A., Martínes, A. C., & Gracia, J. L. (2000). *Enfoques Emergentes en Torno en la Estrucutura de Capital: El caso de la Pyme*. Generalitat Valenciana.

Ariza, L. R. (2011). Enseñando a emprender. *XVI Congreso AECA.*

Armenakis, A. A., & Bedeian, A. G. (1999). Organizational change: A review of theory and research in the 1990s. *Organizational Change, 25*(3), 293–315. doi:10.1177/014920639902500303

Arokiasamy, A. (2013). A qualitative study on causes and effects of employee turnover in the private sector in Malaysia. *Middle East Journal of Scientific Research, 16*(11), 1532–1541.

Arrobas, F., Ferreira, J., Brito-Henriques, E., & Fernandes, A. (2020). Measuring tourism and environmental sciences students' attitudes towards sustainable tourism. *Journal of Hospitality, Leisure, Sport and Tourism Education, 27*, 1–12. doi:10.1016/j.jhlste.2020.100273 PMID:33041660

Arthur, D. (1998). *Recruiting, Interviewing, Selecting & Orienting New Employees* (3rd ed.). Amacom.

Ash, S. L., & Clayton, P. H. (2004). The articulated learning. An approach to reflection and assessment. *Innovative Higher Education, 29*(2), 137–154. doi:10.1023/B:IHIE.0000048795.84634.4a

Asmelash, A. G., & Kumar, S. (2019). Assessing progress of tourism sustainability: Developing and validating sustainability indicators. *Tourism Management*, *71*, 67–83. doi:10.1016/j.tourman.2018.09.020

Association to Advance Collegiate Schools of Business-International (AACSB). (2004). *Ethics Education in Business Schools: Report of the Ethics Education Task Force*. AACSB.

Astebro, T., & Bernhardt, I. (2003). Start-up financing, owner characteristics and survival. *Journal of Economics and Business*, *55*(4), 303–320. doi:10.1016/S0148-6195(03)00029-8

Attridge, M. (2009). Measuring and managing employee work engagement: A review of the research and business literature. *Journal of Workplace Behavioral Health*, *24*(4), 383–398. doi:10.1080/15555240903188398

Aucejo, E. M., French, J., Araya, M. P., & Zafar, B. (2020, November). The impacto f COVID-19 on student experiences and expectations: Evidence from a survey. *Journal of Public Economics*, *191*, 104271. doi:10.1016/j.jpubeco.2020.104271 PMID:32873994

Austin, J., Stevenson, H., & Wei-skillern, J. (2003). *Social Entrepreneurship and Commercial Entrepreneurship: Same, Different, or Both?* Working Paper Series, No. 04-029, Harvard Business School.

Avolio, B. J., Walumbwa, F. O., & Weber, T. J. (2009). Leadership: Current theories, research, and future directions. *Annual Review of Psychology*, *60*(1), 421–449. doi:10.1146/annurev.psych.60.110707.163621 PMID:18651820

Ayala, J., & Manzano, G. (2014). The resilience of the entrepreneur. Influence on the success of the business. A longitudinal analysis. *Journal of Economic Psychology*, *42*, 126–135. doi:10.1016/j.joep.2014.02.004

Aynalem, S., Birhanu, K., & Tesefay, S. (2016). Employment Opportunities and Challenges in Tourism and Hospitality Sectors. *Journal of Tourism & Hospitality (Los Angeles, Calif.)*, *5*(6), 1–5. doi:10.4172/2167-0269.1000257

Backes–Gellner, U., & Werner, A. (2007). Entrepreneurial Signaling via education: Success factor in innovative start-ups. *Small Business Economics*, *29*(2), 173–190. doi:10.100711187-006-0016-9

Baeten, M., Dochy, F., & Struyven, K. (2013). The effects of different learning environments on students' motivation for learning and their achievement. *The British Journal of Educational Psychology*, *83*(3), 484–501. doi:10.1111/j.2044-8279.2012.02076.x PMID:23822533

Bajaelde, O. E., Lauridsen, K., & Lindberg, A. (2018). *Current trends in assessment in Europe – the way forward.* White paper, Coimbra Group Education Innovation Working Group.

Balancho M. J. & Coelho, F. M. (1996). *Motivar os alunos, criatividade na relação pedagógica: conceitos e práticas* (2ª Edição). Texto Editora.

Baloran, E. T. (2020). Knowledge, Attitudes, Anxiety, and Coping Strategies of Studentes during COVID-19 Pandemic. *Journal of Loss and Trauma*, *25*(8), 635–642. doi:10.1080/15325024.2020.1769300

Bao, W. (2020). COVID-19 and online teaching in higher education: A case study of Peking University. *Human Behavior and Emerging Technologies*, *2*(2), 113–115. doi:10.1002/hbe2.191 PMID:32510042

Baptista, R., Karaoz, M., & Mendonca, J. (2013). The impact of human capital on the early success of necessity versus opportunity-based entrepreneurs. *Small Business Economics*, *42*(4), 831–847. doi:10.100711187-013-9502-z

Barai, M., & Adhikary, B. (2013). The Success of Microcredit in Bangladesh: Supplementing 'Group Lending' Explanation with Institutional Understanding. *Review of Integrative Business & Economics Research*, *2*(1), 471–490.

Barata, M. C., Calheiros, M. M., Patrício, J., Graça, J., & Lima, M. L. (2012). *Avaliação do programa mais sucesso escolar*. CISIUL/ISCTE/IUL Edição Direção-Geral de Estatísticas de Educação e Ciência – Ministério da Educação e Ciência.

Baron, R. A., & Markman, G. D. (2003). Beyond social capital: The role of entrepreneurs' social competence in their financial success. *Journal of Business Venturing*, *1*(1), 41–60. doi:10.1016/S0883-9026(00)00069-0

Barrows, H., & Tamblyn, R. (1980). Problem-based learning: an approach to medical education. Springer Series on Medical Education, 1.

Barton, D. C. (2020). Impacts of the COVID-19 pandemic on field instruction and remote teaching alternatives: Results from a survey of instructors. *Ecology and Evolution*, *10*(22), 12499–12507. doi:10.1002/ece3.6628 PMID:32837715

Basardien, F., Friedrich, C., & Parker, H. (2013). The relationship between planning strategies and entrepreneurial success for start-up entrepreneurs in the Western Cape: A psychological approach to entrepreneurship. *International Journal of Entrepreneurship and Innovation*, *14*(4), 281–288. doi:10.5367/ijei.2013.0128

Bass, B. M. (1990). From transactional to transformational leadership: Learning to share the vision. *Organizational Dynamics*, *18*(3), 19–31. doi:10.1016/0090-2616(90)90061-S

Bates, T. (1997). *Race, self-employment and upward mobility: An illusive American dream*. John Hopkins University Press.

Battaglia, M. (2017). Sustainability in the Tourism Business. Symphonya. *Emerging Issues in Management*, *3*, 122-134. doi:10.4468/2016.3.11battaglia

Bauer, T. (2020). *Onboarding new employees*. https://www.shrm.org/foundation/ourwork/initiatives/resources-from-past-initiatives/Documents/Onboarding%20New%20Employees.pdf

Bauer, T., & Erdogan, B. (2011). Organizational socialization: The effective onboarding of new employees. In S. Zedeck (Ed.), APA handbook of industrial and organizational psychology, Vol 3: Maintaining, expanding, and contracting the organization (pp. 51–64). American Psychological Association. doi:10.1037/12171-002

Bauer, T. (2015). *Onboarding: Maximizing role clarity and confidence*. Success Factors.

Baum, J. R., Frese, M., Baron, R. A., & Katz, J. A. (2007). Entrepreneurship as an area of psychology study: an introduction. *The Psychology of Entrepreneurship*, 1-18.

Baumruk, R. (2006). Why managers are crucial to increasing engagement: Identifying steps managers can take to engage their workforce. *Strategic HR Review*, *5*(2), 24–27. doi:10.1108/14754390680000863

Baxter. (2011) *Product design: Practical guide to the design of new products* (3rd ed.). Edgard Blucher.

Bearden, C., Mahan, T., & Nelms, D. (2019). *Work institute 2019 retention report*. https://info.workinstitute.com/hubfs/2019%20Retention%20Report/Work%20Institute%202019%20Retention%20Report%20final-1.pdf

Beck, T., Maimbo, S., Faye, I., & Triki, T. (2011). *Financing Africa Through the Crisis and Beyond*. World Bank. doi:10.1596/978-0-8213-8797-9

Bee, J. (2013). How to keep toxic employees from harming your practice. *Medical Economics*, *90*(23), 38–39. PMID:25272629

Bell, S. (2010). Project-based learning for the 21st century: Skills for the future. *The Clearing House: A Journal of Educational Strategies, Issues and Ideas*, *83*(2), 39–43. doi:10.1080/00098650903505415

Bembem, Santos, & Plácida. (2013). Collective intelligence: A look at the production of Pierre Lévy. *Perspectives in Information Science, 18*(4), 139-151.

Benckendorff, P., & Moscardo, G. (2015). Education for Sustainability Futures. In G. Moscardo & P. Benckendorff (Eds.), *Education for Sustainability in Tourism A Handbook of Processes, Resources, and Strategies* (pp. 271–284). Springer. doi:10.1007/978-3-662-47470-9_17

Bentley, K. J., Secret, M. C., & Cummings, C. R. (2015). The Centrality of Social Presence in Online Teaching and Learning in Social Work. *Journal of Social Work Education, 51*(3), 494–504. doi:10.1080/10437797.2015.1043199

Bergmann, J., & Sams, A. (2012). *Flip your classroom: Reach every student in every class every day* (1st ed.). International Society for Technology in Education.

Berle, D. (2006). Incremental integration: A successful service-learning strategy. *International Journal on Teaching and Learning in Higher Education, 18*(1), 43–48.

Bernard, C. (2012). *Surveying networks of social entrepreneurs.* Retrieved from http://www.kpmgfamilybusiness.com/surveying-networks-of-social-entrepreneurs/

Bernard, R. M., Abrami, P. C., Lou, Y., Borokhovski, E., Wade, A., Wozney, L., Wallet, P. A., Fiset, M., & Huang, B. (2004). How does distance education compare with classroom instruction? A meta-analysis of the empirical literature. *Review of Educational Research, 74*(3), 379–439. doi:10.3102/00346543074003379

Bernard, R. M., Borokhovski, E., Schmid, R. F., Tamim, R. M., & Abrami, P. C. (2014). A meta-analysis of blended learning and technology use in higher education: From the general to the applied. *Journal of Computing in Higher Education, 26*(1), 87–122. doi:10.100712528-013-9077-3

Berne, E. (1964). *Games people play.* Grove Press.

Bertha Centre for Social Innovation & Entrepreneurship. (2018). *Innovative Finance in Africa.* Universidade do Cabo, África do Sul.

Besalú, X. (2002). *Diversidad cultural y educación.* Síntesis.

Biggs, D., Hall, C., & Stoeckl, N. (2012). The resilience of formal and informal tourism enterprises to disasters: Reef tourism in Phuket, Thailand. *Journal of Sustainable Tourism, 20*(5), 645–665. doi:10.1080/09669582.2011.630080

Blondy, L. (2007). Evaluation and application of andragogical assumptions to the adult online learning environment. *Journal of Interactive Online Learning, 6*(2), 116–130. www.ncolr.org/jiol/issues/pdf/6.2.3.pdf

Boley, B. B. (2011). Sustainability in hospitality and tourism education: Towards an integrated curriculum. *Journal of Hospitality & Tourism Education, 23*(4), 22–31. doi:10.1080/10963758.2011.10697017

Boling, E. C., Hough, M., Krinsky, H., Saleem, H., & Stevens, M. (2012). Cutting the distance in distance education: Perspectives on what promotes positive, online learning experiences. *The Internet and Higher Education, 15*(2), 118–126. doi:10.1016/j.iheduc.2011.11.006

Bonk, C. J. (2020). Pandemic ponderings, 30 years to today: Synchronous signals, saviors, or survivors? *Distance Education, 41*(4), 589–599. doi:10.1080/01587919.2020.1821610

Bonwell, C. C. (1991). Active learning: Creating excitement in the classroom. School of Education and Human Development, George Washington University.

Borochovicius, E., & Tortella, J. C. B. (2014). Aprendizagem baseada em problemas: um método de ensino-aprendizagem e suas práticas educativas. *Ensaio: aval. Públ. Educ., 22*(83), 263-294. Retrieved 2021-12-09 from https://www.bing.com/search?q=Borochovicius%2C+E.+e+Tortella%2C+J.C.B.%2C+2014%2C

Borup, J., West, R. E., & Graham, C. R. (2012). Improving online social presence through asynchronous video. *The Internet and Higher Education*, *15*(3), 195–203. doi:10.1016/j.iheduc.2011.11.001

Bourdieu, P. (2007). *El Sentido Práctico*. Siglo XXI.

Bourke, J., & Titus, A. (2020, March 6). The key to inclusive leadership. *Harvard Business Review*. https://hbr.org/2020/03/the-key-to-inclusive-leadership

Bovinet, J. W. (2007). Different skill-set views: A four-year study of marketing students, practitioner and educators. *Journal of Business and Public Affairs*, *1*(1), 1–8.

Bowers, J., & Kumar, P. (2015). Students' perceptions of teaching and social presence: A comparative analysis of face-to-face and online learning environments. *International Journal of Web-Based Learning and Teaching Technologies*, *10*(1), 27–44. doi:10.4018/ijwltt.2015010103

Boyum, G. (2006). *The historical and philosophical influences on Greenleaf's concept of servant leadership: Setting the stage for scientific theory building*. https://www.regent.edu/acad/global/publications/sl_proceedings/2006/boyum.pdf

Bradberry, T., & Greaves, J. (2009). *Emotional intelligence 2.0*. Talentsmart.

Braunsberger, K., & Flamm, R. O. (2013). A mission of civic engagement: Undergraduate students working with nonprofit organizations and public sector agencies to enhance societal wellbeing. *Voluntas*, *24*(1), 1–31. doi:10.100711266-012-9289-6

Brewer, R., & Movahedazarhouligh, S. (2018). Successful stories and conflicts: A literature review on the effectiveness of flipped learning in higher education. *Journal of Computer Assisted Learning*, *34*(4), 409–416. doi:10.1111/jcal.12250

Bridges, W. (1980). *Transitions: Making sense of life's changes*. Addison-Wesley.

Bringle, R. G., & Hatcher, J. A. (1995). A service-learning curriculum for faculty. *Michigan Journal of Community Service Learning*, *2*(1), 112–122.

Brouder, P. (2020). Reset redux: Possible evolutionary pathways towards the transformation of tourism in a COVID-19 world. *Tourism Geographies*, *22*(3), 484–490. doi:10.1080/14616688.2020.1760928

Brown, M., Brown, R. S., & Nandedkar, A. (2019). Transformational leadership theory and exploring the perceptions of diversity management in higher education. *Journal of Higher Education Theory and Practice*, *19*(7), 11–21. doi:10.33423/jhetp.v19i7.2527

Bruderl, J., Preisendorfer, P., & Ziegler, R. (1992). Survival chances of newly founded business organizations. *American Sociological Review*, *57*(2), 227–242. doi:10.2307/2096207

Bruderl, J., & Schussler, R. (1990). Organizational mortality: The liabilities of newness and adolescence. *Administrative Science Quarterly*, *35*(3), 530–547. doi:10.2307/2393316

Bruyne, P. (1991). *Dynamics of Research in Social Sciences*. Francisco Alves.

Buckley, R. (2012). Sustainable Tourism: Research and Reality. *Annals of Tourism Research*, *39*(2), 528–546. doi:10.1016/j.annals.2012.02.003

Bueno, B., & Balestrin, A. (2012). *Collaborative innovation: an open approach to new product development. Business Administration Journal*.

Buhalis, D., Leung, D., & Law, R. (2011). eTourism: Critical Information and Communication Technologies for Tourism Destinations. In Y. Wang & A. Pizam (Eds.), Destination Marketing and Management (pp. 205–224). CAB International.

Bui, B., & Porter, B. (2010). The expectation-performance gap in accounting education: An exploratory study. *Accounting Education, 19*(1-2), 23–50. doi:10.1080/09639280902875556

Bukvova, H., Gilge, S., & Schoop, E. (2006). Virtual collaboration in higher education blended learning arrangements. *Workshop Gemeinschaften in Neuen Medien (GeNeMe) 2006*. http://www-mmt.inf.tu-dresden.de/geneme2006/

Burns, R. A., & Anstey, K. J. (2010). The Connor-Davidson Resilience Scale (CD-RISC): Testing the invariance of a uni-dimensional resilience measure that is independent of positive and negative affect. *Personality and Individual Differences, 48*(5), 527–531. doi:10.1016/j.paid.2009.11.026

Bush-Bacelis, J. L. (1998). Innovative pedagogy: Academic service-learning for business communication. *Business Communication Quarterly, 61*(3), 20–34. doi:10.1177/108056999806100303

Byham, T., & Wellins, R. (2015). *Your first leadership job: How catalyst leaders bring out the best in others*. John Wiley & Sons. doi:10.1002/9781119153849

Byrne, O., & Shepherd, D. A. (2015). Different strokes for different folks: Entrepreneurial narratives of emotion, cognition, and making sense of business failure. *Entrepreneurship Theory and Practice, 39*(2), 375–405. doi:10.1111/etap.12046

Cabello, R., Sorrel, M. A., Fernández-Pinto, I., Extremera, N., & Fernández-Berrocal, P. (2016). Age and gender differences in ability emotional intelligence in adults: A cross-sectional study. *Developmental Psychology, 52*(9), 1486–1492. doi:10.1037/dev0000191 PMID:27570984

Cable, D., Gino, F., & Staats, B. (2013). *Reinventing employee onboarding*. https://sloanreview.mit.edu/article/reinventing-employee-onboarding/

Cable, D. M., Gino, F., & Staats, B. R. (2013). Reinventing employee onboarding. *MIT Sloan Management Review, 54*(3), 23–28.

Caldwell, C., & Peters, R. (2018). New employee onboarding – psychological contracts and ethical perspectives. *Journal of Management Development, 37*(1), 27–39. doi:10.1108/JMD-10-2016-0202

Camisón, C. (2020). Competitiveness and Sustainability in Tourist Firms and Destinations. *Sustainability, 12*(6), 2388. doi:10.3390u12062388

Campanella, S. C., & Sardinha, L. F. (2021). *O efeito da COVID-19 na estratégia de uma instituição de ensino superior: estudo de caso*. Retrieved 2021-12-09 from https://www.researchgate.net/publication/353610866

Campbell-Sills, L., Forte, D. R., & Stein, M. B. (2009). Demographic and childhood environmental predictors of resilience in a community sample. *Journal of Psychiatric Research, 43*(12), 1007–1012. doi:10.1016/j.jpsychires.2009.01.013 PMID:19264325

Canziani, B. F., Sönmez, S., Hsieh, Y., & Byrd, E. T. (2012). A learning theory framework for sustainability education in tourism. *Journal of Teaching in Travel & Tourism, 12*(1), 3–20. doi:10.1080/15313220.2012.650052

Carayol, R. (2011, June 9). *René Carayol: Authentic leadership* [Video]. YouTube. https://youtu.be/g1ACR-odNR4

Cardoso, T., Pestana, F., & Pina, J. (2019). Assessing a b-learning teaching approach and students' learning preferences in higher education. *EDULEARN19 Proceedings*, 10007–10012. 10.21125/edulearn.2019.2502

Cardy, R., & Lengnick-Hall, M. (2011). Will they stay or will they go? Exploring a customer-oriented approach to employee retention. *Journal of Business and Psychology, 26*(2), 213–217. doi:10.100710869-011-9223-8

Career Builder. (2017). *Exclusive Insights From 2017 Candidate Experience Study*. https://resources.careerbuilder.com/guides/candidate-experience-guide

Carree, M. A., & Thurik, A. R. (2003) The Impact of Entrepreneurship on Economic Growth. In Handbook of Entrepreneurship Research. Kluwer Academic Publishers.

Carreta, F. (2019). *Creativity tools for product development* [Master's thesis]. Faculty of Mechanical Engineering, State University of Campinas. Unicamp repository. http://repositorio.unicamp.br/bitstream/REPOSIP/334583/1/Carretta_Fernanda_M.pdf

Carretero, S., Vuorikari, R., & Punie, Y. (2017). *DigComp 2.1: The digital competence framework for citizens with eight proficiency levels and examples of use. EUR, Scientific and technical research series* (Vol. 28558). Publications Office.

Carvalho, L., Backx, A., & Galina, S. (2019). Entrepreneurs' perceptions of business incubator services in Brazil and Portugal. *International Journal of Business Innovation and Research*, *19*(1), 80–100. doi:10.1504/IJBIR.2019.099753

Carver, R. L. (1997). Theoretical underpinnings of service learning. *Theory into Practice*, *36*(3), 143–149. doi:10.1080/00405849709543760

Castillo, A. M., & Abad, I. M. (2003). Enseñanza interactiva y desarrollo de competencias directivas através de la docencia de la administración de empresas. In *XIV Jornadas Luso- Espanholas de Gestão Científica*. Açores.

Caza, A., Caza, B. B., & Posner, B. Z. (2021). Transformational leadership across cultures: Follower perception and satisfaction. *Administrative Sciences*, *11*(32), 32. Advance online publication. doi:10.3390/admsci11010032

Center for Servant Leadership. (n.d.). *The servant as leader*. Robert K. Greenleaf Center for Servant Leadership. https://www.greenleaf.org/what-is-servant-leadership/

CGI-Brazil. (2016, September 13) *Mobile Becomes the Main Internet Access Device*. https://www.cgi.br/noticia/releases/celular-torna-se-o-principal-dispositivo-de-acesso-a-internet-aponta-cetic-br/#:~:text=Entre%20os%20usu%C3%A1rios%20da%20network,e%2076%25%20by%20phone%20cellular

Chams, N., & García-Blandón, J. (2019). On the importance of sustainable human resource management for the adoption of sustainable development goals. *Resources, Conservation and Recycling*, *141*, 109–122. doi:10.1016/j.resconrec.2018.10.006

Chandler, G., & Hanks, S. (1998). An examination of the substitutability of founders human and financial capital in emerging business ventures. *Journal of Business Venturing*, *13*(5), 353–369. doi:10.1016/S0883-9026(97)00034-7

Chandrayanti, T., Nidar, S., Mulyana, A., & Anwar, M. (2019). Credit Accessibility Model of Small Enterprises Based on Firm Characteristics and Business Performance (Case Study at Small Enterprises in West Sumatra Indonesia). *International Journal of Entrepreneurship*, *23*(Special Issue), 1–14.

Chaney, L. H., & Martin, J. (2007). *Intercultural Business Communication*. Pearson Prentice Hall.

Chen, P., Sparrow, P., & Cooper, C. (2016). The relationship between person-organization fit and job satisfaction. *Journal of Managerial Psychology*, *31*(5), 946–959. doi:10.1108/JMP-08-2014-0236

Chen, Y., Wang, Y., & Chen, N. (2014). Computers & Education Is FLIP enough? Or should we use the FLIPPED model instead? *Computers & Education*, *79*, 16–27. doi:10.1016/j.compedu.2014.07.004

Chickering, A. W., & Gamson, Z. F. (1987). Seven principles for good practice in undergraduate education. *AAHE Bulletin*, *39*(7), 3–7.

Child, J., Elbanna, S., & Rodrigues, S. (2010). The political aspects of strategic decision making. In P. C. Nutt & D. C. Wilson (Eds.), *Handbook of decision making* (pp. 105–137). Wiley.

Chin, J. L., Desormeaux, L., & Sawyer, K. (2016). Making way for paradigms of diversity leadership. *Consulting Psychology Journal, 68*(1), 49–71. doi:10.1037/cpb0000051

Chiu, R. K., & Francesco, A. M. (2003). Dispositional traits and turnover intention: Examining the mediating role of job satisfaction and affective commitment. *International Journal of Manpower, 24*(3), 284–298. doi:10.1108/01437720310479741

Chizmar, J. F., & Walbert, M. S. (1999). Web-Based Learning Environments Guided by Principles of Good Teaching Practice. *The Journal of Economic Education, 30*(3), 248–259. doi:10.1080/00220489909595985

Chong, C. S. (2014). Service-learning research: Definitional challenges and complexities. *Asia Pacific Journal of Cooperative Education, 15*(4), 347–358.

Ciucur, D., & Pîrvut, A. F. (2012). The effects of a transactional analysis training programme on team leadership factors in automotive industry. *Procedia: Social and Behavioral Sciences, 33*, 667–671. doi:10.1016/j.sbspro.2012.01.205

Clarke, A. (1997). Survey on employability. *Industrial and Commercial Training, 29*(6), 177–183. doi:10.1108/00197859710178737

Cobanoglu, C., & Berezina, K. (2011). The impact of the use of blogs on students' assignment engagement. *Journal of Hospitality, Leisure, Sports and Tourism Education, 10*(1), 99.

Cobb, S. C. (2009). Social Presence and Online Learning: A Current View from a Research Perspective. *Journal of Interactive Online Learning*, (8), 241–254.

Coffey, B. S., & Wang, J. (2006). Service learning in a master of business administration (MBA) integrative project course: An experience in China. *Journal of Education for Business, 82*(2), 119–124. doi:10.3200/JOEB.82.2.119-124

Colakoglu, S. N., & Sledge, S. A. (2013). The development of critical thinking skills through a service-learning oriented entrepreneurship course. *Journal of Entrepreneurship Education, 16*, 115–124.

Coleman, S. (2007). The role of human and financial capital in the profitability and growth of women-owned small firms. *Journal of Small Business Management, 45*(3), 303–319. doi:10.1111/j.1540-627X.2007.00214.x

Coll, C., Martin, E., & Onrubia, J. (2001). La evaluación del aprendizaje escolar: dimensiones psicológicas, pedgógicas y sociales. In C. Coll, J. Palacios, & A. Marchesi (Eds.), *Desarrollo psicológico y educación. Psicología de la educación escolar* (2nd ed., pp. 549–572). Alianza Editorial.

Collins, H. (2019, October 3). *Take employee onboarding to the next level with the best self kickoff.* 15Five. https://www.15five.com/blog/best-self-kickoff/

Conselho Nacional de Educação. (2019). *Estado da Educação 2018.* Lisboa: Conselho Nacional de Educação. https://www.cnedu.pt/content/edicoes/estado_da_educacao/Estado_da_Educacao2018_web_26nov2019.pdf

Consulting, I. (2018) *VersionOne launches the 12th Annual Report of the State of Ágile.* https://explore.versionone.com/state-of-agile/versionone-12th-annual-state-of-agile-report

Cooks, L., & Scharrer, E. (2006). Assessing Learning in Community Service Learning: A social Approach. *Michigan Journal of Community Service Learning, 13*(1), 44–55.

Cook, T., & Reichardt, C. (1986). *Métodos cualitativos y cuantitativos en la investigación educativa.* Morata.

Cooper-Thomas, H. D., Xu, J., & Saks, A. (2018). The differential value of resources in predicting employee engagement. *Journal of Managerial Psychology, 33*(4/5), 326–344. doi:10.1108/JMP-12-2017-0449

Cope, J. (2011). Entrepreneurial learning from failure: An interpretative phenomenological analysis. *Journal of Business Venturing*, *26*(6), 604–623. doi:10.1016/j.jbusvent.2010.06.002

Corporate Leadership Council. (2004). *Driving performance and retention through employee engagement.* https://www.stcloudstate.edu/humanresources/_files/documents/supv-brown-bag/employee-engagement.pdf

Costa, M. A. (2019). *Maturity in the Use of Web 2.0 Technologies in the Banking Sector in Portugal.* APNOR.

Costa, R. D. (2005). For a new concept of community: Social networks, personal communities, collective intelligence. Interface-communication, health, education. *Scielo, São Paulo, Brazil*, *9*, 235–248.

Costa, T., & Galina, S. (2016). The virtuous relationship between entrepreneurship and social capital: A study on tourism rural businesses in Portugal and Brazil. *Tourism & Management Studies*, *12*(2), 57–69. doi:10.18089/tms.2016.12207

Cote, T. J., & Milliner, B. (2017). Preparing Japanese Students' Digital Literacy for Study Abroad: Is More Training Needed? *The JALT CALL Journal*, *13*(3), 187–197. doi:10.29140/jaltcall.v13n3.218

Covelli, B. J., & Mason, I. (2017). Linking theory to practice: Authentic leadership. *Academy of Strategic Management Journal*, *16*(3), 1–10.

Covin, J. G., & Slevin, D. P. (1989). Strategic management of small firms in hostile and benign environments. *Strategic Management Journal*, *10*(1), 75–87. doi:10.1002mj.4250100107

Cramer, R. A., Alexander-Floyd, N. G., & Means, T. (2019). Balance is a fallacy: Striving for and supporting a life with integrity. *PS, Political Science & Politics*, *52*(1), 35–38. doi:10.1017/S1049096518001154

Cruz, L. M., By, M., & Muller, F. (2016). *Social Epistemology And Democracy Wisdom Of The Crowds X Specialist.* Editora Fi.

Cucculelli, M., & Goffi, G. (2016). Does sustainability enhance tourism destination competitiveness? Evidence from Italian Destinations of Excellence. *Journal of Cleaner Production*, *111*, 370–382. doi:10.1016/j.jclepro.2014.12.069

Dachner, A. M., & Makarius, E. E. (2021). Turn departing employees into loyal alumni. *Harvard Business Review*, *99*(2), 88–97.

Dacin, M. T., Dacin, D. A., & Tracey, P. (2011). Social Entrepreneurship: A Critique and Future Directions. *Organization Science*, *22*(5), 1203–1213. doi:10.1287/orsc.1100.0620

Danes, S. M., Lee, J., Amarapurkar, S., Stafford, K., Haynes, G., & Brewton, K. E. (2009). Determinants of family business resilience after a natural disaster by gender of business owner. *Journal of Developmental Entrepreneurship*, *14*(4), 333–354. doi:10.1142/S1084946709001351

Danes, S. M., Stafford, K., & Loy, J. T. (2007). Family business performance: The effects of gender and management. *Journal of Business Research*, *60*(10), 1058–1069. doi:10.1016/j.jbusres.2006.12.013

Dang, L., & Chuc, A. (2019). *Challenges in implementing the credit guarantee scheme for small and medium-sized enterprises: the case of Vietnam.* Asian Development Bank Institute.

Datta, B. (2015). Assessing the effectiveness of authentic leadership. *International Journal of Leadership Studies*, *9*(1), 19–32. https://www.regent.edu/acad/global/publications/ijls/new/vol9iss1/2-IJLS.pdf

Davidson, B. A. (1997). *Application of adult learning principles for employee training in small manufacturing organizations* [Ph.D. Dissertation, Walden University]. ProQuest.

DeAngelis, L., & Penney, S. (2015). Teaching leaders. *Journal of Leadership Education, 14*(4), 126–137. doi:10.12806/V14/I4/A3

Deans for Impact. (2015). *The Science of Learning*. Deans for Impact.

Deci, E. L., Connell, J. P., & Ryan, R. M. (1989). Self-determination in a work organization. *The Journal of Applied Psychology, 74*(4), 580–590. doi:10.1037/0021-9010.74.4.580

Deci, E., & Ryan, R. (2008). Facilitating optimal motivation and psychological well-being across life's domains. *Canadian Psychology, 49*(1), 14–23. doi:10.1037/0708-5591.49.1.14

Deci, E., & Ryan, R. M. (1985). *Intrinsic motivation and self-determination in human behavior*. Plenum. doi:10.1007/978-1-4899-2271-7

Dehter, M. (2001). *Intrapreneurship*. Retrieved from http://www.justoahora.com/nws/iv02.htm

Del Bosco, B., Mazzucchelli, A., Chierici, R., & Di Gregorio, A. (2019). Innovative startup creation: The effect of local factors and demographic characteristics of entrepreneurs. *The International Entrepreneurship and Management Journal*, 1–20.

Del Solar, S. (2010). *Emprendedores en el aula. Guía para la formación en valores y habilidades sociales de docentes y jóvenes emprendedores*. Fondo Multilateral de Inversiones del Banco Interamericano de Desarrollo.

Delaune, L. D., Rakow, J. S., & Rakow, K. C. (2010). Teaching financial literacy in a co-curricular service-learning model. *Journal of Accounting Education, 28*(2), 103–113. doi:10.1016/j.jaccedu.2011.03.002

Delmar, F., & Shane, S. (2004). Legitimating first: Organizing activities and the survival of new ventures. *Journal of Business Venturing, 19*(3), 385–410. doi:10.1016/S0883-9026(03)00037-5

Demo, P. (2003). *Educating by research (6th ed.)*. Associated Authors.

Dempsey, M., & Brafman, O. (2018). *Radical inclusion: What the post-9/11 world should have taught us about leadership*. Missionday.

Dennen, V. P., Aubteen Darabi, A., & Smith, L. J. (2007). Instructor–Learner Interaction in Online Courses: The relative perceived importance of particular instructor actions on performance and satisfaction. *Distance Education, 28*(1), 65–79. doi:10.1080/01587910701305319

Denyer, D., & Tranfield, D. (2009). Producing asystematic review. In D. A. Buchanan & A. Bryman (Eds.), *The Sage Hand-Book of Organizational Research Methods* (pp. 671–689). Sage Publications.

Dewey, J. (1938). *Experience and education*. Simon and Schuster.

Dey, P. (2006). The rhetoric of social entrepreneurship: Paralogy and new language games in academic discourse. In C. Steyaert & D. Hjorth (Eds.), *Entrepreneurship as Social Change: A Third Movements of Entrepreneurship* (pp. 121–144). Edward Elgar. doi:10.4337/9781847204424.00015

Dilling, J., Varga, M. A., & Mandernach, B. J. (2020). Comparing Teaching and Social Presence in Traditional and Online Community College Learning Environments. *Community College Journal of Research and Practice, 44*(10-12), 854–869. doi:10.1080/10668926.2020.1752852

Dimitratos, P., & Plakoyiannaki, E. (2003). Theoretical foundations of an international entrepreneurial culture. *Journal of International Entrepreneurship, 1*(2), 187–215. doi:10.1023/A:1023804318244

Dittmar, J. (2016, June 30). *Transactional vs. transformational leadership definition* [Video]. YouTube. https://www.youtube.com/watch?v=FtnFKLqhL-Y

Done, A. (2011). *Supply chain knowledge management: A conceptual framework* (Working paper WP-900). IESE Business School, University of Navarra. Retrieved from https://www.iese.edu/research/

Dong, Y., Wei, J., & Li, M. (2014). The influence of mentor network to new employees' career success. *2014 International Conference on Management Science Engineering 21th Annual Conference Proceedings*, 1064–1069. 10.1109/ICMSE.2014.6930346

Dormann, C., & Zapf, D. (2001). Job satisfaction: A meta-analysis of stabilities. *Journal of Organizational Behavior*, *22*(6), 483–504. doi:10.1002/job.98

Doutriaux, J. (1992). Emerging high-tech firms: How durable are their comparative start-up advantages. *Journal of Business Venturing*, *7*(4), 303–322. doi:10.1016/0883-9026(92)90004-B

Dover, P. A., & Dierk, U. (2010). The ambidextrous organization: Integrating managers, entrepreneurs and leaders. *The Journal of Business Strategy*, *31*(5), 49–58. doi:10.1108/02756661011076318

Drucker, P. (1985). *Innovation and entrepreneurship* (1st ed.). Harper Collins.

Drucker, P. (2015). *Innovation and entrepreneurship – Practice and Principles*. Routledge.

Du Toit, C. (2019). *On-boarding: A practical guide to creating extraordinary new employee experiences*. KR Publishing.

Duarte, T., & Ruiz, M. (2009). Emprendimiento, una opción para el desarrollo. *Scienta Et Technica*, *15*(43), 326–331.

Dunne, P., & Hughes, A. (1994). Age, size, growth and survival: UK companies in the 80s. *The Journal of Industrial Economics*, *42*(2), 115–140. doi:10.2307/2950485

Durnalı, M., Orakcı, Ş., & Aktan, O. (2019). The smart learning potential of Turkey's education system in the context of FATIH project. In A. Darshan Singh, S. Raghunathan, E. Robeck, & B. Sharma (Eds.), *Cases on Smart Learning Environments* (pp. 227–243). IGI Global. doi:10.4018/978-1-5225-6136-1.ch013

Early, G. (n.d.). A short history of leadership theories. *Leaders' Quest*. https://leadersquest.org/content/documents/A_short_history_of_leadership_theories.pdf

Eaton, S. E. (2020). Challenging and critiquing notions of servant leadership: Lessons from my mother. In *Women negotiating life in the academy* (pp. 15–23). Springer. doi:10.1007/978-981-15-3114-9_2

Echols, S. (2009). Transformation/servant leadership: A potential synergism for an inclusive leadership style. *Journal of Religious Leadership*, *8*(2), 85–116. http://arl-jrl.org/wp-content/uploads/2016/02/Echols-Transformational-Servant-Leadership-2009-Fall.pdf

Edelheim, J. (2020). How should tourism education values be transformed after 2020? *Tourism Geographies*, *22*(3), 547–554. doi:10.1080/14616688.2020.1760927

Eisenberger, R., Stinglhamber, F., Vandenberghe, C., Sucharski, L., & Rhoades, L. (2002, June). Perceived supervisor support: Contributions to perceived organizational support and employee retention. *The Journal of Applied Psychology*, *87*(3), 565–573. doi:10.1037/0021-9010.87.3.565 PMID:12090614

Eisenhardt, K. M., & Schoonhoven, C. B. (1990). Organizational growth: Linking founding team, strategy, environment, and growth among us semiconductor ventures, 1978-1988. *Administrative Science Quarterly*, *35*(3), 504–529. doi:10.2307/2393315

Eldor, L., & Vigoda-Gadot, E. (2017). The nature of employee engagement: Rethinking the employee–organization relationship. *International Journal of Human Resource Management*, *28*(3), 526–552. doi:10.1080/09585192.2016.1180312

Elliot, A. J., & Harackiewicz, J. M. (1996). Approach and avoidance achievement goals and intrinsic motivation: A meditational analysis. *Journal of Personality and Social Psychology*, *70*(3), 461–475. doi:10.1037/0022-3514.70.3.461

Empresate. (2011). *Emprender en Venezuela*. Retrieved from: https://www.empresate.org/

Englehardt, C. S., & Simmons, P. R. (2002). Creating an organizational space for learning. *The Learning Organization*, *9*(1), 39–47. doi:10.1108/09696470210414818

Etxeberria, M. E. A., & Pike, M. E. (2011). Implantación del aprendizaje basado en proyectos en el análisis de cuentas anuales. XXI Jornadas Hispano-Lusas Gestión Científica.

European Microfinance Network. (2012). *EMN study for Youth entrepreneurship*. European Microfinance Network.

European Microfinance Network. (2015). *European Good Practices in rural microfinance*. European Microfinance Network.

Evans, C. (2008). The effectiveness of m-learning in the form of podcast revision lectures in higher education. *Computers & Education*, *50*(2), 491–498. doi:10.1016/j.compedu.2007.09.016

Evans, C. (2013). Making Sense of Assessment Feedback in Higher Education. *Review of Educational Research*, *83*(1), 70–120. doi:10.3102/0034654312474350

Ewell, P. T. (1997). *Organizing for learning: A point of entry*. National Center for Higher Education Management Systems (NCHEMS).

Eyler, J., & Giles, D. E., Jr. (1999). Where's the Learning in Service-Learning? Jossey-Bass, Inc.

Falasca, M. (2011). Barriers to adult learning: Bridging the gap. *Australian Journal of Adult Learning*, *51*(3), 583–590.

Fal, M. (2013). Accelerating Entrepreneurship in Africa. *Innovations*, *8*(3/4).

Fawcett, S. B., Boothroyd, R., Schultz, J. A., Francisco, V. T., Carson, V., & Bremby, R. (2003). Building capacity for participatory evaluation within community initiatives. *Journal of Prevention & Intervention in the Community*, *26*(2), 21–36. doi:10.1300/J005v26n02_03

Felten, P., & Clayton, P. (2011). Service Learning. *New Directions for Teaching and Learning*, *128*(128), 75–84. doi:10.1002/tl.470

Fenabrave, I. C. D. P. (2019). *The Future of the Concessionaires' Business*. https://online.fliphtml5.com/ordey/wzhl/#p=1

Fernandez-Guerrero, R., Revuelto-Taboada, L., & Simon-Moy, V. (2012). The business plan as a project: An evaluation of its predictive capability for business success. *Service Industries Journal*, *32*(1), 2399–2420. doi:10.1080/02642069.2012.677830

Ferraro, G. P. (1994). *The cultural dimension of international business*. Prentice Hall.

Ferreri, S. P., & O'Connor, S. K. (2013). Redesign of a large lecture course into a small-group learning course. *American Journal of Pharmaceutical Education*, *77*(1), 13. doi:10.5688/ajpe77113 PMID:23459199

Fica, T. (2018). *The new definitive guide to onboarding*. Bamboo HR.

Figueroa-Rivera, A. N. (2016). *Antología de antropología social*. Unideal Universidad Matías Romero de Avendaño.

Finn, D. (2011). Principles of adult learning: An ESL context. *MPAEA Journal of Adult Education*, *40*(1), 34–39.

Flannery, M. J. (1986). Asymmetric Information and Risky Debt Maturity Choice. *The Journal of Finance*, *41*(1), 19–37. doi:10.1111/j.1540-6261.1986.tb04489.x

Flores, M. A., Veiga Simão, A. M., Barros, A., Flores, P., Pereira, D., Lopes Fernandes, E., Costa Ferreira, P., & Costa, L. (2021). Ensino e aprendizagem à distância em tempos de COVID-19: Um estudo com alunos do Ensino Superior. *Revista Portuguesa de Pedagogia*, *55*, e055001. doi:10.14195/1647-8614_55_1

Font, X., & Lynes, J. (2018). Corporate social responsibility in tourism and hospitality. *Journal of Sustainable Tourism*, *26*(7), 1027–1042. doi:10.1080/09669582.2018.1488856

Formichella, M. M. (2004). *El concepto de emprendimiento y su relación con la educación, el empleo y el desarrollo local*. Tres Arroyos.

Formoso, J., Jacubovich, S., Injoque-ricle, I., & Barreyro, J. P. (2018). Resolution of Arithmetic Problems, Processing Speed and Working Memory in Children. Trends in Psychology.

France-Harris, A., Burton, C., & Mooney, M. (2019). Putting Theory into Practice: Incorporating a Community Engagement Model into Online Pre-Professional Courses in Legal Studies and Human Resources Management. *Online Learning*, *23*(2), 21–39. doi:10.24059/olj.v23i2.1448

Franco, M., & Haase, H. (2010). Failure factors in small and medium-sized enterprises: Qualitative study from an attributional perspective. *The International Entrepreneurship and Management Journal*, *6*(4), 503–521. doi:10.100711365-009-0124-5

Freixo, M. (2010). *Metodologia científica, fundamentos, métodos e técnicas*. Instituto Piaget.

Fullerton, A., Reitenauer, V. L., & Kerrigan, S. M. (2015). A grateful recollecting: A qualitative study of the long-term impact of service-learning graduates. *Journal of Higher Education Outreach & Engagement*, *19*(2), 65–92.

Furze, J., Black, L., Peck, K., & Jensen, G. M. (2011). Student perceptions of a community engagement experience: Exploration of reflections on social responsibility and professional formation. *Physiotherapy Theory and Practice*, *27*(6), 411–421. doi:10.3109/09593985.2010.516479 PMID:20946070

Gaglio, C. M. (2004). The role of mental simulations and counterfactualthinking in the opportunity identification process. *Entrepreneurship Theory and Practice*, *28*(6), 533–552. doi:10.1111/j.1540 6520.2004.00063.x

Gallagher, J. M., & Reid, D. K. (1981). The learning theory of Piaget and Inhelder. Academic Press.

Gallien, T., & Oomen-Early, J. (2008). Personalized Versus Collective Instructor Feedback in the Online Courseroom: Does Type of Feedback Affect Student Satisfaction, Academic Performance and Perceived Connectedness With the Instructor? *International Journal on E-Learning*, *7*(3), 463–476. https://www.learntechlib.org/p/23582

Gallup, Inc. (2017). *State of the Global Workplace*. Gallup Press.

Gallup. (2007). *Gallup state of the American workplace report*. Gallup.

García-Canclini, N. (2004). *Diferentes, desiguales y desconectados: mapas de la interculturalidad*. Gedisa.

García-Contreras, R., Faletta, J. P., Krustchinsky, R., & Barnes, P. (2013). A Microcredit Program, a Math Education Initiative and Service-Learning: Matching a University's Mission to Greater Community Needs. *New Horizons in Education*, *61*(1), 11–22.

Gardiner, R. (2011). A critique of the discourse of authentic leadership. *International Journal of Business and Social Science*, *2*(15), 99–104.

Gardner, B. (1997). The controversy over service learning. *NEAToday*, *16*(2), 17–22.

Garrido, F. (2007). *Pensamiento estratégico: la estrategia como centro neurálgico de la empresa*. Editorial Deusto.

Garrison, D. R. (2007). Online Community Inquiry Review: Social, cognitive, and teaching presence issues. *Journal of Asynchronous Learning Networks*, *11*(1), 61–72. doi:10.24059/olj.v11i1.1737

Garrison, D. R. (2017). *E-learning in the 21st Century: A Community of Inquiry Framework for Research and Practice* (3rd ed.). Routledge.

Garrison, D. R., & Kanuka, H. (2004). Blended learning: Uncovering its transformative potential in higher education. *The Internet and Higher Education*, *7*(2), 95–105. doi:10.1016/j.iheduc.2004.02.001

Gegenfurtner, A., & Vauras, M. (2012). Age-related differences in the relation between motivation to learn and transfer of training in adult continuing education. *Contemporary Educational Psychology*, *37*(1), 33–46. doi:10.1016/j.cedpsych.2011.09.003

GEM. (2013). *GEM ANGOLA 2013 – Estudo sobre o empreendedorismo*. Global Entrepreneurship Monitor.

GEM. (n.d.). *Global Report, 2019/20*. London business School.

Gerard, V. (2019). Get on board with offboarding. *Association for Talent Development (ATD) Talent Development, 73*(7).

Getúlio Vargas Foundation IBRE. (2020, October 5) *The difficult resumption after falling: a magnifying glass on the Service Sector during the covid-19 pandemic.* https://blogdoibre.fgv.br/posts/dificil-retomada-apos-tombo-uma-lupa-sobre-o-setor-de-servicos-durante-pandemia-de-covid-19

Gião, R. (2018). *Financiamento das PME- Estudo de caso à Gomes, Sobral & Filhos, lda.* Dissertação de Mestrado manuscript. Instituto Politécnico de Setúbal.

Gil, A. (2002). Como elaborar projectos de pesquisa (4ª edição). São Paulo: Editora Atlas

Gil, A. C. (2008). Métodos e técnicas de pesquisa social (6ª edição). São Paulo: Editora Atlas.

Giles, D. Jr, & Eyler, J. (1998). A service learning research agenda for the next five years. *New Directions for Teaching and Learning*, *73*(73), 65–72. doi:10.1002/tl.7308

Gimeno, J., Folta, T., Cooper, A., & Woo, C. (1997). Survival of the fittest? Entrepreneurial human capital and the persistence of underperforming firms. *Administrative Science Quarterly*, *42*(4), 750–783. doi:10.2307/2393656

Godfrey, P. C., Illes, L. M., & Berry, G. R. (2005). Creating breadth in business education through service-learning. *Academy of Management Learning & Education*, *4*(3), 309–323. doi:10.5465/amle.2005.18122420

Goffee, R., & Jones, G. (2013). Creating the best workplace on earth. *Harvard Business Review*, *91*(5), 98–107. https://hbr.org/2013/05/creating-the-best-workplace-on-earth PMID:23898736

Goffi, G., Cucculelli, M., & Masiero, L. (2019). Fostering tourism destination competitiveness in developing countries: The role of sustainability. *Journal of Cleaner Production*, *209*, 101–115. doi:10.1016/j.jclepro.2018.10.208

Goldberg, L. R., McCormick Richburg, C., & Wood, L. A. (2006). Active learning through service-learning. *Communication Disorders Quarterly*, *27*(3), 131–145. doi:10.1177/15257401060270030201

Goleman, D. (2018). *What is emotional self-awareness?* Korn Ferry Hay Group. https://www.kornferry.com/insights/this-week-in-leadership/what-is-emotional-self-awareness-2019

Gomes, R. M., Brito, E., & Varela, A. (2016). Intervenção na formação no ensino superior: A aprendizagem baseada em problemas (PBL). *Interacções, 42*, 44-57. Retrieved 2021-12-09 from https://www.bing.com/search?q=Gomes%2C+R.M.%2CBrito%2C+E.+e+Varela%2C+A.%2C+2016%2C

Gonçalves, S. P., Sousa, M. J., & Pereira, F. S. (2020). Distance learning perceptions from higher education students—The case of Portugal. *Education Sciences, 10*(12), 374. Advance online publication. doi:10.3390/educsci10120374

Gorgievski, M. J., Ascalon, E. M., & Stephan, U. (2011). Small Business Owners' Success Criteria, a Values Approach to Personal Differences. *Journal of Small Business Management, 49*(2), 207–232. doi:10.1111/j.1540-627X.2011.00322.x

Gössling, S., Scott, D., & Hall, C. (2021). Pandemics, tourism and global change: A rapid assessment of COVID-19. *Journal of Sustainable Tourism, 29*(1), 1–20. doi:10.1080/09669582.2020.1758708

Govekar, M. A., & Rishi, M. (2007). Service learning: Bringing real-world education into the B-school classroom. *Journal of Education for Business, 83*(1), 3–10. doi:10.3200/JOEB.83.1.3-10

Graen, G. B., & Uhl-Bien, M. (1995). Relationship-based approach to leadership: Development of leader-member exchange (LMX) theory of leadership over 25 years: Applying a multi-level multi-domain perspective. *The Leadership Quarterly, 6*(2), 219–247. doi:10.1016/1048-9843(95)90036-5

Graesser, A. C. (2013). Evolution of advanced learning technologies in the 21st Century. *Theory into Practice, 52*, 93–101. doi:10.1080/00405841.2013.795446

Graybill, J. O., Hudson Carpenter, M. T., Offord, J., Piorun, M., & Shaffer, G. (2013). Employee onboarding: Identification of best practices in ACRL libraries. *Library Management; Bradford, 34*(3), 200–218. doi:10.1108/01435121311310897

Gray, M. J., Ondaatje, E. H., Fricker, R. D. Jr, & Geschwind, S. A. (2000). Assessing service-learning: Results from a survey of "Learn and serve America, Higher Education. *The Magazine of Higher Learning, 32*(2), 30–39. doi:10.1080/00091380009601721

Greenleaf, R. K. (1977). *Servant leadership: A journey into the nature of legitimate power and greatness*. Paulist Press.

Gretzel, U., Fuchs, M., Baggio, R., Hoepken, W., Law, R., Neidhardt, J., Pesonen, J., Zanker, M., & Xiang, Z. (2020). E-tourism beyond covid-19: A call for transformative research. *Information Technology & Tourism, 22*(2), 187–203. doi:10.100740558-020-00181-3

Grilo, E. M. (2020). *Não tenham medo do futuro. Ideias para o desenvolvimento de Portugal. As novas oportunidades e desafios do nosso país*. Clube do Autor.

Griner, L., Herron, P. J., & White, S. (2015). Study abroad partnerships: Librarians, business faculty, and in-country facilitator develop an innovative experiential learning program. *Journal of Business & Finance Librarianship, 20*(3), 189–208. doi:10.1080/08963568.2015.1046782

Guan, Y., Deng, H., & Zhou, X. (2020). Understanding the impact of the covid-19 pandemic on career development: Insights from cultural psychology. *Journal of Vocational Behavior, 119*, 103438. Advance online publication. doi:10.1016/j.jvb.2020.103438 PMID:32382162

Guerra-García, E. (2004). La sociointerculturalidad y la educación indígena. In *Cuestión étnica, culturas, construcción de identidades*. México: Universidad Autónoma Indígena de México, Asociación Latinoamericana de Sociología y ediciones el Caracol.

Guerra-García, E., Caro-Dueñas, M. A., & Corrales-Baldenebro, A. L. (2020). Dinámica sociointercultural del surgimiento del puerto de Topolobampo en México. *Revista CoPaLa, Construyendo Paz Latinoamericana, 10*(5), 102-125. Retrieved from http://revistacopala.net/index.php/ojs/article/view/22

Guerra-García, E. (2005). La Anerogogía de la Voluntad, propuesta educativa sociointercultural de la Universidad Autónoma Indígena de México. *Ra Ximhai*, *1*(1), 15–38. doi:10.35197/rx.01.01.2005.02.EG

Gujarathi, M. R., & McQuade, R. J. (2002). Service-learning in business schools: A case study in an intermediate accounting course. *Journal of Education for Business*, *77*(3), 144–150. doi:10.1080/08832320209599063

Gunawardena, C. N., & Zittle, F. J. (1997). Social presence as a predictor of satisfaction within a computer-mediated conferencing environment. *American Journal of Distance Education*, *11*(3), 8–26. doi:10.1080/08923649709526970

Gupta, S., & Mahajan, T. (2012). An analytical study of drivers of employee engagement among executives of a manufacturing organization with special reference to handicraft industry in the Moradabad region. *Saaransh RKG Journal of Management*, *3*(2), 87–92.

Guri-Rosenblit, S. (2005). "Distance education" and "e-learning": Not the same thing. *Higher Education*, *49*(4), 467–493. doi:10.100710734-004-0040-0

Gustafson, S., & Khandker. (2016). *How microfinance has reduced rural poverty in Bangladesh*. IFPRI.

Gyensare, M., Arthur, R., Twumasi, E., & Agyapong, J.-A. (2019). Leader effectiveness – the missing link in the relationship between employee voice and engagement. *Cogent Business & Management*, *6*(1), 1–20. doi:10.1080/23311975.2019.1634910

Haber, S., & Reichel, A. (2005). Identifying performance measures of small ventures – the case of the tourism industry. *Journal of Small Business Management*, *43*(3), 257–286. doi:10.1111/j.1540-627X.2005.00137.x

Hadar, L. L., Ergas, O., Alpert, B., & Ariav, T. (2020). Rethinking teacher education in a VUCA world: Student teachers' social-emotional competencies during the Covid-19 crisis. *European Journal of Teacher Education*, *43*(4), 573–586. doi:10.1080/02619768.2020.1807513

Hai-Jew, S. (2014). *Iff and other conditionals: Expert perceptions of the feasibility of massive open online courses (MOOCs) - A modified E-Delphi study*. IGI-Global. doi:10.4018/978-1-4666-5137-1.ch013

Hale, J., & Granny, J. (2020). *How to get people to actually participate in virtual meetings*. https://hbr.org/2020/03/how-to-get-people-to-actually-participate-in-virtual-meetings

Hallak, D. (2016). Take control of your new job: Proactive development and onboarding success. Academic Press.

Hall, C. (2019). Constructing sustainable tourism development: The 2030 agenda and the managerial ecology of sustainable tourism. *Journal of Sustainable Tourism*, *27*(7), 1044–1060. doi:10.1080/09669582.2018.1560456

Hall, H., & Davison, B. (2007). Social software as support in hybrid learning environments: The value of the blog as a tool for reflective learning and peer support. *Library & Information Science Research*, *29*(2), 163–187. doi:10.1016/j.lisr.2007.04.007

Hall, M., Scott, D., & Gössling, S. (2020). Pandemics, transformations and tourism: Be careful what you wish for. *Tourism Geographies*, *22*(3), 577–598. doi:10.1080/14616688.2020.1759131

Hansen, J. D. (2006). Using problem-based learning in accounting. *Journal of Education for Business*, *81*(4), 221–224. doi:10.3200/JOEB.81.4.221-224

Harding, R. (2006). *Social Entrepreneurship Monitor*. London Global Entrepreneurship Monitor. Retrieved from https://scholar.google.com/citations?user=IKAsBdIAAAAJ&hl=en

Hardin-Ramanan, S., Soupramanien, L. D. B., & DeLapeyre, D. (2018). Project# NuKapav: A Mauritian service-learning case study. *Equality, Diversity and Inclusion*, *37*(2), 167–181. doi:10.1108/EDI-01-2017-0008

Harper, T. (2015, July 16). *Leadership types of power* [Video]. YouTube. https://www.youtube.com/watch?v=2jW1batb_pM&feature=youtu.be

Harter, J. (2018, August 26). Employee engagement on the rise in the U.S. (Survey). *Gallup Poll News Service.* https://news.gallup.com/poll/241649/employee-engagement-rise.aspx

Harter, J. K., Schmidt, F. L., & Hayes, T. L. (2002). Business-unit-level relationship between employee satisfaction, employee engagement, and business outcomes: A meta-analysis. *The Journal of Applied Psychology, 87*(2), 268–279. doi:10.1037/0021-9010.87.2.268 PMID:12002955

Harter, S. (2002). Authenticity. In C. R. Snyder & S. J. Lopez (Eds.), *Handbook of positive psychology* (pp. 382–394). Oxford University Press.

Hashim, K. F., Tan, F. B., & Rashid, A. (2015). Adult learners' intention to adopt mobile learning: A motivational perspective. *British Journal of Educational Technology, 46*(2), 381–390. doi:10.1111/bjet.12148

Hassan, A., & Ahmed, F. (2011). Authentic leadership, trust and work engagement. *International Journal of Humanities and Social Science, 6*(3), 164–170.

Hayton, J. C., George, G., & Zahra, S. A. (2002). National culture and entrepreneurship: A review of behavioral Research. *Entrepreneurship Theory and Practice, 26*(4), 33–52. doi:10.1177/104225870202600403

Headd, B. (2003). Redefining business success: Distinguishing between closure and failure. *Small Business Economics, 21*(1), 51–61. doi:10.1023/A:1024433630958

Hegarty, N. (2011). Adult learners as graduate students: Underlying motivation in completing graduate programs. *The Journal of Continuing Higher Education, 59*(3), 146–151. doi:10.1080/07377363.2011.614883

Hernández, R. (2012). Does continuous assessment in higher education support student learning? *Higher Education, 64*(4), 489–502. doi:10.100710734-012-9506-7

Higgins-Desbiolles, F., Carnicelli, S., Krolikowski, C., Wijesinghe, G., & Boluk, K. (2019). Degrowing tourism: Rethinking tourism. *Journal of Sustainable Tourism, 27*(12), 1926–1944. doi:10.1080/09669582.2019.1601732

Hitt, M., & Ireland, D. (2000). The intersection of entrepreneurship and strategic management research. In D. Sexton & H. Landström (Eds.), *Handbook of entrepreneurship* (pp. 45–63). Blackwell.

Hodges, C., Moore, S., Lockee, B., Trust, T., & Bond, A. (2020). The difference between emergency remote teaching and online learning. *Educause Review.* https://er.educause.edu/articles/2020/3/the-difference-between-emergency-remote-teaching-and-online-learning

Hofstede, G. (2007). *Geert Hofstede Cultural Dimensions.* Retrieved 11/23/2007 from www.geert-hofstede.com

Hofstede, G. (2001). *Cultures and Organizations. Software of the Mind.* McGraw-Hill.

Holmberg, B. (1997). Distance-education theory again. *Open Learning, 12*(1), 31–39. doi:10.1080/0268051970120105

Honeycutt, B. (2016). *Flip the first 5 minutes of class: 50 focusing activities to engage your students.* Flip It Consulting.

Honicke, T., & Broadbent, J. (2016). The influence of academic self-efficacy on academic performance: A systematic review. *Educational Research Review, 17*, 63–84. doi:10.1016/j.edurev.2015.11.002

Hood, S., Barrickman, N., Djerdjian, N., Farr, M., Magner, S., Roychowdhury, H., Gerrits, R., Lawford, H., Ott, B., Ross, K., Paige, O., Stowe, S., Jensen, M., & Hull, K. (2021). "I Like and Prefer to Work Alone": Social Anxiety, Academic Self-Efficacy, and Students' Perceptions of Active Learning. *CBE Life Sciences Education*, *20*(1), ar12. doi:10.1187/cbe.19-12-0271 PMID:33600218

House, R., Hanges, P., Javidan, M., & Dorfman, P. (2004). *Culture, Leadership and Organizations: the GLOBE Study of 62 Societies*. Sage Publications.

Ho, Y., & Wong, P. (2007). Financing, regulatory costs and entrepreneurial propensity. *Small Business Economics*, *28*(2), 187–204. doi:10.100711187-006-9015-0

Hrastinski, S. (2019). What Do We Mean by Blended Learning? *TechTrends*, *63*(5), 564–569. doi:10.100711528-019-00375-5

Hsia, J.-W., Chang, C. C., & Tseng, A. H. (2014). Effects of individuals' locus of control and computer self-efficacy on their e-learning acceptance in high-tech companies. *Behaviour & Information Technology*, *33*(1), 51–64. doi:10.1080/0144929X.2012.702284

Hsiao, S. W., & Chou, J. R. (2004). A creativity-based design process for innovative product design. *International Journal of Industrial Ergonomics*, *34*(5), 421–443. doi:10.1016/j.ergon.2004.05.005

Hsu, C. H. C., Xiao, H., & Chen, N. (2017). Hospitality and tourism education research from 2005 to 2014: "Is the past a prologue to the future? *International Journal of Contemporary Hospitality Management*, *29*(1), 141–160. doi:10.1108/IJCHM-09-2015-0450

Huang, C. K., & Lin, C. Y. (2017). Flipping business education: Transformative use of team-based learning in human resource management classrooms. *Journal of Educational Technology & Society*, *20*(1), 323–336.

Hubackova, S., & Semradova, I. (2014). Research study on motivation in adult education. *Procedia: Social and Behavioral Sciences*, *159*, 396–400. doi:10.1016/j.sbspro.2014.12.395

Hubbs, D. L., & Brand, C. F. (2005). The paper mirror: Understanding reflective journaling. *Journal of Experiential Education*, *28*(1), 60–71. doi:10.1177/105382590502800107

Huggins, R. (2000). The success and failure of policy-implanted inter-firm network initiatives: Motivations, processes and structure. *Entrepreneurship and Regional Development*, *12*(2), 211–236. doi:10.1080/089856200283036

Hull, R. B., Kimmel, C., Robertson, D. P., & Mortimer, M. (2016). International field experiences promote professional development for sustainability leaders. *International Journal of Sustainability in Higher Education*, *17*(1), 86–104. doi:10.1108/IJSHE-07-2014-0105

Hulme, D., & Moore, K. (2007). Why has Microfinance been a Policy Success in Bangladesh? In A. Bebbington & W. McCourt (Eds.), *Development Success*. Palgrave Macmillan. doi:10.1057/9780230223073_5

Hung, H.-T. (2017). The Integration of a Student Response System in Flipped Classrooms. *Language Learning & Technology*, *21*(1), 16–27.

Hussain, A. (2019). Disciplining Microfinance Borrowers in Bangladesh. *Social Change*, *49*(3), 453–468. doi:10.1177/0049085719863890

IAPMEI. (2006). *PME na Estrutura Empresarial Nacional*. www.iapmei.pt

Ide, C., & Thomas, T. (2011). Business students' experience of community service learning. *International Journal of Work-Integrated Learning*, *12*(1), 51–66.

IFC. (2014). *CASE STUDY Garanti Bank SA: Combining SME Banking Excellence with a Proposition for Women Entrepreneurs in Turkey*. World Bank.

IFC. (2020). *Microfinance*. Available on: www1.ifc.org

IIPM. (2006). Case Study on SIDBI – A Successful Financial Institution in SME Financing. Indian Institute of Planning and Management (IIPM) Ahmedabad.

Iliev, I., & Stoyanova, T. (2017). Employee engagement factor for organizational excellence. *International Journal of Business and Economic Sciences Applied Research*, *10*(1), 23–29. doi:10.25103/ijbesar.101.03

Infomoney. (2020, May 19). *The impact of COVID-19 on vehicle sales by state*. https://www.infomoney.com.br/colunistas/o-mundo-sobre-muitas-rodas/o-impacto-do-covid-19-nas-vendas-de-veiculos-por-estado/

Instituto Politécnico de Portalegre. (2020). *Ensino a Distância no Politécnico de Portalegre. Resultados do questionário dirigido aos estudantes*. Relatório final, Observatório Académico, Portalegre: Dezembro.

International Association of Universities & Erasmus Student Network. (2020). *Joint paper: IAU and ESN COVID-19 impact on Higher Education: Institutionak and Students' Perspectives*. Consultado em 18 de novembro de 2021 em https://www.iau-aiu.net/IMG/pdf/joint_paper_iau_and_esn_-_institutional_and_students_perspectives_of_covid-19_impact_on_higher_education.pdf

International Association of Universities. (2020). *Regional/National Perspectives on the Impacto of COVID-19 on Higher Education*. Consultado em 18 de novembro de 2021 em https://www.iau-aiu.net/IMG/pdf/iau_covid-19_regional_perspectives_on_the_impact_of_covid-19_on_he_july_2020_.pdf

Izagirre-Olaizola, J., & Morandeira-Arca, J. (2020). Business management teaching–learning processes in times of pandemic: Flipped classroom at a distance. *Sustainability (Switzerland)*, *12*(23), 1–18. doi:10.3390u122310137

Jacoby, B. (1996). *Service-Learning in Higher Education: Concepts and Practices*. The Jossey-Bass Higher and Adult Education Series. Jossey-Bass Publishers.

Jacoby, B. (2014). *Service-learning essentials: Questions, answers, and lessons learned*. John Wiley & Sons.

Jaén, I., Fernandez-Serrano, J., & Liñan, F. (2013). Valores culturales, nivel de ingresos y actividad emprendedora. *Revista de Economía Mundial*, *35*, 35–52.

Jarillo, J. (1988). On strategic networks. *Strategic Management Journal*, *9*(1), 31–41. doi:10.1002mj.4250090104

Jenkins, A., & Sheehey, P. (2012). A Checklist for Implementing Service-Learning in Higher Education. *Journal of Community Engagement and Scholarship*, *4*(2), 52–60.

Jia, C., Hew, K. F., Bai, S., & Huang, W. (2021). Adaptation of a conventional flipped course to an online flipped format during the Covid-19 pandemic: Student learning performance and engagement. *Journal of Research on Technology in Education*, 1–21. doi:10.1080/15391523.2020.1847220

Johnson-Mallard, V., Jones, R., Coffman, M., Gauda, J., Deming, K., Pacheco, M., & Campbell, J. (2019). The Robert Wood Johnson nurse faculty scholars diversity and inclusion research. *Health Equity*, *3*(1), 297–303. doi:10.1089/heq.2019.0026 PMID:31289788

Johnson, N., Veletsianos, G., & Seaman, J. (2020). U.S. faculty and administrators' experiences and approaches in the early weeks of the COVID-19 pandemic. *Online Learning Journal*, *24*(2), 6–21. doi:10.24059/olj.v24i2.2285

Jones, A. (2010). Generic attributes in accounting: The significance of the disciplinary context. *Accounting Education*, *19*(1-2), 5–21. doi:10.1080/09639280902875523

Jones, A. R. (2013). Increasing adult learner motivation for completing self-directed e-learning. *Performance Improvement, 52*(7), 32–42. doi:10.1002/pfi.21361

Jones, P., Pickernell, D., Fisher, R., & Netana, C. (2017). A Tale of Two Universities: Graduates Perceived Value of Entrepreneurship Education. *Education + Training, 59*(7/8), 689–705. doi:10.1108/ET-06-2017-0079

Jonsen, K., Maznevski, M. L., & Schneider, S. C. (2011). Diversity and its not so diverse literature: An international perspective. *International Journal of Cross Cultural Management, 11*(1), 35–62. doi:10.1177/1470595811398798

Jung-beeman, M., Bowden, E. M., Haberman, J., Frymiare, J. L., Arambel-Liu, S., Greenblatt, R., Reber, P. J., & Kounios, J. (2004). Neural activity when people solve verbal problems with insight. *PLoS Biology, 4*(2), 97. doi:10.1371/journal.pbio.0020097 PMID:15094802

Kahn, W. A. (1990). Psychological conditions of personal engagement and disengagement at work. *Academy of Management Journal, 33*(4), 692–724. doi:10.2307/256287

Kallou, S., & Kikilia, A. (2021). A transformative educational framework in tourism higher education through digital technologies during the COVID-19 pandemic. *Advances in Mobile Learning Educational Research, 1*(1), 37–47. doi:10.25082/AMLER.2021.01.005

Kamau, K. (2011). *Factors influencing SMEs access to finance: A case study of Westland Division, Kenya.* Munich Personal RePEc Archive.

Kandel, E. (2014) Principles of Neuroscience (5th ed.). McGraw Hill.

Kandel, E. (2014). *Principles of Neuroscience*. MCGRAW Hill.

Kandel, E. (2014). Principles of Neuroscience. McGraw-Hill.

Kane, A., Marcus, A., & McDonald, R. L. (1985). Debt Policy and the Rate of Return Premium to Leverage. *Journal of Financial and Quantitative Analysis, 20*(4), 479–499. doi:10.2307/2330763

Karairmak, Ö. (2010). Establishing the psychometric qualities of the Connor-Davidson Resilience Scale (CD-RISC) using exploratory and confirmatory factor analysis in a trauma survivor sample. *Psychiatry Research, 179*(3), 350–356. doi:10.1016/j.psychres.2009.09.012 PMID:20493533

Karambelkar, M., & Bhattacharya, S. (2017). Onboarding is a change: Applying change management model ADKAR to onboarding. *Human Resource Management International Digest, 25*(7), 5–8. doi:10.1108/HRMID-04-2017-0073

Karkockiene, D. (2005). *Creativity: Can it be trained? A Scientific Educology of Creativity. International Journal of Educology.*

Karlsson, T., & Honig, B. (2009). Judging a business by its cover: An institutional perspective on new ventures and the business plan. *Journal of Business Venturing, 24*(1), 27–45. doi:10.1016/j.jbusvent.2007.10.003

Kaye, B., & Jordan-Evans, S. (2014). *Love 'em or lose 'em: Getting good people to stay.* Berrett-Koehler Publishers, Incorporated. https://ebookcentral.proquest.com/lib/bayloru/detail.action?docID=1407851

Kaye, B. L., & Jordan-Evans, S. (1999). *Love 'em or lose 'em: Getting good people to stay.* Berrett-Koehler.

Kay, R., MacDonald, T., & DiGiuseppe, M. (2019). A comparison of lecture-based, active, and flipped classroom teaching approaches in higher education. *Journal of Computing in Higher Education, 31*(3), 449–471. doi:10.100712528-018-9197-x

Keegan, D. (1986). *The foundations of distance education.* Croom Helm /Routledge.

Keegan, D. J. (1980). On defining distance education. *Distance Education, 1*(1), 13–36. doi:10.1080/0158791800010102

Kenworthy, A. L. (1996). Linking business education, campus culture and community: The Bentley service-learning project. *Journal of Business Ethics*, *15*(1), 121–131. doi:10.1007/BF00380268

Khan, Z. A., Nawaz, A., & Khan, I. (2016). Leadership theories and styles: A literature review. *Journal of Resources Development and Management*, 16.

Khan, J., Jaafar, M., Javed, B., Mubarak, N., & Saudagar, T. (2020). Does inclusive leadership affect project success? The mediating role of perceived psychological empowerment and psychological safety. *International Journal of Managing Projects in Business*, *13*(5), 1077–1096. doi:10.1108/IJMPB-10-2019-0267

Kidd, W., & Murray, J. (2020). The Covid-19 pandemic and its effects on teacher education in England: How teacher educators moved practicum learning online. *European Journal of Teacher Education*, *43*(4), 542–558. doi:10.1080/02619768.2020.1820480

Kiely, R. (2005). A transformative learning model for service-learning: A longitudinal case study. *Michigan Journal of Community Service Learning*, *12*(1), 5–22.

Killian, S., Lannon, J., Murray, L., Avram, G., Giralt, M., & O'Riordan, S. (2019). Social Media for Social Good: Student engagement for the SDGs. *International Journal of Management Education*, *17*(3), 100307. doi:10.1016/j.ijme.2019.100307

Kim, B., Kim, H., & Jeon, Y. (2018). Critical Success Factors of a Design Startup Business. *Sustainability*, *10*(9), 29–81. doi:10.3390u10092981

Kim, J. (2020). Learning and Teaching Online During Covid-19: Experiences of student teachers in an early childhood education practicum. *International Journal of Early Childhood*, *52*(2), 145–158. doi:10.100713158-020-00272-6 PMID:32836369

Kim, Y. (1989). Intercultural Adaptation. In M. K. Asante & W. Gudykunst (Eds.), *Handbook of International and Intercultural Communication* (pp. 275–294). Sage.

Kincade, D. H., & Gibson, F. Y. (2012). Retail Classroom Meets Business Practice through a Service-Learning Component. *Journal of Textile and Apparel, Technology and Management*, *7*(3), 1-14. Recuperado de: https://ojs.cnr.ncsu.edu/index.php/JTATM/article/view/2044/1408

King, K. P. (2012). Social Media as Positive Disruption in Education, E Learning and B Learning. In *Handbook of Research on Business Social Networking*. IGI Global. doi:10.4018/978-1-61350-168-9.ch023

Kirschner, P. A., van den Brink, H., & Meester, M. (1991). Audiotape feedback for essays in distance education. *Innovative Higher Education*, *15*(2), 185–195. doi:10.1007/BF00898030

Kiss, A. N., Danis, W. N., & Cavusgil, S. T. (2012). International entrepreneurship research in emerging economies: A critical review and research agenda. *Journal of Business Venturing*, *27*(2), 266–290. doi:10.1016/j.jbusvent.2011.09.004

Knowles, M. (1970). Andragogy, not pedagogy! In S. M. Grabowski (Ed.), *Adult learning and instruction* (pp. 71–80). Adult Education Association of the U.S.A.

Knowles, M. (1973). *The adult learner: A neglected species*. Gulf Publishing Company.

Knowles, M. (1977). Adult learning processes: Pedagogy and andragogy. *Religious Education (Chicago, Ill.)*, *72*(2), 202–211. doi:10.1080/0034408770720210

Knowles, M. (2016). Andragogy: Adult learning theory in perspective. *Community College Review*, *5*(3), 9–20. doi:10.1177/009155217800500302

Knowles, M., Holton, E. F., & Swanson, R. A. (2005). *The adult learner: The definitive classic in adult education and human resource development* (6th ed.). Elsevier. doi:10.4324/9780080481913

Kokubun, K. (2017). Education, organizational commitment, and rewards within Japanese manufacturing companies in China. *Employee Relations*, *40*(3), 458–485. doi:10.1108/ER-12-2016-0246

Kolb, D. A. (1984). *Experiential Learning*. Prentice Hall.

Kolenko, T. A., Porter, G., Wheatley, W., & Colby, M. (1996). A critique of service learning projects in management education: Pedagogical foundations, barriers, and guidelines. *Journal of Business Ethics*, *15*(1), 133–142. doi:10.1007/BF00380269

Kong, X., Si, D., Li, H. & Kong, D. (2021). Does access to credit reduce SMEs' tax avoidance? Evidence from a regression discontinuity design. *Financial Innovation*, *7*(18).

Koontz, H., Weihrich, H., & Cannice, M. (2008). *Administración una perspectiva global y empresarial*. McGraw-Hill Interamericana.

Korner, P. (2006). *The determinants of corporate debt maturity structure: Evidence from Czech firms*. Czech *Journal of Economics and Finance*. Charles University Prague.

Kornis, G. (2013). *Culture in thought (and in action) by Celso Furtado: Development, creativity, tradition and innovation*. CEBRAP.

Kotlyar, I., & Karakowsky, L. (2007). Falling over ourselves to follow the leader: Conceptualizing connections between transformational leader behaviors and dysfunctional team conflict. *Journal of Leadership & Organizational Studies*, *14*(1), 38–49. doi:10.1177/1071791907304285

Kotter, J. P. (2012). *Leading change*. Harvard Business Review Press. https://books.google.com/books?id=xpGX1EWL_EMC

Kouninef, B., Tlemsani, R., Rerbal, S. M., & Lotfi, A. (2012, July). LMS INTTIC system using mobile technology and podcasting in blended learning. *International Conference on Education and E-Learning Innovations*. 10.1109/ICEELI.2012.6360593

Kramer, M. R. (2005). *Measuring innovation: evaluation in the field of social entrepreneurship*. A Publication for Skoll Foundation by Foundation Strategy Group. Retrieves form https://community-wealth.org/content/measuring-innovation-evaluation-field-social-entrepreneurship

Krasman, M. (2015). Three must-have onboarding elements for new and relocated employees. *Employment Relations Today*, *42*(2), 9–14. doi:10.1002/ert.21493

Krausz, M., & Reshef, M. (1992). Managerial job change: Reasons for leaving, choice determinants, and search processes. *Journal of Business and Psychology*, *6*(3), 349–359. doi:10.1007/BF01126770

Kristiansen, S., Furuholt, B., & Wahid, F. (2003). Internet cafe entrepreneurs: Pioneers in information dissemination in Indonesia. *International Journal of Entrepreneurship and Innovation*, *4*(4), 251–263. doi:10.5367/000000003129574315

Kundel, S. W. (1991). *El impacto de la estructura de la estrategia y de la industria en nuevo funcionamiento de la empresa* (Doctoral Dissertatión). University of Georgia Dissertation Abstracts International.

la Velle, L., Newman, S., Montgomery, C., & Hyatt, D. (2020). Initial teacher education in England and the Covid-19 pandemic: Challenges and opportunities. *Journal of Education for Teaching*, *46*(4), 596–608. Advance online publication. doi:10.1080/02607476.2020.1803051

Lage, M. J., Platt, G. J., & Treglia, M. (2000). Inverting the classroom: A gateway to creating an inclusive learning environment. *The Journal of Economic Education, 31*(1), 30–43. doi:10.1080/00220480009596759

Lahiri, I. (2008). *Creating a competency model for diversity and inclusion.* The Conference Board Council on Workforce Diversity. https://www.conference-board.org/pdf_free/councils/TCBCP005.pdf

Lalicic, L., & Weber-Sabil, J. (2020). Stakeholder engagement in sustainable tourism planning through serious gaming. *Tourism Geographies, 23*(1), 185–205. doi:10.1080/14616688.2019.1648543

Lamb, C. H., Swinth, R. L., Vinton, K. L., & Lee, J. B. (1998). Integrating service learning into a business school curriculum. *Journal of Management Education, 22*(5), 637–654. doi:10.1177/105256299802200506

Le Bris, S., Madrid-Guijarro, A., & Martin, D. P. (2019). Decision-making in complex environments under time pressure and risk of critical irreversibility: The role of meta rules. *Management, 22*(1), 1–29.

Leadbeater, C. (2007). *Social enterprise and social innovation: strategies for the next ten years.* Cabinet Office of the Third Sector. Available from: http://www.charlesleadbeater.net/cms/xstandard/social_enterprise_innovation.pdf

Leahey, T. H., Greer, S., Lefrancois, G. R., Reiner, T. W., Spencer, J. L., Wickramasekera, I. E., & Willmarth, E. K. (2014). *History of psychology.* Bridgepoint Education.

Lear, G. (2016, February 18). *The cost of low employee engagement continues to increase.* http://resourcedevelopment-systems.com/seblog/2016/02/the-cost-of-low-employee-engagement-continues-to-increase/

Lee, M. (2017). Interrogating authentic leadership: Identity does matter. *Advances in Developing Human Resources, 19*(4), 347–349. doi:10.1177/1523422317728730

Lee, M. T., & Raschke, R. L. (2016). Understanding employee motivation and organizational performance: Arguments for a set-theoretic approach. *Journal of Innovation & Knowledge, 1*(3), 162–169. doi:10.1016/j.jik.2016.01.004

Leffa, V. J. (1988). Methodology of language teaching. In Topics in applied linguistics: the teaching of foreign languages. UFSC.

Leland, H., & Pyle, D. (1977). Informational Asymmetries, Financial Structure and Financial Intermediation. *The Journal of Finance, 32*(2), 371–387. doi:10.2307/2326770

LePine, J. A., LePine, M. A., & Jackson, C. L. (2004). Challenge and hindrance stress: Relationships with exhaustion, motivation to learn, and learning performance. *The Journal of Applied Psychology, 89*(5), 883–891. doi:10.1037/0021-9010.89.5.883 PMID:15506867

Liburd, J., Hjalager, A. M., & Christensen, I. M. F. (2011). Valuing tourism education 2.0. *Journal of Teaching in Travel & Tourism, 11*(1), 107–130. doi:10.1080/15313220.2011.548745

Li, K., Hall, M., Bermell-Garcia, P., Alcock, J., Tiwari, A., & González-Franco, M. (2017). Measuring the learning effectiveness of serious gaming for training of complex manufacturing tasks. *Simulation & Gaming, 48*(6), 770–790. doi:10.1177/1046878117739929

Liker, J., & Meier, D. (2006). *The Toyota Way fieldbook: A practical guide for implementing Toyota's 4ps.* McGraw-Hill.

Lillo-Bañuls, A., Perles-Ribes, J. F., & Fuentes, R. (2016). Wiki and blog as teaching tools in tourism higher education. *Journal of Teaching in Travel & Tourism, 16*(2), 81–100. doi:10.1080/15313220.2015.1118367

Lim, M. (2020). *Educating despite the Covid-19 outbreak: Lessons from Singapore.* The World University Rankings. Consultado em 18 de novembro de 2021 em https://www.timeshighereducation.com/blog/educating-despite-covid-19-outbreak-lessons-singapore

Lin, C. Y., Huang, C. K., & Ko, C. J. (2020). The impact of perceived enjoyment on team effectiveness and individual learning in a blended learning business course: The mediating effect of knowledge sharing. *Australasian Journal of Educational Technology*, *36*(1), 126–141. doi:10.14742/ajet.4446

Littlefield, H. (2006). Service learning in business communication: Real-world challenges develop real-world skills. *Business Communication Quarterly*, *69*(3), 319–322. doi:10.1177/108056990606900311

Llarena, M. (2013). How not to lose your new employees in their first 45 days. *Forbes*. https://www.forbes.com/sites/85broads/2013/07/19/how-not-to-lose-your-new-employees-in-their-first-45-days/#ff6e9a33be35

Lobos, J. (1993). *Charming Customer: External and Internal* (9th ed.). Hamburg Publishing House.

Lopes, A. P., & Soares, F. (2018). Perception and performance in a flipped Financial Mathematics classroom. *International Journal of Management Education*, *16*(1), 105–113. doi:10.1016/j.ijme.2018.01.001

López-García, P., & Puente, S. (2006, April). Rasgos básicos de la supervivencia de empresas en España. *Boletín Económico del Banco de España*.

Lopez, M. (2009). Incorporating service-learning into the economics curriculum. *The Review of Black Political Economy*, *36*(2), 137–149. doi:10.100712114-009-9040-8

López-Núñez, M. I., Rubio-Valdehita, S., Aparicio-García, M. E., & Díaz-Ramiro, E. M. (2020). Are entrepreneurs born or made? The influence of personality. *Personality and Individual Differences*, 154.

López-Pérez, M. V., Pérez-López, M. C., & Rodríguez-Ariza, L. (2011). Blended learning in higher education: Students' perceptions and their relation to outcomes. *Computers & Education*, *56*(3), 818–826. doi:10.1016/j.compedu.2010.10.023

Lounsbury, M., & Glynn, M. A. (2001). Cultural entrepreneurship: Stories, legitimacy, and the acquisition of resources. *Strategic Management Journal*, *22*(6-7), 545–564. doi:10.1002mj.188

Luca, P., & Presutti, M. (2010). The impact of social capital on the start-ups performance growth. *Journal of Small Business Management*, *48*(2), 197–227. doi:10.1111/j.1540-627X.2010.00292.x

Lugosi, P., & Jameson, S. (2017). Challenges in hospitality management education: Perspectives from the United Kingdom. *Journal of Hospitality and Tourism Management*, *31*, 163–172. doi:10.1016/j.jhtm.2016.12.001

Lukianova, L. (2016). Motivation factors of adult learning. *The New Educational Review*, *44*(1), 223–229. doi:10.15804/tner.2016.44.2.18

Luk, S. (1996). Success in Hong Kong: Factors self-reported by successful small business owners. *Journal of Small Business Management*, *34*(3), 68–75.

Lumpkin, G. T., & Dess, G. G. (1996). Clarifying the entrepreneurial orientation construct and linking it to performance. *Academy of Management Review*, *21*(1), 135–172. doi:10.2307/258632

Luppi, E. (2011). Training to education for sustainable development through e-learning. *Procedia: Social and Behavioral Sciences*, *15*, 3244–3251. doi:10.1016/j.sbspro.2011.04.279

Ma, Q. K., Mayfield, M., & Mayfield, J. (2018). Keep them on-board! How organizations can develop employee embeddedness to increase employee retention. *Development and Learning in Organizations; Bradford*, *32*(4), 5–9. doi:10.1108/DLO-11-2017-0094

Madriz, E. (2000). Focus groups in feminist research. Handbook of Qualitative Research, 2, 835-850.

Madsen, S. R. (2004). Academic service learning in human resource management education. *Journal of Education for Business, 79*(6), 328–332. doi:10.3200/JOEB.79.6.328-332

Madsen, S. R., & Turnbull, O. (2006). Academic service learning experiences of compensation and benefit course students. *Journal of Management Education, 30*(5), 724–742. doi:10.1177/1052562905283710

Magembe, Y. (2017). Credit Access by Small and Medium Enterprises in Tanzania: A Case Study of Dar es Salaam City. *International Journal of Economics & Management Sciences, 6*(5), 1–9. doi:10.4172/2162-6359.1000459

Mahan, J. D., & Stein, D. S. (2014). Teaching adults: Best practices that leverage the emerging understanding of the neurobiology of learning. *Current Problems in Pediatric and Adolescent Health Care, 44*(6), 141–149. doi:10.1016/j.cppeds.2014.01.003 PMID:24981663

Maher, M. W. (2000). Management Accounting Education at the Millennium. *Issues in Accounting Education, 15*(2), 335–346. Advance online publication. doi:10.2308/iace.2000.15.2.335

Mair, J., & Martí, I. (2006). Social entrepreneurship research: A source of explanations, prediction, and delight. *Journal of World Business, 41*(1), 36–44. doi:10.1016/j.jwb.2005.09.002

Major, C. (2020). Innovations in Teaching and Learning during a Time of Crisis. *Innovative Higher Education, 45*(4), 265–266. doi:10.100710755-020-09514-w PMID:32836726

Maldonado, K. (2007). La interculturalidad de los negocios internacionales. *Universidad Empresa Bogotá (Colombia), 6*(12), 261–291.

Malone, T. W. (2018). *Superminds: The Surprising Power of People and Computers Thinking Together*. Little, Brown Spark.

Mancuso, L. C., Alijani, G. S., Kwun, O., & Smith, L. D. (2009). Successful outcomes of teaching minority undergraduate students entrepreneurial business planning concepts using andragogy and service learning. Academy of Entrepreneurship, 15(1), 33.

Mannelly, P. K. (2008). *Managing highly engaged or actively disengaged employees: A phenomenological study of first-level supervisors* (Publication No. 305122694) [Doctoral dissertation, University of Phoenix]. ProQuest Dissertations and Theses.

Manthiou, A., Hickman, E., & Klaus, P. (2020). Beyond good and bad: Challenging the suggested role of emotions in customer experience (CX) research. *Journal of Retailing and Consumer Services, 57*, 102218–102218. doi:10.1016/j.jretconser.2020.102218

Marconi, M., & Lakatos, E. (2003). *Fundamentos de metodologia científica* (5th ed.). Editora Atlas., doi:10.1590/S1517-97022003000100005

Marouli, C. (2021). Sustainability Education for the Future? Challenges and Implications for Education and Pedagogy in the 21st Century. *Sustainability, 13*(5), 2901. Advance online publication. doi:10.3390u13052901

Marques, J. (2016). Shaping morally responsible leaders: Infusing civic engagement into business ethics courses. *Journal of Business Ethics, 135*(2), 279–291. doi:10.100710551-014-2465-4

Marston, S., Li, Z., Bandyopadhyay, S., Zhang, J., & Ghalsasi, A. (2011). Cloud Computing: The business perspective. *Decision Support Systems, 51*(1), 176–189. doi:10.1016/j.dss.2010.12.006

Martin, D. (2020). Exploring the relationship between the framing of cultural diversity and the strategies used in its management among educational leaders. *Canadian Journal for New Scholars in Education, 11*(2), 125–129.

Martínez Domínguez, B., Martínez Domínguez, I., Alonso Sáez, I., & Geruzaga Amundarain, M. (2013). *El aprendizaje-servicio, una oportunidad para avanzar en la innovación educativa dentro de la Universidad del País Vasco*. Academic Press.

Martínez-Jiménez, R., & Ruiz-Jiménez, M. C. (2020). Improving students' satisfaction and learning performance using flipped classroom. *International Journal of Management Education, 18*(3), 100422. Advance online publication. doi:10.1016/j.ijme.2020.100422

Martínez, V. (2017). Educación presencial versus educación a distancia. *La Cuestión Universitaria, 9*, 108–116.

Martín, S., Gil, R., Díaz, G., Sancristobal, E., Castro, M., & Peire, J. (2008). From e-learning to m-learning through b-learning and s-learning. *50th International Symposium ELMAR-2008*, 10–12.

Martins, J., & Nunes, M. B. (2016). The temporal properties of e-learning: An exploratory study of academics' conceptions. *International Journal of Educational Management, 30*(1), 2–19. doi:10.1108/IJEM-04-2014-0048

Mateo, J., & Martínez, F. (2008). *Medición y evaluación educativa*. Editorial La Muralla.

Maxwell, J. (2007). *The 21 irrefutable laws of leadership: Follow them and people will follow you*. Harper Collins.

Mayer, K. (2019). When quitting doesn't have to be a bad breakup: The importance of offboarding - and other vital lessons I've learned during my time at EBN. *Employee Benefit News, 33*(4), 8.

McAndrew, A. (2001). *Service-learning: Benefits, challenges, and strategies for success*. Recuperado de: http://www.unco.edu/ AE-Extra/2001/1/ServiceLearning.html

McClelland, D. C. (1961). *The achieving society*. Van Nostrand. doi:10.1037/14359-000

McCleskey, J. A. (2014). Situational, transformational, and transactional leadership and leadership development. *Journal of Business Studies Quarterly, 5*(4), 117–130.

McClusky, H. (1965). Psychology and learning. *Review of Educational Research, 35*(3), 191–200. https://www.jstor.org/stable/1169825

McClusky, H. (1970). An approach to a differential psychology of adult potential. In S. M. Grabowski (Ed.), *Adult learning and instruction* (pp. 80–95). Adult Education Association of the U.S.A.

McGoldrick, K. (1998). Service-learning in economics: A detailed application. *The Journal of Economic Education, 29*(4), 365–376. doi:10.1080/00220489809595929

McKenzie, D., & Paffhausen, A. L. (2019). Small Firm Death in Developing Countries. *The Review of Economics and Statistics, 101*(4), 645–657. doi:10.1162/rest_a_00798

McKenzie, D., & Sansone, D. (2019). Predicting entrepreneurial success is hard: Evidence from a business plan competition in Nigeria. *Journal of Development Economics, 141*, 141. doi:10.1016/j.jdeveco.2019.07.002

McMahon, R. G. P. (2001). Growth and performance of manufacturing SMEs: The influence of financial management characteristics. *International Small Business Journal, 19*(3), 10–28. doi:10.1177/0266242601193001

MEC – Ministério de Educação e Ciência. (2015). *Experiências de Inovação Didática no Ensino Superior*. Lisboa: Setembro.

Medina, A. (2006). El reto de la interculturalidad: Adaptaciones del centro y del currículo. *Revista Currículo*, (19), 17–57.

Mei, X. (2019). Gaps in tourism education and workforce needs: Attracting and educating the right people. *Current Issues in Tourism, 22*(12), 1400–1404. doi:10.1080/13683500.2017.1402870

Mendonça, M. C., Schmiegelow, S. S., Almeida, F. S., Filho, F. A. P., & Sousa, R. P. L. (2017) Design Thinking, Media, Knowledge and Innovation: Reflections on a Didactic Activity Applying Persona Design and the User Journey Map. *VII International Congress on Knowledge and Innovation Proceeding*.

Merriam, S. B., & Bierema, L. L. (2013). *Adult learning: Linking theory and practice*. John Wiley & Sons.

Merriam-Webster. (n.d.). Sociocultural. In *Merriam-Webster.com dictionary*. Retrieved January 2, 2021, from https://www.merriam-webster.com/dictionary/sociocultural

Meyer, S. (2018). Continuous feedback during change supports success. *Bonfyre*. https://bonfyreapp.com/blog/continuous-feedback-during-change

Meyers, S. A. (2009). Service learning as an opportunity for personal and social transformation. *International Journal on Teaching and Learning in Higher Education*, *21*(3), 373–381.

Miller, J. L. (2017). Managing Transitions: Using William Bridges' Transition Model and a Change Style Assessment Instrument to Inform Strategies and Measure Progress in Organizational Change Management. *Scholarship and Professional Work*, *74*, 9.

MindTools. (n.d.). *Adams' equity theory: Balancing employee inputs and outputs*. https://www.mindtools.com/pages/article/newLDR_96.htm

Ministério da Economia e do Planeamento (2018). PRODESI. Available on: https://prodesi.ao/

Minuano, C. (2019, October 3). *Power of collective intelligence will increase*. Folha de São Paulo. Press Observatory. https://www.observatoriodaimprensa.com.br/e-noticias/poder-da-inteligencia-coletiva-vai-aumentar/

Miro. (2020, October 10). *Car APP, by Francelma Macêdo*. https://miro.com/app/dashboard/

Mishra, L., Gupta, T., & Shree, A. (2020). Online Teaching-Learning in Higher Education during Lockdown Period of COVID-19 Pandemic. *International Journal of Educational Research Open*, *1*, 100012. Advance online publication. doi:10.1016/j.ijedro.2020.100012 PMID:35059663

Mitchell, R. K., Busenitz, L. W., Bird, B., Marie Gaglio, C., Mcmullen, J. S., Morse, E. A., & Smith, J. B. (2007). The central question in entrepreneurial cognition research 2007. *Entrepreneurship Theory and Practice*, *31*(1), 1–27. doi:10.1111/j.1540-6520.2007.00161.x

Mockus, H. (2018). Training beyond onboarding: Filling the gaps in food manufacturing. *Food Manufacture*, *31*(2), 11.

Modigliani, F., & Miller, M. H. (1963). Corporate Income Taxes and the Cost of Capital: A Correction by. *The American Economic Review*, *53*(3), 437–447.

Mok, H. N. (2014). Institutional Knowledge at Singapore Management University Teaching tip : The flipped classroom Teaching Tip. *The Flipped Classroom.*, *25*, 7–11.

Mokoena, P. P. (2018). Analysis of the research design used in a Tourism Management service learning project. *African Journal of Hospitality, Tourism and Leisure*, *7*(4), 1–13.

Mollah, M. (2020). *Loan Disbursement Procedure of Grameen Bank*. Daffodil International University.

Montgomery, B. L. (2020). Academic leadership: Gatekeeping or groundskeeping? *The Journal of Values Based Leadership*, *13*(2), 135–151. doi:10.22543/0733.132.1316

Moore, H. (2006). Employee retention: The high cost of turnover: Attracting, retaining good staff key to success. *Automotive Body Repair News*, *45*(10), 46.

Moore, J., Dickson-Deane, C., & Galyen, K. (2011). E-learning, online learning, and distance learning environments: Are they the same? *Internet and Higher Education, 14*(2), 129–135. doi:10.1016/j.iheduc.2010.10.001

Moore, M. (1990). Recent contributions to the theory of distance education. *Open Learning, 5*(3), 10–15. doi:10.1080/0268051900050303

Moore, M. G., & Kearsley, G. (2005). *Distance education: A systems view*. Wadsworth Publ.

Moreira, J., Henriques, S., Barros, D., Goulão, M. F., & Caeiro, D. (2020). *Educação Digital em Rede: Princípios para o design pedagógico em tempos de pandemia*. Universidade Aberta.

Morozini, A. (2013). *Adding Individual Intelligences Does Not Always Result In Collective Intelligence*. Academic Press.

Moscardo, G. (2015). The Importance of Education for Sustainability in Tourism. In G. Moscardo & P. Benckendorff (Eds.), *Education for Sustainability in Tourism A Handbook of Processes, Resources, and Strategies* (1st ed., pp. 1–24). Springer. doi:10.1007/978-3-662-47470-9_1

Moustakas, L. (2018). Motivation and obstacles to adult participation in lifelong learning programs: The effect of gender and age. *Open Journal for Educational Research, 2*(1), 45–56. doi:10.32591/coas.ojer.0201.04045m

Mpofu, E. (2007). Service-Learning Effects on the Academic Learning of Rehabilitation Services Students. *Michigan Journal of Community Service Learning, 14*(1), 46–52.

Mueller, S. L., & Thomas, A. S. (2000). Culture and entrepreneurial potential: A nine country study of locus of control and innovativeness. *Journal of Business Venturing, 16*(1), 51–75. doi:10.1016/S0883-9026(99)00039-7

Müller, F. A., & Wulf, T. (2020). Technology-supported management education: A systematic review of antecedents of learning effectiveness. *International Journal of Educational Technology in Higher Education, 17*(1), 47. Advance online publication. doi:10.118641239-020-00226-x

Musa Al-Momani, M., & Pilli, O. (2021). The Impact of Integrated Mobile System on Students' Academic Achievement, Interaction and Satisfaction. *TEM Journal*. doi:10.18421/TEM103-50

Mussio, S. (2020). Reflexões sobre as modalidades de estudo na educação a distância: Benefícios e limitações. *Revista EDaPECI São Cristóvão (SE), 20*(1), 119–129. doi:10.29276/redapeci.2020.20.112187.119-129

Muzzio. (2017). *Individual, Leadership and Culture: Evidence of Creativity Management.* https://www.scielo.br/scielo.php?script=sci_arttext&pid=S1415-65552017000100107

Myers, S. C. (1977). Interactions of Corporate Financing and Investment Decisions - Implications for Capital Budgeting. *The Journal of Finance, 29*(1), 1–25. doi:10.1111/j.1540-6261.1974.tb00021.x

Myers, S. C. (1984). The Capital Structure Puzzle. *The Journal of Finance, 39*(3), 575–592. doi:10.2307/2327916

Myers, S. C., & Majluf, N. S. (1984). Corporate Financing and Investment Decisions. When Firms have information that investors do not have. *Journal of Financial Economics, 13*(2), 187–221. doi:10.1016/0304-405X(84)90023-0

Nadeem, T., & Rasool, R. (2018). Marketing: the crucial success factor for Pakistan's credit guarantee scheme. Asian Development Bank Institute.

Naffziger, D., Hornsby, J., & Kuratko, D. F. (1994). A proposed research model of entrepreneurial motivation. *Entrepreneurship Theory and Practice, 18*(3), 29–43. doi:10.1177/104225879401800303

Nart, S., Yaprak, B., Yildirim, Y. T., & Sarihan, A. Y. (2018). The relationship of diversity management and servant leadership with organizational identification and creativity in multinational enterprises. *Finans Politik ve Ekonomik Yorumlar*, *55*(637), 31–47.

National Academies of Sciences. (2018). *How people learn II: Learners, contexts, and cultures*. The National Academies Press. doi:10.17226/24783

National Service-Learning Clearinghouse. (2009). What is service-learning? Nikolova, N., & Andersen, L. (2017). Creating shared value through service-learning in management education. *Journal of Management Education*, *41*(5), 750–780.

Nelson, B. (2018, September 25). How learning & development impacts employee engagement. *Training Industry*. https://trainingindustry.com/blog/performance-management/how-learning-development-impacts-employee-engagement/

Nerantzi, C. (2020). The use of peer instruction and flipped learning to support flexible blended learning during and after the COVID-19 Pandemic. *International Journal of Management and Applied Research*, *7*(2), 184–195. doi:10.18646/2056.72.20-013

Ng, S. (2010). Motivation for lifelong learning: Role of positive environments and supportive relationships. *International Journal of Learning*, *16*(12), 417–429.

Niewiadomski, P. (2020). COVID-19: From temporary deglobalization to a re-discovery of tourism? *Tourism Geographies*, *22*(3), 651–656. doi:10.1080/14616688.2020.1757749

Niñerola, A., Sánchez-Rebull, M., & Hernández-Lara, A. (2019). Tourism Research on Sustainability: A Bibliometric Analysis. *Sustainability*, *11*(5), 1377. doi:10.3390u11051377

Northouse, P. G. (2019). *Leadership: Theory and practice*. Sage Publications.

O'Flaherty, J., & Phillips, C. (2015). The use of flipped classrooms in higher education: A scoping review. *Internet and Higher Education*, *25*, 85–95. doi:10.1016/j.iheduc.2015.02.002

O'Meara, K., & Niehaus, E. (2009). Service learning is… How faculty explain their practice. *Michigan Journal of Community Service Learning*, *16*(1), 1–16.

OCDE. (2015). *New Approaches to SME and Entrepreneurship Financing: Broadening the Range of Instruments*. OCDE.

Ochoa-Zazueta, J. Á. (2006, March). Entrevista personal. *Los Mochis, Sinaloa*, (Mayo), 16.

Odria, A. M. (2007). Service-learning o aprendizaje-servicio: la apertura de la escuela a la comunidad local como propuesta de educación para la ciudadanía. *Bordón. Revista de pedagogía, 59*(4), 627-640.

OECD. (2020). *Mitigating the impact of COVID-19 and preparing for recovery*. . doi:10.1787/23071672

Ogoy, H. (2016). *Strategies for Accessing Credit by Small and Medium Enterprises* (Unpublished master's thesis). Walden University.

Ojah, K., & Mokoteli, T. (2010). Possible Effective Financing Models for Entrepreneurship in South Africa: Guides from Microfinance and Venture Capital Finance. *African Finance Journal*, *12*(1), 1–26.

Olafsen, E., & Cook, P. A. (2016). *Growth Entrepreneurship in Developing Countries: A Preliminary Literature Review*. The World Bank Group.

Omri, A., Frikha, M., & Bouraoui, M. (2015). An empirical investigation of factors affecting small business success. *Journal of Management Development*, *34*(9), 1073–1093. doi:10.1108/JMD-07-2013-0088

Onyalla, D. B. (2018). Authentic leadership and leadership ethics: Proposing a new perspective. *The Journal of Values Based Leadership*, *11*(2), 1–10. doi:10.22543/0733.62.1226

Opazo, H., Aramburuzabala, P., & Cerrillo, R. (2016). A review of the situation of service-learning in higher education in Spain. *Asia Pacific Journal of Cooperative Education*, *17*(1), 75–91.

Orakcı, Ş. (2020). The future of online learning and teaching in higher education. In Global Approaches to Sustainability Through Learning and Education. Hershey, PA: IGI Global. doi:10.4018/978-1-7998-0062-0.ch003

Ormrod, J. (2020). Human learning (8th ed.). Pearson Education.

Osman, M. E. (2020). Global impacto f COVID-19 on education systems: The emergency remote teaching and Sultam Qaboos University. *Journal of Education for Teaching*, *46*(4), 463–471. doi:10.1080/02607476.2020.1802583

Ostgaard, T. A., & Birley, S. (1994). Personal networks and firm competitive strategy: A strategic or coincidental match? *Journal of Business Venturing*, *9*(4), 281–305. doi:10.1016/0883-9026(94)90009-4

Páez Sánchez, M., & Puig Rovira, J. M. (2013). La reflexión en el aprendizaje-servicio. *Revista internacional de educación para la justicia social.*

Paldês, R. (2017). Method 6-3-5: A productive format for Brainwriting. *Networking Requirements.*

Palvia, S., Aeron, P., Gupta, P., Mahapatra, D., Parida, R., Rosner, R., & Sindhi, S. (2018). Online Education: Worldwide Status, Challenges, Trends, and Implications. *Journal of Global Information Technology Management*, *21*(4), 233–241. doi:10.1080/1097198X.2018.1542262

Paphitis, S. A., & Pearse, N. J. (2017). Developing and implementing a service-learning course into an MBA programme: Critical perspectives from students. *Journal for New Generation Sciences*, *15*(1), 140–156.

Parent, J. D., & Lovelace, K. J. (2018). Employee engagement, positive organizational culture, and individual adaptability. *On the Horizon*, *26*(3), 206–214. doi:10.1108/OTH-01-2018-0003

Park, M., & Jones, T. (2021). Going virtual: The impact of COVID-19 on internships in tourism, events, and hospitality education. *Journal of Hospitality & Tourism Education*, 1–18.

Parte, L., & Herrador-Alcaide, T. (2021). Teaching Disruption by COVID-19: Burnout, Isolation, and Sense of Belonging in Accounting Tutors in E-Learning and B-Learning. *International Journal of Environmental Research and Public Health*, *18*(19), 10339. doi:10.3390/ijerph181910339 PMID:34639635

Paschen, J. (2016). Choose wisely: Crowdfunding through the stages of the startup life cycle. *Business Horizons*, 1–10.

Pasin, F., & Giroux, H. (2011). The impact of a simulation game on operations management education. *Computers & Education*, *57*(1), 1240–1254. doi:10.1016/j.compedu.2010.12.006

Paulo, A., Carvalho, L., Costa, T., Lopes, J., & Galina, S. (2017). Mapping Open Innovation: A bibliometric review to compare developed and emerging countries. *Global Business Review*, *18*(3), 291–307. doi:10.1177/0972150916668600

Peixoto, J. M., & Moura, E. P. (2020). Map of Empathy in Health: Elaboration of an Instrument for the Development of Empathy. *Brazilian Journal of Medical Education.*

Pellicer, L. (2008). *Caring enough to lead: How reflective practice leads to moral leadership* (3rd ed.). Corwin Press.

Peña, I. (2002). Intellectual capital and business start up success. *Journal of Intellectual Capital*, *3*(2), 180–198. doi:10.1108/14691930210424761

Peredo, A. M., & Mclean, M. (2006). Social entrepreneurship: A critical review of the concept. *Journal of World Business, 41*(1), 56–65. doi:10.1016/j.jwb.2005.10.007

Perkmann, M., Tartari, V., McKelvey, M., Autio, E., Broström, A., D'Este, P., Fini, R., Geuna, A., Grimaldi, R., Hughes, A., Krabel, S., Kitson, M., Llerena, P., Lissoni, F., Salter, A., & Sobrero, M. (2013). Academic engagement and commercialisation: A review of the literature on university industry relations. *Research Policy, 42*(2), 423–442. doi:10.1016/j.respol.2012.09.007

Persson-Fischer, U., & Liu, S. (2021). What Is Interdisciplinarity in the Study of Sustainable Destination Development? *Sustainability, 13*(7), 3639. doi:10.3390u13073639

Pesce, L., & Hessel, A. M. G. (2021). Ensino superior no contexto da pandemia da COVID – 19: Um relato analítico. *Revista Práxis Educacional, 17*(45), 1-19. Retrieved 2021-12-09 from https://periodicos2.uesb.br/index.php/praxis/article/view/8323/5692

Peters, O. (2000). Digital learning environments: New possibilities and opportunities. *International Review of Research in Open and Distance Learning, 1*(1), 22–39. doi:10.19173/irrodl.v1i1.3

Petry, J. F., Sebastiao, S. A., Martins, E. G., & Barros, P. B. A. (2019). Innovation and Diffusion of Technology in Lowland Agriculture in the Amazon. *Rev. Adm. Contemp., 23*(5), 619-635.

Pettigrew, T. F. (1971). *Racial separate or together?* McGraw-Hill.

Pfeffer, J., & Veiga, J. F. (1999). Putting people first for organizational success. *The Academy of Management Executive, 13*(2), 37–48. doi:10.5465/AME.1999.1899547

Phaal, R., Farrukh, C. J. P., & Robert, D. R. (2006). Technology management tools: Concept, development and application. *Technovation, 26*(3), 336–344. doi:10.1016/j.technovation.2005.02.001

Pham, H. (2017). Determinants of New Small and Medium Enterprises (SMEs) Access to Bank Credit: Case Study in the Phu Tho Province, Vietnam. *International Journal of Business and Management, 12*(7), 83–99. doi:10.5539/ijbm.v12n7p83

Piaget, J., Lazarsfeld, P., & Castrillo, P. (1976). Tendencias de la investigación en las ciencias sociales. México. *Alianza, 42*(001), T43.

Pinchot, G. III, & … . (1999). *Intrapreneuring in Action*. Berrett-Koehler Publisher.

Pokhrel, S., & Chhetri, R. (2021). A literature review on impact of COVID-19 pandemic on teaching and learning. *Higher Education for the Future, 8*(1), 133–141. doi:10.1177/2347631120983481

Polvillo, C. F., & Montaño, J. L. A. (2011): Enfoques de aprendizaje: Un estudio comparativo de las titulaciones de la escuela universitária de Osuna. XXI Jornadas Hispano-Lusas Gestión Cientifica.

Pontes, S. A. E. (2020). Mathematics in early childhood education: An educational look from the perspective of creativity. *Diversitas Journal, 5*(2), 1166–1176.

Ponzio, A. P, & Machado, A. S. (2015). *Use of Creative Methods Envisioning Innovation on Teaching Architectural Design*. LUME.

Poon, J. (2012). Use of blended learning to enhance the student learning experience and engagement in property education. *Property Management, 30*(2), 129–156. Advance online publication. doi:10.1108/02637471211213398

Poon, P., Chan, T. S., & Zhou, L. (2011). Implementation of service-learning in business education: Issues and challenges. *Journal of Teaching in International Business, 22*(3), 185–192. doi:10.1080/08975930.2011.653746

Porter, M. E. (1985). *Competitive advantage: Creating and sustaining superior performance*. Free Press.

Porumb, E. M., & Analoui, F. (2008). How to use KM effectively in a European context: The case of BCT in Romania. *International Journal of Business Information Systems, 3*(6), 609. Advance online publication. doi:10.1504/IJBIS.2008.018993

Poupore, G. (2014). The influence of content on adult L2 learners' task motivation: An interest theory perspective. *Canadian Journal of Applied Linguistics, 17*(2), 69–90.

Preisman, K. A. (2014). Teaching Presence in Online Education: From the Instructor's Point-of-View. *Online Learning, 18*(3). Advance online publication. doi:10.24059/olj.v18i3.446

Priego, R. G., & Peralta, A. G. (2013). Engagement factors and motivation in e-Learning and blended-learning projects. In F. J. García-Peñalvo (Ed.), *Proceedings of the First International Conference on Technological Ecosystem for Enhancing Multiculturality - TEEM '13* (pp. 453–460). ACM Press. 10.1145/2536536.2536606

Programa da Unidade Curricular de Simulação Empresarial. (2020/2021). Retrieved 10-06-2021 from http://www.esce.ips.pt

Protogerou, A., Caloghirou, Y., & Vonortas, N. S. (2017). Determinants of young firms' innovative performance: Empirical evidence from Europe. *Research Policy, 46*(7), 1312–1326. doi:10.1016/j.respol.2017.05.011

Psico, J. (2010). *Microfinanças - Solução para o Combate à Pobreza?* Escolar Editora.

Putre, L. (2015). Onboarding for the "on demand" generation or, how to keep millennials from bailing on day one. *Industry Week, 264*(6), 27.

Quezada, R. L., Talbot, C., & Quezada-Parker, Q. B. (2020). From Bricks and Mortar to Remote Teaching: A Teacher education Programme's Response to COVID-19. *Journal of Education for Teaching, 46*(4), 472–483. doi:10.1080/02607476.2020.1801330

Rahman, A., & Ley, A. (2020). Micro-credit vs. Group savings – different pathways to promote affordable housing improvements in urban Bangladesh. *Habitat International, 106*, 106. doi:10.1016/j.habitatint.2020.102292

Rahman, W. (2011). Comparison of Microcredit Models in China and Bangladesh – the Implication for Institutional Sustainability. *World Applied Sciences Journal, 14*(2), 245–255.

Ramirez-Orellana, A., Martinez-Romero, M., & Mariño-Garrido, T. (2017). Measuring fraud and earning management by a case of study: Evidence from an international family business. *European Journal of Family Business, 7*(1-2), 41–53. doi:10.1016/j.ejfb.2017.10.001

Rauch, A., & Frese, M. (2007). Let's put the person back into entrepreneurship research: A meta analysis on the relationship between business owners'personality traits, business creation, and success. *European Journal of Work and Organizational Psychology, 16*(4), 353–385. doi:10.1080/13594320701595438

Razmerita, L., Kirchner, K., Hockerts, K., & Tan, C.-W. (2020). Modeling Collaborative Intentions and Behavior in Digital Environments: The Case of a Massive Open Online Course (MOOC). *Academy of Management Learning & Education, 19*(4), 469–502. Advance online publication. doi:10.5465/amle.2018.0056

Recomendação da Comissão. (2003). *361/CE, de 6 de Maio de 2003*. Comissão Europeia.

Remedios, R., & Richardson, J. T. E. (2013). Achievement goals in adult learners: Evidence from distance education. *The British Journal of Educational Psychology, 83*(4), 664–685. doi:10.1111/bjep.12001 PMID:24175688

Reuber, A. R., & Fisher, E. (1999). Understanding the consequences of founders' experience. *Journal of Small Business Management, 37*(2), 30–45.

Rhodes, P. (2019, September 19). *What is radical inclusion?* The Good Men Project. https://goodmenproject.com/featured-content/what-is-radical-inclusion-kvnw/

Richard, P., Devinney, T., Yip, G., & Johnson, G. (2009). Measuring Organizational Performance: Towards Methodological Best Practice. *Journal of Management, 35*(3), 718–804. doi:10.1177/0149206308330560

Ritchie, J., & Crouch, G. (2010). A model of destination competitiveness/ sustainability: Brazilian perspectives. *Brazilian Public Administration Review, 44*(5), 1049–1066. doi:10.1590/S0034-76122010000500003

Rivas, M. T., & Donovan, P. (2001). La evaluación participativa. Ediciones Abya-Yala, segunda edición, Quito.

Roberson, Q., & Perry, J. L. (2021). *Inclusive leadership in thought and action: A thematic analysis. Group and Organization Management.* Sage Publications., doi:10.1177/10596011211013161

Rodrigues, F. S. M., Errante, P. R., Lima, R. Y., Carmo, A. O., Silva, E. F., Gehrke, F., Carvalho, D. S., Tikazawa, E. H., Ferraz, R. R. N., Neto, A. C., & Taha, M. O. (2019). Vantagens da utilização do método de aprendizagem baseada em problemas (MABP) em cursos de graduação na área da saúde. *RIAEE – Revista Ibero – Americana de estudos em educação, 14*(2), 340-353. Retrieved 2021-12-09 from https://www.researchgate.net/publication/348077833_Boletim_10_-_Revista_Ibero-Americana_de_Estudos_em_Educacao

Roesler, R. (2012). Web 2.0, social interactions and knowledge building. *VII SIMPED - Pedagogical Symposium and Research in Education.*

Rourke, L., Anderson, T., Garrison, R., & Archer, W. (2001). Assessing Social Presence In Asynchronous Text-based Computer Conferencing. *Journal of Distance Education, 4*(3), 51–70.

Rovai, A. P. (2007). Facilitating online discussions effectively. *The Internet and Higher Education, 10*(1), 77–88. doi:10.1016/j.iheduc.2006.10.001

Rovai, A. P., & Jordan, H. M. (2004). Blended learning and sense of community: A comparative analysis with traditional and fully online graduate courses. *International Review of Research in Open and Distance Learning, 5*(2). Advance online publication. doi:10.19173/irrodl.v5i2.192

Rueda, L., Benitez, J., & Braojos, J. (2017). From traditional education technologies to student satisfaction in Management education: A theory of the role of social media applications. *Information & Management, 54*(8), 1059–1071. doi:10.1016/j.im.2017.06.002

Ruiz-Corbella, M., & García-Gutiérrez, J. (2019). *Aprendizaje-Servicio: los retos de la evaluación* (Vol. 155). Narcea Ediciones.

Rumbley, L. (2020). *Coping with COVID-19: International higher education in Europe. European Association for International Education.* Acedido em 18 novembro de 2021 em https://eaie.org/our-resources/library/publication/Research-and-trends/Coping-with-COVID-19-International-higher-education-in-Europe.html

Saarinen, J. (2018). Beyond growth thinking: The need to revisit sustainable development in tourism. *Tourism Geographies, 20*(2), 337–340. doi:10.1080/14616688.2018.1434817

Sabbaghi, O., SJ, G. F. C., & SJ, T. H. (. (2013). Service-learning and leadership: Evidence from teaching financial literacy. *Journal of Business Ethics, 118*(1), 127–137. doi:10.100710551-012-1545-6

Saks, A. M., Uggerslev, K. L., & Fassina, N. E. (2007). Socialization tactics and newcomer adjustment: A meta-analytic review and test of a model. *Journal of Vocational Behavior, 70*(3), 413–446. doi:10.1016/j.jvb.2006.12.004

Sales, D., Cuevas-cerveró, A., & Cuevas-cerveró, A. (2020). *Perspectives on the information and digital competence of Social Sciences students and faculty before and during lockdown due to Covid-19.* doi:10.3145/epi.2020.jul.23

Salum, M., Gomes, M. & Ramires, D. (2018). As desvantagens do ensino à distância para curso de graduação em Direito. *Revista Electrónica Científica da FAESB, 1*(5), 135-150.

Sanchez-Runde, C., Nardon, L., & Steers, R. M. (2011). Looking beyond Western leadership models: Implications for global managers. *Organizational Dynamics, 40*(3), 207–213. doi:10.1016/j.orgdyn.2011.04.008

Sandmann, L. R., Kiely, R. C., & Grenier, R. S. (2009). Program Planning: The Neglected Dimension of Service-Learning. *Michigan Journal of Community Service Learning, 15*(2), 17–33.

Sandoval-Forero, E. A., Guerra-García, E., & Delgado-Buelna, R. A. (2008). Una visión sociointercultural del ausentismo intermitente de yoremes y mestizos en la UAIM. *Tiempo de Educar, 9*(17), 9–34.

Sanmartí, N. (2007). 10 ideas clave: Evaluar para aprender. Coleccion ideas clave (España).

Santos, M. R. C., Nunes, S., Dominguinhos, P., Mourato, J., Mata, C., & Teixeira, N. M. (2021). Financial Capacity During a Pandemic Crisis: Insights From the Non-Profit Sector. In N. M. Teixeira & I. Lisboa (Eds.), Handbook of Research on Financial Management During Economic Downturn and Recovery (pp. 59–76). IGI Global. doi:10.4018/978-1-7998-6643-5.ch004

Santos, Z. M. M. L. (2020). Os impactos da pandemia do Coronavirus no ensino superior. *VII Congresso Nacional de Educação*. Retrieved 2021-12-09 from https://editorarealize.com.br/index.php/artigo/visualizar/69228

Santos, F. J., Roomi, M. A., & Liñán, F. (2016). About gender differences and the social environment in the development of entrepreneurial intentions. *Journal of Small Business Management, 54*(1), 49–66. doi:10.1111/jsbm.12129

Santos, M. R. C., Laureano, R. M. S., & Moro, S. (2020). Unveiling Research Trends for Organizational Reputation in the Nonprofit Sector. *Voluntas, 31*(1), 56–70. doi:10.100711266-018-00055-7

Sanusi, N. M., Kamalrudin, M., & Mohtar, S. (2019). Student Engagement using Learning Management System in Computer Science Education. *International Journal of Recent Technology and Engineering, 8*(2S11). doi:10.35940/ijrte.B1121.0982S1119

Sathishkumar, V., Radha, R., Mahalakshmi, K., Kumar, V. S., & Saravanakumar, A. R. (2020). E-Learning during Lockdown of Covid-19 Pandemic: A Global Perspective. *International Journal of Control and Automation, 13*(4), 1088–1099.

Sautter, P. (2007). Designing discussion activities to achieve desired learning outcomes: Choices using mode of delivery and structure. *Journal of Marketing Education, 29*(2), 122–131. doi:10.1177/0273475307302014

Scagnoli, N. I., Choo, J., & Tian, J. (2019). Students' insights on the use of video lectures in online classes. *British Journal of Educational Technology, 50*(1), 399–414. doi:10.1111/bjet.12572

Schaufeli, W. B., & Bakker, A. B. (2004). Job demands, job resources, and their relationship with burnout and engagement: A multi-sample study. *Journal of Organizational Behavior, 25*(3), 293–315. doi:10.1002/job.248

Scherer Bassani, P. B. (2011). Interpersonal exchanges in discussion forums: SStudy of learnitudy of learning communities in distance ng communities in distance learning settings. learning settings. *Computers & Education, 56*, 931–938. doi:10.1016/j.compedu.2010.11.009

Scholtz, D. (2018). Service Learning: An Empowerment Agenda for Students and Community Entrepreneurs. *International Journal of Work-Integrated Learning, 19*(1), 69–79.

Schuckert, M., Kim, T., Paek, S., & Lee, G. (2018). Motivate to innovate: How authentic and transformational leaders influence employees' psychological capital and service innovation behavior. *International Journal of Contemporary Hospitality Management*, *30*(2), 776–796. doi:10.1108/IJCHM-05-2016-0282

Schumpeter, J. A. (1961). *The theory of economic development*. Oxford University Press.

Schutjens, V. A. J. M., & Wever, E. (2000). Determinants of new firm success. *Papers in Regional Science*, *79*(2), 135–159. doi:10.1007101100050040

Schwartz, G. (2010). Marrying employee engagement with customer satisfaction. *Strategic HR Review*, *9*(3), 40–41A. doi:10.1108hr.2010.37209cab.010

Schwartz, S. H. (1999). A Theory of Cultural Values and Some Implications for Work. *Applied Psychology*, *48*(1), 23–47. doi:10.1111/j.1464-0597.1999.tb00047.x

Schwartz, S. H., & Bardi, A. (1997). Influences of adaptation to communist rule on value priorities in Eastern Europe. *Political Psychology*, *18*(2), 385–410. doi:10.1111/0162-895X.00062

Sears, L. (2017). 2017 Retention report: Trends, reasons & recommendations. Workinstitute.com/retentionreport

Senge, P. (2006). *The fifth discipline: The art and practice of the learning organization*. Crown Business.

Serra, F. (2004). Reorientação das actividades de ensino/aprendizagem nas instituições de ensino superior: Uma abordagem sistémica. In *XIV Jornadas Luso-Espanholas de Gestão Científica*. Açores.

Shah, S. H. H., Lei, S., Ali, M., Doronin, D., & Hussain, S. T. (2019). Prosumption: Bibliometric analysis using HistCite and VOSviewer. *Kybernetes*, *49*(3), 1020–1045. doi:10.1108/K-12-2018-0696

Shane, S., & Venkataraman, S. (2000). The promise of entrepreneurship as a field of research. *Academy of Management Review*, *25*(1), 217–226. doi:10.5465/amr.2000.2791611

Shapero, A. (1975). The Displaced, Uncomfortable Entrepreneur. *Psychology Today*, *9*(6), 83–88.

Sharma, K., & Teper, Y. (2008) The Gifted and Talented: Creativity, Cultural Perspectives and Skills. *International Conference on Creativity in Mathematics and the Education of Gifted Students*, *5*, 211-215.

Sheafer, V. (2014). Using service learning to teach classic learning theories. *Psychology Journal*, *11*(2), 77–82.

Sheldon, P., Fesenmaier, D., & Tribe, J. (2011). The Tourism Education Futures Initiative (TEFI): Activating change in tourism education. The Critical Turn in Tourism Studies: Creating an Academy of Hope, 75-95.

Shneor, R., Zhao, L., & Flåten, B. (2020). *Advances in Crowdfunding - Research and Practice*. Palgrave MacMillan. doi:10.1007/978-3-030-46309-0

Shuck, B. M., Rocco, T. S., & Albornoz, C. A. (2011). Exploring employee engagement from the employee perspective: Implications for HRD. *Journal of European Industrial Training*, *35*(4), 300–325. https://doi.org/10.1108/03090591111128306

Shuck, B., & Wollard, K. (2010). Employee engagement and HRD: A seminal review of the foundations. *Human Resource Development Review*, *9*(1), 89–110. doi:10.1177/1534484309353560

Siegle, D., Rubenstein, L., Pollard, E., & Romey, E. (2010). Exploring the relationship of college freshmen honors students' effort and ability attribution, interest, and implicit theory of intelligence with perceived ability. *Gifted Child Quarterly*, *54*(2), 93–101. doi:10.1177/0016986209355975

Sigala, M., & Baum, T. (2003). Trends and issues in tourism and hospitality Higher Education: Visioning the future. *Tourism and Hospitality Research*, *4*(4), 367–376. doi:10.1177/146735840300400409

Silva, S., Aleixo, C., & Teixeira, A. B. (2016). A contabilidade e as finanças em Simulação Empresarial, um ensino de sucesso. In *I Congresso Internacional de Contabilidade Pública*. ESCE do IPS.

Silva, E., & Menezes, E. (2005). *Metodologia da pesquisa e elaboração de dissertação* (4th ed.). Universidade Federal de Santa Catarina.

Simer, D. (2017). *Onboarding the next generation workforce in manufacturing. In Manufacturing Business Technology*. ProQuest.

Simonson, M., Schlosser, C., & Orellana, A. (2011). Distance education research: A review of the literature. *Journal of Computing in Higher Education*, *23*(2–3), 124–142. doi:10.100712528-011-9045-8

Sinyan, P. (2018). *Gallup: The holy grail of employee engagement in 2018*. https://www.servicefutures.com/gallup-holy-grail-employee-engagement-2018

Siqueira, J. (2010). *Creativity and innovation*. http: // creativity.com

Slevin, D. P., & Covin, J. G. (1990). New venture strategic posture, structure, and performance: An industry life cycle analysis. *Journal of Business Venturing*, *5*(2), 123–135. doi:10.1016/0883-9026(90)90004-D

SMEFINANCE. (2020). *Improving SMEs' access to finance and finding innovative solutions to unlock sources of capital*. World Bank.

Smith, N. (1999). *Expansive data collection, focused analysis: Combining oral history and grounded theory procedures as research methodology for studies in race, gender and class* [Conference paper]. Race, Gender, and Class Project Conference, Southern University of New Orleans.

Smith, J., Kielly-Coleman, N., & Meijer, G. (2010). Assurance of learning: The role of work-integrated learning and industry partners. *Australian Collaborative Education Network National Conference: Work Integrated Learning (WIL)-Responding to Challenges (ACEN 2010)*, 409-419.

Smith, K., & Clegg, P. (2017). Experiencing Business Start? Up Through an Enterprise Placement Year. In *Entrepreneurship Education: New Perspectives on Entrepreneurship Education. Contemporary Issues in Entrepreneurship Research London* (pp. 307–334). Emerald Group Publishing Ltd. doi:10.1108/S2040-724620170000007018

Smith, M. (2003). *Research methods in accounting*. Sage Publications. doi:10.4135/9781849209809

Smith, S. S., Peters, R., & Caldwell, C. (2016). Creating a culture of engagement—Insights for application. *Business and Management Research*, *5*(2), 1–11. doi:10.5430/bmr.v5n2p70

Smith-Tolken, A. R., & du Plessis, J. M. J. (2013). *Service-Learning across the globe-Paper Series*. Academic Press.

Snell, A. (2006). Researching onboarding best practice: Using research to connect onboarding processes with employee satisfaction. *Strategic HR Review*, *5*(6), 32–35. doi:10.1108/14754390680000925

Sole, K., & Landrum, R. E. (2015). *Academic research and writing: A guide for the social sciences*. Bridgepoint.

Solomon, M. (2016) *Consumer Behavior: Buying, Owning and Being*. Bookman Editora ltda.

Souza, S. C., & Dourado, L. (2015). Aprendizagem baseada em problemas (ABP): Um método de aprendizagem inovador para o ensino educativo. HOLOS, 31(5). Doi:10.15628/holos.2015.2880

Sriram, K., Joseph, J., Mathew, A., & Rai, A. (2019). Factors affecting high employee attrition in manufacturing firms: A case study. *Calitatea*, *20*(169), 23–28.

Stam, W., Arzlanian, S., & Elfring, T. (2014). Social capital of entrepreneurs and small firm performance: A meta-analysis of contextual and methodological moderators. *Journal of Business Venturing*, *29*(1), 152–173. doi:10.1016/j.jbusvent.2013.01.002

Steinberg, K., Hatcher, J. A., & Bringle, R. G. (2011). The civicminded graduate: A north-star. *Michigan Journal of Community Service Learning*, *18*(1), 19–33.

Steinke, P., & Fitch, P. (2007). Assessing service-learning. *Research & Practice in Assessment*, *2*, 24–29.

Stuart, R., & Abetti, P. A. (1987). Start-up ventures: Towards the prediction of initial success. *Journal of Business Venturing*, *2*(3), 215–230. doi:10.1016/0883-9026(87)90010-3

Studer, Q. (2003). *Hardwiring excellence: Purpose, worthwhile work, making a difference*. Fire Starter Publishing.

Suárez, L. M. C., & Ramos, C. F. (2011). Um procedimento de evaluación del estilo de liderazgo en la docência. XXI Jornadas Hispano-Lusas Gestión Cientifica.

Sullivan, G., Weerawardena, J., & Carnegie, K. (2003). Social entrepreneurship: Towards conceptualization. *International Journal of Nonprofit and Voluntary Sector Marketing*, *8*(1), 76–88. doi:10.1002/nvsm.202

Sullivan, W. M., & Rosin, M. S. (2008). *A new agenda for higher education: Shaping a life of the mind for practice*. Jossey-Bass.

Sundgren, M. (2017). Blurring time and place in higher education with bring your own device applications: A literature review. *Education and Information Technologies*, *22*(6), 3081–3119. doi:10.100710639-017-9576-3

Sun, P. C., Tsai, R. J., Finger, G., Chen, Y. Y., & Yeh, D. (2008). What drives a successful e-Learning? An empirical investigation of the critical factors influencing learner satisfaction. *Computers & Education*, *50*(4), 1183–1202. doi:10.1016/j.compedu.2006.11.007

Swan, K. (2002). Building Learning Communities in Online Courses: The importance of interaction. *Education Communication and Information*, *2*(1), 23–49. doi:10.1080/1463631022000005016

Swierczek, F. W., & Ha, T. T. (2003). Entrepreneurial orientation, uncertainty avoidance and firm performance: An analysis of Thai and Vietnamese SMEs. *International Journal of Entrepreneurship and Innovation*, *4*(1), 46–58. doi:10.5367/000000003101299393

Taylor, S. E., & Brown, J. D. (1994). Positive illusions and well-being revisited: Separating fact from fiction. *Psychological Bulletin*, *116*(1), 21–27. doi:10.1037/0033-2909.116.1.21 PMID:8078971

Teixeira, A. B., Aleixo, C., & Silva, S. (2012). Simulação Empresarial e as novas metodologias de ensino: Estudo de Caso. In XV Encontro AECA – Novos caminhos para a Europa, o papel das empresas e do governo. Obra digital.

Teixeira, N., & Brites, R. (2020). A estrutura de capital das empresas portuguesas exportadoras para o mercado comunitário. Jornadas Luso-Espanholas de Gestão Científica; Bragança.

Teixeira, A. B., Silva, S., Aleixo, M. C., & Mata, C. (2015). A contabilidade e as finanças na gestão empresarial: uma prática simulada. *V Congresso OTOC*.

Teixeira, N., & Rodrigues, E. (2013). Microfinanças - Sustentabilidade Financeira versus Alcance Social na África Subsariana. *XIII Congresso do Instituto Internacional de Custos*.

Terano, R., Mohamed, Z., & Jusri, J. (2015). Effectiveness of microcredit program and determinants of income among small business entrepreneurs in Malaysia. *Journal of Global Entrepreneurship Research*, *5*(1), 1–14. doi:10.118640497-015-0038-3

Thompson, J. L. (2002). The world of the social entrepreneur. *International Journal of Public Sector Management*, *15*(5), 412–431. doi:10.1108/09513550210435746

Thoms, C. L. V., & Burton, S. L. (2016). Learning, development, and training: The influence of synergies through educational evolution. *International Journal of Adult Vocational Education and Technology*, *7*(4), 85–104. doi:10.4018/IJAVET.2016100106

Thornhill, S. (2006). Knowledge, innovation and firm performance in high- and low-technology regimes. *Journal of Business Venturing*, *21*(5), 687–703. doi:10.1016/j.jbusvent.2005.06.001

Tims, M., Bakker, A. B., & Xanthopoulou, D. (2011). Do transformational leaders enhance their followers' daily work engagement? *The Leadership Quarterly*, *22*(1), 121–131. doi:10.1016/j.leaqua.2010.12.011

Titman, S., & Wessels, R. (1988). The Determinants of Capital Structure Choice. *The Journal of Finance*, *43*(1), 1–21. doi:10.1111/j.1540-6261.1988.tb02585.x

Tiwari, P., Séraphin, H., & Chowdhary, N. R. (2020). Impacts of COVID-19 on tourism education: Analysis and perspectives. *Journal of Teaching in Travel & Tourism*, 1–26.

Tolkach, D., & Pratt, S. (2021). Travel Professors: A YouTube channel about tourism education & research. *Journal of Hospitality, Leisure, Sport and Tourism Education*, *28*, 100307. doi:10.1016/j.jhlste.2021.100307

Tölkes, C. (2018). Sustainability communication in tourism – A literature review. *Tourism Management Perspectives*, *27*, 10–21. doi:10.1016/j.tmp.2018.04.002

Toor, S. R., & Ogunlana, S. O. (2010). Beyond the 'iron triangle': Stakeholder perception of key performance indicators (KPIs) for large-scale public sector development projects. *International Journal of Project Management*, *28*(3), 228–236. doi:10.1016/j.ijproman.2009.05.005

Touraine, A. (2000). *Igualdad y diversidad: las nuevas tareas de la democracia*. Fondo de Cultura Económica.

Tracey, P., Phillips, N., & Jarvis, O. (2011). Bridging institutiona lentrepreneurship and the creation of new organizational forms: A multilevel model. *Organization Science*, *22*(1), 60–80. doi:10.1287/orsc.1090.0522

Tranfield, D., Denyer, D., & Smart, P. (2003). Towards a methodology for developing evidence-informed management knowledge by means of systematic review. *British Journal of Management*, *14*(3), 207–222. doi:10.1111/1467-8551.00375

Uden, L., & Damiani, E. (2007). *The future of B-learning: B-learning ecosystem*. IEEE DEST.

UNESCO. (2012). *Sustainable Development*. Retrieved from: https://en.unesco.org/themes/education-sustainable-development/what-is-esd/sd#:~:text=Sustainability%20is%20a%20paradigm%20for,an%20improved%20quality%20of%20life

Unesco. (2020). *Suspensão das aulas e resposta à COVID19. Unesco - Organização das Nações Unidas para a Educação, a Ciência e a Cultura*. Acedido em 15 outubro de 2020 em https://unesdoc.unesco.org/ark:/48223/pf0000373305_por

Unger, J. M., Rauch, A., Frese, M., & Rosenbusch, N. (2011). Human capital and entrepreneurial success: A meta-analytical review. *Journal of Business Venturing*, *26*(3), 341–358. doi:10.1016/j.jbusvent.2009.09.004

United Nations. (2015). *Sustainable Development Goals*. Retrieved from: https://www.un.org/sustainabledevelopment/education/

UNWTO & UNDP. (2017). *Tourism and the Sustainable Development Goals – Journey to 2030*. UNWTO.

UNWTO. (2005). *Making tourism more sustainable – A guide for policy makers*. UNWTO.

UNWTO. (2013). *Sustainable Tourism for Development Guidebook*. UNWTO.

Urbano, D., Toledano, N., & Soriano, D. R. (2010). Analyzing social entrepreneurship from an institutional perspective: Evidence from Spain. *Journal of Social Entrepreneurship*, *1*(1), 54–69. doi:10.1080/19420670903442061

Vaghjee, H., & Panchoo, S. (2016, August). Applying the Community of Inquiry Framework to explore sense of community on Moodle. *2016 IEEE International Conference on Emerging Technologies and Innovative Business Practices for the Transformation of Societies (EmergiTech)*. 10.1109/EmergiTech.2016.7737370

Van Beveren, L., Roets, G., Buysse, A., & Rutten, K. (2018). We all reflect, but why? A systematic review of the purposes of reflection in higher education in social and behavioral sciences. *Educational Research Review*, *24*, 1–9. doi:10.1016/j.edurev.2018.01.002

Van de Ven, A. H., Hudson, R., & Schroeder, D. R. (1984). Designing new business start-ups: Entrepreneurial, organizational and ecological considerations. *Journal of Management*, *10*(1), 89–107. doi:10.1177/014920638401000108

van Eck, N. J., & Waltman, L. (2010). Software survey: VOSviewer, a computer program for bibliometric mapping. *Scientometrics*, *84*(2), 523–538. doi:10.100711192-009-0146-3 PMID:20585380

Van Praag, C. M. (2003). Business survival and success of young small business owners. *Small Business Economics*, *21*(1), 1–17. doi:10.1023/A:1024453200297

Van Praag, C., & Cramer, J. (2001). The roots of entrepreneurship and labour demand: Individual ability and low risk aversion. *Economica.*, *68*(269), 45–62. doi:10.1111/1468-0335.00232

Van Wingerden, J., & Van der Stoep, J. (2018). The motivational potential of meaningful work: Relationships with strengths use, work engagement, and performance. *PLoS One*, *13*(6), 1–11. doi:10.1371/journal.pone.0197599 PMID:29897935

Vargas-Hernández, J. G., Guerra García, E., & Zepeda, V. (2017). *La nueva gobernanza instrumental del estado de bienestar: transformaciones y retos*. Editorial Universitaria: Universidad de Guadalajara, Centro Universitario de Ciencias Económico Administrativas, Guadalajara, Jalisco.

Vargas-Hernández, J. G. (2005). Emergencia de la nueva cultura institucional: Impacto en la transformación del escenario de la globalización económica. *Economía, Sociedad y Territorio*, *5*(17), 27–61. doi:10.22136/est002005316

Vasconcelos, S., & Balula, A. (2019). Do You Speak Digital? A Literature Review on Language and Digital Competences in Tourism Education. *ToSEE Tourism in Southern and Eastern Europe*, *5*, 729-737.

Vásquez, O., Fernández, M., & Álvarez, P. (2014). La aportación de los grados al desarrollo de la sensibilidad y competencia intercultural. Perspectiva comparada entre Trabajo Social y Psicología *Revista. Cuadernos de Trabajo Social*, *27*(2), 307–317.

Venkatraman, N. (1989). The concept of fit in strategy research: Toward verbal and statistical correspondence. *Academy of Management Review*, *14*(3), 423–444. doi:10.2307/258177

Veríssimo, S., Godinho, V., Casas, L., & Luengo, R. (2017). Evaluation of Changes in Cognitive Structures after the Learning Process in Mathematics. *International Journal of Innovation in Science and Mathematics Education*, *25*(2), 17–33. https://openjournals.library.sydney.edu.au/index.php/CAL/article/download/11295/11122

Vlachopoulos, D., & Makri, A. (2019). Online communication and interaction in distance higher education: A framework study of good practice. *International Review of Education*, *65*(4), 605–632. doi:10.100711159-019-09792-3

Wach, D. (2010). Defining and measuring entrepreneurial success. In M. Lukes & M. Laguna (Eds.), *Entrepreneurship. A psychological approach* (pp. 89–102). University of Economics.

Wallace, I., & Moore, C. (2012). Providing in-depth and personalised feedback to online students using audio recording. *IPEDR*, *27*, 53–58.

Walter, N., Ortbach, K., & Niehaves, B. (2015). Designing electronic feedback – Analyzing the effects of social presence on perceived feedback usefulness. *International Journal of Human-Computer Studies*, *76*, 1–11. doi:10.1016/j.ijhcs.2014.12.001

Ward, C. (1996). Acculturation. In D. Landis & R. Bhagat (Eds.), *Handbook of intercultural training* (pp. 124–147). Sage.

Wei, F., Li, Y., Zhang, Y., & Liu, S. (2018). The interactive effect of authentic leadership and leader competency on followers' job performance the mediating role of work engagement. *Journal of Business Ethics*, *153*(3), 763–773. doi:10.100710551-016-3379-0

Weisberg, Y. J., DeYoung, C. G., & Hirsh, J. B. (2011). Gender differences in personality across the ten aspects of the Big Five. *Frontiers in Psychology*, *2*, 178. doi:10.3389/fpsyg.2011.00178 PMID:21866227

Werner, T., & Weckenmann, A. (2012). Sustainable quality assurance by assuring competence of employees. *Measurement*, *45*(6), 1534–1539. doi:10.1016/j.measurement.2012.02.025

West, J. T. (2018). *Organizational socialization: The role of onboarding in employee longevity* [Ph.D. Dissertation, University of Texas at Arlington]. ProQuest.

Westall, A., & Chalkley, D. (2007). *Social enterprise futures.* Retrieved from: http://www.smith-institute.org.uk/pdfs/social_enterprise.pdf

West, G. III, & Noel, T. (2009). The impact of knowledge resources on new venture performance. *Journal of Small Business Management*, *47*(1), 1–22. doi:10.1111/j.1540-627X.2008.00259.x

Wiese, N. M., & Sherman, D. J. (2011). Integrating marketing and environmental studies through an interdisciplinary, experiential, service-learning approach. *Journal of Marketing Education*, *33*(1), 41–56. doi:10.1177/0273475310389154

Will, E. (2017). *Onboarding in the manufacturing boom. In Manufacturing Business Technology.* ProQuest.

William & Susan. (2005). Fundamentals of Business: Starting a Small Business. McGraw-Hill/Irwin.

Witter, M. (2011). *Financing sustainable development in small island developing states.* Tools for Mainstreaming Sustainable Development in Small States.

Wittmer, D. P. (2004). Business and community: Integrating service learning in graduate business education. *Journal of Business Ethics*, *51*(4), 359–371. doi:10.1023/B:BUSI.0000032514.05498.2b

Wollard, K. K., & Shuck, B. (2011). Antecedents to employee engagement: A structured review of the literature. *Advances in Developing Human Resources*, *13*(4), 429–446. doi:10.1177/1523422311431220

Woodland, A. M. (2009). Using service-learning in graduate auditing courses: A standards-based framework. *Advances in Accounting Education*, *10*, 61–80. doi:10.1108/S1085-4622(2009)0000010005

World Economic Forum. (2018). *The Future of Jobs Report 2018.* https://es.weforum.org/reports/the-future-of-jobs-report-2018

World Economic Forum. (2021). *Technology Futures: Projecting the Possible, Navigating What's Next.* https://www3.weforum.org/docs/WEF_Technology_Futures_GTGS_2021.pdf

Wuffli, P. A. (2016). *Inclusive leadership: A framework for the global era.* Springer. doi:10.1007/978-3-319-23561-5

Wu, W.-C. V., Hsieh, J. S. C., & Cang, J. C. (2017). Creating an Online Learning Community in a Flipped Classroom to Enhance EFL Learners' Oral Proficiency. *Journal of Educational Technology & Society*, *20*(2), 142–157. https://www.jstor.org/stable/10.2307/90002170

Xiao, H., & Smith, S. L. J. (2006). The making of tourism research: Insights from a social sciences journal. *Annals of Tourism Research*, *33*(2), 490–507. doi:10.1016/j.annals.2006.01.004

Yin, R. K. (2018). *Case study research and applications: Design and methods* (6th ed.). SAGE Publications, Inc.

Yu, D. D. (2011). Achieving Service-Learning Goals in a Financial Accounting Class Project. *New Horizons in Education*, *59*(1), 95–105.

Yu, Y., Li, Y., Zhang, Z., Gu, Z., Zhong, H., Zha, Q., Yang, L., Zhu, C., & Chen, E. (2020). A bibliometric analysis using VOSviewer of publications on COVID-19. *Annals of Translational Medicine*, *8*(13), 1–11. doi:10.21037/atm-20-4235 PMID:32793661

Zadek, S., & Thake, S. (1997). *Practical people, noble causes. How to support community-based social entrepreneurs.* New Economics Foundation.

Zait, D. (2002). *Management intercultural. Valorizarea diferenţelor culturale*. Editura Economică, Bucureti.

Zaman, H. (2004). The Scaling-Up of Microfinance in Bangladesh: Determinants, Impact, and Lessons. World Bank Policy Research Working Paper 3398.

Zamora, V. L. (2012). Using a social enterprise service-learning strategy in an introductory management accounting course. *Issues in Accounting Education*, *27*(1), 187–226. doi:10.2308/iace-50102

Zhang, A. (2020). Dive into Deep Learning. Academic Press.

Zhao, H., & Seibert, S. E. (2006). The big five personality dimensions and entrepreneurial status: A meta-analytical review. *The Journal of Applied Psychology*, *91*(2), 259–271. doi:10.1037/0021-9010.91.2.259 PMID:16551182

Zigarelli, M. (2013, August 17). *Ten leadership theories in five minutes* [Video]. YouTube. https://youtu.be/XKUPDUDOBVo

Zika, L. (2017). Student perceptions of ethics, CSR, and sustainability (ECSRS) in hospitality management education. *Journal of Teaching in Travel & Tourism*, *17*(4), 254–268. doi:10.1080/15313220.2017.1399497

Zimmerman, M. A., & Zeitz, G. J. (2002). Beyond survival: Achieving new venture growth by building legitimacy. *Academy of Management Review*, *27*(3), 414–431. doi:10.2307/4134387

About the Contributors

Luísa Cagica Carvalho holds a PhD in Management in University of Évora, Portugal. Professor of Management on Department of Economics and Management, Institute Polytecnic of Setubal, Portugal. Guest professor in international universities teaches in courses of master and PhDs programs. Researcher at CEFAGE (Center for Advanced Studies in Management and Economics) University of Evora – Portugal. Author of several publications in national and international journals, books, and book chapters.

Pedro Pardal is a PhD in Accounting Professor of Institute Polytechnic of Setúbal, Investigator and Consulter in Finance, Accounting, and Management Control Systems.

* * *

Cristiano Alves is a PhD in Mechanical Engineering from Technical University of Lisbon — Higher Technical Institute, Master and Bachelor in Industrial Design from Paulista State University Júlio de Mesquita Filho (UNESP). Member of the research groups Lignocellulosic Composites (UNESP/Botucatu), IN+ Center for Innovation, Technology and Policy Research (Technical University of Lisbon) and Grupo LOGO (UFSC) in lines of research on the development of technical components for the automotive and railway industries, and Ecodesign and sustainability management systems for products and processes. He has experience as an automotive designer (Mercedes Benz do Brazil), design manager (Jacto Agricultural Machines) and R&D director (Ancel — Composite Technology) teacher of Design at Euripides University of Marília (UNIVEM), University of Sorocaba-SP and Faculty of Administration and Arts of Limeira (FAAL). He acted as coordinator of the Design course of UFRN, as creator and coordinator of the research group ECOAR - Design, Innovation and Sustainability and of the Design, Innovation and Sustainability Center of UFRN (NDIS). Likewise, he is currently an adjunct teacher of design at the Federal University of Santa Catarina (UFSC) and a permanent teacher at UFRN's Professional Master's program in Science, Technology, and Innovation (MPInova). Likewise, he works in the area of Industrial Design, with emphasis on Product Development and Management, acting mainly on the following themes: Sustainable Strategic Design, Natural Composite Materials, Eco-Design, Sustainability, Sustainable Product Development, Life Cycle Analysis (ACV/LCA) of Products and Processes and Strategic Environmental Assessment.

João Alves is a PhD in Sociology. Coordinating Professor at the School of Education and Social Sciences of the Polytechnic Institute of Portalegre. Researcher integrated in VALORIZA (Research centre for endogenous resources valorisation). Associate researcher at CIES-Iscte (Centre for Research and Studies in Sociology - (Higher Institute of Labour and Business Sciences).

Filipe Bacalhau is Guest Assistant of the Department of Accounting and Finance at School of Business and Administration of the Polytechnic Institute of Setubal (IPS), Portugal. Undergraduate degree in Accounting and Finance, School of Business Administration, Polytechnic Institute of Setúbal. Certified Public Accountant.

Jude Berman has a doctorate in education, with focus on cross-cultural communication and humanistic education, from UMass Amherst. She lives in the San Francisco Bay Area and works as a freelance editor and writer.

Carolina Castro holds a degree in Accounting and Finance in Institute Polytecnic of Setubal, Portugal.

Paulo Costa is Guest Adjunct Professor of the Department of Accounting and Finance at School of Business and Administration of the Polytechnic Institute of Setubal (IPS), Portugal. Master's degree in Accounting and Finance, School of Business Administration, Polytechnic Institute of Setúbal. Specialist in Accounting and Taxation. Specialist in Income Taxes (OCC). Certified Public Accountant.

Alexandre Cotovio is a PhD in Sociology. Assistant Professor at the School of Education and Social Sciences of the Polytechnic Institute of Portalegre. Integrated Researcher in CICS.NOVA (Centre for Research in Social Sciences of the Universidade Nova de Lisboa). Researcher at VALORIZA (Research Centre for the valorisation of endogenous resources).

Salvador Cruz Rambaud was born in Cádiz, Spain, in 1957. He received the degree in Mathematics from the University of Granada, Spain, in 1981; later, he received the degree in Economics and the Ph. D. degree in Economics and Business from the Open University, Madrid, Spain, in 1991 and 1994, respectively. In 1992, he joined the Department Accounting and Finance, University of Almería, as a lecturer, where he became an Associate Professor in 1996, and a Professor in 2010. His current research interests include anomalies in intertemporal choice, mathematical analysis of financial operations and elicitation of new statistical distributions in Finance.

Zulmara V. de Carvalho is Associate Professor at the Federal University of Rio Grande do Norte - UFRN, Brazil; coordinator of the Graduate Program in Science, Technology and Innovation at UFRN (2018-2022); co-founder and member of the Deliberative Council of the Incubator of Applied Academic, Scientific and Technological Processes (inPACTA) at UFRN. Creator of the Sci2Biz methodology (from Science to Technological Business) for the dissemination of the Culture of Innovation. Her research is situated in the field of technological business, with a special focus on innovation culture and ecosystems, highlighting the themes: economic engineering; triple helix; creativity, communication and connectivity.

Maria Eduarda Franklin da Costa de Paula Neuroscientist and Master in Neuroengineering, Master's Student in Science, Technology and Innovation, Bachelor in Biomedical Engineering and is a Computer Technician from the Agricultural School of Jundiaí-EAJ, Federal University of Rio Grande do Norte (2016). She was a CAPES scientific initiation fellow, Monitor of Experimental Physics at the

School of Science and Technology, as well as a tutor in the same department. She has experience in computer science, bioinformatics, robotics, neuroengineering and computational neuroscience, neurodynamics, machine learning

Rosa Galvão is Guest Adjunct Professor of the Department of Accounting and Finance at School of Business and Administration of the Polytechnic Institute of Setubal (IPS), Portugal. Researcher, and Consultant in Finance and Accounting. Master's degree in Accounting and Finance, Polytechnic Institute of Setúbal. Doctoral student in Management at the University of Évora. Finance Specialist (DL 206/2009).

Veronica Keiffer-Lewis is an organizational equity and cultural humility specialist with close to three decades of experience. She received her EdD from Mills College in 2010 and holds certifications as a diversity professional, integral coach, and community and workplace conflict mediator. She was the inaugural equity director at De Anza College in Cupertino, California, where she led the development of the college's equity framework, lens, and rubric, in addition to developing systems approaches to deepening institutional equity. She teaches at both De Anza College and California State University at San Francisco and is also the CEO of Allied Path Consulting, LLC, which she founded to carry equity work into educational institutions, social justice nonprofits, public health organizations, and other community and professional settings.

Debra Lacy has more than twenty years of extensive experience in strategic and tactical leadership, training and professional development, consulting, coaching, and mentoring. Debra attained her doctorate in education from Baylor University with a focus on Learning and Organizational Change. She has a Bachelor of Science degree in Training and Development with a minor in Leadership from the University of Houston, and a Masters in Business Administration from the Crummer Graduate School at Rollins College in Winter Park, FL.

Francelma Macedo graduated in Administration from the Federal University of Piauí (2017). Sales consultant at Nissan dealerships from 2015 to 2020. Currently, she is a master's student in Science, Technology and Innovation at the Federal University of Rio Grande do Norte. He has experience in the Administration area, with an emphasis on direct factory sales and financial products. Holds certifications in Banking Self-Regulation; Fraud Prevention and Money Laundering from Bank Votorantim.

Carla Melo graduated in Management and Planning in Tourism, Master in Information Management, Specialist in Tourism and PhD student in Tourism at the Tilburg School of Social and Behavioral Sciences, Tilburg University, Netherlands. She is currently an Adjunct Guest Professor at the School of Hospitality and Tourism of the Polytechnic of Porto. Her priority areas of research are transformative tourism experiences, creative tourism, yoga tourism, gastronomic tourism, and tourism education.

Sandrina B. Moreira (PhD) is Professor of Economics at the Instituto Politécnico de Setúbal (ESCE / IPS) and a researcher of BRU - IUL (Business Research Unit, Instituto Universitário de Lisboa). She coordinates the Management and Economics Department at ESCE/IPS and is the Vice-President of the School Pedagogical Council (since 2018); also Former School Coordinator of International Mobility (2013-2017). Her broad research and teaching interests are Macroeconomics, Economic Growth and

Development, and International Economics. List of publications available in E415-8386-EB73 (Ciência ID) or at https://orcid.org/0000-0003-2124-8366.

Helena Morgado is a PhD student in Social Work - Lusíada University of Lisbon. Social Worker at Polytechnic Institute of Portalegre. Integrated Researcher at CLISSIS (Lusíada Centre for Social Service Research).

Isabel Mourato has a Master's degree in political science, citizenship and governance. Coordinator of the Evaluation and Quality Office of the Polytechnic Institute of Portalegre.

Scott Nelmark earned his doctoral degree in Education, Learning and Organizational Change from Baylor University. He also holds a Bachelor of Arts and Master of Arts in Organizational Leadership from the University of Oklahoma and a Master of Science in Learning Technologies from the University of North Texas. As a learning organization leader, he enthusiastically promotes quality adult learning in the workplace while enabling the best in contributing members in support of employees and customers as adult learners.

Piedad Ortiz Fernández was born in Almería, Spain, in 1986. She received the degree in Business Administration from the University of Almería, Spain in 2009 and the PhD in 2021 also in the University of Almería. She is lecture in the Department of Econonomics and Business, University of Almería. Her current research interests include anomalies in intertemporal choice and active methodologies in Economics and Business education.

Nicole Palan is a post-doc researcher and lecturer of economics at several universities and universities of applied sciences across Austria. She has been lecturing both beginner and advanced economics courses to full-time and part-time students for 15 years. Since 2017 she has experience in online teaching and the specific requirements for well designed online classes. In her research, she is interested in structural change, globalization, the effects of digitalization and measuring inequality.

Maria Pammer is head of the department "Business Administration Online" at MCI, Austria, where she teaches mainly in the fields of organizational development and change management, workplace learning, and business ethics. Her research interests can be summarized with the question of how new technologies affect learning and work processes.

Adelaide Proença is a Ph.D. in Education Sciences. Master in Probabilities and Statistics by the Faculty of Science of the University of Lisbon. Adjunct Professor at the School of Education and Social Sciences of the Polytechnic Institute of Portalegre. Collaborating researcher of VALORIZA (Research centre for endogenous resources valorisation).

Jamersom Queiroz is a Ph.D. in Production Engineering from the Federal University of Santa Catarina (2003), master's degree in Industrial Economics from the Federal University of Santa Catarina (2000) and graduated in Economic Sciences from the University of the Amazon (1996). Teacher at the University of the Extreme South of Santa Catarina (UNESC) from 1999 to 2009. He is currently an adjunct teacher at the Federal University of Rio Grande do Norte, a teacher of the Master's in Production Engineering at UFRN, and a teacher at the Open University of Brazil (UAB) linked to the Public Administration course at UFRN. He has experience in Economics and Production Engineering, with emphasis on elaboration and analysis of national and international funding projects, innovation and entrepreneurship management, university and hospital management. Likewise, he is an Institutional and course evaluator for INEP/MEC, and leader of the Research Group, linked to UFRN's graduate program, "Competitiveness, Innovation, and Management Strategies." Ad-hoc appraiser for the Coordination for the Improvement of Higher Education Personnel (CAPES), as well as for FAPERN (Foundation for the Support of Research of the State of Rio Grande do Norte). Researcher member of the Brazilian Research Network in Wind Energy RBPEE. Leader of the research group Science, technology and management in wind and solar energy.

Márcia R. C. Santos (PhD) is an Assistant Professor at the Escola Superior de Ciências Empresariais at Instituto Politécnico de Setúbal (ESCE-IPS) and a researcher at the Information Sciences and Technologies and Architecture Research Center (ISTAR-IUL) at Instituto Universitário de Lisboa (ISCTE-IUL), Portugal, with interests in the fields of non-profit management, accounting and business intelligence & analytics. She is author of scientific publications (see https://ciencia.iscte-iul.pt/mrcss/en and ORCID:0000-0001-8741-0122).

Jorge Tarifa-Fernandez is Research Fellow in the Department of Economics and Business at the University of Almería since 2014. He received the MBA Degree in 2012 from the University of Almería and the PhD in 2017 also in the University of Almería. His research interests include supply chain management, environmental management, strategy, and digital technologies.

Ana Teixeira is Professor of the Department of Accounting and Finance at School of Business and Administration of the Polytechnic Institute of Setubal (IPS), Portugal. Holds a PhD in Accounting. Researcher in Accounting and Management Control Systems. Author of several papers in journals and conferences in her areas of research.

José G. Vargas-Hernández, M.B.A., Ph.D., Member of the National System of Researchers of Mexico and a research professor at University Center for Economic and Managerial Sciences, University of Guadalajara. Professor Vargas-Hernández has a Ph. D. in Public Administration and a Ph.D. in Organizational Economics. He has undertaken studies in Organisational Behaviour and has a Master of Business Administration, published four books and more than 200 papers in international journals and reviews (some translated to English, French, German, Portuguese, Farsi, Chinese, etc.) and more than 300 essays in national journals and reviews. He has obtained several international Awards and recognition.

Sofia M. Veríssimo Catarreira is a PhD in Mathematics - Didactics of Mathematics. Guest Adjunct Professor at Polytechnic Institute of Portalegre. Teacher of Basic and Secondary Education. Researcher of CiberDidact- Official Group of the Universidad de Extremadura.

Julia Waldegger is Research & Teaching Assistant at the department "Business Administration Online" at MCI. In her daily work, she supports both lecturers and (inter)national students to overcome challenges in the online-studying environment. Her research interests include responsible management education and (organizational) learning.

Wendi Walker-Schmidt has been responsible for all stages of the learning and development cycle including design, delivery, and evaluation. As a key leader, she develops strategic learning and development programs, while and managing day-to-day training activities for client organizations. Wendi conceptualizes creative learning and execution solutions and leads projects through to completion. In previous roles she has led successful learning and organizational development programs that include leadership development, engagement performance interventions, psychometric evaluations, professional enrichment, and executive and management coaching. Wendi has two Bachelors degrees from Houston Baptist University, a Masters degree from Texas Christian University, and is currently working on her Doctorate in Learning and Organizational Change at Baylor University. She holds certifications in instructional system design, mediation and as a certified facilitator. Additionally, she holds a position as a CLO Learning Elite judge, serves on the local TCU Alumni board and is on the Talent Management Human Capital Executive Research Board.

Telmo Wergikosky is Guest Assistant of the Department of Accounting and Finance at School of Business and Administration of the Polytechnic Institute of Setubal (IPS), Portugal. Undergraduate degree in Accounting and Finance, School of Business Administration, Polytechnic Institute of Setúbal. Postgraduate in Taxation. Certified Public Accountant.

Index

F

G

I

L

M

O

P

R

S

T

U

V

W

www.ingramcontent.com/pod-product-compliance
Lightning Source LLC
LaVergne TN
LVHW062135300926
849161LV00010B/2534
* 9 7 8 1 7 9 9 8 8 2 3 9 8 *